Person County North Carolina

DEED BOOKS
1792–1825

Abstracts
by
Katharine Kerr Kendall

CLEARFIELD COMPANY

Printed for
Clearfield Company, Inc. by
Genealogical Publishing Co., Inc.
Baltimore, Maryland
1994

International Standard Book Number: 0-8063-4518-7

INTRODUCTION

Person County, North Carolina, was formed from the eastern part of Caswell County 1791. The first meeting of the County Court was March 1792. Deeds recorded for present Person County from 1777-1791 appear in the Caswell County Deed Books. Abstracts were published in 1989. Prior to 1777, both Person and Caswell were the northern part of Orange County.

Person County is bounded by Caswell County on the west, Granville County on the east, Durham and Orange Counties on the south, and by the state of Virginia on the north, mainly Halifax Co. Deed Books are at the office of the Register of Deeds, Roxboro, NC, 27573. Books A through G total 2899 pages covering 33 years of land transfers, some grants from State of North Carolina, deeds of slaves and other personal property, powers of attorney, division of land to inheritors, and migration of inhabitants.

ABBREVIATIONS USED IN ABSTRACTS

A Acre(s)
adj adjoining
adm administrator(trix)
CC Caswell County
Co County
Commrs: Commissioners
div division
exec executor(trix)
inv inventory
ND No Date
Wit witness(es)

Water Courses
 Br branch
 Cr Creek
 R River

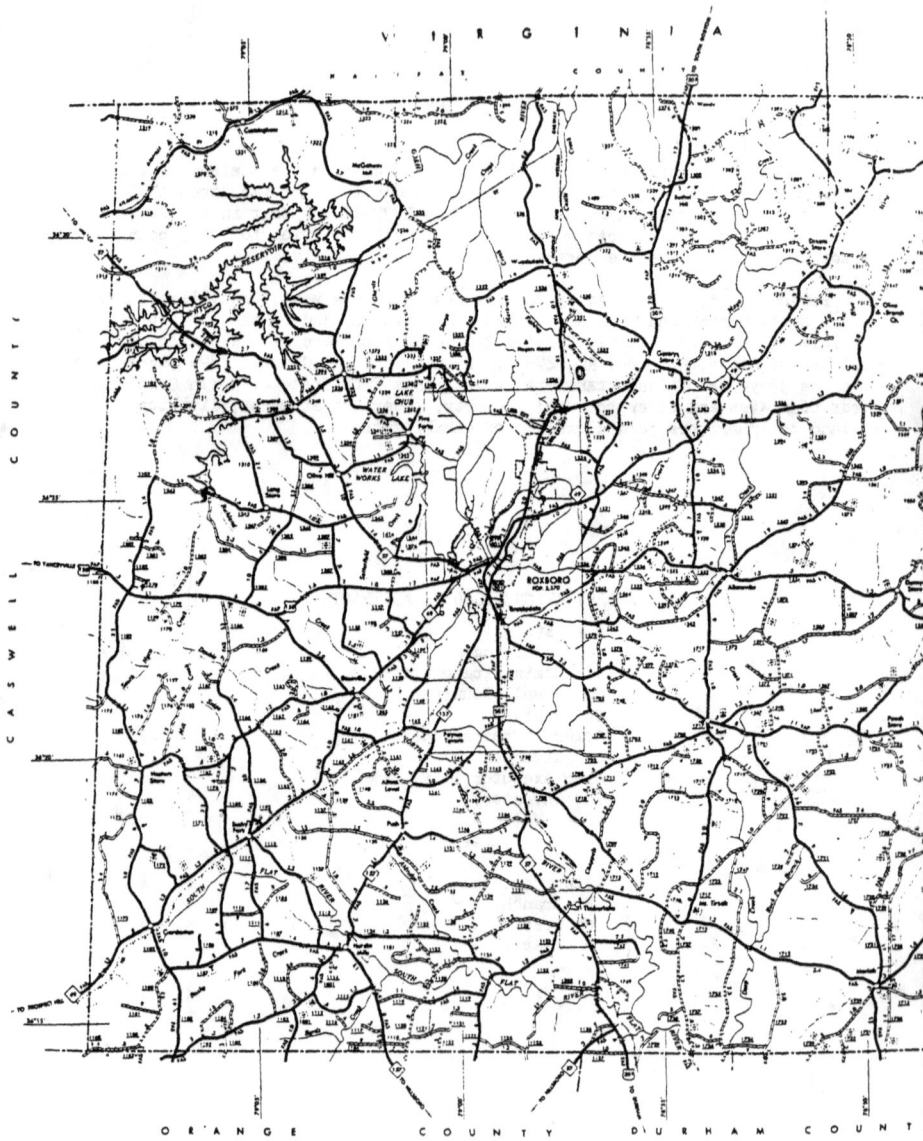

PERSON COUNTY
NORTH CAROLINA

BOOK A

Page

1-3 Osborn Jeffreys to John Commons, for 3 lbs 19sh, 114 A in CC on the River adj Robert Dickens. 24 Dec 1789. Wit: Thomas Vanhook, James Compton, Ephraim Hawkins.

3-4 Edmund Lewis to John Walters, for 100 lbs, 167.75 A on Stories Cr. 20 Mar 1792. Wit: John Barnett, William Barnett.

4-6 David Mann of CC to Yancey Bailey of same, for 50 lbs, 150 A n fork Flat R adj Maj. John Paine, Vanhook - being part of tract purchased of Henry McNeill 20 Jan 1790. 26 Feb. 1791. Wit: Robert A. Dickens, Tinsley Wade.

6-7 Gideon Patterson Sen. of CC to James Patterson of Richmond Co., NC, for 64 lbs, 440 A on Flat R, Adams & Rosemary Creeks adj William Hinton, David Mitchell. 9 Nov 1789. Wit: Tho Miles, Abel Howard.

7-8 James Wilson to Lewis Parrott, for 80 lbs, 200 A on Mayo Cr adj Genl. Person. 16 Mar 1792. Wit: Richd Sanders, James Archdeacon.

9-10 Byrd Wall to Josias Dixon, for 300 lbs, 235 A on Marley Cr & Hico adj Burgess Haralson old line, William Stone old line (now Josias Dickson), John Chambers old line (now Atkinson) - said land purchased of Robert Parker 19 Oct 1791. 20 Mar 1792. Wit: Josias Chambers, James Davy.

10-2 Archibald Murphey of CC to Tobias Williams of Person Co., for 12 lbs, 15 sh, 12.75 A s prong Cain Cr both sides public road adj Murphey, James Hamlett, said Williams. 18 June 1792. Wit: Thomas M. Hamlett, H. Haralson.

12-4 John Chambers to Robert Walker of Campbell Co., VA, for 160 lbs VA currency, 369 A both sides Gents Cr of Hico being 2 surveys granted Chambers by State - 300 A in Dec 1779 and 67 A in 1774 adj Thomas Robertson, Thomas Nash. 8 May 1792. Wit: H. Haralson, D. McFarland, Tho Douglas.

14-5 John Norton of Henry Co., VA, to Robert Allen of Person Co., for 50 lbs, 152A on Adams Cr adj James Currie. 23 May 1792. Wit: Joseph Stovall, William Huston.

15-7 Thomas Brooks late sheriff of CC to Josias Dickson (who brought suit against Richard Finch Oct 1790), for 83 lbs, 12 sh. 5p., 440 A on w side Adams Cr adj William Sergeant, Mitchell. 16 Feb 1792. Wit: John Rogers, Jane Brooks, Jona Brooks.

17-8 James Stuart of CC to son-in-law Julius Justice of same, for love & affection, 100 A in CC adj William Barnett, John Justice, William Huston. 13 Dec 1791. Wit: Robert Seymore, John Justice.

18-9 Phillip Webber & Tappanes his wife by their atty Richard Webber of Cumberland Co., VA, to Catharine Brown wife of William Brown of CC, for love & affection of their sister & for her children, negroes James, Rachel, Annis, Ben. 7 Jan 1792. Wit: William Hayne, William Waite.

19-20 Samuel Neeley to Paul Jeffreys, for 100 lbs, 100 A on Richland Cr adj Roberts. _ June 1792. Acknd.

20-1 Daniel Malone of CC to Jesse Evans of same, for 100 lbs, 130 A in Person Co on S Hyco a part of State grant to Malone. 31 Mar 1792. Wit: John Wilkerson, Staples Malone, J____ Malone.

Page
21-2 Jesse Fuller of CC to John Fuller of Person Co., for 40 lbs, all right to
116 A s fork Stories Cr in Person Co. - said tract conveyed him by Henry Fuller
19 Jan 1791 registered in CC, Book G, page 106. 18 June 1792.
Wit: Zachariah Evans, Henry Fuller.

23-4 Robert Dickens to Moses Springfield, for 40 lbs, 100 A on Mayhoe Cr adj
Moses Street, John Lawson, Davey. 1 June 1792. Wit: Isaac Vanhook, Moses Street.

24-5 Robert Dickens of CC to Drury Allen of same, for 12 lbs pd by John Urquhart,
640 A on Flat R & Double Cr. 25 Dec 1791. Acknd.

25-6 Robert Dickens of Person Co. to James Jay, for 100 lbs in gold, 290 A on Hyco
adj Hall, Waite, McNeil, Cadel. 4 Apr 1792. Wit: Benjamin Jones, Sally Jeffreys.

26-7 John Clayton of CC to Daniel Clayton of same, for 50 lbs, 300 A on Mayho Cr
adj A. Allen. 3 May 1790. Wit: John Clayton Jr., Richd Clayton.

27-8 Daniel Malone of CC to Lewis Malone of same, for 100 lbs, 170 A in Person Co
on S Hyco adj Christion Burgus, John Rainey . 19 June 1792. Wit: Isaac McCullen,
William McKissack.

29-30 John Blake to John Thomas, for 50 lbs, 102 A n side Double Cr of Hyco adj
William Waite, William Brown, John McMurray. 19 June 1792. Wit: William Waite,
David Bracken.

30-1 William Paine of CC to Coleman Clayton of same, for 50 lbs, 640 A on Mill
Cr in CC adj Joseph Gill, David Mitchell, John Man. 11 Dec 1789. Wit: David
Burton, William Clayton.

32-3 James Rankins to Isaac Satterfield, for 100 lbs, 240 A on Richland Cr adj
Hosea Tapley, James Hunt, Andrew Cadel, Edward Clay - it being tract devolved
from his father William Rankin who died intestate. 19 June 1792. Wit: Jab
Vanhook, Benj Hatcher.

33-4 William Tapp to John Carrington of Orange Co., NC, for 100 lbs, 50 A on
Flat R with mill and formerly belonged to Thomas Gibson. 10 Apr 1792.
Wit: Robert Dickens, James Walker.

34-5 State of NC - #1043 - to Osborne Jeffreys, for 10 lbs per 100 A, 29 A in
CC on Tapley's Cr adj Robert Dickens. 16 Nov 1790. Alexr Martin, Governor.

35-7 State of NC - #989 - to John Black, for 50 shillings per 100 A, 33 A in CC
on Hico adj his own line, Robertson, Johnston, excluding part of mill.
18 May 1789. By Saml Johnson, Governor.

37-8 William Sergeant to James Long, for 6 lbs 13 sh 4p., 10 A adj Reuben Newton,
Thomas Robertson. 10 Sept 1792. Wit: William Long, Benj Cochran.

38-9 William Lea Sen. to William Brown, for 11 lbs 10 sh, 38 1/3 A on S Hyco adj
Anness McNeill, said Brown. 18 Sept 1792. Wit: James Cochran, Henry Newton.

40 John Smith Hurst to daughter-in-law Sarah Parker, for love & affection & 5 sh.,
negroes Venus. Bob, Moses, Winters; sorrel mare & horse; cattle; furniture.
8 June 1792. Wit: Jno Sneed, Tho Sneed.

40 John Smith Hurst to daughter-in-law Anne Parker, for love & affection & 5 sh.,
negroes Bett, Sarah, Jack, Fanny; 2 bay mares, colt; cattle; furniture.
8 June 1792. Wit: John Sneed, Thomas Sneed.

41-2 Yancey Bailey to John Paine, for 50 lbs, 150 A n fork Flat R adj said Paine,
Vanhook - it being part of tract purchased of David Mann (see deed from Henry
McNeill to Mann 20 Jan 1790). 18 Sept 1792. Wit: Isaac McCollum, William Paine.

42-3 John Kennon of Granville Co., NC, to Absalem Johnston of same, for 120 lbs,
421 A on head Flat R at Hillsboro Rd adj Taylor, Burch, Daniel Malone, Shadrick
Roberts. 7 Sept 1792. Wit: Charles Kennon, James Johnston.

43-4 Abraham Brown to William Jopling, for 30 lbs, 71 A n side Bushy Fork of Flat R adj George Brown. 6 Sept 1792. Wit: Josiah Brown, John Brown, John Moore.

44-5 Abraham Brown to son John Brown, for love & affection, 160 A on Bushy Fork of Flat R adj Thomas Farmer, Richd Hargis, Peter Farrow, Abraham Moore. 18 Sept 1792. Wit: Josiah Brown, John Price, William Jopling.

45-6 John Hall to Philip Hall Sen., for 100 lbs, 398 A on Flat R adj Robert Dickens, John Wilson, Jacobs, Howel, Jones, Reuben Taylor. 20 Sept 1792.

47-8 Hayden Pryor of CC to John Gwinn of same, for 100 lbs, 179 A on Mill Cr (being plantation whereon Edmund Jones formerly lived)adj John Baird, Gun, Davis, Street, Pool, Robert Dickens. 23 Nov 1784. Wit: David Allen, Catey Allen, Lucey Wade.

48-9 Daniel Hicks to John Gwinn, for 200 lbs, 200 A on Adams Cr. 30 Mar 1792. Wit: Robert Wade, Seth Moore.

49-50 Daniel Hicks to John Gwinn, for 500 lbs, 483 A on Adams Cr adj John Wilson, Josiah Dickson, John Mitchell, Ambrose Hudgens, John Mann, William Mann. 30 Mar 1792. Wit: Robert Wade Jr., Seth Moore.

50-1 Joseph Barnett to Thomas Barnett, for 112 lbs, 210 A adj Silvs Stokes, William Barnett, John Chambers - being tract willed Joseph Barnett by his father. 4 Aug 1792. Wit: John Chambers, John Warrin, Elizabeth Chambers.

51-2 Drury Allen to William Forest, for 50 lbs, 100 A on Flat R adj Robert Dickens, Thomas Hargis. 12 Sept 1792. Wit: John Guin, Robert Paine.

52-4 William Tapp of CC to son Lewis Tapp of same, for love & affection, 239 A both sides Flat R adj Hosea Tapley, James Jay. 13 Sept 1791. Wit: Robert Dickens, Jonathan Cragg, Jesse Dickens.

54-5 John Baird of Prince George Co., VA, to David Barnett of Person Co., for 5 shillings, 308 A on Spoonwater br of Mayo Cr adj Agness Barnett, said Baird, Charles Halliburton, Richard Andrews. 17 Sept 1792. Wit: John Glenn, David Ervin.

55-6 State of NC - #1027 - to Charles Bostick, for 10 lbs per 100 A, 100 A in CC on Maho adj John Paine. 16 Nov 1790.

56-7 State of NC - #1046 - to Robert Dickens, for 50 sh per 100 A, 200 A in CC on Flat R adj Payne, Peter Farrow, John Farrow. 20 Dec 1791.

57-8 State of NC - #1052 - to Robert Dickens, for 10 lbs per 100 A, 200 A in CC on Flat R at Orange Co. line adj Glenn. 20 Dec 1791.

58-9 State of NC - #1047 - to Robert Dickens & William Waite, for 50 sh per 100 A, 442 A on Hico adj John Chambers, Jackson, Terrell, John Atkinson, Lawrence Vanhook. 20 Dec 1791.

59-60 State of NC - #1044 - to Robert Dickens, for 50 sh per 100 A, 393 A on Flat R adj Lyon, Robert Johnston Steel, Osborne Jeffreys. 20 Dec 1791.

60-1 State of NC - #1053 - to William Tapp, for 10 lbs per 100 A, 617 A on Deep Cr & Tar R adj Robert Dickens, William Waite, his own line. 20 Dec 1791.

62 State of NC - #1028 - to Peter Cozart - 272 A on Nappy Reed Cr adj Arthur Moore, the Granville Co. line, Paul Collins former line. 16 Nov 1790.

63 State of NC - #1020 - to Ailsey Winstead, for 50 sh per 100 A, 50 A adj Gabriel Davey, Thomas Day. 18 May 1789.

64 State of NC - #1055 - to John Beard, for 10 lbs per 100 A, 644 A on Mayo & Bluewing adj his own line, Jesse Ragan. 20 Dec 1791.

65-6 Dempsey Moore to James Jones, Saml Woods, John Womack, & Stephen Moore, all commrs to build a courthouse for Person Co., for good will & 5 shillings, 6 A on Adams Cr being part of 200 A purchased of David Mitchell originally a grant from

65-6 cont. State of NC to John Cooper. 11 Dec 1792. Wit: Thomas Moore, Paul Jeffreys.

66-7 John Paine to grandson James Paine Miller of Warren Co., NC, for love & 5 shillings, 1040 A adj David Allen, Mitchell, Robert Paine, William Waite; if Miller die without heirs, same to return to his mother Polly a daughter of John Paine. 19 Dec 1791. Acknd.

68-9 William Southard of CC to Robert Southard of same, for 29 lbs, 6 sh, 200 A on Stories & Adams Creeks adj Benjamin Long, William Sergeant. 15 Dec 1792. Wit: Robert Mitchell, Benj Long, Reuben Long.

69-70 Josias Dickson to Thomas Barnett, for 90 lbs, 150 A on Ghents Cr adj James Patterson, Burgess Haralson old line now Elizabeth Haralson, James Chambers, Stephen Woods old line. 15 Nov 1792. Acknd.

70-1 Henry Wilson to William Caddel, for 50 lbs, 100 A on Flat R adj Abraham Brown, Robert Dickens, Shadrack Roberts. 4 July 1792. Wit: Lewis Green, Andrew Caddel, John Caddel.

71-2 James Kanady of CC to Thomas Mason of same, for 20 lbs, 133 A on Cobb Cr adj Zachariah Baughn. 7 Nov 1788. Wit: John Bowler, Walter Oakley.

72-3 Thomas Barnett to James Pulliam of Mecklenburg Co., VA, for 150 lbs, 210 A on Gents Cr. 2 Nov 1792. Wit: Hez Stone, William Shephard.

73-5 Daniel McFarland to John Johnston (son of Larkin Johnston), for 200 lbs, 200 A s side Hyco & e side Sergeant's Cr adj Archibal Campbell, Joseph Turner - said land surveyed 11 Oct 1748 for Robert Jones Jr & conveyed by him to John McFarland, then to Daniel McFarland. 6 Sept 1792. Wit: John Stone, Tho Barnett, Wm. Tunks.

75-6 William Barnett to Theodorick Johnston, for 60 lbs, 141 A on McFarland Cr of Hyco adj John Chambers, widow Love, Joseph Barnett. 10 June 1792. Wit: John Johnston, W. Barnett.

76-7 Cheslay Bostick to Reuben Long, for 100 lbs, 86½ A e side S Hyco adj Joseph Gold, James D. Hendley on Fish Trap Br. 9 Oct 1792. Wit: John Johnston, William Sargeant.

78-9 William Gately to William Murry of Orange Co., NC, for 30 lbs, 54 A n side Flat R adj Richard Hargis, Vincent, John Urquhart - said land part of grant to Nathl Aldridge 9 Nov 1762 from the Honourable John Earl Granville and conveyed by Aldridge to Gately 1 May 1764. 22 Nov 1792. Wit: William Hargis Sen., Jos Gately.

79-80 Joseph Barnett to William Stanfield of Halifax Co., VA, for 150 lbs, 198 A on Hico. 14 May 1792. Wit: Thomas Barnett, Theod Johnston, John Slade.

80-1 State of NC - #1061 - to Benjamin Newton 300 A in CC on Stories Cr adj Nehemiah Fuller, John Fuller, Henry Fuller, John Atkinson, Long. 27 Nov 1792.

81-2 State of NC - #1057 - to Drury Allen, for 50 sh per 100 A, 218 A in CC s fork Flat R adj Allen, William Gately, Richard Hargis. 20 Dec 1791.

82-3 Richard Coleman to John Harris, for 33 lbs, 17 A on Mayo Cr adj both men. 5 Mar 1793. Wit: Mandly Winstead, Constance Winstead.

83-4 Benjamin Douglas to Richard Eskridge, for 110 lbs, 110 A both sides S Hico on Kelley Br adj Joseph Carney purchased of Douglas, Roger Atkinson. 23 Feb 1793. Wit: Matthew Price.

84-5 Thomas Neeley to John Newton, for 160 lbs, 150 A both sides Bushy Br of S Hico adj William Lea Sen., Lawrence Vanhook. 15 Dec 1792. Acknd.

85-6 Joseph Pogue of CC to Ephraim Hawkins, for 55 lbs, 137 A on Flat R adj John Farrar. 23 Nov 1791. Acknd.

86-7 John Tapley to Robert Hester, for 120 lbs, 200 A on Grier's Cr adj David Mitchell, Daniel Brown, David Herndon. 29 Dec 1792. Wit: George Burch, Jesse Womack, Richd Burch.

87-8 John Ravens Sen. to James Ravens, for 120 lbs, 250 A on Stories Cr adj James Broach, William Glenn, David Mitchell. 15 Mar 1792. Wit: Henderson Trim, Lewis Green.

88-9 William Brecken to Charles Fooshe, for 40 lbs, 73½ A on Double Cr of S Hico being part of tract conveyed by State to Cooper adj Fooshe. 19 Jan 1793. Wit: Robert Stanfield, John Fooshe.

89-90 Robert Frazer to Benjamin Cozart of Granville Co., for 40 lbs, 109 A adj Anthony Cozart, George Anderson, Willis Roberts. 8 Dec 1792. Wit: Peter Cozart, Thos Mallard.

90-1 Drury Allen to Richard Hargis, for $77 1/3, 100 A s fork Flat R adj Hargis, William Murry. 18 Feb 1793. Acknd in court.

91-2 John Guin to John Baird of Prince George Co., VA, for 50 lbs, 178 A on Mill Cr adj widow Guin, Gabriel Davie. 18 Mar 1793. Acknd in court.

92-3 Robert Bright and his brother Isaac Bright of CC to Joseph Pitman of same, for 300 lbs, 200 A on Davie? Cr adj Humphries spring br. 20 Sept 1791. Wit: Robert Humphries, James Wilson.

93-4 John Womack to John Paine, for 6 lbs, 16½ A 24 perches, n side Flat R adj Paine. 23 Feb 1793. Acknd.

94-5 Drury Allen to William Morrow, for $77 1/3, 59 A. 12 Mar 1793. Wit: Robert Paine, Millenton Blalock.

95-6 Josias Dickson to James Mitchell, for 15 lbs, 60 A on Adams Cr adj William Shepherd, Michael Dickson - said tract Dickson purchased of Thomas Brooks, sheriff, 16 June last. 15 Dec 1792. Wit: Tinsley Wade, Walter McFarland.

96-7 William Chambers Jr to Thomas Morton of Prince Edward Co., VA, for 25 lbs, 20 A on Marlow's Cr adj Harrelson. 21 Dec 1792. Wit: Jos Dickson, William Morton, John Carlton.

98 James Patterson to Arthur Brooks Sen., for 80 lbs, 440 A on Flat R, Adams Cr, Rosemary Cr adj David Mitchell, Hinton old line. _ Mar 1793. Acknd.

99 John Baird of Prince George Co., VA, to Daniel Hughs, for 5 shillings, 101 A near Spoonwater Cr adj Baird, Agness Barnett. 29 Sept 1792. Wit: James Jones, David Barnett, Francis Ford, Philip Vass, Robert Stuart.

100-1 Thomas Hinton of CC to Daniel Clayton of same, for 50 lbs, 200 A on Rosemary Cr - said land granted by State 10 Nov 1784. 10 Mar 1791. Wit: John Fuller, William Fuller.

101-2 Reuben Long & Benjamin Long to Henry Fuller, for 150 lbs, 105 A adj Benj Long decd old line, John Crutcher, Peter Bennett. 18 Mar 1793. Wit: Hezekiah Stone. Acknd.

102-4 John Douglas of CC to John Blake of same, for 200 lbs, 270 A on Double Cr of Hico adj William Lea, William Brown, William Wait, McMurry, Sarrott. 21 Oct 1791. Wit: William Lea.

104-5 Yancey Bailey to Richard Deshazo, for 120 lbs, 200 A head waters Dishwater a br of Mayo & Castle Creeks of Hico adj Roger Atkinson, Charles Bostick. 25 June 1793. Wit: John Guin, William Deshazo.

105-6 Owen Ragan to Richard Howson of Halifax Co., VA, for 20 lbs, 17/9 which Ragan owes Joseph Jones of Dinwoody Co., VA, for 5 shillings, 80 A adj Robert Jones, said land purchased of Stephen Jones. Wit: Wm. Bawley, Syl Adams, Moses Street.

107 John Pryor of ? to John Baird of Prince George Co., VA, for 100 lbs, 400 A
on Mayo Cr in CC- said land his grandfather John Pryor purchased of Josiah Adley
& Robert McFarland adj land Baird purchased of William Hawkins Jr. & that purchased of Pryor legatees. 14 Dec 1791. Wit: Wm. Baird, (2 names unreadable).

108 John Warren Sen. to David Foard (Ford), for 10 lbs, 5 A on Robert Holt Mill Cr
adj VA line to Dry Cr. 7 Jan 1793. Wit: John Warren Jr., Mason Foley.

109 Dempsey Moore to Peter Badget, for 100 lbs, 240 A on Flat R adj William Hawkins, Robert Dickens, Humphrey Barnett - said land granted by David Mitchell.
17 Dec 1792. Wit: Isaac McCollum, William Badgett.

110-1 Thomas Halliburton & Martha his wife to James Jones, for 80 lbs, 100 A on
Bluwing Cr adj Daniels. 23 Feb 1792. Wit: Charles Halliburton, John Humphries,
Robert Jones.

111-2 William Sergeant to Solomon Draper Sen., for 40 lbs, 60 A on Sergeant Cr
adj James Long, Thomas Robertson. 14 June 1793. Wit: Reuben Newton, William Long.

112-4 Philip Vass late sheriff of Person Co. to James Robertson of CC - due to
writ from Superior Court at Hillsborough to sell tenements of Stephen Stuart to
pay damages to Robertson - for 20 lbs - 300 A   adj William Huston, John Barnett,
on Adams Cr. 31 May 1793. Wit: Alexander Boyd, William Rainy.

114-5 Mary Duncan to Roger Williams, for 60 lbs, 250 A on Milstone Cr adj Rosebrough, James D. Henley old line. 20 Oct 1792. Wit: J. Campbell, William
Warrin, John Newton.

115-6 James Dunbar Henley to John Clift, for 50 lbs, 100 A on Henley mill cr adj
Edmond Lewis, Wilson Varmillion, Charles Bostick. 18 June 1793. Acknd.

117-8 Daniel McFarland to David Bazwell, for 109 lbs, 109 A s side Hico adj Allen
Love old line, John Johnston, crossing Campbell rd, Robert Moore. 18 Dec 1792.
Wit: H. Haralson, Chs Holdman.

118-9 Charles Mitchell to William Shepard, for 200 lbs, 168½ A on Adams Cr adj
Sarah Barnett, Kinchen Finch on Hillsboro Rd. 4 June 1792. Acknd.

119-20 Richard Sanders to Francis Lawson, for 100 lbs, 100 A adj John Baird,
John Byas, Isaiah Blackwell, crossing Andrew Br, John Gunn deed to Hico Cr -
it being land where Sanders lives. 17 June 1793. Wit: Hugh Stone, John Neal,
Nathan Ragan.

120-1 John Warren to David Ford (Foard) of Halifax Co., VA, for 50 lbs, 82 A
s side Holt mill cr adj State of VA, Allen Love, Hedgeman Warren. 17 June 1793.
Acknd in open court.

121-3 James Dunbar Henley to Joseph Gold, for 16 lbs, 17 A s side S Hyco adj
Gold. 18 June 1793. Acknd.

123-4 William Chambers Jr. to James Dunbar Henley, for 16 lbs, 19½ A s side
Henley Mill Cr. 18 June 1793. Wit: William Sergeant, John Clift.

124-5 Benjamin Newton to William Hamlin Jr., for 50 lbs, 100 A both sides Stories
Cr adj Hamlin, Atkinson, George Hall. 17 June 1793. Acknd.

125-6 Shadrack Owen to Abel Howard, for 30 lbs, 36 A e side Gent's Cr a part of
large grant to Johnston adj Henry Howard. 18 June 1793. Wit: William Allen.

126-7 James McCover of CC to Thomas Neeley, for 100 lbs, 200 A on S Hico adj
Henry Cooper, William Hughes, Aaron Christenbeery - said land supposed to run
in the Moravian land for which grantor is not answerable for. 18 Apr 1791.
Wit: Law Vanhook, Benjn Douglas.

127-8 John Carlton to Abel Howard, for 35 lbs 10sh, 34½ A on ridge path between
Marlow & Gents Cr adj Robert Dickens, Joseph Beadles, James Patterson, Haralson,
Henry Howard. 15 June 1793. Wit: Hiram Howard, Thos Barnett.

128-9 Stephen Jones & Mary his wife to Robert Jones, for 30 lbs, 150 A on little Bluewing Cr adj John Turner, Dixon, John Baird, Robert Chamberlain, James Jones. 12 Feb 1793. Wit: James Jones, Robert Chamberlain.

130 Joseph Palmer to William Caddel, for 15 lbs, 130 A on Flat R - being part of 260 A of Thomas & Joseph Palmer adj Commons. 19 Jan 1792. Wit: Andrew Caddel, Thomas Palmer.

131-2 Charles Hallibruton and Sarah his wife to Benjn Cotnam, for 30 lbs, 77 A on Bluewing Cr adj Conaway, Buckner Brooks, John Baird, Jacob Dixon, Thomas Halli-Burton. 8 Aug 1792. Wit: John Dixon, Bendictus Cotnam, Thos H. Burton.

132-3 Stephen Jones & Mary his wife to Owen Ragan, for 10 lbs, 80 A adj Robert Jones, Robert Chamberlain, James Jones, Mary Ragan. 14 Feb 1793. Wit: James Jones, Robert Jones, Robert Chamberlain.

133-4 Stephen Jones & Mary his wife to Robert Chamberlain, for 3 lbs, 50 A adj John Baird, Robert Jones, Owen Ragan. 15 Feb 1793. Wit: James Jones, Robert Jones, Owen Ragan.

134-5 Edward Doyle to Simon Doyle, for 50 lbs, 60 A w side S Hico adj Daniel Sergeant. 14 June 1793. Wit: D. Vanhook, Joseph Carney.

135-6 State of NC - #1060 - to Dempsie Moore, for 50 sh per 100 A, 460 A in CC on Flat R adj John Paine, Jeffreys. 27 Nov 1792.

136-7 Richd Andrews of Orange Co., NC, to Jesse Ragan of Person Co., for 40 lbs, 400 A on Bluewing Cr adj John Baird, Eleazer Andrews - it being tract granted by State 10 Nov 1784. Wit: ? Ballard, James Jones, Amy Jones.

137-8 Jarrett Wright to Adam McNeeley, for 210 lbs, 307 A on Double Cr of S Hico adj claims of Jesse Jones, James Smith, Aron Christenbury. 11 Feb 1793. Wit: Pemberton Burch, John Willingham.

139-40 James Stuart Sen. to John Williams, for 250 lbs, 540 A both sides Gents Cr being part of 640 A granted from State 13 Oct 1783 adj Thomas Bennett, Howard. 17 Sept 1793. Wit: H. Haralson. Land sold by court order.

140-2 Thomas Neeley late coroner of Person Co. to James Stuart Sen, for 120 lbs, 540 A lands & tenements of Stephen Stuart to pay damages - adj Thomas Bennett, Howard. 17 Sept 1793. Acind.

143-4 William Lockhart of Orange Co. to John Roundtree of Person Co., for 180 lbs, 200 A on Flat R adj John Cates - said land purchased of Robert Cates 11 Sept 1779. Also signed by Sarah Lockhart. 17 Apr 1793. Wit: James Baldridge, Thomas Rountree.

144-6 Philip Vass, late sheriff of Person Co, to Benjn Dixon - due to suit against Michael Dixon Sept 1792 for 72 lbs - 195 A & 310 A, for 17 lbs, on Adams Cr adj Benjamen Edgerton, Josias Dixon, Charles Allen, Lawrence Vanhook, William Paine, John Wilson. 17 Sept 1793. Acknd.

146 Henry McNeil of Person Co. to Alex McNeil of Dunwoody Co., VA, for 40 lbs, negro girl Jane age 10 yrs a daughter of Cloe now in possession of Henry McNeil and formerly of John Pryor decd. 7 Jan 1793. Wit: John H. Pryor, Danl Archdeacon, Polly Pope.

147-8 Matthew Carter and Ann his wife of Mecklenburg Co., VA, to Frederick Going of same, for 100 lbs, 250 A e side Bluewing Cr adj George Moore to Cattail Br.

148-9 Nathan Scoggin to Daniel Sergeant, blacksmith, for 100 lbs, 95 A on S Hico adj William McDaniel. 16 Sept 1793. Wit: David Vanhook, Joseph Johnson.

149-50 William Guthrie of Laurens Co., Ninety-Six District, SC, to Absolom Guthrie of Person Co., for 20 lbs, 125 A on Adams Cr after death of his parents. 27 Nov 1792. Wit: Timothy Holt, Benjamin Haralson, Nathaniel Guthrie.

Deed Book A
Page
150-2 Repeat of pages 144-6 - Vass to Dixon.

152-3 John Blake to John Broadaway, for 40 lbs, 88 A adj William Brown, Capt. William Lea, Joseph Jarrett, John McMurry, John Thomas. 19 Sept 1793. Wit: James Cochran, William Brown.

153-4 James Brooks to James Cochran, for 75 lbs, 285.4 A e fork Stories Cr - being part of land of Joshua Browning granted by State 18 May 1789 & conveyed to Brooks 6 Nov 1790 adj Benjn Hatcher, John Browning, Elmore, Roger Atkinson. 13 Apr 1793. Wit: Edward Clay, Moses Bradsher.

155 James Smith of CC to Richard Minser of Person Co., for 200 lbs, 200 A n side Bird's Cr of Flat R adj Joseph Aldridge. 17 May 1793. Wit: David Mitchell, Anne Mitchell.

156 William Nash of Russell Co., VA, to Benj Cochran of Person Co., for 50 lbs, 200 A adj Thomas Barnett, William Sergeant, Mrs. Pinkerton, John Chambers. 3 July 1792. Wit: John Chambers, William Tunks.

157 Samuel Winstead to Mandley Winstead, for 200 lbs, 200 A both sides Mayo Cr adj Robert Gill, Winstead. 27 Aug 1793. Wit: John Winstead, Charles Brown Winstead.

158 Stephen Norton of Orange Co., NC, to Mary Scoggins of Halifax Co., VA, for 25 lbs, 152 A on Adams Cr of Hico adj James Currie. 3 Dec 1770. Wit: John Wilson, John Hamilton, William Goodman, John Hooper.

159-60 James Roberson of CC to Holloway Pass of same, for 200 lbs, 340 A in Person Co. both sides Fishing Br of Adams Cr under n side of Aspyl Mountain - it being part of tract deeded to Edward Chambers by Earl Granville - from Chambers to Burges Haralson, then to Elkanah Haralson, then to John Henry Pryor, to Stephen Stuart - and sold at sheriff sale to Roberson - adj Hugh Barnett, John Barnett, Howard, William Houston. 1 Dec 1793. /s/ James Robinson. Acknd.

160-1 Stephen Stuart of CC to Thomas Hunt of Halifax Co., VA, for 300 lbs, 300 A adj William Barnett - being part of 520 A. 10 Nov 1786. Wit: George Wiley, Josias Chambers, Benjn Long.

161-2 Richard Eskridge of CC and Matthew Price of Person Co to Nicholas Delone, for 75 lbs 9 p paid to Joseph Culberson by Nicholas Delone of CC, 110 A in Person Co where Price lives both sides S. Hico on Kelly's Br adj Joseph Carney which he purchased of Benjamin Douglas - a deed of trust. 19 Oct 1793. Wit: Zach Evans, Thomas Wright.

162-3 Matthew Price of Person Co. to Nicholas Delone, by deed of trust to Samuel Johnston, for 12 lbs 13 sh 4p, a gelding, a bald eagle mare 13 hands high, a colt. 19 Oct 1793. Wit: Zachariah Evans, Jesse Evans.

163-4 John Serratt to Simon Doyle, for 60 lbs, 150 A on the Moravian line adj widow Dollarhide, Christenberry - said tract granted by State to James Stevenson 10 Nov 1784, later conveyed to Pulliam Williamson and by him to John Burch 4 Feb 1789 and by Burch to Joseph Lewis 9 Feb 1789 and then to Sarrett 26 Aug 1791. 3 Dec 1793. Wit: E. Atkinson, Daniel Sergeant.

164 James Bell to Benjamin Douglas, for 9 lbs 8 sh 10 p, a cow, hogs, furniture. 4 Nov 1793. Wit: William Douglas, Alex Rose.

165 State of NC - #1048 - to Robert Dickens and William Waite, for 50 sh per 100 A 400 A in CC on Stories Cr adj John Cooper, Paul Waters(Walters), Loyd Vanhook, Patterson, William Man. 20 Dec 1791.

166-7 Benjamin Deboe to Sylvanus Stokes, for 190 lbs, 158.2 A on Hyco adj Saml Glaze, Frederick Deboe, McCain, John Johnston. 25 Nov 1793. Wit: Dl McFarland, H. Haralson, James Pulliam.

8

167-8 William Morrow to Michle Robinson of Orange Co, for 65 lbs, 113 A s fork Flat R adj Drury Allen, Richard Hargis. 18 Sept 1793. Wit: John Wilson, John Morrow, Catharine Robinson.

168-9 Robert Dickens to Mills Durden, for 70 lbs, 200 A adj Tap, Lunsford. 29 July 1793. Wit: John Bowles.

169 John Oakley to John Cash, for 75 lbs, 300 A a part of 640 A on Cub Cr adj John Cash to Peters Br. 14 Sept 1793. Wit: Robert Dickens, Martha Daniel; Jesse Dickens, Clerk of Court.

170-1 State of NC - #1050 - to Osborn Jeffreys Jun., for 50 sh per 100 A, 400 A in CC on Flat R adj Osborn Jeffreys Sen., Robert J. Steel, Robert Dickens, Benton, Ragsdale, James Messer. 20 Dec 1791.

171-2 State of NC - #1091 - to Stephen Sargeant, for 10 lbs per 100 A, 410 A in CC on S Hico adj Nathaniel King, Rochard Lea, on the Moravian line, John Lea, Edmond Lea. 26 Nov 1793.

172-3 Robert Dickens to Thomas F. Blalock, for 60 lbs, 200 A adj Pyron, Peter Farrow, Abraham Murry. 31 Oct 1793. Wit: Millington Blalock, Richard Jacobs.

173-4 John Black to Littleton Johnston, for 25 lbs, 30 A adj William Houston, John Johnston, Joseph Turner. _ Jan 1794. Wit: Sylvanus Stokes, John Stone.

174-5 Hezekiah Stone to William Allen, for 30 shillings, 2 A on Mill Cr. 17 Mar 1794. Acknd.

175 Michael Robinson of Orange Co. to Charles Robinson of CC, for 100 lbs, 208 A on Bird's Cr of Flat R adj William Briant, James Smith, Waite & Robert Dickens claim - land surveyed & entered in Lord Earl Granville office. 28 Oct 1788. Wit: David Robinson, Charles Rountree.

176 John Lawson Sen. to Francis Lawson, for 100 lbs, 136 A on Mayo Cr adj Moses Street, Patrick O'briant, John Baird, Robert Donaldson. 17 Mar 1794. Acknd.

176-7 Daniel Hughes to Daniel Ramsey, for 5 shillings, 101 A adj John Baird, Agnes Barnett. 12 Feb 1794. Wit: John Parish, Canor Parish, William Stuart.

178 John Henry Pryor to Yancey Bailey, for 250 lbs, 100 A on Hico Cr adj Bailey, William Stone, Lawrence Rambo. 1 June 1793. Wit: Hezekiah Stone, John Gwin.

179 John Henry Pryor to Yancey Bailey, for 200 lbs, 100 A both sides Castle Cr of Hico adj Bailey. 1 June 1793. Wit: Hez Stone, John Gwin.

180 John Henry Pryor to Yancey Bailey, for 100 lbs, 37 A adj David Womack, Gideon Patterson, Roger Atkinson - it being all the lands owned by Pryor & his father on S side Hico. 1 June 1793. Wit: Hezekiah Stone, John Gwin.

181-2 John Henry Pryor to Yancey Bailey, for 250 lbs, 375 A both sides Hico to Country Line. 1 June 1793. Wit: Hez Stone, John Gwin.

182-3 Peter Cozart to Benjamin Partee, for 50 lbs, 150 A on the Orange Co. line adj Veasey. 26 Dec 1793. Wit: John Ballard, Fowler Jones.

184 Robert Donaldson to Francis Lawson, for 145 lbs, 157½ A both sides Mayo Cr adj John Baird. 17 Mar 1794. Wit: John Gwin.

185-6 Reuben Taylor of CC to Samuel Smith Jr. of Granville Co.,for 34 Spanish milled dollars, 8½ A on Sergeant's Cr. 10 Feb 1794. Wit: Archd Murphey, H. Haralson, Robert Black.

186-7 Arthur Brooks to George Gregory, for 100 lbs, 156 A on Mayo adj Baird, Mrs. Donaldson old line, Holloway, Atkinson, Bailey. 15 Mar 1794. Acknd.

187-8 John Yarbrough to Samuel Yarbrough, for 50 lbs, 75¼ A on Mayo. _ _ 1794. Acknd.

Deed Book A
Page

188-90 John Black & George Black exec of Thomas Black decd to Samuel Smith of Granville Co., for 206 lbs, 217 A s side Sergeant's Cr adj Reuben Taylor, Abraham Turner, Joseph Turner, crossing the great road, William Farrar. 10 Feb 1794. Wit: H. Haralson, Robert Black.

190-1 Adam McNeeley to Hardy Wells, for 100 lbs, 153½ A adj Jones. 10 Feb 1794. Wit: Risdon Fisher, Richd Burch.

191-2 Thomas Barnett to Richard Bearden, for 65 lbs, 118 A on Jents Cr. 4 Nov 1793. Wit: Peter Bennett, Silvanus Stokes, John Chambers.

192-3 Seth Moore to William Allen, for 100 lbs, 375 A adj James Davey, Davy Allen, Hezekiah Stone, Yancey Bailey, Gabriel Davy decd. 7 Jan 1794. Wit: Hezekiah Stone, Memucan Allen.

193-4 Hugh Barnett Jr. to Arthur Brooks Sen., for 100 lbs, 202 A both sides Adams Cr adj John Barnett. 5 Feb 1794. Wit: Hez Stone, Jno Barnett.

194-5 Theodorick Johnston to Thomas Jeffreys of CC, for 40 lbs 18 sh 9p, 141 A on McFarland Cr of Hico adj John Chambers, widow Love, Joseph Barnett. 5 Mar 1794. Wit: J. A. Gunn, Robert Black.

196 James Jay to Paul Jeffreys, for 120 lbs, 68 A both sides Flat R adj Green, Cameron, Neeley. 18 Mar 1794. Acknd.

196-7 Coleman Clayton to Robert Paine, for 40 lbs, 180 A on Adams Cr adj John Mann, Dempsey Moore - said land purchased of William Paine who had grant from State 10 Nov 1784. 12 Feb 1794. Wit: William Paine, James Paine.

198 Robert Mitchell of CC to Daniel Malone of same, for 50 lbs, 120 A in Person Co. on Bushy Fork of Flat R adj Orange Co. line, Aldridge, William Waite, Going, Burch, Durham, Benjamin Wheeley - it being ½ of tract granted Mitchell 18 May 1789. 27 July 1793. Wit: Jno Douglas, Ben Douglas, Will Lea.

199 James Jay to Paul Jeffreys, for 230 lbs, 130 A n fork Flat R & Richland Cr adj John Satterfield, William Neeley, William Jay Sen. 18 Mar 1794. Acknd.

200 Henry Fuller of CC to Nehemiah Fuller, for 5 shillings & valuable consideration, a gift of 116 A on Stories Cr adj Jesse Fuller, William Fuller. ND -Acknd.

200-1 John Browning of Green Co., GA, to John Ravant of CC, for 133 lbs 6 sh 8 p, 526 A on Stories Cr adj Jesse Watson, Edward Clay, Benjamin Hatcher, David Mitchell. 2 Nov 1791. Wit: David Boring, Joshua Browning.

201-2 David Halliburton of Wake Co., NC, to Charles Halliburton of Person Co., for 100 lbs, 356 A on Mayo Cr adj Jesse Rogers, Richard Andrews, John Baird. 20 Dec 1792. Wit: John Humphries, John Halliburton, David Delk.

203-4 William Paine & Prudence his wife to John Sneed, for 200 lbs, 650 A on Adams Cr adj Joseph Gill, John Wilson, Drury Abbott, James Paine - said land a grant from State 10 Nov 1784. 14 Feb 1794. Wit: Thomas Moore, Gabriel Bumpass.

204-5 Edward Atkinson, sheriff of Person Co., to Jacob Cozart of Granville Co., for 40 lbs 1 sh, 300 A on little Cr of deep cr of Flat R adj James Anderson, Willis Roberts, Jesse Meadows - sold by court order for sale of tenements of James Burch & Blackmore Parker to satisfy judgment obtained by Arthur Moore. 2 June 1794. Acknd.

205-6 Littleton Johnston to Edmond Bennett Deshazo, for 52 lbs, 105 A on Castle Cr adj Charles Allen, William Guthrie, James Guthrie, John Neel. 27 May 1794. Wit: J. Johnston. Thed Johnston.

207 John Carlton to James Patterson, for 20 lbs, 20 A on Gents & Marlows Creeks adj Abel Howard, said Patterson. 8 Aug 1793. Wit: Josias Chambers, Joseph Gregory.

208-9 John Warren to James Patterson, for 302 lbs, 233 A both sides Hico Cr adj David Ford, Hedgeman Warren, Henry Fulcher, William Stanfield, Henry Howard. 12 Sept 1793. Wit: H. Haralson, Thos Barnett.

209-10 Levi Sweeney to Abraham Davis of Orange Co., for 34 lbs, 17 sh, to satisfy debt due Davis, 3 feather beds, blankets, sheets, kitchen utensils; trunk, 2 chests, cattle; horse; 550 A adj Millington Blalock, John Cash, Merrit Stone, John Sweeny Jun. & Sen. 2 June 1794. Wit: William Dickens.

211-2 Roger Atkinson the Elder of Dunwoody Co., VA, to son Roger Atkinson Jun. of Chesterfield Co., VA, for love & affection, 172 A on Holt's mill cr n side Hico R adj Roger Atkinson Jun where John Rogers & Joseph Glenn now live - said land purchased of James McIntire Jr decd 29 May 1766 & recorded in Orange Co. 28 May 1793. Wit: Joseph Ponsonby, John Dodd.

212-3 Benjamin Cotnam to Benedictus Cotnam, for 5 lbs 10 sh, 25 A on Bluwing Cr adj John Baird, Buckner Rooks. 17 May 1794. Wit: Thomas Halliburton, Jacob Dickson, Buckner Rooks.

213-4 Benjamin Cotnam to Thomas Halliburton, for 18 Spanish milled dollars, 18 A e side Bluwing Cr adj Sandford, Dickson. 14 May 1794. Wit: James Jones, Robert Jones, John Halliburton.

215-6 Andrew Ferguson to William Tapp, for 300 lbs, 261 A on N Hico. 24 Mar 1794. Wit: Robert Dickens, William Dickens.

216-7 Benjamin Dickson to John Dickson, for 30 lbs, 310 A on Adams Cr adj Benjamin Egerton old line, Josias Dickson, Charles Allen old line, Lawrence Vanhook old line, William Paine, John Wilson - said land Dickson purchased of Philip Vass, sheriff. 3 Feb 1794. Wit: Josias Dickson, Josias Dickson Jun.

218-9 Edward Atkinson, late sheriff, to Simeon Cochran, for 60 lbs, negro fellow Punch - sold by court order against estate of Vincent Degrafenred & John Henry Pryor in suit favoring Josias Dickson to recover 30 lbs 7 sh. 24 May 1794. Wit: P. Bennett. On 24 May 1794, 40 lbs pd by James Cochran; balance due 60 lbs.

220-1 Jesse Ragan to Buckner Rooks, for 40 lbs, 125 A w side Bluewing Cr adj John H Burton, 1 May 1794. Acknd.

221-2 John Sneed & Suckey his wife to Charles Moore Jun. & Thomas Moore, for 89 lbs, 8 sh, 640 A on Adams Cr adj Joseph Gill, John Williams, Drury Abbott, James Paine - said tract granted to William Paine 10 Nov 1784 by State. 22 Apr 1794. Wit: Elizabeth Redd, Lemuel Sneed.

223 Richard Phillips of Lunenburg Co., VA, to Drury Jones, for 50 lbs, negro fellow Peter. 5 Oct 1794. Wit: Thos McNeil, Agness McNeil, Wilson Jones.

224-5 John Lea to Daniel Sergeant son of Joseph Sergeant decd, for 45 lbs, 13 sh, 4 p, 133 A on Cobb Cr adj John Campbell, James Sergeant. 13 Aug 1794. Wit: George Lea, William Lea.

225-6 James Patterson to Walter McFarland, for 175 lbs, 112½ A e side Gents Cr adj Joseph Beedles, Abel Howard, John Carlton, Ezekiel Haralson. 21 Oct 1793. Wit: Hez Stone, Tho Barnett.

227 John Rogers Sen. to grandson John Allen Debow (son of Frederick & Rachel Debow) for love, affection, & 5 sh, negro child Ned age 2 yrs now possessed by Rachel Debow. 29 May 1794. Wit: Arch Murphey, H. Haralson.

228 John Rogers Sen. to granddaughter Nancy May Debow (daughter of Rachel & Frederick Debow), for love & 5 sh, negro Sucke now in their possession. 29 May 1794. Wit: Arch Murphey, H. Haralson.

229 John Rogers Sen. to granddaughter Lucy Rogers Debow (daughter of Frederick & Rachel Debow), for love & 5 shillings, negro girl Easter about 7 yrs old. 29 May 1794. Wit: Archd Murphey, H. Haralson.

230 John Rogers to grandson Solomon Debow (son of Frederick & Rachel Debow), for love & 5 shillings, negro boy Mack about 6 mos old. 29 May 1794. Wit: Archd Murphey, H. Haralson.

231 John Rogers Sen. to granddaughter Milley Rogers Debow (daughter of Frederick & Rachel Debow), for love & 5 sh, negro boy Absolom about 5 yrs. 29 May 1794. Wit: Archd Murphey, H. Haralson.

232 John Rogers Sen. withdraws all claim to negroes Hanah & her children Nice, Phillis, Tom, & Jack and delivers same to Herndon Haralson (clerk) & Robert Black who has since married one of the orphans of Peter Gill decd - a result of court case brought by Herndon Haralson guardian of orphans of Peter Gill. 7 Oct 1793. Wit: Benjn Debow, Boswell Turner, Robert Walker.

233 John Rogers delivers above named negroes for sum of 800 lbs to lawful owners. 17 Oct 1794. Wit: Lark Johnston, Moses Turner.

234 Thomas Pool of Granville Co. to John Lawson of Person Co., for 20 lbs, negro woman Betty and her child Rose. 26 Jan 1793. Wit: James Wilson, Robt Sandford.

235 George Farrar of Edgefield Co., SC, to Robert Howard of Person Co., for 67 lbs, negro man David. 1 Nov 1793. Wit: J. Howard, Hiram Howard.

236 Mason Foley to Larkin Warren of CC, for 582 lbs, 6 negroes: man Carolina, woman Terry, boy Prince, mulatto boy Sol, small boy George & child Isham; also cattle; furniture; 2500 lbs good tobacco; 24 turkeys; plantation utensils. 21 Oct 1794. Wit: Stephen Stuart, Henrietta Foley.

237-8 Hardy Crews to Jacob Mooney, for 100 lbs, 291 A on Flat R & Deep Cr to Richland Spring Cr adj John Paine. 14 Nov 1794. Wit:R. J. Pool, John Cix.

238-9 Philip Hall Sen. to Burwell Green, for 50 lbs, 109 A on Sergents Cr adj John Fuller, William Sergeant, Seamore. 17 Dec 1793. Wit: M. Hall.

240-1 Joseph Palmer to Elijah Denby, for 500 lbs (rating each silver dollar at 10 shillings) 640 A adj Claim of Neal McAllister & including plantation where Palmer lives. 16 Sept 1793. Wit: James Walker, Joseph Traylor, William Prewit.

242-4 John Atkinson of Granville Co to Robert Dickens of Person Co., for 100 lbs which he owes Dickens, negro boy Glasgow; if sold over amt pd to Atkinson. 13 June 1794. Wit: Osborn Jeffreys, David Roberts.

245 Thomas Person of Granville Co. to Edward Atkinson of Person Co., for 50 lbs, negro boy Moses who was willed to Elizabeth Person his wife by John Atkinson decd of Person Co. 16 Oct 1794. Wit: David Womack.

246 Samuel Sneed to John Sneed, for ? , 137 A on Flat R adj James Rutherford. 2 Sept 1794. Wit: John SHurst, Phillip Sneed.

247-8 Hezekiah Dueast to Isaiah Dueast, for 100 lbs, 150 A on Gents Cr adj John Williams, Bird Pulliam. 29 Mar 1794. Wit: Hezekiah Stone, James Barnett.

249-50 John Ravens of CC to Henry Williamson of Person Co., for 100 lbs, 282 A on Stories Cr adj William Glenn, Jesse Watson, Edward Clay, Benj Hatcher, James Ravens. 18 Mar 1794.

251-2 Mary Ragan (or Rogers) to John Halliburton, for 21 lbs, 70 A s side Bluwing Cr at Dixon's Br. 21 May 1794. /s/ Mary Ragan. 26 May 1794. Wit: James Jones, Robert Jones, Owen Ragan.

Deed Book A
Page

253-4 Willis Nichols to Micajah Nichols, for 50 lbs, 362 A on Flat R adj Alexander Coughran, Osborn Jeffreys to Dry Br, Stephen Moore - said land granted 3 Mar 1779. Also signed by Priscilla Nichols. 26 Aug 1794. Wit: Anna Harrison, Jesse Satterfield.

255 Robert Wilson of Chester Co., Pennsylvania, to John Womack of Person Co., for $362, 181 A on Flat R. 29 Nov 1794. Wit: Jesse Womack, Thomas Wilson.

256-7 Joel Ledbetter of CC to Elijah Denby of Franklin Co., NC, for 150 lbs, 130 A on rocky fork Deep Cr of Flat R; also 50 A adj this to be taken from 350 A granted by State 10 Nov 1784. _ _ 1791. Wit: William Brechen, Meret Stone.

257-8 Roger Williams to Vincent Brann of CC, for 100 lbs, 250 A on Millstone Cr adj Rosebrook, James D. Hendley old line, Skeen. 31 Oct 1794. Wit: James Cochran, Robertus Carney.

259 Power of attorney - William Malone & Frances Malone his wife to father Daniel Malone to receive their part of estate of Edward Sanders father of Frances Malone. 3 Mar 1795. Wit: Joseph Taylor.

260-1 Josias Dickson to Seth Moore, for 100 lbs, 380 A on Adams Cr adj James Mitchell, Shephard now Charles Bostick, Charles Mitchell. 12 Aug 1794. Wit: John Dickson, Stephen Wood.

262-3 Miles Wells of Granville Co. to George Eubanks of Person Co., for 400 lbs, 423 A on S Hico adj Orange Co. line, Aron Christenbury, Archibald Hodges, John Rainey.. 2 Dec 1794. Acknd.

264-5 Dempsey Moore to James Williams, for 1000 lbs, 210 A on Flat R. 9 May 1793. Wit: John Gwin.

266 Abraham Brown to beloved son Josiah Brown, for love & affection, negroes Joe about 38 yrs, Obedience about 14 yrs; furniture; livestock. 20 Mar 1793. Wit: Isham Malone.

267-8 John Sweeney Sen. to Richard Holsomback of Orange Co., NC, for 100 lbs, 100 A on Deep Cr being part of tract surveyed for James Blackley in Orange Co., now Person. 18 Nov 1794. Wit: Levy Sweeney, Mary Walker.

END OF BOOK A

Page

1 Power of attorney - William Gregory of York Co., SC, to brother Joseph Gregory of Person Co. to reciver slave James willed him by his grandfather George Thompson of Goochland Co., VA from Robert Donaldson of Person Co., 24 Jan 1793. Wit: Abram Gregory, Samuel Mathews, James Hurtt.

2 William Gregory of York Co., SC, to brother Joseph Gregory of Person Co., for 75 lbs, negro man James. 24 Jan 1793. Wit: Abram Gregory, Samuel Mathews, James Hurt.

2 Robert Dickens to Jesse Dickens, for 49 lbs, 5 sh, negro slave Ebol. 6 Feb 1795. Acknd.

3 Solomon Duty of Lawrence Co., SC, for 10 lbs, to William Duty of CC, his right and claim to land agreeable to will of Matthew Duty. 9 Nov 1791. Wit: J. M. McGehee, Jacob Fuller.

3 Jacob Fuller to William Duty, for 10 lbs, his right & claim to land of Matthew Duty decd. 2 Jan 1795. Wit: Littleton Duty, B. Douglas.

4 Stephen Moore to Jesse Dickens, for love & affection, negro girl Silvia. 25 Dec 1792. Acknd.

4 Littleton Duty of Wilks Co., GA, to William Duty of Person Co., for 10 lbs, his right & claim to land of Matthew Duty. 29 Dec 1794. Wit: Reuben Ballard, Jacob Fuller.

4-5 Abraham Brown to son Josiah Brown, for love & affection, 190 A on Spring Br to Bushy Fork Br adj Jopling, Farrar. 9 Aug 1794. Wit: Clayton Jones, Isham Malone.

5-6 Frances Jones, Drury Jones, Wilson Jones, & John Brown - to Goodrich Jones, for 90 lbs, negro girl Nancy. 21 Aug 1794. Wit: Isham Malone, Henry Graves.

6 Thomas Petters Sen. of Mecklenburg Co., VA, to Thomas Petters Jun. of same, for 200 lbs, 247 A on Castle Cr in Person Co. 9 June 1794. Wit: (unreadable)

7 Samuel McMurray to Charles McMurray, for 110 lbs, 231 A adj Moravian Line, John McMurray, William Lowther. 26 Feb 1795. Wit: Martin Douglass, William McMurray.

8 Samuel McMurray to John McMurray Jr., for 100 lbs, 178 A adj Charles McMurray, William Duty, William Lowther. 26 Feb 1795. Wit: Loyd Vanhook, Joseph Gold.

9-10 Frederick Debow to John Davey, for 190 lbs, 215 A both sides s fork Cain Cr adj Solomon Deboe now Yancey Bailey, Stephen Oliver, Archd Murphey, widow McCain. 8 _ 1794. Wit: H. Haralson, Jos White, ? Davey.

10-11 Frederick Deboe to Stephen Olliver, for 77 lbs, 77 A on Cain Cr of Hico adj said Olliver. 2 Dec 1794. Wit: James Robertson.

11-2 Thomas Petters Sen. of Mecklenburg Co., VA, to Thomas Petters Jun. of same, for 200 lbs, 200 A on Castle Cr adj Ezekiel Haralson, Hurley old line, Fielding Lewis, John Hurley, Robert McFarling. 9 June 1794. Wit: William Huston, ? Huston, Sarah Huston.

13 William Shepherd to James Williamson, for 68 lbs, 19 sh, 6 p, which he owes Williamson, negro girl Lucy about 15 yrs. 17 Feb ? . Wit: Ed Atkinson, P.Bennett

14-5 Div land of Patrick Carnal decd among male heirs agreeable to his last will: to Richard Carnal 101 A adj Douglas Olliver; Hubbard Carnal 100½ A; Flemming Carnal 103½ A; Archd Carnal 102½ A adj Joseph Gholston, Douglass Olliver.
Total value 171 lbs - each child 42 lbs, 15 sh. 27 Nov 1794.
Commrs: H. Haralson, Jeremiah Warren, Goodloe Warren, Robt Moore, Mumford Megehee.

16 James Dowell to Levy Swainey, for 70 lbs, 476 A in new territory of Tenesy on Cumberland R adj Jesse Spilyard, John Turner, at Bear Cr. 3 Mar 1795. Wit: Richard Holsomback, William Dickens.

17 Mathew Daniel to James Saterfield, for 58 lbs, 200 A being all the tract granted by State 20 Dec 1779 on Flat R adj Robert Dickens. 2 Mar 1795. Wit: Jno Hall, Isaac Saterfield.

18-9 David Bazwell to Harison Standfield, for 109 lbs, 109 A e side Hico adj Allen Love, John Johnston, Robert Moore. 28 Feb 1795. Wit: J. McGehee, Danl McFarland, John Slate.

19 Elijah Denby of Franklin Co. to Joseph Palmer, in trust. for 300 lbs, 640 A where he did live in Person Co adj Johnston Steel, Robert Dickens, William McKissack, Benjn Jacobs - if debt not pd by Christmas 1796, it is to be sold. 18 Jan 1795. Wit: J. Dickens.

20-1 Thomas Petters of Mecklenburg Co., VA, to Samuel Cox of same, for 250 lbs, 200 A on Castle Cr in Person Co adj Ezekiel Haralson, Hurley old line, Fielding Lewis on the Chapel Path, John Hurley, Robert McFarland. 22 Dec 1794. Wit: Mary Crowder, Daniel Hix.

21-2 Robert Dickens to William Waite, for 250 lbs, 320 A n fork Double Cr of S Hyco adj William Brown, John Moore, John Blake, Samuel McMurry, Martin Cooper, John Hall - being grant #234 from State to Dickens & Waite in CC. 3 Mar 1795. Wit: Daniel Sergent, Jno Hall.

22-3 William Chambers Sen. to Hugh Barnett Jun, for 80 lbs debt due Barnett, for 10 shillings, 174 A on Stories Cr adj Henry Willis old line now Jacob Bull, Benj Haralson now Ezekiel Haralson, Paul Haralson. 3 Dec 1794. Wit: Josias Dickson, W?Beddles, ? Barnett. (Faded & torn edges)

24-5 Daniel McFarland to Harrison Standfield, for 107 lbs 10 sh, 107 A e side Hico adj David Bazwell, John Johnston, Joseph Turner, William Huston, on Campbell road, Robert Moore. 13 Jan 1795. Wit: J. Moore, J. M. Megehee, John Slate.

25-6 Joseph Traylor to James Hicks, for 50 lbs, 77 A on Deep Cr - said tract deeded him by Thomas Morrow. 17 Nov 1794. Wit: Mathew Griffin, Samuel Boggus, Daniel Hicks.

26-9 John Johnston (in debt to William Rainey for 116 lbs & to Thomas Jeffreys for 110 lbs plus other debts) to William Jeffreys of CC, for 5 sh, 200 A s side Hico said tract purchased of Daniel McFarland. 25 Feb 1795. Wit: B. Johnston, William Sergent.

29-30 Alexander Cochran & Samuel Cochran of Newberry Co. SC, to John Cochran of Person Co., for 135 lbs, their part of 262 A on Flat R which Alexander Cochran their father bequeathed to Alexander, Samuel & Mathew Cochran adj Stephen Moore, Robert Cates, Willis Nichols, Osborne Jeffreys, Micajah Nichols, James Cochran. 20 Nov 1794. Wit: James Cochran, Samuel Brown.

30-1 Abraham Brown to daughter Sarah Brown, for love & affection, negro woman Cloe about 36 yrs old and girl Amy about 19 yrs; feather bed, furniture. 20 Mar 1793. Wit: Isham Malone.

31 Abraham Brown to daughter Margret Brown, for love & affection, negro woman Dolly about 34 yrs old & Lucy about 15 yrs; feather bed, furniture, cow & calf; Dolly to serve Abraham Brown for his life. 20 Mar 1793. Wit: Isham Malone.

32 Thomas Petters Jun. of Mecklenburg Co., VA, to Samuel Cox of same, for 250 lbs, 247 A on Castle Cr. 22 Dec 1794. Wit: Godfrey Crowder, Mary Crowder, Danl Hix.

33-4 William Chambers to sons Davison Chambers & Benjn Chambers, for love & affection, all property & tenements. 28 Feb 1795. Wit: Mar? Haralson, Jacob Bull.

Deed Book B
Page

34-5 Joseph Palmer of Montgomery Co., NC, to William McKissack of Person Co.,
for 25 lbs, 51 A on Double Cr of Hyco adj John McCallister, Badget, Jones.
24 Jan 1795. Wit: Thomas McKissack, Thomson McKissack.

36 Francis Scoging to Alexander Graham, for 50 lbs, 50 A on Flat R adj Robert
Paine. 17 Mar 1794. Wit: David Vanhook, William Paine.

37-9 Henry Fuller to Henry Howard of CC, for 300 lbs, 100 A on Stories Cr adj
Wm. Carver, Marthew Long; 105 A adj John Crutcher, Peter Bennett - to be pd for
by 1796. 3 Mar 1795. Wit: Littleton Johnston, James Boswell, Peter Badgett.

40-1 Powel Parker to Richard Jones, for 27 lbs, 10 sh, 50 A on Tar R adj Isaac
Day, on wagon path from John Day to Jones; said land part of tract of Jonas Parker
decd. 10 Dec 1794. Wit: John Harris Jun., William Winsted.

41-2 Benjamin McNeill to Richard Duty of Granville Co., for 17 lbs, 87 A both
sides S Hico adj Duty, the Moravian line. 27 Nov 1792. Wit: Geo Duty, Thomas
McNeill.

42-3 Solomon Draper to Thomas Brann, for 83 lbs, 6 sh., 60 A on Sergent's Cr adj
Long, Thos Robertson. 6 Feb 1795. Wit: William Long, James Long, Abner Long.

43-4 Stephen Wood to John Wood Sen., for 150 lbs, (frayed) A e side Jents Cr
adj William Allen, Alen Love. 27 Jan 1795. Wit: Josias Chambers, Major Wood.

45 John Malone to William Mitchell, for 12 lbs, 12 A e side S. Hico adj David
Mitchell Sen.. 8 Jan 1795. Wit: George Burch, David Mitchell.

46 John Long to Jacob Bull, for 25 lbs, 100 A on Stories Cr & Adams Cr adj Bull
old line, Giles Trickey, Hugh Barnett, John Atkinson, Artha Brooks, James Long.
1 June 1795. Acknd.

47-8 William Lea Sen. to James Cochran, for $118, 116 A on S Hico adj William Brown,
John Bradsher, Cochran former land by deed of conveyance to his wife Anniss,
said land granted 3 Mar 1779. Wit: Ism Edwards, Namah Lea.

48-50 Thomas Barnett, sheriff Person Co., to Edward Atkinson, for 17 lbs, 10 sh,
200 A on Flat R adj Alexander Rose, John Payne, David Mitchell - sold by court
order to satisfy debt of William Glenn due Walter Alvis - 100 A with his home
plantation sold first to James M. Burton for 40 sh. 30 Oct 1794. Acknd.

50-1 John Paine to Robert Vanhook, for 500 lbs, 55½ A on Flat R adj William Glenn-
it being part of tract granted to Hosea Tapley by James Inness & Francis Corbin
who sold to Aron Vanhook and came to Laurence Vanhook by descent - then granted
to Robert McRaynolds, to Dempsey Moore & then to Payne. 2 Mar 1795. Wit:
Kindle Vanhook.

51-2 Henry McNeill of Person Co. to Hector McNeill of Dinwiddie Co., VA, in trust,
9 negroes: Patience, George, Buck, Jesse, Coleny, Cloe, Bithen, Phillis, Nance;
furniture; 200 A on Hico adj Burch, Dollarhide; livestock. 10 Mar 1795.
Wit: Alexr McNeill, Angus McNeill.

53-4 William Hunt to Henry Graves, for 200 lbs, 220 A except 1 A sold to Peter
Bennett to build a mill - it being part of tract purchased of Benjn Long Jan 1784
adj John Trickey. 1 Aug 1794. Wit: James Cochran, Wm. McKissack.

54-5 Sylvanus Stokes to Thomas Hargis, for ? , negro boy Roger of dark complexion.
7 Mar 1795. Wit: James Cochran, Thos Neeley.

55-6 Thomas Douglas to Benjamin Douglas, for 100 lbs, 100 A on S Hico adj Kindel
Vanhook. 7 Sept 1795. Wit: John Douglas.

56-7 Benjamin Douglas to Thomas Douglas, for 40 lbs & for 90 lbs due Thomas Douglas
Sen., 100 A adj Kindel Vanhook. 5 Sept 1795. Acknd.

16

Deed Book B
Page

57 Benjamin Williamson & Edward Williamson exec of Stephen Williamson decd to Henry Cooper, for 125 lbs, negro Harcolas age 18 yrs. 2 Jan 1795. Wit: Thos Neeley, L. Lea.

58 Buckner Wall of CC to Henry Cooper, for 55 lbs, negro boys Anderson age 8 and Jim age 6. 15 Sept 1790. Wit: Benjn Douglas, Jos Atkinson.

58-9 Richard Duty of Wilks Co., GA, to William Duty of Person Co., for 10 lbs, his claim & title to land willed by Matthew Duty. 29 Aug 1792. Wit: James McMurry, John McMurry.

59 John Sanders Whitley to George Lea, for 55 lbs, negro girl Phebe about 13 yrs of age. 18 Mar 1795. Wit: Henrietta Garrot, B. Douglas.

60 Gabriel Gunn to Samuel Glaze, for 75 lbs, negro man Jacob about 24 yrs. 28 Dec 1795. Wit: ? Holloway, James Robinson.

60-1 John Gordon & Thomas Pool of Granville Co., to William Duty of Person Co., for 180 silver dollars, negro girl Hettha. 22 May 1795. Wit: Sim Cochran, William Pool, Geo Duty.

61 John Gordon & Thomas Pool of Granville Co., to James Cochran of Person Co., for 230 silver dollars, negro Solomon. 22 May 1795. Wit: Sim^n Cochran, William Pool, Geo Duty.

61-2 John Gordon of Northumberland Co., VA, & Thomas Pool of Granville Co., NC, to Samuel McMurry, for 52 lbs, 10 sh, negro woman Cate. 3 June 1795. Wit: Drury Jones, John Gwin.

62-3 Thomas Pool of Granville Co. & John Gordon of Northumberland Co., VA, to Drury Jones, for 125 lbs, negroes Betty & her child Julle about 3 yrs old. 3 June 1795. Wit: William Rainey, James McMurry, Wilson Jones. Thomas Pool signs for self & for John Gordon.

63-5 John Armstrong of Orange Co. to Thomas Douglas of Person Co., for 90 lbs, 227½ A both sides of br of Cobb Cr near Hico the waters of Dan R - said tract described by deed from Lord Granville to William Churton 1 July 1755 & registered at Hillsborough; on 8 Mar 1756 was assigned to Francis Corbin, then from Thomas Douglas to Armstrong 1777 and registered in CC 1799, Book A page 274. 17 Mar 1795. Wit: Geo Lea, John Whitley.

65-6 Henry Lyon to John Phillips, for 40 lbs, 35 A on Flat R at Aldridge Cr. 7 Sept 1795. Acknd.

67-8 Paul Haralson to his son Lea Haralson, for 50 lbs, 103 A on Marlowe Cr of Hico. 1 Mar 1795. Acknd.

68-9 Paul Haralson to his son Major Haralson, for 50 lbs, 59 A on Adams & Marlowe Creeks of Hico adj Ezekiel Haralson old line. 3 June 1794. Wit: H. Haralson, Abner Haralson.

69-70 Wrice Beedles to Bradley Haralson, for 130 lbs, 155 A w side Stories Cr at school house br adj Hezekiah Duest, William Allen, Thomas Barnett, George Vaughan, Ezekiel Haralson, William Chambers. 1 Dec 1794. Acknd.

71-2 Ezekiel Haralson to Paul Haralson, for 40 shillings, 2.4 A w side Stories & Marlowe Creeks. 3 June 1795. Wit: H. Haralson, Eunicy Haralson.

72-3 John Newton to Moses Bradsher, for 47 lbs, 2 sh, 6p., 53½ A e side Rushy Br of S Hico adj Laurence Vanhook, Will Lea. 27 Apr 1795. Wit: Thos Neeley, Tho Carver.

73-4 Thomas Rainey to James Hamblet, for 20 shillings, 1 A on Cain Cr adj Moore. 1 June 1795. Wit: James Rainey, H. Haralson.

75-6 Charles Bostick to Matthew Daniel, for 166 lbs, 210 A on Henley Mill Cr of S Hico adj Darby Henley. 28 Jan 1795. Wit: Wilson Vermillion, Edwd Clay.

76-7 William Rainey of CC to John Campbell of Person Co., for 50 lbs, 65 A on Hico adj Fielding Lewis decd, Ponsonby, Haralson. 14 June 1794. Wit: Henry Priest, Patience Wilkerson, John Morgain.

77-8 William Hunt to Henry Graves, for 50 lbs, 30 A on Stories Cr adj William Carver - said land willed to Thomas Barnett by Benj Long decd & conveyed to Hunt 14 Jan 1791. 22 Apr 1795. Wit: Peter Bennett, Jas Cochran.

79-80 Andrew Buchanon to Shadrack Gentry of Halifax Co., VA, for 100 lbs, 200 A on Castle Cr adj John Neal, Garrot Gutry, Edmond Deshazzor. 8 Oct 1794. Wit: J. A. Buchanon.

80-1 William Hargis to Abraham Hargis, for 100 lbs, 100 A on Flat R. 10 May 1795. Acknd.

81-2 Artha Brooks Sen. to Joseph Tatom, for 42 lbs, 10 sh, 63 3/4 A on VA line; for 11 lbs, 13 sh 4 p., ? A. 14 Apr 1795. Wit: James Ray, David Brooks, John Brooks Sen.

83-4 Joseph Tatom to Artha Brooks Sen., for 11 lbs, 13 sh, 4 p, 17½ A adj David Brooks. 14 Apr 1795. Wit: James Ray, Robert Brooks, David Brooks.

84-5 John James to Andrew Buchanon Sen., for 50 lbs, 50 A on Gray's Br adj Charles Allen, James Tatom. 30 Sept 1794. Wit: James Buchanon.

86-7 Robert Cate to John Cate, for 10 lbs, 227 A adj James Dickens in black pond of snrong of Flat R - said land conveyed by deed from John Cate 10 Apr 176? and to John Cate from Earl Granville 20 Aug 1759. 29 May 1795. Wit: John Womack.

87-8 James Wilson to Nathan Ragan, for 100 lbs, 200 A on Mayo adj Lewis Parrot, Gabriel Davie - it being remainder of tract surveyed by William Waite for Wilson. 23 Apr 1795. Wit: Lewis Parrot, Reubin Parrot.

88-9 John Bairden to David Nutt, for 120 lbs, 100 A on Flat R adj Jones Griffin - it being part of tract granted by Earl Granville to Charles Williams who conveyed to Griffin & from him to John Knight. 2 Dec 1794. Wit: Alexr McMullen, John Carrington.

90-1 James Robinson to Josiah Dickson, for 50 lbs, 75 A on Hico & Cain Creeks adj Archibald Campbell old line, Debow old line. 25 May 1795. Wit: John Bozwell, Stephen Oliver.

91-2 Richard Oakley to William Oakley, for 35 lbs, 320 A on Little Cr adj Noles. 16 May 1795. Wit: Willis Roberts, Thomas Oakley.
93 Jesse Saterfield to William Saterfield, for a bond due Dyer Pierce for 25 lbs, negrp bpy Charley. 3 June 1795.

93-4 Mason Foley to Baird & Weisiger, for 112 lbs 13 sh 5 p., negro fellows Carolina about 35 yrs old and Thomas About 50 yrs - to repay debt due.15 Apr 1795. Wit: John Camp, Stephen Stuart.

94-5 John Gwin to John Walker, for 200 lbs, 200 A on Adams Cr crossing said cr. 2 May 1795. Wit: James Williamson, Isham Melone.

96-7 John Gwin to John Walker, for 200 lbs, 440 A on Adams Cr adj John Wilson, Josias Dickson, John Mitchell, Ambrose Hudgeon, John Man, William Man. 2 May 1795. Wit: James Williamson, Isham Malone.

97-8 George Johnston to William Lea, for 20 lbs, 30 A on S Hico adj Simon Doyle. 20 Mar 1795. Wit: J. Campbell, James Simmons.

Deed Book B
Page
98-100 George Johnston to James Simmons, for 20 lbs, 25 A on Cobs Cr adj Robert
Mitchell. 20 Mar 1795. Wit: J. Campbell, William Lea.

100-1 Benjamin Newton to William Farrar, for 50 lbs, 200 A both sides Stories Cr
adj Nehemiah Fuller, John Fuller, Henry Fuller, Atkinson, James Fuller.
10 Sept 1795. Wit: H. Haralson, Jacob Fuller.

102-3 Edward Clay to grandchildren Nancy May Rogers, Magdelon Tribue Rogers,
Rachel Essom Rogers, & Irlee Rogers - all children of Bird Rogers & Sarah W.
Rogers - for 10 sh & love, female negro Nance & her child Jane now possessed by
Bird Rogers & were delivered to them before Frederick Debow & Mary Clay 1 Oct
1794; said negroes to remain there until young son of Bird Rogers comes of age;
if any child die, negroes go to surviving children. 3 June 1795. Wit: Wm. Cocke,
B. Douglass, Frederick Debow.

103-4 Charles Pyron to Joshua Cate, for 200 lbs, 365? A on Flat R crossing Aldridge Cr it being tract granted by State. 8 Sept 1795. Wit: Thomas Ragsdale,
William Pyron, Isaiah Cate.

104-5 Div lands of George Rosebrook decd between his 2 grandsons: (1) George
Southard 102 A adj Vincent Brand, Edmund Hendley, Joseph Gold, value 40 lbs;
(2) Allen Fuller 102 A adj Edmund Lewis, George Southard, Joseph Gold, Wilson
Vermillion, value 60 lbs & he to pay 10 lbs to Southard; personal estate div
among these 2 also. 16 July 1795. Commrs: William Sergent, Wilson Vermillion,
Joseph Gold, Jas D. Hendley, Wm. Trotter

106-7 Robert Davis (Davies) to Richard Coleman, for 50 lbs, 150 A on Tar R adj
William Tapp, Thos Person. 6 Jan 1795. Wit: Samuel Bumpass, John Harris.

106a George Malone to Isaac Johnston of Granville Co., NC, for 40 lbs, 100 A on
Hico adj Woods, Willingham, Malone. 8 Sept 1795. Wit: Wm. Waite, Benjamin
Harrison.

107a George Malone to Isaac Johnston of Granville Co., for 105 lbs, 200 A on S
Hico adj Nathaniel Malone, Daniel Malone, Samuel Woods. 8 Sept 1795. Wit: Wm.
Waite, Benjamin Harrison.

108-10 Roger Atkinson of Dinwoody Co., VA, & Ann his wife to John Ponsonby of
same, for 400 lbs, 1880 A in 10 tracts in CC on Hico & its branches; 363 A
conveyed by Francis Wright 14 Oct 1772; 145 A conveyed by William Sergent & his
wife 28 Jan 1773; 55 A conveyed by William Sergent 21 Sept 1771; 356 A conveyed
by Samuel Bell & his wife 5 Sept 1771; 127 A conveyed by Samuel Bell & wife 24
Sept 1771; 155 A conveyed by David Maxwell 22 Oct 1771;; 106 A conveyed by Peter
Rogers 9 ? 1772; 147 A conveyed by Samuel Bell date unknown; 123 A conveyed by
Francis Wright date unknown; 303 A bought of John Wright date unknown.
17 Mar 1790. Wit: Thomas Atkinson, Daniel Cordell, Stephen Dixon.
Acknd in open court by Roger Atkinson 13 Jan 1795. Wit: Thomas Atkinson, John
Dodd, Robert Atkinson.

111-2 John Womack to Jesse Womack, for 1 lb., 181 A both sides Flat R. 8 Jan
1795. Wit: Shadrack Roberts, Hosea Tapley.

112-3 William Waite & Robert Dickens to George Malone, for 30 lbs, 100 A on Hico
adj Woods, Malone, Willingham. 26 Mar 1793. Wit: Isaac McCollum, James Willaimson.

113-4 Nathan Ragan to John Baird of Prince George Co., VA, for 131 lbs, 166 A
where Ragan lives with mill adj said Baird, Moses Street, William P. Pool, John
Holoway; also 6 A purchased of William P. Pool. 13 Apr 1795. Wit: Jno Glenn,
John Camp, Benedicktus Cotnam.

115-6 Benedictus Cotnam to Thomas H. Burton, for 6 lbs, 25 A w side Blewing Cr.
19 Dec 1794. Wit: Buckner Rooks, Jacob Dixon, Mary Jones.

Deed Book B
Page
116-7 Daniel Clayton to Artha Brooks, for 100 lbs, 200 A on Rosemary Cr.
10 Sept 1795. Wit: Richard C. Fuller, John Fuller.

117-8 James Long to Joseph Royster, for 62 lbs, 15 sh, 50 A on Sergents Cr.
1 Sept 1795. Wit: Wm. Long, Presley J. Draper.

119 James Long to Joseph Royster, for 12 lbs 15 sh, 10 A adj Reubin Newton, Thos
Robertson. 1 Sept 1795. Wit: Wm. Long, Presley J. Draper.

120-1 John Johnston Jun to Henry Fuller both of CC, for 50 lbs, 100 A on Stories
Cr adj Wm. Carver, Martha Long. 15 Jan 1788. Wit: J. Hurly, Reubin Long.

121-2 Richard Burch Sen. to Baylor Burch, for 50 lbs, 100 A on Hico adj George
Malone, Thomas Wilkerson, George Burch. 7 Sept 1795. Wit: Richard Burch Jun.,
Edmd Burch, Geo Burch, Philip Watkins.

123-4 Henry Lyon to Miles Wells of Granville Co., for 125 lbs, 353 A on Flat R
at Aldridge Cr adj Hargis, Dickens, Joshua Cates. 8 Sept 1795. Wit: Shadrack
Hargis, John Phillips.

124-5 David Ford to Mumford Ford, for 100 lbs, 82 A on the VA line adj Allen
Love, James Patterson, Hedgeman Warren. 2 Mar 1795. Wit: Josias Chambers,
H. F. Chambers.

126 Power of attorney - Zachariah Hill to John McMurray Jun. to transact all
business concerning land in Wilkes Co. on Clouds Cr, Oglethorpe Co., GA, which
Hill purchased of Obediah Bosworth - 275 A and to receive deed to sell land.
3 Mar 1796. Wit: James McMurray, Ben Douglass.

127-8 Hezekiah Stone to William Allin, for 100 lbs, 225 A both sides fork of
Adams Cr adj Charles Moore, Robert Allen, to Nory's Br. 30 Oct 1795. Wit:
Nancy Stone, Allin Cooper.

128-9 Hezekiah Stone to William Allin, for 100 lbs, 150 A on Mill Cr adj Drury
Allin. 31 Oct 1795. Wit: Nancy Stone, Allin Cooper.

129-30 Henry McNeill to Hector McNeill of Dinwoody Co., VA, in trust, 9 negroes
Peter, George, Jesse, Beck, Coloney, Cloe, Bythen, Philis, Nancy; also furniture
& 200 A on Hico adj Burch, Dolarhide mill; horses. If sold, money to satisfy
1050 lbs 6 sh 8p due Hector McNeill. 2 9 Aug 1795. Wit: Alexr McNeill,
Thomas Dyer, Angus McNeill.

131-2 Archibald Murphey of CC to John Campbell of Person Co., for $9, 9¼ A on
Hico Cr adj both men. 2 Dec 1795. Wit: John Pierson, Thomas M. Hamblett,
James Hamblett.

132-3 Jesse Dickens to William Cocke, for 117 lbs 10 sh, 100 A purchased at sheriff
sale 7 Dec 1795 where Hardy Crews now lives on Deep Cr of Flat R; also 640 A adj
the other on Tar R, Deep Cr of Mayo. 7 Dec 1795. Acknd in open court.

134-6 William Cocke sheriff to Jesse Dickens, for 186 lbs 14 sh, 100 A on Deep Cr
of Flat R; also 640 A on Tar R & Deep Cr of Mayo for 117 lbs 10 sh; sold by
court order as land of Hardy Crews favoring John Mutter. 7 Dec ? . Acknd.

136-7 Gabriel A. Gunn to Daniel Gunn & Nathan Scoging, for 500 lbs, negro fellow
Jacob about 24 yrs old, negro Moll age 17; livestock; negro boy Jack age 7;
furniture. 5 Mar 1794. Wit: Matthew Pitman.

137-8 Benjamin Douglas to Thomas Douglas, for 100 lbs, 100 A on S Hico adj Kindel
Vanhook. 27 Feb 1796. Acknd.

139-40 Thomas Douglas to Joseph Carney, for (amt unreadable), 10 A on Cobs Cr
adj Jos Douglas. 24 July 1795. Wit: Rhobartis Carney, B. Douglas.

140-1 John Walters to James Cochran, for 43 lbs, 167 A on Stories Cr - said tract
granted Edmund Low by State 30 Oct 1783 & purchased 20 Mar 1792 by Walters.
30 Oct 1795. Wit: Thos Neeley, Garnet Neeley.

142-3 Benjamin Newton to James Cochran, for 50 lbs, 108 A on Stories Cr adj Henry Fuller - said tract conveyed to Robert Paine by Robert Lytle, sheriff, 24 May 1774 & from Paine to Newton 18 Dec 1780; also 60 A adj Hamblin, Wm. Carver. 16 Nov 1795. Wit: Ism Edwards, Danl Chandler.

143-4 Peter Farrar to Benjamin Jopling, for 130 lbs, 350 A on Flat R adj Thomas Robinson. 1 Dec 1795. Wit: Jno Farrar, Nancy Jacobs.

145-6 William Pyron of CC to Benjamin Jopling of same, for 160 lbs, 150 A on a br of Flat R adj Person, Douglas, William Gately, Peter Farrar, Richard Jacobs. 12 Oct 1787. Wit: James Smith, Peter Farrar.

146-7 Roger Atkinson of Dinwoody Co., VA, to Joseph Jones of same, for 100 lbs, 240 A on Bold Br adj Thomas Person, said Jones, Robert Donaldson, Athy Brooks being land purchased of Meshack Gentry 24 Dec 1787 & registered in CC. 20 May 1794. Wit: Joseph Daniel, ? Warren, Roger Atkinson.

148-9 James Robinson to Josias Dickson, for 114 lbs, 189 3/4 A both sides Cain Cr of Hico adj Stephen Oliver, Frederick Debow, Campbell old line, William Gold, Patrick Carnal - said land purchased of Woolsey Pride 3 May 1784. 5 June 1795. Wit: H. Haralson, Byrd Wall.

150 John Farrar and Elizabeth Farrar his wife to Abraham Moore, for 100 lbs, 240 A on Flat R adj Josiah Brown, down Bushy Fork, James Farquhar. 2 Dec 1795. Wit: John Brown, Clayton Jones, John Moore.

151-2 Reubin Newton Sen. to Solomon Draper, for 60 lbs, 50 A both sides Sergent Cr adj James Long, Mary Duncan. 4 Dec 1795. Acknd in open court.

152-3 William Allin to Hezekiah Stone, for 100 lbs, 300 A on Stories Cr adj Allin Love, William Chambers, Hezekiah Duest, Henry Howard. 31 Oct 1795. Wit: Nancey Stone, Allin Cooper.

153-4 John Day to Sion Turner of Granville Co., for 50 lbs, 200 A on Tar R adj William Tapp, William Day. 4 June 1794. Wit: Robert Davie, Coleman Clayton.

154-6 James Patterson to Richard Carter of Halifax Co., VA, for 157 lbs 5 sh 6p, 233 A both sides Hico adj David Ford, Allen Love, Hedgeman Warren, Henry Fulcher, William Standfield, Henry Howard, Roger Atkinson. 17 Nov 1795. Wit: James A. Gunn, William Murrey, John Carter, William Scott.

156-7 Owen Ragan of Wake Co., NC, to Robert Jones of Person Co., for 7 lbs, 56 A adj said Jones, Robert Chamberlain, James Jones, John Halliburton. 2 Oct 1795. Wit: Benjamin Cotnam, John Halliburton.

157-8 George Darbey to daughter Elizabeth Darby, for love & affection & 5 sh, all household goods & wares now in her possession. 6 Aug 1795. Wit: William Phelps, George Elliott, Hugh Hemphill.

159-60 Joshua Johnston to daughter Anne Johnston, for love & affection, 300 A on Camp Br adj George Anderson, Vessey; the widow's dower excepted. 13 Mar 1795. Wit: Benjn Partee, Susanna Mincey.

160-1 Gideon Patterson of CC to grandsons Heartwell Miles, Thomas Miles, Byrd Miles, & Patterson Miles and to granddaughters Nancy Miles, Betsy Miles, Fanny Miles, for love & affection & 5 sh, negro woman Hannah, girl Nulty, boy Peter. 25 Sept 1795. Wit: B. Johnston, Robt Walker.

161-3 John Campbell, John Womack, Thomas Neeley, James Fuller, & Samuel McMurry - all commrs to sell part of land at the Court House it being part of 6 A conveyed 11 Dec 1792 by Dempsey Moore to James Jones, Goodloe Warren, Samuel Woods, John Womack, & Stephen Moore commrs to fix place for building CH & gaol on 29 Jan 1795- to Thomas Hargis, for 60 lbs 16 sh, 1.9 A adj CH lot, Nicholas Nelone, Dempsey Moore. 10 Sept 1795. Wit: Jas Cochran.

Deed Book B
Page

164-5 Risdon Fisher to James Rimmer, for 125 lbs, 200 A adj Wm. Gilson. 13 Oct 1795. Wit: Shadrack Roberts, Joshua Step.

165-7 Paul Jeffreys to Osborne Jeffreys, for 100 lbs, 520 A both sides s spring Flat R adj Samuel Sneed, Robert Cates, on Hoop Br at Orange Co. line, Coonrod Messer Smith - said land granted from State 4 Nov 1784. 6 Dec 1795. Acknd.

167-8 Powel Parker to William Winstead, for 30 lbs, 73 A on Tar R adj Richard Jones, Isaac Day at Meadow Br, John Day on wagon path, Bumpass old fields - it being part of tract surveyed for legatees of Jonas Parker decd. 10 Mar 1795. Wit: James Wilson, William Wilson.

169-70 Drury Allen to James Cochran, for 100 lbs, 249 A - parts of 190 A conveyed by Robert Dickens 25 Dec 1791, and 59 A a part of grant from State - on Flat R where Allen usually resides adj James Allin, William Forrest. 5 Jan 1796. Wit: Wm. Waite, John Brown.

170-1 Drury Allin to James Cochran, for 80 lbs, negro slave Charles. 4 Jan 1796. Wit: John Bradsher, William Brown.

171 Abner Robertson, in right of wife Nancy, to William Duty, for 10 lbs, all his right & claim to land of Matthew Duty decd agreeable to last will. 11 Sept 1795. Wit: Isham Edwards, Daniel Chandler.

172 Power of attorney - Charles Bostick to son Chesley Bostick to transact all matters in his interest as he is about to leave the State; especially in suit with Delilah South on acct of son Richard Bostick begetting a base begotten child. 13 Jan 1796. Wit: B. Douglas, Anness Cochran.

172-3 Articles of agreement between Benjamin Douglass & Christian Webb widow of Robt Webb decd & Watson Webb; Christian Webb to give up house & plantation where she lives to Benjn Douglas and all interest Christian & Robert Webb have in any of his estate who lived on said land - for 10 lbs proclamation money or $20 in hard money; land to be div between Loyd Vanhook & them within 3 weeks; B. Douglas to take possession after div. 26 Oct 1795. Wit: Mildred Hughs, Thos Douglas.

174 Joseph Beadles, William Beadles, William Stanfield, & Patsy Beadles to William Harding of Laurence Co., SC, two VA born negro girls Till & Milly for 122 lbs, 10 sh. 25 Feb 1797. Wit: Thos Barnett, Thos J. Chambers.

174-5 Henry McNeill to Alexander McNeill of Dinwiddie Co., VA, for 60 lbs, 150 A on Mayo which he purchased of James Buchanon adj Bedwell Satterfield, Hardy Crews, Thomas Claton, John Yarbrough. 14 Sept 1795. Wit: John Sykes, Angus McNeill.

176 Robert Jurdon of Orange Co., NC, to Ambres Harison Duncan of Granville Co, for 60 lbs, 100 A on Jents Cr of Hico adj Robert Walker. 28 Oct 1795. Wit: William McKissack, Pegy Pinkerton.

177-8 Herndon Haralson to John Delahay, for $49, 49 A on Castle Cr it being a grant from State 13 Oct 1783 adj Ezekiel Haralson old line, Robert McFarland old line. 1 Mar 1796. Acknd in open court.

178-9 Robert Dickens to Anthony Brown, for 300 lbs, 326 A near Deep Cr adj Charles Taylor, Genl Moore, Blalock. 1 Feb 17??. Acknd.

179-81 Hugh Barnett Jun. to William Chambers Sen., for 30 lbs, 104 A on Stories Cr adj Henry Willis, Jacob Bull, Burgus Haralson now Ezekiel Haralson, Paul Haralson - said land part of grant purchased of Earl Granville & recorded in Orange Co. 9 Dec 1762. 9 Mar 1796. Wit: Jos Dickson, B. Douglas.

181 Daniel Sargent to Edward Doyle, for 85 lbs, negro woman Lucy about 23 yrs of age, girl Sarah about 1 yr. 6 Jan 1796. Wit: B. Douglas.

22

Deed Book B
Page

182-3 Edward Doyle to Daniel Sargent Sen., for 116 lbs, 104½ A on Cobbs Cr of
N Hico adj Barnett Lea formerly William Lea, Stephen Sargent, James Lea, William
Lea. 6 Jan 1796. Wit: B. Douglas.

183-4 Stephen Sargent to Daniel Sargent Sen., for 10 lbs, 11 5/8 A adj Doyle old
line where he now lives. 6 Jan 1796. Wit: B. Douglas.

184-5 James Buckanon to Henry McNeill, for 50 lbs, 150 A on Mayo - said tract
purchased of Francis Scoging adj Hardy Crews, Thomas Claton, Yarbrough. 4 June
1795. Wit: Wm. Cocke, Beverly Glenn.

186-7 William Shepherd to Charles Mitchel, for 100 lbs, 168½ A on Adams Cr adj
Andrew Barnett, Richard Finch old line, James Mitchel on Hillsborough Rd.
7 Mar 1796. Acknd.

187-8 William Southward to James Williamson, for 100 lbs, 200 A on Stories &
Adams Creeks it being ½ of grant from State adj Robert Southward. 9 Oct 1795.
Wit: P. Bennett, Saml Hargis.

188-90 Goodloe Warren to John Pearson (Pierson), for 50 lbs, 200 A on Cain Cr adj
Hannah Farley, Samuel Johnston, Richard Carnal, Stephen Oliver, Hugh Hemphill.
2 Mar 1796. Wit: H. Haralson, Wm. Penick, John Davey.

190-1 Peter Fuller to Robert Allin, for 25 lbs, 28 3/4 A on Adams Cr adj William
Mann, John Gwin, said Allin. 27 Feb 1795. Wit: Hezek Stone, C. L. Mitchel.
Proved by oath Charles Mitchel.

191-3 Thomas Palmer Jun. & Joseph Palmer both of CC, to John Wheeley of same, for
15 lbs, 72 A on Flat R adj Daniel Malone, said Wheeley, Terrel, Edward Goins, Kelly.
31 July 1786. Wit: Richard Burch Sen., Ewd Goins.

193-4 Ambrose Hudgins to Francis Scoging (Scoggin) both of CC, for 40 lbs, 150 A
on Rosemary Cr adj William Southward former line, Jno Dinwoodie, Long - said
land purchased by grant from State of 300 A, 10 Nov 1784. 12 Oct 1787.
Wit: Jos(ias) Dickson, William Barnett.

195 John Wilson to Richard Wilson, for 50 lbs, 100 A on Flat R adj Dickens & Waite,
William Caddel, Thomas Farmer. 5 Mar 1796. Wit: Edward Goins, Jas Horton.

196-7 Mason Foley to Julius Justice of Halifax Co., VA, for 50 lbs, 100 A on
Whetstone Br adj Thos Johnston, John Justice, William Huston - it being part of
the land where James Stuart Sen. formerly lived. 6 July 1793. Wit: Y. Bailey,
John Gwin.

197-8 Seth Moore to Ann Walker, for 100 lbs, 380 A on Adams Cr adj James Mitchel,
Shepherd now Chesley Bostick. 1 Jan 1796. Wit: James Williamson, William P. Pool.

199 Ezekiel Haralson to Henry F. Chambers, for 50 lbs, 40 A on Stories Cr adj
Thomas Barnett, Paul Haralson. 21 Dec 1795. Wit: William Tulloh, Hzek Stone.

200-1 John Campbell, John Womack, Thomas Neeley, James Fuller, & Samuel McMurry -
commrs appointed by General Assembly 1793 in Fayetteville & in Raleigh in 1794
to sell part of land appropriated for use of Public Buildings for Person Co -
to Robert Paine, for 150 lbs(sold at public auction), 6½ tenth of an A at the CH
being part of 6 A conveyed 11 Dec 1792 by Dempsey Moore adj the gaol lot.
10 Sept 1795. Wit: Jas Cochran, J. Womack.

201-3 Drury Allin to Stokes Allin, for 50 lbs, 150 A on Double Cr of S Hico at the
dividing ridge of Flat R adj Robert Dickens, McKissack. 29 Dec 1795.
Wit: Charles Fooshe, R. Vanhook.

203-4 William Standfield to Robert Dickens, for 10 lbs 10 sh, 10½ A on Hico adj
said Dickens. 9 Mar 1796. Acknd.

204-5 Daniel Malone of CC to John Wheeley of same, for 30 lbs, 100 A on branches of S Hico adj John Terrel, Kelley. 13 June 1785. Wit: John Terrel, Isaac Rainey.

206-7 John Johnston to Edmund Dixon of Halifax Co., VA, for 180 lbs VA money or 300 lbs current money of NC, 200 A s side Hico Cr at e bank Sergent Cr to Debow ford adj Archibald Campbell, Joseph Turner. 29 Dec 1795. Wit: Ad Murphey, Robt Moore, Thos White.

207-9 Joseph Beadles to William Tulloh, for 100 lbs, 100 A on Hico adj Byrd Wall, William Standfield, James Gregory. _ _ 1796. Acknd in open court.

209-10 Abraham Rogers Turner to Samuel Smith Jun., for 80 lbs, 100 A on Sargent Cr adj Joseph Turner - also 1 A joining the mill. 16 Feb 1796. Wit: Phillip Vass, Littleton Johnston, Joseph Turner, B. Johnston.

210-2 Simpson Warrin of Laurence Co., SC, to Timothy Holt of Halifax Co., VA, for 20 lbs, 50 A n side Holt's Mill Cr& Dry Cr at Country Line Cr - it being land willed by his father. 6 Nov 1795. Wit: James Warrin, William Chambers, Nathaniel Guttrie.

212-3 Willis Nichols to Wright Nichols, for 10 lbs, 170½ A adj Osborne Jeffreys. Also signed by Priscilla Nichols. 5 Mar 1796. Wit: John Cate, Jno Sneed.

213-4 Joshua Cate to Richard Lyon, for 100 lbs, 200 A on Aldridge Cr adj Robt Dickens, John Lyon - a part of grant from State 16 Nov 1790 and part conveyed by Thomas Ragsdale. 8 Mar 1796. Wit: Isaiah Cate, John Pyron, Thos Kindrick.

214-5 John Lawson Sen. to John Lawson Jun., for 270 lbs, 250 A on Hico at Ramboe Br adj Roger Atkinson, Lord Lord. 8 Mar 1796. Wit: Robert Harris, David Lawson.

216-21 John Carrington of Orange Co. (in debt to John MacRae of Petersburg, VA, for 1230 12 sh 7 p. gold or silver) to John McRae Jr & Duncan MacRae, trustees, for 5 sh, 750 A in Person Co. purchased from Abraham Davis on Little Cr adj Glen, Moses Moore, Dickens, Evans on county line. Also 250 A in CC purchased of Arthur Moore on Nap of Reed at Granville Co. line adj Jacob Cozart, Abraham Maheris, David Roberts, Thomas Yokeley; also 300 A in Orange Co. on Flat R at the mill pass where it crosses the great rd adj William Ashley & purchased of James Carrington. If debt unpaid by 1 Apr next, ad placed in NORTH CAROLINA GAZETTE 20 days beforehand. 15 May 1795. Wit: William McQuiston, James Watson, Samuel Hill. Proved 22 Mar 1796 before John Estis in Orange Co; registered CC 28 July 1796; in Person Co 29 July 1796.

221-2 State of NC - # 79 to Robert Payne, for 30 sh per 100 A, 125 A on Adams Cr adj John Pain, Demsey Moore. _ 1794. Tract surveyed by William Waite, county surveyor; John Ravens & Coleman Clayton, sworn chain carriers.

222-3 Jesse Ragan to Lewis Wilkerson, for 33 lbs, 115 A both sides of br of Donaldson Cr adj Parish, Baird. 7 June 1796. Wit: John Dixon, Abel Parish.

223-4 John Atkinson of Montgomery Co., NC, to Edward Atkinson of Person Co., for 100 lbs, negro boy Glasgow about 16 yrs of age. 20 Feb 1796. Wit: Rd Atkinson.

224-5 George Fuller to Edward Atkinson, for 100 lbs, 125 A both sides Richland Cr of Hico adj John Atkinson old line. 4 Oct 1795. Wit: Isham Malone, Phillip Morgan, Rd Atkinson.

226 John Williams to Richard Bearden, for 8 lbs 6 sh 8 p, 10 A on Jents Cr adj Bearden. 6 May 1796. Wit: Cary Williams, John Williams Jun.

227-8 Simon Doyle to David Brechen, for 66 lbs, 150 A on the Moravian line adj widow Dollarhide, Chrisonberry. 7 Nov 1795. Wit: Baylor Burch, Phillip Watkins.

228-30 William Cocke, sheriff, to John Camp, for 15 lbs, 50 A adj Ben Wheeley, on Bushy Fork, Daniel Durham, Phillip Watkins. (Sold as good & chattels of Robert Humphreys to satisfy Baird & Weiseger.) 4 June 1796. Acknd in open court.

Deed Book B
Page

230-1 John Sykes to William Moore, for 75 lbs, 111 A on S Hico adj Henry McNeill, Burch, Hargis, Wilson Jones, Herndon Haralson. 23 Mar 1796. Wit: Wm. Cocke, Elijah Daniel.

232 William Chambers Sen. to Abner Chambers, for 100 lbs, 100 A on Stories Cr adj Hugh Barnett. 10 Mar 1796. Wit: Benjn Chambers, Divison Chambers.

233 Ezekiel Haralson to John Beadles, for 50 lbs, 50 A on Stories Cr adj Bradley Haralson. 8 Jan 1796. Wit: Hezh Stone, Abner Chambers.

234-5 Drury Allen to Josiah Allen, for 60 lbs, 200 A on Flat R adj Robt Dickens, Stokes Allen. 29 Dec 1795. Wit: Charles Fooshe, R. Vanhook.

235-7 John Carrington of Orange Co. to Zebulon Veazey of Granville Co., for 1000 lbs, 200 A on Nap of Reed Cr being part of large tract of Thos Person on the county line; 640 A on Nap of Reed Cr & Cubb Cr adj Peter Cozart, Joshua Johnston, Claims of John Cock, Abraham Medares, Jacob Cozart now Carrington; 20 A on Nap of Reed Cr on Granville Co. line adj Jacob Cozart, John Cocke. 6 Mar 1796. Wit: Alexr McMullen, Jas Carrington Jun, Robert Dickens.

237-9 Augustin Bumpass for himself & as atty in fact for Dabney & Sarah Brooks and Elizabeth & James Bumpass of State of SC - all legatees of Edward Bumpass decd - to Anthony Brown of Person Co., for $600, 291 A on Tar R adj Samuel Bumpass. Power of attorney granted Bumpass registered Granville Co., Book C, p 295-6. 31 Mar 1796. Wit:Robert Dickens, Jesse Dickens, William Hicks.

240-1 John Justice of Rutherford Co., NC, to Littleton Johnston of Person Co, for 145 lbs, 118 A on McFarland Cr of Hico adj William Huston formerly Hugh Barnett, former land of Julius Justice, William Barnett old line, Walker. 15 Sept 1795. Wit: John Sanders, Julius Justis.

241-2 William Standfield to William Chambers of Lunenburg Co., VA, for 500 lbs, 209 A both sides Hico Cr adj Bird Wall. 26 Apr 1796. Wit: Josiah Dickson, Thos J. Chambers.

243-4 State of NC - #80 - to Loyd Vanhook & Watson Webb, for 30 sh per 100 A, 183 A on S Hico adj Matthew Price, James McMurray, James Johnston, Thomas Neeley, Thomas Wilson. 26 Mar 1795.

244-5 Reuben Parrot of CC to Francis Scoging, for 100 lbs, 106 A on Hico - a part of tract purchased of Richard Wright as by grant from State 10 Nov 1788, adj Chesley Bostick, Carter Lea, the Moravian line, Charles Bostick, Darba Henlie, James Dunbar Henlie. 1 Sept 1791. Wit: Wilson Vermillion, Carter Lea.

246 Michael Robinson of Orange Co., NC, to David Robinson of Person Co, for 72 lbs, 353 A on lick Cr of Flat R adj Charles Robinson, William Cocke, William Armstrong. 1 June 1796. Wit: Wm. Cocke, Charles Robinson.

247 John Price to Richard Burch Jun., for 100 lbs, 200 A on Double Cr of Hico adj Wilson Jones, Reubin Taylor, Richard Burch Sen., George Burch. 17 Feb 1796. Wit: Wm. Mitchell, Thos Wilkerson, John Hargis.

248-9 Thomas Rainey of CC to William Rice of Halifax Co., VA, for 250 lbs, 356 A on Cain Cr adj Archibald Murphey, orphans of Joseph Moore decd, James Hamblet. 22 July 1796. Wit: Isaac Johnston, Byrd Rodgers, Y. Bailey.

249-50 James Rainey to Thomas Rainey, for 200 lbs, 357 A on Cain Cr whereon Thomas Rainey lives adj Archibald Murphey, John Moore (son of Joseph Moore decd), Thomas M. Hamblet, Frances Hamblet. 24 Nov 1793. Wit: William Rainey, Betty Rainey, James Hamlett.

250-2 George Black to Edmund Dixon exec of John Black decd, for 5 lbs, 5 A on Hico adj Samuel Smith - it being tract John Black decd onveyed to George Black by mistake - conveyed for use of orphans of John Black decd. 18 July 1796. Wit: H. Haralson, J. Campbell, Robert Moore.

252-3 William Waite to Richard Carnal, for 34 lbs 5 sh, 68½ A on Cane Cr adj widow Carnal, Goodloe Warren. 5 Sept 1796. Wit: Thos White, James Hamblett.

253-4 John McVay to William Morrow, for 60 lbs, 100 A on Tar R adj John Day. 3 Mar 1796. Wit: William Wilson.

254-5 John Wood Sen. to Richard Holloway, for 75 lbs, 100 A on Gents Cr adj Hezekiah Stone, Allen Love. 4 Feb 1796. Wit: Hezh Stone.

256-7 Reubin Long to Peter Bennett, for 159 lbs 5 sh, 209 A on Stories Cr. 2 Feb 1793. Wit: Jno Johnston, Samuel Harris.

257-8 Abraham Moore to Obadiah Pearce, for 250 lbs, 200 A on Flat R adj Peter Farrow, Abraham Brown at the Bushy Fork. 8 Sept 1796. Acknd.

258-9 John Robertson to John Pearson, for 75 lbs, 93 A on Hico on main rd - being part of large tract willed him by Hugh McKain adj Robert Black, John Oglesby, Joseph Moore, Wirght's old path. 16 Mar 1796. Wit: William Rainey, H. Haralson, George Black.

260-1 Edmund Dixon **exec** John Black decd & (no name) of Halifax Co., VA, to Henry Mitchel of same, for 171 lbs, 320 A on Sergent Cr adj Samuel Smith, Joseph Turner, crossing McFarland Cr, Joseph Dixon, Robert Walker, Thomas Roberson, Benjamin Johnston - excluding part of mill seat. 23 Aug 1796. Wit: Thos White, Hubbard Carnal, Archd Carnal.

261-2 Thomas Moore Hamlett of CC to James Hamlett of Person Co., for 100 lbs, 138 A on Cain Cr - said land allotted him from estate of James Hamlett decd adj Hugh Hemphill. 25 July 1796. Wit: Ad Murphey, Alex Murphey, H. Haralson, Rice, James Hamlett, Joseph Moore.

263 John Wheley(Wheeley) to Absolem Johnson, for 65 lbs, 171½ A on Flat R adj Shadrack Roberts, Daniel Malone, Durram. 1 Sept 1796. Wit: Wm. Mitchel, Elisabeth Mitchel.

264-5 Robert Mitchel of CC to Benjamin Wheeley of Person Co., for 36 lbs, 120 A adj Durham, Christenbury, Wells,to county line. 19 Feb 1794. Wit: Phillip Wadkins, Sally Wadkins.

265-6 Burrell Green to Benjamin Douglas, for 50 lbs, 109 A on Sergent Cr adj George Hall, Carver, William Sergent. 2 Sept 1796. Wit: Jno Hall.

266-7 John Douglas to Pulliam Williamson, for 100 lbs, 94½ A both sides Cobb Cr in Person & Caswell Cos adj Carney, John Armstrong, Burch old shop. 5 Sept 1796. Acknd.

267-8 State of NC - #83 - to William Carver, for 50 sh per 100 A, 50 A on Stories Cr adj said Carver, James Cochran. 20 Dec 1796. Surveyed 22 Nov 1796. Ben Carver & Robert Carver, sworn chain arriers.

269-70 Commrs to sell part of land at CH to Nicholas Delone,of CC, for 106 lbs, 6½ tenth A at east corner ofCH(sold at public auction) near Dempsey Moore's chimney adj Thomas Hargis. 10 Sept 1795. Wit: James Cochran.

271 John Jones of Halifax Co., VA, to Josias Carver of Person Co., for 20 lbs, 100 A on Jents Cr. 7 July 1796. Wit: Thomas Barnett, Mary Barnett.

272-3 John Holloway Jun. & William Holloway to John Holloway Sen., for 100 lbs, 640 A both sides Dish Water Cr adj Nathan Ragan. 5 Dec 1796. Wit: William McDaniel.

273-4 John McMurry Jun. to William Cocke, for 104 lbs 8 sh, 178 A on Double Cr adj Charles McMurrey, Wm. Duty, William Souther. 20 Oct 1796. Wit: Thos Rountree, James Wilson.

Deed Book B
Page
275-6 William Rice to Archibald Murphey of CC, for 77 lbs, 6/8, 119 A s fork Cain Cr adj Joseph Moore decd, heirs of Danl Duncan decd, on great rd from red house to Deboe fork on Hico adj said Murphey, Herndon Haralson. 8 Nov 1796. Wit: William Rice, Alexr Murphey.

276-7 Archibald Murphey of CC to William Rice of Person Co., for 44 sh, 3¼ A on Cain Cr adj said Rice, Murphey old line. 8 Nov 1796. Wit: Alexr Murphey, William Rice.

277-8 William Farrar to John Harris Jun., for 87 lbs 10 sh, 102 A on Hico Cr adj Thomas Black, George Black, Andrew Forgason. 7 Mar 1796. Wit: Moses Bradsher, Tho Neeley, John McFarland.

278-9 Thomas Miles to William Standfield, for 100 lbs, 192 A on VA line, adj William Stuart, Bird Wall, Samuel Warren. 17 June 1796. Wit: Epenetus Winders, Joseph Bearden, Hezh Stone.

280 Zebulon Veazey to John Baldwin of Orange Co., NC, for 60 lbs, 200 A on Camp Cr on Orange Co. line adj George Anderson, Brown, Peter Cozart, Kiddy Johnston. Also signed by Anne Veazey. 14 Nov 1796. Wit: James Veazey, Josiah Stephenson.

281 Robert Jones & Mary his wife to John Halliburton, for 10 sh, 28 A adj James Jones, Robert Chamberlain, Robert Jones. 17 Jan 1796. Wit: Benjamin Cotnam, Ambrose Jones.

282 Zebulon Veazey to Benjamin Partee, for 12 silver dollars, 11 1/3 A on Camp Cr on Orange Co. line adj said Partee. 11 Mar 1796. Wit: James Veazey, John Veazey, Earle Partee.

283-4 Samuel McMurry & Elisabeth his wife to Thomas Sneed, for 405 lbs, 10 sh, 411 A on Double Cr of Hico adj Thomas Badget, John McMurry, the Moravian line, Adam McNeeley. 15 Oct 1796. Wit: John Pharoah, William McMurry, William Duty, William Badgett.

284-5 David Nutt of Orange Co., NC, to John Bairden of Person Co., for 75 lbs, 100 A on Flat R adj Long, Jones Griffin - being part of tract granted by Earl Granville to Charles Williams & from Williams to Jones Griffin, and from him to John Knight, then to Robert Dickens & Johnathon Parker, from Dickens to John Bairden and then to David Nutt. 3 Dec 1786. Wit: Joshua Cate, John Knight.

285-6 Edward Atkinson to Matthew Daniel, for 25 lbs, 200 A on Flat R it being tract sold by Thomas Barnett, sheriff, to Atkinson 10 Dec 1794 adj Alexander Rose, John Paine, David Mitchel. 25 Jan 1796. Wit: G. A. Gunn, Anselem Bugg.

286-7 Benjamin Partee to William Brown, for 100 lbs, 200 A on Camp Cr on Orange Co. line adj Peter Cozart, land purchased of Veazey. 24 Nov 1796. Wit: Zebulon Veazey, James Veazey.

288-9 James Williamson to William Hamlen, for $110, 200 A both sides Stories Cr adj Nehemiah Fuller, John Fuller, Henry Fuller, Atkinson. 30 Nov 1796. Wit: Francis Howard, Jacob Fuller, William Hamlin Jun.

290 Matthew Price of CC to John Dinwoodie of same, for 40 lbs, negro girl Gude. 6 Sept 1796. Wit: Zachariah Evans, John Melear.

290 John Lemay of Granville Co. to David Barnett of Person Co, for 65 lbs, negro soman Liddy age 25 yrs. 12 Dec 1796. Wit: Wm. Scott, Jesse Ragan.

291 Ralph Williams to Benjamin Tolar, for 40 lbs 18 sh., negro boy Harry. 4 Oct 1796. Wit: R. Vanhook, Jab Vanhook. This obligation void if Toler repay debt due Williams.

292 Benjamin Tolar to Mary Williams daughter of Ralph Williams & granddaughter of Ann Tolar my wife, for affection & 5 shillings, negro girl Jude age about 14 yrs - possession to take place at death of wife or at her pleasure. 9 Mar 1797. Acknd.

27

Deed Book B
Page

293-4 Robert Dickens to William Dickens of Granville Co., for 700 lbs, 1/5, 18 negro slaves:Luke, Jacob, Pertina, Nan, Dol & her child Ben, Fanny and her child Anderson, Philip, Daphne, Tresey, Tom, Seth, Ruth, Phillis, Lieia, Abraham, Perline; one white horse,; if debt pd by 1 Jan 1804, this bill of sale void. 29 Sept 1796. Wit: Anthony Browne.

294-5 Jesse Womack to John Brown, for $500, 181 A on Flat R. 9 Sept 1796. Wit: J. Womack, Danl Farmer, Jno Hall.

295-6 John Fuller Sen. to Josias Cerver, for 20 lbs, 150 A on Stories Cr adj William Carver, Thos Carver. 15 Apr 1796. Wit: Wm. Long, Joseph Royster.

297 Richard Hargis to Robert Hester, for $42, 42 A on S Hico adj Hester. 6 Mar 1797. Wit: William Hargis Jun., Joseph Hargis.

298 Charles Bostick to Thomas Hood of Dinwoodie Co., VA, for 10 lbs, 100 A on Mayo adj John Pain. 16 Nov 1795. Wit: Samuel Cox, Richard Allen.

299 David Brechen to Elizabeth Fenn, for 40 lbs, 70 3/4 A on S Hico which he purchased of Simon Doyle adj Adam McNeeley. 17 Feb 1797. Wit: Henry McNeill, Angus McNeill, Gabriel Fenn.

300-1 Littleton Johnston to Julius Justice, for 70 lbs, 148 A adj William Huston, Wm. Barnett old line, Walker. 9 Jan 1796. Wit: Richd Beardon, Nancy Beardon.

301-2 John Carlton to Walter McFarland, for 50 lbs, 42 A on Marlowe Cr. 7 Mar 1796. Wit: Hezkh Stone, Thos Barnett.

302-3 Julius Justice to Josias Dickson, for 50 lbs, 148 A on Hico adj William Huston, Theod Johnston old line, Robert Walker; said land purchased of Littleton Johnston 9 Jan 1796. 5 May 1796. Wit: John Camp, Elijah Daniel.

304 Reuben Long to John Long, for 41 lbs 10 sh, 100 A on Stories Cr. 29 Nov 1796. Wit: Samuel Harris.

304-5 John Cash to Moses Cash, for 70 lbs, 200 A on Little Cr, Cubb Cr, & Camp Cr adj Joshua Johnston, Arthur Moore. 6 Mar 1797. Acknd.

305-6 John Clift to William Saterfield, for 50 lbs, 100 A on Henley's Mill Cr adj Edmund Lewis old line, Wilson Vermillion, Charles Bostick. 8 Oct 1796. Wit: Jas Cochran, Isaac Saterfield.

307 William Green of Warren Co. to Charles Taylor of Person Co., for $600, 150 A e side Deep Cr. 21 Dec 1796. Wit: Stephen Moore, Anthony Browne.

308 Lewis Wilkerson to William Lowhead, for 5 lbs, 2 A adj Wilkerson. 7 Mar 1797. Wit: Robert Harris, Elizabeth Harris.

309-10 Robert Dickens to Charles Taylor, for $100, 107.4 A on Deep Cr adj Green, Stephen Moore. 28 Oct 1795. Wit: Osborne Jeffreys, John Clixby.

310-1 Benjamin Johnston to William Trotter, for 40 lbs, 99 A on Skeen's Mill Cr & S Hico adj Vincent Brann, Solomon Draper, said Trotter. 11 Nov 1796. Wit: J. Campbell, Sharp Willingham, John Johnston.

311-2 Vincent Brann to William Featherstone, for 55 lbs 13/4, 85 A on Hico adj Thos Talbart, William Trotter, Solomon Draper, William Sergent. 28 Jan 1797. Wit: H. Haralson, Wm. Trotter.

313-4 Joseph Turner to Samuel Smith, for 200 lbs, 220 A on McFarland Cr adj Hugh Robertson, John Black, McFarland. 26 Oct 1796. Wit: J. Campbell, Sharp Willingham

314-5 James Cochran to John Smith Hust, for 120 lbs, 249 A in two tracts: 190 A is same conveyed to Drury Allen by Robert Dickens 25 Dec 1791; 59 A part of tract granted Allen by State on Flat R where Allen lived adj Josiah Allen, Stokes Allen, William Forrest. 28 Jan 1797. Wit: Samuel Sneed, Thomas Sneed.

Deed Book B
Page

315-6 John Brown to Josiah Brown, for 140 lbs, 181 A on Flat R. 20 Sept 1796.
Wit: J. Harris, Clayton Jones.

316-8 William Cocke, sheriff, to Thomas Jeffreys of CC (to sell goods & chattels
of Wm. Phelps to pay debts due Jefferys), for 25 lbs, 1sh, 100 A on Winne Cr adj
George Elliott, Hugh Hemphill. 1 June 1796. Acknd in open court.

318-20 Commrs to sell part of land appropriated for public bldgs, to Thomas Hargis,
for 30 lbs, 1.1 A at the CH being part of 6 A conveyed 11 Dec 1792 by Demsey
Moore adj Jail lot. 10 Sept 1795. Wit: Jas Cochran.

320-1 Thomas Brann to his son John Brann & his wife Catherine Brann, for 5 lbs,
60 A on Sergent's Cr adj Joseph Royster, Thomas Robertson. 9 Jan 1797. Wit:
Solomon Draper, Joseph Royster, Wm. Long.

321-2 Benjamin Cochran to George Duncan, for 65 lbs, 200 A adj Thomas Barnett,
Sergent, Mrs. Pinkerton, John Chambers. 20 Feb 1796. Wit: William Shepherd,
Thos Jeffreys.

323-4 John Clixby to William Barton of Granville Co., for 100 lbs which he owes
Barton & for 5 shillings, 200 A conveyed Clixby by Robert Dickens; if debt pd
deed is void. 10 Oct 1796. Wit: Thomas Hargis, La. Hargis.

325-6 Sylvanus Stokes to James Mullins, for 19 lbs, 158.2 A n side Hico adj Yancey Bailey, John Davey, Edmd Dixon. 20 Mar 1796. Wit: Wm. Penick, Sally Bailey.

326-8 James Mullins to John Person, for 190 lbs, 158.2 A on Hico adj Yancey
Bailey, John Davie, Edmd Dixon. 7 Feb 1796. Wit: Richard Bearden, P. Bennett,
Davison Chambers.

328-9 Samuel McMurry to Drury Jones, Goodrich Jones & Wilson Jones, for 20 lbs,
40 A on Double Cr adj Jesse Jones decd, Thomas Sneed. 18 Nov 1796. Wit: Hardy
Wells, Josiah Brown.

329-30 Josiah Brown to John Brown, for 71 lbs 10 sh, 137 A on Bushy Fork adj
Abraham Moore, Thomas Farmer, Wm. Jopling. 30 Sept 1796. Wit: J. Farrar,
Clayton Jones.

331-2 Ezekiel Haralson to Henry F(elson) Chambers, for 5 lbs, 16 sh, 10 A on
Marlowe Cr adj said Chambers, Thomas Moten Junr. 6 Mar 1797. Wit: Epenetus
Winders, Richd Bearden.

332-3 Ezekiel Haralson to Thomas Morten(Moten), for 16 lbs, 15 A on Marlowe Cr.
1 Mar 1797. Wit: Richd Bearden, Epenetus Winders.

333-5 William Stuart to Munford Megehe, for 55 lbs, 100 A n side Hico adj both
men, Bird Wall. 13 Feb 1797. Wit: John M. Mdgehe, Joseph Megehe.

335-6 Moses Street Senr to William Street, for 100 lbs, 260 A both sides Mayho Cr
adj William P. Pool, John Baird, Francis Lawson near the place of Baptizing.
31 Jan 1797. Wit: Isaac Vanhook, John Scoging, Elisabeth Vanhook.

336-8 Moses Street Sen. to Moses Street Junr., for 100 lbs, 312 A on Mayo Cr adj
William Street, Francis Lawson, John Lawson, Moses Springfield, widow Davie, John
Baird, Wm. P. Pool. 31 Jan 1797. Wit: Isaac Vanhook, John Scoging, Elizabeth
Vanhook.

338-9 Jesse Ragan to William Lowhead (or Lovehead) of Mecklenburg Co., VA, for
50 lbs, 320 A on Donaldson Cr adj Charles Halliburton, John Parish, Lewis Wilkerson. 20 Nov 1796. Wit: Josiah Mitchell, Robt Harris.

340-2 Stephen Sargent to John Campbell, for $616.50, 616½ A on S Hico & Cobb Cr
in two tracts - one part of grant from Granville of 206½ A, the other grant from
State for 410 A on 26 Nov 1793 adj Daniel Sargent Jun., David Sargent Sen., James
Lea, Richard Lea, the Moravian line, John Lea, John Mason. 27 Feb 1797. Wit:
H. Haralson, John McFarland, Art Mitchel.

29

343-4 Elijah Daniel to William Cocke, for 45 lbs 5 sh., 100 A on Gents Cr adj William Allen, Allen Love, it being tract owned by Stephen Wood & sold by execution brought by Baird & Weisiger. 1 Feb 1797. Wit: John Washington

344-8 William Cocke, sheriff, to Elijah Daniel (due to court order to sell goods & chattels of Stephen Woods for debt due of 39 lbs 14/5, in suit brought by Baird & Weisiger) 100 A on Gents Cr was taken in by sheriff adj William Allen, Allen Love and sold to Daniels for 45 lbs. 5 Mar 1796. Wit: John Watlington.

348-9 State of NC - # 84 - to William Hamlin, for 30 sh per 100 A, 100 A on Stories Cr adj William Hamlin Jun., George Hall, William Carver, said Hamlin. 20 Dec 1796. George Hall & William Carver, sworn chain carriers.

350-1 State of NC - #85 - to Benjamin Newton, for 30 sh per 100 A, 60 A on Stories Cr adj his own line, William Hamlin, William Carver. 20 Dec 1796. Geo Hall & Absn Walters, sworn chain carriers.

352-3 James Rankin & Elizabeth Rankin his wife to Edward Davis of Mecklenburg Co., VA, for 500 lbs, 460 A on Flat R both sides Dry Cr adj Gabriel Davey, John Payne, Robert Paine, John Womack. 3 Nov 1796. Wit: J. Womack, John Clixby, John Paine.

353-4 John Smith Hust to James Cochran, for 75 lbs, negro woman Sarah. 28 Jan 1797. Wit: Samuel Sneed, Thos Sneed. (Note: On some records this name is Smithhus†

354-5 John Holloway Sen. to William Holloway, for 100 lbs, 422 A both sides Dish Water Cr adj Nathan Ragan. 5 Dec 1796. Wit: William McDaniel.

355-6 Richard Bland Jun. of Nottoway Co., VA, to Robert Dickens of Person Co., for 165 lbs, 275 A on Flat R adj Paul Jeffreys, said Dickens, Tapp, Lyon. 9 Apr 1797. Wit: Anthony Browne, Wm. Waite.

356-8 William Cocke, sheriff, to Robert Gill (to satisfy judgment obtained by Jacob Slaughter against Wm. Dunkin & Ro Davis for 47 lbs 6/9) for 50 lbs, 200 A of William Duncan on Tar R adj William Tapp. 21 May 1796. Wit: Y. Bailey, Robert Howard.

359-60 Robert Gill to William Cocke, for 50 lbs, 200 A on Tarr R adj Wm. Tapp, Wm. Day - said land former property of William Dunkin. 22 May 1796. Wit: Y. Bailey, Robert Howard.

360-1 James Wells to Spence Mitchel, for 45 lbs 3/4, 53 A on Cobb Cr of Hico adj James Simmons, Arthur Mitchel, John Oglesby, William Rainey. 4 Apr 1797. Wit: H. Haralson, Art Mitchel.

362-3 Miles Wells of Granville Co., NC, to James Wells of Person Co., for 100 lbs, 186 A on Cobb Cr. 2 Mar 1795. Wit: John Gwin, R. Dickens.

END OF BOOK B

Page

1 Thomas Barnett Jun. to Jeremiah McEntire, for 50 lbs, 96 A on Ghents Cr on road from Peter Bennett's mill to George Duncan, Josias Carver. 16 Mar 1797. Wit: Josiah Carver, James Long.

1-2 John Paine to Thomas Clayton, for sundry services & 5 shillings, 90 A near Deep Cr adj James Paine Miller, David Allin. 4 Jan 1797. Wit: John Womack, William Browne.

2 Robert Dickens to Richard Bland Junr. of Nottaway Co., VA, for 165 lbs, 170 A on Gent Cr & Hico adj Howard. 9 Apr 1797. Wit: Arthur Brown, Wm. Waite.

3 Benjamin South to Thomas Talbert, for 100 lbs, 100 A on Henley Mill Cr of Hico adj William Trotter. 14 Nov 1797. Wit: B. Johnston, Edmund Henley.

4 Benjamin South to Thomas Talbert, for 50 lbs, 63 A on Henley Mill Cr & Hico adj Joseph Gold, William Trotter. 14 Nov 1796. Wit: B. Johnston, Edmund Henley.

5 Daniel Hicks to Benjamin Toller, for 100 lbs, negro Charles about 10 yrs old. 30 Jan 1797. Wit: P. Jeffreys, Jno Hall, An. Williams, Elisabeth Wade.

5-6 John Parrish to Abel Parrish, for 25 lbs, 50 A on Donaldson Cr adj John Baird, Lewis Wilkerson. 1 Mar 1797. Wit: Nathan Parish, Caner Parrish.

6-7 Josiah Brown to Ephraim Hawkins, for 20 lbs, 53 A on Bushy Fork & Cucumber Br adj Thomas Farmer. 30 Sept 1796. Wit: J. Farrer, Clayton Jones.

7-8 John Halliburton & Martha his wife to James Jones of Halifax Co., VA, for 25 lbs, 50 A on Blewing Cr adj James Jones, Pendergrass. 7 May 1797. Wit: Robert Jones, Thos H Burton, Ambrose Jones.

8-9 George Duncan to James Duncan, for 40 lbs, 80 A on Ghents Cr adj Josias Carver, William Sergent. 3 Sept 1796. Wit: Hezkh Stone, Josias Carver.

9 Peter Cozart to John Lingo of Granville Co., for 26 lbs, 83 A on Duns Cr, the Granville Co. line to the Orange Co. corner. 1 Jan 1796. Wit: John Cozart, Reuben Cozart, Zebulon Veazey.

10 Thomas Barnett Junr. to Josias Carver, for 50 lbs, 105 A on Stories Cr adj William Carver, George Duncan. 17 Mar 1797. Wit: James Long, Jeremiah McEntire.

11 James Hicks to James Cozart of Orange Co., for 150 lbs, 77 A both sides Deep Cr being tract conveyed him by Joseph Traylor. 14 Mar 1797. Wit: Job Green, Nicholas Green.

11-2 Miles Wells to Richard T. Lyon, for 7 lbs, 7½ A on Flat R at Aldridge Cr adj Lyon, John Phillips. 30 May 1797. Wit: William Roberts.

12-4 William Cocke, sheriff, to Elijah Daniel, for 45 lbs, 87½ A adj VA line, Allen Love, James Peterson, Hedgeman Warren - sold by court order to settle debt due Raird & Weisiger by David Ford. 5 Mar 1797. Wit: James Daniel, James Roberts.

14 Elijah Daniel to William Cocke, for 45 lbs, 87½ A adj VA line, Allen Love, James Peterson, Hedgeman Warren. 5 Mar 1796. Wit: James Daniel, James Roberts.

15 Charles McMurry to William Cocke, for 138 lbs 12 sh., 231 A on Double Cr adj Wm. Lowhead, the Moravian line, John McMurry Sen. 18 Oct 1796. Wit: Jane Holeman, Thos Sneed.

15-6 Daniel Farmer to William Cocke, for 210 lbs, 178 A s side Flat R adj Fariss, Richard Holeman, Ro Cates - it being part of tract conveyed Samuel Farmer by Earl Granville 9 Jan 1761 and from him to Daniel Farmer. 30 Aug 1796. Wit: John Commins, Stephen Farmer.

Deed Book C
Page

16-7 Henry Mitchel of Halifax Co., VA, to Samuel Smith of Person Co., for 171 lbs, 320 A on McFarland & Sergent Creeks adj said Smith, Joseph Turner, Josias Dickson, Robert Walker, Thos Robertson, Benjn Johnston (including part of a mill seat). 30 Oct 1797. Wit: Edmund Dixon, Mason Foley.

18-9 Matthew Cochran to John Cochran, for 87 lbs, his part of 262 A being one-third of land which his father Alexander Cochran bequeathed to be equally div between Alexander Cochran, Samuel Cochran, & Matthew Cochran - on n side Flat R adj Stephen Moore, Robert Cate, Willis Nichols, Osborne Jeffreys, Micajah Nichols, James Cochran. /s/ Matthew Coughran. 9 Jan 1798. Wit: John Hanks, James Cochran

19-20 Samuel Dickens to Robert Dickens, for 200 lbs to be pd in land & 5 sh, 100 A adj Jesse Dickens, Samuel Dickens, Tap; negro boy Evergain. _ May 1797. Acknd.

20 Robert Dickens to Daniel Hicks, for $300, 150 A n side Tapley's Cr adj Jefferson, Traylor, Person. 12 Nov 1797. Wit: William Hicks, Sally Dickens.

21 John Hicks to Johnathon Jackson, for 45 lbs, 150 A being a part of 600 A purchased of Levy Swainey on Cubb Cr & little Rocky Ford adj Millington Blalock, John Cash. 2 Aug 1797. Wit: Millington Blalock Sen., John Blalock, Fanny Hicks.

22-3 John McMurry Sen to John Farrar, for 56 lbs, 45½ A on Double Cr of S Hico adj Joseph Sarratt, John Broadaway, David Brechen. 30 Oct 1797. Wit: B. Douglas, Jas McMurrey, Edward Gaines.

23 William Frazer of Granville Co.to Moses Cash of Person Co., for 50 lbs, 119 A adj Benjamin Cozart on road crossing Collings Br to Little Cr, William Oakley, William Blalock. 2 May 1798. Wit: Millington Blalock, John Cash Sen.

24 Stephen Stuart to Mason Foley - sale of negro boy Isaac. 20 Jan 1795. Wit: Jos Howell.

24 Joseph Lunsford to Jesse Lunsford, for $119, 119 A at a spring adj John Bumpass Sen., Mills Durden, Wm. Ryley. 7 Feb 1798. Wit: Jesse Dickens, John Cash.

25 Elijah Denby of Franklin Co., NC, to Nathaniel Norfleet of Nasemond Co., VA, for 500 lbs, 640 A adj claim of Neal Mecalister including plantation Denby purchased of Joseph Palmer. 23 Oct 1797. Wit: Jas Milner, A. Villines. 23 Oct 1797. Proved before J. Haywood, Judge Superior Court.

26 Edmund Deshazo to Shadrack Gentry, for 61 lbs, 13/4, 105 A on Castle Cr adj Charles Allin, Guttrice, Charles Bostick former line. 15 Feb 1799. Wit: Andrew Buckanon, Dean Buckanon.

27 John Ponsonby of Dinwiddie Co., VA, to John Oglesby of Person Co., for 20 sh per A plus $5 in hand, 1535½ A or 6 tracts on S & N Hico being contiguous: 396½ A called Francis Wright tract, 316 A the Morgan tract, 114 A the Peter Rogers tract, 354 A the Saml Bell tract, 142 A the Saml Bell Jr tract, 216 A the Sergent tract - all tracts conveyed to Ponsonby by Roger Atkinson Sen. dated 17 Mar 1790. Surveys by H. Haralson & Wm. Waite. 20 May 1798. Wit: Gideon Patterson, James Sanders, Thomas Atkinson, Richd Ogilby.

28 John Campbell to Richard Ogilby, for 50 lbs, 56 A on N Hyco adj Fielding Lewis decd, Ponsonby, H. Haralson. 12 Nov 1796. Wit: John Ogilby, John Moore, Wm. Morgan.

29 Nicholas Delone of CC to John Thomas of Person Co., for 200 lbs, 110 A both sides S Hico on Kelley Br adj Joseph Carney new line now Alexander Rose of 10 A Rose purchased of Benjamin Douglas, Roger Atkinson now B. Douglas; said land purchased of Matthew Price 19 Oct 1793. Wit: William Lea, B. Douglas.

30 John Thomas to son Jacob Thomas, for 100 lbs & natural love, 110 A both sides S Hico on Kelley Br adj Alexander Rose formerly Joseph Carney, Roger Atkinson now B. Douglas - said land purchased of Nicholas Delone. 5 Mar 1798. Wit: Maneil Garrot, B. Douglas.

32

31 Jeremiah McEntire to Josiah Carver, for 50 lbs, 96 A on Stories Cr adj George Duncan, said Carver, Thomas Barnett. 18 May 1798. Wit: Richd Beardin, Nancy Bearden.

31-2 James Holt of Halifax Co., VA, to John Pulliam of Person Co., for 65 lbs, 200 A on Jents Cr adj Byrd Pullam, Robt Walker. 4 June 1798. Wit: William Rainey, John Sergant, Wm. McFarland.

32-3 John Clixby to Thomas Moore, for 100 lbs, 321 A on Deep Cr adj Robert Dickens, William Cocke, being part of grant from State. 30 Apr 1798. Wit: Samuel Sneed, William Rice.

33 Memucan Allen to Charles Mitchel, for 500 lbs, 275 A both sides Adams Cr adj Michel Dixon, Andrew Barnett. 23 May 1798. Wit: J. Green, William Huston.

34 Timothy Holt of Halifax Co., VA, to James Holt of same, for 45 lbs, 200 A adj Rachel Barnett, John Chambers, William Barnett, Hezekiah Duest - said land conveyed him by Thomas Tunks in trust for payment of debt due Lewis Mabry & William Holt & recorded in CC. 1 Oct 1794. Wit: William Hobson, James Warren, Byrd Wall, John Parrott, John Warren.

34-5 James Dunbar Henley to Joseph Gold, for 5 lbs, 6 A w side S Hico adj Gold - it being part of land granted Benjamin South by State 10 Nov 1784. (Actually a lease for 97 yrs after which heirs of Henley can repossess.). 5 June 1798. Wit: H. Haralson, Tho Neeley.

35-6 James Williamson to James Cochran, for 95 lbs, 270 A on Stories & Gents Cr adj John Chambers, James McKnight, Hezekiah Dueast, Jacob Bull, Thomas Carver - said land purchased of William Barnett 15 Dec 1791. 12 Dec 1797. Wit: Edward Clay, John Malone.

36-7 Demsey Moore to James Williamson, for 400 lbs, 400 A on Flat R adj William Rankin - said land part of grant to John Paine from State. 6 June 1797. Wit: James Minge Burton, Jesse Dickens.

37 Munford Megehe (McGhee) to John Moore McGhee, for $370, 185 A e side Hico adj Richard Pendergrass, John Woods. _ _ 1797. Acknd in open court.

38 John James Sen. to Nimrod Ellis, for 20 lbs, 85 A on Frays Br adj William Allin. 6 Mar 1795. Wit: James Buckanon, Richd Sanders Jun.

38-9 Daniel Sergant son of Joseph Sergant decd of Pendleton Co., SC, to George Lea of Person Co., for 100 lbs, 133 A on Cobb Cr adj John Campbell, Jos Sergant old corner. 2 Jan 1798. Wit: John McFarland, William Lea.

39 Benjamin Douglas to Burwell Green, for 60 lbs, 109 A on Sergant Cr adj George Hall, Carver, William Sargent. 6 Nov 1797. Wit: James Paine.

40 Nimrod Ellis to Artha Buckanon of Warren Co., NC, for 20 lbs, 85 A on Frays Br adj William Allen. 30 Aug 1797. Wit: Willis Roberts, Richard Sanders Jun.

40-1 Burwell Green to Nathan Scoging, for 60 lbs, 94 A on Double Cr of S Hico adj John Caddel, James Jay. 2 Sept 1797. Wit: Tho Neely, E. Douglas.

41-2 Thomas Talbert to James Dunbar Henley, for 50 lbs, 63 A on Henley Mill Cr & S Hico adj Joseph Gold, William Trotter. 5 Dec 1797. Wit:R. Vanhook, B. Douglas.

42-3 Thomas Barnett to Wm. Cocke, for 90 lbs, 180 A on Gents Cr adj Burgess Haralson old line now Ezekiel Haralson, James Chambers old line, said Cocke - it being part of tract Josias Chambers purchased of Thomas Barnett. 7 June 1798. Wit: Joseph D. McFarland.

43 Robert Seymore to William Duty, for $100, all right & title in right of his wife Amey to land on Hico willed to her by her former husband Matthew Duty decd (Seamore gives bond for $500 debt due for land; if pd by 25 Dec, this deed void. 9 Apr 1798. Wit: Jas Cochran, J. Campbell.

Deed Book C
Page

43-4 Miles Wells to Jane (or Jean) Lyon, for 13 lbs, 26 3/4 A on Flat R adj Hargis, John Phillips at Aldridge Cr. 13 May 1797. Wit: William Roberts, Richd Lyon.

44-5 Thomas Neeley to Benjamin Douglas, for 50 lbs, 200 A on Stories Cr adj Robert Seymore, George Hall, John Atkinson. 2 June 1798. Wit: J. Campbell.

45-6 Robert Dickens to James Anderson, for $400, 200 A on Cub Cr of Tar R adj Oakley. 20 Oct 1796. Wit: Walter Oakley, William Dickens.

46-7 Davison Chambers & Benjamin Chambers to William Chambers Sen., for 300 lbs, all land their father William Chambers Sen. deeded them 8 Feb 1795. 6 Mar 1798. Wit: B. Douglas.

47-8 Goodloe Warren to James Standfield of Halifax Co., VA, for 161 lbs 13/4, 200 A on Stuart's Cr of Hico adj Edmund Dixon, Daniel Glenn, Charles Boulton. 3 Apr 1797. Wit: H. Haralson, Wm. Stanfield.

48-9 James Simmons to Henry Royster, for 83 lbs 6/8, 105 A both sides Mitchel Br adj Arthur Mitchel, George Johnston, William Lea, James Wells. 19 July 1797. Wit: H. Haralson, Joseph Royster.

49-50 James Dunbar Henley to Benjamin Wheeler, for 133 lbs 6/8, 100 A on Henley mill cr of Hico adj Reubin Long, Francis Scoggings. 5 June 1798. Wit: H. Haralson Willis Roberts.

50-1 Hubbard Kernal to lawful heirs of Jeremiah Warren decd (intestate), for 8 lbs 7/6 pd by Warren, 9 3/4 A on Warrin's mill Cr of Hico adj Warren. 4 Sept 1797. Signature is Hubbard Carnal. Wit: H. Haralson, Richd Carnal.

51-2 Peter Bennett to Thomas Owen of Granville Co., NC, for 515 lbs, 406 A on Stories Cr including land purchased of Reubin Long & John Johnston. 22 Aug 1798. Wit: Alex Cunningham, Burgess Haralson.

52 Peter Bennett to Thomas Owen of Granville Co., for 15 lbs, 1 A on Stories Cr adj Benjamin Long decd old line. 22 Aug 1798. Wit: Thos Owen, John Pompratt.

53 John Bumpass Sen. to Gabriel Bumpass his son both of Orange Co., for love & affection, 96 A on Deep Cr adj Lunsford, Cocke. 24 Feb 1798. Wit: William Riley, John Bumpass.

53-4 Sanford Dixon to Jacob Dixon, for 25 lbs, 100 A on Blewing Cr adj Thomas H. Burton. 4 Jan 1798. Wit: Thos H Burton, Martha H Burton, Sarah Johnston.

54 Spence Mitchel to John Mason, for 100 lbs, 123 A on Cobbs Cr adj Stephen Sargent. 17 Oct 1796. Wit: Ephraim Sargent, Miles Wells.

55 Pleasant F. Warrin of Halifax Co., VA, to Mary Fulcher of Person Co., for 20 lbs, negro boy Gilbred about 4 yrs old. 2 Jan 1798. Wit: E. J. Winders, Robert Warren.

55 Samuel Wheelas to John Winstead, for 65 lbs, 100 A adj Robert Gill, Manley Winstead, Samuel Winstead, William Waite or Robert Dickens. 18 Jan 1798. Wit: Manley Winstead, Benjamin Wheelas.

56 William Brechen to Abraham Moore, for 166 lbs, 206½ A on Double Cr of Hico adj John Cooper, Charles Fooshe, Vanhook. 24 Aug 1797. Wit: Charles Fooshe, Obadiah Pierce.

57 Thomas Sneed to Benjamin Fowler, for 366 lbs, 13/4, 411 A on Double Cr of Hico adj Thomas Badgett, William Cocke, the Moravian line, Adam McNeeley. 5 June 1798. Wit: Samuel Cox, Absolem Johnston.

57-8 Andrew Buckanon Sen. to James Redwood of Warren Co., NC, for 15 lbs, 15 A on Frays Br adj Cs Allen, James Layton; 10 yds around Mrs James' grave excepted. 15 July 1797. Wit: William Buckanon, Arthur Buckanon.

Deed Book C
Page
58-9 John McMurray to Thomas Snipes of Granville Co., NC, for 200 lbs, 200 A on Double Cr of Hico adj John Farrar, John Blake, Samuel McMurry, Alexr Rose. Also signed by Elizabeth McMurry. 20 Oct 1797. Wit: John Sarrar, John Farrar.

59-60 Hardy Wells to Simeon Cochran, for 30 lbs, 53½ A on Double Cr of S Hico adj Adam McNeeley, Goodrich Jones, H. Haralson. 13 June 1798. Wit: Thos Burch, Barnard Kemp.

60 John Browning of Green Co., GA, to David Mitchel of Granville Co., for 40 lbs, 137 A on Stories Cr adj Hatcher, said Mitchel. 21 May 1786. Wit: J. Atkinson, Jos Browning. Registered Sept 1798 by oath of Richard Atkinson who proved hand-writing of John Atkinson decd; Jos Browning now dead or outside the county.

61 Henry Fuller to Paul Walters, for 140 lbs, 205 A on Stories Cr adj Wm. Carver, Peter Bennett, John Long, James Couthran. 1 Nov 1796. Wit: William Shepherd, Paul Walters, Daniel Walters, John Long.

61-2 State of NC - # 86 - to Robert Dickens and William Waite, for 30 shillings per 100 A, 150 A on Flat R adj William Hawkins near Orange Co. line, said Dickens & Waite. Survey 1 Apr 1795; registered 2 Dec 1797. Chain carriers: Edwd Goins, Joshua Step,

62-3 State of NC - # 87 - to Robert Dickens & William Waite, ? A on Flat R adj Elizabeth Step, James Rimmer, Edward Goins. 2 Dec 1797. Chain carriers: Edwd Goins, Joshua Step.

63 Benjamin Towler to Ralph Williams, for 45 lbs, negro boy Harry. 3 July 1797. Wit: Augustin Harris, Chas Mitchell, James Boswell.

63-4 Benjamin Jopling to John Brown, for 20 lbs, 21 A on Bushy Fork adj Richard Hargis. 3 July 1797. Wit: James K. Daniel, William Farrar.

64-5 Thomas Farmer Sen. & Mary Farmer to John Brown, for 106 lbs, 212 A on Bushy Fork of Flat R adj Richard Hargis, John Urquhart, Dickens, Waite, Brown. 23 Feb 1797. Wit: Obediah Pearce, Thos Farmer.

65-6 Holloway Pass to John Barnett, for 300 lbs, 340 A both sides Fishing Br of Adams Cr under n side of Espy Mountain - it being part of tract granted Edward Chambers by Earl Granville, from Chambers to Burgess Haralson, to Elkanah Haral-son, to John Henry Pryor, to Stephen Stuart and sold at sheriff sale to James Robertson who sold to Holloway Pass 1 Dec 1793 adj Hugh Barnett, John Barnett, Howard, William Huston, Petters, Haralson orphans. 5 Dec 1797. Wit: Artha Brooks, B. Douglas.

66-7 John Atkinson of Montgomery Co., NC, to Artha Brooks of Person Co., for 17 lbs, 12 s, 88 A on Adams Cr adj John Barnett, Elizabeth Green Pryor, Ambrose Long, Hugh Barnett. 17 Nov 1797. Wit: Lewis Milam, Matthew Brooks, Buckley Walker.

67-8 William Chambers to Thomas J. Chambers, for 500 lbs, 209 A both sides Hico. 7 June 1797. Wit: R. Howard.

68-9 John Rogers & Jane Rogers his wife to William Haralson & Burgess Haralson, for 60 lbs, 193 A on Marlowe & Castle Creeks adj Paul Haralson old line, Josias Dickson - said land Jane Rogers purchased of State by name of Jane Haralson. 15 Dec 1797. Wit: Josias Dickson, Isaiah Dewese.

69-70 William Haralson & Burgess Haralson to John Rogers, for 300 lbs, 336 A both sides Marlowe Cr of Hico adj Henry Howard fromerly Michael Dickson, Josias Dickson, said land willed them by their father Ezekiel Haralson decd. 4 Nov 1797. Wit: Jos^s Dickson, Thos Barnett.

70-1 William Haralson & Burgess Haralson to John Rogers, for 100 lbs, 193 A on Marlowe & Castle Creeks adj Paul Haralson old line, Josias Dickson - said land they purchased of Rogers 15 instant. 28 Dec 1797. Wit: Jos^s Dickson, Isaiah Dewese.

Deed Book C
Page

71-2 Spence Mitchell to John Darby, for 26 lbs 10 sh, 53 A on Cobb Cr of Hico
adj Henry Royster, said Darby, Ogilby, William Rainey. 4 Oct 1797.
Wit: William McDaniel, B. Douglas.

72-3 Arthur Mitchell to John Darby, for 150 lbs, 320 A on Stony Cr of Cobb Cr adj
John Ogilby formerly Roger Atkinson, Royster, George Johnston. 4 Oct 1797.
Wit: William McDaniel, B. Douglas.

73 Mary Fulcher to Henry F. Chambers, for 40 lbs, her whole estate of 1 bay horse,
furniture, property she purchased of her father's estate 26th instant; negroes
from her father William Fulcher decd. 27 Dec 1797. Wit: E. P. Winders,
Pleasant F. Warren.

74 Ralph Williams to John Williams, for 100 lbs, negro boy Harry about 10 yrs of
age. 6 Aug 1798. Wit: Benjn Towler. Condition of sale requires John Williams to
turn over to Ralph Williams negro boy Peter who was left John by his grandfather
when he attain 21 yrs. 6 Aug 1798.

74-5 Power of attorney - William Howard of Knox Co., TN, to John Thorp of Granville Co., NC, to convey to John Oliver all land on Adams Cr formerly held by
Francis Howard decd in Person Co which will come to him as a legatee when div
made. 16 Sept 1797. Wit: Francis Howard, William Huston.

75 Henry Williamson to Jesse Watson, for 40 lbs, tract on Stories Cr adj Burwell
Green, said Watson. 23 Nov 1797. Wit: James Hunt, Ambrose Dollar.

76 Robert Dickens & William Waite to Josiah Brown, for 41 lbs 13/4, 178 A on Bushy
Fork of Flat R adj James Farquhar, James Rimmer, Shadrack Roberts, Caddel, Wilson,
Farmer. 16 June 1797. Wit: Drury Jones, Thos McKissack.

77 Richard Wilson to Hiram Wilson, for 50 lbs, 100 A on Flat R adj Dickens & Waite,
William Caddel, Thos Farmer. 7 Nov 1797. Wit: Andrew Caddel Senr., Andrew
Caddel Junr.

78 Joseph Gholston of Pittsylvania Co., VA, to Hubbard Carnal of Person Co., for
75 lbs, 107 A adj Goodloe Warren, Thomas White, Patrick Carnal. 2 Sept 1797.
Wit: Thos Wood, William Glenn, William Brandon.

79 Zebulon Veazey to James Cozart of Orange Co., for 150 lbs, 500 A on Nap of Reeds
Cr - part formerly belonged to Thomas Person and part to Arthur Moore adj Jacob
Cozart on the Granville Co. line, Peter Cozart. 15 Apr 1797. Wit: William
Brinkley, Absolem Weaver, Peter Cozart.

79-80 John Parish to Elkanah Parish, for 15 lbs, 50 A on Donaldson's Cr adj Henry
Humphries, Patterson. 4 Nov 1797. Wit: Lewis Wilkinson, Jesse Ragan.

80-1 Jesse Ragan to Elkanah Parish, for $20, 50 A both sides Blewing Cr adj Hum-
phries. 4 Nov 1797. Wit: Robert Harris, John Dixon.

81 Richard Atkinson exec last will of Edward Atkinson decd to Thomas Talbert,
for 30 lbs, 60 A n side Richland Cr of S Hico adj Moravian line. 12 June 1798.
Wit: Thos McNeill, Benjn McNeill.

82 John Sarrett to George Eskridge, for 333 1/3 silver dollars, 150 A on S Hico
adj Lawrence Vanhook, James McMurrow. 15 Sept 1797. Wit: Loyd Vanhook, James
Simmons, B. Douglas.

82-3 John Ogilby to Thomas Atkinson of State of VA - for debt due John Ponsonby
for 584 lbs - 6 tracts Ogilby purchased of John Person on N & S Hico. 22 May 1798.
Wit: John Winters, Richd Ogilby, Henry Elam.

84 Richard Burch Sen. to Simeon Cochran of Caswell Co., for 65 lbs, 95 A on S Hico
adj Baylor Burch, Isaac Johnson, Absolem Johnson, Widow Woodie. 18 Oct 1797.
Wit: Abselom Johnson, George Burch, Edmond Burch.

Deed Book C
Page

85 John Baldwin to Benjamin Partee of Granville Co., for $237, 200 A on Camp Cr adj Peter Cozart, Wm. Brown on Orange Co. line, George Anderson, Johnston. 13 Feb 1798. Wit: Earbe Partee, Sarah Allingthorp.

85-6 John Thomas to John Blake, for 50 lbs, 102 A n side Double Cr of Hico adj William Waite, Wm. Brown, John Broadaway, John McMurry. 30 Jan 1797. Wit: Jacob Thomas, B. Douglas.

87 Wilson Vermillion to Roger Tilman, for 145 lbs, 200 A on Hendley Mill Cr adj William Saterfield, Edmund Lewis. 4 Aug 1797. Wit: Wm. Trotter, Thomas Talbert.

87-8 Stokes Allen to John Goodloe Warren, for 50 lbs, 150 A on Double Cr of S Hico at ridge of Flat R adj Robert Dickens, William Forrest, McKissack. 20 Sept 1797. Wit: Robert Stanfield, William Forrest.

88-9 William Lowhead to Jesse Ragan, for 50 lbs, 230 A on Donaldson's Cr adj Charles H. Burton, John Parish, Lewis Wilkerson. 25 Oct 1797. Wit: Robert Harris, John Wilkerson.

89-90 James Pulliam to Bird Pulliam, for 50 lbs, 50 A on Ghents Cr adj Richard Beardin. 16 Mar 1797. Wit: James Pulliam, John Pulliam.

90-1 Patrick Moore to John Moore, for 100 lbs, Nat, a negro man of yellow color about 23 yrs; Ester a girl 20 yrs old; all his legacy & claim as a legatee from estate of his father John Moore decd. 20 Sept 1797. Wit: H. Haralson, James Trotter, Mary Haralson.

91 John Bumpass Sen. to John Bumpass Jr. (his son), for love & affection, 243 A both sides Deep Cr adj Gabriel Bumpass, Wm. Cocke, John Coleman, William Riley. 1 Mar 1798. Wit: William Riley, Gabriel Bumpass.

91-2 Alexander Asken of Nottaway Co., VA, to John Bumpass Sen. of Person Co, for 100 lbs, 339 A both sides Deep Cr adj Wm. Waite, Joseph Lunsford, Wm. Cocke, Daniel Coleman, Wm. Riley. 20 Nov 1797. Wit: Daniel Coleman, Gabriel Bumpass.

92-3 George Gregory to Martin Jones, for 58 lbs 6/8, 156 A on Mayho Cr adj Baird, Mrs. Donaldson old line, Holloway, Atkinson, Bailey. 1 Mar 1798. Acknd in court.

93 Elijah Denby of Franklin Co., NC, to Job Green of Person Co., for 150 lbs, 130 A on Rocky Fork of Deep Cr of Flat R; also 50 A of the 350 A granted to Joel Ledbetter by State 10 Nov 1784. _ _ 1796. Wit: Richd Holsomback, James Walton.

94 Stephen Farmer & Nathan Farmer to Joshua Cate Jun., for 150 lbs, 303 A being part of tract willed by their father adj William Farmer to Quarrel Cr. 4 Oct 1797. Wit: Chas Holeman, James Wilson.

95 John Caddel to John Scoging, for 60 lbs, 60 A on Double Cr of Hico adj James Jay, Andrew Caddel Jun., Nathan Scogging. 2 Oct 1797. Wit: Hosea Tapley, Burwell Green.

95-6 Henry Fulcher to George Gregory, for 60 lbs, 100 A on Hico adj Hedgman Warren, James Petterson, William Stanfield. 5 Mar 1798. Acknd in open court.

97 Richard Hargis to James Broche, for 81 lbs, 208 A on S Hico adj Robert Ester, William Moore, William Marshel, William Mitchell. 23 July 1797. Wit: Richard Burch, Joseph Hargis, George Burch.

97-8 George Southard to Daniel Clayton, for 50 lbs, 102 A on Millstone Cr adj Allen Fuller - it being tract George Rosebrook bequeathed to George Southard his grandson adj Mary Lewis, James D. Hendley, Vincen Brann, Joseph Gold. 26 Aug 1798. Wit: Joseph Southard, Robt Southard.

98 Thomas Jeffreys of CC to George Elliott of Person Co., for 100 lbs, 100 A on Wynns Cr adj said Elliott, Hugh Hemphill. 2 Sept 1797. Wit: Hugh Hemphill, David Hemphill.

99 Matthew Daniel to Samuel Wheelor, for 241 lbs 6/8, 210 A on Henley Mill Cr of S. Hico adj Darby Hendley. 15 Dec 1798. Wit: Nathan Ragan, Samuel Winstead.

99-100 Daniel Malone of CC to Thomas W. Price of Orange Co., NC, for 50 lbs, 120 A on Bushy Fork of Flat R adj Aldridge, the county line, Wm. Waite, Ed Goins old line, Ph Burch, D. Durham - it being half of a grant to Robert Mitchel. 15 Nov 1796. Wit: William Lea, Samuel Love.

100 Douglas Oliver to David Pinar of Halifax Co., VA, for 75 lbs, 100 A on VA line. 21 Nov 1797. Wit: Edmund Dixon, Thos White. Conway Garlington, Hubbard Carnall.

101 Paul Haralson to John Delahay, for 133 lbs, 133+ A on Castle Cr of Hico adj John Haralson, McFarland, Edmund Delahay. 5 Mar 1798. Wit: Edmund Delahay, Major Green.

101-2 Paul Haralson to Edmund Delahay, for 182 lbs, 182½ A on Castle Cr of Hico adj John Delahay, McFarland, Moses Walker, Major Green, John Rogers. 5 Mar 1798. Wit: H. Haralson, John Dellahay, Major Green.

102-3 John Darby to George Darby & Hugh Darby (his brothers), for 85 lbs, 170 A on Cobb Cr adj Major John Ogleby, William Rainey, Henry Royster, Arthur Mitchel. 5 Mar 1798. Wit: H. Haralson, B. Douglas.

103-4 Charles Fooshe to Wright Nicholas, for 208 lbs 7/6, 324 A on Double Cr of S. Hico adj Thomas Graves, Stanfield, McNeill, Vanhook, Moore, Cooper. 10 Mar 1798. Wit: R. Vanhook, Jno Sneed.

104 -6 Div estate of Francis Howard decd - 500 A with 50 A each to:
 1. Henry Howard adj Artha Brooks, John Barnett. 2. Francis Howard adj John Barnet
 3. William Badgett & Betsy his wife adj John Barnett, Will Huston.
 4. Peter Badgett & Rebeccah his wife on the mountain br adj William Huston.
 5. John Tharp & Patsey his wife on the Mountain Br.
 6. Groves Howard on Mountain Br adj Andrew Barnett.
 7. Johnston Howard adj Andrew Barnett, Micke Allen.
 8. Larkin Howard adj Memacan Allen. 9. Nancy Howard. 10. William Howard.
Total value 212 lbs 10 s. Henry Howard was guardian to Larkin Howard; Henry Fuller guardian to Johnston Howard & Nancey Howard.
Commrs: William Huston, John Barnett, H. Haralson, Dempsey Moore. 4 Sept 1798.

107 John Holloway Sen. to John Holloway Jr., for 100 lbs, 292 A on Dish Water Cr, 4 Dec 1798. Wit: Anderson Haralson, Lewis Rainey.

107-8 John Guttrey of Lawrence Co., SC, to Josias Carver of Person Co., for ? , 150 A on Stories Cr adj William Carver, Thomas Carver. 21 June 1797. Wit: William Carver, Edwd Nash.

108-9 William Cocke to William Duty, for 4 lbs, 4 A on Double Cr adj his fence - said tract part of one conveyed by John McMurry Jun. 5 Dec 1798. Acknd in court.

109-10 Thomas Robinson of Green Co., TN, to Ambrose Foster of Halifax Co., VA, for $655, 393 A adj Johnathan Skeen old line now Draper, Robert Walker. 1 Nov 1798 Wit: H. Haralson, J. Yancey.

110-1 Andrew Caddel Junr. to Isaac Saterfield, for 90 lbs, 160 A on Richland Cr - being tract granted from Earl Granville to James Anderson 10 Jan 1761 adj William Brechen. 15 Nov 1798. Wit: Edward Clay, Alexr Rose.

111-2 Abraham Moore to John Moore, for 200 lbs, 206½ A on Double Cr adj John Cooper, Vanhook, Abraham Hargis. 23 Nov 1798. Wit: Obediah Pearce, David Robinson, John P. Womack.

112-3 Coleman Clayton to David Allen, for 65 lbs, 460 A both sides Mill Cr adj Joseph Gill old line, Robert Paine, John Man - being part of tract purchased of William Paine who had grant from State. 27 Nov 1798. Wit: Robt Paine, James Paine.

Deed Book C
Page

113-4 William Tulloh to Thomas Jones Chambers, for 100 lbs, 100 A on Hico Hills adj Byrd Wall, William Standfield, William Cocke, Joseph Beedles, said Chambers. 16 Nov 1798. Wit: R^d Bearden, John Carlton.

114-5 Josiah Allen of Green Co., GA, to William McKissack of Person Co., for 100 lbs, 212 A on Flat R adj Robert Dickens, John Goodloe Warren, John Smith Hust. 12 Nov 1798. Wit: Thos McKissack, Wm. Waite, Jas Milner.

115-6 Miles Wells of CC to Stephen Wells of Person Co., for love to his son, 318 3/4 A on Flat R adj Richard Lyon, Jane Richardson, John Phillips, Shadrack Hargis - said land purchased of Henry Lyon. 4 Dec 1798. Wit: James Farquhar, John Clixby.

116-7 James Jones of Halifax Co., VA, to Robert Harris of Person Co., for 300 lbs, 399 A both sides Crooked Fork adj said Harris. 9 Oct 1798. Wit: William Oliver, Robert Jones, Thos Burch.

117 John McKissack to William McKissack, for 100 lbs, 311 3/4 A on Double Cr of Hico adj Thomas Badget, Nathaniel Norfleet, Thomas McKissack, Standfield. 3 Dec 1798. Wit: Thos McKissack.

118 Robert Dickens to Thomas Oakley Jr. of Granville Co., for $125, 160 A on Cub Cr adj Vaughn, Robert Dickens, Kennedy. 28 Oct 1798. Wit: Wm. Cakly.

118-9 Robert Dickens to Thomas McKissack, for $93, 83 A adj Allen former corner, Palmer old corner. _ _ 1798. Acknd.

119-20 James Guttrie of Union Co., SC, to Absolem Guttrie of Person Co., for $100, 100 A on Hico at Aspin mill cr where widow Barnett lives adj Charles Allen - said tract part of 250 A of Jerrat Guttrie. 6 Nov 1798. Wit: Henry Cogburn, Elisabeth

120-1 Richard Bland Jun. of Nottaway Co, VA, to William Cocke of Person Co., for 170 lbs, 170.2 A on Gents Cr adj Gregory old corner. 2 Jan 1799. Wit:Robert Dickens, Abner Williams.

121 Thomas Douglas to daughter Jennet Lea alias Douglas wife to Geo Lea, for love and affection, negro girl Sall about 13 yrs of age. 5 Apr 1798. Wit: Abner Lea, William Lea.

121-2 Richard Bland of Nottaway Co., VA, to George Connally of same, for 400 lbs, 679 A on Flat R adj Henry Lyon, Robert Dickens, Black old survey - said land purchased of Robert Dickens 11 Feb 1790. 4 June 1798. Wit: Henry W. Lawson, Edwd Bland.

122-3 Thomas Douglas to John Whittly, for 100 lbs, 85 A on Cob Cr of N Hico adj William Hargis, Hamelton Renolds. 2 Mar 1799. Wit: Ben Douglas. Pulliam Williamson.

123-4 John McKissack to Thomas McKissack, for 100 lbs, 328 A on Double Cr of Hico adj Nath Norfleet, William McKissack, Stanfield, Robert Dickens. 3 Dec 1798. Wit: Jas Milner, William McKissack Junr.

124-5 Josiah Carver to Jery McEntire of Halifax Co., VA, for (not given),100 A on Gents Cr. 15 Oct 1798. Wit: Richd Bearden, Robt. Seymore.

125 Richard Holloway to William Cocke, for 100 lbs, 100 A e side Gents Cr it being the land of Stephen Wood who deeded same to John Wood and then to Holloway & sold by sheriff to Elijah Daniel who sold to Wm. Cocke adj William Allen old line, Allen Love. 5 Jan 1799. Wit: Artha Browne, Nath Norfleet.

126 James Jay to children of his wife Martha Jay to wit: Elisabeth Turner, Frances Fuller, Sarah Wisdom, John Wisdon, James Wisdom, Martha Wisdom, Lewis Wisdom, & Delpha Holsonback, for affection & 5 shillings, negro man Ned age 38 yrs; mare & saddle, feather bed, furniture; livestock - all came to wife excepting she may use all for her life unless applied to debts wife may contract

in her widowhood or of her former husband in his lifetime; slave Ned to remain with James Jay for his life then belong to Lewis Wisdom & at his death divided to all children - but to go to Lewis Wisdom's children if he has any. 22 Jan 1799. Wit: William Brown, B. Douglas.

127 Francis Scoggin to James Cochran, for 45 lbs, 150 A on Rose Mary Cr adj William Southard former line, John Dinwiddie decd formerly Hudgens, Long - being part of tract Ambrose Hudgens sold to Scoggin 12 Oct 1787. 7 Feb 1799. Wit: Thos McNeill, Thos Talbert.

128 Daniel Malone of CC to Mark Malone of Person Co., for 100 lbs, 156 A on S Hico adj Jesse Evans, Wheeley, Absolem Johnston. 1 Jan 1799. Wit: Jesse Evans, Eunice Evans.

128-9 John Caddel to Lewis Wisdom of CC, for 153 lbs, 102 A on n br of Double Cr adj Lewis Green decd, William Brecheen, Andrew Caddel, John Scoggin, Nathan Scoggin, Elijah Watson. 31 Oct 1798. Wit: James Jay, Abraham Holsomback.

129 Samuel Davis of Lincoln Co., GA, to Hamilton Reynolds of Person Co., for 98 lbs, negro woman Nancy. 29 June 1798. Wit: J. McMullen, Elijah Reynolds, Betty Hughs.

130 State of NC - # 90 = to John Petty Pool, for 30 sh per 100 A, 280 A on Aron & Blewing Creeks adj Richard Bland, William Montague, Phillip Vass, James Daniel. 13 Dec 1798. Surveyed by Wm. Waite 23 Mar 1797. David Wilkerson & William Petty Pool, sworn chain carriers.

131 Barnett Lea to Thomas Carver, for 150 lbs, 138.2 A on S Hico adj Duty, William Warren. 28 Feb 1799. Wit: Geo Lea, S. Warrin.

131-2 James Cochran to Isaac Fuller, for 60 lbs, 100 A on Stories Cr a part of land purchased of John Walters adj John Long, Paul Walters. 5 Mar 1799. Wit: Isham Edwards, P. Bennett.

132-3 Barnet Lea to James Dollarhide, for 150 lbs, 138½ A on S Hico adj Duty, William Warrin. 4 Dec 1798. Wit: Geo Lea, S. Warrin.

133-4 William Stuart of CC to Charles Boulton of Halifax Co., VA, for $980, 420 A on Stuarts Cr of Hico adj Montford McGhee, Goodloe Warren, James Standfield, Daniel Glenn, William Hobson. 22 Aug 1798. Wit: H. Haralson, Thos White.

134-5 Joseph Beedles to Christopher Bass late of Amelia Co., VA, for $1666 1/3, 410 A both sides Gents Cr of Hico adj Allen Love, Richd Pendergrass, John Wood, Byrd Wall, Thos Chambers, Wm. Cocke. 12 Jan 1799. Wit: Joss Dickson, Mary Dickson

135-6 David Poyner to Alexander Cunningham of Halifax Co., VA, tor 125 lbs, 100 A on main rd from red house to Petersburgh on the VA line adj Thos White, Richard Carnal, William Dixon Senr., Joseph Flipps - being plantation where David Pinar lives. 16 Feb 1799. Wit: Richard Holloway, Hubbard Carnal, Stephen Mason.

136 William Waite to Alexander Cunningham of Halifax Co., VA, for 50 lbs, 112 A adj Richard Carnal, the VA line, Warren, Thos White, Hannah Farley, John Pierson, Wm. Dixon. 4 Mar 1799. Wit: Jas Cochran.

137 Francis Scoggin to Charles Winstead, for 160 lbs, 106 A on Hico & fish trap br adj Reubin Long, Samuel Whitehead, Carter Lea, Wm. Jones, Benj Wheeler, Wm. Saterfield. Also signed by Jemimah Scoggin. 4 Feb 1799. Wit: Matthew Daniel, William Saterfield.

137-8 Nathaniel Malone to CC to Thomas Malone of Person Co., for 100 lbs, 250 A both sides S Hico adj Woods, Isaac Johnston, Rainey. 24 Aug 1797. Wit: W. Muzzall, John Malone.

Deed Book C
Page
138-9 William Duty to John Sarratt, for 204 Spanish milled dollars, 102.8 A on Double Cr of S Hico - This includes 4 A deeded from Wm. Cocke 5 Dec 1798. 5 Mar 1798. Wit: Moses Bradsher, James Hunt.

139-40 Daniel Ledbetter of CC to James Walker of same, for $466, about 500 A on Deep Cr of Flat R adj Abram Davis, Stephen Moore. 10 Nov 1791. Wit: Stephen Moore. Proved Mar 1799.

140-1 Ephraim Hawkins to Jobe Blackard, for 76 lbs 12/11, 137 A on Flat R adj Abraham Moore. 7 Dec 1798. Wit: John Phillips, Shad Hargis.

142-3 Bradley Haralson to Robert Deshazo, for 150 lbs, 155 A w side Stories Cr at school house br adj Hezekiah Dewese, William Allen, Thomas Barnett, George Vaughn, Ezekiel Haralson, William Chambers. 31 Dec 1798. Wit: Anderson Haralson, Rochard Deshazo.

143-4 John Christianbery to James Eubank, for 200 lbs, 354 A on Hico adj Samuel McKonkey. 17 Feb 1796. Wit: Clayton Jones, William Rainey, Reubin Jones.

144-5 State of NC - # 88 - to Benjamin Johnston, for 50 sh per 100 A, 13 A on Sargent Cr adj said Johnston, Samuel Smith, Thomas Robinson. 14 July 1796. Recorded 2 Dec 1797. Chain Carriers: John Johnston, Benj Johnston.

145-6 Hosea Tapley to William Brechen, for 300 lbs, 420 A on Double Cr of Hico adj Rankin. 10 Nov 1797. Wit: John Caddell, John Brechen.

146-7 John Whitley to Richard Eskridge Jr. of CC, for $258, 86 A on Cobb Cr of N Hico on the great road adj Pulliam Williamson, William Hargis, Gabriel Lea, Hamilton Reynolds. 2 Sept 1799. Wit: B. Douglas.

147 George Darby to his son James Darby, for 100 lbs, 100 A adj Hugh Hemphill, George Elliott. 31 Dec 1798. Wit: H. Haralson, John Darby.

148 State of NC - # 1111 - to John Petty Pool, for 30 sh per 100 A, 200 A on Arons Cr in CC adj Whitehead, John Harris, James Jones. 1 Jan 1795. Survey by Robt. Mitchel D. S. (deputy surveyor) 5 Sept 1794. Sworn chain Carriers: Wm. Petty Pool, Stephen Petty Pool.

149 John Campbell to Joseph Rice, for 100 lbs, 209 A on S Hico & Cobb Cr adj Daniel Sargent, Junr., Daniel Sergant Senr., James Lea, John Mason. 29 May 1799. Wit: Currie Barnett, Andrew Lea.

150 George Connally of Nottaway Co., VA, to William Cocke of Person Co., for 203 lbs 14 s, 679 A on Flat R being part of tract deeded by Robert Dickens to Richard Bland Jr. & from Bland to Connally adj Jeffreys, Lyon. 1 June 1799. Wit: James Daniel, Elijah Daniel.

150-1 Robert Dickens to McFarland Oakley, for $280.56, 202 A on Tar R adj Walter Oakley, John Bumpass. 22 Oct 1798. Wit: William Dickens, Saml Dickens.

151-2 Robert Dickens & William Dickens to Henry Knollner of Orange Co., NC, for $200, 200 A on Flat R adj Glenn, on Orange Co. line - it being land William Dickens purchased at sheriff sale. 5 Oct 1798. Wit: Beverly Glenn, William Phillpot, Saml Dickens.

152 William Carver to Benjamin Carver, for 50 lbs, 100 A on Stories Cr. 19 Oct 1799. Acknd in open court.

153 John Goodley Warren to Josiah Fike, for $250, 150 A on Double Cr of Hico on dividing ridge of Flat R adj Robert Dickens, William Forrest, McKissack. 4 June 1799. Wit: Nathl Norfleet, William Muzzall.

153-4 Benjamin McNeill to Moses Fuller, for 40 lbs, 82 A n side Richland Cr of S Hico adj William Fuller, Atkinson. 4 June 1799. Wit: Loyd Vanhook, Stephen P. Pool.

Deed Book C
Page

154-5 William Glenn of CC to Beverly Glenn of same, for 100 lbs, 100 A both sides Deep Cr. 23 Jan 1784. Wit: David Roberts, Daniel Ledbetter. Proved June 1799 by oath David Roberts.

155 Frederick Deboe to Yancey Bailey, for 90 lbs, 108½ A on ridge between Cain Cr & Hico adj Benj Deboe old line, James Robertson. 12 July 1795. /s/ Debow. Wit: H. Haralson, Mary Harralson, J. Holloway Junr.

156 John Campbell to John Rice, for 500 lbs, 510 A on S Hico adj Edmund Lea, Nathaniel King, Richard Lea, the Moravian land, John Lea - this being original grant to Stephen Sergant who sold to John Campbell. 29 May 1799. Wit: Currie Barnett, Andrew Lea.

157 Josias Dickson to John Dickson, for 10 shillings, 148 A on Hico adj Wm. Huston, Willaim Rayney, Robert Walker. 1 Mar 1799. Acknd in open court.

157-8 Yancey Bailey to William Penick, for $416, 208 A on Cain Cr & Hico adj John Pearson formerly James Mullens, John Davies formerly Fred Deboe, Stephen Oliver, Josias Dickson, Archibald Campbell old line, 4 June 1799. Acknd in open court.

158-9 Joshua Cate Jun. to William Cocke, for 13 lbs 10 s, 20 A on Flat R at achoolhouse br adj Charles Holdman. 4 June 1799. Wit: Thos Moore.

159-60 James Walker to James Cozart, for $500, about 500 A on Deep Cr of Flat R adj Abraham Davis, Stephen Moore. 4 Jan 1798. Wit: Phillips Moore, Thos Moore.

160-1 Zebulon Veazey to Jeremiah Moore of Granville Co., NC, for 39 lbs, 130 A being part of tract of Arthur Moore adj said James Cozart, Blalock, Johnston, Benjemin Partee. 3 June 1799. Wit: Thos Moore, James Cozart.

161 Roger Atkinson Sen. of Dinwoody Co., VA, to James Cochran of Person Co., for 409 lbs 7/6, 655 A on Stories Cr - said land conveyed him by Joseph Tolbert 19 Sept 1767 and recorded in Orange Co., NC. 13 Dec 1798. Wit: Thomas Atkinson, Robert Atkinson, Roger Atkinson. Proved by oath Roger Atkinson Jun. Sept 1799.

162 Roger Atkinson, Thomas Atkinson, & Robert Atkinson, for 5 shillings, release any claim to deed for 655 A made to James Cochran 13 Dec 1798. Proved Petersburgh, VA, 13 Apr 1799; proved Person Co. Sept 1799.

163 Joseph Jones and Jane his wife of Dinwoodie Co., VA, to James Cochran of Person Co., for 4 shillings, release all claim to land deeded by Roger Atkinson decd dated 13 Dec 1798. 17 Aug 1799. Wit: Rochard Howson, Edwd Wade, Roger Atkinson.

163-4 State of NC - # 91 - to Millington Blalock, for 30 sh per 100 A, 100 A on Cub Cr adj his corner, Levy Swainey. 7 June 1799.

164-5 Absolem Johnston to Robert Wiles(Willis), for 69 lbs, 171½ A on Flat R adj Jakins, Shadrack Roberts, Daniel Malone, Daniel Durom. 31 Dec 1798. Wit: Reubin Jones, Richd Burch, Clayton Jones.

165-6 John Terrell of CC to James Williamson of Person Co., for 100 lbs, 200 A on Flat R adj Risdon Fisher. 28 Sept 1797. Wit: Absolen Johnston, Isaac Johnston.

166-7 William Winstead to Benjamin Morrow, for 50 lbs, 73 A on Tar R adj Richard Jones, Isaac Day, John Day on wagon path to Bumpass old field. 30 Aug 1799. Acknd in open court.

167 Arthur Brooks Sen. to Francis Lawson, for 30 lbs, 149 A crossing Dishwater Cr adj Ragan, Baird, Holloway, Bailey, Pryor orphans. /s/ Artha Brooks. 17 Mar 1799. Wit: Ep. Winders, Will Street.

167-8 Robert Harris to Overton Harris of Granville Co., for 120 lbs, 236 A both sides Crooked Fork. 16 Mar 1799. Wit: William Huston, Geo Duty.

Deed Book C
Page
168-9 Jesse Ragan to William Winstead, for 60 lbs, 230 A on Donaldson Cr adj
Charles H. Burton, John Parish, Lewis Wilkerson. 1 Mar 1799. Wit: Thos Halliburton, Eleanor Parish. Proved by oath Thos H. Burton.

169-70 William Cocke, suceeding sheriff of Edwd Atkinson, late sheriff of Person Co.
to Thomas Hargis - goods & chattels of John Douglas atty for John Urquhart to
satisfy suit against Thomas Gately 1 Sept 1794 - 50 A of John Urquhart sold to
Hargis for 45/6 adj Benjamin Jopling, William Robinson. 31 Aug 1799. Acknd in
open court.

170-1 Roger Atkinson Sen. of Dinwoodie Co., VA, to Loyd Vanhook of Person Co., for
150 lbs, 150 A on Hico R said tract conveyed him by Abraham Miles 18 July 1767
and registered in Orange Co. 13 Dec 1798. Wit: Thomas Atkinson, Robert Atkinson,
Roger Atkinson, Jun.

171-2 Roger Atkinson, Thomas Atkinson, Robert Atkinson sons of Roger Atkinson decd
to Loyd Vanhook, release of all claim to previous deed made by their father.
13 Apr 1799. Proved Petersburgh, VA, 13 Apr 1799. Proved Person Co. Sept 1799.

172 Joseph Jones & Jane his wife of Dinwoody Co., VA, to Loyd Vanhook, for 5 shillings, release all claim to deed made by Roger Atkinson Sen. 17 Aug 1799. Wit:
Richard Howson, Roger Atkinson, Edwd Wade.

173 William Chambers to Jacob Bull, for 20 lbs, 10 A s side Stories Cr adj both men
on the trading road. 3 Mar 1800. Wit: Benjn Chambers, John Carlton, Byrd Wall.

173-4 Thomas Owen Sen. of Granville Co., to Robert Brooks & Jacob Bull of Person
Co, for 15 lbs, 1 A on Stories Cr - said land deeded him by Peter Bennett adj
Benjamin Long old line. _ Mar 1799. Wit: H. Haralson, William Duty.

174-5 Thomas Owen of Granville Co. to Jacob Bull & Robert Brooks of Person Co.,
for 500 lbs, 406 A both sides Stories Cr being land conveyed by Reubin Long to
Peter Bennett & then to Owen.13 Mar 1799. Wit: H. Haralson, William Duty.

175-6 John Wynn Pulliam to Byrd Pulliam, for 100 lbs, 100 A on Gents Cr of Hico
adj widow Pulliam, Cochran, Kary Williams, Richard Bearden. 31 Aug 1799.
Wit: H. Haralson, James Long.

176-7 William Rice of Halifax Co., VA, to Joseph Hall of CC, for 292 lbs, 11 s.,
234 A in Person Co. adj John Moore, James Hamblett, Fanny Hamblett, Archibald
Murphey. 26 Oct 1799. Wit: H. Haralson, James Hamblett, Thos White.

177-8 Hannah Farley of Halifax Co., VA to Thomas Jeffreys of CC, for 125 lbs, 301
A in Person Co. on Dan R & Winds Cr adj the VA line, Goodloe Warren. 24 Nov 1798.
Wit: Jacob Thomas, John Farley.

178-9 Power of attorney - Nicholas Delone of Richmond, VA, to Gabl Lea of CC &
John McFarland of Person Co to transact all business, to convey property to pay
debts; any remaining to be div equally to wife Edy Delone & daughter Frankey
Delone. 5 June 1798. Wit: Wm. Glayne, Fedrick Ayton. Registered CC Oct 1799.
Registered Person Co. Dec 1799.

180 George Eskridge to Richard Eskridge of CC, for 50 lbs, negro boy Charles about
14 yrs old; sale void if debt owed Richard Eskridge is paid. 30 Mar 1799.
Wit: Samuel Eskridge, Thomas Eskridge.

180-1 William Forrest to John Fooshe, for 75 lbs, 100 A on Flat R adj Drury Allen
former corner, Robert Dickens, Thomas Hargis. 18 June 1800. Wit: John Cooper,
John Moore.

181-2 John Scoging to Thomas Rainey, for 120 lbs, 60 A on Double Cr of Hico adj
James Jay, Andrew Caddel Senr., Nathan Scogging. 26 July 1799. Wit: John Hall,
Nathan Scogging.

182 James Hunt to Jacob Fuller, for 160 lbs, negro boy Sharper about 14 yrs old. 9 Sept 1799. Wit: Rd Atkinson.

182-3 Samuel Smith to Lofton Walton, for 136 lbs, 4 s, 134 A on Sergant's Cr adj Reubin Taylor - including the mill & 1.4 A west side of Cr. 22 Oct 1799. Wit: Hubbard Carnall, Demsey Moore, Isaac Saterfield.

183-4 James Eubank to William Whitfield, for 25 lbs, 50 A on Bushey Fork adj Ben Wheely, Daniel Durham, Philip Wadkins. 3 Dec 1799. Wit: Wm. Norwood.

184-5 George Duncan to his son Ezekil Duncan, for love & good will & 5 shillings, 120 A being all land whereon George Duncan lives adj William Sergent, Robert Walker, McEntire, Josias Carver. 29 Oct 1799. Wit: John Lea, B. Douglas, Frances Douglas.

185 Thomas Douglas to Elisha Roark, for 101 lbs, 10 s, 100 3/4 A on S Hico, adj Joseph Carney, Kindel Vanhook. 22 Oct 1799. Wit: Pulliam Williamson, John Melear.

186 John James of South Carolina to Arthur Buckhannon of Person Co., for 100 lbs, 100 A on Byas mill cr adj said Buckhannon on Fray's Br, Nimrod Ellis, Wm. Allen, James Davie. 10 Dec 1798. Wit: William Petty Pool, Phillip Petty Pool.

186-7 John McFarland & Gabriel Lea, attys for Nicholas Delone, to Demsey Moore, for 300 lbs, 6½ tenths of an A at the CH being part of 6 A lot conveyed 11 Dec 1792 to Commrs for building a court house & Joal adj Demsey Moore's chimney, Thomas Hargis. 10 Dec 1799. Wit: George Lea, William Lea.

187-8 Martin Cooper to Wm. Cocke, for 130 lbs, 259 A on Double Cr of Hico adj Wm. Duty former corner now Cocke, Thomas Badget, Robert Standfield, Phillip Hall, John Hall, Wm. Waite, Saml McMurry - it being part of 2 tracts granted to Wm. Badget # 285 & 682. 4 Jan 1800. Wit: B. Douglas, L. Hargis.

188-9 Allen Love of Brunswick Co., VA, to Wm. Cocke of Person Co., for 150 lbs, 200 A both sides Gents Cr of Hico being a tract deeded to McCall Elliot by Ebenezer Moss & wife. 5 Dec 1799. Wit: David Robinson, Saml Lockhart.

189-90 Power of attorney - Richel Dinwiddie to Thomas Neeley for self & as guardian to orphans of John Dinwiddie decd to recover all debts & attned to all business. _ _ 1799. Wit: William Lea, Vincent Lea.

190-1 Thomas Hargis to William Penn of Granville Co., for $500, lots near Person CH; 1 lot of 1.1 A adj Joal; other of 1.9 A on road from CH to the spring adj Nicholas Delone, Demsey Moore. 3 Dec 1799. Acknd in open court.

191 State of NC - # 92 - to Francis Lawson, for 50 sh per 100 A, 21 A both sides Mayo Cr adj John Baird. 31 Mar 1798. Also # 23 entered 5 Sept 1798. Registered 12 Aug 1799.

192 Henry Cooper to John Russell of Warren Co., for $1920, 576 A both sides S Hico in CC & Person Co. adj Thomas Neeley. 6 Oct 1798. Wit: Tho Neeley, Loyd Vanhook.

192-3 Isaac Johnston of Person Co. to Mary Currie of CC, for 125 lbs, 10 s, 200 A on S Hico adj Nathaniel Malone, Samuel Woods. 16 Nov 1799. Wit: Thomas Talbert, Wm. Mitchel.

193 Isaac Johnston to Mary Currie of CC, for 62 lbs, 10 s, 100 A on S Hico in Person Co. adj Malone, Woods, Willingham. 16 Nov 1799. Wit: Thomas Tolbert, Wm. Mitchel.

194 Benjamin McNeill to Richard Duty, for 85 lbs, 220 A both sides S Hico adj John Bradsher, Fuller, Lea. 4 Sept 1799. Wit: Aaron Fuller, Geo Duty.

Deed Book C
Page
195 Charles Mitchell, Thomas Mitchell, & John Mitchell all of Granville Co.,
to Elisha Mitchell of same, for 100 lbs, all their claim to 640 A in Person Co
adj John Payne - said land they obtained as heirs from David Mitchell Sen. decd.
11 June 1800. Wit: L(eonard) Henderson.

195 William P. Pool to John Baird of Prince George Co., VA, for a certain sum,
7 A on Mill Cr adj Moses Street, Nathan Ragen. 2 Sept 1799. Wit: Wm Huston,
Robert Allen.

196 Stephen Wells to James Wilson, for $426, 345½ A on Flat R at Aldridge Cr
adj Hargis, R. Dickens, Joshua Cate now Richd Lyon. 8 Jan 1800. Wit: Richd
Lyon, Benjamin Wells.

197 Ephraim Hawkins to James Farquhar, millwright, for $ 60, 62 A s side Bushy
Fork. 13 Jan 1800. Wit: Elisha Askew, William Farquhar.

197-8 Isaac Hodge, Samuel Hodge, & David Hodge of CC to James McMurry Sen. of
Person Co, for 60 lbs, 150 A on S Hico on Kelly Br adj Alexander Rose formerly
Joseph Sarrett, Benj Douglas formerly Atkinson, James Johnston, Joseph Carney
formerly Alexr Rose. 27 Nov 1799. Wit: Loyd Vanhook, Samuel McMurry, Benajmin
Stephens.

198-9 Isaac Hodge, Samuel Hodge, & David Hodge all of CC, to James McMurry Sen.
of Person Co, for 60 lbs, 166 A on S Hico adj Jacob Thomas formerly John Douglas,
Alexander Rose formerly Joseph Sarrett, Lawrence Vanhook, Joseph Carney - said
land was granted by State to Johnston Webb 10 Nov 1784 & conveyed to John Hodge
their father. 27 Nov 1799. Wit: Benjamin Stephens, Loyd Vanhook, Saml McMurry.

199-200 David Brechen to Burwell Green, for 40 lbs, 80 A on Double Cr of Hico
adj the Moravian line, Hardymond Wells. 29 Oct 1796. Wit: Charles Fooshe,
B. Douglas.

200-1 Jacob Vanhook sheriff of Person Co. (to satisfy court order against John
Atkinson decd in hands of Robert Dickens exec brought by James Williamson for
sum of 27 lbs 16 s., due since 1792) to Richard Atkinson, for various sums,
negro slaves: Paul about 24 yrs, Isaac about 40 yrs, Ephraim age 6, Lucy about 30
and her child a sucking infant, Lett age 15, Doll age 13, Stephen age 6, Solomon
about 4 yrs, Fillis age 38 - total sales 62 lbs, 13/4. 4 Dec 1799. Acknd in
open court.

201 William Lea to Allen Johnston & George Johnston, for 20 lbs, 30 A on S Hico
adj Simon Doyle. 16 Oct 1799. Wit: J. Campbell, John Lea, Joseph Gold.

202 Robert Johnston Steele of Richmond Co., NC, to Alexander Gray Sen., for 250
lbs, 200 A on Double Cr of Hico adj Howel, Thomas Palmer, McKissack, Jones; also
250 A adj Thomas Palmer, John McAlister, Jones - said land in 2 tracts he purchased of John McAlister & Francis Howell. 25 Nov 1799. Wit: William McKissack,
Nancy Gray.

203 Josiah Brown to Ephraim Hawkins, for 20 lbs, 178 A on Bushy Fork of Flat R
adj James Farquhar, James Rimmer, Shadrack Roberts, Caddel, Wilson, John Brown.
30 Sept 1797. Wit: Obediah Pearce, John Brown, George Whitefield.

203-4 Jesse Dickens to Granville Vaughn, for 22 lbs, 8/6, 74 3/4 A adj Clixby,
Dickens. Wit: Jesse Lunsford.

204 William Lea of Russell Co., VA, to Ambrose Lea of Person Co., for 150 lbs,
119 A n side Bear Br. 15 Oct 1799. Wit: William Lea, Abner Lea, Andrew Lea.

204-5 William Lea of Russell Co., VA, to William Lea & Reuben Lea of Person, for
150 lbs, 141 A s side Bear Br adj Rice. 15 Oct 1799. Wit: Ambrose Lea, Abner Lea,
Andrew Lea.

Deed Book C
Page

205 Granville Vaughn to Mills Durden, for 15 lbs, 84 3/4 A adj Clixby, Jesse
Dickens. Wit: Jesse Dickens, William Riley.

206 Isaiah Duest of Cabarrus Co, NC, to Cary Williams of Person Co., for 100 lbs,
150 A on Jents Cr of Hico adj John Williams, Byrd Pulliam. 30 Dec 1799.
Wit: Isham Edwards, Richd Bearden.

206-7 William Petty Pool to William Street, for 500 lbs, 160 A both sides of
Mill Cr & purchased of Robert Dickens adj Moses Street, William Beard. 10 Oct
1799. Wit: J. Holloway, John Dillehay.

207-8 William Hamblin Sen. to Richard Hamblin, for 10 lbs, 56 A on Stories Cr being
part of Land where grantor lives adj Jacob Fuller. 23 Dec 1799. Wit: W. Jeffreys.

208 William Holloway of Spartenburg Co., SC, to William Ramsey, for $600, 422 A
both sides Dishwater Cr adj Nathan Ragan. 8 Jan 1800. Wit: J. Holloway, John
Lawson, Junr.

208-9 Thomas Talbert to Samuel Garrott, for 50 lbs, 60 A n side Richland Cr of
S Hico adj Moravian line. 25 Feb 1800. Wit: Isham Edwards, William Paine.

209-10 David Barnett to Jesse Ragan, for 150 lbs, 308 A on Spoonwater Cr a br of
Mayo adj John Baird, Agness Barnett, Chalres Halliburton. 8 Oct 1799.
Wit: William Street, William Allen.

210 State of NC - # 94 - to Job Blackard, for 50 sh per 100 A, 40 A on Flat R adj
Thomas Blalock, Thomas Person;6 Dec 1799. Sworn chain carriers: Thomas Hudgins,
.? Hargis.

211 State of NC - # 93 - to Thomas Hudgins, for 50 sh per 100 A, 50½ A on Flat R
adj Thomas Hargis, John Paine, Shadrack Hargis. 6 Dec 1799.Johnathon Hargis &
Carter Hudgins. sworn chain carriers; William Waite, surbeyor.

211-2 William Farmer of Person Co., to William Daniel of Sumner Co., TN, for
100 lbs, 100 A both sides Flat R adj John Commons, James Mercer. 24 Apr 1800.
Wit: Wm. Cocke, Nathan Farmer.

212-3 Absolem Johnston to Simeon Cochran, for 46 lbs, 10sh., 93 A on Flat R adj
Taylor Burch, said Cochran. 4 Mar 1800. Wit: Wm. McKissack, Ambrose Arnold,
John Durram, John Malone.

213 Elizabeth Davy, Isaac Vanhook, Robert Davy, Robert Gill, Gabriel Davy,
Edward B. Davy, John Davy & Ashburn Davy - release and give quit claim to 298 A
to William Davy which he now possesses. This done as last will of Gabriel Davy
5 Oct 1791 devised to each of his sons then of age the tract whereon said son
lived of about 400 A each; tract of William Davy contains only 100 A - for love
& affection to their brother & to prevent any dispute - this land is deeded.
4 June 1800. Wit: Hardy Johnston, Moses Springfield, Ashburn Davy.

214 Power of attorney - Burwell Green of Person Co., to brother John Green of
Orange Co., NC, to sell his land on S Hico: 91 A on Double Cr & 109 A on Sergant
Cr; to make deed to John Baynes for 150 A as Baynes has bond for same for80 lbs;
to make deed for 100 A for bonds due Wm. Freysure & Manuel Garrott. 25 Feb 1797.
Wit: Joseph Stephenson.

215 Lewis Shepherd of CC to James Cochran of Person Co, for 100 lbs, negro slave
Sancoe. 6 May 1800. Wit: Solomon Debow, Nathan Williams.

215-6 Thomas Morton to Paul Haralson, for 7 lbs, 4 3/4 A s bank Marlows Cr adj
said Haralson, Walter McFarland, John Rogers. 1 Mar 1800. Wit: H Haralson,
J. Howard

216 John Hicks to James Cozart of Orange Co, for 50 lbs, 186 A adj Jackson, John
Blalock, Marrit Stone, Johnathon Jackson. 4 Dec 1797. Wit: Richd Holsomback,
Marrit Stone, Job Green.

Deed Book C
Page
217 John Haralson to Alexander Cuningham of Halifax Co., VA, for160 lbs, 228 A on Castle Cr it being tract willed by Ezekiel Haralson and known by name of Cross Road Ordinary adj Saml Cox, John Barnett on Douglas Rd, Peggy Barnett. 25 Apr 1800. Wit: Edmund Dixon, J. Haralson.

217-8 Joseph Pulliam of Halifax Co., VA, to son Joseph Pulliam of Person Co., for 110 lbs, negro slave Tom. 24 Feb 1800. Wit: J. Campbell, Joseph Hicks.

218-9 John Wynn Pulliam to John Seymore, for $200, 100 A both sides Gents Cr adj James Cochran, Robert Walker, Elizabeth Pulliam, Byrd Pulliam. 3 May 1800. Wit: H. Haralson, Moses Street.

219-20 Roger Atkinson to Joseph Jones both of Dinwiddie Co., VA, for 300 lbs, 700 A on Rambo Cr which he purchased of Lawrence Rambo on Castle Cr and known as Rambo patent entry; 166 A on Hico Cr purchased of David Womack 7 Oct 1784. 10 June 1793. Wit: Cela Barroe, Joseph Daniel. Proved Petersburgh, VA, 15 Mar 1800 when both witnesses made oath they saw Atkinson sign deed. Proved Person Co., Sept 1800

220-1 Jacob Cozart of Granville Co. to his son Thomas Cozart of Person Co, for 150 lbs, 300 A adj Thomas Goss, John Cash, Moses Moore. 10 Mar 1796. Wit: Thomas McNeill, Benjamin

221-2 Benjamin Johnston to William Trotter, for 263 lbs, 263 A on Sergant Cr & S Hyco adj Samuel Smith Thomas Robison, Johnathon Skeen. 18 Apr 1800. Wit: Jas Trotter,Reubin Walton, Phillip Walton.

222-3 John Bowles Sen. of Granville Co, to Bennett Williams of same, for 50 lbs, 150 A on Cubb Cr adj Anderson. 5 Apr 1800. Wit: John Bowles Jun., Jordon Bowles.

223-4 William Paine to William Trotter, for 5 lbs, 3 A adj said Trotter. 3 June 1800. Wit: J. Holloway, Jas Trotter.

224 Eleanor Parrish to Joseph Pitman, for 10 lbs 10 sh., 20 A on Donaldson Cr adj John Parish. /s/ is his mark. 27 Apr 1799. Wit: Robert Hargis, Abel Parish.

225 John Beadles to Matthew Brooks, for 60 lbs, 50 A both sides Stories Cr adj Robert Deshazo. 28 Aug 1800. Wit: Jos^S Dickson, Artha Brooks.

225-6 Josiah Carver to William Carver, for $67, 67 A on Stories & Sergant Creeks adj William Carver. 3 June 1800. Wit Richd Bearden, John Rogers.

226-7 Joseph Wood of Person Co. Robert Brooks, Nancy Wood & Sarah Wood of Halifax Co., VA - all legatees to the estate of John Wood decd - to William Wood & John Tucker of Halifax Co., VA, for 50 lbs, 63 A both sides Hico in Person Cr being part of tract of John Wood decd adj Munford Megehee, Byrd Wall, Christopher Bass, Joseph Wood. 13 Feb 1800. Wit: Hardy Ball, Richd Holloway.

227-8 Moses Cash to Millington Blalock Sen., for 70 lbs, 180 A on Little Cr, Camp Cr. & Cub Cr adj Joshua Johnston, Arthur Moore. 28 Nov 1800. Acknd in open court.

228-9 David Parker to CC to Powell Parker of same, for 50 lbs, 254 A on Tar R adj Jones, Day. 17 Feb 1792. Wit: Jesse Allen, Abner Parker.

229 James Cochran to John Cochran, for $162, 46 A on Flat R adj Blakeley on the Great Rd - said land willed James Cochran by his father Alexander Cochran and part of grant from John Earl Granville to James Blakeley 28 June 1761 and contained 362 A. 27 May 1800. Wit: Micajah Nichols, John Cochran Jun.

230 James Cochran to exec of Stephen Moore namely Grizey Moore, Robert Moore, Phillips Moore all of Person Co., for $46.50, 13 3/4 A on Flat R adj Blakeley on Meadow Br on the great rd.Said land part bequeathed by his father Alexander Cochran, decd, and taken from 2 tracts - 10 A from grant of John Allenthorp 6 Dec 1761 from John Earl Granville; the other to James Blakeley by John Earl Granville 28 June 1761. 28 May 1800. Wit: John Clixby, Richd A. Holland.

Deed Book C
Page
231 Richard Hargis to Joseph Hargis, for 50 lbs, 111½ A on Long Br of Flat R adj John Brown, Robert Dickens. 24 July 1799. Wit: Benjamin Jacobs, Nathl Norfleet, W. Hargis.

232-3 Frederic William Marshall of Salen, Stokes Co., NC, to Thomas McNeill of Person Co - concerning deed between William Churton & Charles Metcalf register-ed in Orange Co., Book L, page 106 and in Roan Co(Rowan Co.) book E, #5 page 452 and then conveyed to Charles Metcalf and vested in said Marshall in trust - for $104, 104 A on Richland Cr of S Hico adj Benjamin McNeill. 29 Nov 1800. Wit: Benjamin McNeill.

233-4 Demsey Moore to James Williamson, for 300 lbs, 460 A on Flat R adj John Paine, Jeffreys. 30 Mar 1799. Wit: J. Holloway.

234-5 Yancey Bailey late sheriff Person. to William Dickens - by court order to sell goods & chattels of James Critcher for debt of 343 lbs recovered by Robert Dickens - sold to William Dickens for 57 lbs, 17/,two tracts total 500 A on Flat R adj Glen, along the county line. 4 June 1800. Acknd in open court.

235-6 State of NC - #99 - to Robert Dickens & William Waite for 50/ per 100 A, 261 A on Cub Cr & Deep Cr adj John Cash, Millington Blalock, Luke Moore, John Burford, Cozart. 17 July 1779. Chain carriers: Saml Dickens. Registered 20 Feb 1801; entered 17 July 1779.

236a State of NC - #100 - to William Waite, for 50/ per 100 A, 100 A on Deep Cr at Gabs Br adj John Paine, Craven. 14 Nov 1800. Sworn chain carriers: Wm. Hargis Jun., Carter Hudgins.

236a - State of NC #97 - to Robert Dickens & William Waite, for 50/ per 100 A, 220 A on Deep Cr adj Stephen Moore, John Carrington, Thomas Marshall, William Ring, Walker, Daniel Ledbetter. Entered 17 July 1778. Recorded Nov 1800. Chain carriers: Geo Hall, Wm. Craven.

237 State of NC - #103 - to Thomas Hudgins, for 50/ per 100 A, 220 A on Ald-ridge Cr adj William Cocke, Shadrack Hargis, Michael Robinson. 27 Fev 1800. Chain carriers: Nathan Hargis, Wm. Wilson.

237-9 Jacob Vanhook late sheriff to James Trotter(to comply with suit that James Cochran brought against Robert Seymore late of Person Co), for 47 lbs, 200 A adj William Sergant, James Henley, John Fuller. Acknd in open court.

239-40 Yancey Bailey late sheriff to William Dickens by his agent Jesse Dickens, due to court order to sell property of Robert Dickens - for 211 lbs 9/8, 1000 A adj Wm. Tapp; 500 A adj Paul Jeffreys, Darden. 10 Jan 1798. Wit: Elizabeth Lawson, Betsy Bailey, Rainey Thomson.

240-1 John Ogilby to his son Richard Ogilby, for 500 lbs, 347 A both sides Cobb Cr in fork of Hico adj John Campbell, Herndon Haralson, Gabriel Gun, Tract pur-chased of John Ponsonby known as Rogers tract, John Darby, William Rainey. 2 Mar 1800. Wit: Christopher Bass, Chas Moore, G. A. Gunn.

241-2 Jacob Vanhook sheriff to William Dickens of Granville Co. (to satisfy judg-ment brought by Robert Burton adm of Robert Ballard decd against Anthony Browne) for 410 lbs,1/, 3 negroes : Ephraim, George, Ben; 290.9 A on Tar R adj Saml Bum-pass. 26 Sept 1800. Acknd in open court.

242-3 William Dickens of Granville Co. for $200, 27 A on Tarr R at Cattail Br adj Brown, Gabl Davy. 3 Mar 1801. Acknd in open court.

243 John Lea to George Lea, for 100 lbs, 100 A both sides Cobb Cr adj Barnett Lea, Wilson, Stafford. 15 Nov 1800. Wit: Abner Lea, William Lea.

244 Jacob Fuller to John Ravens, for $320 in silver, negro boy Sharper about 16 yrs of age. 3 Mar 1801. Wit: Duncan Rose.

Deed Book C
Page
244 Simon Doyle of SC to Daniel Sergeant of NC, for $100, 60 A w side S Hico.
13 Jan 1801. Wit: James Dollarhide, Jesse Bradsher.

245 Ann Wilson to Buckner Sims her son, for ? , 66 3/4 A on Long Br of Flat R
where Sims lives. 4 Feb 1801. Wit: Jean Caddel, Eunice Caddel. Proved on oath
Andrew Caddel.

245-6 Ann Wilson to Johnathon Terrel of CC, for 20 lbs, 63 3/4 A on Flat R adj
Richard Wilson, John Brown - it being part of dowery of John Wilson decd.
7 Feb 1801. Wit: David Mitchell, Richard Burch.

246 James Eubank to Henry Burch, for 100 lbs, 200 A on S Hico & Bushy Fork adj
Daniel Durram, widow Wadkins, George Eubank, Charles Allen. 8 Apr 1800.
Wit: George Eubank, Isaac Rainey.

247 Stephen Parker to Abner Parker, for 100 lbs, 100 A on Tar R adj Jonas Parker,
the Cattle Br. 9 Sept 1799. Wit: John Day Junr.

247-8 Thomas Jeffreys of CC to Joel Newman of Person Co., for 200 silver dollars,
141 A on head waters McFarland Cr adj Julius Justice, Robert Wilkerson, widow
Pulliam. 16 Nov 1800. Wit: Cary Williams, James Rainey, Joseph McCain.

248 William Brechen to James Williamson, for 300 lbs, 420 A on Double Cr of Hico
adj Rankin. 25 Feb 1800. Wit: Wm. Jeffreys, John Raven.

249 Benjamin Douglas to Thomas Neeley, for 50 lbs, 200 A on Stories Cr adj Robert
Seymore, George Hall - said tract deeded Doublas by Thomas Neeley 2 June 1798.
Wit: Garnett Neeley.

249-50 Loyd Vanhook to Benjamin Douglas (for Douglas exonerating Vanhook for
payment of $250 to Mssrs Yates & Day attys in fact for Younger & Wilkerson)
75 A on Hico - said tract conveyed to Vanhook by Roger Atkinson Sen. decd,18 Dec
1798 and conveyed to Atkinson by Abram Miles 18 July 1767. 28 July 1800.
Wit: William Yealock, James McMurrey.

250-1 Benjamin Douglas to James McMurrey, for $450, 75 A on S Hico & Ned's Cr
being part of tract deeded by Loyd Vanhook adj Thomas Neeley, Cooper now John
Russell. 28 July 1800. Wit: Loyd Vanhook, William Yealock.

251-2 John Dixon to Edward O. Chambers, for 62 lbs 10/, 310 A on Adams Cr adj
Benjamin Edgerton old line, Josias Dixon, Charles Allen old line, Lawrence
Vanhook. 1 Dec 1800. Wit: Isham Edwards, Moses Fuller.

252-3 William Hargis Sen. to William Cocke, for 196 lbs 11/9, 740 A on Flat R adj
Abraham Hargis, Thomas Hargis, Norsworthy. 10 Nov 1800. Wit: L. Hargis, Wm. Wilson.

253-4 John Hall to Andrew B. Wood, for $610, 183½ A on Double Cr of Hico adj
William Waite. 30 Oct 1800. Acknd in open court.

254 Jesse Ragan Sen. to Jacob Dixon Jun., for $100, 78½ A w side Blewing Cr adj
Charles Halliburton, William Winstead,said Dixon, Thomas Halliburton. 19 Nov 1800.
Wit: James Thomson, James Lawson.

254-5 Jacob Vanhook to William Dickens of Granville Co., for 16 lbs 11/6,
640 A known as Urquhart old field and sold by court order - land both sides Flat R
adj Richard Hargis, Hall, Norfleet. 3 Dec 1800. Wit: Cs Moore Jun.

256 Robert Dickens exec of John Atkinson decd to William Baswell, for$75, 100 A
w side Stories Cr. 2 Dec 1800. Wit: J. Campbell, Antho Browne.
Rochard Atkinson, legatee of John Atkinson decd and exec of his brother Edward
Atkinson who was exec of John Atkinson, relinquishes all title to said land.

257 Hezekiah Duest (or Dewest) to Davison Chambers & Benjamin Chambers, for 135 lbs,
450 A on Story's Cr adj William Chambers, Jacob Bull, McKnight old line,
Isaiah Dewest, Howard, Hezekiah Stone old line. 23 Dec 1797. Wit: Jos Dickson,
William Barnett.

Deed Book C
Page
258 George Eubank to Danial Malone Sen. of CC, for 270 lbs, 221 3/4 A head waters
S Hico adj Thomas Eubank, Rainey, near Orange Co. - it being half of 443½ A
willed to Eubank & His brother, Thomas. 3 Mar 1801. Wit: Robert Malone, Loyd
Vanhook, Thomas Malone.

258 John Ogilby to John Carrington, for $600, 4 negro slaves: Lucy, Nelson, Matilda
Annais. 2 Jan 1801. Wit: Robert Dickens, Peter Howson.

259 Thomas Jeffreys of CC to Stephen Oliver of Person Co., for 130 lbs, 301 A adj
VA line, Goodloe Warren. 22 Dec 1800. Wit: Joseph McCain, Jas Trotter.

259-60 William Lea & Reuben Lea to David Bazwell, for $282, 141 A on Bear Br of
S Hico adj Joseph Rice, Daniel Sargent. 5 Sept 1800. Wit: Henry Royster,
H. Haralson.

260-1 James Darby to Samuel Curles, for $150, 100 A both sides main trading road
at head Wynne's Cr adj Hugh Hamphill, John Darbey, George Darbey, George Elliott.
8 Sept 1800. Wit: H. Haralson, David Hemphill.

261-2 James Lewis of Franklin Co., KY, to Gabriel Gunn of Person Co., for $50,
19¼ A on Hico adj Fielding Lewis, Abner Duncan, Joseph Moore, John Ogilby - it
being land allotted James Lewis as legatee of his late father Fielding Lewis decd.
24 Apr 1799. Wit: H. Haralson, Sally Bennett, Polly Haralson.

262-3 Lawrence Vanhook Sen. of CC to Thomas Hargis of Person Co., for $296 & for
parental respect & affection, all his lands in Caswell & Person Counties on Cobb
Cr including tracts purchased of Henry Black, 10 A purchased of William Lea Jun.,
5¼ A of Nicholas Delone, 95½ A of Pulliam Williamson; 15 out lots drawn by sundry
Persons in Delone & Lea lottery & 10 in lots each with 90 ft length - total
137½ A. 15 Nov 1800. Wit: William Rainey, Vincent Lea, Loyd Vanhook.

263 Robert Dickens & John Womack to Thomas Gibson, for $100, 100 A adj Douglas
former line, Buchanon. 15 Aug 1801. Wit: William Huston, Saml Dickens.

264 Lewis Parrott to Robert Davey, for 36 lbs, 100 A adj Ragan. 1 Mar 1800.
Wit: P. Williamson, J. Holloway.

264-5 Baylor Byrd of CC to Baylor Burch of Person Co., for 60 lbs, 250 A at
Hillsborough Rd adj Reubin Taylor, John Wilson, Ezekiel Haralson. 30 Nov 1800.
Wit: Thos Wilkerson Phillip Wadkins.

265 Zachariah Denny to John Harris Sen. of Granville Co., for 100 lbs, 200 A in
Person & Granville on Aron's Cr adj said Harris, Daniel. Wit: 14 May 1799.
Wit: Jno P. Smith, Starling Harris, Charles Smith.

266 Matthew Daniel to William Glenn, for 70 lbs, 217 A on Flat R adj A. Rose,
Jesse Watson, Mitchel, John Browning - it being tract granted to State to William
Glenn & sold by Thomas Barnett, sheriff, to Edward Atkinson & then to Daniel.
22 Apr 1800. Wit: Alexander Graham, Robert Glenn.

266-7 The heirs of Francis Howard to wit: Henry Howard, Francis Howard, William
Badgett, Peter Badgett, John Thorp and Patsy his wife, Groves Howard, Larkin
Howard, & William Howard - to Archibald Heggie & Thomas Heggie of Granville Co.,
for 120 lbs, all land excepting 50 A or #7 & 9 held by Johnston Howard & Nancy
Howard both underage - 500 A on Adams Cr adj John Barnett, Prior, Mitchell Dixon,
widow Barnett, Robert Huston. 3 Oct 1800. Wit: Wm. Person, Isaiah Fuller,
James Baswell.
Names of Betsy Badgett, Rebecca Badgett & Polly Thorp were inserted before
assigned.

267-8 Thomas Hargis to William Carney, for 107 lbs 8/9, 93 A adj Hargis, Thomas
Douglas to road across the county line on Cobb Cr, Burch old shop on main road.
17 Feb 1801. Wit: Robert Thomas, Joseph Carney, William Donoho.

Deed Book C
Page
268-9 Joseph Hargis to Ephraim Hawkins, for 31 lbs, 10/, 111½ A on Long Br
of Flat R adj John Brown, Robert Dickens. 23 ___ 1801. Wit: Obediah Pearce,
Nathan Farmer, Anraham Moore.

269 Edmund Goin to William Baird, for 86 lbs, 124 A on Blewing Cr adj Waite,
Francis Ford, Frederick Goin on Cattail Br. 8 Apr 1801. Wit: James Thomson,
Starling Hudgins, Sharp Willingham.

270 Ambrose Harison Duncan of Granville, to Jacob Slaughter of same, for $40, 100
A both sides Jents Cr adj William Sargent, George Duncan. 11 Mar 1801. Wit:
M. Saterwhite, Isaac Slaughter.

270 Stephen Parker to William Morrow, for 70 lbs, 25 A on Tar R at Cattail Br adj
Abner Parker. 3 Mar 1801. Wit: Jacob Vanhook, Jane Laton.

271 Thomas McNeill to Samuel Garrott, for $150, 104 A on Richland Cr of S Hico
being land conveyed McNeill by Frederick William Marshall 29 Nov last, adj Ben
McNeill. 3 Dec 1800. Wit: Jas Cochran, Richd Duty.

271-2 Clayborn Denny to Thomas Webb of Granville Co., for 30 lbs, 100 A adj Harris,
Daniel. 12 Mar 1801. Wit: Henry Humphries, John Harris.

272-3 John Blake to William Brown, for 65lbs, 102 A on Double Cr of Hico adj
James Cochran formerly William Waite, John Broadaway, John Farrar formerly John
McMurry - said tract Blake sold to John Thomas 19 June 1792 & then sold by
Thomas to Blake. 13 Mar 1801. Wit: John Farrar, David Brechen.

273 Charles Glenn & Beverly Glenn to John Barden, for 69 lbs, negro woman
Cate sometimes called Jug. 27 Jan 1801. Wit: James Cathron, John Cate.

274 Joseph Hall of CC a supposed legatee of John Drury decd, to Robert Moore,
relinquishment of all right & title to estate of Drury now in possession of Robert
Moore. Robert Moore obliges to make said Hall an equal heir with other formal
heirs or daughters. 20 Apr 1801. Wit: Mumford McGehee, John M. McGehee.

274 Robert Moore to Joseph Hall - obligation to pay $2000 as his equal share with
female heirs or daughters. 20 Apr 1801. Wit: John M. McGehee, Mumford McGehee.

275 Ralph Williams - deed of trust to James Williams for 101 lbs, 3/11 due him:
3 negroes Quiller, Luce, Rachel. 14 Mar 1801. Wit: Jesse Gunn, Benjn Towler.

275-6 William Warren to John Miles, for $300, 150 A on Hico Cr adj Carver.
17 Jan 1801. Wit: Starling Warren. James Dollarhide.

276-7 Joseph Pitman to Clayborn Denny, for 25 lbs, 100 A adj Harris, Daniel, Person.
24 July 1799. Wit: Robert Thomas, Robert Harris.

277 John Clayton to Henry Day Jun., for 50 lbs, 150 A on Rocky br of Mayo adj
Henry Day Sen. 29 May 1801. Wit: John Day Jun.

278 Micajah Nichols to William Coughron, for $130, 62 A on Dry Br of Flat R adj
Coughran, Osborn Jeffreys - said land is sw corner of 362 A granted Willis Nichols
by State 3 Mar 1779. 28 May 1801. Wit: Phillips Moore.

278-9 Thomas Vass of Granville Co. to William Baird of Person Co., for $300, 321 A
on Blewing Cr adj Matthew Carter, Phillip Vass, John Turner, Thomas Burton,
Joseph Blanks. 11 Mar 1801. Wit: James Lawson, James K. Daniel.

279 Ralph Williams to Isaiah Fuller, for 318 lbs, 15/6, negro woman Cloe, boy
George; 13 cattle, mare, colt; 3 feather beds. 22 Apr 1801. Wit: Jacob Fuller,
James Mitchell.

280 Hubbard Carnal to Richard Carnal, for 60 lbs, 100½ A adj Pat Carnal, Fleming
Carnal - it being his tract divided among male heirs of Patrick Carnal decd.
13 May 1801. Wit: Alexr Cunningham, Thos White.

Deed Book C
Page

280-1 Frederick Goin of Mecklenburg, VA, to Edmund Goin of Person Co., for 6/,
124 A on Bluewing Cr adj Waite, Francis Ford, on Cattail Br to Baird line. 11 Mar
1801. Wit: Jeremiah Johnston, Francis Ford, Wm. Thaxton.

281-2 Richard Bearden to Byrd Moore, for $100, 128 A both sides Gents Cr of Hico
adj John Williams, Numan. 20 Apr 1801. Wit: P. Bennett, J. P. Bennett.

282-3 State of NC - #81 - to Nathan Scoging, for 50/ per 100 A, 99½ A on Castle
Cr adj Mary Gunn, John Baird formerly Nathan Scoging, Shadrack Gentry, Guttery,
Allen. 16 Nov 1795. Sworn chain carriers: Thomas Gunn, Sherwood James.

283 State of NC - #102 - to John Womack, 40 A on Flat R adj Joel Pope, Robert
Dickens, said Womack. Entered 9 Dec 1799. Registered 18 Nov 1800. Sworn chain
carriers: Green Womack, John Johnston; Wm. Waite, surveyor.

284 William Paine to Francis Day, for 150 lbs, 144 A on Deep Cr adj Craven.
24 July 1801. Wit: Wm. Yarborough Sen., Wm. Yarborough Jun.

284 Benjamin Towler to Henry Naltines of Orange Co., for 100 lbs, negro boy
George about 26 yrs old. 20 Jan 1801. Wit: John Carrington, Benj Carrington.

285 William McKissack to James Byrd of Franklin Co., NC, for 180 lbs, 212 A on
Flat R adj Robert Dickens, John G. Warren, John Smith Hurst, Richard Hargis.
15 Oct 1800. Wit: Jno Maleer, Thos McKissack, Thomas Badgett, James Badgett.

285 Stephen Stuart & Lucy Towns alias Lucy Stuart of Halifax Co., VA, to William
Duty of Person Co., for 55 lbs, negro boy slave Barney sometimes called John
Barney about 8 yrs & 4 mos old of black complexion rather than yellow. 5 Sept
1801. Wit: John Sargent, Littleton Duty.

286 Ann Towler wife of Benjamin Towler to Mary Paine wife of James Paine, for
good will & affection & 5/, negro woman Jude about 18 yrs old. 26 Aug 1801.
Wit: Edmund Shelton, Martha Shepherd, Polly Shelton.

286 Hiram Lewis adm of Edmond Lewis decd to James Chandler of Halifax Co., VA,
for 112 lbs, 81 A e side Henley Mill Cr adj Saterfield, Roseborough. 10 Aug 1801.
Wit: John McFarland, John Winstead.

287 John Bowles of Granville Co., NC, to Robert Dickens of Person Co., for 20 lbs,
140 A on Cobb Cr adj Walter Oakley & being land where James Anderson now lives.
1 Nov 1797. Wit: Allen Morgan.

287-8 William Waite to John Davis, for $400, 400 A on Deep Cr adj Bumpass, Jesse
Dickens. 7 Feb 1801. Wit: Jesse Dickens.

288 William Paine to William Yarborough Jun., for 50 lbs, 100 A on Mayo Cr adj
John Yarborough, Clayton. 13 Aug 1801. Wit: Wm. Yarborough, Francis Day.

289 Robert Paine to James Paine, for 6/, 267 A on Richland Spring Cr adj
Alexander Graham former line, John Saterfield, James Saterfield, Robert Dickens.
7 Sept 1801. Acknd.

290 John Layton to Charles Mitchel, for 50 lbs, 196 A on Fray's Br of Mayo adj Lawrence Vanhook old line, Michael Dickson, Charles Allen. 8 Apr 1801. Wit: Andr
Buchanan, William Huston.

290-1 Frederick Gowen of Mecklenburg Co., to William Thaxton of Halifax Co., VA,
for 40 lbs, 120 A on Blewing Cr adj Francis Ford, Reubin Jones, William Baird.
6 July 1801. Wit: James Thomson, Zachariah Averett, Charles Thaxton.
291-2 Jacob Vanhook, sheriff, to William Dickens of Granville Co. - to satisfy
judgment brought by Alex Campbell against Robert Dickens - for 33 lbs 3/6, 232 A
adj Wm. Tapp, John Bumpass. 21 Feb 1801. Wit: Samuel Dickens.

292-3 Daniel Hicks Sen. to Samuel Dickens,for $358, 129 A adj Joseph Traylor at
Tapley Cr, Jeffreys. 10 Feb 1801. Wit: Wm. Hicks, Toler Hicks.

Deed Book C
Page

293-4 Samuel Dickens to James Daniel, for $358, 129 A adj Joseph Traylor, at Tapley Cr, Jeffreys. 7 Sept 1801. Wit: John Clixby.

295 Ralph Williams to Benjamin Towler, for 71 lbs, negro boy George about 12-3 yrs of age. 17 Apr 1801. Wit: Jacob Vanhook. Said sale to satisfy Toler as security for Williams in bond given to Rachel Dunwoody exec of John Dunwoddy.

295 Benjamin Douglas to son John Douglas, for love, goodwill & 6/, negro boy David about 2 yrs old, the son of negro Dinah and born since she was given as deed of gift. 7 Dec 1801. Acknd in open court.

296 Jane Greenwood to her son Yancey Greenwood, for affection, goodwill & 5/, negro woman Daphny about 50 yrs old; woman Cate 21 yrs; George about 20, Lucey 15, boy Lighten age 12, James age 3, Randill 2; 50 A where she lives adj Mark Malone, Jesse Evans, Mary Currie; all furniture; cattle; 1500 weight of tobacco; negroes and land deeded for her lifetime and no longer; other property is at her disposal now. When 2 sisters of Yancey Greenwood namely Susannah Greenwood & Tabby Greenwood marry or come of age, he must divide property equally. 24 Nov 1801. Wit: Jesse Evans, Jun., B. Douglas.

297 Thomas Neeley to Vincent Warren, for $188, 125.4 A on S Hico adj Wm. Huse, Russell. 2 Apr 1801. Wit: John Maleer Sen., Garnett Neeley.

297-8 Thomas Duty to William Duty, for 19 lbs, his 8th part of 233 1/3 A willed by Matthew Duty decd - actually 29 1/8 A on Hico. 14 Nov 1801. Wit: Byrd Moore, James Stuart, Osborne Jeffreys.

298-9 Isabellar Rodgers to James Cozart, for 75 lbs, 40 A w side Deep Cr adj John Swainey, Moore, Henry Ledbetter old line - it being part of tract granted to David James by State & conveyed by James to her 24 Sept 1785. 20 Apr 1801. Wit: James Hicks, Samuel Rodgers, Benjn Partee, Phillips Moore.

299-300 Michael Robinson (the younger) of Orange Co., NC, to Samuel Bryan of Person Co., for $160, 167 A on Flat R at Harbour spring br adj Reubin Taylor, Robert Dickens, Wilson. 5 Dec 1801. Wit: Wm. Waite, Davie Robinson.

300-1 Paul Haralson to Major Haralson, for 75 lbs, 50 A on Marlowe Cr adj Lea Haralson, John Rogers. 24 Sept 1801. Wit: H. Haralson, Vincent Haralson.

301 State of NC - #107 - to William Davey, for 50/ per 100 A, 100 A on Mayo adj Winstead. 5 Dec 1801. Sworn chain carriers: Robert Davey, Ashborn Davey.

302 State of NC - #108 - to Samuel Jones, for 50/ per 100 A, 70 A on Tar R adj Person, said Jones, Nathan Ragan. 5 Dec 1801. Sworn chain carriers: Nathan Rogers, Joseph Pitman.

302 Robert Dickens to Jesse Dickens, for sundry services rendered & for 5/, negroes Adam & Molly, children of woman Frank or Fanney and purchased of James Norfleet 1777. 5 Feb 1798. Wit: Saml Dickens.

303 Ambrose Foster of Halifax Co., VA, to John Foster of same, for $200, 101 A in Person Co. adj Joseph Royster, William Sargent, Duncan, Brann. 22 Feb 1802. Wit: Alex Cunningham.

304 John Bumpass Sen. to Gabe Bumpass, for $50, 100 A on Deep Cr being part of tract where he lives adj John Davis, John Bumpass Jun. 25 Feb 1802. Wit: Jesse Dickens, Thomas Webb.

304-5 Wright Nichols to Woodson Hubbard, for 195 lbs, 170½ A adj Osborne Jeffreys. 19 Feb 1802. Wit: Wm. Jeffreys, L. Hargis.

305 John Moore Juh of Prince Edward Co., VA, to Joseph McGehee of Person Co., for $1500, 728 A on Cain Cr adj James Hamblett, Hugh Hemphill - it being tract willed

305 cont. - him by his father Joseph Moore who purchased it from George Black & Josiah Cole. 5 Dec 1801. Wit: J. M. McGehee, Edmund Dixon, J. Moore.

306 Daniel Sargent to Abner Lea, Richard Lea, & Benjamin Lea, for $200, 106 A on S Hico & Cobs Cr adj James Lea, Rice. 1 Feb 1802. Wit: John McFarland, Geo Lea.

306-7 John Miles to Richard Lea, for $275, 150 A adj Carver. 4 Feb 1802. Wit: Moses Bradsher, John B. Lea.

307-8 Nathan Scoggin to Duncan Rose Jun., for 20 lbs 5/8, 99½ A on Castle Cr adj Mary Gunn, John Baird formerly Scoggin, Shadrack Gentry - it being grant from State to Scoggin 16 Nov 1795. Wit: Alexr Rose Jun., B. Douglas. 17 Oct 1801.

308 John Sarratt to William Cocke, for 61 lbs 10/, 102.8 A on Double Cr of Hico 1 Mar 1802. Wit: John Gwin, David Roberts.

309 William Penn to Thomas Hargis, for $600, 2 lots near Person CH: one adj Jail lot with 1.1 A; the other adj CH lot & former lot of Nicholas Delone, Demsey Moore with 1.9 A. 17 Dec 1801. Wit: Jesse Gunn, R. Dickens, Demsey Moore.

310 John Carrington to John Gooch of Nottaway Co., VA, for 100 lbs, 50 A with mill seat both sides Flat R - it being former property of Thomas Gibson. 21 Jan 1802. Wit: Daniel Gooch, Thomas Sneed.

310-1 Artha Brooks Sen. to Artha Brooks Jun., for 40 lbs, 55 3/4 A on Hico adj Robert Brooks, David Brooks. 20 Feb 1802. Acknd in open court.

311-2 Robert Chamberlain to James Thomson (faded ink.) Wit: James Lawson, Jeremiah Johnston.

312 Thomas Sneed to John Gooch of Nottaway Co., VA, for 214 lbs, 515 A on n side Flat R adj John Bearden, Robert Cate, Stephen Moore, Thomas Menchew, John Carrington mill tract. 21 Jan 1802. Wit: Wm. Mitchell, Daniel Gooch.

312-3 James Ravens to Burwell Green, for 100 lbs, 250 A on Stories Cr adj Henry Williamson, Benjamin Hatcher, Mitchel. 10 Feb 1795. Wit: Edwd Atkinson. The witness & grantor are dead; Yancey Bailey proved writing of witness & John Ravens for grantor. Ordered registered Mar 1802.

313 James Jones of Halifax Co., VA, to Joshua Cates, for 5/, 184 A both sides Aldridge Cr adj Land purchased of Benton, Charles Pyron, Dickens. 5 June 1797. Wit: Robt Jones, Richd Camp, Betsey Wade.

314 Ralph Williams to daughter Martha Fuller, for love & affection, negro girl Vilet. 1 Dec 1801. Wit: Andw Buchanon.

314-5 William Warren to Starling Warren, for 100 lbs, 100 A on S Hico & Cobs Cr adj Carver. 8 Feb 1802. Wit: George Eskridge, John Miles.

315 James Farquhar to Ephraim Hawkins, for 222 lbs 10/, 190 A s of Bushy Fork of Flat R. 16 Jan 1802. Wit: Joseph Hargis, William Farquhar.

316 John Green atty for Burwell Green of Orange Co., NC, to James Cochran, for 150 lbs, 150 A on Stories Cr - said land purchased of James Ravens - adj Mitchel, James Hunt formerly Williamson. 2 Dec 1800. Wit: P. Williamson, Jas Hunt.

316-7 Isaac Vanhook to William Glenn, for 100 lbs, 100 A on Flat R adj John Paine, Robert Vanhook, Samuel Vanhook, Lawrence Vanhook - it being part of tract conveyed to Samuel Vanhook by exec of Aron Vanhook decd. 26 Jan 1799. Wit: R. Vanhook, Joseph Courtney, Barton Wood.

317 Lawrence Vanhook Sen. of CC to Loyd Vanhook of Person Co., for $475.70 & for paternal respect or affection, 380 A s fork Bushy Br adj Wm. Lea, George Eskridge, James McMurrey, Joseph Carney, Kindel Vanhook, John Newton, land purchased of Thomas Neely. 15 Nov 1800. Wit: William Rainey, Vincent Lea, Thos Hargis.

Deed Book C
Page

318 James Jones of Halifax Co., VA, to Joshua Cates of Person Co.,for 5/, 200 A both sides Aldridge Cr near Black Br adj Thomas Redmon former line, Goorley former line. 5 July 1791. Wit: Richd Camp, Patsey Wade, Robt Jones.

318-9 John Harris Sen. of Granville Co., to Abel Parish of Person Co., for 75 lbs, 150 A both sides Aron Cr. 5 Jan 1802. Wit: Overton Harris, Starling Harris.

319 Thomas Tolbert to William Pain, for 166 lbs 3/4, 100 A on James Henley Mill Cr of Hico adj William Trotter. 19 Feb 1799. Wit: James D. Henley, Jacob Vanhook.

320 William Dickens of Granville Co. to Samuel Dickens of Person Co., for $1000, 1250 A on Rocky Fork adj Land the late Charles Taylor purchased of William Green, Tapp, Joseph Lunsford, Jesse Dickens. 1 Mar 1802. Acknd in open court.

320-1 Robert Davie to Robert Gill, for 15 lbs, 13 A on Mayo adj Harrison, said Gill. 1 Mar 1802. Wit: James Paine, James Wilson.

321 Joseph Layton to Nathaniel Painter, for 50 lbs, 99 A adj Sarah Barnett, John Mitchell, Josias Dickson. 8 July 1802. Wit: John Guin.

322 Robert Davie to Edwd Bumpass Davie, John Davie, & Ashbourn Davie, for 1000 lbs, 500 A on Mayo adj Swepston Sims, Gabriel Davie at meeting house tract, Isaac Vanhook. 19 Jan 1802. Wit: Gabriel Davie, A. Vanhook.

322-3 Robert Davie to Swepston Sims, for 1000 good money, 600 A on Mayo adj Gabe Davie old line, the meeting house, James, Wilson, Ragan, Harrison. _ Jan 1802. Wit: J. Williamson, Samuel Jones.

323-4 Edward Clay Sen. to Edward Clay Jr., for love & affection, 300 A on Richland Cr including land purchased of Benjamin McNeill adj Atkinson, Isaac Saterfield, McNeill. 11 Aug 1801. Wit: Jas Cochran, Thomas Graves.

324 Yancey Greenwood relinquishes to his mother Jane Greenwood all land, property, & slaves she deeded him. (see Book C, page 296). 3 Mar 1802. Wit: Patrick Flynn, Daniel Malone.

324-5 Janey Greenwood to Daniel Malone, for $300, negro man George. 7 June 1802. Wit: Jesse Evans, John Malone.

325 Thomas Douglas to John Douglas, for 71 lbs, 71 A on Cobb Cr adj Richard Eskridge Junr., Elisha Roark. 26 June 1801. Wit: John Ogilby, Martin Duncan, B. Douglas.

325-6 Anthony Lumkin of Granville Co. to Thomas Sneed of Person Co., for 100 lbs, negro man slave Tom. 9 June 1802. Wit: Robert Wade.

326 William Cocke to Zachaus Hunt, for 216 lbs, 180 A on Gents Cr - it being called the Bennett place adj Burgess Haralson old line now Ezekiel Haralson, James Chambers late line. 20 Jan 1802. Wit: Isham Edwards, Wm. McKissack.

326-7 William Cocke to Zachaus Hunt, for 300 lbs, 200 A on Gents Cr of Hico called Morse old field. 20 Jan 1802. Wit: Isham Edwards, Wm. McKissack.

327 William Cocke to Zachaus Hunt, for 129 lbs, 100 A e side Gents Cr known as Woods place adj Morse old field, Wm. Allen former line, Allen Love now Cocke. 20 Jan 1802. Wit: Isham Edwards, Wm. McKissack.

328 Robert Wiles to William Lea Sen., merchant, of CC, for $98.45, 171½ A on Flat R adj Shadrack Roberts, Daniel Malone, Daniel Duram - deed of trust for $99.45 owed Lea. 9 Nov 1801. Wit: L. Lea, Wm. Donoho.

328-9 Robert Donaldson & Buckley Walker to Magar Haralson, for $80, negro woman Judy. 2 Mar 1802. Wit: Joseph McCain, David Hemphill.

329 James Jay to grandson Barzilla Jay, for love & affection, cattle, furniture, household equipment. 14 May 1802. Wit: Isaac Saterfield, Robert Trim.

Deed Book C
Page

329-30 Martin Duncan to Thomas Jeffreys of CC, for $493, 116 A on Hico adj Herndon Haralson, Abner Duncan. 7 Aug 1802. Wit: H. Haralson, Joseph McCain.

330 James K. Daniel to William Baird, merchant, for 35 lbs, negro woman Amy about 20 yrs and her child - for deed of trust for 35 lbs owed Baird. 8 Oct 1801. Wit: Robert Jones, Thos Halliburton.

331 Jacob Moonett to Mathew Daniel, for 500 Spanish milled dollars, 296 A on Flat R & Deep Cr adj Hardy Crews old line to Richland Spring Cr, John Pain. 1 Nov 1799. Wit: Wm. Jeffreys, Hardy Crews.

331-2 John Thomas to Jacob Thomas, for $104, 120 A on Bushy Fork of Flat R on Orange Co. line adj Aldridge, Edward Goins old line, Phillip Burch, D. Durram, reserving a dividing line to 100 A to Thomas & balance to Robert McNabb and was sold to McNabb by Thos Price - tract conveyed John Thomas by Thomas Price & to Pric by Daniel Malone. 8 Jan 1802. Wit: John Farrar, B. Douglas.

332 Absolem Johnston to Wilson Jones, for 70 lbs, negro girl Jane and girl Nutty. 23 Nov 1801. Wit: Jacob Vanhook, Drury Jones, John Brown.

333 Thomas Carver to Hiram Combs, for 58 lbs, 99 A adj Warren, Reynolds, Johnston. 2 Mar 1802. Acknd in open court.

334 Thomas Webb of Granville Co. to John Norman of same, for 30 lbs 12/, 100 A adj Harris, Daniel Persons. 5 Dec 1801. Wit: Lewis Parrot, Saml Blackwell.

334-5 Archibald Murphey of CC to Herndon Haralson of Person Co., for $866, 266 A on Hico adj Joseph Hall, widow Hamblett, Tobias Williams, Martin Duncan, Abner Duncan, Joseph McGhee. 1 July 1802. Wit: Sol Debow, Nancy Murphey.

336 Tobias Williams to Archibald Murphey, of CC, for 52 lbs 10/, 35 A on Hico in Person Co. adj said Murphey, CC line. 29 June 1802. Wit: James Rainey, H. Haralson, Sol Debow.

337 John Lingo to George Carey of Orange Co., for 45 lbs, 83 A on Dunns Cr in Person Co. adj Granville Co. line & corner of Orange Co. line. 7 Oct 1801. Wit: Charles Glenn, William Lingo.

338 Peter Cozart to George Cary, for 25 lbs, 25 A on Duns Cr adj Carey, Brown at Orange Co. line. 8 Oct 1801. Wit: William Brown, Charles Glenn.

338 Betsey Hamblett to mother Frances Hamblett, for $1, 4 negro slaves: Jenny & Chleery with her 2 children, Douglas & Juy. 13 Feb 1802. Wit: Thos Rainey, James Hamblett.

338-9 Lucy Green to Aron Cash, for 33 lbs, 85 A on Little Cr adj Daniel Meadows on Collings Br, Moses Cash, Benjamin Cozart, Ceddeth Johnson, Thos Cozart. 24 Mar 1802. Wit: Millenton Blalock, Sarah Allentharp.

339-40 Samuel Bumpass to John Bumpass (TR), for 100 lbs, 400 A on Tar R adj Antho Brown, Gabriel Davey, Robert Dickens, Wm. Tapp, McFarland Oakley, Thos Person, John Bowls - said land left them by heirship. 29 July 1802. Wit: Jesse Dickens, Samuel Dickens.

340 John Bumpass (TR) to Samuel Bumpass, for 100 lbs, 200 A in 2 tracts: one on Tar R adj Anthony Brown, Gabriel Davey, Wm. Yarbrough, said land left by his father; the other 140 A adj Wm. Tapp, Gabriel Davey, Robert Dickens. 29 July 1802. Wit: Jesse Dickens, Samuel Dickens.

341 State of NC - #105 - to William Waite, for 50/ per 100 A, 500 A on Flat R adj John Phillips near Aldridge Cr, Joshua Cate, James Farquhar, Blackart, Thomas Blalock, Thomas Hudgins. Entered 22 Nov 1800. Registered 26 Feb 1801. Chain carriers: Nathan Hargis, Wm. Hargis.

Deed Book C
Page

342 State of NC - #104 - to William Waite, 500 A both sides Tapley Cr adj Traylor,
Elijah Daniel, Jeffreys, Pain. Entered 22 Nov 1800. Chain carriers: Robert
Waite, Danl Hix.

343 Nathan Scoggin to John Atkinson, for $282, 94 A on Double Cr of S Hico adj
Thomas Rainey, James Jay. 17 Apr 1802. Wit: John Fooshe, James Cochran.

344 Samuel Neeley of CC to George Roberts of Person Co., for 15 lbs, 93 A on
Tapley Cr being part of grant from State of 296 A adj former line of Wm. Neeley
& Wm. Waite, Paul Jeffreys, Robert Pain east of Muddy Br; also 5 A adj Wm. Jay
now George Roberts. 2 Oct 1798. Wit: Isham Edwards, Robt Paine, James Jay.

344-5 Power of attorney - John Campbell to John McFarland to recover & receive any
debts or demands due him. 4 Dec 1802. Wit: A. D. Murphey.

345 Paul Haralson to Vincent Haralson, for $350, 100 A both sides Adams Cr adj
Abner Chambers, Hugh Barnett, Cox at Fepps Br, Ezekiel Haralson. 1 Oct 1802.
Wit: H. Haralson, Isaac Neeley.

346 Susannah Williamson exec of Henry Williamson to Pulliam Williamson, for 100
lbs, 190 A on Stories Cr adj Burwell Green, Jesse Watson, Edwd Clay, Hatcher.
18 Nov 1802. Wit: R Vanhook, Ja Vanhook, Jacob Fuller.

346 Power of attorney - Charles Allin of Franklin Co., KY, to William Huston,
William Allen, & Robert Allen all of Person Co. to demand & receive money & to
sell 696 A adj William Huston, Absolem Guttery - it being part of grant from
State; to make conveyance to Robert Steles. 28 Sept 1802. Wit: John Huston.

347 William Payne to Jeremiah White Fletcher, for $300, 97 A on James Henley mill
cr of Hico - it being part of larger tract conveyed by Thomas Talbert to Payne
19 Feb 1799 adj William Trotter. 2 Oct 1802. Wit: Edwd Clay Jun., B. Douglas.

347-8 Jacob Cozart of Granville Co. to Hubbard Cozart of same, for 45 lbs, 220 A
on Nap of Reeds Cr adj James Cozart, the Granville line. 1 Dec 1802. Wit: David
Roberts, Reubin Cozart.

348 James Byrd of Person Co., to Abraham Villines of CC, for 150 lbs, 212 A on
Flat R adj Robert Dickens, John Goodley Warren, John Smith Hust, Richard Hargis.
21 Oct 1802. Wit: Wm. McKissack, John M. McKissack.

348-9 Alexander Gray Sen. to son Alexander Gray Jr., for love & affection, 150 A
adj Ben Jacobs, Norfleet, Wm. McKissack. _ Dec 1802. Wit: James Byrd, William
McKissack.

349 Merritt Stone to John Swaney, for 135 lbs, 365 A e side Deep Cr - it being
part of tract that Samuel Fulton obtained from Lord Granville in 1762 on Rocky
Fork adj John Swaney Sen. - said tract part of that Joel Ledbetter purchased of
Henry Ledbetter. 24 Dec 1801. Wit: Job Gwin, James Swaney.

350 William Dickens of Granville Co. to Jesse Browne of Southampton Co., VA, for
$1500, 3 negro men slaves: Ephraim, George, Ben; also 280 A on Tar R adj Gabriel
Davie, William Morrow to Cattail Br, Persons, Samuel Bumpass - said land belonged to Edward Bumpass & purchased by Anthony Browne & sold by court order to Dickens.
16 July 1802. Wit:Anth Browne.

350 James Redwood to Lucy Hawkins Buckanan daughter of Arthur Buckanan, for love
& affection, 50 A on Fray's Br adj Charles Allin, James Layton; 1 mare, cattle,
furniture; all personal estate. 27 Oct 1802. Wit: John Gwin, J. Gwin.

351 Robert Cate Sen. to Robert Cate Jun., for 10 lbs, 180 A on Flat R. 6 Dec
1802. Wit: Micajah Nichols, W. Hubbard.

351-2 Samuel Neeley of CC to Robert Paine of Person Co., for 15 lbs, 93 A on Tap-
ley Cr - it being part of 296 A granted Neeley from State on Hillsborough Rd, adj
Paul Jeffreys on Mud Br, Robert Pain. 2 Oct 1798. Wit: Isham Edwards, Geo Roberts,
James Jay.

Deed Book C
Page

352 Samuel Neely of CC to Paul Jeffreys of Person Co., for 41 lbs 15/10, 93 A on Flat R - it being part of grant from State for 296 A adj George Roberts, Robert Pain. 2 Oct 1798. Wit: Isham Edwards, Geo Roberts, Robt Paine.

352-3 Nancy Darby admx of George Darby decd, John Darbey, Daniel Darbey, Hugh Darbey, George Darbey, James Darbey, John Dyson for his wife Elizabeth, Joseph Robertson for his wife Margaret - all heirs of estate - to Joseph Hall, for 100 lbs 150 A on Wynn's Cr adj Thomas M. Hamblett, Bluford Warren, George Elliott, Samuel Curles, John Darby. 10 Oct 1802. Wit: Gabriel Lea, Robt Thomas, John Warrick, William Lea Jun.

353-4 Osborne Jeffreys to William Cochran, for 15 lbs, 8 A n side Flat R at Dry Br adj Cothran - said tract granted to Osborne Jeffreys Sen. of Franklin Co. & willed to Osborne Jeffreys Jun of Person Co. 23 Nov 1802. Wit: Micajah Nichols.

354 Allen Fuller to Thomas Tolbert, for 125 lbs, 102 A adj James Chandler, Daniel Clayton, Joseph Gold, Roger Tillman. 24 Jan 1803. Wit: Jas Williamson, R. Long.

355 Jeremiah McIntire to Cochran, Haralson, & Co., for $100, 100 A on Gents Cr of Hico. 3 Jan 1799. Wit: William Fuqua, Thomas Henshaw.

355-6 Herndon Haralson & Isham Edwards, 2 co-partners in Co. with James Cochran - quit claim to James Cochran, for 36 lbs, their proportionate part of land purchased of Jeremiah McIntire. 14 Aug 1799. Wit: Davison Chambers, Henry Graves.

356 Ezekiel Haralson to Isham Edwards, for 300 lbs, 230 A both sides Stories Cr adj Zacheus Hart, Robert Deshazo, Walter McFarland - said land where Ezekiel Haralson lives. 8 Mar 1803. Wit: Solomon Cate, Phillip Hall Jun.

357 John Walker of Granville Co. to Benjamin Toler of Person Co., for $1200, 640 A adj Charles Mitchell, Thomas Man - said tract purchased of John Gwyn. 9 Sept 1802. Wit: Antho Browne, William Dickens.

357-8 William Aldridge, Joseph Aldridge, & Henry Hamric all heirs & legatees of Joseph Aldridge decd to Peter Aldridge a legatee & adm of Joseph Aldridge decd, for $200, 154.7 A adj Farquhar, Isham Aldridge at Bird's Cr to the River to Rocky Br. 9 Dec 1802. Wit: John Rountree, James Farquhar Jun.

358 Edmund Dixon to Henry Gray of Halifax Co., VA, for 70 lbs, 116½ A adj Thomas White on the State line, William Dixon, Elizabeth Gray, Daniel Glen, Allen Wade, Warrin. 7 Mar 1803. Acknd in open court.

358-9 Charles Allen of State of KY to John E. Watson of NC, for $108, 108 A on Castle Cr adj Robert Huston old line, Charles Bostick. 27 Sept 1802. Wit: Andw Barnett, Robert Allen.

359-60 Benjamin Jopling to Obediah Pierce, for 20 lbs 5/, 21¼ A on Flat R adj John Brown. 15 Feb 1803. Wit: Wm. Farquhar. Acknd in open court.

360 Laban Stafford of CC to James Stafford of Person Co., for 100 lbs, 100 A on drains of Cobb Cr including house & plantation where James Stafford lives adj John Campbell, George Lea. 11 Nov 1802. Wit: James Rainey, H. Haralson.

360-1 John Halliburton to Robert Halliburton, for 150 lbs, 150 A on Bluewing Cr adj Thomas Halliburton on Dixon Br, Beard. 20 Dec 1802. Wit: M. Halliburton, John Halliburton Jun.

361-2 Robert Walker to Cary Williams, for $1000(silver) or 500 lbs, 367 A both sides Gents Cr of Hico (it being survey granted to John Chambers by State for 300 A on 20 Dec 1779 & 67 A on 10 Nov 1784 - adj Thomas Robertson, Thomas Nash, Joseph Barnett now Pulliam. 20 Sept 1802. Wit: Ish Edwards, Joel Newman.

362 William Hamblin Senr to Richard Hamblin, for 12 lbs 10/, VA money equal to 20 lbs 16/8 money of NC, 100 A on Stories Cr adj William Hamblin Jun., George Hall William Carver. 9 Nov 1802. Wit: Peter Barrott, William Hamblin Jun.

58

Deed Book C
Page
362-3 Henry McNeill to John Scoggin, for 67 lbs, 10/, 150 A on Mayo being part of tract purchased by Scoggin of James Tolbert and part where Bedwell Saterfield lives adj Hardy Crisp, Thomas Alston, John Yarbrough. 14 Oct 1802. Wit: Nathan Scogin, Saml Burk.

363-4 Benjamin Wheelor to Hardy Hubbard, for 115 lbs, 100 A both sides Hendley Mill Cr of Hico adj Reubin Long, Francis Scoggin. 28 Sept 1802. Wit: John Garrott, William Saterfield.

364 State of NC - #101 - to William Blalock, for 50/ per 100 A, 93 A adj Moses Cash, William Oakly, Richard Oakly, Anthy Cozzart, Ben Cozzart. Entered 31 July 1778. Issued 14 Nov 1800.

365 State of NC - #96 - to Paul Jeffreys, for 10 lbs per 100 A, 34½ A n side n fork Flat R at Rattlesnake Br adj his own line. Entered 2 Dec 1784. Registered 14 Nov 1800.

365-6 William Cocke, sheriff, to Elijah Daniel, for 42/, 28 A of Allen Love on Hico at VA line - sold for non-payment of taxes - adj William Cocke formerly David Ford, Roger Atkinson, called Foley place. 5 Mar 1796. Wit: Richd Lyon.

366 Elijah Daniel to William Cocke, for 42/, 28 A on VA line adj Cocke, Atkinson. 5 Mar 1803. Wit: Richd Lyon.

367 Richard Holloway to William Cocke, for 100 lbs, 100 A on Gents Cr adj Robert Deshazo, widow Stone, Moss old field. 5 Jan 1799. Wit: Walter McFarland, Thos Barnett.

367-8 William Cocke to Thomas Chambers, for $850, 170.2 A on Hico & Gents Cr adj Gregory old corner. 6 Sept 1803. Wit: Thos M. Megehe.

368-9 George Cary to Benjamin Partee, for 20 lbs, 113 A on Duns Cr adj Granville Co. line, Charles Glenn, the Orange Co. line. 5 Dec 1801. Wit: Charles Glenn, Yearby Partee.

369 Benjamin Wheeley of Orange Co. to Nancy Watkins of Person Co., for $100, 80 A on road to schoolhouse on Whitfield line adj Ubanks, Chrisonberry, Wells, the county line. 9 Feb 1800. Wit: William Keeling, Betsy Watkins.

370 William Bailey to son Henry Bailey, for love & affection, negro boy Scott - but not in force until after death of grantor. 16 Sept 1802. Wit: John Holloway.

370 Vincent Haralson to Meredith Cox, for $500, 100 A both sides Adams Cr adj Abner Chambers, Hugh Barnett, on Fipps Br, Ezekiel Haralson. 4 Aug 1803. Wit: Joseph D. McFarland, Joseph McGehee. Proved by oath William D. McFarland.

371-2 James Byrd to Stokes Allen, for $211, 111 A on Long br of Flat R adj John Brown, Robert Dickens. 5 Sept 1803. Wit: Duncan Rose, Andrew B. Wood.

372 John Drury Moore relinquishes to his mother a legatee of Robert Moore any claim to 125 A. 6 Sept 1803. Wit: James Fraken, Richd Ogilby.

372-3 Daniel Merritt to heirs of John Dunwoody decd, for 100 lbs, 100 A on Rose Merry Br adj Paul Walters, Benj Toler, Dinwoodie. 7 Sept 1803. Wit: Wm. Jeffreys, Loyd Vanhook, John Russell.

373-4 Robert Moore to his son John Drury Moore, for 5 lbs, 175 A on Hico adj William Huston, Harrison Stanfield, Archibald Campbell old line. 22 Mar 1803. Wit: Richd Ogilby, Fraken.

374 Hiram Combs to Elisabeth Johnston, for 18 lbs, 20 A on Cobb Cr adj William Warren, Carver, Reynolds. 6 June 1803. Wit: Starling Warren, William Johnston.

374-5 Nehemiah Fuller to William Fuller, for 20/, 2 A on Stories Cr being part of tract conveyed by Henry Fuller. 18 Aug 1803. Wit: Jas Cochran, Benj Wheelor.

375 James Currie, Mager Haralson, William Black, surviving exec & legatees of George Black decd; also Nancy Black, Polly Black, Peggy Black children & legatees of George Black attest they have recd their share of his estate. 3 Sept 1803.
Wit: Saml Smith.

376 John Campbell to John Ogilby, for $3521.66, 704 1/3 A both sides Cobb Cr in fork of Hico adj William Rainey, Archd Murphey, Branch. 10 Nov 1802.
Wit: H. Haralson, John McFarland.

377-8 Abner Chambers to Davison Chambers & Benjamin Chambers - deed of trust - for $266 in debts due them, 100 A adj Paul Haralson, Matthew Brooks, Robert Deshazo - said land purchased of William Chambers decd. 11 Apr 1803. Wit: Leonard Morris, Matthew Brooks.

378 Philip Hall to James Bryant, for 158 lbs 6/8, 338 A both sides Flat R adj Robert Dickens, John Wilson, Benjamin Jacobs, Gray, Jones, Reubin Taylor.
9 June 1803. Wit: Wm. Hall, Josiah Fike.

379 David Roberts to Richard Peed of Granville Co., for 123 lbs 12/, 206 A on Cubb Cr adj Abraham Maderas on Ren spring br. 16 Aug 1802. Wit: George Roberts, Arthur Roberts.

379-80 James Bryan to Thomas Saulman, for $90, 45 A on Flat R adj Samuel Bryan, Jacobs. 9 June 1803. Wit: Wm. Hall, Josiah Fike.

380 Michael Robinson to Joseph Hargis, for 115 lbs, 113 A on Flat R adj John S. Hust, Thomas Hargis. 13 June 1803. Wit: Obediah Pierce, Sally Pierce.

381 David Roberts to Andrew Peed, for 36 lbs, 100 A on Cubb Cr to Rens spring br up Fluke Br - said land a part of grant from State. 18 Aug 1803.
Wit: George Roberts, Jeremiah Roberts.

381-2 Benjamin Jopling to Thomas Blalock, for 112 lbs 10/, 90 A on Flat R adj Abrah Moore, Thomas Moore, said Blalock, Henry McIntire. 4 June 1803.
Wit: Thomas Blalock, Henry McEntire.

382 David Roberts to Arthur Roberts, for 120 lbs, 150 A on Cubb Cr at Flukes Br adj Richd Peed, Andrew Peed. 3 Sept 1802. Wit: George Roberts, Jeremiah Roberts, Willie Roberts.

383 David Bazwell to John Lea, for 158 lbs 8/4, 141 A on Bear Br of S Hico adj Joseph Rice, Daniel Sergent. 6 Apr 1803. Wit: H. Haralson, Geo Lea.

383-4 Dempsey Moore to William Jeffreys & James Williamson, for $200, 1 A adj Robert Pain storehouse, near Dickens' house. 9 Oct 1802. Wit: Robert Wade, Richd Allen.

384-5 Benjamin Douglas to little daughter Jenett Brown Douglas, for love & affection & 5 lbs, negro boy Peter about 7 yrs of age; he is son of Dinah given to said Douglas by his father Thomas Douglas; if she die withour issue, Peter to revert to grantor or his heirs. 19 Apr 1803. Wit: Elizabeth Dison, Ann Darbey.

385-6 Benjamin Douglas to daughter Rebekah Evins Douglas, for love & affection, & 5 lbs, negro girl Lucy age 10 yrs - a daughter of Dinah given him by his father Thomas Douglas. 19 Apr 1803. Wit: Elizabeth Dison, Ann Darby.

386 Thomas Williams to Richard Holdman of Orange Co., for $150, negro boy James about 10 yrs old. 21 Mar 1803. Wit: Charles Holdman, Thomas Rountree. Boy sold to satisfy debt.

387 Herndon Haralson to William S. Branch, for $1550, 309 1/6 A both sides N Hico adj Archibald Murphey now Haralson, Thomas Jeffreys, Richard Ogilby, John Campbell to Mineral spring br. 13 Oct 1802. Wit: John Ogilby, J. Campbell.

Deed Book C
Page
388 Jesse Gunn to Francis Lawson, for 210 lbs, 498 A adj Baird on mill cr, Davey, widow Davey, Crossing Dry Br. 13 Oct 1802. Wit: William Street, Moses Street.

388-9 Elisha Roark to Kindal Vanhook, for $120, 49½ A on Rushy Br S Hico adj John Dyson, Douglas. 19 Feb 1803. Wit: Loyd Vanhook.

389 Overton Harris of Granville Co. to Starling Harris of same, for 120 lbs, 256 A in Person Co. on Crooked Fork. 26 Oct 1802. Wit: Starling Hughs, Charles Smith.

390 James Chambers to sons Josias Chambers, William Woodson Chambers, & James Chambers, for love & affection, all property he possesses reserving enough to pay debts; negro men Ben & Hall; women Beck, Nann; boys Esriel, George, Sam, Arter; cattle, curniture. 22 Apr 1803. Wit: William Parrish, John Pierson.

390-1 Ephraim Hawkins to James Byrd, for 104 lbs 10/, 111½ A on long br of Flat R adj John Brown, Robert Dickens. 6 June 1803. Wit: Nathaniel Norfleet, George Broche.

391-2 William Brown to Charles Glenn of Granville Co., for 100 lbs, 200 A adj Orange Co. line, Peter Cozart. 9 Mar 1801. Wit: John Lingo, Peter Cozart.

392-3 Millington Blalock Senr. to William Blalock, for 40 lbs, 350 A on Rocky Fork adj Madaires to Muddy Br, Johnathon Jackson, Dickens. 4 June 1803. Wit: Moses Cash, Robert Blalock, Millington Blalock Jun.

393 James Farquhar, millwright, to William Farquhar, planter, for 110 lbs, 232 A on Bushy Fork Flat R adj Watts, Hawkins. 10 July 1803. Wit: James Farquhar Jun., John Farquhar.

394 Millinton Blalock Sen. to Millington Blalock Jun., for 85 lbs, 320 A on Rocky Fork adj Swainey, Person, Moore, Levi Swainey former line. 4 June 1803. Wit: John Blalock, Robert Blalock, William Blaylock.

394-5 Benjamin Jopling to William Moore, for $250, 265 A head of Flat R adj Obediah Pearce, John Brown, Thomas Farrar. 10 Apr 1803. Wit: Patsey Hargis, Abraham Moore.

395-6 John Harris Sen. of Granville Co. to Starling Harris of Person Co., for 50 lbs, 165 A on crooked fork Aron's Cr adj Overton Harris, John P. Pool, John Harris, Wm. Waite. 6 June 1803. Wit: Overton Harris, R. Harris.

396-7 William Waite to James Cochran, for 875 lbs,320 A n fork Double Cr of Hico adj William Brown, John Blake, Samuel McMurry, William Cock, John Hall, Wood; 313 A adj William Brown, James Jay, Wood, Hall. 26 Nov 1800. Wit: David Brechen, William Roberts, Sol Debow.

397-8 Thomas Jeffreys of CC to Herndon Haralson of Person Co., for $493, 116 A in Person Co. adj Haralson, William Branch on Hico Cr, Abner Duncan. 6 Jan 1803. Wit: Martin Duncan, William McCain, Joseph McCain.

398 Edmund Dixon to John Pearson, for $4, 1 A n side Hyco on wagon rd. 31 Aug 1803. Wit: Thos Tolbert.

399 William Lea Senr. of Leasburg, to Robert Wiles of Person Co., for $95.45, quit claim to following conveyance of land. 24 Oct 1803. Wit: Wm. Donoho, William Lea Jun.
Robert Wiles to Nathaniel Norfleet, for 85 lbs, 171½ A on Flat R adj Jackson, Shadrack Roberts, Absolem Johnston, Daniel Malone, Daniel Durram. 25 Oct 1803. Wit: Elisha Roark, Rebekah Roark.

400 Robert Dickens & William Waite to Joshua Step, for $37½, 50 A adj Step, James Rimmer. 22 Oct 1796. Wit: William Dickens, James Rimmer.

Deed Book C
Page

400 Robert Dickens and William Waite to Elizabeth Step, for $94 2/9, 100 A.
22 Oct 1796. Wit: William Dickens. James Rimmer.

401 Elisabeth Stepp to her son Joshua Stepp, for love, affection, & 5/, 100 A on
Bushey Fork of Flat R adj William Waite, James Rimmer, James Farquhar. 18 Mar
1800. Wit: Wm. Waite, James Jones, James Rimmer.

402 John Clixby to Ro Moore, for 160 lbs, 321 A on Deep Cr adj Clixby, Thomas
Moore, Stephen Moore - said land part of that granted Clixby by State. 24 Aug
1803. Wit: Abner Williams, Ga Davey.

402 Thomas Sneed to Jesse Womack of Sumner Co., TN, for $290, negro girl Letty
about 15 yrs old. 25 Sept 1802. Wit: John Womack, Jas Sneed.

403 Lucy Coleman exec and Valantine Corely exec of Edgefield Dist. SC, to George
Kirk of Person Co, for $110, 100 A on Deep Cr- being part of 594 A adj Bumpass
old line, Bedwell Saterfield, John Saterfield. 15 Nov 1803. Wit: Jesse Dickens,
John Saterfield.

403a William Duty to John Thomas, for $1420, 233 A on Hico Cr adj Stuart, Roberts,
Moore on Millstone Br, Julius Justice, John Williams. 12 Oct 1803. Wit: Edmund
Dixon, Patrick Carnell.

403a-4 John Wilson to Thomas McNeill, for $150, 144 A on Meeting House Br of
Adams Cr adj Joseph Gill. 24 July 1802. Wit: Benjn Fowler, John Moore.

404 Henry P. Chambers to Walter McFarland, for 50 lbs, 50 A w side Marlow Cr adj
Zacheus Hurt, Paul Haralson. 8 Jan 1803. Wit: Daniel Walters, Benjn Chambers.

405 Dempsey Moore to Benjamin Towler, for 640 lbs, 640 A on Storeis Cr adj John
Pain, Joshua Browning, Gideon Patterson, David Mitchell. 3 Oct 1803.
Wit: Robt Wade, Richd Allen, Thos Badgett.

405-7 Bethsheba Norsworthy exec of William Noyal Norsworthy decd of Warren Co.,
NC; to James Frame, for 92 lbs 7/, 440 A on Flat R adj John Womack, John Paine,
Thomas Hargis - said land Norsworthy acquired 20 Nov 1784 and 200 A sold to John
Paine. 20 July 1803. Wit: Allen Miller, James Paine.

407-8 Dempsey Moore to Benjn Towler, for 800 lbs, 200 A on Adams Cr adj John Moore,
Wm. Mann, reserving 7 A where courthouse now stands with lots adj. 4 Oct 1803.
Wit: Robt Wade, John Williams, D. Merritt, Thomas McNeill.

408-9 James Williamson to Joseph Hubbard, for 100 lbs, 640 A on Richland Spring
Cr adj Hubbard, John Pain, Demsey Moore. 1 May 1803. Wit: Robert Wade.

409 Robert Dickens to Jesse Dickens, for services rendered & 5/, negroes boy
Adam, girl Molly - the son & daughter of woman Frank or Fanny which he purchased
in 1777 of James Norfleet. 5 Feb 1798. Wit: Saml Dickens.

409 Alexander Gray Sen., Alexander Gray Jr. & John Gray to John Rountree, for
$249 2/3, negro boy George. 10 Apr 1800. Wit: Nathl Morfleet, Nancy Gray.

410 John Pearson to Abraham Dunaway of CC, for $1272, 159.2 A on Hico adj Yancey
Bailey former line now Penix, John Davey. 13 Oct 1803. Wit: H. Haralson,
Samuel Dunaway.

410 Dempsey Moore to Benjamin Towler, for 500 lbs, 6 negro slaves left by his
father-in-law John Walker decd: Call, Thomas, Anderson, Smith, Sarah, Frank.
3 Oct 1803. Wit: Robt Wade, Danl Merrit.

411 Daniel Sargent to Barnett Lea, for $455, 104½ A on Cobbs Cr adj said Lea
formerly William Lea line, Stephen Sargent now Rice, James Lea. 3 Mar 1804.
Wit: Geo Lea, F. Douglas.

Deed Book C
Page
411-2 Daniel Sargent to Barnett Lea, for $50, 11 5/8 A adj Edwd Doyle former line now Sargent, Joseph Rice formerly Stephen Sargent. 6 Mar 1804. Wit: Ebenezer Whitehead, B. Douglas.

412 Richard Lea to John Bradsher, for $158 1/3, 100 A on S Hico adj Carver. 6 Mar 1804. Wit: Abner Lea, B. Douglas.

413 Nathan Ragan to Jesse Ragan, for 15 lbs, 50 A adj Gabriel David decd, Doctor Symes. 5 Mar 1804. This deed void if Jesse Ragan sells land while grantor still lives. Acknd in open court.

413-4 Elisha Sarratt to Abner Bradsher, for $485, 97 A e fork Double Cr of Hico adj John Farrow, Wm. Lea Sen., John Broadway. 20 Dec 1803. Wit: Moses Bradsher.

414 James Williamson to William Singleton, for 200 lbs, 200 A on Stories & Adams Creeks adj Robert Southward - said land purchased of Southward who had grant from State. 26 Feb 1804. Wit: James Paine, L. Hargis.

414-5 John Cash to Billetha Oens, for 45 lbs, 200 A being part of 640 A on Cubb Cr adj Cozart, Jackson, John Swainey. 24 Mar 1803. Wit: James Burk, John Blalock.

415 Charles Allen of Franklin Co., KY, to John Moore McGehe, for 208 lbs 4/, 706 A on Adams Cr adj William Huston, Thomas Haggie, Andrew Barnett, Edward Chambers, Bearden, Garrot, Guttrie, John Watson. 6 Dec 1803. Wit: H. Haralson, Joseph D. McFarland.

416 Daniel Clayton, William Clayton, Thomas Clayton, & Richard Clayton - to David Clayton Sen., for 15 lbs, 430 A e side Richland Spring Cr adj Joseph Hubbard, Matthew Daniel, John Paine, Robert Paine. 27 Feb 1804. Wit: Hardy Crews Sen., Hardy Crews Jun.

416-7 Samuel Garrett to John Garrett, for $110, 60 A n side Richland Cr of S Hico adj Moravian line. 4 July 1803. Wit: Joseph Coleman, Betsey Coleman.

417 Richard Eskridge to Nicholas Thompson to CC, for $258, 86 A in Person Co. on Cobb Cr adj Thos Douglas, William Carney, William Lea Sen., above the brodge, William Lea Jun., Hamilton Reynolds, John Dyson. 2 Feb 1804. Wit: James Holder, John Tapley, Jesse Womack.

417-8 Thomas Tolbert to Benjamin Wheeler, for 25 lbs, 102 A adj James Chandler, Daniel Clayton, Joseph Gold, Roger Tillman. 3 Mar 1804. Acknd in open court.

418-9 William Black to Edmund Dixon, for $900, 155 A on Hico Cr adj Dixon, Samuel Smith, John Harris, George Tapp. 27 Dec 1803. Wit: Saml Smith, William Dixon.

419 James Stuart to Alexander Cuningham, for 36 lbs, all his right as a legatee of James Stuart Jun. decd in land or any sale of it whereon Mrs. Agnes Stuart now lives containing 200 A - his part being 1/5 on Hico adj John Moore McGehee, Richard Pendergrass Sen., John Williams Sen., John Thomas, Robert Moore. 14 Jan 1804. Wit: Edmund Dixon, William Warrin.

419-20 William Stuart Jun. to Alexander Cuningham, for $120, his 1/5 interest in 200 A as legatee of James Stuart Jun. decd on Hico. 13 Oct 1803. Wit: Nathl Cuttrie, Thomas Bohanon.

420 Robert Standfield Jun. adm of James Standfield decd of Halifax Co., VA, to Allen Wade of Person Co., for 180 lbs, 200 A where Wade lines on Stuart's Cr of Hico adj Edmund Dixon, Daniel Glenn, Charles Boulton. 2 Mar 1804. Wit: H. Standfield, Richd M. Covington.

421 John Newton to James Cochran, for $250, negro man age 32 yrs named Leven. 4 Feb 1804. Wit: Hosea McNeill, Nancy Scoggin.

421 Farish Carter of Hancock Co., GA, to Isham Edwards & Co., for $285, negro woman Eady age about 35 yrs; boy Prince 2 yrs. 15 Apr 1803. Wit: Hosea McNeill, Nancy Scoggin.

421-2 Burwell Green of Pendleton Co., SC, fy his atty John Green, to John Tapley of Person Co., for $100, 80 A on Double Cr of Hico adj the Moravian line, Hardy Wells. 17 Oct 1803. Wit: John Womack, Henry Womack, John P. Womack.

422 Thomas Barnett of Iredell Co., NC, to Henry Graves of Person Co., for 166 lbs, 13/4, 98.1 A adj James Cochran, John Clayton, Josiah Carver. 20 Feb 1804. Wit: Isham Edwards, Benjn Chambers.

423 John Pearson to Solomon Draper Jr., for 94 lbs, 94 A w side Hico adj John Ogilby, Robert Black, widow McCain, Joseph McCain - said tract conveyed by John Robertson 16 Mar 1796. 10 Dec 1803. Wit: H. Haralson, A. L. Clayton.

423-4 Daniel Ramsey Jun. to William Ramsey, for 50 lbs, 101 A adj John Baird, Agness Barnett. 20 Dec 1803. Wit: John Holloway, Lewis Ramsey.

424-5 Gabriel Gunn to Aaron Haskins of Halifax Co., VA, for 20 lbs, 19½ A e side Hico adj Fielding Lewis, Abner Duncan, Joseph McGehee, John Ogilby - said tract allotted James Lewis as legatee of Fielding Lewis decd & by him conveyed to Gunn. /s/ G. A. Gunn. 20 Oct 1803. Wit: H. Haralson, Richard Ogilby, Creed Haskins.

425 George Hall of Halifax Co., VA, to Thomas Jeffreys of CC, for 50 lbs, 133 A near Doctor Parker adj William Hamlin, William Carver, on road from Clay to Edwards store, Robert Walker. 11 Feb 1804. Wit: Joseph McCain, Thomas Tolloh.

426 James Wells of CC to John Mason of Person Co., for 125 lbs, 100 A on Cobbs Cr adj Hugh Darby, Henry Rogers, Robert Mitchell former line. 25 Jan 1804. Wit: Henry Sergent, Miles Wells.

426-7 William Singleton to James Long, for 200 lbs, 200 A on Stories & Adams Creeks - said tract part of grant from State to William Southard & sold by him to James Williamson adj Robert Southward. __ __ 1804. Acknd in open court.

427 Christopher Bass to Joseph D. McFarland, for 500 lbs, 405 A n side Gents Cr of Hico adj Allen Love, Richard Pendergrass, William Barnett, Byrd Wall, Thomas J. Chambers. 1 Mar 1804. Wit: J. Moore, William McGehee.

428-9 Alexander McCain to John McCain both of CC to Joseph McCain, James McCain & William McCain of Person Co., for 400 lbs, 546 A being all property left them in Person Co. by Hugh McCain decd adj Archibald Murphey, John Davie crossing Cain Cr, claim of Robert Black, Solomon Draper. 25 Feb 1804. Wit: Thomas J. Moore, Tho Jeffreys.

429-30 State of NC - #69 - to James Whitehead, for 50/ per 100 A, 300 A in Granville & Caswell Counties both sides crooked fork Aaron's Cr adj Blanks. 24 Sept 1779. Sworn chain carriers: William Hart, William Page. Registered Person Co. 13 June 1804.

430 State of NC - #1197 - to Thomas Hargis, for 10 lbs per 100 A, 309 A on Flat R adj William Gately, John Urquhart, Thomas Person, Abraham Hargis, Drury Allen. Surveyed 14 June 1787. Chain carriers: John Douglas, Joseph Gately. 21 Dec 1803.

431 Frederick William Marshall of Salem, Stokes Co., NC, to Benjamin McNeill of Person Co., for $187.50, 150 A on Richland Cr of S Hico - part of 688 A of original tract obtained by deed of bargain 20 Apr 1764 between William Churton & Charles Metcalf, registered in Orange Co, Book I, page 106 & in Rowan Co., book 5, page 452 and was conveyed by Metcalf in deed of trust to Marshall. 31 May 1799. Wit: Jas McMurry.

432 James Eubank to Daniel Durrum(Durham), for 50 lbs, 57½ A on Bushy Fork adj Charles Allison purchase of Eubank. 15 Aug 1799. Wit: Isaac Rainey, Charles Allison.

432-3 Elisha Roark to James Johnston of Orange Co., for $120, 51 A on Rusha Br of S Hico adj meeting house on Joseph Carney line, Thomas Douglas. 2 Sept 1803. Wit: Loyd Vanhook, Nicholas Thomson.

Deed Book C
Page

433 Thomas Douglas to William Carney, for 41 lbs, 2/, 34.3 A on Cobb Cr on road from Leasburg to the bridge on S Hico adj James Johnston, Joseph Carney. 10 Dec 1803. Wit: Geo Lea, Thomas Allin.

433-4 Benjamin Towler to William Cocke, for $225, 411 A on Double Cr of Hico adj Thomas Badgett, said Cocke, the Moravian line, Adam McNeeley. 6 Sept 1803. Wit: Solomon Moore, James McAden.

434-5 David Robinson to William Cocke, for 262 lbs 10/, 190½ A on lick cr of Flat R adj Michael Robinson, David Robinson old line; also 35 A adj first tract. 13 Oct 1803. Wit: John Reeves Jun., John McKissack.

435-6 William Cocke to Edmond Shelton, for $300, 87½ A on VA line adj Allin Love, James Patterson, Hedgeman Warren; also 28 A on VA line adj Cocke formerly Ford, Roger Atkinson at Foley old place. 19 Dec 1803. Wit: John Paine, Benjn B. Cocke.

436 William Sargent to Archibald Lipscomb, for 210 lbs, 349½ A adj Solomon Draper, John Brann, Joseph Royster, Dunkin, James Cochran, Robert Carver, Hall, William Trotter. 17 May 1804. Wit: Moses Bradsher, William Sargent Jr.

437 Richard Pendergrass to Edward O. Chambers, for $20, 4 A adj said Chambers. 12 Dec 1803. Wit: Jno M. McGehee.

437 Edward Wortham of Dinwiddie Co., VA, to Major Haralson of Person Co., for $600, negro slaves Beckey, Joe, Rosanne. 4 Feb 1804. Wit: Abner Jackson, Isaac Neely.

438 Jacob Vanhook, sheriff of Person Co., to Samuel Smith, for 121 lbs 18/1, 295 A adj Robert Walker, Solomon Draper - sold by deed of trust & court order in suit Thomas Roberson vs Ambrose Foster to collect 115 lbs 14/4 favoring Roberson. 14 June 1802. Wit: Jas Cochran.

438 Benjamin Towler to Isaiah Fuller, for 100 lbs, negro girl Nance about 15 yrs old. 6 Dec 1803. Wit: Andrew Buchanan, Tho McNeill.

438-9 Thomas Vass Sen. of Granville Co. to John Turner of Person Co., for 72 lbs 10/, 200 A on Bluewing Cr adj Robert Jones, Stephen Jones, John Baird, Wm. Baird. 5 May 1804. Wit: David Allen, James Holloway, Ambrose Jones.

439-40 Thomas Hargis to Lawrence Hargis, for $600, 2 lots near Person CH: 1.1 A adj jail lot on road to spring; 1.9 A adj Nicholas Delone on road to spring, Demsey Moore. 2 June 1804. Wit: Matthew Daniel.

440-1 John Walsh to Richard Parker, trustee, of Halifax Co., VA, for 238 lbs,1/, which Welsh owes Joseph Jones of Dinwoody Co., VA, for 5/, Jack, Judy & her children: Barnett, Winny, Phebe, Janey, Fanny. 1 Oct 1802. Wit: John Baynham, Benj Ferrell.

441 James Long to William Singleton, for 200 lbs, 100 A on Stories & Adams Creeks adj John Trickey, Artha Brooks, Henry Graves - said land his father Ambrose Long willed him. 6 Mar 1804. Wit: B. Long.

441-2 James Daniel to Elijah Daniel, for $358, 179 A adj Joseph Traylor, to Tapley's Cr, Jeffreys. 5 June 1804. Wit: Richard Holdman.

442 George Howard to Robert Howard, for $500, all coming to him from estate of Henry Howard decd. 6 June 1801. Wit: J. Howard, Adams Sanders.

443 John Howard to Robert Howard, for $500, all land that will fall to him as a legatee of Henry Howard decd. 16 Mar 1804. Wit: Henry W. Howard, Thos J. Chambers.

443 Daniel Clayton to Stephen Crews, for 25 lbs, 100 A on Richland Spring Cr adj Joseph Hubbard, Matthew Daniel. 19 May 1804. Wit: John Daniel, Matthew Daniel.

444 William Allen (who married Sarah Howard) to Robert Howard, for $80, all his right as legatee of Henry Howard decd & in the land where Priscilla Sanders now lives - 357 A adj Jno Rogers, Walter McFarland, Thos J. Chambers; land on Hico, Marlowe & Gents Creeks; also all his right to 300 A where Edwd O. Chambers now lives adj Richard Pendergrass, Mary Stone, John Williams, Cary Williams - the part of William Allen being 1/14. 4 June 1804 Acknd in open court.

444-5 William Lewis to Robert Howard, for 26 lbs, all his right as legatee of Henry Howard decd & land where Equilla Sanders lives - 350 A adj John Rogers, Walter McFarland, Thos J. Chambers on Hico, Marlowe & Gents Creeks. 31 Mar 1804. Wit: Thos J. Chambers, Ab Stafford.

445 William Carter who married Peggy Howard to Robert Howard, for 27 lbs, all his right as legatee of Henry Howard decd & to tract where Mrs. Priscilla Sanders lives - 357 A on Hico, Marlow, Gents Creeks; also his right to tract where Edward O. Chambers lives - 300 A on Gents Cr - his part being 1/14. 13 Apr 1804. Wit: Thos J. Chambers, Joseph D. McFarland.

445-6 Thomas J. Chambers who intermarried Devina Howard to Robert Howard, for 24 lbs, all his right to land where Priscilla Sanders lives about 300 A on Gents Cr adj John Rogers, Walter McFarland; also all right as a legatee of Henry Howard decd to the 300 A where Edward O. Chambers now lives adj Robert Pendergrass, Mary Stone, John Williams, Cary Williams on Gents Cr. 13 Apr 1804. Wit: John Hawkins, Joseph D. McFarland.

446-7 Shadrack Hargis to his son William Hargis, for love & affection, 390 A on Flat R adj Nathan Hargis, Thomas Hargis, Thomas Hudgins, John Paine, John Womack, Dickens. 3 June 1804. Acknd in open court.

447 Joseph Traylor to John Hix (Hicks), for $100, 100 A on Tapley Cr adj said Traylor. 2 June 1804. Wit: James Paine.

447-8 Magor Haralson to William Moore, for $436, 109 A adj John Rogers, Lea Haralson. 9 Mar 1804. Wit: John E. Watson, Isaac Neeley.

448-9 Julius Justice to Josias Dickson, for 400 Spanish milled dollars, 131 A on Whetstone Br adj Joel Newman, William Huston, Duty old line. 29 Sept 1803. Wit: Thos Dickson, Jno Dickson.

449 Robert Dickens to Joseph Traylor, for $200, 200 A on Tapley Cr adj Daniel Hicks. 25 May 1798. Wit: William Hicks.

449-50 Thomas J. Chambers to Robert Howard, for 50 lbs 15/3 & 3 farthing, 37½ A on e side Hico at Gents Cr adj grantor. 11 Jan 1804. Wit: Benjn Chambers, Joseph D. McFarland.

450-1 John Russell to Martha Richardson, widow, for $664, 200 A on S Hico adj Thomas Neeley. 5 June 1804. Wit: Loyd Vanhook, Tho Neeley, Samuel Woods.

451-2 Robert Jones of Halifax Co., VA, to John Halliburton of Person Co., for 226 lbs 3/1½, 675½ A both sides Blewing Cr adj Baird, said Halliburton. 25 Feb 1804. Wit: Martin Halliburton, Matthew Pickett.

452 McCall Elliott & Co. by their atty Thomas Gholson Jun. to Robert Jones of Halifax Co., VA, for 610 lbs, 670 A both sides Hyco & Cain Creeks adj Goodloe Warren, Woolsey Pride, Daniel McFarland, Benj Debow, Robert Moore. Archibald Campbell on 9 June 1783 conveyed in trust 670 A in CC to Allen Love one of the co-partners of McCall Elliot & Co. for debt due by Campbell & Superior Court ordered foreclosure. 5 June 1804. Wit: Thomas Vaughan.

453 Thomas Douglas to daughter Janett Lea wife of George Lea, for goodwill & affection, negro woman Agg & her child Dulea. 19 Jan 1804. Wit: John McFarland, William Lea.

Deed Book C
Page

453 Edmund Gowen to William Baird of Prince George Co., VA, for 90 lbs 17/2 as debt is due for this amt., negro girl Patty age about 14 yrs; horses, cattle. 5 June 1804. Wit: Samuel Ward, Anselem Bugg, James Thomson.

454 B. Douglas to son John Douglas, for $160, negro Dinah, said negro given him by his father Thomas Douglas; reserving right for him & his wife Frances Douglas to have use of slave if they need her. 13 June 1804. Wit: D. Dickie, Mary Logue Dickie.

454-5 Benjamin Douglas to Thomas Douglas, for 66 lbs 7/2, negro boy Charles about 6 yrs of age; if Charles die before money is paid, he may have Peter. 11 Dec 1802. Wit: Geo Lea, Kezie Robertson. On Nov 30 1803, Thomas Douglas assigns bill of sale to John Douglas. Wit: Geo Lea, Frances Douglas.

455-6 Shadrack Hargis to son Nathan Hargis, for love & affection, 100 A on Flat R adj Michael Robinson, James Wilson. 19 July 1804. Wit: Richd Lyon, Wm. Hargis.

456 Loyd Vanhook to son Alfred Vanhook, for love & affection, 100 A on S Hico adj Capt. William Lea, Duest. 4 Sept 1804. Wit: Nathan Hargis, Geo Lea.

456-7 James Rainey of CC to Thomas J. Moore, for $20, 5½ A adj Col. Murphey. 22 Aug 1804. Wit: H. Haralson, John Ogilby.

457-8 James Rainey to Christopher Bass, for $5, 1 A adj Bass. 22 Aug 1804. Wit: Thomas I. Moore, H. Haralson.

458 Thomas Neeley to Vincent Warren, for $32, 16 A on S Hico adj land John Miles purchased of David Brechen, William Hughs, Warren land purchased of Thomas Neeley. 3 Oct 1802. Wit: Gabriel Lea, William McDaniel.

458-9 John Ogilby to Christopher Bass, for $2375, 471 A both sides Cobb Cr of Hico adj Thomas I. Moore, James Rainey, Wells, Laban Stafford. 3 Sept 1804. Wit: H. Haralson, James Rainey.

459-60 John Ogilby to Thomas Ivy Moore, for $1145, 229 A both sides Cobb Cr of Hico adj Archibald Murphey, William Branch, Richard Ogilby, Christopher Bass, James Rainey. 1 Sept 1804. Wit: H. Haralson, Christopher Bass.

460 Thomas Carver to John Carver, for 100 lbs, 104 A on S Hico adj Duty, Starling Warren, James Dollarhide. 18 Aug 1804. Wit: Starling Warren, Ebenezer Whitehead, Joseph Neeley.

461-2 John Spencer West, Marshall for District of NC, to John Tomkins of Din-widdie Co., VA, - by virtue of execution against Duncan Rose by Buchanan Dunlap & Co. for $9243.22 heard in Circuit Court - for $100, 99½ A adj Mary Gunn, John Baird formerly Nathan Scoggin, Shadrack Gentry, Allen. 19 June 1804. Wit: Wm. Norwood, Dun Cameron.

462 Ralph Williams to son John Williams, for $310, negro slave Harry about 14 yrs of age. 4 Sept 1804. Wit: Is Edwards.

462-3 James McMurray and John McMurray exec of Samuel McMurray decd to William Bell, for $42, 14 A on Double Cr adj John Blake, James Cochran - said land purchased of Saml McMurray heretofore. 16 Dec 1802. Wit: John Blake, William Ragon.

463-4 William Joblin to Ephraim Hawkins, for 30 lbs, 71 A n side Bushy Fork of Flat R - said land already possessed by Joblin. 8 Aug 1797. Wit: John Brown, Thos Palmer Jun.

464 Demsey Moore to William & Samuel Dickens, for $600, 6½ tenths A nw corner of CH lot near Demsey Moore's chimney adj Hargis. _ _ 1801. Wit: John McFarland; proved Sept 1804.

465 Samuel Warren to John Franklin, for ? , 100 A on Hico adj Henry Fulcher, William Warren, the VA line - said land for Franklin to sell to attain 89 lbs 2/2. 25 Aug 1804. Wit: Thos J. Chambers, Jacob Vanhook, J. Williamson.

Deed Book C
Page

465-6 Thomas Neely, in debt to Samuel Pittard Jun. of Granville Co., for $500,
to Samuel Pittard Jun. in trust, 275 A on S Hico adj Loyd Vanhook, Mathew Richardson. 9 Jan 1804. Wit: John McFarland, Wm. McFarland, John Newton.

466-7 Div land: ½ to William Waite & ½ to heirs of Robert Dickens to wit: Jesse
Dickens, William Dickens, Samuel Dickens, Sally Dickens, L. Dickens, Martha
Dickens, Parthenia Dickens, Ann Bland, Elizabeth Ridley Bland, Sally Dickens
Bland, Peter Randolph Bland - the last 4 claiming in right of their decd mother
Elizabeth Bland a daughter of Robert Dickens decd who married Richard Bland.
To Dickens heirs: part of land adj Daniel Merritt, Loyd Vanhook, Brooks formerly
Hinton, Walters; remainder of tract to Waite adj former Hinton land on Rosemary
Br. Tracts on Little Cr & Cobb Cr adj John Burford, Luke Moore, John Cocke,
Moses Moore: 130 A to Dickens heirs and remainder to Waite adj Cash, John Cocke.
Land on Deep Cr adj Genl Moore, Thos Minshew - 120 A to each; land on Byrd's Cr
divided plus other tracts. 18 Aug 1804. Commrs: Thomas Hargis, Shadrack Hargis,
James Wilson, Thomas Blalock, Nathan Hargis.

467-8 Christian Lewis Berzean, exec & devisee of Frederic Wm. Marshall of Salem,
Stokes Co., NC, to William Jones of Person Co. - sold by court order land purchased 20 Apr 1764 of William Churton & Charles Metcalf - for $150, 100 of 632 A
on Richland Cr of S Hico adj Benjamin McNeill, Samuel Wheeler, Charles Winstead,
Carter Lea. 13 Jan 1804. Wit: Christian Lott, John Miles.

468-9 John Brown to Stephen Wells, for 13 lbs 10/, 8¼ A adj Wells; also 3 3/4 A.
1 Sept 1804. Wit: Obediah Pearce, Ephraim Hawkins.

469-70 John Foster of Halifax Co., VA, to Joseph Royster of Person Co., for $200,
101 A adj William Sergant, Duncan, Brann. 11 May 1804. Wit: Richard M. Cuningham, Henry Mitchell, Alexr Cuningham.

470 James Yancey of CC to George Lea of Person Co., for $220, negro boy Tom.
17 Apr 1804. Wit: James Birk Sen., William Lea.

470 Jesse Dickens to Jos Lunsford Jun., a gift of ½ of a spring on land purchased of William Dickens adj Lunsford & former shop of William Hicks. 24 Aug
1804. Acknd in open court.

470-1 Benjamin Jones & Samuel Jones of Person Co. & Anthony Lumpkin of Granville,
Co. to James Webb of Granville Co., for $100, 91 A n side Tar R adj Parker,
Morrow, on Meadow Br. 10 Sept 1804. Wit: Thomas Webb, James Smith, Thomas Owen,
Edmund Lumkin.

471 Jacob Vanhook a legatee of estate of Richard Jones decd relinquishes to
Benjamin Jones his interest in said estate. 4 Dec 1804. Wit: James Smith.
Proved by oath Samuel Smith.

472 Thomas Mason to Miles Wells of Granville Co., for 20 lbs, 133 A on Cobb Cr adj
Zachariah Vaughn near Cubb Cr. 4 Apr 1795. Wit: John Bowles, James Wells.
Cobb Cr or Cubb Cr?

472-3 Vincent Brand to William Trotter, for 206 lbs 5/, 165 A adj said Trotter,
William Featherston, Jeremiah Fletcher, Claton Fuller, James Hendley old line.
1 Dec 1804. Wit: Alexr Cuningham, Jas Trotter.

473 Francis Howard & James Patterson of Elbert Co., GA; Hiram Howard & Wm. H.
Howard of Oglethrope Co., GA - to Robert Howard of Person Co., for $80 for each,
their parts of lands of estate of Henry Howard decd of NC. 27 Oct 1804.
Wit: William Allin, Howard Allin.

474 Hamalton Reynolds to Moses Bradsher, for $840, 240 A both sides Cobb Cr of
N Hico adj William Johnston decd, Thos Carver formerly Thos Neely, heirs of
Zachariah Lea decd, John Dyson formerly Thos Douglas, John McFarland formerly
Saml Johnston - said land granted Reynolds by State 10 Nov 1784. 17 Nov 1804.
Wit: Abner Bradsher, Archibald Lipscomb, B. Douglas.

Deed Book C
Page

475 Maston Powell of Halifax Co., VA, to Thomas Jones Chambers of Person Co., for 25 lbs, his right as a legatee of Richard Carter decd of Halifax Co., VA - said Maston Powell married Polly Carter a daughter of Richard Carter decd - land being 233 A where William Carter lives on Hico adj Robt Howard, George Gregory, said Chambers - the part of Maston Powell is one-eighth. 4 Oct 1804. Wit: Alexr Cunningham, Jas Franklin.

475-6 Benjamin Jones to James Webb of Granville Co., for $1000, 127 A n side Tar R adj Tap, Parker, Bumpass. 25 Aug 1804. Wit: Thomas Webb, James Smith, Thos Owen.

476-7 Thomas Rainey to James Jay Jr., for 150 lbs, 60 A on Double Cr of Hico adj Jay, Andrew Caddel, John Atkins. 20 Nov 1804. Wit: James Jay Sen., Isaac Saterfield.

477 James Wells to Miles Wells, for 60 lbs, 200 A on Cubb Cr at Granville Co. line adj John Bowles, James Kanady. 15 Dec 1794. Wit: John Bowles, John Bowles Jr.

478 John Mason to James Yokeley, for 128 lbs, 120 A adj Hugh Darbey, Wm. Rainey, Henry Royster. 2 Nov 1804. Wit: Henry Royster, McFarland Yokeley.

478-9 Artha Brooks Sen. to Laurence Hargis, for 25 lbs 6/3, 67½ A on Adams Cr adj John Williams, John Pain. 4 Dec 1804. Wit: Ephraim Hawkins, Wm. Carney.

479-80 John Pierson to Samuel Blake, for 120 lbs, 200 A on head waters Cain & Wynn Creeks adj Stephen Oliver, Richard Carnel, Durret Oliver, Hugh Hemphill, Samuel Johnson. 29 Dec 1802. Wit: Wm. Penick, Anna Duty, Jesse B. Carver, Harrison Stanfield.

480 John Turner to Stephen Jones, for 200 lbs, 200 A on Blewing Cr adj Ambrose Jones, formerly James Jones, John Baird formerly James Boswell. 12 Sept 1804. Wit: Allen Morgan, Anselem Bugg, James Thomson. Mrs. Elizabeth Turner relinquishes her dower right to said land.

481 William Dickens of Granville Co. to Joseph Lunsford of Person Co., for $170, 167½ A on Tapley Cr adj Joseph Traylor. 8 Mar 1804. Wit: Samuel Dickens.

481-2 Samuel Dickens to William Yarborough, for $53.75, 53¼ A on Tar R adj William Tapp, Gabriel Davy, said Yarborough. 29 June 1804. Wit: Benjamin Morrow, John Morrow.

482-3 Richard Burch Jun. to Baylor Burch, for 100 lbs, 150 A on Gracie Cr of Hico adj Wilson Jones, Reuben Taylor, Richd Burch Sen., Wm. Mitchel, Robert Hester. 3 Dec 1804. Wit: William McKissack, Simeon Cochran, Thos Wilkerson.

483 Ephraim Hawkins to Stephen Wells, for 130 lbs, 220 A on n side Bushy Fork of Flat R adj Wilson, James Rimmer. 16 Jan 1802. Wit: Obediah Pearce, Jos Hargis.

484 Thomas Wilkerson to Baylor Burch, for $100, 25 A on Hico adj widow Currie. 29 May 1804. Wit: Simeon Cochran, Joseph Traylor, Edmund Burch.

484-5 George Vaughan to Robert Deshazo, for $2, 2 A adj Isham Edwards, Zachaus Hunt. 22 Nov 1804. Wit: John M. Megehee.

485 Thomas Badgett Sen. to David Hunt of Granville Co., for $700, 212¼ A on Double Cr adj Wm. Cock, Hall. 29 Oct 1804. Wit: Loyd Vanhook, John Raven.

486 State of NC - #116 - to Edmund Dixon, for 50/ per 100 A, 11 A e side Hico adj Dixon, William Tapp. Entered 17 Mar 1804. Surveyed 31 Aug 1804 by Wm. Waite, county surveyor. Chain carriers: Herndon Harralson, William Black. Registered 14 Feb 1805. Edmund Dixon paid 5/6 for said land.

487 State of NC - #113 - to Nathan Ragan, for 50/ per 100 A, 36 3/4 A on Tarr R adj Samuel Jones, Person, Davie. Entered 4 Mar 1801. Chain carriers: Ashbourn Davey, Josiah Wade.

Deed Book C
Page

487 State of NC - #118 - to Jesse Ragan, for 50/ per 100 A, 8½ A on Blewing Cr adj his line, Jacob Dixon Jun., Thomas Halliburton. Entered 3 Mar 1802. Registered 8 Mar 1805.

488 State of NC - #117 - to Thomas Hood, for 50/ per 100 A, 109½ A on Mayo adj David Allen, said Hood, Osborn Jeffreys, Winstead, Day. Entered 6 Mar 1804.

488-9 State of NC - #119 - to Robert Carver, for 50/ per 100 A, 31 A on Gents Cr of Hico adj William Carver, George Duncan, William Sergent. Entered 28 Sept 1803. Registered 8 Mar 1805.

489 Benjamin Douglas to son John Douglas who has paid debts for his father of 40 lbs 13/11, all cattle, household & kitchen furniture, house & plantation; working tools; property to be returned if debt pd in 2 yrs. 25 Dec 1804. Wit: James McMurry, Jemima McMurry.

489-90 Jeremiah W. Fletcher to William Trotter, for 166 lbs 13/4, 97 A on Hendly Cr adj William Carver, Trotter. 9 Feb 1805. Wit: Nancy Trotter, James Trotter.

490-1 Thomas Neely to Robert Wade of Granville Co., for 313 lbs 8/10, 301½ A both sides S Hico Cr adj widow Richardson, Vincent Warrin, John Miles, John McMurrie, Loyd Vanhook, John Russell. 31 Jan 1805. Wit: H. Haralson, Jas W. Smith

491 Thomas Williams to Richard Holdman, for 100 lbs, mulatto boy Jim. 2 Feb 1805. Wit: Wm. McKissack.

491-2 Power of attorney - Elisabeth Carmon of Washington Co., TN, to uncle Caleb Carmon of CC to demand & recover from Elijah Carmon or any person adm of estate of Hezekiah Carmon decd. 16 Feb 1805. Wit: Adam Stafford, Joseph Britten, James Chambers.

492 Jacob Fuller to Isaiah Fuller, for $320, 128 A w side Stories Cr adj William Hamblin Sen., Richard Hamblin, John Harris - said land willed him by Henry Fuller. 25 Feb 1805. Wit: Ish Edwards, John McKissack.

493 Richard Burch Sen. to Baylor Burch, for 100 lbs, 75 A adj Simeon Cochran, Mitchel, Baylor Burch. 4 Mar 1805. Wit: Wm. Mansfield, Edm Burch, Thos Burch.

493 John Sneed to Lewis Tapp, for 50 lbs, negro boy James about 6-7 yrs old. 20 June 1801. Wit: Thomas Sneed.

493-4 William Chambers to daughter Elizabeth Chambers, for love & affection, 7 negroes: Else & her 3 children Nelson, Joe, Gabriel; small negroes Lucy, Amy, Isaac. 15 Dec 1805. Wit: Edwd O. Chambers, Jno M. McGehee.

494 Robert Moore to John M. McGehee, for 401 lbs 1/, 200 A both sides Hico adj Richard Pendergrass, said Moore. 23 Oct 1804. Wit: Harrison Standfield, William McGehee.

495 Elisha Sarrott to John Pittard, for $500, 114 A both sides S Hico adj Thomas Snipes, Alexr Rose, Robt Vanhook, Abner Bradsher. 29 Oct 1804. Wit: Saml Pittard, B. Douglas.

495-6 Richard Atkinson to Thomas Goins, for 52 lbs 10/, 100 A both sides Hendley Mill Cr adj Samuel Wheelor, Tillman. 7 Feb 1805. Wit: Joseph Goins.

496 John Garrott to Samuel Garrott, for 60 lbs, 60 A n side Richland Cr of Hico. 24 Nov 1804. Wit: Richd Atkinson, Parthena Atkinson.

496-7 John Sneed to Lewis Tapp, for $400, negro woman & her 2 children: Saluda, David, Aston - she about 35 yrs old. 12 Jan 1801. Wit: Samuel Sneed, James Saterfield.

497-8 George Roberts to Robert Paine, for 375 lbs, 348 A on Richland Cr adj James Satterfield, Thomas Person former line, William Jay & his son William Jay, crossing Mud Br, Paul Jeffreys, Neely. 12 June 1804. Wit: James Thomson, James Daniel; also all interest to 1 A a part of land of Paul Jeffreys decd laid off for mill. 12 June 1804.

Deed Book C
Page

498-9 Jacob Vanhook, sheriff, to Henry Atkinson of CC, for various sums, 5 tracts of about 2800 A sold by court order: Thomas Gholston adm of Allen Love decd sued Henry Atkinson & Richard Atkinson heirs of John Atkinson decd; land adj Edward Clay Jun., James Cochran; included 300 A where John Atkinson lived purchased by Henry Atkinson. 3 Mar 1805. Acknd in open court.

499 John Harris to Seth Coleman, for 80 lbs, 70 A on Mayo adj Coleman, Allen. 5 Jan 1805. Wit: Thomas Clayton Jun., Thomas Clayton Sen.

500 Reubin Smith of Granville Co. to Lewis Tapp of Person Co., for $310, negro girl Cherry about 14 yrs old. 24 Aug 1804. Wit: Jab Vanhook, Mandley Winstead.

500-1 James Cochran to John Harris, for $336, 108 A on Stories Cr adj Henry Fuller (now Paul Walters); 60 A adj Ben Newton former corner, Hamblin, William Carver. 9 Jan 1805. Wit: Ish Edwards, John Daniel.

501-2 Peter Lyon of Sumner Co., TN, to John Tapley of Person Co., for $125, 100 A adj Hargis, Wilson, Person. 1 Sept 1803. Wit: B. Seawell, J. Seawell, William Lyon, James Paine. Proved Mar 1805.

502 Samuel Wheelor to William Saterfield, for $250, 70 A adj Charles Winstead, Benjamin McNeill, Wm. Jones. 6 Feb 1805. Wit: R. Long, Joseph Goins.

502-3 Baylor Burch to Thomas Burch, for 75 lbs, 50 A on Grier Cr of Hico adj Robert Hester, Wilson Jones, Wm. Mitchel. 5 Mar 1805. Wit: Wm. Mansfield, Edm Burch.

503 Reubin Taylor of CC to Solomon Draper Junr. of Person Co., for $10, 2 A both sides Sergent Cr adj Henry Black former mill - said land Taylor purchased of Benjn Johnston. 17 Jan 1805. Wit: Saml Smith, Joshua Partee.

504 William Brechen to James Paine, for 252 lbs, 252 A on Richland & Double Crs - it being part of tract granted by Earl Granville to James Anderson 10 Jan 1761 adj Isaac Saterfield, James Williamson, Lewis Green, John Atkinson, Thomas Rainey. 14 Jan 1805. Wit: James Saterfield, John Curtis.

504-5 Baylor Burch to Edmond Burch, for 150 lbs, 100 A on Grier Cr of Hico adj William Mitchel, Wilson Jones, Reubin Taylor. 4 Mar 1805. Wit: Wm. Mansfield, Thomas Burch.

505 Thomas White Sen. of Halifax Co., VA, to Alexander Cunningham of Person Co., for 100 lbs, 107 A adj VA line, Archibald Carnel, Henry Gray. 4 Mar 1805. Wit: Richd Carnel, Goodloe Warren.

505-6 Abel Howard of Oglethorpe Co., GA, to Robert Howard of Person Co., for 75 lbs, 75 A on the Ridge Path netween Marlow & Jents Crs adj Henry Howard old line, Thomas Chambers, Joseph McFarland, Walter McFarland, John Rodgers. 17 July 1804. Wit: Thos J. Chambers, Jno Howard.

506-7 William Waite to James Farquhar, for $60, 68 3/4 A on Flat R adj Farquhar, Abraham Moore. 5 Mar 1805. Wit: Michal Robinson, Lawrence Hargis.

507-8 John Foshe to Joseph Hargis, for 125 lbs, 100 A on Flat R adj Drury Allen, Robert Dickens. 7 Jan 1805. Wit: Sally Pearce, Obediah Pearce.

508 Abel Howard & Groves Howard of Oglethorpe Co., GA, to Robert Howard of Person Co., for $1000, all land that is due them as legatees of Henry Howard decd. 17 July 1804. Wit: Thomas J. Chambers, John Howard.

508-9 John Smith Hust to Thomas Rainey, for $500, 249 A in 2 tracts: 190 A deeded to Drury Allen by Robert Dickens 25 Dec 1791; 59 A part of grant to Allen by State on Flat R where Allin lives adj Stokes Allen, William Forrest. 20 Nov 1804.

509-10 Thomas Hargis to John Fooshe, for 166 lbs 13/4, 103 A on Flat R adj Wm. Moor. 18 Aug 1804. Wit: Obediah Pearce, Stokes Allen.

71

Deed Book C
Page

510-1 Joseph Hargis to John Foshe, for 155 lbs, 113 A s fork Flat R adj Richard Hargis former line. 7 Jan 1805. Wit: Sally Pearce, Obediah Pearce.

511-2 Samuel Bryant to Nathaniel Norfleet, for $330, 293 A both sides Flat R. adj Wm. Dickens, John Wilson, Thomas Saulman, Benjamin Jacobs,Gray, Jones, Robert Taylor. /s/ Samuel Bryan. 12 Dec 1804. Wit: Henry McNeill, Thomas Wilkerson.

512-3 Christian Lewis Benzien of Salem, Stokes Co., NC, to Charles Brown Winsted - whereas Frederic William Marshall of Salem in his will dated 16 Dec 1801, proved Mar 1802, gave to grantor all lands conveyed from William Churton to Charles Metcalf & vested by General Assembly 1782 - for $224, 224 A on Richland Cr & Henely's Mill Cr of S Hico which is tract 6 of 632 A adj Benjamin McNeel, Wheeley, Atkinson, Garrot. 10 Nov 1804. Wit: Nicholas Thompson, Frederick Meinung.

513-4 James Bryan of Orange Co., NC, to Samuel Bryan of Person Co., for $332, 293 A both sides Flat R adj Wm. Dickens, John Wilson, Thomas Solmon, Benjamin Jacobs, Gray, Robert Taylor. 14 Mar 1804. Wit: Jonathan McKissack, B. N. Milner.

514-5 Thomas Solmon to Thomas Rainey, for $95, 45 A on Flat R adj James Jacobs. /s/ Thomas Saulmon. 8 Feb 1805. Wit: Josiah Fike, John Cooper.

515 William Cocke adm of James Bedford of Granville Co, to John Rountree, for $400, negro boy Nadon. 30 Apr 1805. Wit: James Cocke.

515 Jane Mann widow & exec of John Mann decd to Thomas Mann orphan son of William Man decd, for 50 lbs pd by Thomas Mann, 200 A on Adams Cr adj John Mann, David Mitchell. 30 Mar 1793. Wit: John Gunn, John Fike.

516 Creed Haskins to John Moore, in trust, for $500 which he owes Ogilby, negroes girl Jenny, woman Crease; horses, furniture. 3 Jan 1805. Wit: Francis T. Oglesby, Thomas H. Moore.

516 Joseph O'Briant to John Lawson Sen., for 90 lbs, 100 A on Mayho Cr adj John Baird, Vanhook. 24 Apr 1805. Wit: Lewis Parrot, Thomas Lawson.

517 William Carver to Henry (or Hosey) Carver, for 70 lbs. 130 A on Story's Cr adj Joseph Carver, John Claton, Henry Graves. 3 June 1805. Acknd in open court.

517 William Huston to Manly Winstead, for $1333 1/3, 425 A on fishing br of Adams Cr adj Thomas Heggie at the mountain br, Jno Barnet, Saml Cox, Charles Allin. 4 June 1805. Wit: H. Haralson, J. Layton, Andrew Barnett.

518 Byrd Wall & Elizabeth his wife to Davidson Chambers & Polly his wife daughter of Byrd & Elizabeth Wall, for love & affection, negroes Jack, Creese and her child Tom 18 mos old; negroes given in 1799 at 7 or 10 yrs & said value to be taken from their part of grantor's estate. 15 Apr 1804. Wit: Ep Winders, Trailky Winders.

518 James Layton to John E. Watson, for 20 lbs, 100 A on turkey pen br of Adams Cr adj Lawrence Vanhook, Charles Allen. 1 June 1805. Wit: Andrew Barnett, James Pool.

519 James Layton to John E. Watson, for 40 lbs, 200 A on Byas Cr. 1 June 1805. Wit: Andrew Barnett, James Pool.

519 Henry Atkinson of CC to John Lewis of Pittsylvania Co., VA, for $100, 450 A on Henly Mill Cr adj James Fuller, Boswell, Parker, Neely, Richard Atkinson. 10 May 1805. Wit: H. Haralson, Rd Atkinson.

519 James Jones of Mason Co., KY, sold to Benjamin Jones of Person Co his right & claim to property of Richard Jones decd. 7 Mar 1799. Proved June 1805.

520 Walter McFarland to Zachaus Hurt, for $1000, 272 A on Gents Cr adj Hunt, Isham Edwards, Paul Haralson, John Rogers, Robert Howard, Thomas Chambers, Joseph McFarland. 27 Mar 1805. Wit: Joseph D. McFarland, Benj Chambers.

Deed Book C
Page

520 Charles Boulton of Halifax Co., VA, to William McGehee of Person Co., for $1260, 420 A both sides Stewart's Cr on n side Hico adj Mumford McGehee, Goodloe Warren, James Stanfield, William Hopson. 2 Nov 1804. Wit: Jno M. McGehee, Richard Carnal, Thomas McGehee.

521 Nehemiah Fuller to Sampson M. Glenn, for $210, 105 A on Stories Cr adj William Fuller, James Cochran. 5 Sept 1803. Wit: G. A. Davey Jr., John Day, junior.

521 Fleming Carnal to Archibald Carnal, for $200, 103½ A adj Carnal. 8 Mar 1805. Wit: Alexr Cuningham, Rich M. Cuningham.

521 Sweptston Sims to Nicholas Lewis, for $425, negro man John. 8 May 1805. Acknd in open court.

522 Vincent Warrin to John Miles, for 50 lbs, 50 A adj land Miles purchased of John McMeneway, William Hughs. 19 Apr 1805. Wit: Loyd Vanhook, Robt Wade.

522 State of NC - #109 - to Robert Davey, for 50/ per 100 A, 13 A adj Robert Gill, Harrison, Davey. Entered 18 Aug 1801. Registered Aug 1805.

523 State of NC - #115 - to Robert Gill, for 50/ per 100 A, 25 A on Mayo adj Gill, Pendleton Thomas, Swepston Simms. Entered 7 Sept 1802. Rigistered Aug 1805.

523 State of NC - #110 - to James Cochran, for 50/ per 100 A, 104 A on Story Cr adj Hatcher, Cochran. Entered 3 Jan 1801. Registered 1805.

524 State of NC - #114 - to John Parrish, for 50/ per 100 A, 34 A on Wing & Donaldson Creeks adj William Winstead, John Baird, Henry Humphrey. 28 Dec 1803.

524 Patrick Carnal to Richard Carnal, for $900, 236 A on Cain Cr adj Stephen Oliver, Dixon, Gwin, Warren, Archibald Carnal. 14 Mar 1805. Wit: Alex Cuningham, Wm. S. Parker.

525 Benjamin Johnston to John Durham, for 60 lbs, 30 A on Hico adj John Ogilby, Reubin Taylor. 21 Aug 1805. Wit: H. Haralson, Jas Trotter.

525 Vincent Warrin to Robert Wade of Granville Co., for $500, 98 A adj Mrs. Martha Richardson, Wm. Hughs, Russel. 19 Apr 1805. Wit: Loyd Vanhook, Lawrence Vanhook, John Miles.

526 Samuel Warrin to James Franklin, for 100 lbs, 100 A s side Dan R & n side Hico adj William Warren on VA line, Byrd Wall, Henry Fulcher. _ Sept 1805. Wit: Byrd Wall, William Hobson.

526 Thomas Douglas to John Dyson, for $136, 41½ A on Cobb Cr adj Nicholas Thomson, Kindle Vanhook, James Johnston to great road. 10 Oct 1804. Wit: Loyd Vanhook, Geo Lea, B. Douglas.

527 Artha Brooks Sen. & Anna his wife to John Lawson Jr., for 227 lbs 4/2,1 farthing, 218½ A both sides bold br of Hico adj David Brooks, Artha Brooks Junr., Robert Brooks, Baird, Joseph Tatum. 31 Aug 1805. Wit: James Paine, Edmond Shelton.

527 Jacob Slaughter of Granville Co. to grandson John Duncan son of Ambrose Harrison Duncan, for love & affection, & 5/, 100 A in Person Co. adj John Chambers. _ July 1805. Wit: Thomas Scott, Ambrose H. Duncan.

528 John Lewis of Franklin Co., KY, to Gabriel Gunn of CC, for $125, 25 A e side Hico Cr adj John Ogilby, Abner Duncan - it being a part of land of his father Fielding Lewis who died intestate. 8 Feb 1805. Wit: John McFarland, Wm. McFarland.

528-9 Jesse Ragan Junr. to Nathan Ragan, for $85, 50 A adj Sims, Davis. 17 Apr 1805. Wit: Ashburn Davey, William Street.

529-30 William Gold to John Gwin, for $800, 165 A on Cane Cr of Hico adj John Harralson. 1 June 1805. Wit: Henry Sergent, Barnett Dollason.

Deed Book C
Page
530 William Singleton to Meredith Cox, for 60 lbs, 100 A on Story's Cr adj Jesse
Long, Artha Brooks, Jacob Bull, John Trickey. 4 May 1805. Wit: Benjn Chambers,
Wm. McFarland.

531 Baylor Burch to Joseph Taylor, for $250, 250 A adj Reubin Taylor, John Cooper,
on Hillsborough old road. 4 June 1804. Wit: Thomas Burch, Thos Wilkerson.

531 Nathan Ragan to Swepston Sims, for 200 lbs, 200 A on Mayo adj Saml Jones,
said Sims. 28 May 1805. Wit: Ashburn Davey, William Street.

531 James Wells of CC to Hugh Darby of Person Co., for $40, 10 A adj Jno Mason.
11 Aug 1804. Wit: Loyd Vanhook, George Darby.

532 Bluford Warren to Joseph Pulliam, for 14 lbs 12/6, 19½ A on Wynn's Cr adj
Pulliam, Asque Price. 16 July 1805. Wit: H. Haralson, Asque Price.

532 William Waite to Robert Harris, for $65, 65 A on crooked fork of Aaron's Cr
adj Harris. 21 Feb 1805. Wit: David Ragsdale, Peter Ragsdale.

532 Lowry Booker to Meredith Cox, for 500 lbs, negroes Sam, Delfa, Chiston; Lucy
and her 2 children Amey & Susa, Cloy. 28 Nov 1804. Wit: Samuel Cox, Wist Cox.

533 Robert Allen to William Jeffreys, for $762, 258 A on Adams Cr adj Benj Towler,
Edward O. Chambers, Thos McNeal. _ _ 1805. Wit: Samuel Cox, James Williamson.

533 William Waite to Jesse Lunsford, for $145, 144 A on Deep Cr adj John Bumpass,
Mills Durden, William Cock. 23 Feb 1805. Wit: Gabriel Bumpass, John Cochran.

533-4 Abel Parrish to Overton Harris of Granville Co., for 87 lbs, 150 A both
sides Aaron's Cr. 26 Aug 1805. Wit: R. Harris, Sterling Harris.

534 Dennis Obriant of Granville Co. adm of Patrick Obriant decd of Granville Co.
to Joseph Obriant (or Reubin Ragland), for 180 lbs, 350 A adj John Baird,
Donaldson, Isaac Vanhook. 29 July 1805. Wit: B. W. Daniel, John Obriant,
Phillip Obriant.

534 Thomas Barnett of Iredell Co., NC, to John Claton of Person Co., for 120 lbs,
114 A on Stories Cr adj James Cochran, Josiah Carver. 20 Feb 1804.
Wit: Banjn Chambers, Isham Edwards.

535 David Ford to Edmund Shelton, for 6 lbs, 5 A on Holt's mill cr on VA line
to dry cr adj Timothy Holt. 24 Aug 1805. Wit: Lewis Shaperd, John Shelton.

535 Nathan Ragan to Ashburn Davie, for kindness rendered, 31 3/4 A on Tar R adj
Samuel Jones, Person Davie. 12 Aug 1805. Wit: Swepn Sims, Samuel Self.

535 Alexander Rose Sen. & his wife Mrs. Eunice Rose to their son Alexander Rose Jr,
for natural affection, 118 A on rocky & Chapel branches of S Hico adj land Mrs.
Agnes Cochran was willed by her father Wm. Lea decd., Wm. Brown. 2 Sept 1805.
Wit: Loyd Vanhook.

536-8 Power of attorney - Thomas Graham of Glasgow, Scotland, & Mathew Montgomerie
of same, witnesses to Robert McCall, merchant of Glasgow, Scotland for heirs of
John McCall decd of Glasgow & John Campbell, general of his Majesty customs in
Scotland & assignee of David Elliott by Margaret Niven relict of Alexander Elliott
decd & Alexander Bomar; McCall , Elliott & Co. in Britain & John Gordon & Co.
in America who is retired & Allen Love & Hugh Love managed same - suit for said
co. to pay debts for various cargoes of goods shipped from Britain. John Gholson
merchant of Petersburg, VA, & Robert Colquihoun of Petersburg failed to take
action - power given to Robert Gordon merchant of Richmond, VA, to prosecute all
claims. 27 May 1802. Wit: Thomas Graham, Mat Montgomerie.

539-40 Whereas John Glolson mentioned in above letter of attorney hath lately
departed this life, Robert Colquihoun, merchant of Petersburg, VA, appoints
Thomas Gholson of Brunswick(Co., VA?) his atty in fact to transact business for

74

539-40 cont -the two companies and to collect money due from Mrs. Fanny Love adm with will annexed of Allen Love decd & of Hugh Love decd. 20 Dec 1804. Wit: Walter Colquohoun, Willis Cousins.

540 Pulliam Williamson to Humphrey Pitterd, for 100 lbs, 109 A on Story Cr adj Burrel Green, Jesse Watson, Hatcher, James Raven - said tract conveyed by Susannah Williamson exec of Henry Williamson decd 18 Nov 1802. 12 Oct 1805. Wit: L. Hargis, Samuel Pitterd Senr.

541 James Johnston Senr of CC to David Brachen of same, for $400, 129¼ A in Person Co. adj James McMurry, Joseph Carney, John Russell. 15 June 1805. Wit: Loyd Vanhook, William Brecken.

541-2 Thomas Gibson Sen. to Thomas Gibson Jun., for $100, 35½ A on dry br adj Richard Deshazo. 18 Sept 1805. Wit: Andr Buchanon Senr, Edmund Deshazo, Thomas Bohannon.

542-3 William Murrow to Abner Parker, for 120 lbs 6/, 52 A on Tar R at Cattail Br adj Brown, Gabe Davey, said Parker. 4 Nov 1805. Wit: J. Williamson.

543-4 Priscilla Williams to Tobias Williams, for $100, 40 A on Cane Cr adj Archibald Murphey, heirs of James Hamlet. 19 Nov 1805. Wit: Abner Duncan, Robt Seymour.

544 Gabriel Gunn of CC to Thomas Jeffreys of same, for $125, 25 A e bank Hico adj Jno Ogilby, Abner Duncan. 19 Nov 1805. Wit: Geo M. Willson, John Willson.

544 Sterling Warrin to Hiram Lewis, for 54 lbs, 54 A adj Thomas Carver on road from Warrin to Leasburg. 14 Oct 1805. Wit: John B. Lea, Warner Lewis.

545 Sterling Warren to John B. Lea, for 13 lbs 10/, 13½ A adj Warren. 23 Sept 1805. Wit: Moses Bradsher, Hiram Lewis.

545 Arthur Buchannon to Joseph Davis, for 20 lbs, 85 A on Fray's Br adj William Allin. 27 Aug 1805. Wit: Thomas Gibson, David Buchannon.

545-6 Thomas Douglas to beloved daughter Janet Lea & her husband George Lea, for the trouble & expenses he has caused them, all property he possesses at this time; 2 negro girls, Jemimah & Lethe; feather bed, furniture. 9 Oct 1805. Wit: John McFarland, William Lea, Abner Lea.

546 Thomas McNeill to John Barnett, for $160, 144 A on meeting house br of Adams Cr adj Gill. 26 Nov 1805. Wit: W. Jeffreys, Milton Rose, Chas Mitchel.

546 McFarling Oakley to John Bumpass, for $400, 200 A on Tarr R adj Walter Oakley, said Bumpass. 24 Sept 1805. Wit: Samuel Douglas, Walter Oakly Jr., Jesse Bumpass.

547 Walter McFarland & Joseph D. McFarland to William McFarland, for 200 lbs, all willed to them by their father Robert McFarland decd being 2/3 of 602 A both sides Castle Cr adj Moses Walker, John Dillaha. 21 Sept 1805. Wit: John McFarland, Thos Morton.

547 William Blalock to Millenton Blalock, for $175, 175 A on rocky fork adj Moore, Dickens. 13 Dec 1804. Wit: John Clixby.

548 Thomas Gibson Senr. to Henry Gibson, for 50 lbs, 64½ A on dry br adj Deshazo near Thomas Gipson Junr, Bendego Gentry. 18 Sept 1805. Wit: Andrew Buchanon, Sen., Edmond Deshazo, Thomas Bohanan.

548 Joseph Hubbard to John Daniel, for $100, 112 A on Richland Spring Cr adj John Pain. 2 Dec 1805. Wit: Jeremiah Hubbard, Duncan Rose.

548 Jenny Greenwood to loving friend John Blackwell of Granville Co., a gift of all goods & chattels plus 50 A land; 8 negroes: Dopery, Cate, Lucy, Big Jim, Randel, Robin, John. 2 Dec 1805. Wit: Jno Malone.

Deed Book C
Page

549 Richard Pendergrass to William Moore, for $1000, 256½ A on Hico adj John McGehee, John Williams, Edward Chambers, Joseph Woods. 7 Nov 1805. Wit: Benj Chambers, John M. McGehee.

549 Lewis Parrott to Samuel Jones, for 50 lbs, 100 A adj said Parrott. 21 May 1799. Wit: John McVey, John Day. Proved Dec 1805.

549 Davison Chambers & Banjamin Chambers to Abner Chambers, for $300, quit claim to 100 A on Stories Cr adj Jas Barnett. 19 Oct 1805. Wit: Ish Edwards.

550 Ambrose Lea to William Brechen, for 95 lbs 4/, 119 A n side Bear Br. 12 Oct 1805. Wit: Ervin Johnston, James Brechen.

550 John Davies to John Russel, for 120 lbs 16/2, 2 negro boys James & Ephraim; deed void if Davies repays debt of same amt by 25 May 1807. 13 May 1805. Wit: Hiram McDaniel, Loyd Vanhook.

550 Nathaniel Norfleet to Jacob Vanhook, for $225, negro girl Beck. 5 Oct 1805. Wit: Wm. Cocke.

551 William Pool & Robert Davie to Sarah Vanhook, for 145 lbs, 3 negroes: Pheby, Sucke, Traveller. 30 July 1803. Wit: Ashburn Davie.

551 James Rimmer to Ephraim Hawkins, for $400, 206½ A both sides Bushy Fork of Flat R adj Joshua Step, Fisher, Sim Cochran. 30 Jan 1805. Wit: Loyd Vanhook, Joshua Step.

551 State of NC - #973 - to Thomas Person, for 10/ per 100 A, 300 A in CC both sides Flat R at Aldridge Cr adj Jones, Ragsdale, Pryant, Lockhart, Alston, Holdman. 20 Nov 1788. Sworn chain carriers: Thomas Ragsdale, Benjn Ragsdale.

552 Power of attorney - Ezekiel Penington & Catherine Penington formerly Catherine Hughs of Salisbury, NC, to William Crockett of Person Co. to take possession of negroes Vines & her children Henry, Charles, Jess, Peter, Nelson; the first 2 were purchased by Catharine Hughs at sale of her father Joseph Hughs decd formerly of Salisbury; the remainder are increase of Vines since the purchase; they were taken & sold illegally by debt of her brother Hudson Hughs; 4 are in possession of William Hampton of Salisbury. 3 Feb 1806. Wit: John D. Moore, J. Moore.

552 Buckner Rooks to Robert Halliburton, for 35 lbs 12/6, 95 A on Bluewing Cr adj Baird, Thomas Hallyburton at Henderson Br. 20 Feb 1806. Wit: Thos Halliburton, David Halliburton, Martha Halliburton.

553 James Farquhar to son John Farquhar, for love & affection, 233 A on Bushy Fork Flat R adj John Brown, Moore, Wait. 25 Feb 1806. Wit: Jab Vanhook, Thomas Hargis.

553 Charles Thaxton of Halifax Co., VA, to William Jones of Person Co., for 90 lbs, 124 A on Bluewing Cr adj Ambrose Jones, Francis Foard. 19 Jan 1806. Wit: Ambrose Jones, Lovey Jones, Wilie Jones.

553 Joseph D. McFarland to Thomas J. Chambers, for 500 lbs, 410 A n side Gents Cr of Hico adj Zachaus Hart, Edward O. Chambers, Richd Pendergrass, William Woods. 30 July 1805. Wit: Alexander Cuningham, Henry Gray.

553-4 Bird Moore of Halifax Co., VA, to James Pulliam of same, for 150 lbs, 164 A both sides Gents Cr of Hico adj John Williams, Newman. 27 Feb 1806. Wit: Alex Cunningham, Richd Carnell, Wm. Penick.

554-5 Alexr Rose exec of William Lea Senr. decd to James Cochran, for 421 lbs 6/8, 160 A w bank S Hico adj Moses Bradsher, Sarett. 7 Mar 1805. Wit: William Brown, William Ragan, Edwd Clay Jun.

556 Herndon Haralson to William Scott Branch, for $625, 132 A on N Hico adj said Branch, Abner Duncan - said land was conveyed to Martin Duncan by his late mother. 26 Sept 1805. Wit: Thos Jeffreys, Geo Lea.

Deed Book C
Page

556-7 Samuel Black to Stephen Oliver, for 120 lbs, 200 A on Cain & Winn Creeks adj said Oliver, Hugh Hemphill, Samuel Johnston. 5 Oct 1805. Wit: Thomas Burch, Durrett Oliver, Jno. Daniel.

557 Richard Carnal to Durrett Oliver, for 3 lbs 2/10, 5.1 A adj Stephen Oliver, Saml Black. 8 Mar 1805. Wit: Stephen Oliver, Robt Oliver.

557 Philip Vass of Halifax Co. VA, to Ambrose Jones of Person Co., for 232 lbs, 10/2, 306 A adj Francis Foard at the State line to Granville Co. line, Bowles, Thaxton. 5 Sept 1805. Wit: Stephen Jones, Francis Foard, William Thaxton.

557 Jesse Evans to William Allin of Mecklenburg Co., VA, for $200, 105 A on Flat R adj John S. Hall, former property of Richd Hargis, Hust - excepting 1 A with Catawba spring sold to John Scoggin. 28 Feb 1806. Wit: James Paine, Thomas Rainey.

558 Thomas Rainey to William Allin of Mecklenburg Co., VA, for $500, 249 A on Flat R adj Josiah Allen, Stokes Allen, William Forrest. 28 Feb 1806. Wit: James Paine, Jesse Evans.

558 Archiblad Murphey of CC to John Daniel of Person Co., for $1130, 323 A both sides middle fork Cain Cr adj Goodloe Warren, Henphill, McGhee, Frederick Debow old line, Oliver. 22 Jan 1806. Wit: H. Haralson, Henry Day, junior.

558 Thomas Jeffreys of CC to William S. Branch of Person Co., for $125, 25 A on e bank Hico adj Major John Ogilby, Abner Duncan. 31 Dec 1805. Wit: H. Haralson, Thomas Rainey.

558-9 Powel Parker to William Morrow, for 300 lbs, 167 A on Tarr R adj Benjamin Morrow, James Webb, McVey. 9 Nov 1805. Wit: Charles Davis, Josiah Mangum, Jones Parker.

559 George Hall of Halifax Co., VA, to Thomas Parker of Person Co., for 60 lbs, 270½ A on Story & Sergent Creeks adj William Hamblin, Richd Atkinson, Thomas Neeley old line, William Trotter, Presly Draper. 30 July 1805. Wit: Benj Chambers, Thos Talbert.

559 John Barnett to Joseph Morton, for $124, 144 A on meeting house br of Adams Cr adj Joseph Gill. 1 Feb 1806. Wit: Ish Edwards, Henry Graves.

559 George Lea to McFarland Oakley, for $532, 133 A on Cobb Cr adj John Campbell, John Mason. 10 Oct 1805. Wit: John Mason, William Lea.

560 William Rainey of CC to Richard Ogilby of Person Co., for 250 lbs, 282 A on Cob Cr which he purchased of Arthur Mitchel 18 Apr 1786 adj Thomas J. Moore, George Darby, Christopher Bass. 1 Nov 1805. Wit: John McAden, Thomas J. Moore, John Ogilby.

560 Jesse Ragan Sen. of Granville Co., to John Breesee, for $300, 308 A adj John Baird, Agnes Barnet, Charles Halliburton, Richard Andrews. 15 Feb 1806. Wit: Stephen Jones, William Winstead, Lewis Wilkerson, James Ligon.

560 Abner Chambers to Benjamin Chambers, for $500, 100 A both sides Stories Cr adj Barnett, Robert Deshazo. _ Oct 1805. Wit: Wm. McFarland, Davison Chambers.

560-1 Andrew Buchannon to Abedago Gentry, for 100 lbs, 200 A on Castle Cr adj Shadrack Gentry, John Neal decd, Richard Deshazo, land purchased of Robt Dickens. 25 Jan 1805. Wit: Thomas Allen.

561 Benjamin McNeill to Moses Fuller, for 80 lbs, 64 A on Richland Cr of S Hico at school house br adj William Fuller, Wm. Jones, Charles Winstead. 17 Oct 1805. Aaron Fuller, Asa Fuller, William Long, witnesses.

561 State of NC - #123 - to William Davy, for 50/ per 100 A, 99 3/4 A on Mayo adj Jefferson, Hood new line. 2 Oct 1805.

END OF BOOK C

77

210

Know it known to all Men whom these Presents may concern that I Richard Clayton of the County of Person & State of No Carolina for & in Consideration of the Sum of ninety five Pounds current & lawfull Money of Virginia the Receipt whereof I do hereby acknowledge have this Day Bargained Sold & delivered & do by these Presents Bargain Sell & deliver unto John Cottran son one Negroe Woman by Name Easther To have & to hold the sd Negroe her Heirs Exers Admrs & Assigns forever and I the said Richard Clayton for himself his Heirs Exers & Admrs shall and will warrant and forever defend against all Persons claiming or intending to claim the said Negroe unto the sd John Cottran his Heirs Exers Admrs & Assigns forever henceforth In Witness whereof he has hereunto set his hand & affixd his Seal this Day of February one year above Sd 1810 & the 34th Year of American Independence   Richard Clayton {Seal}

Signed & in presence of   State of North Carolina Person
Wm Jeffreys (jurat)   County May Term 1810 } The Execution of this Bill of sale was duly
                               proved in open Court by the Oath of Wm Jeffreys a subscribing Witness thereto
                               and ordered to be registered   Test Jesse Dickins CC

Know all Men by these Presents that I Heywood Jones of Person County North Carolina for & in Consideration of the Sum of forty eight Pounds to Me in hand paid by John Witherson of the said County have Bargained & sold to the John Witherson a Negroe Girl named Easter about five Years old To have and to hold the said Girl to the said John Witherson his Heirs or Assigns as his or their Right or Property & warrant to defend to the present the sd John Witherson his Heirs or Assigns against any Claim or Claims or Rolle to the said negroe Girl made by Me my Heirs or Assigns or any other Person or Persons whatever In Witness wherof I have set my Hand & Seal this 28th Day of March 1810   Heywood Jones {Seal}

Signed & in presence of   State of North Carolina Person
John Owen   County May Term 1810 } The Execution of this Bill of sale was duly
David Witherson (jurat)   proved in open Court by the Oath of David Witherson a subscribing
Samuel Jones   Witness thereto & ordered to be registered Test Jesse Dickins CC

State of North Carolina. Whereas John Derby brought his Suit against Henry Register & Debt & obtained a Judgment before a single Magistrate in the County of Person for the Sum of seventeen Pounds 12/9 & Costs and an Execution was issued against the Estate of the sd Henry Register in favour of the sd Plaintiff directed to Thomas Talbert a Constable for the County aforesaid in the following words to wit State of North Carolina Person County to any lawfull Officer to execute & return within three Months. You are hereby commanded that of the Goods & Chattels of Henry Register you cause to be made good the Sum of seventeen Pounds 12/9 which John Derby obtained of him before Henry Sergeant Esqr on the third Day of August 1809 herein fail not Given under my hand this 13th Day of December 1809   Henry Sergeant
And the Constable aforesaid after such Execution being levyed & Return made thereon that he had levyed on a Negroe Woman Slave belonging to the Defendant named Sell and the same by way of publick Vendue on the 4th day of June 1810 after having advertised agreeable to Law & John Mason became the Purchaser at the sd Negroe on one Bill for the sum of one hundred & two Pounds Currency he being the last & highest Bidder Judgment & costs paid the surplus paid the Defendant by the sd Jo. Mason Know all Men therefore that for & in consideration of the sum of seventeen Pounds 12/9 to Me in hand paid by the sd John Mason & by virtue of the sd Execution & the Laws of the Act of our Genl Assembly in that Case made & provided have Bargained & by these presents do sell grant the sd John Mason his Heirs & Assigns forever all the Right Title Interest Claim & Demand which the sd Henry Register had of in & to the aforesaid negroe Sell In Witness whereof I the sd Thomas Talbert have hereunto set my hand & Seal this 16th Day of May Anno Dom 1810   Tho Talbert {Seal}
in presence of State of North Carolina Person County &c...

Page

1 Abraham Villines of CC to Jesse Evans, for $300, 106 A on Flat R adj John Smith Hust, Richard Hargis decd, Thomas Villines, Thom McKissack. 5 June 1805. Proved Mar 1806 in open court.

1 Jesse Dickens to Abner Williams, for 57 lbs, 38 A on Deep Cr at Mud Br adj Gunn. 17 Apr 1805. Wit: Samuel Dickens.

2 Reubin Long to Ebenezer Whitehead, for 160 lbs 6 pence, 129 A e side S Hico adj James D. Hendley, Hubbert, Charles Winstead, Daniel Sargent. _ _ 1804. Wit: William Satterfield, Charles B. Winstead.

2-3 John Beardin to George Roberts, for $700, 100 A adj Long, Jones Griffin. 20 Sept 1803. Wit: John Swaney Jr., John Roberts.

3-4 Benjamin Morrow to James Webb, for $200, 73 A on Tar R adj Jas Webb, Isaac Day, on wagon road, Jno Day. 19 Sept 1805. Wit: Thos Owin, Abel Parrish.

4 Jesse Evans to John Scoggin, for $4, 1 A on Flat R adj Evans. 27 Jan 1806. Proved by oath Nathan Scoggin.

5 Abraham Verlines of CC to John Scoggings of Person Co., for 100 lbs, 105 A on Flat R adj John Goodloe Warren, John Smith Hurst, Richd Hargis. 14 May 1804. Wit: William McKissack, Nathan Scogings.

5-6 John Parrish to Abel Parrish, for 40 lbs, 150 A on Blewing Cr adj Robert Pitman, Joseph Pitman, Parrish. 15 Oct 1805. Wit: James Thomson, R. Vanhook.

6 Div land of Ezekiel Dollarhide into 7 lots of 57 A each to following legatees: Joshua Step, Willm Dollarhide, William Gallagher, Garnett Neeley, John B. Lea, Thomas Dollarhide, Henry Birch. 17 May 1806. Wit: Loyd Vanhook, John McMullen.

7 State of NC - #? - to Reubin Taylor, for 50 / per 100 A, 1 A on Sergent's Mill Cr adj Henry Black grist mill. Entered 29 May 1804.

7 Sterling Warrin to William Warrin, for 18 lbs 2/, 18½ A on S Hico & Cobb Cr. 26 May 1806. Wit: John Newton, Jas Dollarhide, Francis Wright.

8 Richard Oakly to Kedar Powell of Granville Co., for 120 lbs, 100 A on little Cr adj Wm. Oakly, Evans. 8 Jan 1806. Wit: William Oakly, Amos Parker.

8-9 Richard Ogilby to Thomas J. Moore, for 208 lbs, 141 A e side Cobb Cr of Hico adj John Mason, said Moore, Christopher Bass. 4 Mar 1806. Wit: Jas M. Burton.

9 Robert Wade to William Jeffreys, in trust, for 40 lbs 15/2, negroes Belinda & Peter; if debt paid sale void. 5 Apr 1806. Wit: John Gwin.

9-10 Vincent Harrison of State of GA, to Samuel Yarbrough, for $800, negro woman Hanner, children Phill, Harden, Caty, & one young one. 5 July 1803. Wit: W. Jeffreys.

10 Ellen Harrison to Samuel Yarbrough, for $800, negro woman Hanna, boy Phill, boy Harden, Caty, Juder. 20 June 1803. Wit: William Yarbrough, Catherine Yarbrough.

10-11 Edward Clay Jr. to James Cochran, for $1721¼, 270 A +, said tract conveyed him by Edward Clay Sen. adj Richard Atkinson, Saterfield. 11 Jan 1806. Wit: Alexr Rose, James Clay.

11-12 John Broadaway to William Brown, for 88 lbs, 88 A being the tract where Broadaway lives adj Capt. William Lea decd, Joseph Sarratt former line, John McMurry. 13 Mar 1806. Wit: Jas Cochran, James Jay Junr.

12-3 John Ogilby Sen. to William Trotter, for 44 lbs 18/, 11.1 A on Hico adj Trotter. 21 Sept 1805. Wit: Richard Ogilby, Thomas J. Moore.

Deep Book D
Page

13 Thomas Gipson to Richard Deshazo, for $50, 35½ A on Brooks Rd adj Henry
Gipson. 28 May 1806. /s/ Thomas Gibson. Wit: Thomas Bohannon, Anw Bohannon.

13-5 Andrew Barnett to Charles Mitchell, for 750 lbs, 346 A crossing the Cr adj
John McGehee, Thomas Heggie. 2 June 1806. Wit: Ish Edwards, J. Hubbard.

15 Wm. Cocke to John Cochran Sen., for $370, ½ of a tract that belonged to Hardy
Crews on Deep Cr - 370 A & sold by execution of Jesse Dickens. 1 Sept 1806.
Wit: James Thomson.

15-6 Joseph Jones of Dinwiddie Co., VA, to Robert Brooks of Person Co., for $460,
240 A adj both men. 23 May 1806. Wit: Artha Brooks, Lewis Overby, Roger Atkinson.

16 James Messer to Gabriel Bumpass, for $1280, 640 A on Flat R adj Hollman, Farmer,
Ragsdale, Comer, Gentry. 14 July 1806. Wit: Hendon Paine, Allen Twitty.

16 John Clixby to Jesse Lunsford, for $225, negro girl Mary about 10 yrs of age.
26 Dec 1805. Wit: Joseph Lunsford.

17 John Sweany Sen. of CC to John Sweany Jr. of same, for 20 lbs, 120 A on Deep
Cr being a part of 566 A adj Thomas Paine, Stephen Moore, Rogers. 2 Nov 1785.
Wit: Millington Blalock, John Cash.

17 Joseph Pitman to John Wilkerson, for 25 lbs, 100 A adj Baird, Harris, Bright.
25 Aug 1806. Wit: Robt Harris.

18 William Cocke to John Day Jun., for $370, ½ of tract that belonged to Hardy
Crews & sold by execution of Jesse Dickens on Deep Cr, Mayo, & Tar R - 370 A.
1 Sept 1806. Wit: James Thomson.

18 William Winstead to Lewis Wilkerson, for $24, 30 A. _ _ 1806. Wit: Abel
Parrish, Lewis Wilkerson Jr.

19 Gabriel Bumpass to Joseph Lunsford Jun., for 90 lbs, 100 A on Deep Cr adj
Jesse Lunsford, Crews old line. 11 Jan 1805. Wit: Jesse Lunsford, William Paine.

19 John E. Watson to William Bazzel(Bazwell), for 54 lbs, 108 A on Castle Cr adj
Robert Huston old line, Charles Bostick old line. 14 July 1806.
Wit: Wm. Jeffreys, Dennis Hargis.

20 Vincent Warrin to John Miles, for $200, 200 A on Sergent Cr adj John Atkinson,
John Fuller. 13 Nov 1805. Wit: John McFarland, John Russell.

20 Bennett Williams to Samuel Williams, for 100 lbs, 183 A on Cubb Cr adj Wm.
Oakley, widow Vaughan. 29 June 1805. Wit: Wm. Dickens.

20-1 Richard Burch Sen. to granddaughters Jean Burch & Betsy Burch, daughters of
Richard Burch Jr., for love & affection, to each a bed. 8 July 1800. Wit:
Nathl Norfleet, Robert P. Ritchie.

21 Hiram Combs & Sterling Warren to Moses Bradsher, for $310, 93 A on Cobb Cr adj
Elisabeth Johnston, William Warren, on road fom Leasburg to confluence of N & S
Hico. 29 Aug 1806. Wit: Loyd Vanhook, Isaac Satterfield.

22 Thomas Neeley Sen. to Vincent Warrin, for $200, 200 A on Sergent Cr adj John
Atkinson, John Fuller. 21 Feb 1805. Wit: Garnett Neeley, John Miles, Thomas
Neeley.

22 John McFarland to George Lea, for $800, 216½ A both sides Cobb Cr adj Eskridge.
6 Oct 1806. Wit: Abner Lea, Danl Darby.

23 Martin Jones to Lewis Ramsey, for 50 lbs, 156 A on Mayo adj Baird, Mrs. Donaldson old line, Holloway, Atkinson, Bailey. 8 Oct 1806. Wit: John Holloway,
Nancy Briston.

23-4 Lowry Booker to Meredith Cox, for 27 lbs 15/6, negro woman Cloey. 2 Aug
1806. Wit: W. Jeffreys.

24 Joseph Hargis to William Hall, for $200, 100 A on Flat R adj Drury Allin, Robt Dickens, Thos Hargis. 8 Jan 1806. Wit: Phillip Hall, John Byas.

24-5 Arthur Buchanon to Francis Lawson, for $100, 100 A on Byrd Mill Cr at Frays Br adj Joseph Davis, Wm. Allin, James Davey. 5 Jan 806. Wit: Moses Street, Josiah Wade.

25 John Bell of Mecklenburg Co., VA, to William Tapp of Person Co., for $25, 41 A e side Hico adj Tap, Dixon, former Sergent line - it being tract sold by Daniel Weldon for Robert Jones Jun. to Saml Bell in 1761. 6 Oct 1806. Wit: G. W. Brame, Saml Dickens.

25-6 Dennis Obriant adm of Patrick Obriant decd of Granville Co. to Joseph Obriant of Person Co., for 180 lbs, 350 A in Person Co. adj Byrd, Donaldson, Isaac Vanhook, Baird. 1 Dec 1806. NB - This deed made in consequence of name of Reuben Ragland & his heirs named instead of Joseph Obriant in former deed. 29 July 1805. Wit: F. W. Daniel, Allen Howard.

26 Christopher Bass(who gave deed of trust of 22 negroes to Cuningham & Trabern for 547 lbs 9/8) relinquishment of negroes to Bass for payment. 3 Aug 1807. Acknd in open court.

26 Thomas Farrow to William Moore, for $112, 123 A on Flat R adj said Moore. 3 Mar 1806. Wit: Wm. McKissack, William Rainey.

27 Joseph Morton to William Jeffreys, for $144, 144 A on meeting house br of Adams Cr adj Joseph Gill. 24 Mar 1806. Wit: Danl Merritt, Thomas Allin.

27 State of NC - #122 - to James Jay, George Huston & Barnett Lea, trustees for the Rev. Wm. Brown's Church, for 50/ per 100 A, 7 A on middle prong of Rushy Br adj James Johnston, Joseph Carney, Kindel Vanhook. Entered 27 Feb 1805.

28 State of NC - #112 - to William Waite, for 50/ per 100 A, 73½ A on crooked fork Aaron's Cr adj John Halliburton, Robert Jones, Ambrose Jones, Richard Blanks, Harris. Entered 16 Aug 1803.

28 Artha Brooks Jun. to John Lawson, for 83 lbs 5/, 55 3/4 A on Hico on bold br adj Joseph Jones, David Brookes, said Lawson, Robert Brooks. 27 Nov 1806. Wit: Thomas Lawson.

28 Lowry Booker to Meredith Cox, for 264 lbs, 5 negroes: Sam, Doyle, Christian, Lucy, & ? . 2 Aug 1806. Wit: W. Jeffreys.

29 Lowry Booker to William Jeffreys, for 41 lbs,14/4, negro girl Ame. 2 Aug 1806. Wit: Meredith Cox.

29 Thomas Dollarhide of CC and John B. Lea of Person Co., to Henry Burch of CC, 114 A on S Hico adj Garnet Nealy, John Miles, McMullen; 57 A of this they acquired on account of their wives being lawful heirs of Ezekiel Dollarhide late of CC. 24 Oct 1806. Wit: Loyd Vanhook Senr., Moses Bradsher.

29-30 George Eskridge, William Lea & Vincent Lea of CC, trustees, to Nicholas Thompson, 130 A on Double Cr of S Hico adj Thomas Snipes. 27 Oct 1806. Wit: Ish Edwards.

30-1 Thomas Goins to Thomas Keeling, for 26 lbs 5/, 15 A adj Wheeler, Roger Tilman, Allison. _ Sept 1806. Wit: Benjamin Wheeler, Jas D. Henley.

31 William Brechen to Benjamin Wheeler, for 95 lbs, 119 A n side bear br. 1 Dec 1806. Wit: William Saterfield, James Chandler.

31 John Miles to John Russell, for $200, 200 A on Sergent Cr adj John Fuller, John Atkinson. 14 Nov 1805. Wit: Vinson Warren, Downey Wade.

32 John Bressie to Meredith Daniel of Granville Co., for $375, 308 A on Spoon-water Cr adj John Baird, Agnes Barnett, Charles Halliburton, Richd Andrews. 17 Nov 1806. Wit: Mings Yancey, Bressie Lewis.

32 Thomas Rainey to Thomas Saulmon, for $95, 45 A on Flat R adj Benjamin Jacobs. 1 Dec 1806. Wit: Nathan Hargis, Wilson Currie.

33 John B. Lea to Jeremiah Brooks of CC, for $283.75, 113½ A on S Hico adj Carver. 27 Sept 1806. Wit: Thomas Carver, William Carver.

33-4 William Moore to Larkin Brooks, for $545, 109 A adj John Rogers, Lea Haralson. 18 Feb 1806. Wit: H. Haralson, Isaac Neely.

34 Thomas Carver to Archibald Lipscomb, for $920, 230½ A on S Hico adj Hiram Lewis, John Carver, widow Hughs, widow Lea. 2 Dec 1806. Wit: Henry Sergent, Loyd Vanhook.

35 David Evans and wife Polly Evans to Ann Hall, widow of Phillip Hall Sen. decd, for 5/ and knowing she did not apply for her dower of land, a tract for her life with mansion buse including land willed by Phillip Hall to Polly Evans wife of David Evnas. 27 Feb 1807. Wit: Jas Cochran, Wm. Hall.

35 Mabel Gentry & Nancy McIntire to James Williamson, for $100, 100 A n side Flat R adj Thomas Rainey, Thomas Blalock, Benjamin Jopling, Thomas Hargis. 22 Dec 1806. Wit: Thomas Rainey, L. Hargis.

36 Christopher Bass to william Tapp, for $2832, tracts both side Cob Cr of Hico; 421 A adj Thomas J. Moore, Jas Rainey, Wells, Labon Stafford; 1 A adj Bass. 22 Jan 1807. Wit: James Williamson, Alex Cuningham.

36-7 John James of Provence of NC and county of Wake to children George James, John James, Ann Oneal, Mary James, William Johnston James, Thomas James, Abner James, Phebe James, Temperance James Rogers, for love & affection, all negroes, livestock, household articles after death of grantor & his wife. 30 Dec 1772. Wit: Wm. Anderson Fowler, Mosias Jones. Proved March Court 1807 by oath of Nathan Massey as Anderson Fowler & Mosias Jones are both decd.

37 Richard Carnal to Alexander Cuningham, for 81 lbs 12/, 136.8 A adj Archd Carnal, Stephen Oliver. 9 Feb 1807. Wit: H. Haralson, Jas Daniel.

38 Joshua Cate to James Thomson, for $750, 233 A both sides Aldridge Cr including land on which Isaiah Cate now lives adj Taylor, Bumpass, Cocke. 6 Dec 1806. Wit: Chas Holeman, Joel Hicks.

38 Joshua Jacobs to William Allin of Mecklenburg Co., VA, for $100, 54 A s fork Flat R. Also signed by Sarah Jacobs. 12 Sept 1806. Wit: Shadrack Hargis, John Allin. Sarah Jacobs consented to sale of her own free will.

39 Rebekah Burton to Joel Hicks, for $60, 59 A on Richland Spring Cr adj Joseph Hubbard, James P. Miller, Robert Paine. 30 Dec 1806. Wit: Joseph Traler, John Hicks.

39-40 William Featherstone to James Stuart, for 86 lbs, 86 A on Hico adj William Trotter, Solomon Draper, Archd Lipscomb. 27 Jan 1807. Wit: Henry Sergent, James Trotter.

40-1 William Blalock (in debt to Millenton Blalock Jun. for 12 lbs 14/ & for debt due Dickens & Wilson for store goods) to Millenton Blalock, for 5/, 175 A on Cob Cr adj Babista Owin, Millenton Blalock Jun., Jonathan Jackson. 27 Aug 1806. Wit: Saml Yarbrough.

41 Fielding Lewis of Shelby Co., KY, to Benjamin Johnston of Person Co., for $137½, 25 A on N Hico adj Zachariah Lewis, Abner Duncan, John Ogilby, Henry Atkinson - it being his part of large tract of Fielding Lewis his father. /s/ by John Lewis for Fielding Lewis. 2 Feb 1807. Wit: H. Haralson, Archd Haralson.

Deed Book D
Page
41-2 John Foshee to Thomas Rainey, for 100 lbs, 103 A on Flat R adj Wm. Moore.
22 Sept 1806. Wit: Nathl Norfleet, Robt P. Ritchie.

42-3 David Brechen to Hiram Combs, for $430, 129¼ A both sides Neds Cr adj James
McMurry, Joseph Carney, John Russell. 30 Aug 1806. Wit: Moses Bradsher, Loyd
Vanhook.

43 John Foshee to Thomas Rainey, for $339, 113 A s fork Flat R adj John Allin,
Richd Hargis decd. 22 Sept 1806. Wit: Nathl Norfleet, Robert P. Ritchie.

43-4 John Brooks to Baptist Church on Mayo & their survivers for benefit of the
Church, 1 A adj General Jones; including their meeting house called Bethel.
28 Nov 1806. Wit: Thos Halliburton, George Hunt, John Lawson.

44 Humphrey Pittard to Richard Long & Benjamin G. Long, for 100 lbs, 190 A adj
Burrell Green, Jesse Watson, Edward Clay, Hatcher - said tract conveyed Susannah
Williamson exec of Henry Williamson decd on 18 Nov 1802. 30 Dec 1806.
Wit: Samuel Pittard, R. Long.

45 James Cochran to Lozen Carver, for 24 lbs, 66 3/4 A on Stories Cr being part
of tract purchased of John Walters adj Isaac Fuller, John Long. 28 Feb 1807.
Wit: Joseph Neely, Hosea Carver.

45-6 James McMurry to Hiram Combs, for $60, 18 A on Neds Cr adj said Combs.
2 Sept 1806. Wit: Moses Bradsher, Loyd Vanhook.

46 Osborn Jeffreys Sen. to Osborn Jeffreys Jun., for 20 lbs, 700 A on Flat R adj
John Commins, John Cates, Samuel Sneed, Serat land purchased of Jno Allison.
12 Mar 1806. Wit: Allen Miller, James Cochran.

46 Thomas Saulmon to Josiah Fike, for $162.50, 45 A on Flat R adj Benjamin
Jacobs. 1 Dec 1806. Wit: Nathan Hargis, Wilson Currie.

47 William Moore to John Campbell of Abbeville Dist., SC, for $150, his part of
7 negroes willed by his father John Moore to his children after death of his
Mother now wife of John Campbell; negroes: old Lewis, young Lewis, Aaron, Beck
and her increase Will & Dick, Molly. 13 May 1807. Wit: R. Vanhook, Ish Edwards,
Benj Chambers.

47-8 John Ogilby (in debt to Jas W. Smith for 121 lbs 7/9, plus other debts) to
Cary Williams, trustee, for 5/, 200 A s side S Hico adj William Trotter, Tap,
Durham. 2 May 1807. Wit: Currie Barnett, George W. Duncan.

48 John Blake to Thomas Snipes, for $310, 97½ A s side n prong Double Cr of S
Hico adj Wm. Brown, James Cochran, Wm. Lea merchant decd, John McMurry, said
Snipes. 16 Dec 1806. Wit: Loyd Vanhook, Lawrence Vanhook.

48-9 William Gold to Henry Sargent, for ? (not given), 33 A on S Hico adj John
Darbey, said Sargent. 11 May 1807. Wit: Thos Talbert, James Stafford.

49 Henry Sargent to William Gold, for ? (not given), 200 A on Henly Mill Cr adj
George Rosebrock old line. _ _ 1807. Wit: Thos Talbert, James Stafford.

49-50 Henry Atkinson of CC to William S. Branch, for 35 lbs, 19½ A e side Hico
adj Fielding Lewis, Abner Duncan, Joseph McGehee, John Ogilby - it being tract
allotted to James Lewis a legatee of Fielding Lewis decd; was conveyed to Gabriel
Gun, then to Aaron Haskins, & by sheriff to Henry Atkinson. 12 May 1807.
Acknd in open court.

50-1 Swepston Sims to Robert Gill, for $872, 200 A adj Gabriel Davie decd, said
Gill, & was purchased of Robert Davie. 17 Apr 1807. Wit: Thos Halliburton,
John Holloway.

51 James Campbell of Petersburg, VA, merchant, to Elisabeth Green Jeffreys, James Osborn Spiers Jeffreys, David Jeffreys, & Lucy Peters Jeffreys - all orphans of Paul Jeffreys decd - for $500 pd by Paul Jeffreys in his lifetime & residue by his heirs, 500 A on Flat R adj Robt. Kellum, Osborn Jeffreys, James Messer, Robert Dickens; also 200 A on Flat R adj Osborn Jeffreys. 11 June 1807. Wit: Dun Cameron.

51-2 Joseph Obriant to Thomas Lawson, a gift of 100 A on Mayo Cr - said tract conveyed to John Lawson Sen. & given to his son Thomas Lawson by codicil to his will and conveyed by mistake to Obriant. 9 Mar 1807. Wit: Wm. Elixson, John Womack.

52 Ephraim Hawkins to Simeon Cochran, for $400, 206½ A on bushey fork of Flat R adj Joel Step, Fisher. Also signed by Ann Hawkins. 16 July 1806. Wit: Wm. McKissack, Robt McKissack, Richd St. John, Wm. Marshal.

53 Baylor Burch to Simeon Cochran, for $500, 225 A on Hico adj said Cochran's storehouse. 9 Apr 1807. Wit: Thomas W. Thomson, Loyd Vanhook, Wm. Mansfield.

53-4 Henry W. Howard to Robt Howard, for $100, all claim to land as legatee of Henry Howard decd, about 257 A, adj Thomas J. Chambers on Hico, Marlowe, & Gents Creeks; also his right to land where Edward O. Chambers now lives, 100 A. 19 Sept 1806. Wit: Thos J. Chambers, William Carter.

54 Henry Atkinson of CC to Richard Atkinson of Person Co., for 1000 lbs, 800 A both sides Trim's Br & Richland Cr - it being where John Atkinson decd formerly lived adj James Cochran, Edward Clay Sen., Reubin Walton, James Walton, James Fuller, John B. Lewis, Samuel Garret, Thomas Atkinson. 13 May 1807. Acknd in open court.

55-6 Jacob Vanhook, sheriff, to John Williams (due to suit brought by William Moore of Granville Co. against Benjamin Towler of Person Co. for 93 lbs 15/) for 426 lbs, 640 A a part of land sold at the CH adj CH lot adj John Paine, Joshua Browning, Brooks, David Mitchel; also tract adj John Man of 200 A. 15 May 1807. Wit: James Thomson, William Mann.

56-7 Jacob Vanhook, sheriff, to Henry Atkinson of CC, for 35 lbs, 19½ A adj Major John Ogilby, Joseph McGehee, Abner Duncan; sold to satisfy judgment which Richard & Samuel obtained against Aron Haskins. 12 May 1807. Acknd in open court.

57 William Dickens & Samuel Dickens to Jesse Dickens, for $700, 1½ tenths of A at ne corner CH lot adj Dempsey Moore's chimney, Benjamin Toler, Hargis. 4 June 1806. Acknd in open court.

58 William Dickens of Granville Co., NC, to Jesse Dickens of Person Co., for 200 lbs, 685 A on dry br of Deep Cr adj Jos Lunsford, Jesse Dickens, Thomas Moore. 20 Aug 1804. Wit: Ira Lea.

58-9 William Waite of Williamson Co., TN, late of Person Co., to Jesse Dickens, for $56.25, 75 A on Rosemary Cr adj Peterson, Vanhook, Brooks. 8 Apr 1807. Wit: W. Jeffreys.

59 Joseph Pitman to Overton Harris of Granville Co., for 45 lbs, 150 A adj Baird, Humphries, Harris. 25 Aug 1806. Wit: Robt Harris, Lewis Parrott.

59-60 Robert Payne Senr. to James Paine, for 6/, 105 A both sides Adams C adj Jno Mann, David Allin. 3 July 1807. Wit: Wm. Cocke, James Thomson.

60 James Gooch Sen. to Thomas Sneed & wife Nancy Sneed, for 214 lbs, 515 A n side Flat R adj John Bairden, Robert Cates, Phillips Moore, Thomas Minshew - it being tract deeded Gooch by Sneed 21 Jan 1802 & formerly property of Nancy Parker now wife of Thomas Sneed. 6 Aug 1807. Wit: Solomon Cates, Josiah Brown.

Deed Book D
Page
61 James Williamson to Joseph Hargis, for 100 lbs, 100 A n side Flat R adj
Thomas Rainey, Thos Blalock, Benjamin Jopling, Thomas Hargis. 30 May 1807.
Wit: T. Hargis, Saml Satterfield.

61 Joel Newman to Cary Williams, for $400, 141 A head waters McFarland Cr of Hico
adj Joshua Dickson, Julius Justice, widow Pulliam. 1 Mar 1807.
Wit: Ish Edwards, Hugh Woods.

62 Thomas Sneed & his wife Nancy Sneed to John Gooch Sen., for 214 lbs, 515 A
n side Flat R adj John Bearden, Robert Cates, Phillip Moore, Thomas Minshew.
6 Aug 1807. Wit: Solomon Cates, Josiah Brown.

62-3 William Hall to Jno Bowers Sen., for $200, 100 A on Flat R adj Drury Allin,
Robert Dickens, Thos Hargis. 14 Mar 1807. Wit: Dennis Evans, James Frost.

63 Hiram Lewis to Moses Bradsher, for 54 lbs, 54 A on road by William Warren
from Leasburg. 17 Feb 1807. Wit: Henry Lea.

63-4 Thomas W. Price of Orange Co., to William Whitfield Sen., for 10 lbs, 25 A
on Orange Co. line adj Simeon Cochran. 1 Mar 1807. Wit: James Whitfield,
Susannah Whitfield.

64 William McFarland to James Pool, for $400, 196 A both sides Castle Cr adj
John Horley old line, Robert McFarland old line. Wit: James Trotter, Benj Chambers. 11 Nov 1807.

65 Yancey Bailey to Orbourne Jefferson, for 50/ per 100 A, 250 A on Mill Cr adj
Gabl Davey, Nathaniel Cuningham, Seth Moore. 6 Aug 1801. Wit: Thos Hood, John
Carrington, Gl Davey.

65-6 James Pulliam to Byrd Pulliam, for 150 lbs, 164 A both sides Gents Cr of
Hico adj John Williams, Newman. 25 Aug 1807. Wit: Ish Edwards, Wm. Frazer.

66-7 James Mitchell to Charles Mitchell, for 50 lbs, 60 A on Aaron's Cr adj Edward
Chambers - being same land James Mitchell purchased of Josiah Dickson. 5 Aug 1807.
Wit: Jno Willson, W. Jeffreys.

67 Hartwell Marrable of Halifax Co., VA, to Jesse Dickens, for $225, 300 A on
Stories Cr adj Roger Atkinson, John Cooper. 9 Oct 1805. Wit: John Bowles Jr.,
Wm. Moore.

67-8 William Pool of Granville Co. to Ashburn Davey of Person Co., for 32 lbs,
sale of negro Aaron. _ Nov 1807. Wit: William Davey.

68 Osborn Jeffreys Sen. to Lewis Tapp, for $300, negro woman Cassanora age 16 or
17 yrs. Wit: James Thomson, Jno Daniel. 18 Aug 1807.

68-9 Joseph Hubbard Sen. to Joseph Hubbard Jun., for 10 lbs, 360 A on Richland
Spring Cr adj John Daniels, James Williamson. 8 Nov 1807. Wit: W. Hubbard,
Jeremiah Hubbard.

69 Alexander Cuningham to Thomas Webb & Co., for 120 lbs, 228 A on Castle Cr
known by name of the cross road ordinary adj Samuel Cox, John Barnet, Douglas.
31 Jan 1806. Wit: Rich M. Cuningham, John McCall.

69-70 Jacob Vanhook, sheriff, to James Williamson, for 34 lbs 15/, 100 A of Stephen
Crews & sold by court order to collect 75 lbs 10/ to satisfy Burton for judgment-
land on Richland Spring Cr adj Mathew Daniel, Daniel Clayton, Joseph Hubbard.
30 Sept 1807. Wit: Saml Satterfield.

70-1 Martha Richardson to Robert Wade, for $138½, 27.7 A adj Wade, Nealy. 10 Oct
1807. Wit: Francis B. Wright, Staples Malone, Robert Wade Jun.

71 Robert Wade to Downey Wade, for $130 & parental affection, 115 A w side S Hico adj Loyd Vanhook, widow Richardson, John Russell, James McMurry. 10 Oct 1807. Wit: Francis H. Wright, Staples Malone, Robert Wade Jun.

72 Willis Nichols Senr. to Mathias Nichols, for 10 lbs, 191½ A on Flat R adj Jeffreys, Hubbard. 8 Feb 1808. Wit: W. Hubbard, James Cothron.

72-3 Willis Nichols Senr. to Willis Nichols Jr., for 10 lbs, 189 A on Flat R adj Robert Cates, Solomon Cates, Jeffreys, Mathias Nichols. 8 Feb 1808. Wit: W. Hubbard, James Cothran.

73-4 Jacob Vanhook, sheriff, to William Dickens of Granville Co., for 49 lbs 3/9, 640 A on Flat R & formerly property of Robt Dickens adj Joseph Jay former land, James Jay, Ann Pyron, Henry Ford - sold by court order to settle suit brought by James Messer against Dickens. 12 Nov 1807. Wit: Samuel Dickens.

74 John Scogin to James Martin of Mecklenburg Co., VA, for 108 lbs, 105 A on Flat R adj John Goodloe Warrin, William Allin, Dickens. 31 Aug 1807. Wit: James Paine, William Allin.

74-5 Meredith Cox to Hugh Woods, for $500, 100 A both sides Adams Cr adj Abner Chambers, Hugh Barnett. 14 Mar 1807. Wit: Cary Williams, R. Long.

75 Samuel Smith to Samuel Morgan of Nottaway Co., VA, for 1656 lbs, 1039 A both sides Sergent & McFarland Creeks of Hico adj Edmund Dixon, John Dixon, Cary Williams, Joseph Royster, William Trotter, Reubin Taylor, Lofton Walton, John Harris. 25 Dec 1807. Wit: Edmund Dixon, Jos M. McGehee.

75-6 William Dickens of Granville Co. to Thomas J. Moore of CC, for love & affection to him and his wife Lucretia Moore & for 5/, 640 A on Flat R said tract granted to Robert Dickens in his lifetime and sold by sheriff - adj James Jay, Ann Pyron former claim, Henry Ford former land, Joseph Jay former land. _ Jan 1808. Acknd in open court.

76 Willis Roberts to Jesse Oakley of Granville Co., for 90 lbs, 250 A both sides Cub Cr adj David Roberts, Arthur Moore. 19 Nov 1807. Wit: Jno Knott, Samuel Yarbrough, Richard Oakly.

76-7 William Paine to Francis Day, for $160, 80 A on Deep Cr. 23 Nov 1807. Wit: John Day Sr., J. Bumpass.

77 Thomas Craven of Randolph Co., NC, to William Paine of Person Co., for 40 lbs, 80 A on Deep Cr. 22 Oct 1802. Wit: Harden Paine, Joshua Craven.

77 Clayton Fuller to Thomas Talbert, for $156, 36½ A on Hico adj widow Henly, William Trotter. 8 Dec 1807. Wit: James Holloway.

78 Millinton Blalock to William Oakly, for 55 lbs, 93 A on little Cr adj Moses Cash, Walter Oakly, Richd Oakly, Anthony Cozart, Ben Cozart. 28 Feb 1807. Wit: Samuel Dickens, Jno Knott.

78-9 John Trickey to Thomas Duty, for 350 lbs, 120 A both sides Stories Cr adj Jacob Bull, Duty mill pond, William Trickey. 14 Oct 1807. Wit: Ish Edwards, John Thomas.

79 Davison Chambers to William Wood, for 90 lbs, 30 A adj Alex Cuningham land purchased of Thomas J. Chambers to path to Hico Cr at racoon ford, Mumford McGehee. 11 Jan 1808. Wit: Edmund Dixon, Henry Dixon, Warren Dixon.

79-80 Solomon Draper to William Dixon, for 112 lbs 16/, 94 A nw side Hico Cr adj Edmund Dixon, orphans of Robert Black decd, Joseph McGehee, widow McCain - said tract conveyed him by John Pearson. 10 Dec 1803. Wit: Edmund Dixon, Josias Chambers.

Deed Book D
Page

80 Davison Chambers to Benjamin Chambers, for $700, 450 A on Stories Cr adj Jacob Bull, James Cochran, Cary Williams, Robert Deshazo - being same land purchased of Ezekiel Duest in co-partnership; also his right in another tract adj this where their father William Chambers lived & died after death of their mother, Elisabeth Chambers containing 220 A; his interest in negro slave Julie which they owned together; his claim in the mill. 10 Dec 1807. Wit: Ish Edwards, George C. Rogers.

80-1 William Trickey (in debt to Cochran & Edwards for 135 lbs) to Benjamin Chambers in trust, for $1, 100 A adj Henry Graves, Jacob Bull. 2 Mar 1807. Wit: Jas Trotter, Thos Dixon.

81-2 William Penick to Alexander Cuningham, for $1600, 208 A on Cain & Hico adj Abram Dunaway, John Davis, Stephen Oliver, Thomas Dixon, Robert Jones old line. 6 Jan 1808. Wit: Jno M. McGehee, Wm. McKissack.

82 John Gwin to Samuel Smith, for $825, 165 A on Cain Cr of Hico adj John Harralson - said land he purchased of William Gold. 13 Dec 1807. Wit: Robert Wade, Wm. Penick.

82-3 John Ogilby to Edmund Dixon, for $2170, 310 A on N Hico adj heirs of Fielding Lewis decd, widow Black, Solomon Draper, Joseph McGehee, Wm. Branch, Benjamin Johnston. 27 Nov 1807. Wit: William Dixon, Warren Dixon, Robt Seymour, Wiley Jones, Wm. Williams.

83 Daniel Evans to Phillip Hall, for 100 lbs, 60 A on Double Cr of S Hico adj Thos Graves. 12 Jan 1808. Wit: Wm. Hall, James Frost.

83-4 Jacob Vanhook, sheriff, (to settle court case of Person Co. against John Sneed favoring Cain & Ray to collect for 47 lbs 8/3) to Thomas Sneed, negro boy Zack for 23 lbs, another called ? for 30 lbs, girl Dina 15 lbs, woman & child & Reubin for 38 lbs; horses. 13 May 1808. Acknd in open court.

84 Osborn Jeffreys Senr to William Bilbo of Mecklenburg Co., VA, for 3000 lbs, 2759 A on Flat R adj Lemuel Sneed, Willis Nichols, Woodson Hubbard, William Cohoon, estate of Stephen Moore, Jesse Dickens, James Clark, estate of Paul Jeffreys, William Claton, John Commins, Osborn Jeffreys Jun. 7 May 1808. Wit: Thomas Wade, Archer West.

84-5 Osborn Jeffreys Sen. to William Bilbo of Mecklenburg, VA, for 200 lbs, 250 A on Mill Cr adj Gabriel Davie, Nathaniel Cunningham, Seth Moore. 7 May 1808. Wit: Thomas Wade, Archer West.

85 Osborn Jeffreys Senr to William Bilbo of Mecklenburg Co., VA, for 2000 lbs, property: Jacob, Ailse, Tempy, Chany, Dick, Judy, Ailse, Jacob, Penny, Brutus, Rhody, Crawford, Nancy, Mary, Darky, Jenny, Archer, Ely, Elisha, Burwell, Claiborn, Patience, Sarsy, Andrew, Aron, Hinton; all livestock; household & kitchen furniture. 9 May 1808. Wit: Thomas Wade, Archer West.

85-6 Thomas Jay Moore to James Lea, for $1690, 338 A both sides Cob Cr on middle fork of Hico adj Richard Ogilby, John Mason, Thomas Jeffreys, William Tap, James Rainey, Archd Murphey, William S. Branch. 31 Dec 1807. Wit: H. Haralson, Richard Ogilby.

86-7 Sterling Harris to James King of Granville Co., for $1000, 236 A both sides Crooked Fork. 30 Nov 1807. Wit: Overton Harris, Wm. Elixson, Abel Parrish.

87 Sterling Harris of Granville Co. to James King of same, for $30, 165 A on crooked fork of Aaron's Cr adj Overton Harris, John P. Pool, John Harris, William Waite, Robert Harris. 30 Nov 1807. Wit: Overton Harris, Wm. Elixson, Abel Parrish.

Deed Book D
Page

87-8 Andrew Peede to Jeremiah Roberts, for 36 lbs, 100 A on Cub Cr at Rens Spring br. 2 Mar 1807. Wit: John Knott, Milley Knott, A. Roberts.

88 Joseph Lunsford to Granville Vaughn, for $170, 167½ A on Tapley's Cr adj Joseph Traler. 28 Dec 1807. Wit: Jesse Lunsford, Joseph Renn.

89 Josiah Brown (in debt to James Williamson for $625) to James Williamson, in trust for 3/, 181 A on Flat R; also two negroes Daniel & Obedience.

89-90 William Hamblin Sen. to Nathaniel Hamlen, for $300, 102 A on Stories Cr adj Joseph Hamlin, John Parker. 30 Dec 1807. Wit: Benj Chambers, Joseph Hamblen.

90 William Hamblen to Joseph Hamblen, for $200, 66 A on Stories Cr adj John Harris, John Fuller, Richd Hamblen. 30 Dec 1807. Wit: Benj Chambers, Nathaniel Hamblen.

90-1 Jessey Long to Joseph Southard, for $50, 23 1/5 A on Adams Cr adj Charles Mitchell. 4 Feb 1807. Wit: Benj Chambers, Robert Southard.

91 Edmund Dixon to William Scott Branch, for 159 lbs 17/3, 50 3/4 A on n side N Hico adj Thomas Jeffreys, dower land of Elizabeth Gun, said Branch, Joseph McGehee, Solomon Draper. 26 Dec 1807. Wit: H. Harralson, Abraham Dunaway, Arch Harralson.

91-2 James Okeley(Oakley) to John Winstead, for 120 lbs, 128 A adj Hugh Darby, William Rainey, Jno Mason, Henry Royster. 25 Feb 1808. Wit: Samuel Winstead, H. Sergent.

92 John Carver to Richard Duty, for $520, 104 A on S Hico adj said Duty, Moses Bradsher, Brooks, James Dollarhide. 26 Nov 1807. Wit: Moses Bradsher, Charles Winstead.

93 Reuben Newton Junr. of Hardin Co., KY, to legal heirs of Solomon Draper Senr. decd of Person Co., for 125 lbs (75 lbs pd by Draper & 50 lbs by exec), 160 A on Sergent's Cr being tract conveyed Newton by Jonnathan Skeen 14 Dec 1788. 30 Apr 1808. Wit: Jas Cochran, James Cardin.

93-4 George Roberts of Wake Co., NC, to Allen Burton of Person Co., for $700, 100 A on Flat R adj Long, James Griffin. 3 May 1808. Wit: James Cothran, Alex Cothran.

94 Benjamin Wheeler to Roger Tilman, for 105 lbs, 102 A adj James Chandler, Daniel Clayton, Gold, Roger Tilman. 26 Feb 1808. Wit: Henry Sergent.

95 Clayton Fuller to Roger Tilman, for 3 lbs, 2 A adj James Chandler, said Fuller at Rosebrook Br. 6 Feb 1808. Wit: John Parker.

95-6 Jacob Vanhook, sheriff, to George Lea (case of Herndon Haralson who brought suit against John Lea for debt of 65 lbs 5/7), for 52 lbs 5/, 141 A bought at public auction on Bear Cr of S Hico adj Joseph Rice, Daniel Sargent. 9 Nov 1807. Wit: Ish Edwards.

97 Richard Eskridge to CC to George Lea of Person Co., for $20, 18 A w side Cobb Cr adj said Lea, former McFarland land. 19 Mar 1808. Wit: W. A. Lea, William Eskridge.

97 James Jay Junr. to Robert H. Childers, for $300, 60 A adj James Paine, John Atkinson. 11 May 1808. Wit: Isaac Saterfield, John Bradsher.

98 Loyd Vanhook to Moses Bradsher, for $261.62½, 74 3/4 A on Bushy br of S Hico adj Alfred Vanhook, James Cothran, John Newton. 3 Sept 1807. Wit: Jesse Bradsher, James Dollarhide.

98-9 Archibald Lipscomb to Elvira, Matilda, Binion, Geoffre, & Comma Lipscomb - heirs of Thomas Lipscomb decd, for $920, 230½ A on S Hico adj Hiram Lewis, John Carver, widow Hughs, widow Lea. 17 Nov 1807. Wit: John Bradsher, Wm. Frazer.

Deed Book D
Page

99-100 Levi Sweaney (in debt to Dickens & Wilson for 55 lbs 0/2, to Samuel Yarbrough in trust, for 5 /, 108 A e side Deep Cr near Cozzart mill where Sweaney lives adj Cozzart, John Sweaney, including one horse with blaze face 3 yrs old. 11 Apr 1808. Wit: John Parrott.

100 Thomas Cate to Robert Cate, for 400 lbs, 121 A on Flat R adj William Cocke, John Rountree. 21 June 1808. Wit: Saml Satterfield, Hasten Bartlett.

101 James Thompson to James Peters the younger of Wake Co., NC, & Charles Holeman of Person Co. (James Thompson low in bodily health and wishing to provide for his family), for 20/, all his right to land in Person Co. in which his wife has dower interest through her marriage with Paul Jeffreys decd her former husband; also his right to any land purchased from Isaiah Cate; negroes: Ben, Ledora, Winny, Rachel, Joshua, Polly, Mera, Hany, Stephen, Jane & Christy; all livestock, household & plantation equipment; all estate to be conveyed to beloved Susannah or if they have children to the children. 19 May 1808. Wit: James Peters Sen., Elisabeth Oliver.

102 Levi Sweaney (in debt to David Ray & William Cain trading as firm of Ray & Cain of Flat R for 52 lbs 19/. and to Benjamin Bullock & Co. of Flat R) - to Joseph B. Shaw of Orange Co., in trust for 5/, 180 A where he lives & 200 A; also cattle, household equipment. 2 June 1808. Wit: Richd Holsonback, James J. Gooch. Proved by oath of James Jay Gooch.

103 William L. Parker (in debt to Hart & Wright of Petersburg, VA, for 246 lbs 7/) to Alexander Cunningham, in trust for $1, 6 negroes: Lewis, Alie, ? ? page damaged Cloe, Nancy; horses. Household furniture. 22 July 1808. Wit: John Williams, Edwd O. Chambers.

104 Bennett Williams (in debt to Dickens & Wilson for 34 lbs,8/4½) to Samuel Yarborough, in trust for 5/, 300 A being the tract where he lives adj James Anderson, John Washington, Millenton Blalock, heirs of Zachariah Vaughn. Wit: Saml A. Brown. 2 June 1808.

105-6 Jacob Vanhook, sheriff, to Thomas McGehee (due to suit brought by Richard Pendergrass against William Moore & Zachary Hurt for debt of 292 lbs 10/, plus damages), for 205 lbs 1/, 256½ A adj John McGehee, John Williams, Edward Chambers, Joseph Woods - it being tract purchased by William Moore of Pendergrass who had a grant from State. 7 Nov 1805. Acknd in open court.

106 James Jay Senr. to James Jay Junr., for 175 lbs, 91½ A on Double Cr adj James Cochran, Payne. 8 Jan 1808. Wit: James Saterfield, Wm. Jay.

107 William Hall to John Jay, for 200 lbs, 132 A on Double Cr adj James Cochran mill cr, Phillip Hall, Stanfield, Hunt. 23 June 1808. Wit: Robert Stanfield, Stokes Allin.

107 Josiah Fike to John Bowers, for $150, 45 A on Flat R adj Benjamin Jacobs. 14 Jan 1808. Wit: James Frost, James Farquhar.

108 William Waite late of Person Co. but now of Williamson Co., TN, to Jesse Lunsford of Person Co., for $96, 144 A on Deep Cr adj said Lunsford, Mills Durden, John Cochran, William Tap. 31 Mar 1807. Wit: Samuel Dickens.

108-9 Goodloe Warren to Durrett Stanfield, for $100, 100 A on Cain Cr of Hico adj Arch Carnal, Richd Carnal, Saml Smith, Jones. _ _ 1808. Wit: Archibald Carnal, Benj W. Harrilson.

109 Thomas Jay Moore to Thomas Jeffreys, for $125, 37½ A on Cobb Cr of Hico adj John Mason, William Tap, George Lea. 31 Dec 1808. Wit: H. Haralson, Richard Ogilby.

109 Thomas Cate to Robert Cate Jun, for(no amt given),50 A which he obtained of legatees of Thomas Person decd adj Capt. William Cocke. 2 July 1808. Wit: Saml Satterfield, Hartin Bartlett.

Deed Book D
Page

110 Fielding Lewis & Zachariah Lewis, heirs of Fielding Lewis, both of Franklin Co., KY, to Thomas Jeffreys of CC, for $59.50, 59½ A both sides N Hico adj John Ogilby crossing Cobb Cr, Abner Duncan, Richd Ogilby - said land that of Fielding Lewis decd and allotted to widow Elisabeth as her dower after she married Gabriel Gunn. _ May 1808. Wit: H. Haralson, James Howerton.

110-1 Power of attorney - Fielding Lewis of Shelby Co., KY, to brother Zachariah Lewis of Franklin Co., KY, to sell & dispose of property in Person Co. 17 Nov 1807. Wit: Isaac E. Gane, Benjamin Merphin.

111 William Allin to his son Thomas Allin, for love & affection, 140 A on Mill Cr adj James Davie decd - said land part of that of Seth Moore. 18 May 1808. Wit: William H. Allin, Grant Allin.

112 John Thomas to Benjamin Duty, for $1500, 233 A s side Hico Cr adj Stewart, Roberts, Moore, Julius Justice, John Williams. 16 Feb 1808. Wit: Thomas Webb, Thos Dickens.

112 Aggatha Paine to William Miller Marr, for compensation, pay, expense that he had in settling differences between her & exec of her late husband Robert Paine decd, 10 negroes: Jacob, Esau, Buck, James, Peter, Isbell, Cinthy, Betsey, Susannah, Patsy daughter of Felicity; 5 of these are small children and will remain with Aggatha Paine until they are old enough to labor; horses. 21 June 1808. Wit: Jacob Vanhook, John Womack.

113 Daniel Evans to Philip Hall, for 100 lbs, 50 A on double cr of Hyco adj Stanfield, said Hall. Also signed by Mary Evans. 17 May 1808.
Wit: Wm. Hall, Jesse Watson.

113 Jeremiah Brooks of CC to James Dollarhide of Person Co., for $290, 113½ A on S Hico in Person Co. adj Carver. 26 Dec 1807. Wit: Wm. Carver, David Brechen.

114 Joseph C. Obryan to Burgess Pool of Granville Co., for $400, negro man Ben. 24 Apr 1808. Wit: Thomas Webb, Samuel Jones, Thomas Gill.

114-5 Thomas Duty (in debt to Samuel Smith for 519 lbs 5/, plus other debts) to Cary Williams, in trust, for 5/, 242 A on Whetstone Br s side Hico adj Robert Moor, John Williams - said land sold by William Duty to John Thomas who sold to Benjamin Duty - then sold by sheriff & purchased by Samuel Smith; also negro man Peter purchased of Benjamin Duty. 31 Oct 1808. Wit: Mary Hatcher, John Parker.

115-6 Jacob Vanhook, sheriff, to Reuben Long (to settle suit brought by John Ogilby against Gabriel Gunn in Sept 1805 and suit brought by Gunn against John Ogilby & Creed Haskens), for 36 lbs 6/, 63 A allotted to wife of Gunn as dower adj John Ogilby, crossing Cobb Cr on N Hyco, William S. Branch, Richard Ogilby. 17 Nov 1808. Wit: Jas Williamson, James Barnett.

116-7 Jacob Vanhook, sheriff, to Artha Brooks Junr. (whereas Artha & his wife brought suit against Woody Brooks June 1806 for detaining negroes Pat & Bob, value 267 lbs 4/4, - goods & chattels of Woody Brooks to be sold); for 125 lbs 10/, 585 A adj William McFarland sold 30 Apr 1808 adj Pool, Bailey, Gibson, Darby both sides Castle Cr. 17 Nov 1808. Wit: R. Long, LV Hargis.

118 Lucy Black to Alvy Oliver of Halifax Co., VA, for $100, 38 1/3 A on N Hico laid off as her dower from her late husband Robert Black adj Edmund Dixon formerly Solomon Draper. 17 Nov 1808. Wit: H. Haralson, Richd Ogilby.

119 Abednago Gentry of Surry Co., NC, to Simon Gentry of Person Co., for 100 lbs, 167 3/4 A on Castle Cr adj Shadrack Gentry, legatees of John Neal decd, Richd Deshazo - also tract of land Andrew Buchanon purchased of Robert Dickens & a part of tract where Shadrack Gentry lives - total 200 A. 13 June 1808. Wit: Thomas Allin, Edward Martin, William Allin.

Deed Book D
Page
119-20 Ann Moore to Lambert S. Moore (by purchase of and dated 15 Sept 1808 from Ann Moore at ___ Neck in Westchester Co., NY), for $442.40, 21 1/5 A on Deep Cr adj Persons, Abner Williams, Robert Moore - it being all the land allotted Ann Moore in div estate of Genl Stephen Moore decd. 11 Nov 1808. Wit: Phillips Moore, Thos Moore.

120 George Lea to Henry Sergent, for 150 lbs, 141 A on Bear Cr of S Hico adj Joseph Rice, Daniel Sargent. 14 Nov 1808. Wit: William Lea, William A. Lea.

121 Thomas Halliburton to loving niece Martha Wade Jones of Halifax Co., VA, & for $1, negro girl Nancy about 8 or 9 yrs old. 10 Feb 1808. Wit: Thomas Pool, John Dixon.

121 Power of attorney - George James, Elisabeth James, & Robert James to Artha Brooks to demand & recover money and sell land due them as legatees under will of George James late of Wake Co. to whom Elisabeth James alias Elisabeth Brooks was exec. 31 Aug 1808. Wit: John Lawson, Benjamin Tatom.

121 James Dollarhide to James McMurry, for $700, 4 negroes: Mary age 24 and her 3 children: Jimmy, Rhoda, Jerry. 28 May 1808. Wit: R. H. Childers, Nathl Norfleet.

122 Richard Lyon to Lawrence V. Hargis & James Williamson, merchants under firm of Hargis & Williamson, for 428 lbs,11/7, 6 negro slaves: Esther & her 5 children: Burwell, Silvia, Gilbert, Jack, girl Tiller. 15 May 1808. Wit: Ira Lea, T. Hargis.

122-3 Seth Coleman to Thomas Hood, for 39 lbs, 65 A at Coleman spring br adj David Allin, Daniel Clayton. 13 Oct 1807. Wit: Jno Willson, Richard Clayton, William Fuller.

123 Thomas Hudgins to Artha Brooks & Larkin Brooks, for 43 lbs 3/1 & 1 farthing, 100 A on Castle Cr adj William McFarland, Major Green, Buckley Walker - being land allotted as dower to his wife Anny from her first husband Moses Walker. 6 Feb 1809. Wit: William Allen, Robert James.

124 Nicholas Thompson of Leasburg, CC, trustee to George Eskridge, Vincent Lea & William Lea of same, for 64 lbs to satisfy deed of trust, 130 A on Double Cr of S Hico adj Thomas Snipes. 11 Sept 1807. Wit: Gabriel Lea, Jr.

124-5 Joseph Hubbard Senr to James Cochran, for 100 lbs, 150 A adj Williamson. 24 Dec 1808. Wit: W. Hubbard, James Satterfield.

125 Thompson McKissack of CC to John McMurry of Person Co., for $300, negro girl Phebe about 14 yrs old. 21 Oct 1807. Wit: Abraham Villines, Robt McKissack.

125-6 Alexander Rose to Duncan Rose, for $354, 118 A on Chapple Br & rocky br of S Hyco adj land given Mrs. Agness Cochran by will of Capt. William Lea Senr. decd; adj William Brown. 12 Dec 1807. Wit: Beverly Rose, Uriah Newton.

126 Abner Duncan to William Scott Branch, for $1100, 137.2 A on N Hyco adj said Branch, Joseph McGehee - said land willed him by his late mother. 27 Sept 1808. Wit: Hugh Shaw, James Nelson, H. Haralson.

127 Absalom Johnston gives mortgage to Nathaniel Norfleet for 193 lbs 1/10, for 305 A where Johnston lives adj Reubin Taylor, Simeon Cochran, Mark Malone, Cooper Taylor, Joseph Taylor; also negroes fellow Shedrick & woman Jean. 19 Jan 1809. Wit: Robert P, Ritchie, Beverly Rose.

127-8 Paul Walters to son Abraham Walters, for love & affection, two tracts: 200 A on Stories Cr adj Henry Fuller; 200 A on Stories & Rosemerry Creeks adj Edmund Lewis, John Dinwoodie, Thomas Hinton, on Fuller's mountain. _ Feb 1809. Wit: W. Jeffreys.

Deed Book D
Page

128-9 Samuel McMurry of Sumner Co., TN, to George Eskridge of Person Co., for
$400, 130 A on double cr of S Hico adj Thomas Snipes, Wilson, John McMurry,
Cochran, James McMurry; by virtue of power of attorney from his father John
McMurry releases all claim of both to Eskridge. 25 Aug 1806.
Wit: Samuel McMurry, Henrietta McMurry.

129-30 Alva Oliver (or Alvy Oliver) of Halifax Co., VA, to Lucy Black, for $100,
39 A w side Hyco adj Edmond Dixon - it being same tract conveyed him by Lucy
Black as her dower of land of Robert Black decd. 25 Jan 1809. Wit: H. Harralson,
P. Moore, Richd Ogilby.

130 James Walton to Reubin Walton, for 125 lbs, 100 A on west br Stories Cr adj
James Cochran, Hatcher. 18 Nov 1808. Wit: Loyd Vanhook, Jesse Bradsher.

131 Artha Brooks Jun. to John J. Brooks, for 125 lbs 10/, 585 A on Castle Cr adj
Samuel Cox, Wm. McFarland, James Pool, Bailey, Gibson. 15 Feb 1809.
Wit: A. Parker, Caswell Vaughan.

131-2 Benjamin Duty to John Wagstaff of Mecklenburg Co., VA, for $100, all his
undivided right & Claim to 300 A on Hico of Richard Duty decd of Granville Co.;
land should be sold when youngest child reached 21 yrs & money div to all children; testator left 10 children: George Duty, Nancy Duty decd, Richard Duty,
Susannah Duty, Benjamin Duty, Thomas Duty, Jabez Duty, Rachel Duty, Elisabeth
Duty, Samuel Duty, & Sarah Duty. 10 Oct 1808. Wit: Joshua Dickson, Thos Duty.

132 Charles Holeman and James Peters the younger of Wake Co. to Susannah Thomson
of Person Co., for 5/ - by virtue of power of attorney vested in them by deed of
trust of James Thomson late of Person Co. 19 May 1808 - all property mentioned
in deed of trust and purchased by James Thomson of Isaiah Cate; negroes: Ben,
Leden, Winny, Rachel, Winny, Joshua, Polly, Mira, Henry, Stephen, Jane, Critty; all
livestock, furniture. 12 Nov 1808. Wit: James Daniel, Wm. Cocke.

132-3 Phillip Hall to John Atkinson, for $362, 90½ A on Double Cr adj Cochran mill
cr, Wm. Brechen. 24 Nov 1808. Wit: Loyd Vanhook, Jas Atkinson.

133 John Ogilby to Thomas Jeffreys of CC, for $5642, 808½ A both sides S Hico
& Cobb Cr adj dower land of Elisabeth Gun, William S. Branch, Edmund Dixon, Wil-
liam Tap, Reubin Taylor, Durham, Benjamin Johnston, William Trotter, John Darby,
Richard Ogilby. 26 Nov 1808. Wit: Richard Ogilby, Charles Willson.

133-4 Benjamin Stovaul & Samuel Whitehead of Oglethorpe Co., GA; Robert Malone
of Sumner Co., TN; Robert Bullington of Union Co., SC; & Ursula Newton of Davidson Co., TN - to Ebenezer Whitehead of Person Co., for 160 lbs 11/3, 103 A on
Richland Cr adj Carter Lea, Charles Winstead, Vanhook on wagon road. 14 Dec 1808.
Wit: Ira Lea, Carter Lea.

134-5 James Chandler to William Gold, for 81 lbs, 81 A e side Henley Mill Cr adj
Saterfield, Rosebrough. 13 Feb 1809. Wit: Ira Lea, John Parker.

135 John Atkinson to James Jay Senr, for $300, 94 A both sides e prong Cochran
mill cr adj Robert H. Childers formerly Thomas Rainey, James Pain. 16 Jan 1809.
Wit: R. H. Childers, John Jay, William Jay.

135-6 William McFarland to Frances Walker, for 117 lbs 10/, 100 A on Stories Cr
adj James(or Jesse) Long, Artha Brooks, Jacob Bull, Thomas Duty. Sold by power of
attorney - it being land of Meredith Cox conveyed by William Singleton & Cox is
now in another country. 14 Feb 1809. Wit: Thomas Dickson, Buckley Walker Junr.

136 William Fuller to William Jeffreys, for 18 lbs 6/7½, 118 A both sides Stories
Cr adj James Fuller. 26 Jan 1809. Wit: John G. Wilson.

Power of attorney - Osborne Jeffreys Jun. to Lewis Daniel to take to any part of
United States 6 negroes for sale: Ben, Tulip & her children Alee, Jacob, Judy &
small girl 1 yr old. 11 May 1809. Wit: Samuel Dickens.

Deed Book D
Page
137 Articles of agreement between Kidy Johnson & Marmaduke Roberts - Kidy Johnson gives up all she has to Roberts & he should feed her as long as necessary
and she to find him clothing also washing, mending, & making same. 7 Nov 1804.
5 Nov 1804. Wit: Y. Partee, recorded May 1809.

137 William McDaniel of CC to Bartlett Hatchett of Person Co., for $702, 117 A
on William Gold's ford adj George Johnson. 10 May 1809. Wit: H. Haralson,
Duncan Rose.

138 Thomas Jeffreys of CC to William Scott Branch of Person Co., for $35, 3½ A
n bank N Hico adj dower land of Elisabeth Lewis alias Elisabeth Gun, said Branch -
said land part of dower of Elisabeth Gunn. 1 Apr 1809. Wit: Richd Ogilby,
H. Haralson.

138 James Long to Abraham Gregory, for $60, 33 A on Adams Cr adj Frankey Walker,
William Baird. 19 Apr 1809. Wit: B. Johnston, Samuel Bull, Moses Walker.
Proved by oath Benjamin Johnston.

139 William Jeffreys to Charles Mitchel, for 36 lbs, 99 A adj Sarah Barnett,
John Mitchell, Josias Dixon. 26 Dec 1808. Wit: J. G. Willson.

139 William Crockett to Alexander Cunningham, for 158 lbs 2/, negroes Juda about
25 yrs old and her child Mary about 8 yrs old. 3 Mar 1806. Wit: John Williams,
Richd M. Cunningham.

139 Archibald Lipscomb to daughter Elisabeth Frazer, for love & affection, negro
woman Ann & her 3 children: 2 girls Ivy, Frankey and boy Richard - all now in her
possession. 20 Sept 1808. Wit: Jas Cochran.

140-1 William McKissack, sheriff, to Duncan Cameron of Orange Co. (goods & chattels of Osborne Jeffreys Sen. sold to pay 1732 lbs plus other debts), for
1875 lbs, tracts on Flat R including where Jeffreys lives; also land devised
by Osborne Jeffreys the older of Franklin Co., NC; 200 A of 640 A called Blalock
tract. 7 Apr 1809. Wit: Wm. Norwood.

141 Osborne Jeffreys Senr, Osborne Jeffreys Jun. & William Bilbo have executed
bond due Duncan Cameron to Maurice Smith of Granville Co. & Benjamin Bullock
of Orange Co., in trust, for $1, negro slaves Jacob, Elisha, Alsey, big Enoch,
Jerry, Mary, Andrew, Enoch(little), Dorcas, Claiborne, Burwell, Brutus, Rhody,
Crawford, Demsey, Nancy, Perry, Archer, Tom, Simon, Ely, Amey, Simon. 7 Apr
1809. Wit: Samuel Dickens.

141-2 Osborne Jeffreys Sen. conveys all interest in above named slaves to Osborne
Jeffreys Jun & Willima Bilbo after debt to Cameron is paid. 7 Apr 1809.
Wit: Samuel Dickens.

142 Jacob Vanhook, late sheriff, to Millington Blalock Jun (due to suit brought
by Mary Johnston against Marmaduke Roberts for 251 lbs), the widow dower of
Millington Blalock Jun for 30 lbs 10/ & for cost of guardian, 96 A adj widow
Johnston, Anderson, Partee - during natural life of Christian Johnston, widow
of Joshua Johnston. 23 Feb 1809. Wit: Alex Cuningham, Y. Partee, Richd Carnal.

142 James Saterfield to Elisabeth Jeffreys, for 400 lbs, negro slave Tiller age
27 yrs. 18 Feb 1809. Wit: Wm. Cocke.

143 Millinton Blalock Jun. to Benjamin Partee, for $100, all his interest & claim
to dower right in land where Christian Johnston now lives which Blalock purchased at sheriff sale - 96 A adj widow Johnston & the legatees, Anderson - said
deed in force during natural life of Christian Johnston widow of Joshua Johnston.
27 Feb 1809. Wit: Yearbe Partee, Millenton Blalock Sen.

143-4 William McKissack, sheriff, to Samuel Smith (due to suit brought by John
Thomas against Benjamin Duty for debt of 375 lbs plus other debts), for 389 lbs 8/7,

93

143-4 cont - 233 A. livestock, adj Robert Moore on Whetstone Br, Wm. Huston, Joshua Dixon, Jno Williams. 1 May 1809. Acknd in open court.

144 Thomas Keeling to Abner Wallace, for $150, 51 A adj Roger Tilghman, Wheeler, Atkinson. 31 Mar 1809. Wit: Hosea Fuller, Aaron Fuller.

145 William McKissack, sheriff, to Haywood Jones who brought suit as assignee of Jas Harris against Samuel Jones for debt, for 156 lbs 6/6, 308 A & chattels sold of Samuel Jones to Haywood Jones; also negro woman Dol & child; land adj John Baird, Agnes Barnett, Charles Halliburton, Richd Andrews. _ _ 1809. Acknd in open court.

146 George Elliot to David Bazwell, for $250, 107 A on a br adj Jno Warrin, Hugh Hemphill. 19 Apr 1809. Wit: H. Haralson, Wm. Williams.

146 Samuel Cox to Henry Baly, for $1000, 200 A on Castle Cr adj Ezekiel Haralson, James Horley old line, Fielding Lewis on the chapel path, Robert McFarland. 17 Mar 1809. Wit: Hugh Woods, John Holloway.

147 Samuel Cox to Henry Bailey, for $1000, 247 A on Castle Cr. 17 Mar 1809. Wit: Hugh Woods, John Holloway.

147-8 William Jones (in debt to Charles Thaxton for 45 lbs) to William Thaxton, in trust, for $1, 124 A adj Ambrose Jones, Francis Ford. 18 Nov 1808. Wit: Francis Foard, Thomas Thaxton.

148 Reubin Taylor of CC to Solomon Draper of Person Co., for 100 lbs, 150 A on Sergents Cr adj Lofton Walton, Samuel Morgan, Johnston line on Sugartree Cr excluding 2 A - one A of the mill seat and the other belonging to Lofton Walton where Turner's mill stood formerly. 21 Feb 1809. Wit: H. Harralson, John Parker.

148-9 William Brechen to Willis Horton, for 70 lbs, 150 A on Double Cr of Hico adj Robert Dickens, Bowers. 21 Feb 1809. Wit: John Malone, Wm. Hargis.

149 Erwin Johnston & George Johnston (in debt to James D. Henley for $100 for bond executed to Edmond Henly decd, also $5.50 on acct) to William Trotter, in trust, for 5/, 30 A on both sides Bear Br of S Hico adj Daniel Sargent formerly Simon Doyle, Wm. McDaniel; also 50½ A on s end of tract granted George Johnston 20 Dec 1779 & descended to Erwin & George by George Johnston decd. 27 Feb 1809. Wit: R. Long, Thomas Goins.

150 Elizabeth Stanfield to John Gwin, for $500, 69 A adj William Hobson, Byrd Wall, William McGehee. 17 May 1808. Wit: Robert Wade, Thos Hood.

150-1 Goodloe Warrin to Stephen Oliver, for $500, 198 A on Cain Cr of Hyco near Durrett Olliver's house adj John Daniel, Hugh Hemphill. 21 Feb 1809. Wit: H. Haralson, Jno Daniel.

151 Josiah Fike to William Brechen Senr., for 25 lbs, 150 A on Double Cr of S Hico adj Robert Dickens, Jno Fooshe. 28 Apr 1808. Wit: S. Cochran, John Malone.

151-2 Archibald Lipscomb to Thomas Lipscomb a gift of a negro girl Betty. 8 Sept 1808. Wit: Henry Sergent.

152 Daniel Sergent to daughter Polly Lipscomb a gift of negro girl Phillis & her increase. 8 Sept 1808. Wit: H. Sergent.

152 Samuel Smith to Thomas Duty, for 519 lbs, 233 A adj William Huston, Joshua Dixon Jno Williams, Jno McGehee, Robert Moore. 31 Oct 1808. Acknd in open court.

152 Goodrich Jones to Wilson Jones, for 60 lbs 10/, his one-third part or 40 A on McMurry Br of Double Cr of Hico adj Jesse Jones decd, Thomas Sneed. 25 Feb 1809. Wit: Wm. McKissack, Drury Jones.

Deed Book D
Page
153 Thomas McKissack to William McKissack Jun., for 205 lbs 10/, 411 A on Double
Cr of Hico adj Brechen, Saterfield, Norfleet. 14 Nov 1808. Wit: Wilson Jones,
Robt P. Ritchie.

153 Nathaniel Painter to William Jeffreys, for 36 lbs, 99 A adj Sarah Barnet,
John Mitchel, Josias Dixon. 15 Aug 1808. Wit: John G. Wilson, Buckley Walker.

154 Henry Sergent to William Trotter, for 39 lbs 12/, 33 A on S Hico adj Trotter,
John Darby, George L. Johnston, William Gold. 10 May 1809. Acknd in open court.

154-5 Osborne Jeffreys Sen. & William Bilbo to Duncan Cameron, for $3750, 2300 A
on Flat R including where Jeffreys lives and that devised by Osborne Jeffreys the
elder late of Franklin Co., NC plus all other land he purchased excluding 150
or 200 A of the old tract of 640 A called Blalock tract which was conveyed to
Osborne Jeffreys Jun. adj heirs of Paul Jeffreys decd, Josiah Brown, Willis
Nichols, Woodson Hubbard, William Cochran, Micajah Nichols. 7 Apr 1809.
Wit: Osborne Jeffreys Jun., Chas Holeman, B. Bullock.

155 Claibourne Bevil (in debt to Jeffreys for 142 lbs 12/11) & Charles Wilson of
the red house in CC, for $1, to Thomas Jeffreys, in trust, negro woman Nancy
19 yrs old, Alexander 2 yrs, Amelia 1 yr; livestock, crops, furniture.
12 June 1809. Wit: John Moore, Phillip J. Echols.

156 Peter Cozzart to Moses Carnel of Granville Co., for $115.75, 77 A & 6 3/4
chains on Duns Cr adj Charles Glenn, William Cozzart. 21 Oct 1808.
Wit: Samuel Dickens. Charles Glenn.

156 John M. McGehee to Robert Moore Sen., for 18½ A in exchange, 12 3/4 A on Hico
adj Thos McGehee. _ 1809. Acknd in open court.

157 Osborne Jeffreys Sen. to Osborne Jeffreys Jun., for 20 lbs, 700 A on Flat R
adj John Commins, Jno Cates, Lemuel Sneed, Samuel Sneed purchased of John Allison.
12 Mar 1806. Wit: Allen Miller, James Cochran, Jno Comins, Chas Holeman,
Dnl Farmer.

157 Gabriel Bumpass to William Clayton, for $540, 375 A on Flat R adj Taylor for-
merly Person, Commins. 1 June 1809. Acknd in open court.

157-8 Robert Moore to John M. McGehee, for $180, 18½ A e side Hico. 14 Aug 1809.
Acknd in open court.

158-9 William McKissack, sheriff, to Moses Carnel (due to suit brought by Dickens
& Wilson against James Johnston & Peter Cozart for 13/9) - 30 A where Cozart lives
adj Moses Carnel, Charles Glen sold to Carnel for 13 lbs 12/. 15 Aug 1809.
Acknd in open court.

159 William Hamblen Senr to William Hamblen Junr., for $200, 200 A on Stories Cr
adj Nathaniel Fuller, John Fuller, Atkinson. 17 Aug 1809. Acknd in open court.

159 Daniel Clayton to Richard Clayton Fuller, for 100 lbs, 102 A adj James Chandler, Roger Tilman, William Gold, William Trotter. 1 Sept 1807. Wit: R. Long,
Rebecca Long.

159-60 John Brown to beloved daughter Ellinor Brown, for love & affection, negro
girl Priscilla about 11 or 12 yrs old. 2 Feb 1809. Wit: Robert P. Ritchie,
Alfred Brown.

160 John Brown to son Alfred Brown, for love & affection & 10 lbs, 108 A on Bushy
Fork of Flat R adj Moore, Allen, Web, Terrill, Hawkins. 1 Feb 1809.
Wit: John Gray, Beverly Rose, Robert P. Ritchie.

160 Samuel Yarbrough, trustee, to John Sweaney, for 92 lbs, 180 A of Levi Sweaney
sold to satisfy deed of trust - land adj Cozart, John Sweaney. 9 May 1809.
Wit: W. Jeffreys, J. G. Willson.

Deed Book D
Page

161 William McKissack, sheriff, to Haywood Jones (due to court order to sell goods & chattels of Samuel Jones to settle debt of 156 lbs 6/6),308 A and negroes Dot & her children Esther & Nelly, man James - all sold to Haywood Jones the plaintiff and assignee of John Harris who brought suit against Jones for total of 488 lbs 3/9. Acknd in open court.

161 William Jeffreys to Samson M. Glenn, for $230, 118 A both sides Stories Cr adj John Fuller. 28 Feb 1809. Wit: R. Hood, J. G. Wilson.

162 James Cothran & Mary his wife an heir of Benjamin Harrison decd to Lawrence Van Hook Hargis, for $85, 20.4 A on Flat R where B. Harrison died adj Sneed - said land is plot #7 in div land of Harrison. 17 Aug 1809.
Wit: James Cothran, Loyd Vanhook.
Polly Cothran examined apart from her husband & freely agreed to deed.

162-3 Woodson Hubbard & Susannah his wife an heir of Benjamin Harrison decd to Lawrence Van Hook Hargis, for $253, 39.7 A on Flat R designated as plot #4 in div of his land. 17 Aug 1809. Wit: James Cochran, Loyd Vanhook.
Susannah Hubbard examined apart from her husband and testified she voluntarily signed deed.

163-4 Joseph Hubbard Jun. & Elizabeth his wife, she an heir of Benjamin Harrison decd, to Lawrence VanHook Hargis, for $79, 17 1/5 A on Flat R adj B. Sneed, Brown, being plot #6 in div land of B. Harrison. 17 Aug 1809. Wit: Jas Cochran, Loyd Van Hook. Elizabeth Hubbard examined apart from her husband & freely executed deed.

164 James McMurrey to John Whitfield, for $150, 50 A adj Loyd Vanhook. 12 Apr 1806. Wit: John McMurrey, George Whitfield.

165 Samuel Smith to Richard Carnal, for $825, 165 A on Cain Cr of Hico adj Robert Jones, Thomas Dixon, Jacob Vanhook - said land where Smith lives purchased of John Gwin. 4 Aug 1809. Wit: Alex Cuningham, Archd Carnal, Danl C. Townes.

165-6 Joseph Carney to Laurence Lea of CC, for 5 lbs, 10 A on Cobb Cr in Person Co. adj John Douglas, along the old road & crossing the great road. 19 Oct 1807. Wit: A. Vanhook, W. Donoho, Rhobartis H. Carney.

166-7 William Carver to Robert Carver, for 100 lbs, 100 A on Gents Cr adj Gutrey, William Sargent. 21 Aug 1797. Wit: John Hall, John Johnson.

167-8 William Carney to Lawrence Lea, for $300, 93 A in Person Co. on Cobb Cr adj Thomas Douglas old line, Thos Hargis, up main road across the county line & Cobb Cr, Burch's shop. 26 Oct 1807. Wit: Rhob Carney, Bird G. Parker, W. Donoho.

168-9 Joseph Carney to Lawrence Lea of CC, for 5 lbs, 10 A in Person Co. on Cobb Cr adj John Douglas old line. 19 Oct 1807. Wit: A. Vanhook, W. Donoho, Rho Carney

169-70 John Darby to Lucy Black, for $400, 101 A on Winn's Cr adj heirs of Joseph Hall decd, heirs of James Hamlet decd, David Hemphill. 19 Aug 1809.
Wit: Richd Ogilby, H. Haralson.

170-1 Jesse Long (in debt to James Cochran & Isham Edwards for 98 lbs 11/5) to Murrell Breesie, in trust, for $1, 177 A adj Jacob Bull, Robert Smithward, Reubin Long Jun. 3 Dec 1807. Wit: Carlton Nunn, Wm. Trickey.

171 Isaac Day to James Webb, for 90 lbs, 175 A on Tarr R adj John Day, Johnston, William Tap. 28 Aug 1809. Wit: John Bowles Jun., Thomas Gill.

172 Jacob Bull to Samuel Blackwell, for 50 lbs, 100 A on Story & Adams Creeks adj Thomas Duty, Jacob Barnett, James Barnett. 23 Dec 1808. Wit: Samuel Bull.

Deed Book D
Page

172-3 Elijah Daniel to James Williamson, for $400, 179 A adj Joseph Traylor to Tapley Cr, Jeffreys. 11 Oct 1809. Wit: Thomas V. Hargis.

173 William McFarland to Buckley Walker, for $1200, 602 A on Castle Cr adj Moses Walker, Joseph Jones, James Holloway. 30 Sept 1809. Wit: Lord Lord, Richd Howson.

173-4 Clayton Fuller (or Richard C. Fuller) to Thomas Talbert, for 127 lbs, 63½ A on Henley Mill Cr adj William Trotter, on Rosebrook Br adj Roger Tilman, William Gold. 7 Aug 1809. Wit: Thomas Hood, Asa Fuller.

174 Jacob Vanhook to William Lewis (due to execution against William Bull by William Lea Sen., merchant), for 30 lbs, 14 A on Double Cr adj John Blake, James Cochran; said land deeded Bull 16 Dec 1802 by exec of Samuel McMurry decd. 25 Aug 1806. Wit: John Moore, L. Lea.

175 Power of attorney - John McMurry of Sumner Co., TN, to Samuel McMurry of Person Co. to convey land in Person & Orange Counties. 6 July 1806. Proved Person Co., Feb 1810.

175A-6 Hardy Hubbard to Samuel Winstead, for 118 lbs 16/, 99 A both sides Henley Mill Cr of Hyco adj Charles Winstead, Ebenezer Whitehead. 6 Dec 1809. Wit: Alex Winstead, Ebenz Whitehead.

176-7 Loyd Vanhook to William Lipscomb, for $575, 101 A on S Hyco adj Wade, Wilson, McMurry. 1 Oct 1809. Wit: James McMurry, J. Vanhook.

177-8 Cary Williams, assignee & trustee for Thomas Duty who was in debt to Samuel Smith for 519 lbs, to Lewis Amis Junr of Granville Co.,for $713. 242 A of Duty on S side Hyco adj Robert Moore, John Holloway; said tract was sold to William Duty by John Thomas - then to Benjamin Duty & then by sheriff. 8 Jan 1810. Wit: Thomas Talbert, Joseph Royster.

178-9 John Lewis of Franklin Co., KY, to Thomas Jeffreys of CC, for $30, his part in dower land of his mother Elizabeth Gun, formerly Elizabeth Lewis; total of 49 A & John Lewis entitled to one-fourth; land on Hyco & Cobb Cr in Person Co. adj said Jeffreys, William Scott Branch, Richard Ogilby and formerly belonged to Fielding Lewis decd. 22 Dec 1809. Wit: H. Harralson, Ben Johnston, A. Harralson.

179-80 Zachariah Lewis of Franklin Co., KY, to Benjamin Johnston Jun. of Person Co., for $140, 24 A n side N Hyco adj William S. Branch; said land allotted from estate of his father Fielding Lewis decd & designated as lot #2. 23 Dec 1809. Wit: H. Harralson, Ad Harralson.

180 Zachaus Hurt to Robert Howard, for $545, 136 A on ridge between Gents & Marlowe Creeks adj John Rogers. 20 Jan 1810. Wit: H. Harralson, Ish Edwards.

181 Div land of Hezekiah Stone decd to:
1. Anderson Stone adj Edwd P. Chambers, Zachaus Hurt, Benjamin Chambers, 140 A.
2. Bird Stone - 101½ A adj Benjamin Chambers, Zachaus Hurt.
3. John Stone - 101½ A adj Zachaus Hurt, Deshazo.
Surveyed 16 Jan 1810; proved Jan 1810.

181-2 James Peters Sr. & Simon Turner of Wake Co., NC, to Susannah Thompson, for $500, negro man Crawford about 25 yrs old. 1 Feb 1810. Wit: Wm. Cocke.

182-3 Paul Walters Senr. to Daniel Walters his natural born son, for love & affection, 117 A both sidesMiry Cr adj Samuel Harris decd, William Carver, John Long - said tract part of that purchased from Henry Fuller, reserving the right for him or his wife Mary to cultivate the land for their lives. 9 Feb 1810. Wit: Abraham Walters, Benj Chambers.

183 Robert H. Childers to John H. McNeill, for $250, 60 A adj James Jay Senr., James Paine, Wm. Jay former land. 1 Feb 1810. Wit: Duncan Rose, John Bradsher.

97

184 Osborne Jeffreys to John Bumpass Junr., for $450, negro woman Tempy & her 2 children Jacob & Rose. 28 Nov 1809. Wit: Ira Lea.

184-5 Buckley Walker to John Dillihay, for $40, 8 A & 240 links on Castle Cr of Hyco adj both men, Edmund Dillihay. 21 Dec 1809. Wit: Richd Howson, Henry Woody, John Walker.

185-6 John Guin to Tarlton Moore, for $200, 64 A , being land he purchased of Elizabeth Stanfield widow of William Stanfield decd; her dower total of 192 A adj William Hobson, Davidson Chambers, Byrd Wall, William Megee - same to be occupied by widow for her life. 2 Feb 1810. Wit: William Hobson, Betsy Hobson.

186-7 James McMurry to William Lipscomb, for $187, 44 A on S Hyco adj Downey Wade, Web spring. 31 Oct 1809. Wit: Loyd Vanhook, Lemuel Bowers.

187 Fielding Lewis, Zachariah Lewis, & John Lewis to Lawson Neal, for $100, 67½ A at the dower line with 36 A, on the chapple path adj Atkinson, Deshazo; Zachariah Lewis signs for John Lewis as atty. 3 Jan 1810. Wit: Thomas Webb, Thomas Lawson.

187-8 Elijah Watson & Elizabeth his wife to Jesse Watson Sen., 66 A being all dower rights belonging to Lewis Green decd adj James Paine, James Jay Senr., heirs of Lewis Green decd. Elisabeth Watson to have dower land for her life. 24 Feb 1809. Wit: John Raven, Charles Watson.

188 Power of attorney - John Lewis of Franklin Co., KY, to Zachariah Lewis of same, to convey land in Person Co. which was sold by Zachariah Lewis to Thomas Jeffreys. 20 Nov 1809.

188-9 James Long to Jesse Long, for 200 lbs, 200 A on Stories Cr adj Jacob Bull, Robert Southward, Reuben Long Junr., said tract where Jesse Long lives. 3 Dec 1807. Wit: Ish Edwards, Murrell Bressee.

189 Paul Walters Senr. to son Paul Walters Junr., for love & affection, 117 A both sides Stories Cr adj Jacob Bull, Harris orphans, William Carver - said land part of larger tract purchased of Henry Fuller. Paul Walters & wife Mary Walters reserve right to cultivate same. 9 Feb 1810. Wit: Abraham Walters, Benj Chambers.

190 Bartlett Hatchett (in debt to John Darby for $702) to Thomas Jeffreys in trust, for 5/, 117 A where Hatchett lives & purchased of William McDaniel. 18 Aug 1809. Wit: William Rainey, Richd Ogilby.

191 Henry Sargent to John Mason, for 90 lbs, 141 A on Bear Cr of S Hyco adj Joseph Rice, Daniel Sargent. 12 Feb 1810. Wit: Loyd Vanhook.

191-2 Absolem Johnston to Simeon Cochran, for $64, 48 A on S Hico adj Mark Melone. 2 Nov 1808. Wit: Mark Melone, Loyd Vanhook.

192-3 John Russell to Downey Wade, for $343 1/3, 103 A on S Hico adj Martha Richardson, on road from Leasburg to Hillsborough, Wm. Johnston. 25 Sept 1809. Wit: John Douglas, William Lipscomb.

193-4 Samuel McMurry atty for John McMurry both of Sumner Co., TN, to Robert Vanhook of Person Co., for 25 lbs, 15.7 A on Hico adj Vincent Lea, Wilson. 7 Nov 1808. Wit: Wm. Mitchell, Betsy Mitchell, John McMurry.

194 Goodloe Warren to Archibald Carnal, for $183, 55 A on Cane Cr of Hyco adj Durret Stanfield, Jacob Vanhook. 7 Feb 1810. Wit: H. Harralson, John Eskridge.

195 William Carney to L. Lea of CC, for 50 lbs 2/, 34.3 A on Cobs Cr in Person Co. on road from Leasburg to S Hico. 10 Oct 1807. Wit: Saml Hayes, Byrd G. Parker, A. Vanhook. The handwriting of William Carney proved by oaths of Vincent Lea, Reubin Walton & Rhobartus Carney as Wm. Carney has removed from the State; Saml Hayes, Byrd G. Parker, A. Vanhook are all dead.

195-6 Thomas Badgett Sen. to William McKissack Sen., for $50, 22 A on Double Cr adj McKissack. 16 Dec 1803. Wit: Simeon Cochran, Abraham Villines, William Rainey.

196 John Paine to Robert Vanhook, for 6 lbs 13/, 5 A on Flat R adj Vanhook. 25 July 1797. Wit: John Womack, Charles Fooshe. Registered Feb 1810 on oath of John Womack.

196-7 Jacob Vanhook & Kindle Vanhook, surviving exec of David Vanhook decd, to Robert Vanhook, for $300, 61½ A s side N fork Flat R adj Demsy Moore, Henry McNeel - said land part of larger tract granted by State. 17 Nov 1808. Wit: L. V. Hargis, Charles Winstead, John Moore.

197 George Eskridge to Robert Vanhook, for $500, 150 A on S Hico adj Lawrence Vanhook, James McMurry. 18 Apr 1802. Wit: Jab Vanhook, Thomas Rainey.

197-8 Simeon Cochran to Robert Cochran of CC, for 50 lbs, 100 A on Flat R adj Dickens & Waite, Cadwell, Thomas Farmer. 23 Oct 1809. Wit: John Malone, Ira Ellis.

198 William Carney to L. Lea of CC, for 50 lbs 2/, 34.3 A on Cob Cr in Person Co. on road from Leasburg to S Hico adj James Johnston, Joseph Carney, 10 Oct 1807. Wit: Saml Hayes, Byrd G. Parker, A. Vanhook. Proved by oaths of Vincent Lea, Reubin Walton, & Rhobartis Carney as William Carney has removed from the State and all witnesses are decd.

199 James Johnston to Rhobartis Carney, for $112, 51 A on Rushy Br of S Hico adj meeting house lot, William Carney, Kindle Vanhook. 17 Jan 180?. Wit: Daniel Sargent, Gabl Lea, Vincent Lea.

199 Joseph Carney to Rhobartis Carney, for 150 lbs, 150 A on Cob Cr adj Loyd Vanhook, Thomas Douglas old line, McMurry. 25 Aug 1806. Wit: H. Burton, Vincent Lea.

200 James McMurry to Jeremiah Brooks of CC, for $474, 158 A on S Hico adj Rose, Jacob Thomas, Kelly Br, H. Combs, Whitfield, Robert Vanhook. 29 Nov 1809. Wit: Loyd Vanhook, Adam McNeely.

200 State of NC - #128 - to Gabriel Davie (son of William Davie), for 50/ per 100 A, 105 A on Tarr R adj Self, Johnston, Street. 19 Oct 1809.

201 State of NC - #126 - to Gabriel Davie (son of William), for 50/ per 100 A, 300 A on Tar R adj Dickens, Thomas Person,Jun., B. Person. 19)ct 1809.

201 John Mason (for 110 lbs paid part by Solomon Draper) to James Wilkens Royster, William Harrison Royster, Mary Royster, John Royster, & Thomas Royster - the 5 living children of Henry Royster & Frankey his wife, negro woman Lill about 18 yrs of age who was purchased at constable sale 4 Jan 1810. 16 Dec 1810. Acknd in open court.

201 Lawrence V. Hargis of firm ot Hargis & Williamson to James Cochran Jun., for $180, negro boys Jack 8 or 9 yrs old; for $136.50 negro Gilbert. 14 Dec 1809. Proved in open court.

202 Power of attorney - William Huston to Isham Edwards to sell 265.6 A adj Samuel Smith, Harrison Stanfield. 19 Sept 1805. Wit: John Barnett, Henry Graves.

202 James Pettypool to John Lawson, trustee for bond executed by Pettypool with Buckley Walker Sen., security, for 5/, 196 A on Castle Cr, being land purchased of William McFarland. 14 Feb 1810. Wit: Thomas Webb, Gabriel Davey.

203 Henry Atkinson, Capt. 3rd Regt., stationed in New Orleans, to Jesse Carter of CC, for $1000, 921 A on Henley Mill Cr adj John Lewis, Thomas Parker, William Trotter, William Gold, Roger Tillman, Abner Walters, Samuel Wheeler, Charles Winstead. Richard Atkinson & Bartlett Yancey made oath the signature was of Henry Atkinson; ordered recorded. 17 June 1809.

Deed Book D
Page
203 Samuel Jones to Jacob Dixon Jun., for 50 lbs, 70 A adj Nathan Ragan, Person.
13 Dec 1806. Wit: Lewis Parrott, Moses Street.

204 Samuel Jones to Jacob Dixon Junr., for 50 lbs, 100 A. 13 Dec 1806.
Wit: Lewis Parrott, Moses Street.

204 John Bumpass to Jesse Bumpass, for $251, 125½ A on Tar R adj Dickens.
30 Mar 1810. Wit: Alfred Bumpass, Saml Bumpass Junr.

204-5 John Bumpass to Samuel Bumpass, for $407, 205½ A on Tar R adj Dickens.
30 Mar 1810. Wit: Alfred Bumpass, Jesse Bumpass.

205 Woodson Hubbard to Duncan Cameron of Orange Co., for $375, 170½ A on Flat R
adj Osborn Jeffreys, near Cameron corner. 12 May 1810. Wit: L. V. Hargis.

206 Benjamin Johnston Jun. to William S. Branch, for $275, 51 A n side N Hico adj
Branch, John Ogilby now Branch. 15 May 1808. Wit: H. Harralson, Richd Ogilby.

206 Phillip Hall to John Scogins, for $300, 95 A adj Andrew B. Woods, Cocke,
John Jay, being part of large tract of Phillip Hall decd. 7 May 1810.
Wit: R. H. Childers.

207 William Carver to Josias Carver, for 100 lbs, 100 A on Stories Cr. 15 Feb
1810. Wit: Reubin Long, William Sargent, Ish Edwards.

207-8 Lawrence V. Hargis and James Williamson under firm of Hargis & Williamson
brought suit against Benjamin Towler & Ann Towler his wife for 59 lbs 13/5 -
William McKissack, sheriff, to Lawrence Vanhook, for 70 lbs 2/6, negro woman
Hannah & her child Hanner. 14 Feb 1810. Wit: H. Harralson.

209 Jeremiah Roberts to Walter Oakly Junr., for $75, 50 A adj Abram Dunest to
Cub Cr. 22 Dec 1809. Wit: Charles Parrish, Samuel Williams.

209 John Bowers Sen. to Nathaniel Norfleet, for $75, 45 A on Flat R adj Benjamin
Jacobs. 20 Feb 1810. Wit: Beverly Rose, J. Muzzall, Nath Norfleet Jr.

209 Richard Atkinson to Polly Williamson daughter of James Williamson & Susannah
his wife, for love & affection, negro girl Luecy age 4 yrs. 14 May 1810.
Acknd in open court.

210 Richard Clayton to John Cothran Sen., for 95 lbs, negro woman Easter.
_ Feb 1810. Wit: W. Jeffreys.

210 Haywood Jones to John Wilkerson, for 48 lbs, negro girl Easter about 5 yrs
old. 25 Mar 1810. Wit: John Owen, David Wilkerson, Samuel Jones.

210 Thomas Talbert, constable, to John Mason, for 12 lbs 12/9, negro woman Lill -
sold to satisfy suit brought by John Darby against Henry Royster obtained of
him bfore Henry Sergant. 16 May 1810. Wit: Henry Sargent.

211 Jacob Vanhook, sheriff, to Kindle Vanhook (to satisfy suit George Huston
brought against Robert Jones & James McMurry for 22 lbs 10/), 90 A of James McMurry
sold for 25 lbs 12/, adj John Miles, Adam McNealy, the Moravian line, Hardeman
Wells, William Cocke. 12 Sept 1809. Wit: W. Jeffreys, J. G. Wilson.

212-4 Div estate of Paul Jeffreys decd to legatees: Widow 900 A (Mrs. Thompson)
homestead tract on Flat R adj Paine near Richland Cr. To:
David Jeffreys 317 A of 1st quality & 105 A of 2nd quality on Cummins mill
pond; John Lyon & wife Elizabeth his wife 312 A of 1st quality & 87 A of
2nd quality; Lucy Jeffreys 35 or 40 A & 290½ A; James O^S Jeffreys 224 A plus
120 A sold to James Jay adj Neely; also 64 A & 80 A of 2nd quality, on Flat R
& Richland Cr adj John Satterfield.
Commrs: Wm. Cocke, Saml Dickens, James Paine, Charles Holeman, Tho Sneed;
Phillips Moore, CS (county surveyor). 8 Feb 1810.

Deed Book D
Page
215 John Hamlett to Robert Hamlett, for $550, 138 3/4 A on Wynn's Cr adj Thomas Moore, James Hamlett, Lucy Black, said land his moiety of James Hamlett decd as lot #2 in div between widow & several heirs. 30 July 1810. Wit: H. Harrelson, Jane Harrelson.

216 Edmond Burch to James Broche & John Malone, for 400 lbs, 100 A on Grier Cr of Hico adj William Mitchel, Wilson Jones, Reubin Taylor. 27 Jan 1809. Wit: Elijah Hester, Thom Burch, Nihu Hester.

216 Mary Stone & John Gwin to Alexander Cuningham, for $189, 252 A near the CH being land directed by will of Hezekiah Stone decd to be sold adj Howard Allen, Wm. Mann. 12 Apr 1810. Wit: Thos Duty, Lewis Amis, Anderson Stone.

217 Henry Day Jun.to William Jeffreys, for 50 lbs, 150 A on Mayo Cr adj Henry Day Senr. 21 July 1810. Wit: Jno G. Wilson.

217 John Campbell of Abbeville District, SC, to Isham Edwards of Person Co., for $50, lot #28 in Milton, CC. 28 Sept 1809. Wit: Harrison Stanfield, George Duncan.

217-8 George Gregory to William Williams adm of Robert Newman decd, for $112 pd by the decd in his lifetime, 28 A n side Hico adj Alex Cunningham formerly Thomas J. Chambers. 15 Aug 1810. Wit: L. Amis, John W. Stone.

218 William Dickens of Granville Co. to John Allen of Person Co., for $150, 91 A on Flat R adj Norfleet, Palmer old corner now Norfleet. 16 Nov 1808. Wit: Ira Lea, T. Woods.

219 Thomas Burch to Simeon Cochran, for 50 lbs, 50 A on Grice Cr of Hico adj Robt Hester, Wilson Jones, William Mitchell. 22 May 1810. Wit: Thomas Willson, James Broach, Pomfort Melone.

219 James McAden of CC to Melinda Rose daughter of Duncan Rose, now an infant, for goodwill, negro Eunice age 13 yrs. 31 Aug 1809. Wit: Duncan Rose.

220-1 Plat of land surveyed for Thos Hatcher 2 Aug 1810 on Stories Cr, 95.4 A adj James Cochran; also to allot land to legatees of Benjamin Hatcher. Allotment of 95.4 A to John Hatcher on Stories Cr adj James Cochran, Mitchel. John Hatcher entitled to $60 plus his land over that laid off for Thomas Hatcher both legatees of Benjamin Hatcher agreeable to his will. 2 Aug 1810. Commrs: Richd Atkinson, R. Vanhook, Duncan Rose, Isaac Satterfield, John Ravens. Acknd in open court.

221 Allotment of 95.4 A to Charles Hatcher on Stories Cr adj Reubin Walton, James Cochran, Mitchel, he a legatee of Benjamin Hatcher. 2 Aug 1810. Acknd in open court.

222 Allotment of 95.4 A to Hugh Woods w side Stories Cr adj Edward Clay, Walton, Mitchel by commrs to div estate of Benjamin Hatcher decd. 21 Aug 1810. Acknd in open court.

222-3 Allotment of 95.4 A to Polly Hatcher legatee of Benjamin Hatcher decd. 2 Aug 1810. Acknd in open court.

223 Samuel Johnston Senr. of CC, to his daughter Sally Holder & her husband James Holder of same, for love & affection, 150 A in Person Co. on Cain Cr & Wins Cr adj Hugh Hemphill, Phebe Johnston, Oliver. 19 May 1810. Wit: Loyd Vanhook, A. Gordon.

224 Samuel Johnston Senr. of CC to His daughter Phebe Johnston of Same, for parental Love & affection, 150 A on Wynn's Cr adj Oliver, Polly Johnston, James Holder, Hugh Hemphill, Alex Gordon. 19 May 1810. Wit: Loyd Vanhook, A. Gordon.

Deed Book D
Page

224-5 Samuel Johnston Sen. of CC to daughter Susannah Gordon & her husband
Alexander Gordon, for parental love & affection, 150 A on Wins Cr in Person Co
on VA line adj Polly Johnston, Phebe Johnston. 19 May 1810. Wit: Loyd Vanhook,
Phebe Johnston.

225 Samuel Johnston of CC to daughter Polly Johnston of same, for love & affection,
150 A on Wins Cr on VA line adj Oliver, Phebe Johnston, Alex Gordon. 19 May 1810.
Wit: Loyd Vanhook, A. Gordon.

226-8 Francis Nunn & Mary his wife of State of GA - said Mary a sister of John
Rice decd - to Solomon Debow of CC - the will of Rice dated 14 June 1784 said
each of his brothers should have first choice of 5000 A of his land after dis-
posing of Chickasaw tract; each sister should have 5000 A each, then willed
6000 A to Jesse Benton & 5000 A for schooling the poor at Cumberland; the remainder be div to brothers & his exec who were Anthony Bledsow & Jesse Benton who
both died during life of testator. William H. Rice & Elisha Rice then became
exec; grantors have agreed for Solomon Debow, atty, to recover lands. Hence to
Solomon Debow, for his charges to reclaim land and for 10 shillings, 7 full &
equal 10th part; to make conveyances & 3 tenth remain for Francis Nunn & Mary
his wife. 12 Nov 1805. Wit: Shadrack Hargis. Proved Feb 1810.

228-9 Samuel Dickens & James Clark, commrs appointed at Hillsborough District,
to George Gregory - case concerning surviving partner of McCall & Elliott & Co.
was complainant & Henry Fulcher, defendant, to raise 62 lbs 4/9 with interest
from 22 Dec 1773 - for 249 lbs, 136 A n side Hico near Barnett ford adj Gregory,
William Warren, James Franklin, the heirs of Bird Wall decd, Alex Cuningham.
James Thompson also a commr is decd. 16 Nov 1810. Wit: John Seymour, John Dickson

229 John Dickens to William Waite - reconveyance of land & conveyance of tract
in CC in lieu of misunderstanding over 1st deed in which Waite deeded Dickens a
tract on Rosemary stream. 28 Feb 1810. Wit: Hardy Crews, Thos Moore.

229-30 William McKissack, sheriff (whereas Clement Deshazo brought suit against
Thomas Hudgens for 8 lbs 10/7, 100 A & goods & chattels of Hudgens adj Artha
Brooks & Larkin Brooks adj Buckley Walker, Sen. - being the dower of his wife sold
to Moses Walker for 73 lbs 5/. 16 Nov 1810. Acknd in open court.

230-1 Merrell Bressie, trustee, to Isham Edwards (due to debt of Jesse Long to
Edwards for 115 lbs 3/1), for $115 3/1. 10 Oct 1810. Wit: W. Hubbard, L. S.
Moore. Proved by oath Woodson Hubbard.

231-2 William McKissack, sheriff, to Isham Edwards (whereas firm of Cochran &
Edwards brought suit against John Wynn Pulliam for 12 lbs 2/11) an undivided part
of 150 A on Gents Cr belonging to James Pulliam decd adj John Seymour, Cary
Williams - sold for 2 lbs 10/. 16 Nov 1810. Acknd in open court.

232-3 Artha Brooks Sen. (in debt to Thomas Webb for 105 lbs 2/5½) to John Dillehay,
trustee, for 5/, 202 A both sides Adams Cr where Brooks now lives & purchased of
Hugh Barnett; 88 A purchased of John Atkinson; 12¼ A adj John Barnett, Francis
Walker, Saml Blackwell, William Baird, James Heggie; household furniture.
14 June 1810. Wit: James Barnett, Buckley Walker.

233-4 Zachaus Hurt to John Gwin, for 602 lbs 10/, 361¼ A on Gents Cr of Hyco adj
Edward O. Chambers, Stone heirs, Robert Deshazo, Isham Edwards, Robert Howard.
23 Sept 1810. Wit: H. Harralson, Edwd O. Chambers.

234 William Huston of Ohio Co., KY, to Samuel Morgan of Nottaway Co., VA, for
$1328, 265.1 A on Hico adj said Morgan, Harrison Stanfield. 27 Sept 1810.
Wit: John Bradsher, Currie Barnett.

Deed Book D
Page
235 Moses Street Jun. to William Street, for $450, 190 A on Mayo Cr adj land
purchased jointly of Thomas Lawson & William Street from Moses Street adj John
Carr, the baptizing waters near Street meeting house, Thomas Lawson the land
devised him by his father. 14 Nov 1810. Wit: Am Davie, Buckley Walker.

236 Moses Street to Thomas Lawson, for $450, 190 A on Mayo Cr adj Moses Spring-
field, Ashburn Davie decd, Jno Carr, inclusive with the forenamed Wm. Street's
purchase devised by Moses Street Sen. to Moses Street Jun. 14 Nov 1810,
Wit: Am Davie, Buckley Walker.

236-7 Jacob Dixon Jr. to Jesse Ragan of Granville Co., for 40 lbs, 100 A on
Bluewing Cr adj David Halliburton. 17 Sept 1806. Wit: Robt Moore, John Dixon.

237-8 Edward O. Chambers to Thomas Sheppard of Granville Co., for $2000, 485 1/3 A
both sides Gents Cr adj Thomas J. Chambers, Thomas McGehee, John Williams, Cary
Williams, John Green. 27 Oct 1810. Wit: Benj Chambers, James Smith,
Tho J. Chambers.

238 Zachaus Hurt to Edward O. Chambers, for 231 lbs, 128 1/3 A w side Gents Cr
adj Edward O. Chambers, Christopher Bass, Richd Pendergrass. 12 Dec 1802.
Wit: John M. McGehee.

238-9 Robert Howard to Edward O. Chambers, for 300 lbs, 300 A both sides Gents Cr
it being land he purchased of heirs of his father Henry Howard decd adj James
Stuard, Allen Love, Barnett; 50 A of this granted Barnett by State. 9 Aug 1802.
Wit: Thos J. Chambers, Charles S. Hurt, Christopher Bass.

239-40 Abraham Self to Moses Street, for 50 lbs, 150 A on Buck Mountain Cr adj
Waite. 24 Oct 1810. Wit: Gab Davie, John Parrot.

240 George Gregory to Joel Newman, for 136 lbs, 136 A n side Hico adj Wm. Warren,
James Franklin, heirs of Bird Wall, Alexander Cuningham - said tract Gregory
purchased of James Clark & Samuel Dickens. 16 Nov 1810. Wit: L. V. Hargis,
Robert Stanfield.

240-1 William Carver to Lemuel Carver, for $100, 134 A adj Benjamin Carver, Thomas
Parker. 20 Feb 1810. Wit: Josias Carver, Benj Chambers.

241-2 William Hamblin Jun. to Thomas Parker, for $20, 10 A on Stories Cr.
17 Apr 1810. Wit: John Parker, Nancy Parker.

242 John Bowers Sen. to Robert Stanfield, for $100, 100 A on Flat R adj Drury
Allen, Robert Dickens, Thos Hargis. 2 July 1810. Wit: Willis Horton, John
Stanfield.

242-3 Thomas Jeffreys of CC to Vincent Tap, for 70 lbs 17/6, 37½ A on Cobb Cr of
Hyco adj Jno Mason, Wm. Tap, George Lea. 25 Apr 1810. Wit: William Tap, John
Ogilby, Lewis Vaughan, Cha Wilson, Geo W. Jeffreys.

243 John Miles of CC to Nicholas Burch, for $80, 53½ A on Double Cr of Hico adj
Goodrich Jones, Adam McNealy, James McMurry, Herndon Harrel, Robert Huston -
said tract where Wm. E. Fox formerly lived & sale ordered by court. 29 Nov 1809.
Wit: Baylor Burch, Daniel Carney, Joshua Carney.

243-4 James McMurry & John McMurry to Sarah Vanhook, widow, for $500, 196 A adj
Vincent Lea, Wade, Lipscomb, Jacob Thomas. 14 Aug 1810. Wit: Gabriel Davey.

244-5 William McKissack, sheriff, to Jesse Dickens (due to court order of Jesse
Dickens against Daniel Merritt), 41 A of Daniel Merrit adj Artha Brooks sold for
6 lbs 5/. 16 Nov 1810. Acknd in open court.

245 William Carney of Rutherford Co., TN, atty for his father Joseph Carney, to
Moses Bradsher, for $600, 300 A on Cobb Cr adj Gold, Lawrence Lea decd, Wm. Carney,
Broache or Combs. 1 Aug 1810. Wit: Loyd Vanhook, Rho Carney.

Deed Book D
Page

245-6 State of NC - #129 - to Lewis Wilkerson, for 50/ per 100 A, 25.75 A on Aaron's Cr adj Little, John Person, Bob Harris. _ _ 1810.

246 William Bracken to Andrew B. Wood, for $200, 79 A on Double Cr of S Hico adj Phillip Hall, said Wood. 24 Aug 1809. Wit: Duncan Rose, John Raven.

247 John Cooper to Absolem Cooper, for $80, 79 A adj orphans & heirs of Lewis Green decd, Hall, McCoy old line - it being tract conveyed by Robert Dickens 5 Jan 1790. 12 Feb 1808. Wit: Jas Cochran, Thomas Graves.

247-8 Thomas Gaines to Robert Holloway, for $100, 50 A on Henley Mill Cr adj Abner Wallace, Richard Atkinson, Samuel Wheeler. 9 Feb 1810. Wit: Wm. Trotter, Thos Talbert.

248-9 Benjamin Jopling (in debt to Nathaniel Norfleet for $320) to John Malone, in trust, for 25¢, boy George. 21 Nov 1810. Wit: Elizabeth Jopling, Jas W. Muzzall.

249-50 Richard Lyon (in debt to Nathaniel Norfleet for 107 lbs 11/1½) to William McKissack, trustee, for 10/, 200 A adj Robert Dickens, John Lyon old line at Aldridge Cr., Joshua Cate; 7½ A adj John Phillips. 21 Apr 1810. Wit: William Stevenson, Spivy McKissack.

250 William McKissack, sheriff, to Isham Edwards - due to execution against Mary Stone recovered by James Cochran for 27 lbs 15/), for 3 lbs 2/, ? A on Gents Cr adj Cary Williams, John Seymore, Byrd Pulliam. 27 Dec 1810. Acknd in open court.

251 James Cochran to Isham Edwards, for $1500, 270 A on Stories & Gents Cr adj John Chambers former line, James McKnight, Hezekiah Deurast, Jacob Bull, Thomas Carver former line; said tract purchased of James Williamson 12 Dec 1797, 19 Apr 1809. Wit: Josias Carver, John W. Stone.

251 Benjamin Johnston Sen. to Arthur Leath, for $877, 219¼ A on Hico adj John Durham, Wm. Trotter, Solomon Draper. 7 Feb 1811. Wit: Ish Edwards, Morgan Jordon.

252 William KcKissack, sheriff, to James Williamson - due to execution in Granville Co. against John Sneed for 247 lbs 2/), for 180 lbs 2/3, 337½ A in Person Co. adj Jane Sneed, widow, Turrentine formerly Smith, Lemuel Sneed. 13 Feb 1811. Wit: L. V. Hargis, Wm. Norwood.

252-3 Alexander Cuningham to Warren Dixon, for $1200, 208 A on Cain Cr & Hico adj Abraham Dunaway formerly John Pearson, John Davies formerly Frederick Debow, Stephen Oliver, Thomas Dixon, Robert Jones old line formerly Archibald Campbell. 12 Feb 1811. Wit: W. Jeffreys.

253-4 John Winstead to Moses Springfield, for 100 lbs, 111 1/3 A adj Waite, Robert Gill, Manley Winstead. 29 Dec 1810. Wit: Ira Lea, Gabriel Davey.

254 William Waite of Bedford Co., TN, to Thomas Halliburton, for $120, 143.75 A on Bluewing Cr adj Robert Harris, Jesse Ragon, Dixon br. 10 Mar 1810. Wit: Jesse Ragon, Robt Harris, Nancy P. Wade.

254-5 Howard Jones, Allford Jones, & Samuel Jones all of Person Co., to Merydith Daniel, for $400, 308 A adj John Baird, Agness Barnett, crossing Spoonwater Cr, Charles Halliburton, Richard Andrews. 21 Nov 1810. Wit: John Holloway, Isaac D. Vanhook.

255-6 Edmund Dixon to William Dixon, for $130, 108 A on Hico adj orphans of Robert Black decd. 8 Feb 1811. Acind in open court.

256 Edmund Dixon to Henry Dixon, for $100, 170 A on Hico Cr adj Saml Morgan, John Harris, George Tap. 11 Feb 1811. Acknd in open court.

256 William Jeffreys to Thomas Pool of Granville Co., for 90 lbs, negro boy Peter about 9 yrs old. 14 Feb 1810. Acknd in open court.

257 Buckley Walker to Henry Brooks, for 120 lbs, 122 A on Castle Cr adj McFarland old survey, Jones, Larkin Brooks. Henry Woody releases any claim to this land. 9 Jan 1811. Wit: John Lawson.

257 David Bazwell to George Elliott, for $250, 107 A adj John Warren, Hugh Hemphill. 15 Nov 1810. Wit: George Elliott.

258 John Atkinson to James Jay Jr., for $400, 90½ A on br of Cochran mill cr adj Brechen. 5 Nov 1810. Wit: John Jay, R. H.Childers, Jno Scoggin.

258 William Cocke, sheriff, whereas Yancy Bailey, assignee, to William Penick, for 50 lbs, 100 A of Benjamin Debow adj Abraham Dunaway. 11 Feb 1811. Wit:William Norwood.

258-9 Power of attorney - Ellin Harrison to William Allen Jr. to recover boy Ralph now in possession of Benjamin Wheeler. 14 Jan 1811. Wit: William Yarbrough, John Yarbrough.

259 James Jay Jun. to John H. McNeal, for $343.73, 92 A & 1 rod, 10 perches, adj Cochran. 28 May 1810. Wit: John Raven.

259 Joseph P. Obryant to Meredith Daniel, for 150 lbs, 250 A adj Baird, Thomas Lawson, James Vanhook, John Wilkerson, Dennis decd. 18 Jan 1808. Wit: Irvin Lawson, Francis Lawson.

260 Richard T. Lyon to Samuel Pannill of Campbell Co., VA, Jeremiah Pannill, & George Pannill of Orange Co., VA, for $500, tracts on Aldridge Cr - 200 A adj William Cocke formerly Robert Dickens, John Lyon old line now James Wilson; said tract granted by State to Joshua Cate and to Richard T. Lyon Mar 1796; 7½ A adj first tract adj John Phillips and was purchased of Miles Wells June 1797. 2 Mar 1811. Wit: Wm. Dickerson, Thomas McCrowell, Loyd Vanhook, Ira Lea, John Parker.

260-1 William McKissack, trustee, & Nathaniel Norfleet to Samuel Pannill, Jeremiah Pannill, & George Pannill, release of deed of trust given Richard T. Lyon. 12 Mar 1811. Wit: Currie Barnett, Benj Chambers, John G. Newton.

261-2 William McKissack, sheriff, to Simeon Cochran (due to execution against Thomas Wilkerson for 148 lbs & recovered by Simeon Cochran, Wilson Jones, Danl Durham, Nicholas Thompson, & Nathaniel Norfleet - 175 A on Grier's Cr adj Mary Currie, John Malone sold to Cochran for 115 lbs. 23 Apr 1811. Wit: John Bradsher.

262-3 Joshua Blanton of Prince Edward Co., VA (in debt to Thomas McGehee for $500), to John M. McGehee, in trust, for $1, 256½ A on Hico adj McGehee, John Williams, Edwd O. Chambers, Joseph Woods. 29 Dec 1809. Wit: William McGehee, George Melton.

263 Davidson Chambers & Polly Chambers his wife to Thomas McGehee, for $500, release all interest in land by virtue of last will of Claud Muirhead decd - being an undivided 9th part; said land on Hico adj William Woods, Mumford McGehee, George Gregory. 17 May 1811. Wit: Benjn Chambers, Wm. McGehee. Polly Chambers examined apart from her husband and freely executed deed.

263-4 Lewis Amis to John Wagstaff of Granville Co., for $760, 242 A on Hico adj Jno Williams, John M. McGehee, Robert Moore on Whetstone Br, Samuel Morgan, Joshua Dixon. 29 Mar 1811. Wit: John Bradsher, William Puryear.

264 Byrd Wall & Elizabeth Wall his wife to Davidson Chambers, for $500, tract on Hico adj Wm. Woods, Mumford McGehee, George Gregory - being the land of Claud Muirhead the first husband of Elizabeth Wall devised to her in his will except 50 A sold to Mumford McGehee. 10 Dec 1807. Wit: Ish Edwards, Benj Chambers. Elizabeth Wall examined apart from her husband & freely executed deed.

Deed Book D
Page

264-5 John Gwin to Elisabeth Henriette Wade, for 50 lbs, negro girl Jenny about 9 yrs old. She was purchased at sheriff sale by Jacob Vanhhok, Sheriff. 23 Mar 1809. Wit: Richard Clayton.

265 Davidson Chambers to Thomas McGehee, for $500, tract both sides Hico adj Wm. Woods, Mumford McGehee, George Gregory being whole of lands owned by Claud Muirhead at his death & devised by him to his widow Elisabeth Muirhead, now Elisabeth Wall for her life & sold by her & her husband Byrd Wall to Chambers, 10 Dec 1807 excepting 20-30 A sold to Wm. Woods. 17 May 1811. Wit: Benj Chambers, William McGehee.

265 Joseph Lunsford relinquishes land to Samuel Lunsford his son if the son settles all debts he owes - tract on Deep Cr; cattle excepting 9 hogs, furniture. He must maintain his mother Elizabeth Lunsford for her life. 15 May 1811. Wit: Benjn Chambers, John Paine.

266 Thomas Norman Jr. of Granville Co. to William Daniel of same, for $100, 100 A all land he purchased of his father formerly land of Claborn Denny, Thomas Webb adj Harris, Daniel. 9 Feb 1811. Wit: Saml Hart.

266 Hugh Wood,whose wife is a legatee of Benjamin Hatcher, to John Byasee, for $230, 95.4 A adj Edward Clay, Walton Cochran, Mitchel. 29 Dec 1810. Wit: Cary Williams, Thomas Byasee.

267 Benjamin Wheeler to William Trotter, for 105 lbs, 119 A n side Bear Br. 18 Dec 1810. Wit: Jas Trotter, George L. Johnston.

267 Joshua Dickson to Currie Barnett, for $400, 131.4 A adj Jno Dickson, Morgan, Wagstaff, Jno Williams, Cary Williams - said land conveyed by Josias Dickson. 15 May 1811. Wit: Cary Williams, Spivy McKissack.

268 Power of attorney - Benjamin Wheeler to John Darby to collect debts due and to represent him in court to plead any suits. 30 Mar 1811. Wit: Tabitha Vaughan, H. Haralson.

268 Samuel Wheelor to son Benjamin Wheelor, all right & title to negro Ralph now in possession of Elender Harrison. 18 Mar 1808. Wit: H. Sergent, Margan Sergent.

268-9 William Hamblin to John Parker, for $273, 91 A on Stories Cr adj Nathaniel Hamblin, Thomas Jeffreys, Thomas Parker, Richard Atkinson. 16 Nov 1810. Wit: Benj Hamblin, Hugh Woods.

269 Nathaniel Hamblin to John Parker, for $41.66, 28 A on Stories C adj William Hamblin Jr. 17 Nov 1810. Wit: Wm. Jeffreys, Alex Winstead.

269 Legatees of Gabriel Davy decd and Elizabeth Davy to Ambrose Davy, for 108 lbs 12 shillings, negroes Buck & Ester. 1 Aug 1810. /s/ John Davy, Gab Davy, Polly Davy, Robert Gill. Proved in open court.

270 Phillip Hall to Duncan Rose, for $450, 57 A adj Andrew B. Wood, William Brechen, James Jay, John Scoggin. 7 Nov 1810. Acknd in open court.

270 State of NC - #130 - to John Mason, for 50/ per 100 A, 18½ A on S Hico adj Jno Rice, Claburn Bevil. Entered 20 Jan 1810.

271 Power of attorney - William Ramsey & Nancy Ramsey to William Jones to demand their interest & title in estate of James Jones decd, formerly a resident of King & Queen Co., VA, in right of his wife Nancy, daughter of Edmund Jones decd. 14 May 1811. Wit: John Holloway, Jane Holloway, Alex Cuningham.

271-2 Bennett Williams to Thomas Phelps & John Philpot of Granville Co., NC, for 10/, ? A on Cub Cr adj John Washington, James Anderson, heirs of Zachariah Vaughn - deed of trust for debt due John Washington of 80 lbs /3. 1 Feb 1811. Wit: William McKissack, Jno Parker.

Deed Book D
Page

272-3 Martha Richardson to daughter Elizabeth Douglass & her husband John Douglass, for love & affection, 30 A for him to improve adj Robert Wade; is she should will her land, they should receive $150. 21 Mar 1809. Wit: Loyd Vanhook, John Russell.

273 Anthony Brown to Richard Wood of Granville Co., for $1500, 280 A both sides Tarr R adj Gabl Davey, Abner Parker to Cattail Br, Washington, Saml Bumpass. 31 Dec 1810. Wit: John Washington, James Webb, A. Parker.

273 John Lyon of Smith Co., TN, to William Cocke of Person Co., negroes Dick, Burrell, Tom, Olliver, Clony & Anson; this bill of sale null & void if Lyon comply to obligation due Mrs. Thomson with Wm. Cocke, security, for land on Flat R. 21 June 1810. Wit: Benjamin B. Cocke.

274 Jesse Dickens to James Cochran, for $800, 6½ tenth of an A at ne corner CH lot adj John Williams chimney(formerly Densey Moore), Hargis. 13 Aug 1811. Wit: Charles Holeman, Gabl Davy Junr.

274 John Brown to Ephraim Hawkins, for $200, 100 A on Bushy Fork & Flat R adj Steven Wells. 31 Dec 1806. Wit: Loyd Vanhook, Alfred Brown.

275 William McKissack, sheriff, to George Glenn, for 37 lbs 7/9, 200 A adj Benjamin Partee, Moses Currie. 13 Aug 1811. Wit: H. Harralson.

275-6 Osborne Jeffreys Sen. gives to John Frederick the right to live on the land on s side Flat R as long as Frederick lives. 10 Mar 1806. Wit: Richard Oliver, James Cochran, Danl Frederick.

276-7 William Hargis (in debt to James Williamson, merchant, for 70 lbs) to Ira Lea, trustee, for 5/, 390 A on Flat R adj Nathan Hargis, Thomas Hargis, Thomas Hudgens, John Paine, John Womack, Dickens, Shadrack Hargis. 14 Aug 1811. Wit: Beverly Rose.

277-8 William McKissack, sheriff, to James Williamson (court order against William Hamblin Sen. for 10 lbs 12/ recovered by Duncan Rose & William Jeffreys) 50 A adj Joseph Hamblin mill cr, Nathaniel Hamblin, Richard Hamblin sold to Williamson for 15 lbs 17/. 14 Feb 1811. Wit: Ira Lea.

279 Abraham Hargis to Moses Fuller, for $100, 100 A adj William Hargis. 1 Mar 1811. Wit: Duncan Rose.

279-80 David Moore to Millenton Blalock Jun., for $285, 100 A on Cub Cr adj Bennett Williams, Zachariah Vaughn decd. Also signed by Susannah Vaughn. 28 May 1808. Wit: William Oakly.

280-1 Jonathan Terrel of CC to Ephraim Hawkins of Person Co., for $250, 200 A on Flat R adj Cochran, Cadwell, Brown, Webb. 22 Aug 1809. Wit: Simeon Cochran, Churchwell Jones.

281 Thomas Hood to Daniel Cleyton, for $135, 65 A on Mayo Cr adj Coleman, David Allen. 5 Aug 1811. Wit: Wm. Jeffreys, Alex Winstead.

282 Anderson Stone to Isham Edwards, for $400, 140 A adj Thomas Shepherd, Jno Gwin, Byrd Stone. 30 July 1811. Wit: J. Bradsher, John Williams Sen.

282 Millenton Blalock Senr. to his grandson William Blalock son to Millenton Blalock Junr., for love & affection & 5/, 82 A on S fork Flat R adj Thomas Hargis, Robert Blalock - said land deeded by Robert Blalock 1 Oct 1807; Millenton Blalock Senr. reserves a life estate in this land. 27 Feb 1810. Wit: Samuel Dickens.

283 William McKissack, sheriff, to James Williamson (due to court order against William Hamblin Sen. for 31 lbs 8/10 recovered by Hargis & Williamson), for 25 lbs, 100 A on Stories Cr adj Richard, William, & Nathaniel Hamblin. 14 Feb 1811. Wit: Ira Lea.

283 William McKissack, sheriff, to Gabriel Lea & Vincent Lea of CC, (due to court order against James McMurry for 572 lbs 4/ recovered by James Williamson & James Dollarhide), for 143 lbs, 150 A on S Hico adj William Lipscomb, Hiram Combs. 4 Aug 1811. Wit: Wm. Robards.

283-4 William McKissack, sheriff, to Gabriel Lea & Vincent Lea of CC, (due to court order against James McMurry & others for 572 lbs 4/ recovered by James Williamson & James Dollarhide), for 21 lbs, 71 3/4 A on S Hico adj William Gallaugher. 14 Aug 1811. Wit: Wm. Robards.

285 William McKissack to Gabriel Lea & Vincent Lea (due to court order against James McMurry for 272 lbs 4/ recovered by James Williamson & James Dollarhide), for 21 lbs, 21 3/4 A on S Hico adj William Gallaugher. 14 Aug 1811. Wit: Wm. Robards.

286 James Cochran to daughter Susannah Lea & William Archer Lea, for love & affection, negro slaves Pett about 18 yrs, Nutty. 9 Nov 1811. Acknd in open court.

286 Absolom Johnston to Nathaniel Norfleet, for $250, negro man Shadrack about 34 yrs now in possession of Norfleet to secure a debt. 29 Oct 1810. Wit: Wm. Stephenson, Thos Badgett, Jas W. Muzzall.

286-7 William Brown to James Cochran, for 17 lbs 18/, 17.9 A adj Cochran, on road from his dwelling house to his mill. _ May 1809. Wit: William Lea, Stephen Pleasant.

287 Robert Southward Senr. to John Shelton, for $80, 54½ A on Story's Cr adj James Williamson, George Morton. 18 Sept 1811. Wit: Benj Chambers, James Southward.

288 Hiram Combs to Stephen Pleasant, for $600, 147¼ A both sides Ned Cr adj James McMurry, Joseph Carney, John Russell; also 18 A on Ned Cr of S Hico. 11 Dec 1811. Wit: John H. McNeill, Aaron Scoggin.

288 George Lea to son William Archer Lea, for love & affection, negro woman Agg & two of her children Reuben & Amy; Sall & 2 of her children Harry & Agg; negro boy Fill. 2 Nov 1809. Wit: Abner Lea.

289 John Jay (in debt to James Williamson for $294.56) to Ira Lea in trust for 50¢, 132 A on Double Cr adj James Cochran mill, Philip Hall, Stanfield, Hunt. 10 Oct 1811. Wit: Beverly Rose.

289 Richard Pulliam to Isham Edwards, for $60, his right to negro slaves during the life of his mother Elizabeth Pulliam; negroes Stephen, Tempey & her child Paty; the interest of Richard Pulliam is one-tenth. 9 Nov 1811. Wit: John Parker, Wm. McKissack.

290 Robert Cate Jun. to Solomon Cate, for 450 lbs, 182 A on Flat R. 28 Feb 1807. Wit: Woodson Hubbard, Josiah Brown.

290 Jacob Bull to Robert Brooks, for $641.40, 320 A both sides Stories Cr adj Isham Edwards, Thomas Duty, Samuel Smith, Benjamin Chambers. 16 Jan 1811. Wit: Ish Edwards, Benj Chambers.

291 Solomon Cates (in debt to Lawrence V. Hargis & Co., merchants, for $569.37), for 87½ ¢, to Thomas N. J. Hargis, 200 A n prong Flat R adj Robert Cate Sen., Willis Nichols Jun. - land on which Cate & James Coughron now live. 1 July 1811. Wit: Saml Yarbrough.

292 Solomon Cate (further in debt to Hargis & Co. for $160.62) agrees for Thomas NJ Hargis to sell land to pay debt. 18 Nov 1811. Wit: Saml Yarbrough.

292 Samuel Dickens to John Bumpass, for $400, 200 A on Rocky Fork adj Anderson. 21 July 1810. Wit: Jesse Bumpass, Samuel Bumpass Junior.

293 James Williamson to Jesse Lunsford, for $266, 209 A adj heirs of William Lapp decd, Samuel Dickens, Jesse Lunsford, Joseph Lunsford Senr. 12 Feb 1810. Wit: Duncan Rose.

293-4 William Williams adm of Robert Newman decd to Kinchen Newman, for $112, 28 A n side Hico adj Alexander Cunungham - said land sold to benefit the estate for debt due James Warren for $112. 13 Nov 1811. Wit: John Long, John Ingram.

294 John Malone (in debt to Nathaniel Norfleet for $436.20) to William McKissack, Jun., in trust, for 25¢, negro man Jacob about 30 yrs of age 18 May 1811. Wit: Jos W. Muzzall.

295 Jeremiah Moore to Daniel Meaders of Granville Co., for 100 lbs, part of tract of 130 A of Arthur Moore adj James Cozart, Blalock, Johnston, Benjamin Partee. 31 Oct 1806. Wit: Yearby Partee, Charles Glenn.

295-6 Artha Brooks Sen. to James Cochran, for $372.50, 372½ A, being all of tract conveyed by James Patterson excepting part conveyed to Lawrence B. Hargis for 57½ A adj Merritt, John Williams, tract of John Cooper conveyed by State of NC. 15 Nov 1811. Wit: L. V. Hargis, Beverly Rose.

296 Eleanor Harrison to William Allen, for $500, negro man Ralph; the same was recovered from Benjamin Wheeler. 11 Sept 1811. Wit: John Holloway, Thomas Winstead.

297 Joseph Hargis to James Williamson, in trust for debt due Williamson & for 5/, 100 A adj Thomas Rany, Thomas Blalock, Benjamin Jopling, Thomas Morgan. 5 Jan 1810. Wit: Beverly Rose, Thos Atkinson.

297 Zachaus Hart Sen. to beloved son Samuel Hart, for natural love & affection, 3 negroes: Peter, Simon, Tamer. 24 Sept 1811. Wit: John Gwinn, John G. Wade, John W. Stone.

298-9 Thomas Parker (in debt to James Williamson, merchant, for $140) to Ira Lea in trust for 5/, 270½ A on Stories & Sargent Creeks adj William Hamlin, Richard Atkinson, Thomas Nealy old line, William Trotter, Presly Draper; livestock, household articles, crops of corn & tobacco; fodder & cotton. 1 Sept 1811. Wit: Beverly Rose.

299-300 Elijah Day (in debt to James Williamson for $201.80 on 3 notes) to Ira Lea for 5/, trustee, 104.7 A on Flat R at still house br adj Wm. Daniel, Rountree, Coleman, Cocke. 29 Oct 1811. Wit: Beverly Rose.

300 Sarah VanHook to Gabriel Davey, for 142 lbs 5/, 122½ A on Mayho Cr adj Lawson. 28 July 1811. Wit: Wm. Davy.

300 Edmund Dixon Senr to Edmund Dixon Jun., for 300 lbs, 150 A nw side Hico Cr adj Wm. S. Branch, Wm. Dixon. 13 Nov 1811. Acknd in open court.

301 Zachaus Hart to Isham Edwards, for $201, 100½ A on Stories Cr adj John Gwin, Abner Haralson, John Rodgers, Robert Howard. 5 Nov 1811. Wit: H. Haralson, John Parker.

301 William Waite of Bedford Co., TN, to Samuel Dickens of Person Co., for $150, 473 A both sides Tapley Cr adj John Hicks, Traylor, Williamson, Jeffreys. 15 Apr 1810. Wit: J. Bumpass.

302 John Seymore to Isham Edwards, for 100 lbs, 100 A on Jents Cr adj Cary Williams, Elisabeth Pulliam, Byrd Pulliam. 6 Nov 1811. Wit: Cary Williams, John Parker.

302-3 William McKissack, sheriff, to William Jeffreys (due to 2 executions against William Moore recovered by William Jeffreys) for 34 lbs 11/10, 300 A on Adams Cr adj William Jeffreys, James Layton. Charles Mitchel. 13 Aug 1811. Acknd in open court.

Deed Book D
Page
303-4 Lawrence V. Hargis to James Cochran, for $750, 2 lots at Person CH being same lots conveyed by Thomas Hargis; also tract near CH conveyed to Lawrence V. Hargis by Artha Brooks of 67½ A adj John Williams, Jno Paine; 2 lots at CH contain 1.1 A & 1.9 A adj jail, Cochran formerly Nicholas Delone, John Williams formerly Demsey Moore. 14 Nov 1811. Wit: William Lea, James Williamson.

304 Ellen Harrison who brought suit in Court against Benjamin Wheeler to recover negro Ralph - if recovered to be sold to William Allen. 29 Dec 1810. Wit: Francis Day, Allen Morgan.

304 Samuel Bumpass Senr to John Bumpass, for $210, 140 A adj Dickens where his road crosses William Tapp decd, Gabl Davey. 18 Nov 1811. Wit: Alfred Bumpass, John Bumpass.

304-5 Gabriel Bumpass to John Bumpass Jr., for $100, 80 A on Deep Cr adj John Bumpass Jr., John Davis. 5 Oct 1811. Wit: James Satterfield, Joseph Lunsford.

305 George Waite, agent of William Waite of Bedford Co., TN, to John Halliburton, for $30.50, 70 A on Bluewing Cr adj King. 11 Feb 1811. Wit: Thomas Halliburton, Thomas Webb.

305-6 Robert Wade (in debt to Isham Edwards for $147.95) to Cary Williams, trustee for $1, 20 A which he purchased of Davidson Chambers adj Joseph Wood, Thomas McGehee, Alexr Cuningham; negro man Charles; cattle, hogs, sheep, household articles; 1500 lbs tobacco, 30 barrels corn. 7 Feb 1812. Wit: John M. McGehee, John Parker.

306 Elizabeth Pulliam (in debt to Cochran & Edwards for 161 lbs 17/11) to Cary Williams, trustee for 10/, negro girls Jane about 13 yrs, Letty about 9 yrs; mares, cows, oxen; 3 feather beds, furniture. 15 June 1809. Wit: Foster Moore, John Bradsher.

307 Edmund Martin (in debt to James Holloway for $93) to Henry Bailey, trustee, for 5/, a sorrel mare, colt, a mare swapped from James Long, cow & calf; household & kitchen furniture. 18 Feb 1812. Wit: John Holloway, John Crowd.

307-8 Sarah Vanhook, Robert Davey, William Davey, Robert Gill, Elisabeth Gill, Gabl Davey Senr., Edward B. Davey, & John Davey all of Person Co. except Robert Davey who resides in GA, to Moses Street Jun., for $300, 300 A adj William Sims, Abram Selph, Thomas Person. Also signed by Elisabeth Davey, Buckley Walker, Mary Walker, Moses Chambers, Lucy Chambers, Wm. Thaxton, Aley Thaxton. 13 Nov 1808. Wit: John Buchanon, John Williams.

308 James Barnett to Samuel Smith of CC, for $1535, 307 A on Adams Cr adj Jno Barnett, Artha Brooks, Samuel Blackwell, Jacob Bull, Benjamin Chambers, Hugh Woods, heirs of Hugh Barnett. 12 Oct 1810. Wit: Ish Edwards, Thomas Dickson.

309 Robert Wade to Joseph Wood, for $180, 53 A adj Alexander Cuningham purchased of Thomas J. Chambers, Joseph Wood, McGehee mill. 25 Nov 1811. Wit: Ish Edwards, B. Walker.

309-10 Elijah Day to Thomas Sneed in trust for 78¢, 104.1 A on Flat R adj Francis Taylor, Charles Holeman, Charles Rountree - to satisfy debt due Lawrence V. Hargis & Co., merchants, for $120. 18 Nov 1811. Wit: Saml Yarbrough.

310 Elijah Day since deed of trust in debt to L. V. Hargis & Co. for $13.81, being a debt contracted by his wife previous to their marriage. 24 Dec 1811. Wit: Saml Yarbrough.

310 Josiah Brown (in debt to Lawrence V. Hargis for $496.13½, also debt due James Cochran) to Samuel Yarbrough, trustee, for $1, 181 A both sides s fork Flat R adj Thomas Sneed, Lawrence B. Hargis, Solomon Cate; slaves Daniel, Joe; woman Biddy & her 4 children: Hannah, Letty, Silvy, Lucy; wagons, horses, furniture. 14 Dec 1811. Wit: Jonathan P. Sneed.

Deed Book D
Page
311 Thomas Minshew (in debt to Lawrence V. Hargis & Co. for $520) to Ira Lea, trustee, for 50¢, 250 A between Deep Cr & Flat R adj John Gooch Sen., William Dickens, Henry Knolender; negro woman Rose; sorrel mare 8 yrs old, cows, beds, furniture. 4 Dec 1811. Wit: Saml Yarbrough.

311 Power of attorney - Thomas Hatcher of State of GA, to Hugh Woods of Person Co. to sell tract on Stories Cr being part of tract of Benjamin Hatcher Jun. & to make settlement with estate of Benjamin Hatcher decd of Bedford Co., VA. 4 Jan 1812. Wit: Cary Williams, Polly Hatcher.

312 William Chambers of Halifax Co., VA, to John Holloway of Person Co., for $315, negro man Will now in possession of John Holloway. 25 Sept 1811. Wit: Richd E. Bennett, James Holloway.

312 Joshua Cate Jun. to Charles Rountree of Orange Co., for 250 lbs, 221½ A on Flat R at quarrel cr adj Wm. Daniel, Harden Pain, Charles Holeman. 11 Feb 1811. Wit: James Williamson, Jno Rountree.

312 Mary Curry to John Love, for 100 lbs, 3 negroes: Dicey, Price, Celinda. 28 Oct 1811. Wit: John Mitchell, James Mitchell.

313 Mary Curry to son-in-law John Love, for affection, negro Jerry. 5 Feb 1812. Wit: John Mitchell, William Hester.

313 Joseph Stafford of CC to George Lea of Person Co., for $150, 50 A both sides Cobb Cr adj James Stafford, George Lea. 30 Dec 1811. Wit: William A. Lea.

313-4 Joseph J. Gooch (in debt to Lawrence V. Hargis & Co., for $300) to Samuel Yarbrough, for 50¢, negro man Mack. 9 Jan 1812. Wit: Jonathan P. Sneed.

314 John Cothran Jun. (in debt to Lawrence V. Hargis for $46) to Samuel Yarbrough, for 25¢, a bay mare, cows. 30 Dec 1811. Wit: Jonathan P. Sneed.

315 Jesse Evans Senr. to Simeon Cochran, for $390, 130 A on S Hico being part of tract granted Daniel Malone by State. 7 Apr 1809. Wit: Charles Ellison, Robt Jones Junr.

315 Charles Elison (or Charles Allison) to Simeon Cochran, for $3, 1.75 A. 7 Apr 1809. Wit: Jesse Evans, Robert Jones Jun.

315-6 Gabriel Bumpass to Jesse Evans, for ?(not given), 225 A both sides Flat R adj Wm. Daniel, Taylor. _ Sept 1811. Wit: William Clayton, Samuel Evans.

316 William McKissack, sheriff, to Nicholas Thompson of CC (due to court order against John Dixon for 132 lbs 17/10 recovered by Samuel McMurry & William Brown), for 131 lbs, 112 A on Cobb Cr adj Nicholas Thompson, Moses Bradsher. 13 Feb 1812. Wit: Alex Winstead.

316-7 Mary Currie to son-in-law William Mitchel, for affection, negro girl Lucy between 7 or 8 yrs old. 5 Feb 1812. Wit: John Mitchel, William Hester.

317 Mary Curry to William Mitchel, for $500, 2 negroes Caleb & Nicy. 28 Oct 1811. Wit: John Mitchel, James Mitchel.

317 William McKissack, sheriff, to Nicholas Thompson (due to court order against John Thomas for 157 lbs 14/9, recovered by Breesie Lewis), for $50.01, his undivided part of 235 A on Hico adj Richard Duty, Carter Lea, James Dollarhide. 13 Feb 1812. Wit: Alex Winstead, Wm. Jeffreys.

317-8 Ann Williams of CC to Joseph Taylor, for $400, negroes Avey a woman, and Rachel a child. 6 Jan 1812. Wit: Philip J. Echols, John C. Ogilby, E. D. Jones.

318 James Williamson to John Williams, for $255, negro girl Silvia, 12 yrs old. 25 Sept 1811. Wit: Ira Lea.

Deed Book D
Page
318 James Paine to Duncan Rose, for $200, 105 A both sides Adams Cr adj John
Mann, David Allen. 5 Dec 1811. Wit: John Raven, R. H. Childers.

318-9 James Paine to Duncan Rose, for $600, .6½ A at the CH being part of 6 A lot
conveyed by Demsey Moore 11 Dec 1792 to commrs to build CH adj jail. 5 Dec 1811.
Wit: John Raven, R. H.Childers.

319 Jesse Dickens to Phillips Moore, for $300, 288.4 A on Flat R which he obtained
from estate of Gen. Stephen Moore decd as a legatee adj Gooch, said Moore.
3 Feb 1811. Wit: H. Haralson.

319 Joseph Traler to Gabriel Davey, for $300, 100 A on Tapley Cr adj John Hicks,
James Clark, Jesse Lunsford. 2 Mar 1812. Wit: John Kerr.

319 Phillips Moore to Jesse Dickens, for $200, negro girl Cresa. 3 Feb 1811.
Wit: H. Haralson.

320 Gabriel Davey (in debt to Thomas Sneed for $275) to Lawrence V. Hargis &
Alfred Brown, trustees, for $1, 204 A on Tarr R adj William Yarbrough Sen.,
Samuel Bumpass Sen., Richard Wood, James Webb; also 5 negroes Daniel, Dave, Rhoda,
Mary, Lucy. 24 Apr 1812. Wit: Wm. McKissack, Saml Yarbrough.

320-1 Allen Wade (in debt to Alexander Cuningham for $1500) to George Wilson of
Halifax Co., VA, in trust, for $1, 200 A where Wade resides adj Goodloe Warren,
Henry Gray, Wm. McGehee, Danl Glenn, orphans of Jeremiah Warren decd;
negroes Buck, Will, Isbell & her daughter Hannah, Juda & her 2 children Jane
& Frank; furniture, utensils. 19 Feb 1812. Wit: Daniel C. Towns, William Dixon,
Alva Oliver.

321 John Morgan to Alexander Cuningham, for $750, negro woman Anna about 25 yrs old
& her 4 children: Nelson, Peter, Fanny, Jany; 5 horses, cattle, furniture;
crop tobacco. 13 May 1812. Wit: Thomas Word, Daniel C. Towns.

322 John Malone (in debt to Wilson Jones for 167 lbs 7/) to William McKissack,
trustee, for $1, 200 A on S Hico adj David Mitchell, David Carson. 7 Jan 1812.
Wit: A. Brown, Jonnathon McKissack.

322-3 George Lester of Oglethorpe Co., GA, to Alexander Cuningham, for $40, all
his right as legatee of William Stanfield decd to tract on Hico adj James Franklin, Byrd Wall old tract, Wm. Hobson; George Lester married Patsy Stanfield
daughter of said decd - it being the land where Tarlton Moore lives; also right
to dower land during life of Elizabeth Stanfield widow the decd being ¼ part of
said tract. 17 Feb 1812.

323 Power of attorney - John Coleman, William Coleman, Edward Coleman, Seth
Coleman, & heirs of Richard Coleman to wit: John Coleman, James Coleman, Eliza-
beth Coleman, Matthew Coleman - all of Edgefield District, SC, excepting Seth
Coleman of Person Co. - to friends Phillip Jenings, Lucy Jenings, & Valentine
Corly of Edgefield Dist - to dispose of plantation in Person Co. of 596 A on
Deep Cr; above are heirs of John Coleman at his decease; also to make title to
Samuel Yarbrough for as much of land he claims by purchase from Daniel Coleman decd.
Oct 1810. Wit: Hubbard Partace, Peter Badgett, William Mann Jr.
Proved Person Co. May 1812.

324 Coleman heirs listed on page 323 to Samuel Yarbrough, for 160 lbs, 470 A adj
Bumpass, Kirk. 4 Nov 1811. Wit: John Partain, Hubbard Partain. Signed by
John Partain, atty. Proved Person Co. May 1812.

324-5 William McKissack to Wilson Jones (due to court order against John Dixon
for 132 lbs 17/10 recovered by Samuel McMurry & William Brown) for 125 lbs 10/,
127 A on Hico & Double Cr adj Thomas Snipes. 14 Feb 1812. Acknd in open court.

Deed Book D
Page

325 Power of attorney - Samuel Smith & Holland Smith his wife of Person Co. to Pryor McNeill to receive their share of land entered in Bourbon Co., KY, under names of Benjamin Davis & Jordan on Licking R; Holland Smith is one of the heirs of William Davis decd formerly a resident of Isle of Wight, VA. 12 May 1812. Wit: Henry McNeill, Samuel Burk, Joshua Grant.

325 John Brown to Nathl Norfleet, for 105 lbs, negro boy Leban age between 7-8 yrs old. 5 Feb 1812. Wit: D. W. Milner, Nathl Norfleet Jun.

326 John Dillaway, trustee,to Robert Brooks - whereas Artha Brooks was in debt to Thomas Webb for 105 lbs 10/5½ with John Dillaway security - for $562.40, 302½ A adj John Barnett, Francis Walker, Samuel Blackwell, William Bairden, James Heggie - said tract where Artha Brooks Senr. lives. 17 Mar 1812. Wit: Cary Williams.

326-7 William McKissack, sheriff, to Nathaniel Norfleet (due to court order against Absolem Johnson for 78 lbs 15/4 & recovered by Nathaniel Norfleet), for 100 lbs 11/1, 305 A both sides Flat R adj Joseph Taylor, Simeon Cochran, Reuben Taylor. 10 Dec 1811. Wit: Elijah Jacobs.

327 Joseph Stafford of CC to James Stafford of Person Co., for $186, 62 A adj Henry Stafford. 11 May 1812. Wit: E. D. Jones, A. Jones, Chas L. Read.

327 Joseph Rice to John Mason, for $35, 10½ A on Cobb Cr of Hico adj Walter Oakly, Barnett Lea. 30 Apr 1812. Wit: H. Haralson, Henry Royster.

328 Jonathan McKissack (in debt to Wilson Jones for 115 lbs 9/1.75) to William McKissack, in trust, for $1, negro boy Joe age 5-6 yrs; 122 A adj Alexr Gray, Benjamin Jacobs. 31 July 1812. Wit: Drury Jones.

328 Jonathan McKissack (in debt to Nathl Norfleet for $334.38) to William McKissack, in trust, negro girl Milly about 6 yrs old. 7 Jan 1812. Wit: James Milner, Joseph W. Muzzall.

329 John Davey (in debt to Alexr Cuningham for $1028.34) to George Wilson, in trust, for $1, 216 A on Cain Cr whereon Davey lives adj Stephen Oliver, Warren Dixon, Abraham Dunnaway, James McCain, William McCain, Jno Daniel; negro boy Robin about 18 yrs, woman Phillis about 35 yrs. 21 Feb 1812. Wit: Daniel C. Towns, Thos White.

329-30 Henry Gray (in debt to Alexander Cuningham for $1227) to James Rainey, in trust, negro Betty about 16 yrs old, Abram about 26 yrs, Peter about 20; 116½ A where Gray lives adj Cuningham, the State line, Daniel Glenn, Allen Wade. 18 Apr 1812. Wit: Daniel C. Towns, Sol Debow, Jno W. Glenn, Richd Long, John Brooks.

330 John McMurry (in debt to Nathl Norfleet for 60 lbs) to James Milner, in trust, for 25¢, negro boy Lossen about 6 yrs old. 17 Dec 1811. Wit: Jos W. Muzzall.

331 Alexander Gray (in debt to Nathl Norfleet for 40 lbs 10/11) to Wm. McKissack, Jun., in trust, for 25¢, negro Nelson about 15 yrs. 16 Jan 1812. Wit: James Milner, Jos W. Muzzall.

331 John Minshew to Robert Berry Jun., for $70, 50 A being part of tract where R. Minshew decd lived on Byrd's Cr adj Dickens. Also signed by Elisha Minshew. 3 Feb 1812. Wit: Wm. Cocke, Jacob Paskill.

331-3 Roger Atkinson the elder & Anne Atkinson his wife to Thomas Griffin Peachy, David Buchanon, & Charles Duncan, in trust, 1350 A in Mecklenburg Co., VA, purchased of Edmund Bacon 18 Nov 1763; 915 A in Halifax Co., VA conveyed by Richard Rogers 1 Feb 1763; about 100 A on s side road to Boyd's Ferry; land deeded to son Roger Atkinson was purchased of Peter Rogers 20 Aug 1772; 200 A in Person Co. conveyed by Thomas Barnett 7 June 1773; 200 A conveyed by John Horly 17 Sept 1779.

113

Deed Book D
Page

331-3 cont - Wit: Wm. Mayo Jr., Elizabeth Randolph, Roger Atkinson, Robt Atkinson. 12 Feb 1795. Proved Petersburg, VA, on oaths of witnesses 1811. Proved Person Co. Aug Court 1812.

333 David Buchanon by his atty James Freeland & Thomas Bennett of Petersburg, VA, to Roger Atkinson of Chesterfield Co., VA, for 100 lbs, 200 A on Hico R adj said Atkinson & known as Thomas Barnett place who conveyed it to Atkinson the elder 7 June 1773 recorded in Orange Co. Roger Atkinson late of Mansfield, Dinwiddie Co., VA, father of the former conveyed land in Mecklenburg & Halifax Co., VA & in Person Co. 12 Feb 1795 to Thomas G. Peachy, David Buchanon and Charles Duncan, trustees then of VA,to satisfy debt due Richard Hanson; David Buchanon now sole surviving trustee and resides in Kingdom of Great Britain. 30 Nov 1811. Wit: R. B. Cook, Willis Cousins, Robt Walker, Richd Moore.

333-4 Osborne Jeffreys the younger to Duncan Cameron of Orange Co., for $2500, 738½ A both sides south fork Flat R including Jeffreys old tract and Blalock tract - said land conveyed by Osborne Jeffreys the elder adj Ellison now Sneed, Cate, Cameron, to Hoop Br to Cub Br to Orange Co. line. 15 Sept 1812. Wit: Samuel Dickens.

334 Cary Williams to Curry Barnett, for $43, 18.4 A adj land Barnett purchased of John Dixon. 15 May 1811. Wit: Duncan Rose, Jno Rountree.

335 William McKissack, sheriff, to Cary Williams (by court order against Richard Pulliam for 12 lbs 15/10 recovered by Cary Williams & Doctor Currie Barnett agents for Pulliam), for 5 lbs, the undivided part of 150 A on Gents Cr belonging to Richard Pulliam. 13 May 1812. Acknd in open court.

335 Banister Wall to Thomas McGehee, for $150, any interest he may have in estate of Claud Muirhead decd, it being one undivided 9th part on both sides Hico adj William McGehee, Joel Newman, Alexr Cunningham. 18 Mar 1812. Wit: James Franklin, William McGehee, Robt Seymour.

336 David Wall to Thomas McGehee, for $150, all interest he may have in estate of Claud Muirhead decd, being one undivided 9th part on both sides Hico adj Mumford McGehee, Alexander Cuningham. 26 Sept 1811. Wit: Henry M. Clay, William McGehee, John Hall.

336 Joseph M. McGehee to Thomas McGehee, for 66 lbs, all right he might have in marrying Patsy Wall daughter of Elizabeth Wall widow of Claud Muirhead decd - it being an undivided 9th part. __ 1811. Wit: John M. McGehee, Banister Wall.

337-8 Joseph Moore McGehee trustee to Thomas McGehee - (Joshua Blanton of VA in debt to Thomas McGehee for $1090.13 & conveyed in trust to both McGehees), for $650, 256½ A on Hyco & Gents Creeks adj John Williams, Thomas Shepherd, Joseph Woods; deed of trust not pd. 20 Apr 1812. Acknd in open court.

338-9 Richard Carnal to Jacob Vanhook of Halifax Co., VA, for $1648, 364 A adj Archibald Carnal, Alexander Cuningham, Stephen Oliver, Durret Oliver, Thomas Dickson, Durret Stanfield. 25 July 1812. Wit: R. Vanhook, A. Brown.

339 Hugh Hemphill to David Hemphill, for $30, 26½ A head of middle fork Cain Cr adj Jno Daniel. 8 Aug 1812. Wit: H. Haralson, Herndon Haralson Junr.

339 Polly Royster to James Puryear, for 125 lbs, negroes Cloe and her youngest child Letty. _ June 1812. Wit: Ira Lea, Wm. McKissack.

340 Polly Royster to James Puryear, for 100 lbs, negroes woman Mourning, boy Ralph, boys Milan, Tom. 2 June 1812. Wit: C. Vaughan, Anderson Rose.

340 John & Elizabeth G. Lyon of Smith Co., TN, to Susannah Thompson of Person Co., for $1800, 312 A both sides Tapley Cr near Cameron mill pond adj dower line of Susannah Thompson, Jeffreys. 21 June 1810. Wit: __ Muzzall, Osborn Jeffreys.

Deed Book D
Page

341 William Tapp to James Daniel of Charlotte Co., VA, for $800, negro man Davey about 56 yrs old; woman Isbel about 27 yrs; man Joshua about 26 yrs, boy Sam about 7 yrs. 25 July 1812. Wit: Jno C. Ogilby, Mandley Winstead.

341 William Tapp to James Daniel of Charlotte Co., VA, for $1500, 317 A both sides Cobb Cr at fork of Hyco adj James Rainey, John Lea, Vincent Tap to the mill stone, Laban Stafford. 25 July 1812. Wit: Jno C. Ogilby, Mandley Winstead, Jno Mason.

342 Miles Wells of CC to Samuel Williams of Person Co., for 100 lbs, 333 A on Cub Cr at the Granville Co. line adj William Craven. 8 Aug 1812. Wit: Stephen Ellis, James Brewer.

342 Elisha Minchew to John Cummins, for $40, 40 A adj Peter Aldridge, William Cocke. 2 Feb 1812. Wit: William Cocke, Jno Cocke.

342-3 William Mann to Wyatt Painter, for $100, 50 A on Adams Cr adj Robert Mann. 28 Aug 1805. Wit: H. Haralson, W. Jeffreys.

343 Thomas Parker to Nathaniel Painter, for $300, 270½ A on Stories & Sergant Creeks adj William Hamlin, Richd Atkinson, Thomas Nealy old line, Wm. Trotter, Presly Draper. 10 Aug 1812. Wit: Ira Lea, Charles B. Winstead.

343-4 William McKissack, sheriff, to Daniel Malone Senr.(execution against Mark Malone for 86 lbs 19/8) for 70 lbs 10/, 156 A on Hico adj Simeon Cochran, Nathl Norfleet. 10 Aug 1812. Acknd in open court.

344 Neill B. Rose of Orange Co. to Duncan Rose of Person Co., for $500, 200 A s side Haw R adj Michel Holt. 10 May 1807. Wit: John Raven, Charles Trim.

344 Samuel Dickens to Anthony Brown, for $1000, 280 A both sides Tar R adj Gabriel Davey, Abner Parker formerly William Morrow, Washington formerly Person, Saml Bumpass - being a tract purchased of Jesse Brown 28 Mar 1808. 30 Oct 1810. Acknd in open court.

344 Jesse Brown of Southampton Co., VA, to Samuel Dickens of Person Co., for $1500, 3 negroes Ephraim, George, Ben; also 280 A on Tar R adj Gabriel Davey, William Morrow to Cattail Br, Person, Samuel Bumpass - said land purchased of Wm. Dickson 16 July 1802. 28 Mar 1808. Wit: Anth Browne, R. H. Walker, Saml Browne.

345 Wyatt Painter to Wm. Jeffreys, for 35 lbs 17/6, 50 A on Adams Cr adj Robert Mann, Jno Mann. 9 June 1812. Wit: Wm. McKissack, Alex Winstead.

345 Valentine Corly & Lucy Coleman exec of Daniel Coleman decd both of Edgefield Co., SC, to Samuel Yarbrough of Person Co., for 164 lbs 17/, 471 A adj Bumpass, Kirk. _ Oct 1803. Wit: Jesse Dickens, Gebriel Bumpass.

345-6 James Walton to Reuben Walton, for $75, 50 A both sides w prong Stories Cr adj Atkinson, Cochran. 21 Feb 1812. Wit: Loyd Vanhook, Lofton Walton.

346 James Walton to his daughter Elizabeth Walton, for $232.50, 155 A western prong Stories Cr adj Reuben Walton, Atkinson, Cochran. 21 Feb 1812. Wit: Loyd Vanhook, Lofton Walton.

346 Bennett Smith of Granville Co. to Elizabeth Davie of Person Co., for $420, 2 negroes: Cherry 22 yrs of age & her child Esther. 31 Aug 1812. Wit: Ambrose Davie, Lawson Neal.

346 Peter Cozart to William Cozart of Granville Co., for $70, 40 A on Davie Cr on Granville Co. line adj James Cozart. 15 Sept 1816. Wit: Hubbard Cozart, Absolem Weaver. Proved Person Co. Nov 1812.

347 James Jones to Daniel Malone - his legacy of the widow Step decd. 4 Aug 1812. Wit: R. Henslee.

Deed Book D
Page

347 John Whitfield to James Johnston, for $200, 50 A adj Loyd Vanhook. 27 Aug 1812. Wit: Robartus Carney.

347 Daniel Malone to James Jones, for $200, 80 A on S Hico adj Wheely Meeting House, Simeon Cochran. 20 Aug 1812. Wit: Loyd Vanhook, Sally Malone.

348 Jesse Dickens to Duncan Cameron of Orange Co., for $516.75, 516.75 A on Dry Br of Flat R adj John Moore, Thomas Moore, Stanford, Jesse Lunsford; according to survey made by Samuel Dickens Sept 1812. 10 Oct 1812. Wit: Samuel Dickens, Charles Holeman.

349 Jesse Evans to Francis Epperson, for ? (not given), 225 A on Flat R at still house br adj William Daniel, Taylor. 31 Aug 1812. Wit: Jos Terry, Robert Paine.

349 Power of attorney - John Rainey to son David Rainey to sell land where John Rainey lives, 209 A. 29 Sept ? . Wit: Thomas Hargis, Isaac Rainey. Proved Nov 1812.

350 John Lawson to Buckley Walker Sen. - whereas James Petty Pool on 14 Feb 1810 conveyed in trust to John Lawson 196 A on Castle Cr to pay debt of 210 lbs due Buckley Walker - for 105 lbs, said land conveyed to Walker as highest bidder. 12 Nov 1812. Wit: H. Haralson, Moses Bradsher.

350 Cary Williams to Isham Edwards, for $266, negro woman Jane about 17 yrs old & her child Granderson about 1 yr. 2 Nov 1812. Wit: Wm. McKissack.

350 John Brown to Alfred Brown, for $150, negro girl Chainey about 5 yrs of age. 17 Oct 1812. Wit: Jesse Hargis, Jesse Brown.

351 William Cozart of Granville Co. to Hubbard Cozart of same, for 100 lbs, 257½ A on Nap of Reed & Cub Creeks being part of 2 tracts formerly belonging to Arthur Moore adj Abraham Dennis, Jno Cash, Daniel Meadows, Hiram Cozart. 4 Nov 1808. Wit: A. Partee, Groves Hunt.

351 James Jones to Baylor Burch, for $200, 80 A on S Hico on Wheeley Meeting House spring br adj Daniel Malone, Simeon Cochran, Currie, Taylor. 11 Nov 1812. Wit: Loyd Vanhook, James Broach.

351 John Darby to Bartley Hatchett - release of land on which was deed of trust given to Thomas Jeffreys, 117 A, as debt is paid. 11 Aug 1809. Wit: Edward D. Jones, Jonathan Haralson.

352 William McKissack, sheriff, to Duncan Rose (due to court order against John Parker for 63 lbs 17/6 recovered by William Hamblin Jun.), for 31 lbs 2/6, 119 A on Stories Cr. 13 Nov 1811. Acknd in open court.

352 Jonathan McKissack to Wilson Jones, for $300, negro girl Bet age 15 yrs. 15 Dec 1812. Wit: Wm. McKissack, Ellinor Brown.

353 Lewis Ramsey to William Baird of Prince George Co., VA, for 78 lbs, 156 A adj Mrs. Donnalson old line, Holloway. 14 Nov 1812. Wit: John Holloway, Thomas Townsend.

353 Wright Nichols to Alfred Brown, for $140, 112½ A on Double Cr adj Moore, Vanhook, McNeill, John Moore. 17 Jan 1813. Wit: Jesse Hargis, Benj Chambers.

353-4 George Kirk to Phillip Day, for 90 lbs, 100 A on Deep Cr adj Bumpass, Bedwell Satterfield, John Satterfield. 3 Dec 1811. Wit: John Day Jun., John Cothran Jun.

354 John Malone (in debt to Bartholomew Dameron for $220; debt due Daniel Malone Jr. for $152) to John Vanhook, in trust, for $10, negro boy George. 2 Sept 1812. Wit: Jesse Vanhook.

Deed Book D
Page

354 Loyd Vanhook to son Lawrence Vanhook, for parental affection, & for $62.50, the undivided moiety of 125 A on Stories Cr adj James Cochran, Walton - land was from 250 A granted by State to Loyd Vanhook. 4 Jan 1812. Wit: John Vanhook.

355 John Malone (in debt to James Williamson, merchant, for $383) to Ira Lea, in trust, for 50¢, 131½ A adj Mitchel; negro man Gorge. 11 Sept 1812. Wit: Wm. Hargis.

355 Daniel Meadows to Thomas Cozart, for 100 lbs, 110 A on some creek. 17 Oct 1806. Wit: Millenton Blalock, Senr., Benjamin Cozart.

356 Richard Ogilby to William Cozart, for $418, 209 A on Flat R adj William Oakley, Anthony Cozart, Mangum, Abraham Parker, Cader Parker, at meeting house br. 2 Dec 1809. Wit: Benjamin Cozart.

356 John W. Philpot of Granville Co. to John Washington of same, for 86 lbs, 150 A in Person Co. on Cub Cr adj said Washington, James Anderson, heirs of Zachariah Vaughn - it being tract conveyed to John Philpot & Thomas Philpot by deed of trust of Bennett Williams 1 Feb 1811. 8 Feb 1813. Wit: Millenton Blalock, Solomon W. Philpott.

357 Cary Williams to Byrd Pulliam, for $12.75, 4¼ A near Gents Cr adj John Williams Senr. _ _ 1812. Wit: Ish Edwards, Robt Seymour.

357 Agreement between William Carver and his six sons: Josias Carver, Benjamin Carver, Robert Carver, Landrum Carver, Loosen Carver, Hosea Carver - 6 sons agree to rebuild mill on lands of William Carver & Wm. Carver to take ½ of profits; sons to have ½ profits during life of William Carver; after his death, wife to have his ½ part & at her death 3 daughters Anney, Betsy, & Tempy (now living with him) to draw same share as the father as long as they are unmarried. 23 Jan 1810. Wit: Wm. McKissack.

358 William Carver to Billy Carver, for $200, 201 A on Stories Cr adj Hosey Carver, Jacob Bull, Paul Walters, except the mill plot & pond which was covenantly to his 6 sons. 6 Feb 1813. Wit: Benj Chambers, John Harris.

358 John Hill to Thomas Cozart, for 15 lbs, 14A & 20 poles adj both men, Joshua Johnson. 4 Oct 1809. Wit: R. C. Jones, __ Oakley.

358-9 George Moore to Benjamin Cozart, for 125 lbs, ½ of tract of 500 A formerly belonging to his father Moses Moore decd on n fork of little cr adj Daniel Meadows. 13 Nov 1802. Wit: W. Hubbard, Josiah Brown, Thomas Cozart.

359 Luke Moore to Benjamin Cozart, for 125 lbs, ½ of 500 A belonging to his father Moses Moore decd on little cr. 13 Nov 1802. Wit: W. Hubbard, Josiah Brown, Thomas Cozart.

359 Overton Harris of Granville Co. to Henrietta Wilkerson of Person Co., for 15 lbs, 50 A adj Abel Parrish, Humphries, Harris. 12 Aug 1811. Wit: Abel Parrish, Stephen Pitman.

360 James Daniel to Lewis Daniel, for 240 lbs, 312 A on n fork Flat R adj Green hunting br. 2 Nov 1812. Wit: James Williamson.

360 George Wilson, trustee, of Halifax Co., VA, to Allen Halliburton of same, for $334, 200 A adj Goodloe Warren, Henry Gray, William McGehee, Daniel Glenn, orphans of Jeremiah Warren decd - said land that of Allen Wade who was in debt to Alexander Cuningham for $1500. 9 Feb 1813. Wit: Jno W. Glenn, John S. Vaugan.

360-1 William Hawkins to son-in-law Thomas Blalock, for love & affection, all his estate right to land & property now in his hands. 3 Feb 1813. Wit: Thomas Blalock Jun., Obediah Pearce.

361 Bartley Hatchett to Philip J. Echols of CC, for $400, 117 A on S Hico adj Daniel Sargent, Wm. Gold, being land he purchased of Jno Darby or Wm. McDaniel 5 yrs ago. 18 June 1813. Wit: William E. Ogilby, E. D. Jones, Polly N. Hatchett.

361 James Williamson & John Williams to Charles Mitchell, for $500, negro man Quiller who formerly belonged to estate of Ralph Williams decd. 28 Dec 1812. Wit: Ira Lea.

362 William McKissack, sheriff, to Ira Lea (due to court order against Wm. Anderson & Abner Wallace for 18 lbs 7/11½, which was recovered by McDaniel Vanhook) for 22 lbs 16/1½, 50 A on Henley Mill Cr adj Roger Tilman, Samuel Wheeler. 8 Feb 1813. Acknd in open court.

362 James Cochran to Joseph Scoggin, for $300, 150 A on Stories Cr being land conveyed by James Ravens to Burwell Green by his atty John Glenn, then to Cochran adj Mitchel, Reubin Long. 16 Oct 1812. Wit: Jno Ravens.

362-3 William McKissack, sheriff, to Gabriel Lea & Vincent Lea of CC - (due to court order against Wm. Anderson for 52 lbs 10/, recovered by Joseph Langley & Moses Long), for 77 lbs 12/6, 85 A on Hico adj John Darby, Henry Royster. 12 Nov 1812. Acknd in open court.

363 William Trotter to William Frazer, for 200 lbs, 119 A n side Bear Br. 19 Sept 1812. Wit: James Dollarhide, Arch Lipscomb.

363 Robert Hester to 4 grandchildren: Sally Malone, Robert Malone, Elijah Malone, & Daniel Malone, children of daughter Nancy Malone wife of Stephen Malone of Orange Co., for love & affection, 3 negroes: Hannah age 18 yrs, Nicholas age 3 yrs, Yancy age 2 yrs. 8 Feb 1813. Wit: Elijah Hester, William Hester.

364 Robert Hester to six grandchildren: Henry Malone, Wright Malone, Robt Pomphrey Malone, Nancy Malone, Brandie Malone, & Betsy Malone - all children of daughter Sally Malone wife of Brandie Malone, for love & affection - 3 negroes: Eady age 21 yrs, William 2 yrs, Squire age 6 mos. 8 Feb 1813. Wit: Elijah Hester, William Hester.

364 Reubin Taylor of CC to John Durham & his wife Fanny Durham of Person Co., for $100, 154 A on S Hico adj Solomon Draper, Samuel Morgan, John Harris, Thomas Jeffreys. 31 Oct 1812. Wit: H. Haralson, Robert Hamlet, George Tapp.

364 Allotment of dower to Delpha Sargent widow of Daniel Sargent decd of her one-third of 292 A adj Bartley Hatchett, Vanhook, John Rice, or 97½ A. 23 Nov 1812.

365 Robert Holloway to Wyley Jones, for $115, 50 A on Henley Mill Cr adj Abner Wallace, Richard Atkinson, Samuel Wheeler. 8 Oct 1812. Wit: Arthur Fowler, Thomas Holloway.

365 Martha Richardson to son Lawrence Rochardson, for love & affection, negro boy Mag age 6 yrs & girl Banche 2 yrs. 2 June 1812. Wit: Edward Mitchel, John Russell.

366 Robert Cate (in debt to James Williamson, merchant, for $264.92) to Ira Lea, trustee, for 50¢, 2 tracts on Flat R: 121 A adj William Cocke, Jno Rountree; 50 A which Thomas Cate obtained of legatees of Thomas Person decd. 3 Oct 1812. Wit: Ira Lea.

366-7 William Gold (in debt to James Williamson for $200 equal to 100 lbs), to Ira Lea, trustee, for 5/, negro man David about 23-4 yrs of age. 11 June 1812. Wit: Charles B. Winstead.

367 Samuel Dickens to Michael Cary of Orange Co., for $140, 50 A on Camp Cr adj the county line, Sherman, Johnston, Benjamin Cozart. 20 Oct 1812. Wit: C.Vaughn.

Deed Book D
Page
367 William Waite, late of Person Co. & now of Williamson Co., TN, to Samuel
Dickens, for $200.75, 301 A on Deep Cr adj John Davis, Jesse Dickens. 31 Mar
1807. Wit: Abner Williams, Jesse Lunsford.

368 Samuel Yarbrough,(trustee for Josiah Brown who was in debt to Lawrence V.
Hargis & Co. & to James Cochran) to Duncan Cameron of Orange Co., for $500, 181 A
both sides Flat R adj Thomas Sneed, Hargis. 30 Apr 1813. Wit: Jonathan P. Sneed.

368 Thomas J. Chambers to Alexander Cunningham, for $5470, 1094 A both sides Hico
at Gents Cr adj Thomas Shepherd, Thomas McGehee, Joseph Woods, George Gregory,
Edward Shelton, Roger Atkinson, Robert Howard decd. 1 May 1813.
Wit: J. W. Glenn, Wm. Chambers, Jno M. McGehee.

369 Gabriel Davey Senr. to James Webb, for $190, 19 A n side Tar R adj Bumpass,
Abner Parker - it being part of tract conveyed from Gabriel Davey & John Bumpass
exec of estate of Robert Bumpass 18 Jan 1791. 6 Jan 1813. Wit: Wm. Yarbrough,
Junr., Robert Moore.

369 James Williamson to James Martin, for 100 lbs, 100 A n side Flat R adj Thomas
Rainey, Thomas Blalock, Benjamin Joplin, Thomas Hargis. 17 Dec 1812.
Wit: Francis Epperson, J. G. Williamson.

369-70 Robert Hamlett to Thomas Moore Hamlett, for $414, 103½ A head waters
Winn's Cr adj Addison Hall. 7 Jan 1813. Wit: H. Haralson, Jos Pulliam.

370 Hardy Wells of Surry Co., NC, to Robert Hester of Person Co., for 100 lbs,
100 A on Hico adj Jones. 27 Apr 1802. Wit: Isaac Rainey, Samuel Thomas.

370 Robert Hester to Nicholas Hester, for 100 lbs, 100 A on Double Cr adj Jones.
10 May 1813. Wit: Thomas Burch, E. Hester.

371 Howard Allin son of William Allin Sen. to aforesaid William Allin Sen., for
$240, 225 A on Adams Cr adj Charles Man, William Jeffreys, Wm. Man, David Allin,
Moore - it being same tract Wm. Allin gave to Howard Allin & never recorded.
2 Jan 1813. Wit: Joseph E. O'bryan, Anna O'bryan.

371 Thomas Webb of Person Co., John Webb of Granville Co., & Samuel Smith of CC -
to Thomas Webb, 228 A on Castle Cr known by name of Crossroad Ordinary adj Samuel
Cox, John Barnett, on Douglas Rd. - this deeds all interest in said land to
Thomas Webb. 3 May 1813. Wit: James Webb, Isaac Webb, Josiah Wade.

372 Joshua Step to Simeon Cochran, for $300, 150 A adj James Farquhar, Elizabeth
Step. 24 Oct 1812. Wit: Isaac Rainey, Baylor Burch.

372 Currie Barnett to John Dixon, for $40, 13½ A, part was purchased of Cary
Williams. 30 Mar 1813. Wit: John Bradsher, Thos Shapard.

372 George Simmons of Baldwin Co., GA, to Wilson Jones of Person Co., for $300,
negro woman Mary. 17 Apr 1813. Wit: Drury Jones, Wm. G. Cochran.

373 Thomas Eubank, exec of George Eubank decd, to David Rainey, for 50 lbs, 50 A
on Hico adj John Rainey. 5 Aug 1813. Wit: Joseph Hargis, James Blackwell.

373 Frances Walker to Drury A. Pulliam, for $235, 100 A on Stories Cr adj Jesse
Long, Artha Brooks, Samuel Blackwell, Thomas Duty. 8 Oct 1812.
Wit: Ish Edwards, John Seymour.

373-4 Johnston Howard of Russell Co., VA, to James Heggie of Person Co., for $55,
50 A on Adams Cr adj Andrew Barnett, Mark Allen. 10 Sept 1812. Wit: Ira Lea,
John Malone.

374 Archibald Heggie of Columbia Co., GA, to James Heggie of Person Co., for $400,
200 A on Adams Cr adj John Barnett, Will Baird, Charles Mitchel, Manly Winstead.
7 Aug 1813. Wit: Ira Lea, Wm. McKissack.

Deed Book D
Page

374-5 Samuel Bumpass to James Webb, for 67 lbs, 67 A on Tarr R adj Dickens road, Gab Davey, Samuel Yarborough, Wm. Yarborough, John Bumpass. 10 May 1813. Wit: William Yarborough Jun., Wm. Yarborough Sen.

375 William Rainey to Hasten Bartlett of CC, for $400, 116 A on S Hico adj Jno Rainey. 14 Sept 1811. Wit: Wilson Jones, L. Rainey.

375-6 Joseph Hubbard Jun. of Orange Co. to Jacob Hubbard of same, for 75 lbs, 200 A in Person Co. on Richland Cr adj James Cochran. 17 Jan 1811. Wit: Wm. B. Jameson.

376 John Williams Sen. to Thomas Shapard, for $120, 24 A s side Hico adj Thomas McGehee, Jno McGehee. 9 Aug 1813. Wit: William Williams, John Williams Jun.

376-7 Richard Ogilby to Thomas Jeffreys of CC, for $4705, 535 A in Person Co both sides Cobb Cr of Hico adj William S. Branch, Saml Smith, Lewis Amis, Henry Royster, Hugh Darby, John Darby. 17 Nov 1812. Wit: H. Haralson, Jno C. Ogilby, F. Johnston.

377-8 William McKissack, sheriff, to Simeon Cochran (due to court order against John Malone for 28 lbs 14/, recovered by Wilson Jones), for $354, 200 A on S Hico adj David Mitchell. 9 Aug 1813. Acknd in open court.

378 John Jay to John Wisdom, for $450, 136½ A adj John Scoggins, st Stanfield Cr a br of Double Cr. 8 Aug 1812. Wit: R. H.Childers, Jno Scoggins.

378 John Vanhook to John Johnston, for $350, 100 A on S Hico adj Capt. William Lea decd line. 11 Aug 1813. Wit: Jesse Vanhook.

378-9 James Martin to John Scogin, for $200, 106 A on Flat R adj Willis Horton, William Allen, Dickens. 5 Sept 1811. Wit: Moses Bradsher.

379-80 Benjamin B. Cocke, Rebecca Paine, John W. Williams & Susanna His wife, Sally Cocke, Robert Paine & Polly his wife, John Cocke, Martha Cocke, Henry Womack & Frances his wife - Benjamin, Rebecca, Susanna, Sally, Polly, John, Martha, & Frances are heirs of William Cocke decd of Person Co.- to Jesse Evans, for $632.25, 231 A on Flat R where William Cocke died adj John Cates, Richard Holeman, Charles Holeman, Charles Rountree Jr., to Quarrel Cr. 28 May 1813. Wit: Saml Dickens, Saml Yarbrough, Jonathan P. Sneed, John Womack, James Saterfield, Lewis Daniel. Daughters examined by Jno Holloway & Jno Rountree apart from husbands and freely agreed to conveyance.

380 George Gregory to Edmund Shelton, trustee, for 1/, 72 A n side Hico adj Alex Cuningham, Joel Newman, Kinchen Newman. Deed of trust given for money owed James Franken of $100. 3 May 1813. Wit: Cary Williams, William Williams.

380-1 Mrs. Grizy Moore, Robert Moore, Phillips Moore, Portius Moore, Samuel Moore, Sidney Moore, Saml Moore, Ann Moore Jun. & Jesse Dickens, Mary Stanford - all of Person Co. -to Richard Stanford of Orange Co., for $2200, a tract called Mount Tirzah of 497 A. Mrs. Grizy Moore to retain dower rights. 2 Oct 1813. Wit: Thomas Phillips.

381 Richard Stanford received deed of relinquishment of Mount Tirzah exempting dower right from legatees of Genl Stephen Moore decd. 2 Oct 1813. Wit: Thomas Phillips.

381 Robert Moore to Portius Moore, for $229, 57¼ A on Hillsborough Rd adj Abner Williams, John Clixby. 10 Nov 1813. Wit: James Williamson, Francis Epperson.

381 Allen Halliburton of Halifax Co., VA, to Richard Halliburton of same, for 100 lbs, 200 A on br of Hico where Allen Wade lives & sold by deed of trust to Alex Cunningham & purchased by Allen Halliburton adj Goodloe Warren, William McGehee, Henry Gray, Daniel Glenn. 10 Nov 1813. Acknd in open court.

382 William McKissack, sheriff, to Thomas McGehee (sold by court order as William Jeffrey of Village of Rocksborough brought suit against Robert Wade), for 30 lbs 5/, 20 A adj Robert McGehee, Joseph Woods. 10 Aug 1813. Wit: B. Yancy, H Haralson.

382 James Webb to William Morrow, for $18, 18½ A on Tar R at Buckhorn Br. 10 Nov 1813. Wit: William Yarbrough Jun., John Owen Jun.

382 John Frederick to Duncan Cameron, for $75, all his right & interest in a tract on s fork Flat R which he claims on conveyance of Osborn Jeffreys Sen.; also crops now growing. 14 Sept 1812. Wit: Jesse Evans, Jno Cumins.

383 William Morrow to James Webb, for $24, 24½ A adj John Day on wagon path to Bumpass, said James Webb. 10 Nov 1813. Wit: William Yarbrough Jr., John Owen Jun.

383 Allotment of dower to Sarah Coleman widow of Richd Coleman decd - total on Mayho 235 A, another tract of 150 A; one-third part to Sarah Coleman adj Daniel Clayton, Paine, Moses Springfield, about 128 A including dwelling house or mansion. 5 July 1813. Wit: Wm. McKissack, sheriff.

383-4 John Davey to Edward B. Davey, for 80 lbs, 240 A on Mayo & Mill Cr - it being an equal moriety of land devised him by his father Gabl Davey decd inclusive with other moiety by said John Davey disposed of to Ashburn Davey; Div land of Gabl Davey was to John Davey, legatee of Ashburn Davey decd. 10 Nov 1813. Wit: Alex Winstead, Richd Howson, Ashburn Davey.

384 Samuel Woods of CC to Thomas Woods of Person Co., for $410, 168 A in Person Co. on S Hico adj Isaac Rainey. 13 Aug 1813. Wit: William Richmond, William Woods.

384 Henry Burch of CC to Jas C. Smith of same, for $263, 169.9 A in Person Co. adj Vincent Lea, McMullin. 10 Dec 1811. Wit: Daniel Jackson, Reubin Walton, John Eskridge.

385 Allotment of dower to Rebecca Paine widow of John Paine decd - 291 A and dwelling house on Flat R on Hillsborough rd adj John Womack, Polly Davis. 28 Sept 1813. Wit: Wm. McKissack, sheriff.

385 John Cummins Sen. (in debt to Duncan Cameron of Orange Co. for $100) to Lawrence V.Hargis, trustee, for 50¢, 319 A on Flat R adj Epperson - said land conveyed him by Robert Dickens. 20 Sept 1813. Wit: Francis Epperson, Lemuel Sneed.

386 Richard Clayton (in debt to Thomas Walton, carpenter, for 61 lbs 5/9) to Reubin Walton, for 5/, tract adj John Scoggins, Samuel Yarborough, being his proportion of land from estate of Thomas Clayton decd; horse, mare, cattle. 9 Aug 1813. Wit: John Day Jun., Wm. Pannill.

386 State of NC - #132 - to Jacob VanHook, for 50/ per 100 A, 488 1/5 A on Flat R & Double Cr of S Hico adj Jno Moore, Vanhook, Nichols, Henry McNeal. Entered 12 Oct 1812.

387 William McKissack, sheriff, to Isham Edwards (by court order against John Parker for 37 lbs 11/7 recovered by James Williamson), for 30 lbs, 119 A on Stories Cr adj William Hamlin, Nathl Hamlin. 10 Aug 1813. Wit: Wm. Hargis, Robert Johnston.

387-8 Samuel Morgan of Nottaway Co., VA, to Charles Sallard, for $1650, 1039 A both sides Sargent & McFarland Creeks of Hico adj Edmund Dixon Senr., John Dixon, Cary Williams, Joseph Royster, William Trotter, Solomon Draper, Lofton Walton, John Harris, Henry Dixon - being all of the land Morgan purchased of Saml Smith. 11 Feb 1814. Wit: Daniel Reese, Robr W. Thomas, Frances L. Moseley.

Deed Book D
Page

388 Henry Graves to Jacob Bull, for $20, 1.1 A on Stories Cr adj his mill, Jacob Bull. __ __ 1807. Wit: Samuel Bull.

388 Samuel Morgan of Nottaway Co., VA, to Charles Sallard, for $1328, 256.6 A on Hico adj Harris Stanfield. 11 Jan 1814. Wit: Daniel Reese, Robt W. Thomas, Frances L. Moseley.

388-9 Lucy Black to John Daniel, for $450, 101 A both sides main road on head waters Cain Cr of Hico of Dan R adj heirs of Joseph Hall decd, heirs of James Hamlet decd, David Hemphill. 25 Aug 1813. Wit: H. Haralson, Richd Ogilby.

389 Peter Badgett to James Heggie, for $40, 50 A on Adams Cr - it being lot #9 in tract of Francis Howard decd. 22 Dec 1813. Wit: Ira Lea.

389 John Dickson (or John Dixon) to Currie Barnett, for $10, 3½ A adj both men. 30 Mar 1813. Wit: John Bradsher, Thos Shepard.

389-90 Thomas Moore to Charles Moore of Robeson Co., NC, for $160, all his right to 640 A on Adams Cr adj Joseph Gill, John Wilson, Drewry Abbot, James Paine. 20 Jan 1814. Acknd in open court.

390 Alexander Cuningham adm of Robert Howard decd with will annexed to Thomas McGehee (in his will devised all land to be sold & equally div between his wife & 2 children namely Polly & Henry Williams), for $1601, 632 A on Hico, Marlowe, & Gents Creeks adj John Gwin, John Rogers, Cuningham. 27 Nov 1813. Acknd in open court.

390-1 William Farquhar & Stephen Wells exec of estate of James Farquhar Sen. decd to James Farquhar Jun., for $704.50, 292½ A on Flat R adj Abraham Moore. 14 Feb 1814. Wit: Lewis Tapp, Obadiah Pearce.

391 Joshua Cate Senr to Charles Cates, for $300, 116½ A on Flat R at Aldridge Cr. 15 Feb 1814. Wit: R. H. Childers, Baylor Burch.

391 Alfred Brown to Ephraim Hawkins, for $140, 108 A on bushey fork of Flat R adj Jno Brown, Moore, Allen, Webb, Hawkins. 15 Oct 1811. Wit: Wright Nichols, Susanna Nichols.

392 Isaac Fuller to Dennis OBryant, for $550, 2 tracts on Stories Cr: 100 A given by his father Henry Fuller; 100 A purchased of James Cochran adj John Long, Walters. 3 Dec 1813. Wit: Ira Lea, Saml Wheeler.

392 Joshua Cate Senr. to Robert Wallis, for $396.50, 122 A on Flat R at Black Br & Aldridge Cr, adj Pannel. 29 Oct 1813. Wit: L. V. Hargis, John Daniel.

393 Henry Day to Nathaniel Smith late of Guilford Co., NC, for $360, 200 A on Mayo Cr adj estate of John Yarbrough decd, David Allin. 22 Dec 1813. Wit: Green Daniel, John Yarbrough.

393 William McKissack, sheriff, to Samuel Dickens (due to court order against George Anderson for 48 lbs 11/5 recovered by Dickens & Wilson & Samuel Dickens), for 46 lbs, 40 A on Camp Cr on Orange Co. line adj Johnston, Benjamin Cozart, Sherman. 11 Feb 1811. Acknd in open court.

394 Thomas McGehee to Alexander Cuningham, for $1601, all his title & claim to 632 A on Marlowe Cr, Hyco, & Gents Cr adj John Gwin, John Rogers. 14 Feb 1814. Acknd in open court.

394 George Wilson, trustee, of Halifax Co., VA, to Alexander Cuningham of Person Co., for $1112.50, 216 A on Cain Cr adj Stephen Oliver, Warren Dixon, Abraham Dunaway, James McCain, William McCain, Jno Daniel. Sold to satisfy deed of trust of John Davey who owed debt to Cuningham. 10 Feb 1814. Wit: M. Wilson, Harrison Stanfield.

Deed Book D
Page

394-5 James Lea to Samuel Smith both of CC, for $1750, 350 A both sides Cobb Cr in Person Co. adj James Raney, Archd Murphey, William S. Branch, Richd Ogilby, Wm. Tap; said land Lea purchased of Thomas J. Moore. 25 Dec 1812. Wit: Charles Wilson, Tho Jeffreys.

395-6 William McKissack, sheriff, to Herndon Haralson (who brought suit against Wiley Jones for $39.73½), for $50.50, 53 A - said land conveyed by Robert Holloway adj Samuel Wheeler, Ira Lea on Henley Mill Cr, Abner Wallis, Col. Richd Atkinson. 14 Feb 1814. Acknd in open court.

396 Goodloe Warren to Archibald Carnal, for $100, 44 A on Cain Cr of Hyco adj Durrett Stanfield, Jones. 10 Feb 1814. Wit: H. Haralson, Herndon Haralson, Jun.

396 Mills Durden to John Moore, for $74½, 74.75 A adj Clixby, Jesse Dickens. 18 Oct 1806. Wit: Thos Moore, Anne Moore. Proved Feb 1814 on oath Thomas Moore.

397 Spivy McKissack & Susan McKissack his wife, late Susanna Thompson, to Lawrence V. Hargis, for $1900, 314.75 A both sides Tapley Cr adj D. Cameron mill pond, Susan Thompson dower line, Jeffreys - being the part of land of Paul Jeffreys decd allotted to his daughter Elizabeth G. Lyon & conveyed by John Lyon & Elizabeth Lyon his wife to Susanna Thompson or McKissack by deed 21 June 1810. 31 May 1814. Wit: Thos V. Hargis.

397 Ephraim Hawkins to Wright Nichols, for 200 lbs, 190 A on Bushy Fork of Flat R. 12 Feb 1807. Wit: William Hester, Robt Hester.

398 Joseph Lunsford Senr to Osborn Jeffreys, for $150, 150 A e side Deep Cr adj Jesse Dickens, Coley old line now Saml Dickens, Durden path now Lunsford, Jesse Lunsford. 12 Nov 1813. Wit: John Day Junr.

398 Joshua Cate Senr to John Cate Junr, for 10 lbs, 161½ A on Aldridge Cr adj Robert Wallis, William Pannell, John Phillips, Waite or Person. _ May 1814. Acknd in open court.

399 Reubin Taylor to Solomon Draper, for $100, 100 A on Flat R adj Joseph Taylor, Simeon Cochran. 6 Feb 1814. Wit: H. Haralson, Jonathan Haralson.

399-400 Richard Duty to James Williamson, for $250, 90½ A on Hyco adj Carter Lea. 24 Apr 1813. Wit: Alex Winstead, Ira Lea.

400 James Paine to James Williamson, for $630, 252 A on Double Cr - it being part of tract granted by Earl Granville to James Anderson 10 Jan 1761 adj Isaac Satterfield, John Stanfield, John McNeill. 24 Dec 1813. Wit: Robert Payne Jun., Ira Lea, Wm. McKissack.

400 Artha Brooks to James Williamson, for 100 lbs, 200 A on Rosemary Cr. 4 July 1812. Wit: Ira Lea.

401 Lawrence V. Hargis to Spivy McKissack, for $1900, 314.75 A both sides Tapley Cr adj D. Cameron, Susan Thompson dower line, Jeffreys - it being part of land of Paul Jeffreys decd allotted to his daughter Elisabeth G. Lyon & conveyed by John & Elisabeth Lyon to Susannah Thompson 21 June 1810 & conveyed by Spivy McKissack & Susannah his wife to Hargis. 31 May 1814. Wit: Thos V. Hargis.

401-2 Jesse Watkins (in debt to Duncan Rose for 155 lbs 5/9) to William McKissack, trustee, for 5/, 200 A on Richland Cr adj John Ravens, Duncan Rose, Reubin Long, Edward Clay Senr, John Gwin. 27 Apr 1814. Wit: Jas Heggie, John W. Graves.

402 Thomas Price of Orange Co. to John Thomas of Person Co., for $100, 120 A on Bushey Fork Flat R adj Orange Co. line, Aldridge, Wm. Waite, Edward Goines, Philip Burch, D. Durham, Benj Wheeley; a line intersects tract as 20 A already sold to Robert McNab; tract conveyed to Price by Daniel Malone. /s/ Thos Wm^s Price. 25 Dec 1799. Wit: Samuel Serrett, B. Douglas. Both witnesses removed from State; proved by oath of John Whitfield who was present when deed was sriten; Cary Williams proved handwriting of B. Douglas.

403 Spivy McKissack to Duncan Cameron of Orange Co., for $1900, 314.75 A both sides Tapley Cr adj Susan Thompson now McKissack dower line, Jeffreys - being part of land of Paul Jeffreys decd allotted to his daughter Elizabeth G. Lyon & husband John Lyon who conveyed it to Susanna Thompson & McKissack. 21 June 1810. Wit: L. V. Hargis, Thos V. Hargis.

403-4 Joseph Clark & Samuel Dickens, commrs, to Lewis Tapp - (due to court order involving Thomas Gholston adm of Allen Love decd in 1805 against Joel Pope & Daniel Burton), for $218, 137 A on Flat R adj Jno Womack, Dickens, Lewis Tapp - said land to satisfy debt of 240 lbs due 22 Mar 1784 to estate of Allen Love. 8 Aug 1814. Wit: Joab Robertson, Roger Tilman.

404-5 John W. Stone to Alexander Cuningham, for 150 lbs, 101+ A adj John Gwin, Isham Edwards, Robert Deshazo, Benj Chambers, Byrd Stone. 15 June 1814. Wit: Harrison Stanfield, Saml Dickens, Richd Ogilby.

405 Buckley Walker Senr to Jno Walker, for $300, 196 A adj Jno Henley old line, Robert McFarland. 30 May 1814. Wit: John Rogers Senr, Thomas Webb.

405-6 Div land of John Warren decd among 3 heirs: 1. John Scott in right of his wife 96 A value $264 adj VA line; 2. John McCain in right of hiw wife 96 A value $264 adj VA line to Winn Cr; 3. Thomas Brandon in right of hiw wife 96 A value $264 on Winn Cr adj Elliott; land already allotted to 3 children in his life-time to wit: Bluford Warren his son 100 A, Stuart Warren 100 A, William Phelps in right of his wife Jane 100 A. 3 May 1814. Commrs; Goodloe Warren, Edmund Dixon, David Hemphill, Jno Daniel.

406 State of NC - #133 - to Thomas Hudgins , for 50/ per 100 A, 53 A on Flat R adj Jopling, Jeffreys, Thomas Hargis. 24 Nov 1813.

406-7 John Cummins Senr to Jesse Evans, for $112, 112 A adj Epperson, Clayton, Cameron. 25 Oct 1814. Wit: Francis Epperson, Robert Cummins.

407 John Cummins Senr to Francis Epperson, for $113.40, 37.8 A n side s prong Flat R. 14 Nov 1814. Wit: Jesse Evans, Robert Cummins.

407-8 William McCain to Edmund Dixon Jun., for $900, 183 A s side Cain Cr adj Black, William Dixon, Joseph McGehee. 6 Oct 1814. Wit: Wm. L. Parker, William Dixon.

408 Edmund Dixon Jun to William Dixon, for 300 lbs, 150 A nw side Hico adj William S. Branch, Wm. Dixon. 16 Nov 1814. Wit: Edmund Dixon Senr.

408 Thomas Heggie of Siogo? Co., NY, to James Heggie of Person Co., for $296, his undivided part of 400 A on Adams Cr in Person Co; the other part of 200 A now owned by James Heggie. 5 Mar 1814. Wit: Alex Winstead, Ira Lea.

409 Abram Self to Moses Street, for 125 lbs, 150 A on Buck Mountain Cr adj John-son, Davey, Gill, Waite. 22 Mar 1812. Wit: Gab Davey, Gideon Patterson.

409 Billy Carver to Henry Carver, for $150, 70 A on Stories Cr adj Josias Carver, Graves, Jacobs, William Carver. 4 Oct 1814. Wit: Wm. Trickey, Benj Chambers.

410 Wright Nichols to John Moore, for $166.66, 100 A on Double Cr adj Alfred Brown, said Moore, Childers, Graves. 7 Sept 1814. Wit: L. V. Hargis, Francis Epperson.

410 Lea Haralson of Halifax Co., VA, to William Allen Sen of David Allen, for $412, 103 A on Marlowe Cr of Hico at Hams Br adj old tract of Paul Haralson decd. 16 Nov 1814. Wit: Hugh Woods.

411 William Gold to Coleman Mitchel of Rockingham, for 140 lbs, 81 A e side Henley Mill Cr adj Satterfield, Tillman. 1 Sept 1814. Wit: Jas Trotter, Solomon Draper.

Deed Book D
Page

411 Charles Rountree Junr to Jesse Evans, for 59 lbs, 59 A on Flat R at Quarrel Cr adj Wm. Daniel, at schoolhouse br. 16 Aug 1814. Wit: Phillips Moore.

411-2 Larkin Brooks to John Rogers Sen., for $500, 109 A on Hams Br at corner of Lea Haralson adj Rogers. 15 Nov 1814. Wit: Wm. McKissack, Wm. G. Cochran.

412 Jeremiah Roberts to Thomas Peed, for 50 lbs, 50 A on Cub Cr at Rice spring be adj Walter Oakley. 26 Oct 1814. Wit: John Bowles Junr., John Peed.

412-3 Vincent Tapp to William A. Lea, for $1300, 188¼ A on Cobb Cr of Hico adj James Stafford, John Mason. 8 Nov 1814. Wit: Geo Lea, Barnett Lea.

413 Joseph McCain of Rockingham Co., NC, to Alexander Cuningham of Person Co., for $785, 157 A s side Cain Cr of Hico adj Edmund Dixon Junr, the Black orphans. 10 Oct 1814. Wit: H. Haralson, William Dixon.

413 William Bell to Thomas Snipes, for $56, 14 A on Double Cr adj Snipes, James Cochran, James McMurry. 29 Sept 1814. Wit: Saml Brown.

414 Clayton Fuller, William Moore, & John Fuller all of Person Co., to Alfred Jones of same, for 100 lbs, 207 A on Stories Cr adj William Hamlin, William Fuller, Sampson Glen, James Cochran, Dickens, Van Hook, Paul Walters. 14 Nov 1811. Wit: Ira Lea, N. Thompson.

414 William Dickens to Thomas Webb both of Granville Co., NC, for 200 lbs, 640 A on Flat R adj Nathl Norfleet, Stokes Allen, & known as Urquhart old field. _ May 1813. Wit: Daniel Gooch, James Cochran, Portius Moore.

414-5 Alfred Jones (in debt to Williamson & Lea, merchants of Roxbrough, for $63.11) to Alexander Winstead, trustee, for 25¢, 207 A on Stories Cr adj Wm. Hamlin, Wm. Fuller, Samson Glenn, James Cochran, Dickens, Van Hook, Paul Walters. 14 Nov 1814. Wit: James Heggie, Joab Robinson.

415 Thomas McGehee to Thomas Shapard, for $897.75, 256½ A adj John McGehee, Jno Williams, Joseph Woods. 13 Dec 1814. Acknd in court.

415-6 Amos Satterfield of CC to William Satterfield of Person Co., for $60, 158 A on Deep Cr adj Yarbrough, Roger Atkinson, Hardy Crews - it being part of tract of 316 A conveyed by Francis Scogin 16 Nov 1784. 20 Dec 1814. Wit: Char⁵ B. Winstead, Ira Lea.

416 Goodrich Jones to Drury Jones, for $83.66, 28½ A on Double Cr adj Samuel P. Ashe. 5 Nov 1814. Wit: H. Milner, William McKissack.

416 Richard Duty exec & heir of Richard Duty Sen. decd to Nicholas Thompson, for $50, ? A on S Hico adj James Williamson, James Dollarhide, heirs of David Vanhook - it being his undivided part of tract left to heirs of his father Richard Duty Sen. decd. 8 May 1813. Wit: Jno G. Wilson, R. B. Wilson.

417 William Satterfield to Samuel Winstead, for $53.33, 10 2/3 A on Henley Mill Cr adj Roger Tilman. 23 Nov 1814. Wit: James Rainey, Philip J. Echols, Roger Tilman.

417 Wilson Jones to Drury Jones, for $384, 128 A on Double Cr of Hico adj Lea, Vanhook, Thomas, Snipes, Rose. 19 Oct 1814. Wit: Wm. McKissack, Jas Milner.

418 John Cates Sen. to Francis Epperson, for $5, 1 A s side s fork Flat R adj Duncan Cameron. 6 Feb 1815. Wit: Robert Wallace, J. Bumpass.

418 Drury Jones & Wilson Jones to Goodrich Jones, for $66.66, 40 A on Double Cr adj Goodrich Jones, Thos Badgett, heirs of Wm. Cocke, Adam McNealy. 21 Oct 1814. Wit: A. Brown, Wm. McKissack.

418 Robert H. Childers to Duncan Rose, for $350, 152 A on Double Cr adj Abram Hargis, Jno Moore, James Jay Jun., Thomas Graves decd, Andrew B. Woods, Duncan Rose mill tract. 30 Nov 1814. Wit: John Raven, Jesse Satterfield.

Deed Book D
Page

419 Archibald Lipscomb to James Hannah, for $700, 349½ A on Sargent Cr adj Solomon Draper, John Bran, Joseph Royster, Duncan, James Cochran, Robert Carver, Hall, William Trotter - it being a tract purchased of Wm. Sargent 17 May 1804. 27 Mar 1812. Wit: Jno M. McGehee, Wm. McKissack.

419 Herndon Haralson to Nicholas Thompson of town of Leasburg, NC, for $180, 113 A on dividing ridge between S Hico & Double Cr in Person Co. adj Vincent Lea, Ezekiel Dollarhide, Henry McNeal, Nicholas Burch. 8 Mar 1814. Wit: Nathaniel Wier, Thornton Black.

420 John Allen of Person Co. to Thomas N.S. Hargis & Dennis Hargis of Hillsborough, for 100 lbs, 91 A adj Norfleet, Palmer old corner. 24 Sept 1814. Wit: William Allen Senr.

420-1 Alexander Cuningham to Edmund Dixon Senr., for $392.50, 78½ A on s side main rd from red house to Dixon's bridge on Hico adj Abram Dunaway, heirs of R° Black - it being tract purchased of Joseph McCain. 14 Feb 1815. Wit: H. Haralson, E. D. Jones.

421 Robert Berry Junr to Laurence V. Hargis & Co., for $90, 50 A on Byrd's Cr adj Dickens, Cocke - it being part of land where Richd Minshew decd lived. 31 Dec 1812. Wit: Thos Sneed, Jas Farquhar Jun.

421-2 James Rainey of CC to Alexander Cuningham of Person Co., for $140, 116 A formerly property of Henry Gray adj the State line, Cuningham, Daniel Glen, Allen Wade, Jeremiah Warren. 11 Feb 1815. Wit: E. D. Jones, William Rainey Junr., James Rainey Junr.

422 John Davis to Robert Downey of Granville Co., for $250, 200 A adj Samuel Dickens, Jesse Dickens, James Yokely. 15 Apr 1815. Wit: Wm. McKissack.

422 John Clixby to Portius Moore, for $975, 200 A on Deep Cr adj Robert Moore. 11 May 1815. Wit: Ish Edwards, Thomas Webb.

422-3 Herndon Haralson to Thomas Thomas, for $50, 50 A on Henly Mill Cr of S Hico adj Abner Wallace, Col. Richard Atkinson, Samuel Wheeler. 2 Jan 1815. Wit: George Q. Johnston, Jas Rainey Junr.

423 Reuben Walden & Louisa Walden his wife, formerly Louisa Lipscomb, to Archibald Lipscomb, for $120, 56 A on S Hico - it being their undivided part of land of Thomas Lipscomb decd which descended to his 5 children: Elisha, Matilda, Bynion, Geoffrey, & Emma which they hold as tenants in common - the 5th part being sold - adj Hiram Lewis, John Carver, widow Hughs, widow Lea - total of 230½ A. /s/ R. Walrond, Eloise Walrond. 15 Mar 1815. Wit: Benj Chambers, Cary Williams.

424 William McKissack, sheriff, to Samuel P. Ashe (due to court order against Hasten Bartlett for 47 lbs 9/3, & recovered by William Rainey), for 54 lbs 4/6, 66 A adj David Rainey now Samuel P. Ash, Christopher Thomas. 26 July 1814. Wit: William Cochran, Wm. Frazer.

424-5 Willaim McKissack, sheriff, to John Phillips (due to court order against Nathan Hargis for 147 lbs 7/6 recovered by James Williamson), for 200 lbs, 100 A adj Tapley, James Wilson, Thomas Hargis. 25 Apr 1815. Wit: Wm. Frazer, Charles B. Winstead.

425-6 William McKissack, sheriff, to Thomas Walton (due to court order against Richd Clayton for 33 lbs 18/3 recovered by Bartley Hatchett - and against Henry Day & Richard Clayton) Clayton's undivided part of 255 A adj David Allin sold to Walton for 7 lbs 10/. 3 May 1815. Acknd in open court.

426 David Rainey to Samuel P. Ashe of Halifax Co., VA, for $976.50, 279 A in Person Co. & CC on S Hico adj John Rainey old line, Bartlett, Isaac Rainey. 20 Oct 1813. Wit: Wm. Sheppard, Egbert Sheppard.

Deed Book D
Page

426-7 Wilson Jones to Samuel P. Ashe, for $1000, 640 A on Double Cr adj Edmd Burch, Robert Hester, Broache, McNeill, Nicholas Hester, Drury Jones, Gray, Nancy McKissack, Norfleet, Taylor. _ Oct 1814. Wit: Wm. McKissack, B. W. Milner.

427 Hasten Bartlett & Christopher Thomas to Samuel P. Ashe, for $138.33 1/3, 40 A on S Hico adj Daniel Malone, Ashe formerly Ellison - said land a part of that purchased by Hasten Bartlett of William Rainey & sold by him to said Thomas but deed never recorded. 7 Dec 1814. Wit: Stephen Jones, Margaret Sheppard.

427-8 Charles Rountree Jun. (in debt to Jesse Evans for $450 & $350.50) to Thomas Sneed, trustee, 300 A on Flat R adj John Cothran, Wm. Cothran, Duncan Cameron. 28 Jan 1815. Wit: Jo Rountree.

428-9 Samuel McMurry & Matilda McMurry his wife to Archibald Lipscomb, for $120, 46 A on S Hico being the undivided part of a tract which on death of Thomas Lipscomb descended to his 5 children & heirs at law to wit: Eloisa, Matilda, Binion, Geoffrey, & Emma - adj Hiram Lewis, Jno Carver, widow Hughs, widow Lea - total of 230½ A. 15 Mar 1815. Wit: R. Vanhook, James Hannah.

429 Goodloe Warrin to Richard Halliburton, for $100, 40 A on Cain Cr adj Richard HBurton. 2 Mar 1815. Acknd in open court.

429-30 Jesse Evans to Francis Epperson, for $130, 112 A on Congrove Br adj Clayton, Cameron. 16 Mar 1815. Wit: Charles Rountree, John Frederick.

430 Thomas Rainey to Richard Blalock, for $250, 103 A on Flat R adj Wm. Moore. 4 Feb 1808. Wit: Samuel Dickens.

430 Millinton Blalock Jun. to Robert Blalock, for 31 lbs 7/3, 30 A on n side s fork Flat R. 1 Mar 1809. Wit: Thomas Blalock Jun., Millinton Blalock Sen.

430-1 Millentin Blalock of Granville Co. to Nathan Oakley, for 101 lbs 5/, 100 A on Cub Cr adj Bennett Williams. 23 Feb 1812. Wit: Thomas Philpot, Hardy Johnston.

431-2 William McKissack, sheriff, to James Williamson (due to court order against Wm. Lumkin for 22 lbs 3/, recovered by Gabriel Davey)an undivided tract on Mayho adj David Allen, Richard Coleman heirs, Moses Springfield - including Lumkin's undivided part of 500 A sold to Williamson for 10 lbs. 4 May 1815. Acknd in open court.

432 Charles Sallard to Simon Sallard of Nottaway Co., VA, for 150 lbs, 200 A adj James Jordan, Thomas Edmonson, Loften Walton, John Dixon. 6 Apr 1815. Wit: Wm. McKissack, Charles Tucker.

432 James Fuller of CC to Sampson M. Glenn of Person Co., for $277.50, 110 A on Stories Cr adj James Cochran, William Boswell. 11 May 1815. Wit: Lord Lord, Benj Chambers.

433 Edmund Shelton to Alexander Cuningham, for $650, 130 A at the State line where it crosses Holt mill cr adj Roger Atkinson, Timothy Holt, William Warren. 16 Mar 1815. Wit: James Franklin, Wm. Penick, Wm. Bailey, H. Stanfield.

433 Cary Williams to Currie Barnett, for $29.25, 9.75 A - it being part of tract purchased of Joel Newman adj said Barnett. 10 Mar 1815. Wit: L. V. Hargis, Ira Lea.

434 Elijah Mitchell of City of Raleigh (in debt to Stephen Sneed of Granville Co. for $400 & Sneed bound to Robert Burton, John Hare, James Hamilton, & Leonard Henderson on indemnity for $775 for debt Mitchell owed Bank at Newbern) to Thomas Sneed of Person Co., a tract in Person Co. adj James Williamson, being land David Mitchell the elder owned & Elijah inherited & purchased from heirs of his brother David; also negroes: Cropsy & her 3 children Erasmus, Newburn, Mary. Stephen Sneed had already purchased of Elisha Mitchell slaves Judy & her 3 children Wallace, Ritter, Caleb for $775. 11 May 1815. Wit: Junius Sneed for Mitchell; Wm. Robards for Thos Sneed.

Deed Book D
Page

435 Charles Sallard to Thomas Edmondson, for 150 lbs, 200 A e side Sergent Cr
adj Wm. Trotter, Solomon Draper, Lofton Walton, Simon Sallard, James Jordan.
1 June 1815. Wit: Edmund Dixon Senr., Jeremiah Dixon.

435 James Anderson to John Washington of Granville Co., for $450, 200 A on Cub
Cr of Tarr R adj Oakley. 24 Oct 1814. Wit: James Terry, Samuel Davis.

436 Herndon Haralson to William McGehee, for $2160, 280 A head waters Cain Cr of
Hico adj Wm. L. Parker, Frances Hamlett, Archd Murphey, Wm. S. Branch, Joseph
McGehee. 15 June 1815. Wit: James Rainey, Joseph McGehee, Jonnathan Haralson.

436 Meredith Daniel to Francis Lawson, for $650, 250 A adj Baird, Thomas Lawson,
Gabriel Davey, John Wilkerson, Ben Denny decd. 16 Aug 1815. Wit: Thomas Lawson,
W. Jeffreys.

436-7 John Bumpass (Tarr R) to his son John Bumpass, for $400, 200 A on each
side Rocky Fork on Dickens rd adj James Anderson. 25 Mar 1812. Wit: Alfred
Bumpass, William Bumpass.

437 John Duncan of Granville Co. to Garrot Tingean of same, for $200, 100 A on
Gents Cr adj John Chambers. 24 June 1815. Wit: Howell L. Ridley, Charles Durkin.

437-8 John Daniel to James Daniel, for $600, 101 A on head waters of Cain Cr of
Hico & Wins Cr of Dan R adj heirs of Joseph Hall decd, heirs of James Hamlett,
David Hemphill. 27 May 1815. Wit: George Elliot Jun., Robert Hamlett, John
McAden.

438 John Daniel to Stephen Oliver Senr., for $1305.25, 323 A on Cain Cr adj Goodloe
Warrin, David Hemphill, Frederick Debow, Oliver. 31 May 1815. Wit: H. Haralson,
Durrett Oliver, Jonathan Haralson.

438-9 Daniel Malone to Caleb Jacobs, for $140, 76 A on S Hico adj Wheeley Meet-
ing House br at Malone fence, Baylor Burch. 26 Sept 1813. Wit: Duncan Rose,
Jeoffrey Lipscomb.

439 Samuel Dickens to John Bumpass (DC) (possibly Deep Cr?), for $400, 200 A on
Deep Cr adj Jesse Dickens, said Bumpass. 5 Apr 1815. Wit: Thos Moore.

439 Robert Moore Senr to Alexander Moore, for parental affection, 156 A on Hyco
adj John M. McGehee, John Wagstaff, John D. Moore. 19 Feb 1813. Wit: W. McGehee,
John D. Moore.

439-40 Richard Hamblin to John Hudgins, for $95, 100 A on Stories Cr adj John
Harris, William Hamblin Junr. 23 Nov 1813. Wit: Richd Harris.

440 William Jones to John Clixby, for $300, 100 A on Richland Cr of Hico adj
Aaron Fuller, Charles Winstead, William Saterfield, Carter Lea. 1 Aug 1815.
Wit: Charles B. Winstead, John Parr.

440-1 Moses Cash & Daniel Cash to Bennett Williams Junr., for 42 lbs, 133½ A on
Cub Cr adj George Pead, being a tract laid out of lands of Jno Cash Sen. decd for
his legatees called lot #2 allotted to Daniel Cash. 25 Nov 1814.
Wit: Jesse Peed, Abraham Medaris.

441 James Martin to William Moore, for $8, 2 A s fork Flat R at Moore mill pond.
3 Apr 1815. Wit: E. W. Milner, John Brown.

441-2 Robert Paine to Lewis Daniel, for $400, 51 A on Richland Cr adj heirs of
Paul Jeffreys. 17 Nov 1813. Wit: Henry Womack, Lewis Graves, John Vanhook,
Samuel Holeman.

442-3 Ebenezer Whitehead to Ira Lea, for $400, 103 A on Richland Cr adj Carter Lea,
Charles Winstead, Vanhook. 18 May 1815. Wit: John Parrott, Carter Lea.

443 Baylor Burch to Simeon Cochran, for $100, 80 A on S Hyco adj Wheeley Meeting
house br, Daniel Malone, Currie, Taylor. 6 Mar 1815. Wit: E. Hester, Wm. G.Cochran

Deed Book D
Page

444-5 William Wilkerson & Martha Wilkerson his wife of Granville Co. to Richard
Blanks of same, for $200, 280 A on Aaron & Bluewing Creeks in Person Co. adj
Blanks, William Montague, Phillip Vass, James Daniel, James Jones, Benjamin
Whitehead. 30 Oct 1815. Wit: John Holloway, Thos Haliburton.
Martha Wilkerson certified she voluntarily agreed to deed.

445-6 Thomas Blalack to Jeremiah Rimmer, for 100 lbs, 180 A on Flat R - it being
part of tract granted by William Hawkins to James Bryan & to Bryan from Richard
Caswell, Governor, Captain, General Commander in chief at Kingston, 1 Mar 1780.
2 Oct 1815. Wit: John Blalack, Hasten Blalack.

446 Thomas Allen to Edward Mitchell, for $350, 140 A on Mill Cr adj James Davey -
said tract William Allen gave to Thomas Allen.15 Nov 1815. Acknd in open court.

446-7 Phillip J. Echols to Archibald Lipscomb, for $650, 122 A on S Hyco adj
heirs of Daniel Sarjent decd, William Gold - said land he purchased of Bartley
Hatchett decd. 11 Oct 1815. Wit: James Rainey, John G. Willson, J. McMullen.

447 John W. Graves to Jacob Couch, for $100, 52 A on Stories Cr adj Jas Cochran,
Nancy Graves, Josias Carver, Isham Edwards. 29 Nov 1814. Wit: Ish Edwards,
Currie Barnett.

448 Lewis Amis to Douglas Fulcher, for $400, 128 A on Mitchie Br of Cob Cr adj
Hugh Darby, Wm. Rainey, John Mason, Henry Royster. 29 Aug 1815.
Wit: Cary Williams, George Gregory.

448-9 Roger Atkinson & Agnes Atkinson his wife of Chesterfield Co., VA, to Jacob
Faulkner of Halifax Co., VA, for $1911, 273 A on n bank of Hico R at Holt Mill
Cr adj Cuningham, Timothy Holt. 29 Sept 1815. Wit: Joseph Jones, David Woody,
James Faulkner. Agnes Atkinson examined apart from her husband & freely signed
deed.

449 James Holder of Milton, CC, to Richard Carnal of Person Co., for $500, 150 A
on Cain & Wins Creeks adj Hugh Hemphill, Phoebe Johnston, Oliver. 3 Feb 1816.
Wit: Robt Jones, Ch Wilson, Richd Vanhook.

449-50 Robert Jones to John D. Moore, for $15, 3½ A adj both man. 30 Nov 1815.
Wit: Thomas Dixon, Solomon Walker.

450 Moses Fuller to Aaron Fuller, for $206, 70 A on S Hico adj John Clixby,
Carter Lea, William Fuller, Moses Fuller, at still house br, Charles Winstead to
CH road. 16 Dec 1815. Wit: Asa Fuller.

450-1 Dennis Hargis to Benja W. Milner, for 100 lbs, 100 A both sides Flat R adj
Robert Blalack, Webb. 23 Sept 1809. Wit: Jos Hargis, Beverly Rose, Richd Hargis.

451 Charles Gregory to Samuel Michel, for $75, 65 A on head waters Mayho Cr adj
Thomas Hood, David Allen. 1 Jan 1816. Wit: Wm. McKissack, Cary Williams.

452 Thomas Dixon to Robert Jones, for $105.50, 33 A on Cain Cr adj Capt. Richard
Carnal. 6 F b 1815. Wit: Edmund Dixon Junr., Solomon Walker.

452-3 John Boswell of Wilkes Co., GA, to John W. Williams of Person Co., vacinity
of Roxborough, for $300, all his interest in land & slaves willed by Jno Walker
decd to heirs & representatives of Ralph Williams decd; Boswell in right of his
wife Elizabeth Boswell is heir to said tract on Adams Cr between 300-400 A;
also slaves James & Caty his wife, Ned, Daniel, Charles, Abram, Patt; Boswell
& wife entitled to one-ninth of said land & slaves. 4 Sept 1815.
Wit: Ira Lea, John G. Wade.

453 William Deshazo, Robert Deshazo, Edmund Deshazo, & Clembernet Deshazo - all of
Person Co. - to James Holloway of same, for $275.10, 233 1/3 A on Dishwater Br of
Mayo & Castle Creeks of Hico adj Atkinson, Neal, Dickens. /s/ Robt Bohannon
Deshazo, Clement Barnet Deshazo. 15 Aug 1815. Wit: Mos Walker, Jesse Munday.

Deed Book D
Page

453-4 John Gibhard Cunow of Bethlehem, Northampton Co., PA, to Moses Fuller of Person Co., for $67.50, 54 A on Richland & Henley Mill Creeks of S Hico adj former tract of Benjn McNeal, William Jones, Wheeley. /s/ by his atty in fact, Lewis Der Schweinitz. 10 Oct 1815. Wit: Barza Graves, Asa Fuller.

454 Lewis Wilkerson to Abel Parish, for $37.12½, 24 3/4 A on Aaron's Cr adj Little, John Person, Harris. 1 Feb 1815. Wit: Robert Harris, Wm. Harris.

454-5 Rebekah Paine to William Yarbrough Jun., for $250, 200 A on Tar R adj Wm. Tap, Wm. Day - said land former property of William Duncan & sold by execution to Robert Gill. 3 Feb 1816. Wit: Jno W. Williams, J. Bumpass.

455 John Darby to Samuel Smith of CC, for $1463, 418 A on Cobb Cr & S Hico adj Thomas Jeffreys, Mitchel, Henry Royster, George Johnson, Wm. Trotter. 28 Apr 1814. Wit: H. Haralson, Jesse Bradsher, A. Haralson.

455-6 John Durham of CC to John Harris of Person Co., for $1200, 179 A on S Hico adj Solomon Draper, George Tap, Thomas Jeffreys, Arthur Leath. 23 Jan 1816. Wit: Solomon Draper.

456 John Durham to Churchwell Jones both of Person Co., for $300, 200 A on Bushey Fork adj Caleb Jacobs, Charles Allison, Norfleet. 22 Dec 1815. Wit: B. W. Milner, John Jones.

456-7 Moses Fuller to Charles B. Winstead, for $100, 41 A on S Hico on Leasburg Rd adj John Clixby, William Satterfield, Samuel Wheeler. 28 Dec 1815. Wit: James Williamson, Aaron Fuller.

457 Herndon Haralson, an exec of Paul Haralson decd; James Haralson & David Haralson of State of TN; Jonathan Haralson of State of GA; & Paul Haralson of the Illinois Territory - to Abner Haralson of Person Co., for $667, 81 A both sides Marlowe Cr in fork of Stories Cr & Adams Cr adj William Allin, Larkin Brooks, Isham Edwards, John Rogers, George Rogers. _ _ 1815. Wit: Smith Murphey, Jonathan Haralson. Proved by eath H. Haralson for himself & as atty for others.

458 Herndon Haralson & Abner Haralson, exec last will of Paul Haralson decd, in their own right, James Haralson, Paul Haralson, Jonathan Haralson, David Haralson, all heirs of the decd - to Larkin Brooks, for $2434, 456 A both sides Adams Cr adj heirs of Barnett, Thomas Web, William Allin, Isham Edwards, Hugh Woods on Hams Br. Herndon Haralson & Abner Haralson sign as atty for others named above. 13 Oct 1815. Wit: Thomas Webb, Jno Dillahey, Jno Morgan.

458-9 Harris M. Barnett & Hugh Barnett both of Davidson Co., KY, to James Barnett & John Barnett of Person Co., for $2990, 299 A on Adams Cr adj Thomas Webb, said Barnett, Larkin Brooks, Hugh Woods, Saml Smith - it being all the land left them by their father Hugh Barnett and their grandfather Hugh Barnett Sen. 1 Jan 1816. Wit: Burd Stone, Benj Chambers.

459 Joseph Rice to Reuben P. Comer, for $185, 74 A on S Hico on Leasburg Rd. 30 Jan 1816. Wit: Abner Lea.

459-60 William Brown to Samuel Brown, for 102 lbs, 102 A n side Double Cr of Hico adj James Cochran formerly Wm. Waite, Wm. Brown formerly Jno Broadaway, Jno Farmer formerly Jno McMurry. 12 Feb 1816. Wit: ___ Rainey.

460 Thomas Duty to Nicholas Thompson of CC, for $50, 231 A on S Hico Which is all the undivided share of land of Richard Duty decd late of Granville Co. who devised this tract be sold (except part James Williamson claims) when youngest child is 21 yrs & money div between all children; youngest child is Sarah Harris wife of Willis Harris now of full age; testator left 10 children: George Duty, Richd Duty, Nancy Duty who is decd, Susannah Duty, Benjamin Duty, Thomas Duty, Jabez Duty, Rachel Duty; Elizabeth Duty, Saml Duty, Sarah Duty. 5 Sept 1814. Wit: Robert Johnston, John W. Graves.

Deed Book D
Page
461 State of NC - #131 - to Laurence V. Hargis, for 50/ per 100 A, 73½ A on Flat R adj Josiah Brown, Solomon Cate, Willis Nichols, Lemuel Sneed. Entered 25 Feb 1811. Registered 27 Apr 1812.

461 Div land of Thomas Lipscomb decd - allotment privously made to widow. Five lots of 30 A each to : Geoffra Lipscomb, Matilda Lipscomb, Louisa Lipscomb, Emma Lipscomb, Benion Lipscomb. 31 Oct 1815. Commrs: John Rice, Philip J. Echols, William A. Lea, Carter Lea, James Dollarhide.

461-2 Allotment to Fannie Heggie widow of James Heggie decd who owned 500 A - 166 2/3 A on Adams Cr including dwelling house adj Chas Mitchel, on side of the mountain, Manly Winstead. 27 Oct 1815. Acknd in open court.

462 Allotment to Judith Brown widow of Alfred Brown decd 34 1/6 A with dwelling house adj John Moore; total of 100 A owned by Brown. 29 Jan 1816. Wit: Wm. McKissack, sheriff.

463 John Gooch (in debt to Portius Moore adm of John Gooch decd for $238.52) to Bentley Epperson, in trust, for 25¢, all right & title to estate of his father John Gooch Sen. decd; all livestock. 21 Sept 1815. Wit: L. V. Hargis, Richison Nichols.

463-4 Bentley Epperson, trustee, to Phillips Moore, for $172.50, all right & claim that John Gooch Junr. had in estate of his father Jno Gooch decd. 14 May 1816. Wit: L. V. Hargis, Jas Gooch.

464 Redford Gooch of Granville Co., one of the children & heir at law of John Gooch Senr decd, to Phillip Moore, for $70.20 & 1 dime, one undivided tenth part of 178 A on Flat R adj dower land of Nancy Barton, Robt Cate, Thomas Minchew; excepting the life estate of Judith Gooch widow John Gooch Senr decd. 23 Feb 1816. Wit: Mathias Nichols, Willis Nichols, L. V. Hargis.

465 Mary Jones of Nottoway Co., VA, one of the children & heir at law of John Gooch Senr decd, to Phillips Moore, for $70.20 plus 1 dime, one undivided tenth part of 178 A on Flat R adj dower of Nancy Barton, Robert Cate, Thomas Minchew, to the mill tract which was a grant to Thos Gipson from Earl Granville 2 May 1750 - excepting life estate of Judith Gooch, widow. 12 Mar 1816. Wit: J. B. Shaw, F. M. Cash.

465-6 Jos J. Gooch, one of the children & heir at law of John Gooch Senr decd, to Phillips Moore, for $70.20 plus 10¢, one undivided tenth part of 178 A on Flat R. 6 Feb 1815. Wit: L. V. Hargis, Redford Gooch.

466 Judith A. Reade, a child & heir at law of John Gooch Sen. decd, to Phillips Moore, for $70.20, one undivided tenth part of 178 A on Flat R. 26 Feb 1816. Wit: L. V. Hargis, Jos J. Gooch.

467 Ann Gooch, a child & heir at law of John Gooch Senr decd, to Phillips Moore, for $70.20, one undivided tenth part of 178 A on Flat R excepting estate right of Judith Gooch, widow. 26 Feb 1816. Wit: L. V. Hargis, Jos J. Gooch.

467-8 William Gooch of Nottaway Co., VA, a child & heir of John Gooch Senr decd, to Phillips Moore, for $70.20, one undivided tenth part of 178 A of John Gooch Senr decd excepting life estate of Judith Gooch, widow. 12 Mar 1816. Wit: J. B. Shaw, F. M. Cook.

468 Elijah Jacobs, Thomas Rimmer & Jemima Rimmer his wife, Caleb Jacobs, Polly Jacobs, Nancy Jacobs (widow of Benjamin Jacobs decd) & Moses Jacobs - all of Person Co.(and all heirs of Benjamin Jacobs decd) to James W. Hauxhurst of same, for $161.25, 100 A excepting 4 A already conveyed to Hawxhurst by Benjamin Jacobs in his lifetime. 14 Oct 1815. Wit: Jas Milner, Willis Horton.

468-9 William Gold to James Jordan of Lunenburg Co., VA, for $2327.50, 332½ A both sides S Hico on Henly Mill Cr adj William Trotter, Ebenr Whitehead, Archd Lipscomb, George Johnston - said land willed him by Joseph Gold. 17 Apr 1816. Wit: James Clay, Benjn Chambers.

469 William Gold to James Jordan of Lunenburg Co., VA, for $700, 200 A on Henly Mill Cr adj Thomas Grant, William Trotter, Atkinson, Roger Tillman. 17 Apr 1816. Wit: James Clay, Benjn Chambers.

469-70 James Osborn Jeffreys, James Peters, to Lewis Daniel, for $658, 120 A on Flat R & n side Richland Cr adj James Satterfield; also tract s side Flat R adj Tap, Jay old line. 28 Dec 1815. Wit: S. McKissack, David Jeffreys.
(No explanation as to name of James Peters on this deed.)

470 Benjamin Jacobs to James W. Hawxhurst, for $16.80, 4.8 A on Flat R adj N. Norfleet. 28 June 1813. Wit: A. Brown, B. W. Milner, John Brown.

471 John Mason to Henry Curtis, for $184.50, 41½ A on S Hico. 3 Mar 1816. Wit: R. P. Comer, Moses Fuller.

471 Joseph Rice to Henry Curtis, for $120, 40 A on S Hico. 3 Mar 1816. Wit: Uriah Newton, R. P. Comer.

472 Jno Womack & Saml Dickens, exec of Robert Dickens decd, to Lewis Ramsey, for $372.50, 372½ A on Castle Cr & Dishwater Cr adj Thomas Douglas former land, Bailey, Gentry, Deshazo. 13 Feb 1816. Wit: Wm. G. Cochran.

472 John Rice to Abner Lea, Richard Lea, & Benjamin Lea, for $60, 12 A on S Hico; also all estate right or claim John Rice has to said Leas. 3 Apr 1816. Wit: R. P. Comer, Daniel Sergent.

473 John Gebhard Cunow of Bethlehem, PA, by his atty Lewis D. Schweinitz, to John McMurry, for $400, 530 A on Serratt's spring br. 29 Apr 1816. Wit: Alex Murphey, J. Bagge.

473 George Waite atty in fact for William Waite of Bedford Co., TN, to James King of Person Co., for $245, 245 A on Aaron's Cr adj Robert Harris, Wm. Daniel, Baird. 17 Feb 1816. Wit: Thos Halliburton, Robt Halliburton.

473-4 John McMurry to James Snipes of Granville Co., for $1050, 350 A on Double Cr adj David Brechen, Wade, 3 May 1816. Wit: Saml Brown, Anderson Snipes.

474 Reuben Newton atty in fact for Rachel Ireland & guardian for Elizabeth Dinwiddie & William Dinwiddiw of Hardin Co., KY, to Charles Gregory of Person Co., for $300, 500 A on Adams Cr adj Edgerton, James Cochran, Paul Walters, Benjamin Towler. 13 Mar 1816. Wit: Ira Lea, Robt Wade.

475 George Waite, atty in fact for Wm. Waite of Bedford Co., TN, to Thomas Halliburton of Person Co., for $225, 300 A on Bluewing Cr adj John Halliburton, R. Harris, James Yancey. 15 Feb 1816. Wit: Wilie Jones, John C. Halliburton.

475 William Waite of Bedford Co., TN by his atty in fact George Waite to Moses Springfield, for $330, 330 A on Mayo Cr adj Moses Street, Gill, Winstead, Coleman. 21 Feb 1816. Wit: John Springfield, Frances Springfield.

475-6 George Waite, atty in fact for William Waite of Bedford Co., TN, to Lucy Jones, for $27, 27 A on Bluewing Cr adj her corner. 13 Feb 1816. Wit: Thos Halliburton Senr., John C. Halliburton.

476 John Clayton to Charles Gregory, for $81.25, 65 A on Mayo Cr adj Thomas Hood, Henry Day, Junr., Allin. _ _ 1811. Wit: Saml Blackwell, Robt Wade.

476-7 John W. Williams to William McKissack, for $3000, 2 tracts: 200 A adj John Man old line, Rose, James Cochran; 640 A adj John Pain, James Williamson, Browning old line, James Cochran, Saml Dickens - being total of 840 A deeded by Dempsey Moore to Benjamin Towler & sold by sheriff to John W. Williams. The CH lots &

Deed Book D
Page
476-7 cont - other private lots were taken from these tracts amounting to 7 A.
27 Mar 1816. Wit: Alex Winstead, Benj Chambers.

477 William Jeffreys to Samuel Mitchel, for $159, 159 A on Mayo Cr adj David
Allin, Thomas Hood, at rocky br. 22 Mar 1816. Wit: Benj Cnambers, Alex Winstead.

478 Lewis Wilkerson to Sharp Willingham, for $525, 185 A adj Baird, Chambers,
Burton, Eastwood. 14 Oct 1815. Wit: Robt Harris, Moses Chambers.

478 Jesse Bumpass to Jonas Parker of Granville Co., for $350, 125½ A on Tarr R
adj Dickens at Dickens rd, said Bumpass. 2 Apr 1816. Wit: Saml Bumpass Jr.,
J. Bumpass.

479 Alexander Cuningham to Jeremiah Dixon, for $3000, 216 A on Cain Cr of Hico
formerly owned by Jno Davey & part of tract conveyed by Joseph McCain to Cuningham; 78½ A on Hico n side road from red house to Dixon's bridge - total of 294½ A
adj Stephen Oliver, Warren, Dixon, Abram Dunaway, James McCain, Edmd Dixon Junr.,
Edmd Dixon Senr. 1 Apr 1816. Wit: Edmund Dixon, Jno Garner.

479 Robert H. Childers to Gabriel Fenn of Orange Co., NC, for $150, 50 A adj
Robert Hester, Wilson Jones, Wm. Mitchel. 17 Dec 1815. Wit: S. Cochran,
Wm. G. Cochran.

479-80 Robert Hamlett to John Hamlett, for $202.50, 40½ A on Wins Cr adj James
Daniel, Joseph Addison Hall, Thomas M. Hamlett, Robert Hamlett. 22 Jan 1816.
Wit: Jonathan Haralson, H. Haralson.

480 William Trotter to Thomas Trotter, for $500, 172½ A on Sergent's Cr adj
Arthur Leath, Solomon Draper, Edmundson, Joseph Royster, widow Draper. 4 Mar
1816. Wit: Jas Trotter, Benj Chambers.

480-1 Larkin Brooks to John Dillehay, for $655, 163.75 A on Adams Cr adj Thomas
Web, James Barnett on road from Bailey ford to Person CH. 30 Mar 1816.
Wit: Thomas Webb, Mary J. Webb.

481 Solomon Draper to Simeon Cochran, for $150, 100 A on Flat R adj Jas Taylor.
17 Sept 1815. Wit: Thomas Woods, William McKissack, Wm. G. Cochran.

481 Samuel Williams to Peggy Inscore of Granville Co., for $133 1/3, 133 1/3 A
on Cubb Cr adj William Oakley. 16 Sept 1815. Wit: M. McGehee, William Clemance.

482-4 Div lands of Charles Mitchell decd, 1318½ A on Adams Cr adj Wm. Jeffreys,
John McGehee, estate of James Heggie decd; also 196 A adj Jeffreys, James Layton.
Div to: widow Mary Mitchell 503 A & dwelling house adj Dinwiddie, Robt Southard;
2 tracts one of 1331 A & one of 196 A allotted to:
1. Edward Mitchell 196 A adj Lawrence Vanhook, Michael Dixon old line, John
    McGehee being the whole of tract 2.
2. Samuel Mitchell 222 A adj Hicks old line, Dinwiddie at Rosemary Cr.
3. Mary Russell 222 A adj Robert Southard, John Williams on Rosemary Cr.
4. Elijah Mitchell 222 A adj Joseph Southard.
5. Mathew Mitchell 222 A adj John Williams, John McGehee, William Jeffreys.
6. Martha Bailey 222 A adj Barnett old spring, John Williams.
7. Lucy Lawson 222 A adj Barnet, Jno McGehee, Heggie.
Total value $3976.50; value to each legatee $568.07. Those valued with more than
equal share must pay to others. Commrs: Benj Chambers, Thomas Webb, John Holloway, Mandly Winstead, Ish Edwards. 21 Nov 1815.

484-5 James Trotter to William Trotter, for $300, 200 A on Sergent Cr adj James
Henley, William Sergent, John Fuller. 12 Feb 1816. Wit: Thomas Watts, Benjn
Chambers.

485 Robert B. Scott atty for heirs of Joseph Tatom decd to Benjamin Tatom &
Charles Tatom of Person Co., for $456.13, 100¼ A on Bold Br adj both grantees.
12 June 1816. Wit: William Tatom, David Tatom.

133

486 Robert C. Scott, atty for heirs of Joseph Tatom decd to William Tatom of Person Co., $456.13, 100¼ A on Bold Br adj Benjamin Tatom, Charles Tatom. 12 June 1816. Wit: Abner Tatom, David Tatom.

487-8 Robert Paine & Polly Paine his wife of Giles Co., TN, to Samuel Gooch of Person Co., for $850, 331.7 A s fork Flat R being a part of land allotted to Robert Paine & Polly Paine from lands of William Cocke decd adj Robert Cates, Holeman Bradford old line, to Quarrel Cr, the Mansion tract. 26 Dec 1815. Wit: George Daniel, James Paine. In Giles Co., TN, Polly Paine examined apart from her husband & freely executed deed. Proved Aug 1816 Person Co.

488-9 Moses Bradsher to Thomas Lipscomb, for 108 lbs, 54 A adj Archibald Lipscomb, William Warren. 19 Dec 1815. Wit: Jesse Bradsher.

489-90 William Trotter to James Trotter, for $500, 170½ A on Sergent Cr adj James Stuart, Arthur Leath, Draper. 4 Mar 1816. Wit: Thomas Trotter, Benj Chambers.

490 James Stuart to William Trotter, for 85 lbs, 85 A on Hico adj said Trotter, widow Draper, James Hannah. 15 Apr 1816. Wit: James Trotter, Sterling Trotter.

491 Samuel Bumpass to William Philpot of Granville Co., for $450, 205½ A on Tar R adj Dickens. 2 Jan 1816. Wit: John W. Philpot, Jesse Bumpass.

491-2 Samuel Moore to John Sweaney Sen., for $300, 150 A on Deep Cr adj Sidney Moore, Grizey Moore, said Sweaney. 27 Aug 1812. Wit: Portius Moore, Mary Johnston.

492 Nathaniel Norfleet to treasurer of upper S Hico Church at Wheeley's Meeting House, for convenience of the church & meeting house, 5 A on which the house stands known as Wheeley Meeting House. 3 Feb 1816. Wit: Obediah Pearce, Benj Milner.

493 William Hughs to George Whitefield, for $325, 162 3/4 A on S Hico adj Galaugher, John Eskridge, McMullin, Lea, Vincent Lea. 9 Feb 1816. Wit: John Douglas, Loyd Vanhook.

494 John H. McNeill to James Williamson, for $300, 60 A adj James Jay Senr., said Williamson. _ May 1816. Wit: Isaac Satterfield, James Jay Senr.

494-5 Moses Bradsher to Thomas Lipscomb, for 186 lbs, 93 A on Cob Cr adj Elizabeth Johnston, William Warren, on road from Leasburg to confluence of N & S Hico, heirs of Thomas Lipscomb decd. 19 Dec 1815. Wit: Jesse Bradsher.

495-6 Allotment of dower to Leah Combs widow of Hiram Combs decd - one-third of 45 A on Ned Cr of S Hico adj Webb, Lipscomb. 29 July 1816.

496 Allotment of dower to Judith Gooch, widow of John Gooch decd - his plantation on Flat R of 565 A and she to get 178 A with dwelling house including mill tract adj Nancy Burton, Robert Cates, Thomas Minshew. 7 Mar 1815.

497-8 Div of land (292 A) of Daniel Sergent decd on both sides S Hico into 7 parts & each to have 41½ A: 1. Samuel Winstead, 2. Thos Lipscomb, 3. Stephen Sergent, 4. Delpha Sergent, 5. Daniel Sergent, 6. John Sergent, 7. Henry Sergent. Total value $1099.95. Commrs: Moses Fuller, Benjamin Lea, Abner Lea, James Dollarhide, John Rice. 9 Aug 1816.

498-9 Stephen Pleasant to Elijah Jacobs, for $736.25, 147¼ A both sides Neds Cr adj James McMurry, Joseph Carney, John Russell; also 18 A adj first tract. 23 Sept 1816. Wit: Lawrence Vanhook, Wm. Whitefield.

499-500 Stephen Smith of Rockingham Co., NC, to Lawrence V. Hargis of Person Co., for $15, ¼ undivided part of his father Conrad Messer Smith Jun's undivided one-fifth part of 306 A adj Duncan Cameron, Thomas Sneed, James Williamson. 4 Oct 1816. Wit: Thos Hargis, James Gooch.

500 Robert Cate Sen. to James Cochran Jun., for $17.40, 5.8 A w side n prong
Flat R. 12 Nov 1816. Wit: L. V. Hargis, James Gooche.

501 Stephen Messer Smith of Orange Co., NC, to Lawrence V. Hargis of Person Co.,
for $100, an undivided fifth part of 306 A adj Duncan Cameron, Thomas Sneed to
county line, James Williamson. 2 Oct 1816. Wit: Jacob Waggoner, Bentley
Epperson.

501-2 Reuben P. Comer to George Lea, for $259, 74 A on Cob Cr on Leasburg road.
16 Oct 1816. Wit: Abner Lea, Wm. Satterfield.

502-3 Benjamin Lea to Richard Lea Junr & George J. Lea, for $530, 106 A on Cob
Cr adj Richd Lea. 8 Oct 1816. Wit: Abner Lea, Wm. Frazer?.

503 Robert Moore to Robert Jones, for $15, 3½ A on Hico adj Drury Moore, said
Jones. 29 Nov 1815. Wit: John D. Moore, Thos Winstead.

504 Swepston Sims of Rutherford Co., TN, to Thomas Townsend of Person Co., for
$450, 393 A on Mayo Cr adj Gill, Yarbrough, Street, Dixon, Daniel. By John
Holloway, atty for Swepston Sims. 13 Aug 1816. Wit: Gab Davie, Crowder Holloway.

504-5 Robert Southward Senr. to Joseph Southward, for $50, 50 A on Adams Cr adj
Charles Mitchel, John Shelton. 10 June 1815. Wit: Paul Walters, Reuben Long Jun.

505-6 James Hannah to Thomas Edmondson, for $1300, 349½ A on Sergent Cr adj Mrs.
Draper, John Brann, Joseph Royster, Duncan, James Cameron, Robt Carver, William
Trotter - said tract formerly owned by William Sergent who sold to Archibald
Lipscomb & from him to James Hannah. 21 Sept 1816. Wit: Cary Williams,
John Bran.

506-7 Jeremiah Dixon to Edmund Dixon Jun, for $340, 34 A on Cain Cr adj both men.
14 Nov 1816. Acknd in open court.

507-8 Jacob Couch (in debt to Reuben Long for $80) to Thomas Webb, in trust, for
5/, 40½ A on Stories Cr adj Jacob Bull, James Long, Josias Carver, Polly Graves -
it being lot #5 allotted Couch in div lands of Henry Graves decd. 18 Mar 1816.
Wit: Saml Smith, Thos Webb Jr.

508 Abner Lea & Benjamin Lea relinquish to their brother Richard Lea all right
& claim to 106 A on Cobb Cr where Richard Lea now lives; in return Richard Lea
to relinquish his claim for all lots of land assigned for other land. _ _ 1816.
Wit: John Douglas, Moses Bradsher.

509 Richard Lea & Benjamin Lea relinquish to their brother Abner Lea all right
& claim to 2 tracts: 66½ A where Abner Lea lives adj Benjn Lea at Cob Cr; also
39½ A adj Benj Lea on road to Leasburg; total of 106 A. 2 Oct 1816.
Wit: John Douglas, Moses Bradsher.

510 Power of attorney - Solomon Paine of Smith Co., TN, to Lawrence V. Hargis to
make lawful deed to tract of land on Richland Spring Cr. 27 July 1816.
Wit: William Gregory, Peter Hood, Joel Dyer Jun.

510-1 Abraham Davis of Orange Co., NC, to John Carrington, merchant of same, for
500 lbs, 750 A on little Cr adj Glenn, Moses Moore, Dickens, Evans to county line,
Frazer. 23 Dec 1795. Wit: Alex McMullen, John Knight, Andrew Smith.

511-12 Arthur Moore of CC to John Carrington of Orange Co., for 500 lbs, 2050 A
on Nap of Reed on Granville Co. line adj Jacob Cozart, Abraham Maderias, David
Roberts, Thomas Yockley. 14 Oct 1788. Wit: Alexr McMullen, John Knight.
Proved by oath John Knight 2 Aug 1816.

512-3 Thomas Badget Senr to James Rimmer, for $191.50, 78 A on Double Cr of
Hico adj William McKissack, Jones. 21 Dec 1816. Wit: Will McKissack, John
Roberts.

513 James Broach & John Malone to John Crisp of CC, for 100 lbs, 100 A on S Hyco at Grier Cr adj William Mitchel, Wilson Jones, Reuben Taylor. 3 Sept 1812. Wit: Jos Taylor, Jos Hargis. Proved Feb 1817 by oath Jos Hargis.

514-5 William Hobson (in debt to James Warrin for $1247.12) to Benjamin Adams of Halifax Co., VA, in trust, for $1, 112 A in Person Co. on VA line near Brooks old school house adj William McGehee, Bluford; also slaves Sam about 25 yrs old, woman Moll about 60 yrs, Sarah about 37 yrs, girl Tabby about 12, Judy about 3. 8 Feb 1817. Wit: John Rogers, Saml Adams.

515-6 Edmund Dixon Senr to Henry Dixon, for $300, 57 A on Sergent Cr adj Charles Sallard. 4 Feb 1817. Wit: Joel Boulton, Ransom S. Austin, Edmund Dixon Jr., William Dixon.

516 Edmund Dillahay to James Woody (or Moody), for 575 lbs, 182½ A on Castle Cr of Hyco adj McFarling, Moses Walker, Mager Green, John Rogers. 4 Feb 1817. Wit: John Dillahay.

517 William S. Branch to William Irvine of State of VA, for $9000, 740 A on N Hico adj Archibald Murphey, William McGehee, William Dixon, Thomas Jeffreys, John Campbell. 25 Oct 1816. Wit: James Rainey, Tho Jeffreys.

517-8 Thomas Badget Senr to William McKissack Sen., for $47, 21½ A on double creeks on road to Cochran mill adj David Hunt. 21 June 1814. Wit: John Bradsher, William Badget, Jas Rimmer.

518-9 Joseph B. Shaw & Martha Shaw his wife of Orange Co., - said Martha Shaw being a child & heir of John Gooche decd - to Phillips Moore, for $70.20, an undivided tenth part of tract on n bank Flat R adj Nancy Burton, Robert Cates, Thos Minshew to a mill tract (granted by Earl Granville to Thos Gibson) - total land 178 A excepting life estate of Judith Gooche decd widow of John Gooche. 26 Feb 1816. Wit: Thos Sneed, Thos V. Hargis.
Martha Shaw connot travel to Person Court; when commrs find it convenient to examine her, report made to Court. Certificate registered on page 522.

520 Robartus Carney to Jno G. Willson & Co. of Leasburg, CC, for $153, 51 A on S Hico in Person Co. & Rushey Br adj meeting house lot at Carney line, Wm. Carney, Kindle Vanhook. 16 Aug 1816. Wit: Daniel Darby, Isaac Satterfield.

521 Robartus Carney to Jno G. Willson & Co. of Leasburg, CC, for $1347, 462 A on Cob Cr adj Lawrence Vanhook, Thomas Douglas, Daniel Gold tract known by name of Kilbraick tract. 16 Aug 1816. Wit: Daniel Darby, Isaac Satterfield.

522 Martha Shaw wife of Joseph B. Shaw in private examination agrees to conveyance of her title to deed between her husband & Phillips Moore. 21 Dec 1816. Wit: L. V. Hargis, Thos Sneed.

522 James Jay Jr. to Benjamin W. Milner, for $500, 90½ A on S Hyco adj James Cochran mill cr, Duncan Rose. 16 Oct 1816. Wit: John Nichols, Moore Lawson, Chs Holdman.

523 John Cocke of Chatham Co., NC, to Abraham Moore of Person Co., for $315, 420 A on Flat R adj Henry Womack, Thos Hargis. 29 Nov 1816. Wit: John W. Williams, James Williamson.

523-4 Roger Atkinson of Olive Hill, Chesterfield Co., VA, to George Wade of Person Co., for 306 lbs, 102 A s side Hico R at mouth of Marley Cr adj John Baily, estate of Josiah Dickson, Alexander Cuningham - being the part of Chambers tract including 6 A lowlands on n side Hico. 7 June 1816. Wit: James Jones, Benjn Adams.

524 Robert Cochran to Stephen Wells, for $95, 100 A on Flat R adj said Wells, Saml Rimmer, Ephraim Hawkins. 9 Aug 1815. Wit: John Burch, Wm. Farquhar.

525-6 Andrew B. Wood, Isaac D. Vanhook, George Darby, Samuel Self, Thomas Oakley , Gabriel Davey,.Aaron Vanhook, Ann Vanhook, Jane Vanhook, & Henry Lipscomb - to Henry Lipscomb, for $790.86, 196 A adj Vincent Lea, John McMurray, Wade, Lipscomb, Jacob Thomas. 20 Oct 1816. Wit: William Lipscomb, James McMullen, James McMurry.

526-7 Solomon Paine of Smith Co., TN, to Benjamin Jones of Person Co., for $850, 1109½ A on Richland & Tapley Cr being part of land left by his father Robt Paine adj James Saterfield, James Milner, Saml Dickens, William Hicks, Marcus Oakley, Joel Hicks, George Woods. By L. V. Hargis, atty. 9 Jan 1817.
Wit: Phillips Moore, James Gooche.

527 Carter Lea Sen. to Ira Lea, for $5, 1 A where Carter Lea lives both sides Richland Cr adj both men. 13 Jan 1816. Wit: Carter Lea Jun.

528 Samuel P. Ashe to John Crisp of CC, for $1000, 640 A both sides s fork Double Cr adj Edmund Burch, Childers, Robert Hester, Brookes, McNeel, George Broache, Guthrie Jones, Drury Jones, A. Gray, Nancy McKissack, Norfleet, Taylor - excepting 60 square feet reserved by Mr. Jones for graveyard. 14 Dec 1815.
Wit: Thos Slade, Churchwell Jones.

529 John Halliburton to Thomas Brown of Granville Co., for 110 lbs, 200 A on little Blue Wing Cr adj Baird. 9 Mar 1816. Wit: James King, Moses Cotnam.

529-30 Ira Lea, trustee for Benja Jopling decd (who in his life conveyed to Ira Lea 2 tracts to secure sum due James Williamson) to Thos V. Hargis, for $140, 150 A on Flat R adj Persons, Douglas, Gately, Peter Farrar, Richd Jacobs; the other 50 A on Flat R. 28 Sept 1816. Wit: John Hudgins.

530-1 Henly Gibson, William Brooks & wife to John James Brooks, for $30, 22 A on Dry Br adj James Holloway, Lewis Ramsay. 20 Nov 1816. /s/ for wife is Cathy Brooks. Wit: James B. Buchanon, Jesse Munday.

531-2 Joseph Jones of Cedar Grove, Dinwiddie Co., VA; Roger Atkinson of Olive Hill, Chesterfield Co., VA; Thomas Atkinson, & Robert Atkinson of Dinwiddie Co - all heirs at law of the late Roger Atkinson - recovered 585 A on Castle Cr in Person Co. from Francis Brooks, John James Brooks & Wiley Brooks children of Woody Brooks decd and said land was conveyed to Atkinson by Thomas Douglas in 3 deeds recorded in CC (now Person); 2 lots on 25 Oct 1780 and 1 on 20 Dec 1780 - to Ann Ponsonby their sister, for love & affection, the Atkinsons release all right & title to said land. 3 Aug 1816. Wit: John A. Jones, William D. Hood, William Atkinson, Alexr Cunningham.

532-3 Ann Ponsonby of Dinwiddie Co., VA, to James Holloway of Person Co., for $1053, 3 tracts in Person Co. purchased by Roger Atkinson her father of Thomas Douglas - said land conveyed to her by deed from heirs of Roger Atkinson.
25 Sept 1816. Wit: Alex Cunningham, Thos Atkinson, Jno Verell.

533 John H. McNeill to Aaron Scoggin, for $375, 92 A,1 rod & 10 perches adj Cochran. 1 May 1816. Wit: James Jay Sen., Isaac Satterfield.

534 Samuel Smith of Person Co. to James C. Smith, trustee, of CC, for $1300 which he owes James C. Smith, a tract adj Nich Thompson, Wm. Hughs, 13 Jan 1816.
Wit: H. L. Villines, W. Smith.

534-5 Loyd Vanhook to his son, Lawrence Vanhook, for parental affection, 50 A on middle prong Rushy Br adj Kindal Vanhook, Vincent Lea, George Lea, John Newton, to meeting house tract. 13 Feb 1815. Proved by oaths of Nathl Norfleet, Robt Vanhook, Abner Bradsher that handwriting of signer is Loyd Vanhook.

535-6 Thomas Webb of Granville Co. to George Briggs of same, for $1350, 729 A on Flat R on n side road from Norfleet to High Rock (Hauxhurst corner), Hawkins, Allen. 23 Nov 1816. Wit: B. W. Milner, Nathl Norfleet.

Deed Book D
Page

536-40 Div land of Peter Alldridge decd on Flat R & Bird's Cr, surveyed 13 Dec
1816 by Phillips Moore CS (county surveyor) - 11 div to:
1. John Alldridge 20½ A adj Abraham Moore, Wm. Blalock, James Farquhar.
2. David Allridge 19.75 A adj Blalock.
3. Catherine Alldridge 22 A adj Blalock.
4. George Berry & Susannah 19 A adj Blalock.
5. Joseph Alldridge 12.75 A adj Isham Alldridge, Jas Farquhar.
6. Peter Alldridge 12¼ A adj Isham Alldridge.
7. Jenny (or Janey) Alldridge 12¼ A adj Isham Alldridge.
8. Lilly Alldridge (or Uley) 23 A adj Isham Alldridge, Bird.
9. James Farquhar & Polly Farquhar 13 A adj Isham Alldridge on Bird's Cr.
10. Betsy Alldridge 17 A on Bird's Cr adj Isham Alldridge, Cummins.
11 Sally Alldridge 17.75 A adj Isham Alldridge, John Cummins, Dickens.
Total value $966.87½. Commrs: Obediah Pearce, Samuel Sneed, John   ? .

541-2 John H. McNeill to James Cochran, for $350, his undivided part of two
tracts including one-fourth of the whole of his father John McNeill who died
intestate: 400 A adj Lawrence Vanhook, Edwd Clay, Cochran, Anderson old line,
said tract conveyed to John McNeill by Thomas McNeill; 120½ A conveyed to John
McNeill by Robt Dickens adj William Waite, now Cochran, the mill tract, Andrew
Caldwell old line, James Paine, former line William Lea, William Brown.
John McNeill decd left 4 sons: Hosea McNeill, William L. McNeill, John H.
McNeill, George McNeill - the only heirs under the then existing laws; widow
is entitled to 1/3 of said land for her life and this deed includes one-fourth
part of widow's dower which is now in possession of James Cochran in right of
his wife who is widow of John McNeill decd. 30 Mar 1811.
Wit: William A. Lea, Betsey Hargis.

542-3 William L. McNeill to James Cochran, for $350, his undivided one-fourth
part of land of his father John McNeill decd plus ½ part of widow's dower.
(See previous deed for full description.). 3 Apr 1809. Wit: Carter Lea,
William A. Lea.

543-4 Samuel Dickens to Marcus Oakley, for $300, 150 A both sides Tapley Cr adj
John Hicks to public road, Miller. 28 Sept 1815. Wit: William Hicks, John Hicks.

544-5 Samuel Dickens to John Hicks, for $235, 117½ A both sides Tapley Cr adj
Williamson, Davis or Traylor. 11 Nov 1815. Wit: William Hicks, Anth° Brown.

545-6 Elizabeth Cates of Orange Co. to Laurence Vanhook Hargis of Person Co., for
$40, all her right & claim to an undivided tract left by her late father Conrad
Messer Smith to be div equally to her & other children; total of 306 A on Flat R
adj Thos Sneed, Duncan Cameron, James Williamson. 31 Aug 1815.
Wit: Thos Wilson, Thomas V. Hargis.

546-7 Ira Lea, trustee, for Elijah Day for debt due James Williamson, to
Laurence V. Hargis, for $350, 104.7 A on still house br of Flat R adj William
Daniel, Rountree, Holeman, Cocke, Taylor. Wit: Stephen Dickens, Francis
Epperson. Acknd in open court.

547-8 James Williamson to Solomon Clayton, for $150, 92 A on Stories Cr adj
Sampson M. Glenn, John Fuller, Richd Hamlin, William Hamblen. 15 Mar 1817.
Wit: Ira Lea.

548 Samuel McMurry to Thomas Snipes, for $552.25, 124½ A adj Womack, Ba¹ Hays.
27 Feb 1817. Wit: Samuel Brown, David Hunt.

549 Laurence V. Hargis to Francis Epperson, for $350, 104.7 A s prong Flat R at
still house br adj William Daniel, Rountree, Holeman, Cocke, Taylor. 4 Mar 1817.
Wit: Bentley Epperson, James Gooch.

549-50 Jesse Dickens to Samuel Webb, for love & affection, 300 A on Deep Cr adj Dempsey Clayton, said Dickens, Downey, John Bumpass & including the mill. 29 Mar 1817. Acknd in open court.

550 Thomas Badgett Sen. to John Penn, for $300, 146 A adj William McKissack Senr, David Hunt, Rebecca Pain, Rimmer. 17 Dec 1816. Wit: David Hunt, Samuel Brown.

550-1 James Farquhar to William Blalock, for $200, 113 A on Flat R adj Peter Aldridge, Abraham Moore. 22 Apr 1817. Wit: J. Rountree, Jno Rountree.

551-2 John Hargis to his son Richard Hargis a gift of 60 A on Stories Cr adj Wm. Carver, James Williamson, John Hudgens. /s/ John Harris. Wit: John Hudgins, William Clayton. NB Note on side of page: In this deed the name Hargis is altered to Harris.

552 John Johnston, carpt, to John Vanhook Jr. of Orange Co., for $350, 100 A on S Hico adj Moses Bradsher, James Cochran, Robert Vanhook, Loyd Vanhook - it being same tract sold to John Johnston, carpt, by John Vanhook. 10 Dec 1815. Wit: James Clay.

552-3 William Fuller to Asa Fuller, for $203.50, 37 A on Richland Cr of S Hico adj James Williamson, James Bradsher, Richd Atkinson, near Haw Br. 18 Apr 1817. Wit: Moses Fuller.

553-4 William McKissack to James Cochran, for $200, .2 A being part of tract purchased of John W. Williams adj Cochran; 8 A near CH adj Duncan Rose, Cochran, formerly Brooks. 19 Apr 1816. Wit: Benjn Chambers, Thos Worsham.

555-6 George McNeill to James Cochran, for $392, his undivided one-fourth part of two tracts left by his father John McNeill. 15 Sept 1812. (See pages 541-2 for same description of land & relatives.). 15 Sept 1812. Wit: Samuel Pittard, Addison Cochran.

556-8 Hosea McNelll of CC to James Cochran of Person Co., for $350, his undivided one-fourth part of land left by his father John McNeill. 3 May 1809. (See pages 541-2 for same description of land & relatives.). Wit: David Barker, John H. McNeill.

558-9 Phillip Day to Ambrose Day, for $? , 100 A on Deep Cr adj Bumpass, Bedwell Satterfield, John Satterfield. ND 1817. Wit: John Day Junr.; proved May 1817.

559 Samuel Mitchell to Gabriel Bailey, for $125, 222 A on Adams Cr & Rosemary Cr adj Dunwoody. 14 May 1817. Wit: John Vanhook.

560 Joseph Hubbard Sen. to George Woods, for $422.50, 160 A adj Joseph Lunsford, Joel Hicks, Jones. 13 Aug 1816. Wit: Jesse Bumpass, Matthew Daniel.

561-2 Squire Sheerman b Jacob Cozart, for $66.50, all his right to the dower right of land whereon Christiana Johnson formerly lived which Sheerman purchased of Benjn Partee adj Dickens, at Pine Meadows, on dividing line between Johnson & the legatees - total of 96 A; deed effective during life of Christiana Johnson widow of Joshua Johnson decd & no longer. 4 Mar 1814. Wit: Wm. McKissack, Hubbard Cozart.

END OF BOOK D

Jesse Dickens, CCC (Clerk
County Court)
/s/ Benja W. Milner PR
(Public Register)

413

State of Carolina
Pearson County

Know all men by these presents that I Peavy
Clark of S. County have this day for these considerations of the
sum of five hundred dollars to me in hand paid by
Nicholas Thompson have bargained and sold to him the
S Thompson two negroes warranty by the name of Nancy & her child
Smith 2 & S. Peavy Covenant warrant & secure unto the
Thompson title of the 8 negroes to him & his & his Successors
have this 29th day of Janry AD 1821.

Peavy Clark

J. M. Dickins Nancy 17 years old

State of Carolina
Pearson County

1821. The Execution
of this title of sale was duly proven in Court by the
Oath of Stephen all Dickins a Subscribing witness thereto
to be registered

Page

1. James Cochran to William Clayton, for $500, 150 A on Rosemary Cr adj William Southward former line, John Dinwiddie former line - said land conveyed to Ambrose Hudgins by State, then to Francis Scoggins, and to Cochran. 12 Feb 1816. Acknd in open court.

1-2 Henry McNeill to Hector McNeill of Dinwiddie Co., VA, for $800, 2000 A on S Hico being grant from State to Alexander Caerns, then conveyed to John Smith & by him to Henry McNeill. 5 Dec 1816. Wit: Wm. McKissack, Nathl Norfleet.

2-3 Jesse Dickens & Frances his wife (she being a child & legatee of General Stepehn Moore) to Phillips Moore, for $300, 280 2/5 A , said land allotted to her by court in div land - on Deep Cr of Flat R adj Phillips Moore, Sidney Moore, Cozart or Sweaney, Gooch. 12 Feb 1817. Wit: Thos Sneed, Carter Atkinson. Frances Dickens appeared in court & privately consented to said conveyance.

3-4 Duncan Rose to Stephen Pleasant, for $311.80, 159½ A on Hico adj Vanhook, Pittard, Snipes, Jones, Lipscomb formerly widow Vanhook, Thomas, Brooks. 26 Dec 1816. Wit: John Pittard, Abner Bradsher.

4a William Lawson and Lucy his wife of Rockingahm Co., NC, to Elijah Mitchel of Person Co., for $1350, 222 A on Adams Cr being lot #7 in div land of Charles Mitchel and allotted them as heirs adj Barnett, John McGehee, Heggie. 14 May 1817. Wit: Ira Lea, Gab Davie. Lucy Lawson examined apart from husband and freely executed deed.

5 Div land of John Sweaney Senr decd to heirs:
   1. Edy Sweaney the homestead tract 112 A adj Saml Moore, William Person on Flat R.
   2. 137 A purchased of S. Moore to Joel Sweaney adj Sidney Moore, Richd Stanford.
   3. 86¼ A to Robt Sweaney Jr. adj Sidney Moore, Cozart.
   4. Henry Sweaney 247½ A north end Rocky Fork adj Levi Sweaney, Saml Dickens.
   5. Marit Sweaney 153½ A on s end Rocky Fork adj stone quarry, Levi Sweaney.
   6. Not in lottery - As Marit Sweaney already possesses lot #3 at his father's death, above allotted so as not to dispossess him.
   7. Jane Sweaney 277½ A adj George Burch or Mitchell, Thos Felps.
Commrs: Jesse Evnas, Robt Moore, James Cochran; each paid $24 for 8 days' work; to Phillips Moore for survey 8 days' work $16 plus $7 to make plots. 25 Jan 1817.

8 On 8 Feb 1809 John Sweaney bound to Nathaniel Carrington for $400 to make right & title to land whereon Levi Sweaney lives. Wit: Marit Sweaney, Bennett Williams. On 15 May 1815 for value recd, Nathaniel Carrington assigns this bond to Lawrence V. Hargis as John Sweaney is decd & Portius Moore is him adm; court ordered deed written to Nathl Carrington.

8-9 John Carrington Sen. of Orange Co. to Hubbard Cozart of Granville Co., for 500 lbs, 250 A on Nap of Reed Cr on Granville Co. line adj Jacob Cozart, Abraham Meadows, David Roberts, Thos Oakley. 24 Aug 1815. Wit: John J. Carrington, Benja Cozart.

9-10 Joseph McGehee to William McGehee, for $1256, 157 A on N Hico adj both men. 6 Sept 1816. Wit: Jno M. McGehee, James Rainey, Thos McGehee.

10 Cary Williams to Currie Barnett, for $201, 40 A adj John Dickson, Byrd Pulliam, John Williams. 12 June 1817. Acknd in open court.

10-1 William Marshall of Brunswick Co., VA, to his son Lackey Marshall of Person Co., for love & affection & 42 lbs 10/, 162½ A on S Hico at Mitchel mill adj James Broache, NcNealy, Roberts. 31 Mar 1817. Wit: Isaac Rainey, Jesse Kirk.

Deed Book E
Page

11-2 Jesse Dickens to Demsey Clayton, for $527½, 105½ A on Deep Cr adj Portius
Moore. 13 Mar 1817. Wit: James Clayton.

12 William Boswell to Andrew Buchanan, for $263, 108 A on Castle Cr adj Robert
Huston old line, Charles Bostick old line. 4 Jan 1817. Wit: Robt Wade,
Simon Gentry.

12-4 Allen Williams & Elizabeth his wife, Willis Harris & Sarah his wife of
Granville Co. to James Williamson of Person Co., for $180, their undivided part
of land of Richard Duty decd of Granville Co. who willed 175 A in Person Co. on
S Hico adj James Dollarhide to be sold when youngest child in 21 yrs. Youngest
child is Sarah Harris now of full age; legatees: George Duty, Richd Duty,
Nancy Duty who is decd before this deed, Susanna Duty, Benja Duty, Thomas Duty,
Jabez Duty, Richd Duty, Elizabeth Duty, Samuel Duty, Sarah Duty. 4 Sept 1816.
Wit: John Lemay, John Thomas. Said wives were examined in private and each
voluntarily signed contract.

14-5 Jabez Duty & Samuel Duty of Granville Co. to James Williamson, for $200,
their undivided share of land of Richard Duty decd of Granville Co. 4 Sept 1816.
Wit: John Thomas, Willis Harris.

15 Samuel McMurray to James McMurray, for $260, 90 A. _ Mar 1817. Wit: Jos
McMurray, Henry Womack.

16 John Mason to William Royster, for $35, 10½ A on Cobb Cr of Hycho adj McFar-
land Oakley, Barnet Lea. 16 Oct 1816. Wit: Henry Royster, Frances Royster,
McFarland Oakley.

16-7 David Jeffreys to Duncan Cameron of Orange Co., for $2500, 320½ A both sides
n fork Flat R at Tapley Cr adj Cameron, formerly Elizabeth Jeffreys, Mrs.
McKissack, dower land from Paul Jeffreys decd - it being that part of land where
Paul Jeffreys died & was allotted to said David Jeffreys as lot #1. 23 June 1817.
Wit: L. V. Hargis, Bentley Epperson. Money recd for same 23 June 1817.

18 Hugh Darby to Thomas Jeffreys, for $430, 86 A on Cobb Cr adj Reuben Grinstead,
Jeffreys. 4 Nov 1816. Wit: Geo W. Jeffreys, Geo M. Wilson, James Rainey.

18-9 Mary Currie to Hasten Bartlett, for $400, 200 A on S Hico adj Woods, Rainey,
Ellison, Cochran. 16 Oct 1815. Wit: B. W. Milner, Thos Woods.

19 Nicholas Thompson of CC to James Williamson of Person Co., for $147, two-tenth
of 175 A left by Richard Duty decd on S Hycho adj James Dollarhide, John Rice,
heirs of David Vanhook, said Williamson. Shares are those of Thos Duty & Richd
Duty sons of Richd Duty decd. 11 Jan 1816. Wit: J. G. Wilson, Peter Weir.

19-20 Samuel Garrott to Thomas Westbrook, for $237, 104 A on Richland Cr of S
Hycho & was conveyed to him by Thos McNeill adj Moses Fuller. 7 Mar 1816.
Wit: R. Atkinson, Thomas Byasee.

20-1 Samuel Garrott to Jesse Westbrook of Mecklenburg Co., VA, for $163, 60 A
n side Richland Cr of S Hyco adj Thos Westbrook. 9 Mar 1816. Wit: R. Atkinson,
Thos Byasee.

21-2 Drury A. Pulliam to Isham Edwards, for $500, 100 A on Story's Cr adj James
Long, Robt Brooks, John Brooks, Carver, McKissack. 12 Nov 1817. Wit: W. Jeffreys.

22 Nicholas Hester to George Broach, for 100 lbs, 100 A on Double Creeks adj
John Crisp. 11 Nov 1817. Wit: Nathl Norfleet, Elijah Hester.

23 Thomas Edmondson to John Brand, for $81.73, 4.75 A on Gents Cr & Sergent Cr
at Leasburg Rd. adj Solomon Draper; also 22½ A on Leasburg Rd adj said Brand,
Joseph Royster & is part of tract purchased of James Hannah. 27 Feb 1817.
Wit: James Hannah, Benja Chambers.

142

Deed Book E
Page

23-4 Ebenezer Whitehead to Williamson & Lea, for $500, 130 A on S Hyco adj Ira Lea, Charles Winstead, Saml Winstead, James D. Hendlie, William Gould. 20 Nov 1816. Wit: Robt Wade, John W. Williams.

24-5 Robert Stanfield Jr. of Oglethorpe Co., GA, to John Stanfield Sen. of Halifax Co., VA, for $150, 40 A n side Hyco it being his part as one of the 4 legatees of William Stanfield decd of Person Co. adj Wm. Hobson, Wm. McGehee, Thos McGehee, James Franklin. 18 Feb 1817. Wit: Harrison Stanfield, Ephraim Standfield, Thos Brandon, Jarrel Powell.

25-6 William McKissack, trustee for Jesse Watson Senr decd, to James Clay, for $363.50, 202½ A on Richland & Stories Creeks. 13 Nov 1817. Acknd in open court.

26 Benjamin W. Milner to John Allen, for $400, 100 A on Flat R adj Robt Blalack, George Briggs; reserving 3 A around the grave of Richd Hargis decd & reserved as property of Jane Hargis. 7 Apr 1817. Wit: John Scoggin.

27 Caleb Jacobs to William Norris, for $175, 76 A on S Hyco adj Wheely meeting house br at Daniel Malone's fence, Baylor Burch. _ Oct 1817. Wit: Nathl Norfleet, Thos Badget.

27-8 David Jeffreys to Duncan Cameron of Orange Co., for $200, 105 A adj dower line of the widow of Paul Jeffreys decd, Cameron; it being lot #1 of second quality land allotted to him by County Court. 14 Nov 1817. Wit: Jesse Evans, L. V. Hargis.

28-9 Williamson & Lea to Roger Tilman, for $130, 51 A on Mill Cr adj said Tilman, Wheeley. 27 May 1817. Wit: Robt. Wade.

29 Robert H. Childers to Laurence Richardson, for $150, 30 A adj Downey Wade, formerly Martha Richardson. 23 Aug 1817. Wit: John Douglas, Robt. Jones.

30 Thomas Edmondson to Benjamin Moore, for $350, 100 A on Sergent's Cr adj Thomas Maret, Robert Carver on Clay Rd & Leasburg Rd, John Brann. 24 July 1817. Wit: James Hannah, Benj Chambers.

30-1 John Walters & Lucy Walters his wife of Orange Co.; Charles Eastwood & Sarah Eastwood of Granville Co.; Elizabeth Denny, Nancy Denny, & Thos Denny of Person Co. - to Josiah Wade, for $200, 100 A on Donaldson's Cr adj Meredith Daniel, Thos Person. 15 Apr 1816. Wit: John Day, Ambrose Day. Lucy Walters & Sarah Eastwood examined apart from their husbands & freely consented to conveyance.

32 John Rountree b Samuel Evans of Wilson Co., TN, for $1200, 200 A on Flat R adj Robert Cates, Junr. 23 July 1817. Wit: Thos Rountree, Thos Evans, Jesse Evans.

33 Douglas Fulcher to Terrel Fulcher, for $300, 128 A on Mitchel Br of Cob Cr adj Hugh Darby, William Rainey, John Mason, Henry Royster. 8 Sept 1817. Wit: Lewis Amis, Shartah Amis.

33-4 Jacob Couch to James Long, for $202.50, 40½ A adj Drewry A. Pulliam, Nancy Graves - it being allotted to his wife Martha Couch in div land of Henry Graves decd. 11 July 1817. Wit: Ish Edwards, Jos M. Stanfield. Martha Couch examined apart from her husband & freely consented to conveyance.

34-5 William McKissack, Junr. to James Whitefield Sen., for $1000, 414½ A on Double Creeks of Hico adj Willis Horton, Stanfield, Wm. McKissack Sen., Norfleet. 23 Dec 1817. Wit: Nathaniel Norfleet, Stokes Allin.

35-6 John Scoggin to John Penn, for $300, 78 A on Double Cr of Hico adj Wm. McKissack, said Penn, Jones. 11 Feb 1818. Wit: B. W. Milner.

36-7 Gabriel Davy to Archibald Lipscomb, for $600, 200 A on Tar R branches adj Tapp, Yarbrough. 19 Sept 1817. Wit: Ira Lea, Henry Lipscomb.

37-8 Mandley Winstead to Moses Chambers, for $1500, 425 A on Fishing Br of Adams Cr on head of mountain br a corner of Thomas Hagie adj Howard heirs, John Barnett, Saml Cox, Charles Allen. 12 July 1817. Wit: Thomas Webb, Mary Webb.

38-9 Mandley Winstead to Moses Chambers, for $800, 200 A both sides Mayo Cr adj Samuel Winstead, Robert Gill, 12 July 1817. Wit: Thos Webb, Mary Webb.

39-40 Ira Lea, commissioner for heirs of Ralph Williams decd appointed by Judge Superior Court Mar 1817, to John W. Williams by his agent, Benjamin Chambers, for $1.25 per A totaling $475, 380 A on Adams Cr adj James Mitchell, Matthew Mitchel formerly Sheppard, Charles Mitchel. 1 Nov 1817. Wit: Alexr Winstead.

40-1 George Gregory to James Franklin, for $432, 72 A on Hyco adj Alexr Cunningham, Newman. 19 Dec 1817. Wit: John Garner, James Harrison.

41 Joseph Alldridge to James Farquhar, for $60, 12.75 A w side Flat R adj Isham Alldridge. 28 Jan 1818. Wit: Wm. Hargis, Jas H. Cates.

42 Archibald Lipscomb to Thomas Lipscomb, for $765, 122 A on S Hico adj Daniel Sergent, William Gold - it being same land Bartley Hatchet purchased of John Darby or Wm. McDaniel. 17 Oct 1817. Wit: Jesse Bradsher, Henry Lipscomb, Joel Foley.

42-3 Samuel Dickens exec of Robert Dickens decd to James Jay, Isaac Satterfield, & Wright Nichols, elders of the Baptist Church, for his love & affection for the Church & to promote the Gospel,& 5¢, 2 A on Flat R with buildings. 9 Feb 1818. Wit: Jesse Evans.

43-4 John Stanfield & Jane Stanfield his wife (in debt to Andrew B. Wood for $100 bond) to Robt Vanhook, trustee, for 25¢, 90 A where Stanfield lives on Double Cr of Hyco adj James Jay Sen., Jas Williamson, Abraham Hargis. 13 June 1814. Wit: Duncan Rose.

45-6 Levi Sweany (in debt to Lawrence V. Hargis & Co., merchants, for $268.84) to Lawrence V. Hargis, trustee, for 50¢, 180 A on Deep Cr adj heirs of Hiram Cozart decd,, Jno Sweaney, Maret Sweaney - it being land where Sweaney resides conveyed in 1796 to Job Green by Elijah Denby & from Green to Sweaney. 20 Aug 1817. Wit: James Gooch.

46-7 Jane Gwinn to Samuel Painter of Halifax Co., VA, for $1 & love & affection, negroes Cyrus, Anderson, Phil, Mary, Jack, Benjamin, William; girls Willy, Rachel; also 300 A where she lives - but she to enjoy land & negroes for her life. Said possessions then divided to sister Patsy Painter wife of Samuel Painter (negroes Cyrus, Anderson, Melissa); to children of sister Polly Jones wife of Robt Jones: negroes Phil, Mary, Jack; to Tinsley Wade brother of Jane Gwin: negro boy William; to John G. Wade son of Robt Wade & Ann Wade his wife, boy Benjamin; to Jane Painter daughter of Saml Painter and Patsy his wife, negro woman Willy; to Martha Painter daughter of Samuel & Patsy Painter, 1 dozen silver teaspoons & ½ dozen silver tablespoons; to Elizabeth H. Woody wife of James Woody she a daughter of Robert & Ann Wade, negro Rachel. Her land to be sold with ½ proceeds to John G. Woody & Elizabeth H. Woody his wife; money from remainder of sale to Elizabeth Patterson $150, to Peggy Lawrence wife of William Lawrence $150; balance of sale of ½ of land to Tinsley Wade brother to Jane Gwin; Saml Painter to have 6% of sales for his trouble. 3 Oct 1817. Wit: Ish Edwards, R. Jones, Jas M. Stanfield.

47-8 Vincent Lea of Petersburg, VA, to Robt D. Wade of Person Co., for $296.60, 177.75 A on S Hycho adj Robt Wade decd. 11 Jan 1817. Wit: Thomas Snipes, Wm. Mitchel.

48-9 Vincent Lea of Petersburg, VA, to Robt D. Wade of Person Co., for $83 1/3,
50 A on S Hycho adj former deed, William Snipes. 11 Jan 1817.
Wit: Thos Snipes, Wm. Mitchell.

49-50 James Williamson to Reuben Long Jun., for $200, 77 A on Story's Cr adj
Robt Southard. 8 Jan 1818. Wit: Alex Winstead.

50-1 Jesse Westbrook to Richard Atkinson, for $150, 60 A both sides Trim's Br
of Richland Cr adj Thos Westbrook, Thomas Atkinson, Carter Atkinson. 4 Feb 1818.
Wit: Thos Atkinson, C. Atkinson.

51 James Rimmer to John Scoggin, for $300, 78 A on Double Creeks of Hycho adj
Wm. McKissack, Badget, Jones. 7 Apr 1817. Wit: B. W. Milner.

52 Thomas Edmundson to Cary Williams, for $846, 84.6 A adj James Jordan, Joseph
Royster, Trotter - said land part of tract deeded by Charles Sallard. 16 Jan
1818. Wit: Mary Hatcher, Vines Williams.

52-3 Robert Mann of Randolph Co., NC, to Nathaniel Hamlin of Person Co., for
$278, 85½ A on Adams Cr adj Fowler, Painter. 20 Aug 1815. Wit: John G. Wade,
Wm. Mann Jr.

53 James Osborn Jeffreys of Smith Co., TN, to David Jeffreys of Person Co., for
$1300, 274 A on Richland Cr adj the dower tract, Paine; also his right & claim
to dower lands where Spivy McKissack now lives both sides Flat R - 900 A -
said land allotted to Susan Jeffreys widow of Paul Jeffreys decd now Susan Mc-
Kissack wife to Spivy McKissack. 28 Dec 1815. Wit: S. McKissack.

54 James Daniel to Thomas Walton, for $1262.50, 101 A on main road from red house
to Cuningham store - said land he purchased of John Daniel where William S.
Branch now lives adj David Hemphill, James Hamlett, Robt Hamlett, estate of
Joseph Hall decd. 28 Oct 1816. Wit: John Hamlet, Robt Hamlett, Abram Foard.

54-5 John Aldridge to James Farquhar, for $164, 20½ A e side Flat R adj Abraham
Moore, William Blalack. 6 Dec 1817. Wit: John Farquhar, George Berry.

55-6 Thomas V. Hargis, trustee for Levi Sweany & Lawrence V. Hargis & Co., to
Maret Sweany, for $278.50, 180 A on Deep Cr adj Hiram Cozart decd, John Sweany,
Maret Sweany - being same land conveyed in 1796 to Job Green by Elijah Denby.
5 Jan 1818. Wit: John J. Carrington, Joel Sweany Junr.

56 James Broach to Richard Broach, for $200, 100 A on S Hico adj John Crisp,
Marshal, McNeill. 7 Jan 1818. Wit: Elijah Hester, Edmund Burch, George Burch.

57 Daniel Merit of CC to William Jeffreys of Person Co., for $80, 70 A on Rose-
mary Cr adj Brooks, Benja Fowler, Thomas Mann. 21 Dec 1811. Wit: William Rainey,
E. D. Jones, R. W. Singleton, Robt Wade. Proved Feb 1818 by oath of Robt Wade.

57-8 Gabriel Davy Sen. to Archibald Lipscomb, for $1400, 190 A on Tar R adj James
Webb, William Yarbrough, Saml Yarbrough, Saml Bumpass, Richd Woods. 19 Sept 1817.
Wit: Ira Lea, Henry Lipscomb.

58-60 Div 224 A of Elizabeth Step decd among her 7 legatees: 1. Elizabeth
Jordan 32 A; 2. Joshua Step Sen. 27.4 A; 3. Sarah Hargis 36.6 A; 4. Thomas
Hargis 32 A; 5. Thomas Hargis 32 A; 6. James Jones 32 A; 7. Patsy Berry 32 A.
Benja W. Milner allowed $6 for 3 days surveying and $7 for drawing plats.
Commrs: Wright Nichols, Obadiah Pearce, Stephen Wells each paid $6 for 2 days
dividing land; chain carriers $4 or $2 each. 20 Dec 1817.

60-1 Samuel Wheeler to William Satterfield, for 144 lbs 11/6, 152 A on Henley
Mill Cr of S Hico adj Roger Tillman, Thomas Thomas, heirs of Jesse Carter,
Charles Winstead, said Satterfield - reserving that his step-mother, Jane Wheeler,
relict of Samuel Wheeler Senr decd, should not be disinherited of her part
during her life. 30 Sept 1817. Wit: Ira Lea.

61 Div estate of Ashburne Davy according to his will: to Ambrose Davy & wife one-fifth part adj widow Davey, Francis Lawson, Edward Davey - 145 A & value $290; balance of land worth $1660 with 580 A; remainder to go to Ezekiel, Robert, Jane, & Gabriel Davy children of Ashbourn Davy decd; negroes Phil, Abram, Abraham is 5th part of negroes to go to Ambrose Davy, value $674; also part of cattle. 25 Dec 1817. Commrs: William Street, Thos Halliburton, James Webb, Thos Lawson.

62 David Jeffreys to Spivy McKissack, for $200, tract s side Flat R at Rattle-snake Br adj Lewis Daniel - said land part of dower of Spivy McKissack's wife, Susan, of land of Paul Jeffreys decd excepting right & interest held in said dower by John Lyon & Elizabeth Lyon his wife. 18 Jan 1818.
Wit: Wm. McKissack, John G. Wade.

62-3 Thomas Lipscomb to Rachel Talley of Warren Co., NC, for $765, 153 A e side Cobs Cr of N Hico adj William Warren, James Williamson, Archibald Lipscomb. 17 Oct 1817. Wit: Jesse Bradsher, Henry Lipscomb.

63-4 John Scott of Hillsborough, Orange Co., NC, to Thos N. L. Hargis, of same, for 200 lbs, 100 A on Flat R in Person Co. adj Palmer old corner now Norfleet. 23 Apr 1818. Wit: Herod Hargis, Anthony Horton. Proved before Superior Court 28 May 1818, Thomas Ruffin, judge.

64-5 Thomas N. S. Hargis & Dennis Hargis both of Hillsborough, Orange Co., NC, to John Scott of same, for 200 lbs, 100 A on Flat R adj Norfleet, Palmer old line now Norfleet. 28 May 1818. Proved in Superior Court 28 May 1818.

65 Samuel Winstead, Charles Winstead for self & for Clark Spencer & Katharine Spencer his wife, John Walker, Thos Winstead, James Williamson, Wm. McKissack, Alex Winstead for himself & for heirs of Richd Coleman Decd, Stephen H. Winstead, Rebecca Winstead - all heirs at law of Cotance Winstead decd - to Samuel Davie, for $807, 250 A on Mayo Cr and this conveyed by Samuel Winstead Sen. to Cotance Winstead in 1787 adj David Allen, William Davie; also willed by Samuel Winstead Sen. to Cotance Winstead ? A on Mayo Cr adj David Allen, the former tract, Mandley Winstead. 31 Jan 1818. Wit: Robt Wade, Ambrose Davie.

66 William Baird to Robert Harris, for $547.40, 273.3 A on Blewing & Aaron's Cr adj Henry Humphreys. 12 Nov 1817. Wit: Thos Halliburton Sen., Thos Halli-burton Jun., Moses Woody.

66-7 Archibald Lipscomb to Thomas Webb, for $1700, 190 A on Tar R adj James Webb, William Yarbrough, Saml Bumpass, Richd Woods. 14 May 1818. Wit: John Bradsher, Willis Brooks, Robt Wade.

67-8 Charles Gregory to Thomas Allen, for $100, 100 A on Adams Cr adj Abram Walters, the mountain. 5 May 1818. Wit: Benja Chambers.

68-9 Nicholas Burch of CC to Pryor McNeill of Person Co., for $167, 111 A on S Hyco, said land Burch purchased of John Clark & Elizabeth Moore the heirs of William Moore decd adj Henry McNeill, Marshall, Broach, Wilson Jones, Harrington Haralson. 13 Jan 1816. Wit: Malcom McNeill, John McMurray.

69-70 John G. Wilson & Co. of Leasburg, CC, to William Lipscomb of Person Co., for $1591, 530.9 A in Person Co. on Cobb Cr & Rushy Br adj heirs of Lawrence Lea decd, James Johnson Jun., Jeremiah Brooks, Laurence Vanhook, near the meeting house, Kendal Vanhook, Nicholas Thompson. 1 Jan 1818. Wit: Nicholas Thompson, John H. McNeill.

70-1 Harrison Warren & Jeremiah S. Warren both of Elbert Co., GA, to John Halli-burton of Person Co., for $600, 222½ A at fork Cain Cr adj Goodloe Warren, Richd Halliburton, Alexr Cuningham, Hubbard Carnal, Archibald Carnal, Durrett Stan-field. 11 Feb 1818. Wit: Edmund Dixon, Robert Stanfield, Henry Dixon.

Deed Book E
Page
71 James Williamson to Richd Hamlin, for $160, 85 A on Story's Cr adj John Hudgins, John Harris, Josiah Fuller, Walter Fuller. 14 May 1818. Wit: Robt Wade, John Bradsher.

72 Jesse Brandon & Polly Brandon his wife of Halifax Co., VA, to William McKissack & Josiah Carver of Person Co., for $240, 40 A adj James Long, Currie Barnet, Cary Williams, dower land of Nancy Graves. 13 May 1818. Wit: Jesse Dickens, Jesse Bumpass. Polly Brandon examined apart from her husband & freely conveyed deed.

73 Samuel Dickens, exec of Robt Dickens decd & John Womack to Cornelius Buchanon, for $81, 81 A on Castle Cr & Mayo Cr adj Dickens, Womack old line, Simon Gentry, Shadrack Gentry, Bird, Lawson. 9 Feb 1818. Wit: William H. Allen, John McFarland.

73-4 John Moore to Churchwel C. Delamar of Granville Co., for $150, 74.75 A adj Thomas Moore, Jesse Dickens. 14 Oct 1815. Wit: Dempsey Clayton, James Clayton.

74-5 Joseph Hubbard Sen. of Guilford Co., NC, to Jesse Bumpass of Person Co., for $408, 277 A on Richland Cr adj Ebenezer Morrow, James Cochran, Jacob Hubbard, George Wood. 12 Jan 1818. Wit: George Wood, James Satterfield.

75 Cornelius Buchanon to Francis Lawson, for $120, 60 A on Mayo & Castle Creeks adj Ramsey, Simon Gentry, Bird. 9 Apr 1818. Wit: William Buchanon, Andrew Buchanon.

75-6 John Russell & Mary Russell his wife to Matthew Mitchell, for $836, 222 A on Adams Cr adj Robert Southard, John Williams, to Rosemary Cr. 26 July 1817. Wit: Jesse Bumpass, Will A. Lea. Mary Russell examined apart from her husband and consented to conveyance of her own free will.

76 Thomas Moore of Guilford Co., NC, to James Clayton of Person Co., for $650, 326 A on Deep Cr adj Portius Moore. 10 Jan 1818. Wit: Saml Dickens.

76-7 John Cummins Sen. to Francis Epperson, for $129, 130 A adj Cameron at mouth of a small br. 6 Mar 1818. Wit: Alexr Cummins, John Burton.

77 Daniel Meritt of CC to James Cochran of Person Co., for(amt. not given), 200 A on Rosemary Cr adj Thomas Mann, Brooks. 21 Dec 1811. Wit: William Rainey, E. D. Jones, P. M. Singleton, Robt Wade.

77-8 Francis Lawson to Andrew Buchanon, for 200 lbs, 50 A adj Lawson, William Baird. 10 May 1818. Wit: William Buchanon, William Buchanon Jun.

78 Overton Harris to Robert Harris, for $105, 100 A on Donaldson Cr adj Baird, Parrish, Bright, John Wilkerson. 29 Oct 1816. Wit: William Harris, Isabel J. Street.

78-9 Thomas Duty to Josias Carver & William McKissack, for 700 lbs, 120 A both sides Stories Cr adj Jacob Bull, John Brooks. 3 Sept 1816. Wit: Green W. Brown, Nathl Smith.

79 Thomas Webb to Hugh Woods, for $2280, 228 A on Castle Cr & known as Crossroad Ordinary adj Henry Bailey, on Douglas road, James Barnett, John Barnett. 7 Apr 1818. Wit: Cary Williams, Thomas Duty, Robt Halliburton.

80 Sarah Halliburton to Robert Halliburton, for $100, 286 A on Mayo Cr - it being tract left her by Charles Halliburton decd. 13 Dec 1817. Wit: Thomas Halliburton Sen., William H.Burton, John C. Halliburton.

80 William Tatum to David Woody, for $600, 100¼ A on Bold Br adj Benjamin Tatom, Charles Tatom, William Tatom. 10 Feb 1818. Wit: Robt N. Jones, John Lawson, Junr, Jas M. Daniel.

80-1 David Buchanon, survivor from parrence(parents?) of which were David, T. Groffee, Peachy, & Charles Duncan (by his atty Thos Bennett) - to Henry Bailey of Person Co., for $600, tract sold by John Henley to Roger Atkinson 17 Sept 1779 recorded in CC. This to satisfy deed of trust of Roger Atkinson to David Buchanon, Thomas G., Peachy, & Charles Duncan to secure debt due to Richard Hanson then of Petersburg, VA. 21 Nov 1817. Wit: Edward Atkinson, Richd Atkinson, Alexr Winstead.

81-2 Archiblad Lipscomb to Thomas Webb, for $800, 200 A on branches of Tar R adj Tapp, Yarbrough. 14 May 1818. Wit: John Bradsher, Willie Brooks, Robt Wade.

82 Isaac Satterfield & William Yarbrough to John Yarbrough, for $205, 205 A on Deep Cr adj Francis Day - said land sold by direction of will of John Yarbrough decd. 1 May 1818. Wit: ___ Woods, John Douglas.

82-3 Drucilla Vaughan, Caswell Vaughan for self and as agent & atty for Dilly Vaughan now in VA, Milly Vaughan, Abram Anderson & his wife Dorkus Anderson, Avis Vaughan, & Saml Dickens all of Person Co. - to Nathan Oakley, for $361, 114 A on Cob Cr (or Cub Cr) adj Washington, said Oakley, Dickens, Moore. 1 Jan 1818. Wit: Thomas Phillpot, William Phillpot.

83-4 Samuel Yarbrough Sen. to his son Samuel H. Yarbrough, for love & good will, 532 A both sides Deep Cr adj Bumpass, Day. 7 May 1818. Acknd in open court.

84 John Russell to William Trotter, for $225, 200 A on Sergent Cr adj John Atkinson heirs, Trotter formerly Robert Seymore. 10 Mar 1818. Wit: Arthur Leath, Stephen Pleasant.

84-5 Terl Fulcher to Henry Fulcher, for $187, 60 A on Hyco adj Smith, Wm. A. Lea, John Mason. 8 May 1818. Wit: John Tilman, Burgess Fulcher.

85-6 Pryor McNeill of Christian Co., KY, to Malcom McNeill of same, for $171, 111 A on S Hico being a tract purchased of Nicholas Burch adj Henry McNeill, Marshall, Broach, Wilson Jones, Herndon Haralson. 22 Feb 1817. Wit: Henry McNeill. Proved by oaths of John McMurray & Robt Vanhook.

86 Benjamin Harris to Sampson M. Glenn, for $160.50, 53½ A on Stories Cr adj John Fuller, Solomon Clayton. 28 Apr 1817. Wit: Saml Jones, Benja Chambers.

86-7 John W. Stanfield to John Stevenson of Granville Co., for $425, 90 A on Double Cr adj James Williamson, James Jay, Abraham Hargis, heirs of Lewis Green decd. 8 Dec 1817. Wit: Daniel Gooche, William Watson, Saml Forsythe.

87-8 Jacob Bull to Currie Barnett & Cary Williams, for $3000, 406 A both sides Stories Cr adj Reuben Long, Jesse Long, Robt Southworth, Williamson, Samuel Harris, Walters, William Carver; also 1.1 A which Bull purchased of Henry Graves adj Bull. 1 May 1818. Wit: William Williams, Saml Bull, Robt Jones, Jesse Bull.

88 Jesse Dickens to Sampson M. Glenn, for $250, 143 A on Stories Cr adj Roger Atkinson, John Cooper. 21 Apr 1818. Wit: John G. Wade.

88-9 Henry Lipscomb & Sally Lipscomb his wife to George Lea Junr., for $160, all their interest in undivided tract of land which belonged to Henry Lea decd & held by Henry Lipscomb in right of his wife formerly Sally Lea. 13 July 1818. Wit: R. Vanhook, J. Bradsher. Sally Lispcomb examined apart from her husband & conveyed land of her free will.

89-90 Robert Brooks to Jacob Bull, for 260 lbs, 406 A both sides Story's Cr adj Reubin Long, Jesse Long, Robt Southward, Williamson, Saml Harris, William Carver, Walters - said tract conveyed to Jacob Bull & Robert Brooks jointly by Thomas Owens 13 Mar 1799. 6 Jan 1806. Wit: Ish Edwards, John McKissack.

90-1 John Russell to Charles Wade, for $75, 12½ A s side Hicho adj Wade. _ Oct 1817. Wit: R. H. Childers.

91 Buckley Walker to Henry Woody, for $400, 95.3 A on Castle Cr adj Woody, James Holloway. 18 Apr 1818. Acknd in open court.

Deed Book E
Page

91-2 Thomas Halliburton, Humphries Halliburton, Charles Halliburton, Susanna Halliburton, David Halliburton, Patsy P.Pool, Betsy Dickson - all heirs of Charles Halliburton decd - to Jesse Ragon, for 20 lbs, 50 A on Bluwing Cr adj David Halliburton. Said money paid during life of Charles Halliburton. 14 Oct 1816. Wit: Thos Halliburton, Richd Blanks.

92 James Cochran to John Bradsher Jun., for $286, 100 A near Duty's mill - said land formerly owned by William Tricky & will be conveyed to Cochran by Benjamin Chambers, trustee, after 25 dec next. 31 Oct 1814. Wit: Will A. Lea.

92-4 Benjamin Bullock & Elizabeth Bullock his wife of Granville Co. (she daughter & heir at law of John Gooche decd of Person Co.) to Phillips Moore, for $88.25, their undivided 8th part of a tract on Flat R - it being one-third part of land Gooche possessed & laid off as dower for Judith Gooche, widow, including dwelling house & mill adj Thomas Sneed, Robt Cate Senr. 13 _ 1816. Wit: Robt F. P. Jones, Radford Gooche. Elizabeth Bullock examined in Granville Co. apart from her husband & freely conveyed deed. 2 May 1818. By Thomas Benehan & James Walker.

94-5 Rachel Talley of Warren Co., NC, & Burwell Pitchford, trustee, of same, to Richard Russel of same, for $735, 180 A where Rachel Talley, Joel Talley, & Green Talley now live; for $1 pd by Burwell Pitchford the tract she purchased of Archer Lipscomb of Person Co., 147 A, adj Mrs. Johnson, Mr. Warren; Green Talley, Lizy Talley, Orren Talley, & John Talley infants under 20 yrs children of Robert Talley decd their father have their right to part of this land at age 21 & if they do not agree to convey, this deed void. 10 Nov 1817. Wit: John Marshal, Saml Paschal. Proved before Jon Hall, JSC.

95-7 Thomas N. S. Hargis, trustee, of Orange Co., NC, to James Cochran of Person Co., for $745, 180 A -200 A on Flat R - land sold to satisfy deed of trust given by Solomon Cate 1 July 1811 to pay debt due Laurence V. Hargis & Co. for $569.37 and $106.62½. 16 Jan 1817. Wit: Willie P. Mangum, J. P. Sneed.

97 Roger Tilman to John Tilman, for $130, 51 A adj Roger Tilman, Jane Clay dower line formerly Samuel Wheeler, Thomas Thomson, heirs of Jesse Carter. 16 June 1818. Wit: Jas Tilman, Richd N. Tilman.

97-8 Mathias Nichols to Lawrence B. Hargis, for $815, 191 A n prong Flat R adj Duncan Cameron, Hubbard, Jeffreys old line. 29 July 1818. Wit: Willis Nichols, David Satterfield.

98-9 Charles Tatum & Benjamin Tatum to William Tatum, for $600, 100¼ A on Bold Br adj all 3 men. 13 Feb 1818. Wit: Jas M. Daniel, Robt W. Jones, David Woody.

99-100 Robert Mann to William Mann Junr., for $25, tract on Adams Cr being all his interest in tract laid out for Jane Mann Sen. during her natural life left by her late husband John Mann decd - total being 200 A. 10 Jan 1818. Wit: Ira Lea, Alex Winstead.

100-1 Joseph Scoggin to Joseph Hawks of Mecklenburg Co., VA, for $450, 150 A on Story's Cr - it being land conveyed by Jas Cochran 16 Oct 1812 to Scoggin adj Mitchel, James Hunt now Reuben Long. 16 Dec 1816. Wit: John Raven, Thomas Byase.

101-2 Hugh Woods and William Vanhook to William Street & Lawson Neal, for $200, 183 A on S Hico & Reedy Cr adj George Duty, Nathan Scoggin, Reuben Parrott, Samuel Whitehead to wagon road ford of Richland Cr, Carter Lea; also 5 A on S Hico adj Owen Lea now Mitchel - both tracts were willed to Robert Vanhook & William Vanhook by the decd father David Vanhook. 20 Aug 1817. Wit: Thomas Lawson, S. M. Glenn, Robert Vanhook.

102-3 Coleman Mitchel to Hardy Johnson, for $300, 81 A on Amis Mill Cr adj Satterfield, Tilman. 13 July 1818. Wit: Ira Lea, Addison B. Garrot.

Deed Book E
Page

103-4 Kendal Vanhook to William Gallaugher, for $85, 90 A adj the Moravian land, Hardaman Wells, William Cocke. 17 Dec 1816. Wit: James Johnston, Stephen Pleasant.

104 Thomas Thomas to John Tilman, for $200, 50 A on Henley Mill Cr of S Hico adj heirs of Jesse Carter, Jane Clay dower line, John Tilman. 22 June 1818. Wit: James Tillman, Richd N. Tilman.

104-5 John Clark to Nicholas Burch of CC, for $167, 111 A on S Hyco adj Hargis, Wilson Jones, Harralson, Henry McNeel. 16 Nov 1813. Wit: Elijah Hester, John Mitchel.

105-6 Edward Clay Sen. to his son James Clay, for $500 & for love & affection, 400 A on Richland Cr of Hyco adj James Cochran, Richd Atkinson, Reuben Walton, Byase - land to be taken off west end of tract where Clay lives. 3 Mar 1818. Wit: R. Atkinson, Jno Montgomery.

106-7 Williamson Moore & Nancy Moore his wife of CC to Jacob Couch of Person Co., for $300, 50 1/7 A on Stories Cr adj dower of Nancy Graves, Leah Graves, Hosea Carver, John Carver. 30 May 1818. Wit: Lewis Amis, John W. Williams. Nancy Moore examined apart from her husband & signed conveyance of her free will.

108-9 Samuel Davey to John Lawson, for $1200, 433 A adj Allen, Springfield, Winstead, Davey. 14 May 1818. Wit: William Jeffreys, Henry Bailey.

109 Robert Moore to John Trice of Halifax Co., VA., for $160, 74 A on Stories Cr adj Joseph Hamlin, Parker old line. 8 July 1818. Wit: Ira Lea, James Holloway.

109-10 Joseph McCain of Rockingham Co., NC, to James McCain of Person Co., for $24, 26 A n side Cain Cr adj Edmund Dixon. 26 Oct 1817. Wit: John McCain.

110-1 John Green, atty for Burwell Green to James Jay Sen., for $75, 124½ A on Stories Cr; John Green has power of attorney dated 17 Nov 1797. 22 Jan 1817. Wit: Nancy Turner, John M. Glenn. NB True intent is to convey balance of tract sold by James Raven to Burwell Green adj Mitchel, West, Brooks, Watson, Glenn.

111-2 David Mitchel of CC adm of John Gray decd late of CC to Alexander Gray of Person Co. (John Gray decd was by bond dated 31 Oct 1804 bound to convey to Alexander Gray his undivided share in lands of Alexr Gray decd & conveyance never made), for $250, this share of John Gray decd of 180 A on Double Cr which he held as heir of Alexr Gray decd adj Moss late Benjamin Jacobs, Jonathan McKissack, Jones, Alexr Gray Junr. - it being amt left after allotting to Nancy McKissack 122 A. 12 Nov 1818. Wit: Nathl Norfleet, John Ellison, Robt Jones.

112 Samuel Yarbrough to John Bumpass, for $58.33, 50 A on Deep Cr adj said Bumpass, Day, Sam Wood. 7 May 1818. Wit: John Yarbrough, Robt Bumpass.

112-3 Hardy Johnston to son James Johnston, for love & affection, a tract deeded by Coleman Mitchell 1st of this month adj Roger Tilman, Lewis Amis, S. Winstead. 30 July 1818. Wit: Lewis Amis, Barnet Winstead, Thos Garrot.

113-4 George Waite, atty in fact for William Waite of Bedford Co., TN, to Jesse Lunsford of Person Co., for $125, 238 A on Tar R adj Cochran, Lunsford, Cocke, Tap. 20 Feb 1816. Wit: David Satterfield, Joseph Lunsford.

114 William Waite by his atty George Waite to Ezekiel Jones of Person Co., for $40, 67½ A on Bluwing Cr adj Jones, Jesse Ragen, R. Harris, former Baird line. 27 Oct 1818. Wit: Jesse Ragen, James Ragen.

114-5 Samuel Winstead & Thomas Lipscomb to Stephen Sergent, for $200, two lots #1 & #4 each with 41½ A on Hico adj David Vanhook legatees, Archibald Lipscomb - said land part of tract of Daniel Sergent decd & div to heirs; lot #1 drawn by Winstead & #4 by Lipscomb. Also signed by Eliza Winstead, & Polly Lipscomb who were examined apart from husbands & freely executed deed. 9 Aug 1816. Wit: Benja Lea, Moses Fuller.

Deed Book E
Page
116 Stokes Allen to John Miner, for $500, 111½ A on Long Br of Flat R adj John Brown, Robert Dickens. 23 Oct 1818. Wit: George Briggs, David Hunt.

117 Thomas Falconer exec of last will of Elijah Mitchel of Wake Co., NC, to Robert Vanhook of Person Co., for $210, 195 A both sides n fork Flat R adj William Glenn formerly now Duncan Rose, Paine - sold to pay debts and tract selected by Sally Mitchel to be sold. 11 Mar 1817. Wit: Saml Davy.
Sally Mitchel widow of Elijah Mitchel agrees to sell land to pay debts of estate. Wit: Ad Cochran.

117-8 Henry Sergent & Rachel his wife (late Rachel Lea) of Russell Co., VA, to Vincent Lea of Person Co., for $160, 100 A on S Hyco adj Moses Bradsher - Henry Lea died and said land descended to Rachel Lea, sister of Henry Lea decd - her part being ¼ which Henry Lea held as devisee of Zachariah Lea decd.
5 Oct 1818. In Russell Co., VA, Rachel Sergent privately examined & freely executed deed. Proved Nov 1818 in Person Co. as county seal of Russell Co. affixed.

119 Abraham Dunnaway to son Archibald Dunnaway, for love & affection, 159 1/5 A where he lives on Hico adj Edmund Dixon Senr., Warren Dixon; also negro slave Gilbert about 20 yrs old; grantor to possess land & slave during his life. Wit: Arthur Leath, Chs Sallard. 10 Nov 1818.

119-20 Thomas Blalock Senr to his son Thomas Blalock Junr., for $1, 100 A on Flat R adj Moore. 11 Nov 1818. Wit: Wm. Moore, Hastin Blalock.

120 Lewis Daniel, exec estate of William Daniel decd, to Francis Epperson, for $443.50, 100 A both sides Flat R adj John Cummins Sen., Charles Rountree, Jesse Evans. 4 Sept 1818. Wit: H. Hayes.

121 Thomas McGehee to William McGehee, for $6084?, 473 A both sides Hyco Cr adj James Rainey, William Irvine - being tract where Wm. McGehee lives & heirs of Saml Smith decd. 4 July 1818. Acknd in open court.

121-2 James W. Hauxhurst to William Moore, for $300, 100 A on Double Cr & Flat R adj Nathl Norfleet, Alexr Gray, Nancy McKissack. Also signed by Eliza Hauxhurst. 10 Nov 1818. Wit: Nathl Norfleet, Wm. Whitefield, Alex Gray.

122-3 Garrot Tingen of Granville Co. to Drury Pulliam, for $290.50, 117 A on Gents Cr adj Cary Williams, Jordan, Joseph Royster, John Brand, George Duncan. 18 May 1818. Wit: John Brand, Benja Chambers.

123 Richard Halliburton to Benjamin Halliburton of Halifax Co., VA, for $2484, 221 A on Hyco & Cain Cr being part of land Goodloe Warren decd adj Robt Jones. 28 Oct 1818. Wit: James Rainey, Robert Jones.

123-4 Wyatt Painter to Benja W. Milner, in trust, for 25¢, 150 A on Mayo adj Bedwell Satterfield spring, Hardy Crews, Thos Clayton, John Yarbrough - deeded to satisfy 2 notes due James Rimmer for $85 & for $80 both due Dec 25, 1819. 27 Oct 1818. Wit: Charles Watson, Crowder Holloway.

124-5 Mary Currie to John Allison, for $250, 100 A on S Hyco adj Simeon Cochran. 10 Apr 1815. Wit: Wm. Mitchel, L. Rainey. Proved Nov 1818 by oath Leml Rainey.

125-6 James Paine to Joseph Lunsford, for $506.56, 304 A on Richland Spring Cr adj James Satterfield, Dickens. 2 Mar 1814. Wit: Jesse Lunsford, Wm. McKissack.

126-7 Thomas Hargis Sen. to his son Thomas V. Hargis, for love & affection, 44 A adj Capt. Wm. Hargis. Hargis blacksmith shop, on main rd from Person CH to Hillsboro, John Phillips. 11 Nov 1818. Wit: Wm. Hargis.

127 William Waite (by his atty in fact George Waite) of Bedford Co., TN, to Jesse Ragan of Person Co., for $40, 80 A on Bluewing Cr adj said Ragan, Winstead, Harris, Burton. 27 Oct 1818. Wit: Ezekiel Jones, James Ragan.

127-8 Thomas Williams of Orange Co., NC, to Laurence V. Hargis of Person Co., for $310, coloured girl Celia. 23 Mar 1814. Wit: Thos V. Hargis.

128 Richard Rimmer to Nathan Hargis, for $275.93 3/4, 159¼ A on Bushy Fork of Flat R adj dower line of widow Rimmer, Stephen Wells. 28 Oct 1817. Wit: S. Cochran, Saml Evans.

128-9 John Wagstaff to Currie Barnett, for $1800, 242 A on Whetstone Br adj John Williams, John M. McGehee, Sallard. 24 Dec 1818. Wit: Cary Williams, Byrd Pulliam.

129-30 Reubin Taylor of CC to son Charles Taylor, for parental affection, 425 A on Flat R adj Simeon Cochran, Norfleet. 10 Apr 1818. Wit: Turner D. White, Saml Dunnaway.

130 Samuel Dickens, adm de bonis of William Cocke decd, to John W. Williams, for $360.30, negro boy Adam. 30 June 1813. Proved in open court Feb 1819.

130 Jos Rountree & Jesse Evans, execs estate of John Cate decd, to Ransom Cates, for $350.25, negro girl Nance. 22 Mar 1816. Wit: L. V. Hargis.

131 Nathaniel Painter to Presby Draper, for $800, 170½ A on Stories Cr & Sergent Cr adj William Hamlen, Richd Atkinson, Thos Neely old line, William Trotter. 22 Dec 1818. Wit: Ira Lea, John Draper.

132 Gabriel Lea & Vincent Lea of CC to Reuben Grinstead of Person Co., for $235, 81½ A on Mitchel Br. 6 Feb 1819. Acknd in open court.

132-3 Jos Rountree of Orange Co. & Jesse Evans of Person Co., execs last will of John Cates decd, to Andrew Gray of Orange Co., for $2721, 227 A in Person Co. s fork Flat R adj James Dickens - excepting 1 A formerly sold to Francis Epperson on ne corner of tract adj Duncan Cameron. 24 Dec 1816. Wit: John Satterfield, Wm. Hall, Amos Nichols.

133-4 John Lyon & his wife Elizabeth of town of Carthage, TN, to Spivy McKissack of Person Co., for $500, all their right & interest to 1 undivided fourth part where Spivy McKissack now lives on both sides Flat R adj Duncan Cameron, David Jeffreys, James Milner, Lewis Daniel - said tract allotted to widow in div land of Paul Jeffreys decd, she now wife to Spivy McKissack - total of 900 A. 24 Sept 1818. Elizabeth Lyon examined in Smith Co., TN, & acknowledged she signed deed voluntarily. Proved Person Co. Feb 1819.

135 Patty Taylor of Franklin Co., NC, to Lewis Daniel of Person Co., for $1025, 205.85 A both sides Flat R & Aldridge Cr near Cocke formerly William Allston - said land part of tract purchased of James Goreley by the late Thomas Person. 2 Jan 1817. Wit: John Person, Benja P. Thorp.

135-6 Thomas McGehee to Richard Halliburton, for $4040, 404 A on Cain Cr adj Robert Jones, William McGehee. 10 Oct 1818. Wit: Archd Cearnall, Robert Jones.

136-7 John Bumpass to Sidney D. Bumpass, for $2000, 320 A on Tar R adj Richard Woods, James Webb, Dickens, Jonas Parker, William Philpott, Walter Oakley, Person. 26 Jan 1819. Acknd in open court.

137-8 Joseph Rice to John Mason, for $62.50, 12½ A on road from Leasburg to confluence of N & S Hico adj Henry Curtis, Mason. 22 May 1818. Wit: McFarland Oakley, William Royster.

138 Stephen Pleasant of Person Co. to Nicholas Thompson of CC, for $1600, 159½ A on S Hico adj John Pittard, Thos Snipes, Vanhook, Jones, Lipscomb formerly widow Vanhook, Thomas, Brooks. 6 Apr 1818. Wit: Duncan Rose, Pate W. Milner.

Deed Book E
Page
139 Nathan Hargis & Jenny his wife, Stephen Ellis & Elizabeth his wife, James
Rimmer, Saml Rimmer, Jeremiah Rimmer, Phobe Rimmer, & Polly Rimmer - all heirs
& legatees of James Rimmer decd of Person Co.-to Richard Rimmer , for $261.13,
159¼ A on Bushy Fork of Flat R, said land held by them in right of their father
James Rimmer decd adj widow dower, Stephen Wells. 26 July 1817.
Wit: John Blalock, Thos Hawkins, John Hudgins.

140 Joseph Rice to William Royster, for $51, 10 A adj John Mason, on road from
Leasburg to confluence of N & S Hico. 22 May 1818. Wit: McFarland Oakley,
John Mason.

140-1 Laurence V. Hargis & Co. to Elizabeth Denny, for $200, 50 A s side Bird's
Cr adj Dickens. Berry. 11 Jan 1819. Wit: Ambrose Day, Roben Day.

141-2 James Williamson to John Hudgins, for $50, 15 A on Stories Cr adj Richd
Hamlin, Walter Fuller. 8 Jan 1818. Wit: Robt Wade.

142-3 State of NC - #137 - to Lozen Carver, for 50/ per 100 A, 26 A on Rose Mary
Cr adj Charles Gregory, said Carver, James Williamson, Wm. Clayton. Entered
14 May 1818. Recorded 13 Sept 1819 by B. W. Milner, Register.

143-4 William O'Briant to Kindal Davie, trustee, for $100, negro boy Green about
6 yrs old; sale made as grantor is in debt to Ambrose Davie for $100. 17 May
1819. Wit: Jones Davie, Charles Gill.

144-5 Robert Downey (in debt to Ambrose Davey for $437.50) to Kindal Davie, in
trust, two negroes Sook & Moses. 8 Aug 1817. Wit: J. Bumpass, R. Vanhook.

145-6 Abel L. Parish to Francis Lawson, for $200, 154 A where Parish lives on
Bluewing Cr adj William Bird, Robert Pitman, Joseph Pitman. 15 Mar 1819.
Wit: Overton S. Parish, Lumpkin Winstead.

146 Lewis Ramsey to William Ramsey, for $193, 193 A on Dishwater Cr adj Bailey,
James Holloway. 12 May 1819. Wit: William Street.

147-8 Thomas Sneed, trustee, to Elias Fort of Orange Co., NC, for $450, 300 A
adj Stephen Moore, John Cothran, William Cothran to Dry Br, Duncan Cameron;
land sold to satisfy deed of trust given by Charles Rountree dated 28 Jan 1815
for debts due Mathias Nichols & Jesse Evans, securities. 10 Mar 1817.
Wit: James Williamson, William McKissack.

149 William Evans (in debt to James C. Smith for $162.50) to Downey Wade,
security, for $1, 72½ A on Hyco adj James C. Smith, Adam McNeeley, William
Gallaugher. 21 May 1818. Wit: Samuel Dickens.

149-50 John Harris, Lucy Harris, Richard Harris, Benjamin Harris, Polly Harris -
all orphans of Samuel Harris decd - to Paul Walters, for $112, 80 A adj James
Williamson, Jacob Bull, & one-third part excepted as dower of Ann Hudgins for
her life as she was last wife of Samuel Harris decd - dower is now property of
Jacob Bull. 9 Dec 1815. Wit: Ish Edwards, John Bradsher. Proved May 1819.

150-1 Thomas Hudgins of Sussex Co., VA, to John Hudgins of Person Co., for $50,
53 A on Flat R adj Jopling, Thomas Hargis. 8 Dec 1818. Wit: Thomas Hudgins Jun.

151-2 Thomas Hargis to Laurence Vanhook Hargis, for $512, 512 A being his undi-
vided interest in 2100 A devised by his brother, Shadrack Hargis, in his last
will - said land in Western District & a grant from State of NC 10 July 1788 as
#120 - land on both sides Loochatchee R including a buffalo lick adj Robert
Goodloe #572. 12 Dec 1818. Wit: James Gooch, Francis Epperson. (Now in TN).

152-3 John Brown to Asa Hudgins, for $145.50, 51.75 A on Flat R adj Ephraim
Hawkins, Wm. Moore. 27 Feb 1819. Wit: B. W. Milner, B. Burch, John Farquhar.

153-4 Margaret Vanhook relict of Loyd Vanhook decd to William G. Long of CC, for $250, 156½ A on S Hico in Person Co. adj Lipscomb, Laurence Vanhook, R. Vanhook, Moses Bradsher. 10 Nov 1818. Wit: Saml Johnson.

154-5 Nathan Hargis to Lawrence V. Hargis, for $222, his undivided interest in 2200 A left by his father Shadrack Hargis in his last will; land in the western district granted by State of NC 10 July 1788 as lot #120 on Looshatchee R including a buffalo lick adj Robt Goodloe #572. 12 Dec 1818. Wit: James Gooche, Thos V. Hargis.

155-6 Lord Lord to Thomas Pool, for love & affection, 50 A adj Jones, Pool, John Lawson. 17 May 1819. Wit: John Lawson Sen., B. Jones.

156-7 Joseph Hawks to Sally W. Rogers, for $640, 150 A on Stories Cr said land he purchased of Joseph Scoggin adj Mitchel. 16 Sept 1818. Wit: Thomas Byasse, James Clay, Jno Richmond.

157-8 Robert Vanhook, high sheriff, to Phillips Moore (due to execution issued by court against real estate of Jas J. Gooche decd for $180.55 and said sum recovered by Lawrence V. Hargis), for $180.55, tract on Flat R adj said Moore, Robert Cates Sen., Laurence V. Hargis - said land an undivided share of Jas J. Gooche from his father John Gooche decd. 29 Apr 1819. Wit: L. V. Hargis.

158-60 Robert Vanhook, sheriff, to James Farquhar (due to execution by court against John Cummins Junr. for $84 & recovered by William McKissack Junr, Lewis Daniel, & John Cate) for $86.50, 40 A on Bird's Cr adj Saml Dickens, B. Hayes. 11 May 1819. Wit: Augustin Vanhook, Jesse Bumpass.

160-2 The heirs of William Davie decd to wit: John Scoggin & Catharine Scoggin his wife, Gabriel Davie, Ambrose Davie, Kendal Davie, all of Person Co.; William Davie, Solomon Philpott & Peggy Philpott his wife, Robert Halliburton & Mary A. Halliburton his wife all of Granville Co. - to James Philpot of Granville Co., for $3239.80, 668 A on Mayo Cr adj Edward B. Davie, Mandly Winstead. 1 May 1819. Wit: Alexr Winstead, William Street.
Catherine Scoggin, Mary Halliburton, & Peggy Philpot, separate & apart from their husbands, consented freely to conveyance. Wit: Ira Lea, Alex Winstead.

162 Thomas Pede to Daniel Tucker of Granville Co., for $142, 71 A e side Cub Cr at Rens Br adj Fluke Br, Oakley. 10 Dec 1817. Wit: Danl Gooche, Abraham Madeares.

162-3 Laurence Richardson to John Russell, for ?(not given), 17 A on S Hyco at Wade's ford. 20 Sept 1800. Proved in open court May 1819.

163-4 Arthur Roberts to Hubbard Cozart of Granville Co., for $300, 196 A on Cub Cr at Fluke Br adj Richard Peed, Thomas Peed, Jesse Oakley. 24 Feb 1816. Wit: Hubbard Cozart Jun., Thos Pharrer.

164 Gabriel H. Finn of Orange Co., NC, to James Broach, for $200, 50 A on S Hico adj Robert Hester, John Crisp, David Mitchel. 10 May 1819. Wit: George Burch, Lucinda Burch, Lucy Burch.

164-5 Daniel Tucker of Granville Co. to Hubbard Cozart of same, for $142, 71 A e side Cub Cr at Rens Br & Fluke Br adj Oakley. 20 Dec 1818. Wit: William Cozart, Abraham Madeares.

165-6 William Ramsay to Lewis Ramsay, for $300, 211 A both sides Dishwater Cr. 9 Aug 1819. Wit: Ira Lea, Wm. Street.

166-7 John Pittard to Abner Bradsher, for $1470, 147 A on S Hyco adj Robt Vanhook, Nicholas Thompson, Thos Snipes on Double Cr. 19 Mar 1819. Wit: Jesse Bradsher.

Deep Book E
Page
167 Susannah Turner to Cary Williams - whereas she sold to Williams in 1811 her right & interest in land of her father, James Pulliam Senr decd,for $20 on Gents Cr, total being 160 A adj Byrd Pulliam, Isham Edwards - said deed affirms first deed & her interest is one tenth. 8 Mar 1819. Wit: John Bradhser Jun., David Jeffreys.

167-8 Matthew McMillan of CC to Thomas Winstead of Person Co., for $100, one quarter section of land in Illinois being sw quarter of section 28 of township 15N in Range Rw in the tract appropriated by Congress for military bounties containing 160 A. 25 June 1819. Wit: Edmund Dixon, Robt Jones.

168-9 Thomas Edmundson (in debt to Abel Royster for $476.32) to Cary Williams, trustee, for 5/, negro woman Milly & her 3 children Thomas, Rachel, & a child not named. 13 May 1819. Wit: Alexr Williams, Mary Hatcher.

169-70 Robert D. Wade to Nathaniel Torian, for $2957.50, 455 A on S Hico on road at the ford from Leasburg to Hillsboro adj William Lipscomb including house where Torian lives. 6 Jan 1819. Wit: James Rainey, Henry Gallaugher.

170 Alexander Murphey of CC & Archibald D. Murphey of Orange Co. to Thomas McGehee of Person Co., for $6385, 473 A both sides Hico in Person Co. adj James Rainey, William Irvine, McGehee, devisees of Samuel Smith decd - said land part of estate of Archiblad Murphey who devised it be sold & proceeds to all children. 3 Jan 1818. Wit: James Rainey, H. Haralson.

171 Goodloe Warren to Thomas McGehee, for $4040, 404 A on Cain Cr adj Richd Halliburton, Robert Jones, William McGehee. 9 Oct 1818. Wit: Edmund Dixon, Jno M. McGehee, Durret Stanfield.

171-2 John Minor Sen. of Granville Co., to Lazarus Minor of same, for $500, 111½ A on Flat R in Person Co. adj John Brown, Robt Dickens. 29 Mar 1819. Wit: Radford Gooch, Elisabeth Gooch.

172 Bartholomew L. Hayes to Robert Wallis, for $2000, 380 A on Flat R adj Dickens, Jeffreys, Lyon - it being part of tract owned by William Cocke decd known as Bland's Quarter & allotted to Martha Cocke in div lands of Wm. Cocke. Also signed by Martha Hayes. _ Aug 1819. Wit: Isaac Satterfield, Alex Winstead.

173 William Lipscomb to Stephen Pleasant, for $1137.50, 227½ A adj Brooks, Jacobs, said Lipscomb, Laurence Lea decd, Gabl B. Lea, James Johnson. 30 May 1818. Wit: John H. McNeill, Laurence Vanhook.

173-4 William Lipscomb to Jeremiah Brooks, for $225, 50¼ A on S Hico adj Laurence Vanhook, said Brooks, Elijah Jacobs. 3 Jan 1818. Wit: Jesse Bradsher, Stephen Pleasant.

174 Sarah Allen to beloved son-in-law Reubin Kennon of CC, for love & affection, negro girl Minerva about 6 yrs old, it being part of his legacy in estate of William Allen decd & left to her by her late husband's will for her life; she relinquishes all right. 9 Aug 1819. Wit: William H. Allen.

174-5 William Caddel ot Pendleton Co., SC, to Samuel Rimmer of Person Co., for $110, 100 A on Flat R adj Simeon Cochran, Robt Dickens, James Williamson. 30 Dec 1811. Wit: S. Cochran, Baylor Burch. Proved Aug 1819 by oath of Simeon Cochran.

175-6 Matthew McMillan of CC to Thomas Winstead of Person Co., for $100, 160 A in Illinois, SE Quarter, section 31, township 11 N, Range 3 W & said tract appropriated by Congress for military bounties in territory of Illinois. 25 June 1819. Wit: Edmund Dixon, Robert Jones.

176-7 Francis Epperson to Duncan Cameron of Orange Co., for $388, 37.8 A n side s prong Flat R; also 1 A adj Cameron. 13 Sept 1819. Wit: James Gooche, L. V. Hargis.

178 Rebecca E. Paine to dear child Elizabeth H. Paine, for love & maternal affection, negro woman Amy & her 2 children Lueicy & Hamilton; set silver spoons (table spoons) & set silver tea spoons to be delivered at death of grantor. 3 Oct 1817. Wit: Sally Cocke, Alex Winstead.

178-9 John Seymour (in debt to Isham Edwards for $504.92) to William McKissack, Jun., for $1, 197 A on Stories & Marlow Creeks adj Joseph Southard, Williams, Barnet. 4 Mar 1819. Wit: Cary Williams, Robert Wade.

180-1 Robert Southward Sen. (in debt to Isham Edwards for $99.66) to Samuel Bull, for $1, in trust, 30 A where Southward lives adj John Shelton, Jos Southward; furniture, livestock, pewter dishes. 25 Sept 1819. Wit: Ransom Austin, William Trickey.

181-3 William Southward (in debt to Isham Edwards for $115.78) to Samuel Blackwell, for $1 in trust, 66 A on Marlowe Cr where grantor lives adj Robert Southward Sen., Jos Southward. 25 Sept 1819. Wit: Ransom Austin, William Trickey.

183 Douglas Fulcher (late a private in Dabney's Co. of 43rd Regt of infantry of U. S. Army - but at this time a resident of Person Co.) to John G. Wilson of CC, for $100, 160 A in Territory of Illinois designated as NE Quarter of Section 8 of Township 10 N in Range 4W & was granted for services rendered during the late war, warrant #7883. 10 July 1819. Wit: Carter Atkinson, Addison Cochran.

184 John Atwell (late a private in Capt. McChesney's Cr. of 7th Infantry of U. S. Army byt now resident of CC) to John G. Wilson of same, for $100, 160 A in Territory of Illinois designated as NW Quarter Section 8, township 10 N in Range 4 West & was granted for service rendered in late war, warrant #7886. 16 July 1819. Wit: Jo Wright, John H. McMullin.

184-5 Thomas Edmundson to Loftin Walton, for $1492.50, 115.4 A on Sargent Cr on road of Cary Williams adj Draper mill, Thomas Trotter. 31 Aug 1819. Wit: Cary Williams, Mary Hatcher.

185-6 William Waite by his atty George Waite of Bedford Co., TN; to James Farquhar of Person Co., for $130, 208 A on Flat R adj John Farquhar, Dickens, William Farquhar. 9 Nov 1818. Wit: Jos Alldridge, Thos Blalack.

186 David Allridge to George Berry, for $100, 19.75 A on Flat R adj Blalack. 6 Nov 1819. Wit: James Farquhar.

187 John Harris Sen. of Granville Co. to Overton Harris of Person Co., for 50 lbs, 326½ A on Aaron's Cr adj Smith. 11 May 1818. Wit: Robt Harris, Robt Sandford Jr.

187-8 John Van Hook Jun. of Hillsboro, Orange Co., to Addison Cochran of Person Co., for $800, 100 A adj Robt Vanhook, said Cochran, Moses Bradsher, William Long. 2 Nov 1819. Wit: Joab Robertson, Hannah Bishop.

188-9 Hubbard Carnal to Hardin Winfrey of Milton, CC, for $241.70, 90 A on a br. _ Oct 1819. Wit: Durret Stanfield, James Franklin, John Garner.

189 Currie Barnet & Cary Williams to Jacob Bull, for $1500, 308½ A on Stories Cr being a part of tract purchased of said Bull adj McKissack, Walters, Reuben Long, James Long. 10 Sept 1819. Wit: Jesse Bull, Benja Chambers.

189-90 John Cocke of Chatham Co., NC, to Bartholomew L Hayes of Person Co., for $1250, 480 A on Flat R & Bird Cr adj the mansion tract, James Cocke, James Armstrong - said land allotted him by his father's estate. 14 Oct 1817. Wit: Green Womack, J. W. Williams.

190-1 Vincent Lea & George Lea both of Person Co. to John Bradsher, for $55, 10.1 A adj Kindal Vanhook, Thompson, said Bradsher. 1 Aug 1818. Wit: Jesse Vanhook.

Deed Book E
Page
191-2 Moses Street to Thomas Sheppard, for $1500, 621 A on Buck Mt. Cr adj Yarbrough, Robt Gill, Waite, Johnson, Davis, Person, Townsend. 11 May 1819. Wit: Thomas Townsend, Joseph Gill.

192 William Johnston to Alexander Moore, for $450, negro girl Dicea. 24 Oct 1818. Wit: John Bradsher.

192-3 Edward Clay Sen. to children and to husbands of daughters of his former wife: Edward Clay Jun., John Richmond & Judith his wife, John Montgomery & Martha his wife, Sarah Rogers, Mary Gold, Jemimah Fletcher & Frances his wife, & James Clay - all slaves to wit: Sam, Polly, Eff & her child Hester, Letty & her child Bobb, Deely, Curry, Isaac, Peter, Mason, Veny, Hannah, Ursuly, Amy, Lucy, Esther, Absolem, Washington, Saml, son of Delly, Sarah - all negroes are descendants of Deely & Tabb formerly property of Tribue, father of his late wife; said deed to settle controversey between children & are given them for love & affection. 18 Sept 1819. Wit: Isaac Satterfield, George Satterfield.

193-4 Robert Downey to John Bumpass, for $500, negro slave Bill about 22 yrs old. 1 Sept 1819. Proved by oath Jno Day.

194 State of NC - #140 - to Thomas Hood, for 50/ per 100 A, 250 A on Mill Cr adj Charles Moore, Thomas Moore, David Allen, Cunningham. Entered 20 Nov 1818. Registered Nov Court 1819.

195 Plat of survey of land of Thomas Hood on Mill Cr; survey 23 Feb 1819 by Phillips Moore, CS (county surveyor). Sworn chain carriers: Nathl Smith, Edwd Mitchel.

195-6 State of NC - #141 - to Moses Springfield, for 50/ per 100 A, 150 A on Mayo Cr adj Robert Gill, John Lawson, Coleman, Dickens. Entered 3 Aug 1818. Survey 14 Sept 1819. Sworn chain carriers: Robert Gill, Moor Springfield.

196-8 Robert Vanhook, sheriff, to George Berry (due to execution against Wright Nichols adm of William Blalack decd for $106.80 & this sum recovered by James Farquhar) for $76, 32 A of Blalack being lot #3 in div land of Peter Alldridge decd on both sides Flat R & allotted to Catharine Alldridge & was property of William Blalack when sold. 22 Oct 1819. Wit: Parthenia Vanhook, Mary Vanhook.

198-9 John H. McNeill to Joab Robertson, for $850, 104.6 A in Caswell & Person Counties on S Hico adj Archer Lipscomb, Jacobs, Pleasant, Archer Lea. 27 Oct 1819. Wit: Wm. A. Lea, Will F. Smith.

199-200 George Berry & Susannah Berry his wife, to John Jackson, for $300, 61.75 A n side Flat R being part of tract formerly property of Peter Alldridge adj Samuel Evans, James Farquhar. 10 Nov 1819. Wit: Jesse Evans, Wm. McKissack. Susannah Berry examined apart from her husband & freely agreed to conveyance.

200 John Towler to Robert D. Wade, for $150, 37½ A on S Hico adj George Whitefield, Nathl Torian. /s/ John Tolar. 30 Jan 1819. Wit: L. Richardson, Downey Wade.

200-1   Robert Wills to James Milner, for $540, 2 tracts on Flat R, one bought of George Roberts by Robert Paine Senr, about 295 A excluding the mill of 52 A owned by Lewis Daniel on Richland Cr adj James Satterfield, Robert Paine, William Jay Sen., Wm. Jay Jr., Person, crossing Mud Br, Paul Jeffreys; the second tract purchased by Robert Paine Sen. of Samuel Neely on Hillsboro Rd adj first tract, 93 A. 4 Jan 1816. Wit: Lewis Tapp, James Satterfield.

202 Alexander Winstead to Duncan Rose, for $200, 1 lot in town of Haywood known as lot #51 with 100 ft frontage. 16 Apr 1818. Wit: Jos Gill. NB:Haywood was in Chatham Co., NC.

202-3 State of NC - #144 - to Duncan Rose, for $5 per 100 A, 30 A on Double Cr of Hico adj Jesse Hargis, said Rose, John Moore, Abram Hargis. Entered 2 Jan 1818. Registered 22 Mar 1820.

Deed Book E
Page

203-4 State of NC - #145 - to Samuel Mitchel, for $5 per 100 A, 200 A adj
Mitchel, David Allen. Entered 18 Jan 1817. Registered 27 Mar 1820 by B. W.
Milner, Register.

204-5 State of NC - #138 - to George Waite, for 50/ per 100 A, 767 A on Gabs Br
& Tapley Cr adj Waite, Day, John Paine heirs, heirs Robert Paine, Oakley.
Entered 19 Nov 1818. Registered Feb 1820.

205 Moses Chambers to William Winstead, for $312, 142 A on branches of Mayo adj
Baird, Tap, Halliburton, Josiah Chambers. 5 Feb 1820. Wit: Will Davie.

205-6 George Waite, atty in fact for William Waite of Bedford Co., TN (by power
of attorney of 1 Nov 1815) to Jesse Lunsford of Person Co., for 50¢ per A,
192 A on Cub Cr adj Dickens, John Cash old line, Burford former line, Cozart,
Williams. 24 Mar 1819. Wit: Saml Dickens, John Lunsford.

206-7 Articles of agreement between Laurence V. Hargis & Thos V. Hargis - the
former has leased land of the latter for term of 10 yrs from 1 Dec last on
s prong Flat R adj Thomas Sneed; Laurence V. Hargis to pay $400 at expiration
date & promises to build dwelling house 26 by 16 ft main body and a shed 14X26.
5 Feb 1820. Wit: Harris Wilkerson, Wm. B. Martin.

207-8 George Waite atty in fact for William Waite of Bedford Co., TN, to Jesse
Lunsford, for 42 1/3 ¢ per A, tract on Tar R adj John Day now William Yarbrough,
Moses Street, Dickens. 24 Mar 1819. Wit: Saml Dickens, John Lunsford.

208 Drury A. Pulliam to Bird Pulliam, for $80, all his claim to 160 A on Gents
Cr adj Isham Edwards, Cary Williams - said land that of James Pulliam Sen. decd to
be div after death of his mother Elizabeth Pulliam wife of James Pulliam; the
part of Drury A. Pulliam is one-tenth or 16 A. 29 Jan 1820. Wit: Cary Williams,
Moses Chambers.

208-9 Cary Williams & Currie Barnett to Susannah Turner, for $120, 30 A adj John
Carver, Isham Edwards, Josias Carver. 25 Jan 1820. Wit: John Garner, Benjamin
Chambers.

209 Jacob Couch to John Carver, for $88, 22 A on Stories Cr adj Nancy Graves,
Josias Carver. 7 Feb 1820. Wit: Samuel Bull, Paul Walters.

210 Thomas Edmonson to Artha Brooks son of John Brooks, for $1044, 174 A on
Sargent Cr adj Draper, John Bran, Benjamin Moore, William Trotter. 25 Dec 1819.
Wit: Cary Williams, Matthew Brooks.

210-1 William Hargis to Laurence Vanhook Hargis, for $444, his undivided interest
in land devised by his father Shadrack Hargis, 2100 A in western districe of TN
by grant from State of NC on 10 July 1788 - tract on Looshatchie R including a
Buffalo lick adj Robert Goodloe. 2 Mar 1820. Wit: Richd Holeman, James Gooche.

211-2 Jacob Couch to Reubin Long, for $400, 95 A on Stories Cr adj dower of Nancy
Graves, Josias Carver, near Barnett's Meeting House. 14 Feb 1820. Wit: R. Long,
Williamson Moore.

212-3 Robert Vanhook, sheriff (due to execution from county court against John
Newton for $742 & same recovered by Gabl H. Lea, Jno P. Newton, James McMurry)
to Moses Bradsher, for $750.24, 106½ A on Rushy Br of Hico adj Bradsher, Vincent
Lea. 13 Nov 1818. Wit: P. M. Glenn, A. Vanhook

213-4 Drucilla Vaughan, Caswell Vaughan as agent & atty for Dicy Vaughan now in
VA, Abram Anderson & his wife Darkus, Caswell Vaughan, & Milly Vaughan, all of
Person Co. - to Aris Vaughan, for $200, 2 tracts on Cub Cr, 45 A and 20 A adj
Kennady. 1 Jan 1818. Wit: Thomas Phillpot, William Philpott.

214-5 Thomas Hargis Sen. to Thomas V. Hargis - in exchange for lands in western territory - 303½ A on Flat R. 13 Nov 1819. Wit: Wm. Hargis, Elizabeth Moore.

215 Samuel Moore to Joel Sweaney, for $400, 135 A on Deep Cr adj Portius Moore, Person. 1 May 1819. Wit: Henry Sweaney, James Cozart.

215-6 George Waite, atty in fact for William Waite of Bedford Co., TN, to Jesse Lunsford, for ? , 300 A on Gab's Br adj Day. 30 Mar 1819. Wit: Saml Dickens, John Lunsford.

216 Solomon Draper exec of Solomon Draper Sen. decd, to Thomas Trotter, for $1492.90, 209 A on Sergent Cr adj Joseph Royster, William Trotter, Artha Brooks, John Brand - said land was purchased of Reubin Newton Sen & Reubin Newton Jr. excluding ¼ A for graveyard. 13 Jan 1820. Wit: Cary Williams, Benja Chambers.

217 Richard Halliburton to Thomas Winstead, for $548, 36½ A on Hico adj Benja Halliburton. 9 Feb 1820. Wit: James Rainey.

217-8 Robert Vanhook, high sheriff, to Addison Cochran (due to court order against Wright Nichols adm of William Blalock decd & Samuel Dickens for $40.80 recovered by James Farquhar), for $126, 113 A e side S fork Flat R adj Abram Moore, James Farquhar - being tract where Blalock formerly lived. 12 Feb 1820. Wit: Jos Gill, Augustine Vanhook.

218-9 Currie Barnett & Cary Williams have sold to Hosea Carver 5 A on Stories Cr adj Paul Walton; Carver has paid $5 per A for said land; grantors defend title to said land. 10 Dec 1819. Wit: John P. Jones, Littleton Berry.

219-20 John H. Ingram (in debt to Duncan Rose for $64.30 & $77.37 to Wm. McKissack) to Alexander Winstead, in trust, 160 A being se quarter, section 29, township 10N & granted by Congress in territory of Illinois for military service. 8 Aug 1819. Wit: G. W. Brown.

220 Joseph Rice to Stephen Serghent, for $131, 65½ A on Cob Cr near N & S Hico adj George Lea, Barnet Lea, William Royster. 3 Dec 1819. Wit: Henry Serghent, Daniel Serghent.

221 John Fuller Sen. (in debt to Winstead & Williamson, merchants, at Rockboro, for $60.52) to James Gooche, trustee, for $1, 80 A on Stories Cr adj Isaiah Fuller, Abram Walters. 22 Jan 1820. Wit: Joseph Gill.

222 William Waite of Bedford Co., TN, by his atty in fact, George Waite, to Jesse Lunsford, for 42½¢ per A, 100 A on Long Br adj John Pain former line, Day. 30 Mar 1819. Wit: Samuel Dickens, John Lunsford.

222-3 Allen Phillips & his wife Elizabeth Allen Phillips of Mecklenburg Co., VA, to Byrd Pulliam, for $80, all their interest & claim to 160 A on Gents Cr adj Byrd Pulliam, Isham Edwards, Cary Williams - said land fell to them from James Pulliam Sen. decd, they being legal heirs & entitled to one-tenth part. 15 Feb 1820. Wit: Benjamin Chambers, J. A. Pulliam. Elizabeth Phillips examined apart fom her husband & executed deed without coercion from her husband.

223 Jesse Ragan to Thomas Ragan, for $100, 50 A on Blewing Cr adj Thomas H Burton, David H. Burton, Jesse Ragan. 11 May 1819. Acknd in open court.

223-4 Hardin Winfree of CC (in debt to Willson & Dixon of CC for $96.66) to Edmund Dixon Sen. of Person Co., in trust, for $1, 93 A adj Archibald Carnal, Alex Cunningham. /s/ Hardy Winfree. 25 Nov 1819. Wit: W. M. Sanders.

224-5 Chesterfield Franklin (in debt to Alexander Winstead & James Williamson, merchants at Roxbrough, for $74.60) to James Gooch, for $1 in trust, 61.3 A on Stories Cr; 8 A he purchased of Samuel Jones & 53.3 A from John Fuller adj Sampson M. Glenn, John Fuller. 2 Feb 1820. Wit: Joseph Gill.

225-6 Benjamin Chambers to heirs of James Cochran decd (whereas William Trickey was in debt to Cochran for 135 lbs,13/10 with deed of trust dated 2 Mar 1807 & then transferred to Benjamin Chambers in trust), 100 A adj Ish Edwards, Robert Brooks, Nancy Graves - said land purchased by James Cochran for $250; this land was willed to William Trickey by his father Giles Trickey. 9 Aug 1818. Wit: Jesse Evans, Wm. Word.

226-7 John Seymore & his wife Agnes Seymore to Byrd Pulliam, for $80, all claim to 160 A on Gents Cr adj Pulliam, Isham Edwards, Cary Williams - said land fell to them as heirs of James Pulliam Sen. decd, their part being one-tenth. 15 Feb 1820. Wit: James A. Pulliam, Benja Chambers. Agnes Seymore examined apart fom her husband & freely executed deed.

227 Henry Womack & Frances Womack his wife to John Scoggin, for $208.24, 52.06 A on Double Cr of S Hico adj Dobbins, Hunt, Woods - said land part of estate of William Cocke decd known as Cooper's tract. 9 Aug 1819. Wit: Saml Brown, Isaac Satterfield. Frances Womack examined apart from her husband & freely acknd contract.

228 Pascal Roberts to William Mitchell, for $120, 160 A in the Missouri Territory in NE Quarter, section 35, township 56N, Range 16W - said land appropriated by Congress of the US for service rendered during the last war. 14 Feb 1820. Also signed by Equaley Roberts. Wit: John McMurry, Joseph Marshall.

228-9 Mathew Brooks (in debt to Thomas Webb for $365.02) to Hugh Woods, trustee, for 50¢, 50 A on Stories Cr adj Robert Deshazo, John Edwards, Hugh Woods, Benja Chambers; horses, cows, furniture, sheep, hogs, wagon, gun. 17 Nov 1819. Wit: Thomas Webb Jun., William Webb, Currie Barnett.

229-30 Jesse Ragon to James Ragon, for $150, 72 A, 1 rod, 37 perches, both sides Bluwing Cr adj John Dixon, William Winstead, Elizabeth Jones, Thomas Halliburton. 12 Feb 1820. Acknd in open court.

230-1 Joseph Tanner & Ailsey Tanner his wife of Williamson Co., TN (Ailsey an heir of Benjamin Harrison decd of Person Co.) to Lawrence Vanhook Hargis, for $148, 20.8 A on Flat R being a part of the land where Harrison lived & died adj Solo Cates, Burton, being plat #5 in div lands of Benjamin Harrison. 10 Oct 1818. Privy exam of Ailsey Harrison taken in Williamson.Co., & she freely acknd deed, Sept 1818. Thomas Hardeman Jr. Clerk.

231-3 Murrel Bressee & Nancy Bressee his wife of William Co., TN (Nancy an heir of Benjamin Harrison decd of Person Co.) to Lawrence Vanhook Hargis, for $128, 25.4 A on Flat R being their share of land of Harrison decd adj Brown & known as plat #3 in said div. 12 Nov 1818. Nancy Bressee in privy exam freely acknd contract. Wit: Timothy Shaw, Will Bond.

233-4 George Waite of Bedford Co., TN, to Jesse Lunsford, for 42½¢ per A, 663 A on Tapley Cr to dry br adj Dickens, Paine heirs, Saml Dickens. 30 Mar 1819. Wit: Saml Dickens, John Lunsford.

234 Henry Royster to William Royster, for $500, 105 A on Mitchell Br adj Terrell, Fulcher, Reubin Grinstead, George Johnston, William Frasure. 12 Feb 1820. Wit: Ira Lea, Henry Sergent.

235-7 Sampson M. Glenn (in debt to James Williamson & Ira Lea, merchants, for $772.44½, also to Alex Winstead & Williamson, merchants at Roxborough for $571.30; also debt due State Bank in Raleigh endorsed by Wm. Jeffreys & Alex Winstead & to Bank of New Bern at Milton), to James Gooch, for $1, trustee, 504 A on Stories Cr purchased of Nehemiah Fuller, Wm. Fuller, Chesterfield Franklin, Jesse Dickens adj John Williams, Wm. Boswell, Wm. Hamblin, Solomon Clayborn, Samuel Jones; negroes Tom, Viney; Gooch to sell property to pay debts. 8 Jan 1820. Wit: Joseph Gill.

Deed Book E
Page
237 State of NC - #142 - to James Yarborough, for 50/ per 100 A, 35¼ A on Deep Cr & Mayo adj David Allen, Nathaniel Smith. Entered 22 Apr 1818.

237-8 Samuel Moore to Joel Sweaney, for $400, 135 A on Deep Cr adj Portius Moore, said Sweaney. 1 May 1819. Wit: Henry Sweaney, James Cozart.

238 Kendal Davie to William Davie, for $438.10, negro slave woman Suck about 22 yrs & man Moses about 19 - sold by virtue of deed of trust of Robert Downey 11 Aug last to secure payment of debt due Ambrose Davie. 5 Jan 1820. Wit: John Holloway, Thos Lawson.

238-9 Patty Taylor of Franklin Co., NC, to Benjamin P. Thorp, for $700, 690 A both sides s prong Tar R in Person Co. adj Thomas Person former corner, Bergoon Bird - deducting 100 A sold by Nicholas Murphey to John Day. 24 Nov 1819. Wit: Howel L. Ridley, Howel Briggs, Mims N. Hope, James Johnson. 24 Nov 1819. Proved before Archiblad D. Murphey, Judge Superior Court, 7 Mar 1820 by oath of Howel L. Ridley.

240-1 James McMurry & Elizabeth McMurry to Obediah Pearce, for $2460.50, 483.3 A on double cr of Hico on road fom Hillsborough to Dobbins mill adj Thomas Snipes, Hayes, James Snipes, Henry Lipscomb, Drewry Jones - being tracts purchased of Sml McMurry & one of William McMurry both of which Elizabeth McMurry is entitled to dower; 1 tract purchased of Vincent Lea. 21 Mar 1820. Wit: Duncan Rose, Robt Vanhook, Nath Norfleet.

241-2 Thomas Winstead to James McGehee, Thomas McGehee, Robert Jones, Richard Halliburton, & Archiblad Cearnal, trustees, for $1, ½ A adj Richard Halliburton, Benjamin Halliburton, said Winstead, including passage to spring for purpose of building a Methodist Meeting House to be free to all preachers of the Gospel of respective churches when not occupied by Methodists - also to be occupied as a schoolhouse for the neighborhood; if not built, land to be returned to Winstead. 20 May 1820. Acknd in open court.

242 Joseph Hubbard Senr. of Guilford Co., NC, to Ebeneser Murrow of Person Co., for $291.20, 208 A on Richland Cr adj George Woods, said Hubbard, Joseph Lunsford. 19 June 1820. Wit: Frances Moore, Jacob Hubbard.

243 Jesse Hargis to James Wisdom, for $220, 71 A on Double Cr of Hico adj A. B. Woods, James Jay Sen. 23 Mar 1820. Wit: Robt Vanhook, Augustin Vanhook.

243-4 Nicholas Murphey to John Day, for $250, 100 A being a part of 690 A purchased of Murphey. 20 Mar 1816. Wit: Eli Tapp, Thos Deney. Proved June 1820 on oath Eli Tapp.

244 James Clayton to Dempsey H. Clayton, for $100, 50 A on Deep Cr adj Delamar, Portius Moore, Robert Moore. 29 Dec 1819. Wit: Churchil Delamar.

244-5 Power of attorney - Dicy Vaughan to brother Caswell Vaughan to convey her right & title to 400 A on Cub Cr adj Dickens, Washington, Thos Oakley, Saml Williams, James Kennaday - said tract devised to her & others by her father Zachariah Vaughan in his will. 15 Dec 1817. Wit: James Brewer, Leory Peed.

245-6 Vincent Lea of Petersburg, VA, to James McMurry of Person Co., for $427.50, 130 A on Double Cr of S Hico adj Thos Snipes. 25 May 1817. Wit: John H. McNeill, Gebl B. Lea.

246 Nicholas Thompson of CC to Abner Bradsher, relinquishment of all claim to 4½ A disputed land on Hico adj Thomas Snipes - said land was deeded Thompson by Stephen Pleasant and also to Bradsher by John Pittard. 3 June 1820. Wit: John Bradsher.

246-7 Sidney Moore to James Clack, Saml Webb, Joel Sweaney, Sidney Moore & Portius Moore, all trustees to find suitable site for Methodist Meeting House,

Deed Book E
Page

246-7 cont - for $1, 2 A at the spring adj Moore - said tract being part of Stephen Moore decd land. 10 Nov 1819. Wit: Portius Moore, Griffin Jones.

247-8 William McKissack, sheriff, to William Hargis (due to execution for 15 lbs 15/ against Thomas Cate, Patsy Minshew, & Thomas Hudgins recovered by Henry Turner Senr.), for 5 lbs 1/, 50 A adj Thomas Hargis. 10 June 1809. Wit: Josiah Brown, Richard Holman.

248-9 Duncan Rose (in debt to Andrew B. Wood for $169 & also note due Reubin Walton adm estate of Geoffrey Lipscomb decd for $690.50) to Robert Stanfield, in trust, 220 A adj said Woods, Jesse Hargis, Benja Milner, Jno Scoggin. 19 Feb 1820. Wit: Isaac S. Wood.

249-50 Mathew Brooks to Robert Deshazo, for $500, 50 A both sides Stories Cr adj Hugh Woods, Deshazo. 18 Apr 1820. Wit: Cary Williams.

250 Abraham Hargis to son Jesse Hargis, for love & good will, 71 A on Double Cr of Hico. 24 Apr 1816. Wit: R. Vanhook, Andrew B. Wood.

251 Joseph McGehee of Halifax Co., VA, to Thomas McGehee of Milton, NC, for $8000, 614 A on Cain Cr adj James Hamlett, heirs of Joseph Hall decd, William McGehee, William Dixon, Edmund Dixon Junr., James McCain, David Hemphill. 8 Nov 1819. Wit: Mumford Stanfield, Jno Rogers.

251-2 State of NC - #139 - to Nicholas Thompson, for 50/ per 100 A, 15 A on S Hico in Person Co. adj said Thompson, McNeill. Entered 9 Mar 1818.

252-3 Samuel Bull (in debt to Josias Carver for $300) to William McKissack, trustee, for $1, 100 A on Stories Cr adj Jacob Couch, Isham Edwards, Nancy Graves. 28 Jan 1820. Wit: R. Satterfield.

254 Robert Harris to William Harris, for $547.40, 273.7 A on Blewing & crooked fork of Aaron's Cr adj Henry Hemphill. 20 Dec 1819. Wit: Overton Harris.

254-5 John Frew (in debt to Elizabeth Frew for $30) to Azza Frew, for $1, trustee, 74 A on Stories Cr adj Richard Hamblin, Daniel Clayton, John Hudgins; John Frew to possess same until Jan next. Wit: John Frew. (John Trew)
NB The name Trew was written Frew by mistake of Register, B. W. Milner.

256 Samuel Blackwell (trustee for William Southward in debt due Isham Edwards for $119.97) as debt not paid - 66 A sold to Isham Edwards for $119.97. 1 Apr 1820. Wit: John Barnett, G. W. Willson.

257 Samuel Bull (trustee for Robert Southward Sen. who was in debt to Isham Edwards for $103.50) as debt not paid - to Isham Edwards, for $60, 30 A adj Ruben Long Junr., William Clayton. 18 Mar 1820. Wit: Jesse Bull, Robert Johnston.

258 Billy Carver Jun. to Josias Carver, for $187.50, 120 A on Stories Cr adj Hosea Carver, Walters; excepting land which mill pond covers which is for the benefit of his six brothers: Josias Carver, Robert Carver, Landrom Carver, Losen Carver, Hosea Carver. 4 Nov 1814. Wit: Wm. McKissack, Jeofrey Lipscomb.

259 James Clayton to Griffin Jones, for $560, 225 A on Deep Cr adj Demsey Clayton, Churchwel Delamar, Cameron, Robert Moore. 11 Mar 1820. Wit: Portius Moore, Dempsey Clayton.

259-60 John Day to Isaac Day, for $284.50, 102 A on Deep Cr being part of tract purchased of Wm. Cocke adj Cothran, Satterfield. 21 June 1820. Wit: John Bumpass, Solomon Griffin.

260-1 Lemuel Rainey to Alexander Winstead, trustee (Robert Vanhook endorses for said Rainey to Obediah Pearce on bond for $750), for $1 paid by Winstead, 100 A adj Alexander Gordon, Saml Woods, with mills & tenements. 12 Nov 1819. Wit: Joseph Gill.

261-2 John Ravens to Jesse Satterfield, for $400, 80.7 A on Richland Cr of Hyco adj Clay, Isaac Satterfield. 26 Jan 1820. Wit: Duncan Rose, Isaac Satterfield.

Deed Book E
Page

262-3 Elijah Williams to Caswell Vaughan, for $102, 50 A on Cub Cr adj Samuel Williams, James Cannaday - it being part of an undivided tract belonging to heirs of Zachariah Vaughan decd & drawn by Caswell Vaughan but sold by Robert Vanhook, sheriff, to grantor who resells to Caswell Vaughan. 23 Aug 1820. Wit: Wm. Philpot, Thos Philpot.

263-4 Thomas Jeffreys of CC to his son George Washington Jeffreys, for natural love & affection, 850 A on S Hyco & mouth of N Hyco adj George Tapp, John Harris, Leath, William Trotter, Smith to Mitchel br, Richd Ogilby former land - including all islands. 24 June 1820. Wit: James Rainey, James W. Jeffreys.

264 Ezekiel Duncan to George Duncan, for $250, 125 A on Gents Cr adj Josias Carver, James Cochran, Cary Williams. 19 Nov 1814. Wit: Ish Edwards, John Dixon.

265-6 Moses Bradsher of CC to John Bradsher of Person Co., for $1920, 240 A in Person Co. on Cobb Cr of N Hico adj heirs of William Johnson decd, Thomas Carver formerly Thomas Neely, heirs of Zachariah Lea decd, Nicholas Thompson formerly Thomas Douglas, John McFarland formerly Saml Johnston - said land was granted to Hamilton Reynolds by State 10 Nov 1784 registered in CC & then deeded to Bradsher 20 Nov 1804. 8 Aug 1820. Wit: James O. Bradsher.

266 Joseph Southward to Talton Morton, for $245, 73.20 A on Adams Cr adj Isham Edwards, John Shelton, Mitchel. 17 Apr 1820. Wit: Jesse Bradsher, Isham Edwards.

266-7 Archiblad Carnal to Durratt Stanfield, for $210, 28.9 A. 27 Apr 1820. Wit: Jacob Faulkner, Obadiah Faulkner, Thos J. Terrel.

267-9 Robert Hamlet (in debt to Alexr Cunningham for $236.76) to Archiblad Carnal, trustee, for $1, 128.75 A adj Thomas Walton, Thomas M. Hamlett, John Hamblet; livestock, furniture. 25 Sept 1820. Wit: Jno Garner.

269 Samuel Davey to Birges Walker, for $500 pd by Edward Mitchell decd, 165 A both sides Mill Br adj Allen, said Davie on the CH road. 12 Aug 1820. Wit: Wm. Davie, J. Walker.

270-1 Durrett Stanfield (in debt to Alexr Cuningham for $1113.76) to Archibald Carnal, trustee, for $1, 100 A adj Robt Jones, John H. Burton; negro man Martin about 36 yrs old, negro girl Elizabeth about 10 yrs old; horses, livestock, furniture. 7 Mar 1820. Wit: Thomas Winstead, Robert Jones, J. Garner.

271-2 Henry Lipscomb to William McMurry, for $737½, 196 A adj Obadiah Pearce, James Snipes, Wade, William Lipscomb, Jacob Thomas. 23 Sept 1820. Wit: C. S. McMurry, Jos McMurry.

272-3 Roger Tilman to Richard N. Tilman, for $400, 104 A on Rosebrock Br adj James Johnson, William McKissack, Thomas Grant, heirs of James D. Henley, James Jordan. 19 Sept 1820. Wit: John Tilman, George Tilman.

273-4 Jesse Watson Sen. to John Stanfield & Barbara Green, for $125, all dower right to 66 A belonging to Lewis Green decd adj James Pain, James Jay Senr., heirs of Lewis Green decd - to take effect after death of Elizabeth Watson formerly wife of Lewis Green decd. 29 Oct 1811. Wit: Duncan Rose, John Raven.

274 Archibald Carnal to Durratt Stanfield, for $210, 78.9 A on the creek. 27 Apr 1820. Wit: Jacob Faulkner, Obadiah Faulkner, Thos J. Terrell.

275-6 Robert Hamlet (in debt to Alexander Cunningham for $226.26) to Archiblad Carnal, trustee, for $1, 138.75 A adj Thos Walton, Thos M. Hamlet, Jno Hamlet, plus all his interest in land where Frances Hamlet now lives; livestock, furniture. 25 Sept 1820. Wit: Jno Garner.

276-7 Samuel Dickens, sheriff, to William McKissack (due to execution against Hardy Johnston for $29 recovered by Alex Winstead), for $85, 80 A on Henley Mill Cr adj Saml Winstead, Roger Tilman, Lewis Amis. 22 Sept 1820. Acknd in open court.

277-8 Asa Hudgens to Benja Phillips, for $50, 55 A on Flat R adj Thomas Hargis, 25 Sept 1820. Wit: Peter Wolf, George Duncan.

278-9 George Duncan (in debt to Isham Edwards for $275.88) to William Williams, trustee, for $1, 125 A adj Drury Pulliam, Josias Carver; livestock, furniture, pewter dishes. 25 Sept 1820. Wit: Green W. Brown, Stephen W. Dickens.

279-80 James Williamson to Archibald Lipscomb, for $300, 30 A adj dower of Dorothy Lipscomb; said tract sold by court of equity to James Williamson. 8 Dec 1819. Wit: Alexr Moore.

280-1 John Hamlet (in debt to Alexander Cunningham for $470.07) to Archibald Carnal, in trust, for $1, 40½ A adj Thos Waller, Thomas M. Hamlet; livestock, furniture. 21 Sept 1820. Wit: Jno Garner.

281-2 James Philpot of Granville Co. to John W. Philpot of same, for $3259.80, 668 A on Mayo adj Edwd B. Davie, James Philpot, Winstead; said land purchased of heirs of William Davie decd. 2 June 1819. Wit: Will Philpot, Solomon Philpot.

282-3 William McKissack to Thomas Lawson, for $77.78, 80 A which he purchased at sheriff sale as land of Hardy Johnson on Henly Mill Cr adj Roger Tilman, Saml Winstead, Lewis Amis. 22 Sept 1820. Acknd in open court.

283 Moses Fullar to William Hargis, for $150, 100 A adj Hargis. Delivered 15 Sept 1819. 14 Aug 1818. Wit: Duncan Rose.

284 Moses Chambers to Josias Chambers, for $610, 168½ A on Mayo adj Halliburton, Man, Baird. 27 Dec 1819. Wit: Wm. Davie, Wm. Jeffreys.

284-5 Laurence Richardson to Nathaniel Torian, for $900, 150 A n side Hico adj John Russell, Downey Wade. /s/ L. R. Richardson. 15 Mar 1819. Wit: Chs D. Wade, Downey Wade.

285 Richard Hamlin to John Hudgins, for $100, 85 A on Stories Cr adj Richd Harris, John Harris, Isaiah Fuller, Daniel Clayton, John Frew(John Trew). 11 Jan 1820. Wit: Josias Chambers, Wm. Chambers.

286 Alexander Winstead & Sally Winstead his wife, Bartholomew Hayes & Martha Hayes his wife to William R. Robinson of Orange Co., for $1350, 239 A s prong Flat R adj James Cocke - reserving for themselves the grave yard of 1 A including the yard a small distance n of dwelling house. 27 Sept 1820. Wit: Joseph Gill, Isaac Satterfield, Saml Brown.
Sally Winstead & Martha Hayes examined apart from their husbands & freely executed deed.

287 State of NC - #143 - to Robert Mann, for 50/ per 100 A, 200 A on Cub Cr & Rocky Fork adj Saml Dickens, Riley Suit, William Blalock heirs. Entered 20 Aug 1818.

287-8 Benj. B. Cocke, Rebecca Paine, John W. Williams & Susannah his wife, Sally Cocke, Robt Paine & Polly his wife, John Cocke, Martha Cocke, Henry Womack & Frances his wife - all heirs of William Cocke decd - to Jesse Evans, for $632.25, 230 A on Flat R s side s prong which Wm. Cocke possessed adj John Cates, Richard Holman, Charles Holman, Charles Rountree Jun., to quarrel cr. 28 May 1813. Wit: Samuel Dickens, Saml Yarbrough, Jas Satterfield, Lewis Daniel, Richd Holman.

289-90 William Fullar Senr. to Moses Fullar, for $1600, 130 A on Richland Cr adj Asa Fullar, Richard Atkinson, Carter Lea; William Fullar to possess land for his lifetime & lifetime of his wife Sarah Fullar; Moses Fullar to take immediate possession of mill. 31 Mar 1820. Wit: Aaron Fullar, Jesse G. Fullar, J. A. Pulliam.

Deed Book E
Page

290-1 Thomas Dixon to Warren Dixon, for $350, 50 A w side Hyco adj Robt Jones, on road from Red House to McGehee mill. /s/ Thomas Dickson. 22 Nov 1820. Wit: Jesse Bradsher, Alex Moore, James Stuart.

291 Richard Lea Jun. to George Lea Jun., for $227.50, 55½ A on Cobs Cr being tract conveyed by heirs of James Lea Sen. decd to Benja Lea his brother adj Richd Lea Senr., George Lea, Abner Lea. 7 Dec 1820. Wit: Ira Lea, J. A. Pulliam.

291-2 James Snipes to Anderson Snipes, for $150, 60 A on Double Cr of S Hico adj Wm. Williams, the old Moravian line, near an old schoolhouse. 15 Dec 1820. Wit: Saml Brown, James Snipes Jun.

292-3 Richard Hallibruton (in debt to Edmund Dixon Senr. for $638.12) to William Dixon, in trust, for $1, 150 A adj Robt Jones, Thos McGehee, James McGehee, Thos Winstead. 7 Dec 1820. Wit: Jno Garner, Thos Winstead, Leak Dixon.

294 Aaron Fullar to William Westbrook, for $210, 70 A on S Hico adj John Clixby, Carter Lea, William Fullar, Moses Fullar, Charles Winstead, to CH road. 3 Aug 1820. Wit: Jno Rice, Moses Fullar, Jesse G. Fullar.

294-5 Robert Vanhook, sheriff, to Gabriel B. Lea of Orange Co. (due to execution against Thorndon Black for $177.85 recovered by said Lea) for $177.85, tract on N Hyco in Person Co. adj William Dixon, Edmund Dixon Jun. - it being undivided tract of land which fell to Thordon Black by death of his father. 23 Dec ? . Wit: Parthenia Vanhook, Sally Vanhook.

296 James Clayton to Churchill Delamar, for $130, 87 A on Deep Cr adj Cameron, said Delamar. 5 Mar 1819. Wit: Dempsey Clayton, Susan Holsonback.

296-7 John Towler of CC to John Russell, as trustee, 4 cows to secure payment of $20 due as his part of a judgment where George Towler is principal & George Whitefield & John Towler, securities. 2 Feb 1821. Wit: Wm. Whitefield, J. Bowden.

297-8 Jesse Bull (in debt to Samuel Blackwell for $350.50), to Thomas Webb, for 50¢ in trust, his undivided interest in 319 A which his father possessed on Stories Cr adj James Long, Paul Walters; his undivided interest in 7 negroes: Lucy, Jane, Bill, Isbell, Will, Frank & Blalack; livestock, furniture; all his interest in debts due his decd father. 18 Dec 1820. Wit: Hugh Woods.

298 Thomas Talbert to Lewis Amis, for $272.75, 68.2 A on Henley Mill Cr adj William Trotter, William Gold, Roger Tilman. 20 Aug 1811. Wit: Banja Chambers, Roger Tilman.

298-9 Francis Lawson to Solomon Walker, for $400, 200 A on Fray's Br adj Samuel Davie, James Redwood, Mitchel, Bergis Walker, Wm. Buchanon, Harrison Davie. 25 Nov 1820. Wit: John Melton, Moses Springfield.

299-301 Robert Vanhook, sheriff, to Joseph & Thomas McGehee (due to court order against Hardin Winfree for $108.07½ recovered by McGehee 20 Aug 1820) for $12, 92 A on little Cain Cr adj Archiblad Carnal, John Halliburton, Alexr Cunningham. 20 Aug 1820. Acknd in open court.
This tract of land had been conveyed by Hardin Winfree in deed of trust to Wilson & Dixon of Milton, NC,; debt due McGehee paid and deed of trust transferred to Wilson & Dixon. Wit: Edmund Dixon Senr., Edward D. Bolton.

301 Shadrack Gentry to his son Abednego Gentry, for love & affection, 105 A on Castle Cr adj Charles Allen, Charles Bostick former line, said Gentry. 26 Dec 1820. Wit: Johnson Davis, A. Gentry.

302-3 Benjamin Halliburton of Halifax Co., VA, (in debt to Edmund Dixon Sen. for $789.34) to William Dixon, in trust, for $1, 221 A adj Richd Halliburton, Thos Winstead, Robert Jones, Durret Stanfield, John Halliburton. 7 Dec 1820. Wit: Jno Garner, Thos Winstead.

165

Deed Book E
Page
303-4 Joel Hicks (in debt to Jesse Bumpass for $75) to John Daniel, in trust, for $1, 70 A on Richland Cr adj George Wood, Rebecca Burton. 24 Aug 1820. Wit: Jos Traylor, Hutchins Burton.

304 John Tilman to Richard N. Tilman, for $350, 100 A adj Jane Clay dower line, Roger Tilman, Wm. Satterfield after death of Mrs. Clay. 11 Nov 1820. Proved in open court.

305 John Shelton to Isham Edwards, for $88, 40 A on Stories Cr adj John Seymore, Reuben Long Junr. 15 Nov 1820. Wit: G. W. Wilson, Robt Johnston.

305-6 Mary Winningham to Tryon Yancey of Granville Co., for $150, 54 A on Donelson Cr adj Baird, Winstead; it being tract allotted her as her dower in lands of Sharp Winningham decd her late husband. 8 NOv 1820. Wit: John Brown, Thomas Winningham, Abraham Eastwood, James Ragan.

306-7 John Cummins Senr. to his children Margaret Cummins, Mary Cummins, & Alexander Cummins, for love & affection, 200 A; cattle, furniture, excepting one bed. 25 Dec 1820. Wit: Charles Holeman, Richd Holeman.

307-8 Robert Vanhook, sheriff, to Joel Sweaney (due to court order against Richard Peed to collect $84.35 recovered by Marmaduke Roberts), for $52.50, 206 A on Cub Cr adj Abram Medeares, Bennett Williams Jun. 1 Aug 1820. Wit: John Phillips, Parthenia Vanhook.

309 Robert Blalack to William Fowler, for $250, 210 A on Rocky Fork Cr adj Saml Dickens, William Cocke decd, John Sweaney, James Cozart, Jonathan Jackson. 17 Mar 1820. Wit: Richd Hargis, Edward Villines.

309 Charles D. Smith of CC to James Satterfield of Person Co., for $300, negro girl Sine. 10 Mar 1820. Wit: Stephen Dodson.

310 Edward Martin to Hyram Holt of Halifax Co., VA, for $105.75, 160 A being NW corner of Quarter 35, township 56N in Range 16W in tract appropriated by Congress for military bounties in territory of Missouri; patent dated 10 Apr 1819. 8 Mar 1821. Wit: Robert Brandon.

311 Edward Wilson (in debt to John Holt of Halifax Co., VA, for $30) to Robert Brandon, in trust, for $1, 4 horses, wagon, cow, hogs; furniture. 15 June 1820. Wit: Robt Hblt.

312 James Wrenn to David Jeffreys, for $110, ? A in the Missouri Territory, SW quarter, section 27, township 54N, Range 2W in tract appropriated by Congress in May 1812 for military bounties. /s/ James Renn. 29 Oct 1819. Wit: Duncan Rose, Lewis Tapp.

312-3 Edward Lewis to David Jeffreys, for $180, 160 A in Illinois Territory SW quarter, Section 34, township 3S, Range 6W in tract for military bounties. 30 Oct 1819. Wit: John Douglas, Lewis Daniel.

313-4 James Satterfield (in debt to Sherwood Haywood, agt of Newbern Bank at Raleigh for $700 with Isaac Satterfield & William McKissack, securities; also debt due James Jay Senr for $400: one to Wm. McKissack & Williamson) to Green W. Brown & John Read, in trust, for 75¢, 400 A on Richland Cr adj James Milner, Lewis Daniel; also negro slaves: Cyrus, Isaac, Sally & her 3 children Dick, Mary, Peter. 10 Mar 1821. Wit: S. McKissack, Saml Webb.

314-5 John D. Moore (in debt to Lewis Daniel for $2500) to Isham Edwards, in trust for $1, lot #41 in Milton, CC; also lot #33; his interest in 4 negroes Jack, Saml, Dianner, Washington; horses, cattle, hogs; furniture; 3000 lbs tobacco. 27 Feb 1821. Wit: G. W. Willson, Hugh Woods.

315-6 William Winstead to Jonas Parker, for $243, negro woman Martha. 2 Jan 1821. Proved by oath William Yarbrough.

Deed Book E
Page
316 Carter Atkinson (in debt to Richard Atkinson for several notes & to Bank of NC) to Ira Lea, in trust, for 50¢, negro man Ephraim; also all his part of land willed to him & his brother by Thomas Atkinson their father adj Moses Fuller, James Bradsher; his interest in lot in Milton with brick house thereon on Main St. adj Charles Willson, Warren Williams. 4 Oct 1820. Wit: Duncan Rose.

317 Asa Fullar to Ira Lea, for $115.50, 38½ A on Richland Cr adj James Williamson, James Bradsher, Richd Atkinson near Haw Br. 17 Mar 1821. Wit: Stephen Sergent, Hardy Johnson.

317-8 Willis Nichols to Lemuel Sneed, for $500, 189 A on Flat R adj Robt Cates, James Cochran, Cameron, Clements. 3 Jan 1821. Wit: James Gooch, L. V. Hargis.

318-20 John M. McGehee (in debt to Thomas McGehee of Milton for $2137.66; to McGehee & Stanfield of Milton for $2000; to Bank of New Bern - plus other debts) to George W. Jeffreys, in trust, for $1, 400 A where he lives on Hyco adj Thomas Sheppard; also 706 A called the Allen tract adj Moses Chambers; negro slaves: Henry age 21, Moses 20, Ellick 22, Nat 18, Hall 18, London 12, Richd 4, Billy 10, Sall 45, Milly 30, Leddy 15, Lizzy 15, Betty 6, Frankey 10, Mary 7, Hannah 20 & her child 1 yr. 18 Feb 1820. Wit: Wm. McGehee, Joseph McGehee.

320 Jacob Waggoner of Orange Co. to Laurence V. Hargis, for $47.50, an undivided fifth part of tract of 306 A owned by Conrad Messer Smith decd & same reverted to Valentine Smith his son & heir who is now dead & land reverts to his heirs: Thomas Smith, Leonard Smith. Valentine Smith, Mary Carter wife to Thomas J. Carter all of Elbert Co., GA; Thomas Smith adm estate of Valentine Smith sold his part to Jacob Waggoner 7 Nov 1817 adj Duncan Cameron, James Williamson. 10 Jan 1821. Wit: Jas Gooche, Jas Turner.

321-2 David Jeffreys to William McKissack Jun., for $3179, 374 A n side Flat R near Lewis Daniel mill to Richland Cr adj Milner, Paine, to mouth Rattlesnake Br. 17 July 1820. Wit: G. W. Brown, Sm Dickens.

322 James Clack to Duncan Cameron of Orange Co., for $700, negro woman & 3 children to wit: Farthey, Fanny, John, Becky. 7 Mar 1821. Wit: Henry Sweaney, Jos Lunsford.

322-3 Samuel Forsythe of Granville Co. to Jno Stanfield, for $150 due on notes & credit of $120 plus other notes, all his right & title to 200 A conveyed by said Stanfield & John Stephenson to Forsythe - said land he purchased of Redford Gooch, trustee, on Double Cr of S Hico adj James Williamson, Abm Hargis, Jas Wisdom, Jas Jay; land formerly property of Lewis Green decd and divided to his 2 daughters Jane Stanfield wife of John Stanfield & Barbara Stephenson wife of Jno Stephenson. Jno Stanfield has conveyed his title to Stephenson & he to Redford Gooch in trust. Also signed by Edwd Jones. 26 Jan 1821. Wit: Edmund D. Stanfield, James Forsythe.

323-4 Richard Rogers gives bond as Constable of Person Co. with John Vanhook & James Clay of Milton as securities. To secure indemnity, for $1 pd by John Scott of Hillsboro, all his right & interest to negroes which John Rogers decd bequeathed to children of Byrd Rogers decd subject to support of Littleton Rogers: negro woman Esther, old man Ned, Litt, young Esther & her infant son, Mary & her infant child, Nell, Mark, Lewis, Jude, young Ned, Moses. 14 Mar 1821. Wit: Alex Winstead.

324 David Wall to Thomas McGehee, for $20, an undivided interest in tract both sides Hyco adj Alexr Cunningham & known as Wall tract which fell to him at death of his brother Hampton Wall, he being lawful owner of one-ninth part of 487 A. 20 Dec 1820. Wit: Alexr Moore, Wm. Chambers.

Deed Book E
Page
325 William Dickens & Samuel Dickens, exec of Robert Dickens decd, to Isaac Webb, for $1500, 700 A on Hog Pen Br of Mayo adj Clayton, Scoggins, Jno Day Jun., Lunsford, Moses Street, Springfield, including entire grant from State #1023 dated 15 July 1790 to Robert Dickens & part of grant #1025. 23 Mar 1821. Wit: Henry H. Allen, Riley Suit.

325-6 William McKissack, sheriff, to John Satterfield (due to court order against David Satterfield et al for 24 lbs 15/ & recovered by John Satterfield), for 29 lbs 15/3, 158 A on Deep Cr adj Jno Day Jun., Jno Cochran, heirs of Jno Yarbrough decd, Ambrose Day. 8 Nov 1817. Acknd in open court.

326-7 Obediah Pearce to Abraham Moore, for $600, 221¼ A on Flat R adj Jno Brown old corner, said Pearce to Bushy Fork. 5 Jan 1821. Wit: Stephen Moore, R.Moore.

327-8 David Berry of Orange Co. to Simeon Cochran, trustee, of Person Co. (Berry in debt to Wm. McKissack for $300), for $1, negro girl Emy age 17 yrs now in possession of McKissack. 27 Nov 1821. Wit: R. G. Cummins, Saml Mader.

328 Bennett Williams to Elijah Williams, for 125 lbs, negro boy Luke about 12 yrs old. 13 Nov 1813. Wit: Jno Jacobs, Nathan Oakly.

328-9 John Drury Moore to Alexander Moore, for $1750, 175 A on Hico adj Charles Sallard, Harrison Stanfield, Robt Jones. 24 Feb 1821. Wit: Ish Edwards, R. Long.

329-30 Goodrich Jones to son Eli A. Jones, for love & affection, negro Lawson age 12 yrs. 21 Nov 1820. Wit: Adams G. Richmond, Jas Martin.

330 Goodrich Jones to daughter Sally Richmond & son-in-law Adams S. Richmond, for love & affection, negro girl Betsy age 15 yrs. 21 Nov 1820. Wit: James Martin, Eli A. Jones.

330-1 Jno M. McGehee of Person Co. to Mumford Stanfield of Milton, trustee, for $1, horses, cattle, hogs, sheep; 2 stills; wagon, leather top riding chair; 8 beds & other furniture; bond on Abraham Percy of Lancaster Dist. SC; bond on Warren Williams of Halifax Co., VA; 50 barrels corn, 250 bushels wheat; 3500 lbs tobacco; said deed to secure note of Jno M. McGehee with William McGehee, Thos McGehee, & Joseph McGehee who have signed as securities for note due Bank of New Bern for $1500. 2 Feb 1821. Wit: Thos McGehee, William McGehee.

331-2 Nancy McKissack (in debt to James Milner guardian to orphans of Jonathan McKissack for $150) to James Satterfield, trustee, for 50¢, 120 A where she lives on head waters Double Cr of Hico adj Alexr Gray, Nathl Norfleet, Wilson Jones former tract. 24 May 1820. Wit: S. Cochran, Lewis Daniel.

332-3 James Gooch, trustee for Sampson M. Glenn, to James Williamson, for $801.30, 504 A on Stories Cr adj Jno W. Williams, Wm. Bozwell, Wm. Hamlin, Solomon Clayton, Saml Jones - being 4 tracts:105 A purchased of Nehemiah Fullar, 145 A of William Fullar, 111 A of Chesterfield Franklin, 143 A of Jesse Dickens; Glenn debt to several merchants was unpaid. 27 Mar 1821. Wit: W. Jeffreys, Duncan Rose.

333-4 Downey Wade of Person Co. (in debt to Nicholas Thompson of CC for $437.18¼) to Labon Farley, for $1, trustee, negro boy Harbard age 19 yrs now in possession of Thompson. 24 Aug 1820. Wit: B. C. Allen.

334-5 Ish Edwards to Byrd Pulliam, for $126, 32 A where Elizabeth Pulliam formerly lived on Gents Cr which Edwards purchased at sheriff sale & was former property of Jno W. Pulliam & Mary Stone who were legatees of James Pulliam decd. 26 Feb 1820. Wit: Currie Barnett, Benja Chambers.

335 John G. Wade to Moses Chambers & Robt Jones, for $64.12, all claim & title to following negroes: Rhoda & her children Buck, Ben, Russell, Burwell, Hannah, Esther; he was legatee with brothers & sisters Edmund Tinsley Wade, Jane Mary, Sally, Robt, & James Wade. 6 Mar 1820. Wit: B. Walker, Jesse Walker.

Deed Book E
Page

336-7 David Jeffreys of Person Co. to Duncan Cameron of Orange Co., for $4500, 292½ A on Tapley Cr n side n fork Flat R adj James Milner, Clack field, Ben Morrow old field, Cameron fromerly Elizabeth Jeffreys (lot #2), dower allotted to Susan Jeffreys, lot #4 of James O Jeffreys -it being part of land of Paul Jeffreys decd allotted to his daughter Lucy as lot #3. Proved in open court in TN before Judge Nathl W. Williams 23 Aug 1820. Proved Person Co. Mar 1821.

337-8 John Hudgins to Thomas V. Hargis, for $53, 153 A on Flat R adj Jopling old line, Thomas Hargis. 27 Mar 1821. Wit: J. Bumpass.

338-40 James Daniel of CC (in debt to Bank of Newbern at their Milton office for $920 & for $1600; to State Bank for $750 plus other notes with Mark Wilson & Jno Smith both of CC securities) to William Pleasant Hall of CC, in trust, for $1, 23 Negroes: Jim age 27 yrs, Davy about 60, Irena, Joy & her 3 children Green, Nancy & young Adam, Phill, Phillis, Hall, Lewis, Sucky, Anderson, Randolph, Washington, Nancy, Juda & her child Milly, Mary, Dilsy, Nancy age 11; tenement on Bridge St in Milton adj J. Hubbard & Jno P. Pugh; tenement on Bridge St purchased of R. Sanders adj Shields; livestock; also 336 A on Cob Cr. 13 Nov 1820. Wit: Jno Gordon.

340-1 Drucilla Vaughan, Milly Vaughan, Caswel Vaughan who is empowered to act for Dicy Vaughan & for himself, Abraham Anderson & Dorcas Anderson his wife - all of Person Co. - to Arris Vaughan of same, for $42.50, 11 A former land of Zachariah Vaughan decd on s side Cub Cr adj Nathan Oakley, Arris Vaughan. 23 Dec 1820. Wit: William Philpot, Nathan Oakley.

341-2 Drucilla Vaughan, Milly Vaughan, Caswel Vaughan for self & for Dicy Vaughan, Abraham Anderson & Dorcas Anderson his wife - all of Person Co. - to Nathan Oakley, for $228.75, 61 A & 76 poles on Cub Cr & Vaughan Br - said land former that of Zachariah Vaughan decd. The 76 poles exempted for the graveyard. 24 Aug 1820. Wit: Wm. Philpot, Thos Philpot.

342-3 Spivy McKissack & Susanna McKissack his wife to William McKissack, for $3500, 524 A being part of dower of Susannah McKissack of lands of Paul Jeffreys decd on s side Flat R on Rattlesnake Br adj Lewis Daniel. 9 Feb 1821. Wit: Portius Moore, Jno Reed. Susannah McKissack examined apart fom her husband & executed deed of own free will. John Garner, JP.

343-5 Americus V. Dixon & Lucy Dixon of Smith Co., TN, to David Jeffreys of Person Co, for $3500, 2 tracts on Tapley Cr & Flat R: 296½ A adj James Milner, Clack field, Benja Morrow old field, Duncan Cameron formerly John Lyon & Elizabeth Lyon, the dower line, James O. Jeffreys - it being all land allotted to Lucy Dixon from estate of Paul Jeffreys decd, called lot #3; also ¼ part of undivided tract of dower land of 900 A possessed by Spivy McKissack who married widow of Paul Jeffreys decd. 29 Mar 1820.
Lucy Dixon examined in Smith Co., TN, apart from husband & freely agreed to deed. Proved Person Co. Mar 1821.

345-6 Jno James Brooks to Daniel Briggs, for $50, 22 A on Dry Br adj James Holloway, Lewis Ramsey. 21 Nov 1818. Wit: Gabl Bailey, Wilie Brooks.

346-8 Thomas J. Chambers (in debt to Alexr Cunningham for $1779.33 with Wm. Chambers & Jno M. McGehee, securities) to Cary Williams, trustee, for $1, negroes Allen age 35 yrs, Simon 28, Matt 26, Scot 18, Anderson 14, Richard 12, Molly & her child Sarah, Rachel 21, old Milly 23 with her 3 children, Letty 11, Harrison 7, Martha 5, Sucky 28, Jenny 26, Aggy 45. 13 Jan 1820. Wit: Jno Garner, Jas P. Harrison.

348-9 Asa Fuller (in debt to Ira Lea & James Williamson, merchants, for $309.85¼) to John Bradsher, in trust, for 50¢, negro boy Arter age 15 yrs. 21 Feb 1821. Wit: Hezekiah Morton, James Dollarhide.

Deed Book E
Page

349-50 Polly Wright,exec of last will of Anderson Rose decd,now of CC to Ira Lea of Person Co., for $56.40, 70 A on Stories Cr on road from Roxbrough to Sampson M. Glenn adj Cochran, William McKissack; land sold during lifetime of Anderson Rose & no deed conveyed. 17 July 1820. Wit: Hezekiah Morton.

350-1 James Daniel of CC (in debt to State Bank of NC at Milton office & at Raleigh office for several sums with Richard Ogilby & Wm. Irvine, securities) to Edward H. Ogilby of CC, trustee, for $1, 336 A in Person Co. on Cob Cr adj Richd Ogilby, Saml Smith; part of lot #1 in Milton on Main St with 73 front ft; slaves Adam age 46, Phillis 38, Nancy 10, Irena 8, Lewis 5, Henry 17, Phill 48, Suck 22, Anderson 7, Randolph 6, Washington 4. 17 Oct 1820. Wit: Hugh J. Ogilby, Charles Sims. Proved CC Jan 1821; proved Person Co. Mar 1821.

352-3 Samuel Dickens to Portius Moore, Phillips Moore, James Clayton, Dempsey Clayton, James Clack, Churchwel Delamar, Yancy Moore, Albert Moore, & Sidney Moore - all trustees - 5 A on a branch on Hillsboro Rd to erect a house of worship for Methodist Episcopal Church - grant is void if church is abandoned (which we pray God to forbid).20 Nov 1816. Acknd in open court.

353-4 Cary Williams,exec to last will of James D. Henley decd, to Lewis Amis, for $1500.80, 292 A on br of Hico adj Saml Winstead, Ira Lea, James Jordan, William Trotter. This satisfies contract made with Amis 28 Dec 1815 to sell him this land. 24 Mar 1821. Wit: Wm. McKissack.

354 William Hargis to James Williamson, for $816, 408 A on Flat R adj Thomas Hargis, _ _ 1820. Wit: Wm. Jeffreys, Dennis Obriant.

355 Jesse Peed (in debt to James Gooch for $61.21 with George Peed, security) to Harris Wilkerson, for 25¢, trustee, 100.75 A on Cub Cr adj George Peed, William Cozart, Bennet Williams Jun.; sows, pigs. 20 Jan 1821. Wit: William Fowler.

356-7 Jesse Bull (in debt to Isham Edwards for $129.80) to Benjamin Chambers, for $1, trustee, his interest to negro woman Bet willed by Moses Walker decd to Jesse Bull after death of his father & mother, Jacob Bull & Elizabeth Bull; will probate Sept 1806; also his undivided part of land where his mother now lives; corn, furniture, cattle. 26 Dec 1820. Wit: Jno Hudgins, G. W. Wilson.

357-8 Samuel Dickens to John Lunsford, for $1200, 600 A on Deep Cr adj Jesse Lunsford, Robt Dickens, Saml Webb, Bumpass. 15 Mar 1821. Wit: Eli Tapp.

358 John Winstead to Lewis Amis, for $400, 128 A on Hyco adj Hugh Darby, William Rainey, Jno Mason, Henry Royster. 22 Aug 1811. Wit: Jno Dickson, Leonard Morris.

358-9 Edmund Dixon Jun., trustee, to Willson & Dixon of Milton, CC, for $111, 93 A adj Archibald Carnal, Alex Cunningham - land sold to satisfy deed of trust conveyed to Dixon as trustee by Hardin Winfree. 25 Dec 1820. Acknd in open court.

359 Jesse Dickens to son Stephen Moore Dickens, for love & affection, 300 A on Deep Cr adj Saml Webb, on public road to Mud Br, Samuel Dickens, Osborn Jeffreys. 25 Feb 1819. Wit: Robt Dickens.

359-60 Jesse Bull, constable, received of Duncan Rose $75 for negro boy Burrel property of Robert Wade & sold due to execution at instance of Rose & Chambers. 4 Sept 1819. Wit: Alex Winstead.

360-1 Lewis Ramsey (in debt to John Holloway for $118.11) to James Holloway, for 5/, in trust, 211 A where Ramsey lives said land conveyed him by William Ramsay. 28 Dec 1820. Wit: Crowder Holloway.

361-2 Duncan Rose (in debt to several banks with Richard Atkinson security up to $4000), to James Williamson, trustee, 355 A on Hico adj Addison Cochran, Wm. Brown; also 1 lot at Roxboro & 105 A near said lot. 19 Feb 1820. Wit: C. Atkinson, Atk^n Palham.

362-3 Duncan Rose to Carter Atkinson, in trust, for 25¢, 530 A where Rose lives adj Jno Raven, James Williamson, Robt Vanhook; also 318 A called the Glenn tract adj Robt Vanhook, heirs of Elijah Mitchel; negro blacksmith Dave & Charles; said deed of trust to secure Richard Atkinson as security for former note. Sept 1820. Wit: Atk^n Palham, Green W. Brown.
NB - By consent of Richard Atkinson, slave Peter exchanged for Charles. 17 Nov 1820.

363-4 Downey Wade (in debt to Nathaniel Torian for 2 bonds) to Robert D. Wade, for $1, in trust, negroes Bill, Nutty, Adelina, Nancy. 28 Sept 1820. Wit: Elizabeth Gallaugher.

364 John G. Wade to James Woody, for $160, negro boy Ben who was given him by Jane Gwin & recorded at her death. 26 Apr 1820. No witnesses.

364-6 James Clay & James Clay & Co. of Milton (in debt to State Bank of NC at Milton for notes of $260, $747, $495 with Charles Willson & William G. Cochran of Milton as securities) to Simeon Cochran, trustee, of Person Co., for $1, 400 A in Person Co devised by his father adj Genl Richard Atkinson; the Watson plot of 200 A adj Duncan Rose; also tract in Person Co. devised to Phebe Clay wife of James Clay (alias Phebe Jackson) adj Alex Gordon; 9 negroes: Charles about 30 yrs, Jim 70, George 19, Susanna 40, Rachel & her 3 children Joe, Ben, & Jane; all household & kitchen furniture in Milton; all plantation tools in Person Co; all livestock. The old trust is excepted given to Jno Richmond to secure Cary Williams & Satterfield. 12 Apr 1821. Wit: Saml D. Bolton, W. Willson.

367 Presly Draper bound to Thos Merritt for $1000, to purchase 100 A where Merritt lives adj Wm. Trotter, Benja Carver. 22 July 1819. Wit: Ish Edwards.

367-8 Norris Compton (in debt to Nathaniel Norfleet for $12.40¼, & also for rent of plantation where Compton lives for $20.50) to George Briggs, for 25¢, in trust, a mare, cattle, hogs, 8 geese, 4 feather beds, furniture. 10 Apr 1820. Wit: James Norfleet, B. W. Milner.

369-70 Thomas J. Chambers (in debt to Alexander Cunningham, for $495.56) to Cary Williams, in trust, for $1, negroes Allen age 35, Simon 29, Matt 27, Scott 17, Richd 12, Anderson 14; Molly 25 & her child Sarah; Rachel 20; Milly 20 & her 3 children Letty, Harrison, Martha; Jenny 24, Sucky 29, Aggy 47; a part of property already conveyed to Thomas McGehee & Jno Garner & Cunningham. 4 June 1821. Wit: Thos Stanfield.

370-1 James Clay adm estate of Edward Clay decd & bonded for $200 with Cary Williams & Isaac Satterfield, securities, to secure same & for 5/ pd by John Richmond, 400 A on Richland Cr adj Richard Atkinson, Annis Cochran, said Satterfield, said tract deeded James Clay by his father Edward Clay decd. 10 May 1821. Wit: Jas Montgomery, Isaac Satterfield.

372 Dempsey W. Clayton to Thomas Denny, for $200, 50 A on Deep Cr adj Delamar, Portius Moore, Robert Moore. 10 Nov 1820. Wit: Saml Webb, Major Davis.

372-4 Benjamin Chambers (in debt to Bank of Newbern at Raleigh office for $1800 & to Bank of Raleigh for $1800 with Richd Atkinson & Thos McGehee scurities) to Cary Williams, for $1, trustee, 800 A on Stories Cr where he lives adj Cary Williams, Isham Edwards, Robt Deshazo, James Barnet. 16 Mar 1821. Wit: Alex Williams, Haywood Williams.

374-5 James Clay (in debt to Thomas Trotter for $456) to Cary Williams for this amt. & $1, in trust, 400 A on Richland Cr adj Richd Atkinson, Isaac Sat terfield - said land deeded him by his father Edward Clay; also his interest in 147 A which is one-eighth adj Jno Raven decd; his interest in 150 A adj Richd Carnal which Clay has life estate as land fell to his wife by death of her father, Sam Johnson;

374-5 cont - negroes Jim alias James, Charles; His interest in negroes from estate of Edward Clay decd being one-seventh part agreeable to deed of gift; his one-half interest in negro girl Jane during the life of Jane Clay late widow of Edward Clay decd; livestock. 27 June 1821. Acknd in open court.

375-7 Thomas Dickson (in debt to Alex Cunningham for $405.69 & $73.98) to Alexander Moore, in trust, for $1, 193½ A adj Robt Jones, Warren Dixon, Richd Carnal, Jacob Vanhook, Stephen Oliver. 5 June 1821. Wit: Warren Dixon.

377 Warren Dixon relinquishes all right to Robert Jones, for $80, 8 A n side Hyco adj Claim of Robert Jones - sold to settle suit over said land. 19 June 1821. Wit: James Stuart, Jno Garner.

377-8 Robert Deshazo to Isham Edwards, for $500, 50 A both sides Stories Cr. 2 Jan 1821. Wit: W. Chambers, Benja Chambers.

378-9 Benjamin Adams of Halifax Co., VA, to James Warren of same, for $448, 112 A on VA state line near Brooks old schoolhouse adj James McGehee, Bluford - sold to satisfy deed of trust given to Adams by William Hobson of Person Co. who left debt unpaid. _ Apr 1821. Wit: Richard Halliburton, Thos Winstead.

379-80 Robert Blake (in debt to Nathaniel Norfleet for $33.55) to Green W. Brown, for $1, in trust, 32 A on Bushy Fork where Blake now resides adj Richard Rimmer, Ephraim Hawkins. 22 May 1821. Wit: Stephen Wells, Jno Brown.

380-1 Robert Blake (in debt to Stephen Wells for $18.11) to Green W. Brown, for $1, in trust ,cattle, sheep, bay mare; furniture. 22 May 1821. Wit: Nathaniel Norfleet.

381-2 Benjamin Harris to John Harris (Hico), for $301.50, 67½ A including mill seat on Stories Cr adj S. M. Glenn, Law Vanhook, Abram Walters, Jno Fullar. 27 Apr 1819. Wit: Saml Jones, Haywood Jones.

382 Ezekiel Jones to John H. Jones, for $32, 2 cows, calves, 1 mare; 1 feather bed, furniture. 6 June 1821. Wit: Jno Douglas.

382-3 Ezekiel Jones to John H. Jones, for $30, 70 A on Bluewing Cr adj James Ragan formerly William Waite, Benjn Wade, Wm. Harris, Jno Parish now Abel L. Parish. 6 June 1821. Wit: John Douglas, Joshua Byasse.

383-4 Robert Jones (in debt to Yancey Brooks for $400) to Wilie Brooks for security & $1, 10 head cattle, hogs, sheep, 1 hogshead tobacco, geese; furniture; negro woman Peggy; 1/3 part of quarter A lot in East Milton adj Oliver on Main St; ½ A lot in Milton adj Hugh Wood & Co. on Main St. 13 Apr 1821. Wit: Thomas Walker

384-5 John Kerr (in debt to James Williamson, merchant, for $560) to Ira Lea, trustee, for $1, six beds & furniture; cattle, horses; large quantity earthenware & tin. 5 Sept 1820. Wit: Wm. Kerr.

385-6 Henry Lipscomb to Kendal Vanhook, for $275, 50 A on S Hyco near the meeting house adj heirs of Zachariah Lea, Moses Bradsher, Wm. Long, Wm. Lipscomb. 15 Sept 1820. Wit: J. A. Pulliam, Jesse Bradsher.

386-7 William A. Lea & Susanna Lea his wife to Cary Williams & Currie Barnett, for $430, 107½ A on Gents Cr adj said Williams, Isham Edwards, Josiah Carver, Duncan. 10 Nov 1818. Wit: Geo Lea.

387 Will A. Lea & Susanna Lea his wife to Cary Williams & Currie Barnett, for $132, 88 A on Gents Cr which fell to them as heirs of James Cochran decd adj Geo Duncan, Josiah Carver, Thos Merit. 10 Nov 1818. Wit: Abner Lea, Geo Lea.

388 Susanna Lea examined apart from her husband & she signed of her own free will the above deeds. Nov 1818. Wit: Ira Lea, Jno Bradsher.

Deed Book E
Page
388 Thomas McGehee to Harrison Stanfield, for $4180, 418 A on Cain Cr of N Hico adj Addison Hall, Edmund Dixon. 20 June 1821. Wit: James Rainey, Jos McDowell.

389-90 Nathaniel Painter (in debt to Ira Lea & James Williamson, merchants, for $103) to Martin Morton, for 50¢, in trust, a bay mare, wagon, cows, oxen, steers, hogs; furniture. 5 June 1821. Wit: James Hannah.

390-1 Drury Pulliam to Joseph Royster, for $409.50, 117 A on Gents Cr adj Cary Williams, Jho Brann, Geo Duncan. 13 Apr 1821. Wit: Ish Edwards, Cary Williams.

391-2 Samuel H. Smith & John Smith, exec of Samuel Smith decd of CC, to John Barnett & James Barnett, for $2456, 307 A on fishing br of Adams Cr adj said Barnetts, Artha Brooks, Hugh Woods, Samuel Blackwell, Jacob Bull, Benjamin Chambers, heirs of Hugh Barnett now John & James Barnett. 23 Dec 1820. Wit: Matthew Mitchell, Cary Williams.

392-3 Samuel Dickens, sheriff, to Isham Edwards (sold to satisfy suit against Jesse Bull for $192.66 recovered by Edwards), for $97.25 for goods & chattels & $19.74 collected plus $20, 319 A on Stories Cr adj James Long, Reuben Long Jun. 24 June 1821. Wit: Currie Barnett, Cary Williams.

394-5 Isaac Satterfield (in debt to James Williamson for $643.79) to Ira Lea, for 50¢ in trust, 250 A on Richland Cr adj James Clay, John Dobbins, James Williamson, John Ravens. 2 June 1821. Wit: Duncan Rose.

395-7 Aaron Scoggin (in debt to James Williamson for $403 with James Jay, security) to Isaac Satterfield, in trust, for 50¢, a tract where Scoggin lives. 23 Feb 1821. Wit: Isaac Satterfield Junr.

397-8 Harrison Stanfield to Thomas McGehee, for $2195, 219½ A on Cammel old rd adj Edmund Dixon Senr, Charles Sallard, Alexander Moore, Robert Jones. 3 Apr 1821. Wit: James Rainey, Joseph McDowell.

398-9 William Street & Lawson Neal to Thomas Lawson, for $1000, 183 A on S Hyco & Richland Cr adj George Duty, Daniel Sergent, Nathan Scoggin, Reuben Parrott, Samuel Whitehead, Carter Lea; also 5 A e side S Hyco adj Owen Lea old line now Mitchel; both tracts were willed to Robert Vanhook & William Vanhook by the decd father David Vanhook. 15 Jan 1821. Wit: Robert Gill, W. M. B. Lawson.

399-401 Samuel Dickens, sheriff, to William Robinson, for $51.50, 53 A on Stories Cr adj Benjamin Harris, James Williamson - sold to satisfy deed of trust given by Sampson M. Glenn for debt of $242 recovered by William R. Robertson & Chesterfield Franklin. 26 Sept 1820. Wit: Thomas P. Evans.

401-2 Benjamin Moore to John Brann, for $350, 100 A adj Brann, Artha Brooks, William Trotter Sen. on Clay Rd, Robert Carver to Leasburg Rd. 13 Jan 1820. Wit: Cary Williams, Benj Chambers.

402-3 Thomas Townsend (in debt to Joseph Gill for $65) to David Gill, in trust, a sorrel mare, mule, colt, cattle; furniture. 23 Jan 1821. Wit: Thomas Gill.

403-5 William McGehee to James McGehee of Lynchburg, VA, for $4200, 420 A both sides Sergent Cr & n side Hyco adj Thomas McGehee, Goodloe Warren, Wm. Hopson. 27 Feb 1818. Wit: Th McGehee, Lewis Shirley.

405-6 John H. McNeill (in debt to Jos Currie of CC by bond with Hosea McNeill of CC, security) to indemnify security, to Hosea McNeill, trustee, for $5, all his right & claim under last will of Annis Cochran decd the mother of John McNeill; also all his right under will of Thomas McNeill & in estate of Ann McNeill decd widow of Thomas McNeill. 11 June 1821. Wit: John Douglas.

406-7 John H. McNeill (in debt to Nicholas Thompson of Leasburg, NC, for $353.12) to Nicholas Thompson, this same amt. to be paid by legacy recd from Annis Cochran decd late of Person Co. 1 June 1821. Wit: B. C. Allen.

Deed Book E
Page
407-8 John H. McNeill (in debt to Jos Currie of CC with Hosea McNeill security) to Hosea McNeill, in trust, for $1, all claim to crops on plantation lately property of Annis Cochran decd now property of John M. Dobbin. _ June 1821. Wit: Jno Douglas.

408-9 Lewis Wilkerson of Granville Co. to Abel L. Parish of Person Co., for $37.50, 20.75 A between Donaldson & Aaron Creeks, said tract purchased of Patty Taylor, adj Jno Person, Wm. Little, Harrison, Jones former land. 13 Jan 1820. Wit: Jas Milner.

409-10 William McGehee to James Rainey of CC, for $40, 1 A in Person Co. on n fork N Hyco adj both men. 22 June 1821. Wit: Loften Walton.

410-1 Lumpkin Winstead (in debt to Cary Williams for $100 & as security on bond of $70 for hire of negro payable to Alexr Winstead, plus other debts) to William Williams, for $1, in trust, negro man Dick alias Richard age 20 yrs. 12 May 1821. Wit: Haywood Williams, Alexr Williams.

412 James Whitefield Sen. to William Whitefield of CC, for $100, 80.5 A on Double Cr of S Hico & was purchased of Wm. McKissack Jun. adj Wm. McKissack Sen., Robt Stanfield. 9 June 1821. Wit: Minchew Whitefield, Mary Whitefield.

413 Downey Wade to Nicholas Thompson, for $500, negro woman Nancy, 17 yrs old & her child Smith. 29 Jan 1821. Wit: SM Dickens. Proved by oath Stephen M. Dickens.

413-4 Charles Willson of CC & Jeremiah Dixon to Edmund Dixon Senr., for $220, 93 A. 4 May 1821. Wit: Thos McGehee, Warren Dixon.

414-5 James Williamson to Cary Williams & Currie Barnett, for $600, 150 A on Stories Cr adj Reuben Long, Jno Shelton. 10 Dec 1818. Wit: Isaac Satterfield, Lewis Daniel.

415-6 Joseph B. Shaw of Orange Co. (in debt to James Jackson for $55.50) to Paul Kennon of Orange Co., for $1, in trust, 52 A in Person Co. which is his undivided part of lands of John Gooche. 5 May 1821. Wit: Jas Stag, Isaac Jackson.

416-7 Benjamin W. Milner (in debt to Nathaniel Norfleet for $443.36½ & $120.20) to David Hunt, for $1, in trust, 100 A on Double Cr of Hico adj Robt Stanfield, John Wisdom. 18 Aug 1821. Wit: Pate W. Milner, Edwd Norfleet. Proved by oath Pate Wells Milner.

417-8 Benjamin A. Browder (in debt to James A. Pulliam for $31.37) to Cary Williams, for 50¢, in trust, 1 bay horse, a mahoghany bureau. 6 June 1821. Wit: Robt Newton.

418-9 William Chambers (in debt to Jno Barnet for $300) to Green W. Brown, negro man Olive about 20 yrs old. 7 June 1821. Wit: G. W. Brown.

420-1 John H. McNeill (in debt to A. & R. M. Cunningham, merchants, for $181.65) to John Garner, for $5, in trust, his one-eighth interest in 100 A lately property of Addison Cochran on S Hico adj Robt Vanhook, Abner Bradsher; all his right to one-seventh part of estate of Daniel Darby decd; all debts due him. 24 Sept 1821. Wit: B. Yancey.

421-2 William Chambers (in debt to State Bank of NC, Raleigh, for $1430 & $210 with Cary Williams security) to Haywood Williams, in trust, for $1, slaves Henry about 40 yrs, Dick 25, James 9, Currie 6, Jordan 4, Judesey 3. 28 June 1821. Wit: Thos J. Chambers, Alexr Williams.

422-4 Benjamin Chambers (in debt to Bank of Newbern in Milton for $2000 with Isham Edwards, James Barnet, Moses Chambers & Thomas McGehee, securities; debt due Alex Cunningham with same security) to William Williams, for $1, in trust, 800 A where Chambers lives adj James Barnet, Jno Barnet, Hugh Wood, Robt Deshazo, Isham Edwards; also slaves Julius about 70 yrs old, Dick about 56, little Dick 28,

422-4 cont - Molly 45, Amy 20 with 2 children Henderson 5 & John 2; Eliza 18 yrs
& 2 children a girl 4 yrs & a boy 18 mos; Harry 15, Viney 10; lots in Milton both
sides Bridge St; horses, cattle, 80 hogs, 1 still, 3 feather beds, furniture;
a quantity of goods worth $300; wagon, carryall; crops; quantity of lumber at
saw mill value $150. 28 Aug 1821. Wit: Alexr Moore, A. Pelham.

424 William Cates (in debt to Thomas P. Evans for $50 of Orange Co.) to John New
of Person Co., for $1, in trust, his part of tract adj James Armstrong, Jeremiah
Rimmer. 10 Apr 1821. Wit: David Murdoc.

425-6 Benjamin Chambers, co-partner of Rose & Chambers (in debt to Bank of Newbern
at Milton for $876 with Jno Barnet, Hugh Woods, Geo C. Rogers, Moses Chambers &
Byrd Rogers, securities) to William Williams, for $1, in trust, 800 A where he
lives. 21 Sept 1821. Wit: Jno Hudgins, Josias Chambers.

426-7 William Chambers (in debt to Alexr Cunningham for $599.26) to Alexander
Moore, in trust, negro Hall 35 yrs old, Dick 25, James 9, Currie 7, Jordan 5,
Juda 3, Oliver 37. 14 Sept 1821. Wit: Jno Garner.

428 Meredith Daniel to William Daniel of Granville Co., for 100 lbs, 253 A on
Mayo adj Gill, Davy, Person, Dixon, Ragon. 22 Mar 1820. Wit: J. P. Davis, Mark
Davis.

429 Edmund Dixon Sen. to Archibald Carnal, for $200, 93 A on a branch. 9 July
1821. Wit: Warren Dixon, Thos Trotter, Levi Dixon, Jno Garner.

429-30 Richard Duty to James Cochran - power of attorney to sell one-seventh part
of undivided estate of Thomas McNeill Senr decd to wit: negro woman Juda & her
4 children Rachel, Sarah, Rose, Charles; these free of encumbrances excepting
conformity with last will of Thomas McNeill decd which said estate div after
death of widow; claim of Duty through wife Lois Duty. 20 Nov 1811. Wit: Wm.
Street, Sharp Winningham.

431-2 Samuel Dickens to Thomas Hunt of Granville Co., for $13665, 1365 A on Deep
Cr where Dickens resides except ½ A with family graveyard, adj Abner Williams,
Jesse Dickens, Osborne Jeffreys, Jesse Lunsford, Eli Tapp, heirs of Robert Dickens.
3 Apr 1821. Wit: Robert Dickens, James Clack, Wm. Dickens.

432-3 Jesse Dickens to son Robt Dickens, 276 A adj Saml Webb, Saml Dickens, Jesse
Lunsford, Cameron, Clayton, Downey, to Dry Br. 24 Nov 1820. Acknd in open court.

433-4 Thomas Grant (in debt to Ira Lea & James Williamson, merchants, for $111)
to Barnet Winstead, for 50¢, in trust, 178 A on Henley Mill Cr adj William Trotter,
Mrs. Henley, James Jordan; livestock, furniture. 5 July 1821. Wit: Thomas
Douglas, Wm. Satterfield.

434-5 Abraham Gregory (in debt to Isham Edwards for $110.16) to Samuel Bull, for
$1, in trust, cattle, furniture. 12 Apr 1821. Wit: G. W. Willson.

436-7 Joel Hicks (in debt to James Williamson & Wm. McKissack for $70.39) to
John Reed & Radford Satterfield, for $1, in trust, 70 A on Richland Cr adj Geo
Wood, Rebecca Burton. 11 Apr 1820. Wit: Wm. Jeffreys.

437 Benjamin Halliburton of Halifax Co., VA, to Kinchen Newman of same, for $700,
100 A on Cain Cr adj Richard Halliburton, Robert Jones. 30 July 1821. Wit:
Richd Halliburton, Thos Winstead.

438-9 William Hargis (in debt to Thomas V. Hargis for $43 & to Hargis & Sneed for
$9.27½, plus other notes to L. V. Hargis & Dudley Sneed) to James Gooche, for
25¢, in trust, cow & yearling, sheep, wagon, gears; 100 A on Flat R adj Thomas
Hargis Sen., McNeill, Henry Womack. 14 July 1821. Wit: Thomas Hargis, Jesse Evans.

439-40 William Hamlin Jun. (in debt to Isham Edwards for $71.11) to James A.
Pulliam, for $1, in trust, 120 A on Stories Cr adj Solomon Clayton, Jno Clayton.
20 June 1821. Wit: G. W. Willson, Lucy Crocket.

Deed Book E
Page

440-2 Asa Hudgins (in debt to Green W. Brown for $120.33 & for staying execution on judgment which John Allin obtained against Hudgins & Baylor Burch; for staying execution which Charles D. Wade assignee of Nath Norfleet obtained against Hudgins) to Stephen Wells, for 75¢, in trust, 41.75 A adj John Brown, Ephraim Hawkins; negroes Matilda 8 or 9 yrs old; livestock, furniture. 1 Sept 1821. Wit: Miles Wells, Benja Wells.

442-3 Robert Johnson (in debt to Isham Edwards for $93.77¼) to Samuel Bull, for $1, in trust, his undivided part of 319 A where Elizabeth Bull lives formerly property of Jacob Bull decd on Stories Cr adj James Long, Paul Walters; furniture; undivided part of crops made on land of James Barnet & Jno Barnet as an overseer consisting of one-sixth part. 15 Sept 1821. Wit: G. W. Wilson, Wesley Carver.

443-5 William Jeffreys (with James Williamson & Jno Williams securities for several notes due banks in Newbern & Raleigh) to William McKissack, for 50¢ to secure them from any liability, 258 A on Adams Cr; 300 A bought at sheriff sale belonging to William Moore; 144 A purchased of Joseph Morton - total of 703 A all adj each other & adj Edwd Mitchel decd, Jno Williams, Matthew Mitchel, Benja Towler, William Mann, heirs of William Allen. 24 Sept 1821. Wit: Ira Lea.

445-6 William Jones to Samuel Davy, for 75 lbs, 124 A on Bluewing Cr adj Lucy Jones, Mary W. Jones, Francis Foard, William Loftis, at Cattail Br. 11 Aug 1821. Wit: John Humphries.

446 Power of attorney - Polly Lea, William Hawkins & Elizabeth Hawkins his wife formerly Elizabeth Lea to Abner Lea of Jackson Co., TN, to collect & receive any property they are entitled to as heirs of Ambrose Lea decd & to settle any business with Col. George Lea. 24 Aug 1821. Wit: Thos Talbert.

446-7 Thomas Lawson to William Street, for $1200, 183 A on S Hico & Richland Cr adj George Duty, Daniel Sergent, Reuben Parrot, Saml Whitehead, Carter Lea; also 5 A on e side S Hico adj Owen Lea old line now Mithcell - said tracts were willed to Robert Vanhook & William Vanhook by their decd father David Vanhook. 24 Jan 1821. Wit: Robert Gill, Lawson Neal, R. Lawson.

448 Benion P. Lipscomb of Smith Co., TN, to Archibald Lipscomb of Person Co., for $15, part of dower of his mother Dorothy Lipscomb. 11 Sept 1821. Wit: John Bradsher, H. B. Dollarhide.

448-9 Jesse Lunsford to daughter Polly Tapp wife of John Tapp, for love & affection, & 50¢, negro woman Charlotte & her child Nancy. No date. Wit: Matthew Griffin, John Lewis. Proved Sept 1821.

449-50 John Long (in debt to William McKissack for $108.11) to Green D. Satterfield & Jno Reed, for 75¢ in trust, 100 A adj Polly Walters, Lozen Carver; livestock. 7 May 1821. Wit: Green W. Brown, Jesse Bumpass.

450-1 Thomas McNeill to James Cochran, for $43.75, all his right & title to negroes from undivided estate of his father Thomas McNeill decd to wit: Juda & her 3 children Ritty, Sarah, Rose. 14 Feb 1801. Wit: Rho Carney, William Carney. Proved Person Co. Sept 1821 by oath of Duncan Rose who proved handwriting of Rhobartus Carney; the other witness resided out of State; Rose also proved handwriting of Thomas McNeill Jr as he & Rhobartus Carney are dead.

451-2 Benjamin W. Milner (in debt to Jacobina Milner for $476 who advanced him this amt.) to David Hunt, for $1, in trust, negro woman Gill age 32 & her 2 children Ellick & Isaac. 1 Sept 1821. Wit: G. W. Brown, Pate W. Milner.

452-3 John Mansfield of Person Co. (for note due Lemuel Rainey) to Christopher Thomas of CC, for $1, in trust, a bay mare, 4 head cattle, 14 hogs; household furniture; his part of crops of wheat, tobacco & corn made with Lemuel Rainey. 9 July 1821. Wit: Elizabeth Towler, G. W. Brown.

176

Deed Book E
Page

453-4 Philip Obriant of Grandville Co. to Samuel Jones of Person Co., for $100,
73 1/3 A adj Jno Waite, Jno Parish, William Winstead. 16 Nov 1806. Wit: Gideon
Roberts. Proved Sept 1821 by oath Gideon Robertson.

454-5 William L. Parker (in debt to Bank of Newbern at Milton office for $490
with Josiah Oliver as endorsor) to Reuben Oliver, for $1, in trust, crops of
corn, wheat, oats, cotton. 15 Apr 1821. Wit: Archer Bell Grant. Proved by
oath Archd Grant.

455-6 Drury A. Pulliam (in debt to Alex Cuningham, amt not given) to ___ (name not
given),trustee, for $1, horses, cattle, hogs, furniture; 2 lots in East Milton.
16 Aug 1821. Wit: Jno Garner, Jno Ward. Also signed by Archd Carnal.

457 Drury A. Pulliam (in debt to Isham Edwards for $214.63) to William Williams,
trustee, for $1, hroses, cattle, hogs, furniture; corn, wheat; 2 shot guns; lots
17 & 84 in East Milton. 27 July 1821. Wit: G. W. Willson.

458-9 Drury A. Pulliam (in debt to Alexander Moore for $105) to Thomas McGehee,
in trust, for $1, horses, cattle, hogs, furniture; 2 lots in Milton. 16 Aug
1821. Acknd in open court. 2 witnesses unreadable.

459-60 Charles G. Rose (in debt to Bank of Newbern at Milton for $350 endorsed by
Richard Atkinson & Ira Lea) to Thomas Atkinson, in trust, horses, cows; windsor
chairs, silver spoons, candlesticks; other furniture. 19 June 1821.
Wit: Jno Barnett. Duncan Rose has these articles in his possession & will deliver to Thomas Atkinson, trustee.

460-1 Jesse Ragan to Thomas Ragan, for $150, 58½ A w side Bluewing Cr adj Baird,
Winstead. 26 Aug 1820. Wit: Robt Harris, Wm. Harris.

461 Edmund Roberts to Anne McNeill & Wilson Vermillion exec of Thos McNeill decd,
for them to deliver to James Cochran, his proportion or dividend (one-seventh part
of undivided share of estate of Thos McNeill decd now remaining in hamds of said
Anne McNeill consisting of a negro woman Jude & her younger child now with her.
9 Apr 1797. Wit: H. Haralson, Jno Hall. Proved Sept 1821 by oath of Duncan Rose
who proved writing of H. Haralson & Jno Hall who are now residents of other states.

461-2 Durett Stanfield to Archibald Carnal, for $202.25, 22.75 A; also 3½ A.
27 Apr 1820. Wit: Jacob Faulkner, Obediah Faulkner, Thos J. Terrell.

463-4 Samuel Dickens, sheriff, to Nathaniel Norfleet (to recover $43.29 in case
against Nancy McKissack & sold by court order), 130 A on Double Cr adj Alexr Gray,
Jno Crisp,for above amt. & $2.75. 25 Apr 1821 Acknd in open court.

464-6 James Trotter (in debt to Ira Lea & James Williamson, merchants, for 2 notes:
$115.72 & $71.45½; also in debt to Ira Lea, guardian, for Leah Graves $27.40½) to
Cary Williams, in trust, for $1, 122½ A on Hico adj Arthur Leath heirs, Thomas
Trotter, William Trotter Jun. - said land is where James Trotter lives. 30 Apr
1821. Wit: Jas Hannah, Thos L. Douglas.

467-8 Thomas Townsend (in debt to William Street, agt. for Moses Street, for $138)
to William Street & Joseph Gill, for $1, wagon, cart, oxen; 217½ A on Oak Sapling
Br adj Robert Gill, Jno Townsend, Thomas Sheppard - said land tract purchased of
Jno Holloway as agt for Sweptston Sims. 8 Feb 1821. Wit: Charles G. Gill.

468 Downey Wade to Robt D. Wade, for $158, yellow negro boy named Reuben.
Wit: Nathl Torian. 10 Feb 1821.

469 William Williams to Hugh Wood, in trust, for love for Elizabeth Woods daughter
of Hugh Woods (she 7 yrs old), negro girl Louisa age 13 yrs. 24 Sept 1821.
24 Sept 1821. Acknd in open court.

470 Downey Wade to Robt D. Wade, for $100, negro boy Sam. 2 Sept 1820. Wit:
Nathl Torian.

Deed Book E
Page

470 Charles D. Wade to Robt D. Wade, for $600, negro man Anderson. 4 Sept 1820.
Wit: Nathl Torian.

471 Downey Wade to Robt D. Wade, for $450, negro girl Theny. 2 Sept 1820. Wit:
Nathl Torian.

471 John Washington of Granville Co., to James Webb of Person Co., for $1531.31,
371½ A on Tar R in Person & Granville Counties on the Goshen Rd adj Richd Woods,
Bumpass old corner, to Cattail Br, McVay, Thorp. 8 Sept 1821. Wit: Lewis G. Lanie
Jno McVay.

END OF BOOK E

Page
1-3 William Chambers (in debt to Alexr Cunningham for $550) to John Garner, for
$1, in trust, slaves Dick age 25 yrs, James 8, Currie 6, Judy 5, Judsy 3, Oliver
30, Lucy, 24, Davy 6, Reuben 3, Lewis 1, Mary 24, Ann 4, Sarah 2, 24 Dec 1820.
Wit: Harrison Stanfield.

3-4 Duncan Rose (in debt to Bank of Cape Fear in Hillsborough with Isaac Satterfield & John Raven, securities) to Charles G. Rose, all title & interest in negro
boy Burrel; carriage, horses. Wit: B. W. Milner. (Date unreadable)

4-5 Jacob Faulkner Sen. of Halifax Co., VA, to son Obediah Faulkner, for love &
affection, 273 A in Person Co. on Highco R said land purchased of Roger Atkinson.
8 Aug 1821. Wit: Jacob Bland, Wm. Bailey, Wm. Williams, Jno Bailey.

5-7 James Martin (in debt to Nathaniel Torian for $109.43) to Anderson Snipes,
for $1, in trust, sorrel mare, colt; cattle, furniture; large Bible; other
equipment. 26 Nov 1821. Wit: D. Wade, Jas Snipes.

7-9 Ezekiel Jones to Benjamin Wade, for $69, 72½ A on Bluewing Cr adj Robt Harris,
said Jones. 24 May 1821. Wit: Robt Harris, Lawson Harris.

9-11 David Brooks & his wife Nancy Brooks; Edmd Dillahay & his wife Johanna
Dillaway; Elizabeth Dillaway; John Dillaway & his wife Sally Dillaway - all of
Person Co. - to Thomas K. Mayler of Sussex Co., VA, for $720, all their right
& interest in 240 A in Sussex Co. which John Dillaway formerly of Person Co. possessed & bequeathed to Edmund, Elizabeth, Nancy, & Arthur Dillahay who decd intestate without issue; John Dillaway was entitled to one-fourth part of said land
adj Wm. Robinson, Robt Wells, Peter Rainey, heirs of Jno Powel. 24 Sept 1821.
Wit: Wm. Jones, Wm. Allen.

12-4 Samuel Dickens, sheriff, to Lewis Tapp (due to execution against James Milner
for $1079 recovered by Wm. McKissack , Thomas McGehee, Rose & Chambers, Richd
Holeman) for $301.25, 388 A on Flat R adj Lewis Daniel, James Satterfield.
16 Oct 1821. Wit: Wm. McKissack, Radford Satterfield.

15-6 Richard Atkinson to Ira Lea, for $600, 236 A on Richland Cr adj Wm. West-
brook, Carter Lea, James Williamson - said land was 2 tracts belonging to Moses
Fuller & purchased of Wm. Fuller Sen. who reserved it for his lifetime.
5 Nov 1821. Wit: Jas Williamson, C. Atkinson.

17-8 Samuel Dickens to William Hicks, for $1, all his title & interest to 50 A
which Dickens purchased of Solomon Paine whereon Hicks now resides on Tapley Cr
adj Paine old corner, Durden, Oakley. 23 Mar 1821. Wit: Marcis Oakley.

18-9 James Draper to John Hudgins, for $13, all his interest & claim to 171½ A
on Stories Cr which was his father's property adj Wm. Trotter - his interest
as an heir of Presley Draper decd. 8 Nov 1821. Wit: Hardy Walters, Richd Harris.

19-20 Thomas Talbert to Lewis Amis, for $150, 36½ A on Hyco adj William Trotter,
Lettuce Henley, said Amis. 9 Jan 1813. Wit: James Trotter, Jas Talbert.
Proved Dec 1821.

21-3 John H. McNeill to William F. Smith, for $150, one-seventh part of undivided
estate of Daniel Darby decd consisting of negroes Jude & her child (name not re-
called); his interest in any notes, bonds bequeathed to him & his wife Ann McNeill;
Smith given power of attorney to seize same. 23 Aug 1821. Wit: Hannah Bishop,
Anne Evans.

23-4 Richard Hamlin to Richard Harris, for $60, 30 A on Stories Cr adj Jno Harris,
Jno Hudgins - said land part of larger tract purchased of James Williamson.
31 Mar 1819. Wit: Benjn Chambers, Hardy Walters.

Deed Book F
Page
24-5 Wilie Jones to William Loftis, for $600, 144½ A on Blewing Cr adj Samuel
Davey, William Jones to Granville Co. line & then to VA line, Francis Foard.
18 June 1821. Wit: Overton Wiles, William Jones.

26-8 John Barnett, sheriff Person Co., to Alexr Winstead (due to judgment obtained by Lucretia Sharp against James Clay for $749) 400 A on Richland Cr adj Richd
Atkinson, Isaac Satterfield; land belonged to Clay & sold to Winstead for $900.
26 Dec 1821. Wit: Will McKissack, Richd Nichols.

28-30 Tryon Yancey of Person Co. (in debt to George Brown & Thomas Brown for
$301.94) to Joseph Hart of Granville Co., for $1, in trust, all his interest in
53 A purchased of Mrs Mary Winningham where he lives adj Wm. Baird, Saml Dickens
on Mayo & Spoon Cr; negro man Harry, woman Jane; furniture, livestock; crops of
corn, fodder, cotton, tobacco. 24 Sept 1821. Wit: Saml F. Spence Jun.,
Henry M. Daniel.

30-2 John Bowles Junr (in debt to Solomon Griffin for $45) to Henry H. Allen, for
$1, in trust, furniture; 1 feather bed; an undivided crop of corn & fodder.
9 Sept 1821. Wit: Henry Sweaney.

32-3 Ira Lea adm of Presly Draper to Thomas Merritt, for 5/, 100 A on Sergent Cr
adj William Trotter, Thos Jeffreys. Sold to satisfy bond executed by Draper to
convey title to Merritt. 9 Nov 1821. Wit: Barnett Winstead, John Douglas.
Bond registered on page 365, Book E.

34 Phillips Moore to William Davie, for $208, negro boy George about 13 yrs of age
of sound health. 26 Dec 1821. Wit: James Webb.

34-5 John Draper to John Hudgins, for $27½, all his right & title to 170½ A on
Stories Cr where his father Presly Draper decd lived & left to his heirs adj
William Trotter. 8 Nov 1821. Wit: Alex Winstead, Green W. Brown.

35-7 Gabriel Bailey to Matthew Mitchell, for $225, 272 A on Adams Cr adj Hicks
old line, Dinwiddie to Rosemary Cr. 13 Mar 1821. Wit: C. Haoloway.

37-8 Isaac Satterfield Senr (in debt to Isaac Satterfield Junr assignee of Duncan
Rose for $182.72) to William Satterfield, in trust, negro man Lewis about 50 yrs
of age. 15 Sept 1821. Wit: George Satterfield.

39-40 Benjamin Carver of Rockingham Co., NC, to Hosea Carver of Person Co., for
$115, 100 A on Stories Cr adj Lemuel Carver. 28 July 1821. Wit: Ish Edwards,
G. G. Willson.

40-2 Samuel Jones (in debt to John H. Jones for $36) to Reuben Walton, in trust,
73.3 A on Bluewing Cr adj Jno Wait, Jno Parrish, William Winstead - said land
already conveyed to Reuben Walton to secure debt due Thos Byase for $22 & must
be pd first if land sold. 27 July 1821. Wit: Richd Hamlin, Hardy Walters.

42-4 Samuel Jones (in debt to Thos Byasse for $22) to Reuben Walton, in trust,
73.3 A on Bluewing Cr adj Jno Waite, John Parrish, William Winstead. 27 July 1821.
Wit: Richd Hamlin, Hardy Walters.

44-8 David Jeffreys of Person Co. to Duncan Cameron of Orange Co., for $4500,
several tracts on Tapley Cr n side Flat R: 290½ A called the Jeffreys tract adj
James Milner, Clack, said Cameron, formerly Elizabeth Jeffreys lot #2, Susan
Jeffreys allotment to dower line, Jas Jeffreys allotment; said tract was allotted
to Lucy Jeffreys from estate of Paul Jeffreys decd as lot #3; 234 2/5 A allotted
to James O. Jeffreys as lot #4. 7 __ 1820. Wit: Will H. Haywood Jr. Proved before
Jno Louis Taylor CSC, Raleigh, NC, 14 Jan 1822.

48-9 William Polk of Wake Co., NC, to Duncan Cameron of Orange Co., for $80, 80 A
in Person Co. adj Spivy McKissack, the allotment to Lucy Dixon in div estate of
Paul Jeffreys decd. 1 June 1821. Wit: Rufus Haywood, Leonidas Polk.

Deed Book F
Page

50-1 William Chambers (in debt to James Franklin for $1563.61) to John Garner, for $1, in trust, negroes Lucy about 24 yrs & her 3 children Davy, Reuben, Lewis; Mary & her 2 children Ann & Sarah. 29 Sept 1821. Wit: Thos Stanfield, Arch Carnal.

51-4 Andrew Gray (in debt to Duncan Cameron for $1313.90) to Lawrence V. Hargis & Saml Yarbrough, for $1, in trust, 277 A s fork Flat R where Gray lives adj said Cameron, Richd Holeman formerly Dickens; said land lately of the estate of Jno Cates decd; negroes Daniel & Phillis. 21 Jan 1822. Wit: Jas Cochran, Geo Staly.

54-6 John King Jun. of Lincoln Co., KY, to John M. Smith & Sally Smith his wife of Smith Co., TN, for love & affection, one-half of an undivided estate of Elizabeth Keller of State of VA who was grandmother of Elizabeth King wife of John King; also ½ of all estate from Jno King's father-in-law Osborne Jeffreys of NC; excepting negro man Crawford conveyed to John King from William Bilboa. Sally Smith is step-daughter of Jno King. Proved Lincoln Co., KY, 12 Sept 1821.

56-7 John Morgan (in debt to James Franklin for $200) to John Garner, for $1, in trust, negro girls Milly 7 yrs old & Polly 5 yrs. 6 Feb 1821. Wit: Jas P. Harrison, Jos Pulliam.

58-9 William Chabmers bound jointly with his father Thomas J. Chambers to Cary Williams as guardian for Thos J. Chambers; Cary Williams also bound by bond with Thos J. Chambers & Wm. Chambers payable to Unice Farley - to William Williams, for $1, negro girl Marie age 8; cattle, hogs, 20 barrels corn; household furniture. 10 Dec 1821. Acknd in open court.

59-60 Millington Blalock Sen. to his son Robert Blalock, for regards & 5/, 210 A on Cub Cr & Rocky Fork adj Samuel Dickens, William Cocke, James Cozart, Jonathan Jackson. 7 Feb 1813. Wit: William Moore.

60-2 Benjamin W. Milner, trustee, to Cary Williams & Isaac Satterfield, for $131, 150 A on Mayo Cr adj Bedwell Satterfield, Hardy Crews, Thomas Clayton, Jno Yarbrough; sold to satisfy deed of trust of Wyatt Painter to Milner & debt not paid. 27 Mar 1822. Acknd in open court.

62-4 Thomas J. Chambers who executed deed of trust to Cary Williams on negroes Simon 28 yrs, Mat a man 26 yrs, Scott 17, Anderson 13, Richard 11, Milly 23 with 3 children, Rachael 21, Ellen 35, Lucy 27 - to secure Jno Garner & Thomas McGehee his securities on note due Bank of NC for $3000; also deed of trust on Molly & child, Sarah, Sucky 28, Jenny 26, Aggy 45 - to secure payment of $1779.33 due Alex Cuningham plus other debts - agreement to sell said negroes & apply proceeds to notes. 24 Dec 1821. Wit: Jno Garner, Currie Barnett.

64-5 William Royster to Polly Grinstead for her life & then to heirs of her body, for good will & affection, gift of negro girl Matilda; Edmund Grinstead may not sell, trade, or hire out said slave. 21 Sept 1821. Acknd in open court.

65-7 John Sergent to Stephen Sergent, for $207.50, 41½ A on S Hyco, it being lot #2 in div lands of Daniel Sergent decd. 25 Mar 1822. Wit: Ira Lea, J. A. Pulliam.

67-9 John Montgomery (in debt to Andrew B. Woods for $365.26) to Isaac Satterfield, in trust, for $1, negro boy Arch age 17 yrs. 19 Jan 1822. Wit: R. Vanhook.

69-70 Phillips Moore to Hubbard Cozart of Granville Co., for $134.02, 76½ A on Deep Cr adj said Cozart & land he purchased of Sidney Moore - said land part of tract purchased of Jesse Dickens. 25 Mar 1822. Acknd in open court.

70-1 James W. Jones to Alexander Elixson, for $425, 164½ A on Cattail Br adj Robt Jones, Richd Blanks, Ary Jones, Lucy Jones. 1 Sept 1821. Wit: James King, Jas C. Halliburton.

Deed Book F
Page

71-2 Cary Williams & Isaac Satterfield to Isaac Webb, for $190, 150 A on Mayho adj Bedwell Satterfield, Hardy Crews, Thos Clayton, Jno Yarbrough. 27 Mar 1822. Wit: Thos Sheppard, Saml Webb.

72-3 Sidney Moore to Hubbard Cozart of Granville Co., for $200, 100 A on Deep Cr adj Phillips Moore, Joel Sweaney, Cozart. 13 Dec 1821. Wit: Pinckney Cozart.

74 Thomas Meritt & Polly Meritt his wife to Jno Hudgins, for $15, all their right & claim to 171 A of Presley Draper decd on Stories Cr adj William Trotter. 24 Mar 1822. Wit: Richd Harris, Hardy D. Royster.

74-6 Saml Davey & Emilia Davey to Alexr Elixson, for $425, 144½ A on Granville Co. line adj William Loften on Cattail Br. 9 Nov 1821. Wit: James King, Reuben Jones. Emilia Davey examined apart from her husband & freely relinquished this land.

76-7 Isham Edwards to Benjamin Moore, for $650, 100 A on Stories Cr adj James Long, Robert Brooks, John Brooks, Samuel Blackwell, Carver, McKissack. 8 Mar 1822. Wit: Josias Dixon, Jno Barnett.

77-8 Robert Stanfield & Andrew B. Wood to Duncan Rose, for $570, relinquishment of all right & title to 172 A which Rose conveyed them by deed of trust for land on Double Cr of Hico adj Benj W. Milner. 16 Feb 1822. Wit: B. W. Milner, P. W. Milner.

78-80 Samuel Dickens, sheriff, to John Holloway & Isham Edwards (due to execution by David S. Young & Isham Edwards against Lewis Ramsay for debt of $233.06½), for $300, 207 A on Dishwater Cr adj William Ramsay. 23 July 1821. NB John Holloway erased before assigned. Wit: B. W. Milner, J. A. Pulliam.

80-1 George Elliot to Yancey Oliver & Wilson Oliver, for $535, 107 A adj John Warrin, Hugh Hemphill. 18 Mar 1822. Wit: Salmon Jackson.

82-3 William Jeffreys to William Mann Sen., for $100, 50 A on Adams Cr adj Nath Hamlin, James Mann. 6 Mar 1822. Wit: John W. Williams.

83-4 William Mann to Nathl Hamlin, Lewis Amis, Byrd Pulliam, Thomas Mann, & Jacob Wright - all trustees for the Methodist Church known as Cool Spring Meeting House near Roxbrough, for propagation of the Gospel & 25¢, about 2 A adj said Mann, said Hamlin. 26 Mar 1822. Acknd in open court.

84-5 James McMurry to Obediah Pearce, for $5 per A, 202½ A on Double Cr of S Hico adj Saml McMurry, Martha Hays, Thos Snipes. 11 Mar 1822. Wit: B. W. Milner.

86-7 Joab Robertson to Henry Lipscomb, for $691.50, 104 A in Caswell & Person Counties on S Hico adj Archer Lipscomb, Jacobs, Pleasant, Lea. 7 Feb 1822. Wit: John Bradsher, Wm. McKissack.

87-8 Charles Sallard to James Jordan, for 200 lbs, 200 A adj Cary Williams, Duncan, Painter. 26 Mar 1822. Wit: Ira Lea, Lewis Amis.

89-90 Div negroes of Charles Taylor who in his will gave to wife Elizabeth for her life & then to 2 daughters Easter Scutchens & Elizabeth; Abner Williams his intermarried with Elizabeth widow of said Charles; Henderson Chandler has married Easter Scutchens; Jesse B. Drake has married Elizabeth Ridley (Taylor?) daughter of Charles Taylor. To Abner Williams & wife Elizabeth: negroes Milbro & Sylvia; Henderson Chandler & Easter his wife: Nancy & Harriet; Jesse B. Drake & Elizabeth his wife: Milly, Lethy, Julia. 1 Mar 1822. Wit: Portius Moore, Yancey Moore, Churchwell C. Delamar, Robt Kennedy.

90-2 Francis Raven (in debt to Lewis Amis Sen. of Granville Co. for $226 & for $1510) to Isaac Satterfield & Lewis Amis Jun., for $1, in trust, negro woman Jane & her 8 children: James, Green, Hannah, Smith, Mary, Jackson,   & , Dick. 25 Mar 1822. Wit: Wm. Snipes.

92-4 William Fullar Sen. to Bradsher Fuller, for $1000, 130 A both sides Richland
Cr of Hico adj Asa Fullar, Richd Atkinson, Moses Fullar, Carter Lea. 25 Mar 1822.
Wit: Barnett Winstead, Jesse G. Fullar.

94-5 Samuel Dickens to Jesse Durden, for $310, 150 A on Tapley Cr adj Jones, Wm.
Hicks, Milner, Cameron, Jno Hicks, Williamson, Marcus Oakley; Jesse Durden to
hold said promises in trust for benefit of his mother Polly Durden during her life
& after her death must divide land with his brother James Durden & he to pay for
½ of it. 31 Mar 1821. Wit: Jno Satterfield.

96-7 Robert Hamlet of Person Co. to Thomas M. Hamlet of CC, for $380, 138.75 A in
Person Co. adj Reuben Taylor, James Hamlet, Thomas Walters - said tract purchased
of Jno Hamlet 16 July 1810. 22 Mar 1822. Wit: James Rainey.

97-8 George L. Johnson to Thomas Lipscomb, for $288.75, 57.75 A on Hyco adj James
Jordan, on road to Leasburg, William Frazer, Jno Mason, Henry Sergent. 27 Feb 1821.
Wit: Lewis Amis, Delpha Lipscomb.

98-9 Robert Hamlet to Thomas M. Hamlet of CC, for $220, 72 A in Person Co. adj
William McGehee, Addison Hall. 22 Mar 1822. Wit: James Rainey.

99-101 Benjamin A. Browder (in debt to Jesse Woodson of Pittsylvania Co., VA, for
$41.75) to Drury Woodson of Pittsylvania Co., trustee, for $1, negro woman Tamar.
24 Jan 1822. Wit: Wm. Trotter.

101-2 Benion P. Lipscomb of Smith Co., TN, to George Lea of Person Co., for $220,
30 A adj Archiblad Lipscomb. 11 Sept 1820. Wit: John Bradsher, H. B. Dollarhide.

102-4 Jesse Satterfield to Richard Jones & Stephen Wilkerson, for   ?(not given),
83 A on Richland Cr of Hyco adj Clay now A. Winstead, Isaac Satterfield.
26 Mar 1822. Wit: John Montgomery, Isaac Satterfield.

104-5 Thomas Hallibruton Jun., Charles Halliburton, Susanna Hallibruton, John
Dixon & Elizabeth Dixon his wife - to Robert Halliburton, for $200, all their
right & claim to 286 A on Mayo Cr adj Baird, Winstead, Chambers, crossing Spoonwater Br - all are legatees of Charles Halliburton decd. 25 Oct 1820.
Wit: Thos Hallibruton, Martha Hallibruton, Margaret H. Merony.

105-6 Ebenezer Morrow to Joseph Lunsford, for $250, 208 A on Richland Cr adj George
Wood, Joseph Hubbard, said Lunsford. 24 May 1821. Wit: Wm. Jones, George Wood.

107 George Wood to Joseph Lunsford Jun., for $76, 60 4/5 A on Richland Cr adj
Lunsford. 25 June 1821. Wit: George Wood, Phillips Moore.

108-9 Duncan Rose to James Wisdom, for $517.26, 172.42 A on Double Cr of S Hyco
adj Benj A. Milner, Woods, Jno Moore. 18 Oct 1820. Wit: Jno Roberts, B. W. Milner.

109-1 James O. S. Jeffreys of Smith Co., TN, to William Polk of Wake Co., NC, for
$60, 80 A adj Spivy McKissack & land allotted to Lucy Dixon in div land of Paul
Jeffreys decd. 13 Dec 1820. Proved Person Co. June 1822 after accepting acknow-
ledgment from Nath W. Williams, Judge, State of TN.

111-3 Washington Blackard (who purchased sorrel horse of Thomas Clayton with
Thomas V. Hargis security for $58) to Asa Hargis, for 25¢, in trust, the same
sorrel horse, bay mare & saddle. 20 Feb 1821. Wit: Edmd D. Stanfield.
On May 24, 1822 this sorrel horse exchanged for a bay mare Ned to be placed on
deed of trust; Thomas B. Hargis to pay $18 in swap of horses. 20 Feb 1821.

114-7 Giles Rogers (in debt to Jno Vanhook of Hillsboro, Otway B. Rogers of Person
Co. & James Clay of Milton guardian of Littleton Rogers for various amounts) to
John Scott of Hillsboro, for $1, in trust, all his right & claim to negroes of
estate of Byrd Rogers decd subject to life estate interest of Littleton Rogers of
Person Co. under will of Jno Rogers decd: negroes Esther about 75 yrs, Ned 60,
Let 36, young Ester about 18, Mary 16, Nelly 16, Mark 12, Lewis 7, Jude 5, Ned son
of Let 3, Moses son of Ester 1. 3 Feb 1820. Acknd in open court.

Deed Book F
Page

117-8 Enos Ross,(in debt to Robert D. Wade for $60) to Nathaniel Torian, for $1, trustee, 1 cow & yearling, feather bed & bureau made of gum plank. 14 Nov 1821. Wit: Archd Lipscomb, Downey Wade.

119-20 William A. Lea of CC to John Mason of Person Co., for $82, 18½ A on S Hico in Person Co. adj Mason, Jno Rice, Claborn Bevil. 26 Oct 1820. Wit: Jesse A. Dollarhide, William Lea.

120-1 Charles Wade to Robert Wade, for $876, 146 A on S Hico adj Nathl Torian, ford at Jno Russell along the road. 13 Nov 1821. /s/ C. D. Wade. Wit: Jas H. Cates, Nathaniel Torian.

121-3 James Johnston to Lawrence Vanhook, for $127.12½, 30½ A on S Hico adj John Wilson, Loyd Vanhook, Robert Vanhook, Jeremiah Brooks. 27 Oct 1817. Wit: Jesse Bradsher.

123-4 Wright Nichols, George Broach & Elijah Hester, exec of Nicholas Burch decd, to James H. Cates, for $120, 53½ A on Double Cr of Hico adj Guthrie Jones, Adam McNeeley, Herndon Haralson, Robt Hester - it being the tract of Nicholas Burch decd. 10 Oct 1821. Wit: Jas McMullin, Willie Snipes.

124-6 Edward H. Ogilby of Milton to William Irvine of CC, for $2500, 317 A on Cob Cr adj James Rainey, Jno Lea, Vincent Tapp, Labon Stafford; said land sold to satisfy deed of trust of James Daniel on land which he purchased of Wm. Tapp. 6 Apr 1821. Wit: J. G. Lewis, Jno Garland.

126-8 James Webb to Thomas Webb, for 67 lbs, 67 A on Tar R near Dickens road adj Gabriel Davy, Saml Yarboro, William Yarbro, Jno Bumpass. 5 Apr 1822. Wit: Wm. Riley, Isaac Webb.

129-30 Richerson Nicholas of Orange Co. to John Hix of Person Co., for $59.50, 100 A on Flat R - with encumbrance of dower of Nancy Davy for one-third thereof during her life; said Nancy widow of Gabl Davy decd; land he purchased of Jos Traylor adj James Clack. 24 June 1822. Wit: Green W. Brown, Jno Barnett.

130-2 Samuel Dickens, sheriff, to Nathaniel Norfleet (for debts of William Fowler due Nancy Graves & Norfleet), for $50, 210 A on Rocky Fork adj Robert Cannaday, Robt Sweaney, Saml Dickens. 25 Apr 1821. Acknd in open court.

132-3 Thomas Jeffreys of CC to his son George W. Jeffreys of Person Co., for love & affection, 133 A at cross roads near Doctor Parker adj Wm. Hamlin, Wm. Carver, on road from Clay to Edwards store, Robert Walker. 15 Mar 1822. Wit: Jno Sergent, Maurice Smith.

134-5 Reuben Grinstead (in debt to Thomas Jeffreys as security for notes due McGehee & Stanfield for $25.52 & for $25 note due Jeffreys) to Thomas Jeffreys & Alexr M. Long, for $1, in trust, 1 bay horse, 26 hogs, cattle, household furniture & articles, plantation tools. 21 May 1822. Wit: Geo W. Jeffreys, William Dunnaway.

135-6 Reuben Grinstead to James W. Jeffreys of CC, for $300, 81½ A on Mitchel Br in Person Co. adj Thos Jeffreys, Henry Royster. 20 June 1820. Wit: Geo W. Jeffreys. Alexr M. Long.

136-7 Logustin P. Pool of Granville Co. to Lemuel Smith of same, for $90, 180 A on Aaron Cr adj Blanks, King, Harris. 24 Apr 1822. Wit: Irby Smith, Gabl C. Jones.

138-9 Thomas Webb to James Webb, for $300, 74 1/5 A both sides Tar R on the great road adj James Webb. 5 Apr 1822. Wit: Wm. Riley, Isaac Webb.

139-40 Thomas McGehee to John Pass, for $637.50, 129½ A on the State line between VA & NC adj James Franklin, William Runnels, James Warrin. 16 May 1822. 16 May 1822. Acknd in open court.

Deed Book F
Page

140-4 George Wood (in debt to Williamson & McKissack for $79.60½) to Green D.
Satterfield, in trust, for $1, 100 A where Wood lives. 30 Jan 1822.
Wit: Radford Satterfield.

144-6 William Lawson & wife Lucy Lawson; Samuel Mitchel & wife Susan Mitchel;
Gabrile Bailey in right of his children by his wife Martha Bailey decd; Jno
Russell & wife Mary Russell; exec of Edwd Mitchel decd & his wife Rebecca Mitchel;
adm of Elijah Mitchel decd & his wife Sally Mitchel; Matthew Mitchell & his wife
Elleanor Mitchell; and Mary Mitchel relict of Charles Mitchell decd - all the
heirs at law of Charles Mitchell decd - to Richard Russell of Warren Co., NC, with
power of attorney, to ask for & receive of Christopher Haskins Sen. or his exec
all sums of money that may be due in consequence of their interest as heirs of
Charles Mitchell decd in the ferry known as Haskins & Mitchell Ferry on Roanoke
R - their interest being one-third part of estate of Edwd Mitchel decd of Mecklenburg Co., VA. 12 Mar 1822. Wit: W. McKissack, Chs M. Lawson, Moses Chambers,
William Street exec, Thos Webb adm.

146-8 William McMurray of Pendleton District, SC, to James McMurry of Person Co.,
for $700, 210½ A on Double Cr of S Hico adj Samuel McMurry; also his share of
the mills erected by Samuel McMurry Senr decd. 15 Dec 1821. Wit: C. G. McMurry,
James Bowden, Ann McMurry. Proved by oath Charles G. McMurry.

148-50 Thomas Atkinson & Ira Lea exec of Richard Atkinson decd to Edward Davis
of Orange Co., for $5, transfer of all interest in following land for purpose of
indemnifying them as securities of Carter Atkinson. Carter Atkinson had
executed to Ira Lea for use of Richd Atkinson a tract in Person Co. willed by
father of Carter Atkinson to him & his brother Thomas Atkinson adj Moses Fuller,
James Bradsher for purpose of securing Richard Atkinson for debt due State Bank
of NC. Davis now becomes endorser of Carter Atkinson for said debt. 27 Apr 1822.
Wit: Thos L. Douglas, Hezekiah Morton. Proved before Leonard Henderson, Judge
of Supreme Court of NC 19 Oct 1822.

150-2 Harris Wilkerson to Stephen Inscore of Granville Co., for $68, 100.75 A
on Cub Cr adj James Hill, Bennett Williams Jun., Cozart, to new road, David Peed.
14 Feb 1822. Wit: Wyat Cannaday, Jesse Jones.

152-3 Laurence Vanhook to Nicholas Thompson of CC, town of Leasburg, for $88.50,
30½ A on S Hico adj Lipscomb, Loyd Vanhook decd, Robt Vanhook, Jeremiah Brooks.
17 Nov 1821. Wit: Will A. Lea, Wm. Lipscomb.

153-4 William Stanfield of Oglethorpe Co., GA, to Thomas McGehee of Person Co.,
for $137.50, all his interest in 192 A adj James Franklin, Wm. Runnals, James
Warren, James McGehee, Thos McGehee; said land came to him as heir of William
Stanfield decd & is an undivided fourth part of said land. 4 Feb 1822.
Wit: Jno Garner, Geo M. Hamlet.

154-7 Samuel Dickens, sheriff, to Ira Lea, for $62.50, 78 A on Stories Cr adj
Samp M. Glenn; sold to satisfy execution against Benjamin Harris for $54.67 3/4
which was recovered by Wm. McKissack, Isham Edwards, Benja Chambers. 25 July 1821.
Acknd in open court.

158 Andrew B. Wood to Milton Rose of Petersburg VA, for $198.25, 20 A on Double
Cr which he purchased of Robt Stanfield with mill,adj Jno Scoggin, James Wisdom,
Benja W. Milner. 16 Sept 1822. Wit: Robt Stanfield, C. G. Rose.

158-60 Robert Stanfield to Andrew B. Wood (Duncan Rose on 19 Feb 1820 conveyed
to Robert Stanfield 220 A in trust for Andrew B. Wood on Double Cr adj Jesse
Hargis, Benja W. Milner; said Stanfield sold 200 A to James Wisdom; the remainder
contains the grist mill) - Stanfield conveys residue of tract of 20 A to Wood
with timbers & mill. 30 Sept 1822. Wit: Charles G. Rose, Milton Rose.

Deed Book F
Page

160-3 Milton Rose of Petersburg, VA (in debt to Bank of Newbern for $1452.59)
to Sherwood Haywood of Raleigh, NC, for $1, trustee, 350 A on Hyco Cr adj Addison
Cochran, Wm. Brown; a lot in Roxbrough; 105 A near said lot conveyed by James
Payne to Duncan Rose. 13 Sept 1822. Wit: Charles G. Rose, Ira Lea.

163-5 James Williamson, trustee, to Sherwood Haywood of Raleigh, NC, for $815,
350 A on Hyco adj the late Addison Cochran, Wm. Brown; lot in Roxbrough & 105 A
nearby; said land sold to satisfy deed of trust given to Williamson by Duncan
Rose to secure debts. 13 Sept 1822. Wit: C. G. Rose.

165-6 Sherwood Haywood of Raleigh, NC, to Milton Rose of Petersburg VA, for $1452,
all lands in Person mentioned on preceeding deed. 13 Sept 1822. Wit: Charles
G. Rose.

166 John Barnett, high sheriff Person Co.,(ordered by court to sell goods &
chattels of Phillip Burch decd to pay debt of $190) to James Williamson, for
$80.10, 230 A on Bushy Fork Flat R adj Churchwell Jones, Robt Jones. 4 Apr
1822. Acknd in open court. **Note** - This deed is divided with the last half
included on pages 170-1.

167-9 John Barnett, sheriff (by court order to sell lands of Lewis Ransay for
debt of $230.06½ recovered by Isham Edwards, Jno Womack, & David Young plus costs
& other charges) to John Holloway & Isham Edwards, for $300, 211 A on Dishwater
Cr adj William Ramsey; Samuel Dickens has moved from the State before executing
this deed; John Barnett his successor executed deed for sale 31 May 1821.
26 Sept 1822. Acknd in open court.

170-1 are remainder of page 166. See above.

172-3 James E. Flack (in debt to Edmund Whitman of Meadsville, Halifax Co., VA,
for $44.83¼) to Robert Vanhook, for $1, in trust, a horse, gig, 1 bed, 2 walnut
tables. 17 Apr 1822. Wit: N. Compton, Robt Vanhook, Henry Womack.

174-5 William A. Lea & Susanna Lea his wife to John W. Williams, for $8640,
1080 A on Stories Cr adj Hatcher, Browning, Benja Harris, Glenn. 23 May 1818.
Wit: Geo Lea, Abner Lea. Susanna Lea examined apart from her husband & she is
satisfied with conveyance.

176-7 William McKissack to Ebenezer Morrow (or Murrow), for $200, 100 A adj
Abraham Walters on a side of the mountain. 26 Sept 1822. Wit: John Douglas,
John Barnett.

177-8 Richard Jones to John Lunsford, for $175, negro boy Daniel about 2 yrs old.
24 Sept 1822. Wit: Dennis Obriant.

178-9 Mary Morrow to John Morrow & Samuel Yarbrough, for $400, negro man Tom.
11 Apr 1820. Wit: William Yarbrough Jun.
179-81 Thomas Townsend (in debt to Thomas Shepard for $35.56) to Joseph Gill,
for 25¢, in trust, a sorrel mare, colt, cattle; household & kitchen furniture.
28 May 1822. Wit: Thomas Gill.

181-3 William Person of Warren Co., NC, to John Bumpass of Person Co., for $850,
393 A on Granville Co. line adj Brown, said Bumpass, Washington, Williamson,
Anderson, Oakley. 5 Apr 1822. Wit: Sherwood Haywood, Samuel Holman.

183-5 Thomas Edmondson (in debt to Cary Williams for 2 bonds for $114.79 &
$238; debt due Isham Edwards $26.76, to Wm. McKissack & Samuel Davey) to William
Williams, for $1, trustee, 393 A; negro woman Milly & her 2 children William &
Moses. 21 Aug 1822. Wit: Haywood Williams, Alexander Williams.

185-6 John Brooks Sen. to Daniel Brooks, for 56 lbs 10/, 193 A on Mayo Cr.
2 Sept 1822. Wit: Reuben P. Brooks.

186

Deed Book F
Page
186-8 Charles D. Wade (in debt to Nathaniel Torian for $75.75 & for $27.40 plus 3 other notes as assignee) to James Martin, for $1, negro woman Hannah & boy Lewis; horse, pony; furniture. 27 Aug 1822. Wit: Mary Wade, Downey Wade. Ordered registered 14 Feb 1823.

189-90 James Royster, William Royster, Edmund Grinstead & Polly Grinstead his wife relinquish unto Frances Royster wife of Henry Royster, for $1500, the negro woman Lett & her increase which was purchased 16 May 1810 by legatees of Frances & Henry Royster; said negro to remain with Frances Royster for her life & her increase div among above legatees including Parthenia Royster who was not named in bill of sale. Wit: Ira Lea. 1 Mar 1821.

190 Henry Royster relinquishes all claim to negroes named in foregoing deed. 22 May 1822. Wit: Ira Lea.

191-2 Samuel Davy to John Y. Wilkerson, for $250, 124 A on Cat Tail Br of Blewing Cr adj Lucy Jones, Mary W. Jones, Francis Foard, William Loftis, Alexr Ellison. 23 Sept 1822. Wit: R. Vanhook, Willie Jones.

192-4 William Mitchel of CC (in debt to John McMurray Sen. for $331.34) to John McMurray Jun, trustee, 130 A on S Hyco adj George Whitefield. 1 June 1822. Wit: Unicy Grider, Thos Villines.

195-7 John Barnett, sheriff, (due to court order to collect of Thomas Allen,BS, debt of $80.97½ recovered by Wm. McKissack) to Wm. McKissack, for $85, 100 A on Rosemary Cr adj Charles Gregory. 5 Sept 1822. Wit: John Douglas.

198-9 James Franklin to Joel Newman, for $17.50, 3½ A n side Hico adj said Newman. 16 Apr 1822. Wit: Cary Williams, Jno Barnett.

199-200 Martin Morton to John McMurray (due to execution against Downey Wade by John McMurray) for $32.60, negro boy Reuben sold to John McMurray. 26 Apr 1821. Wit: Ira Lea.

200-3 Samuel Dickens, sheriff, to Richd Atkinson (due to 10 executions from county court against Moses Fuller for $747.21 recovered by Williamson & Lea, Carter Lea Jun., Ira Lea & Co., George Huston, Jno Rice, Jno Flinn, & Lewis Amis against Moses Fuller) for $260, 250 A on Richland Cr adj Asa Fullar, Carter Lea. 24 July 1822. Acknd in open court, Mar 1823.

203-5 John W. Philpott of Granville Co. to Pleasant Henderson of Orange Co., for $1500, 668 A on Mayo Cr adj Edward B. Davie, Winstead. _ _ 1821. Wit: Nathl Robards.

205-6 John Morrow to Samuel Yarbrough, for $250, all his claim to negro man Sam formerly property of William Morrow decd. 26 Aug 1822. Wit: Archd Morrow.

206-8 John Barnett to Isham Edwards (due to court order against Thomas Merrit for $99.21 recovered by Isham Edwards plus other debts), for $50, 100 A on Gents Cr adj Robert Carver, heirs of Presly Draper. 26 Sept 1822. Wit: Jno Douglas.

209-11 William Frazer (in debt to William Satterfield as his security for debts due Kindle Vanhook, James Pulliam, Lea & Vanhook, Martin Morton, Lewis Amis, Carter Lea & Co.) to James Hannah, for 50¢, trustee, 119 A on Hico where Hannah lives adj Geo L. Johnson, Thos Lipscomb, Jno Mason, Royster; livestock. 4 June 1822. Wit: Wm. Watson, Thos L. Douglas.

212 Henry Berry & David Berry of Orange Co. to William McKissack sen. of Person Co., for $350, negro woman Amy. _ Sept 1821. Wit: Thos P. Evans, Robt G. Cummins, William Lipscomb, Jno Cummins.

212-3 Laurence Vanhook of CC to Nicholas Thompson of same, for $62½, 295.6 A on Stories Cr adj Walters. 23 May 1822. Wit: B. W. Milner, Jno Rimmer.

214-5 Addison Cochran to Jno Jackson, for $250, 113 A on Flat R adj Abraham Moore, James Farquhar. 9 Oct 1820. Proved by oath Saml Evans.

215-6 John Halliburton & Letty Halliburton his wife to Thomas Terrill, for $600, 220½ A on Cain Cr adj Hubbard Carnal, Richard Halliburton. 8 Nov 1822. Wit: Benja Halliburton, Jos Terrill, Thos Winstead.

217 Plat of survey for John Halliburton on Cain Cr as conveyed above. 15 May 1819. Wm. Davie, surveyor; chain carriers: R. Halliburton, J. Halliburton.

218-9 Thomas Durham & Satsy Tapley of Jones Co., GA, to Thomas Lawson of Person Co., for $125, 100 A adj Hargis, Wilson, Person; Thomas Durham atty for Satsy Tapley. 26 Nov 1822. Wit: John Lawson, James Wilkerson.

219-22 Jesse Evans to Harman Royster of Granville Co., for $2,250, 319 1/8 A on Flat R adj Richard Holman, Andrew Gray to Quarrel Cr, Epperson to school house br, heirs of Charles Holman decd, Holman meeting house. 9 Oct 1822. Wit: Jno Douglas, Wm. Hall.

222-4 Archibald Carnal, trustee for deed of trust executed by Durret Stanfield to Alexander Cunningham, to William Terrill, for $750, 100 A on Cain Cr adj Carnal, Robert Jones Sen., Thomas J. Terrel, Kinchen Newman. 23 Dec 1822. Wit: Jno Garner, Richd C. Word.

224 John Penn to daughter Elizabeth Penn, for love & affection, negro girl Piety about 3 yrs old. 16 Aug 1822. Wit: Green W. Brown, Geo Briggs.

225 John Sanders of Franklin Co., NC, acting as agent for Jacobina Milner by power of attorney dated 3 Apr, purchases from David Hunt, trustee, for $523, 3 negro slaves: Gelly, Ellick, & Isaac; Sanders relinquishes all claims to Jacobina Milner. 8 Apr 1823. Wit: J. Person, Jno Wilson. Proved Franklin Co. in Superior Court.

226-7 Jacobina Milner of Franklin Co., NC, to Benjamin W. Milner, for $280 on the amt of execution which Nathl Norfleet brought against Jacobina Milner & now in hands of sheriff of Person Co. for collection -(said B. W. Milner to pay amt of execution & to prevent sale of her negro Harry) - 3 negroes Gilly & her 2 children Isaac & Allex. 8 Apr 1823. Wit: Jno G. Wilson, Jno Sanders.

228-9 Joshua Byasee to Sally Rogers, for $10, 170 A on Cobb Cr adj John Bradsher, Col. George Lea; sold to satisfy deed of trust Asa Fullar gave to Joshua Byasee to secure debt due Watkins Rogers by Fullar - sold at house of Thomas Byasee. 24 Dec 1822. Wit: Maurice Smith, Alex Winstead.

230-1 John Barnett, successor to Samuel Dickens late sheriff of Person Co., to Lewis Tapp, for $301.25, 388 A adj Lewis Daniel, James Satterfield; sold by court order against James Milner to collect for $1029.1765 recovered by William McKissack Thos McGehee, Richd Holman, Chambers. 5 Nov 1822. Wit: Wm. McKissack, J. A. Pulliam.

232-3 Asa Fullar (in debt to Watkins Rogers for $32.75) to Joshua Byasee, in trust, for $1, all his interest in 170 A on Cobb Cr adj Jno Bradsher, Col. George Lea. 24 Aug 1822. Wit: Alex Winstead, Maurice Smith.

234-5 George W. Jeffreys to Charles Sallard, for $150, 123 A near Doct. Parker now Presley Draper, William Hamlin, William Carver, on road from Clay's to Edwards store, Robert Walker. 2 Oct 1822. Wit: William Eskridge, Henry Dixon.

235-7 James Woody to Allen Woody, for $1234, 154¼ A on Bold Br. _ Dec 1822. Wit: Jos Gill.

237-8 Abner A. Dixon to George Wade, for $20, 1 A adj Jno Bailey, said Wade; also use of spring known as factory spring. 23 Dec 1822. Wit: Stanford Long, Robert Brooks, Moses Chambers. Jno Rogers.

Deed Book F
Page

239 Ransom Cates, exec to estate of Robt Cate Sen. decd, to Robert Cates, for $458, negro woman Milly. 2 Nov 1823. Wit: Joseph Hicks.

239-42 Joseph Gill, guardian to heirs of Mandley Winstead decd, to Jno Lawson Sen., for $700, 200 A both sides Mayo Cr adj said Lawson, Robt Gill; excepting 69 A for Cothran Winstead for his life it being dower in said land. 1 Oct 1822. Wit: Thos Gill, Wm. Gill, B. W. Lawson.

242-4 William Winstead Junr. to John Morrow, for $200, 152 A on Mayo Cr adj Chambers, Baird, Halliburton at CH road. 14 Dec 1822. Wit: Josias Bumpass.

244-5 George Richardson to Harris Wilkerson, for $50, one-fourth of 160 A being sw quarter, section 3, township 7N, in range 11W in territory of Arkansas appropriated for military bounties. 20 Feb 1822. Wit: L. V. Hargis, Jonas Parker.

246-7 Hastin Bartlett of Person Co. to Alexander Gordon of CC, for $60, 60 A on S Hico adj Leml Rainey, Thomas Woods, Jno Ellison, Simeon Cochran. 27 Nov 1821. Wit: Thomas Woods, Nelson Bartlett.

247-9 Thomas McGehee to Charles Sallard, for $1500, 219½ A adj Edmund Dixon, said Sallard, Alexr Moore, Robert Jones, near Campbell old road. 20 Feb 1823. Proved by oath Jno Barnett.

249-50 Archibald Morrow to John Morrow, for $134, all right & interest in estate of his father late decd & of Mary Morrow his mother now living. 26 Oct 1822. Wit: Kindal Davie, Wm. Davie.

250-1 Peggy Inscore to Aris Vaughan & her heirs, for $100, 133½ A on Cubb Cr adj William Oakley. 7 Feb 1823. Wit: C. Vaughan, Jno Oakley.

251-3 George Peed to Jesse Lunsford, for $44, 100 A being part of 640 A on Cub Cr adj Cozart, Jackson. 27 May 1822. Wit: Henry H. Allen, David Peed, Gaton Suit.

253-4 Maurice Smith & Martha Smith to Isabella L. Hayes the daughter of Martha Smith by her former husband Bartholomew Hayes decd, for love & affection & 10/ paid by Wm. L. Hayes next friend of Isabella Hayes who is now an infant, negro girl Lizzy about 8 or 9 yrs of age and negro boy Jackson about 6 yrs; both negroes were property of Martha Smith before her marriage. 25 Dec 1822. Wit: Alexr Winstead.

255-6 Joseph Stanfield of Oglethrop Co., GA, to Thomas McGehee of Person Co., for $139.60, 192 A adj Franklin, William Warren, William Runnals, James Warren, Jas McGehee, Thomas McGehee; said tract was one-fourth part of land of William Stanfield decd & Joseph Stanfield is heir at law. 30 Dec 1822. Wit: Jas McGehee, Wm. M. McGehee.

257-9 Andrew Gray (in debt to Alexander Gray Sen. for $560) to Robert F. Murdock of Randolph Co., NC, trustee, for $1, 226 A on Flat R adj Duncan Cameron, Richd Holman former Dickens; said land where Andrew Gray resides formerly land of John Cates decd. 14 Dec 1822. Wit: Ezl Morgan, Andrew Gray Jun. Proved before Frederic Nash, Judge Superior Court.

260-1 Isaiah Fullar to children John Fullar, Abraham Fullar, Elizabeth Fullar, Mary W. Fullar, Solomon Fuller, James M. Fuller, Roana Fuller & Ralph W. Fuller, for love & affection, all claim & right to negro slaves to wit: Charles, Nancy, Viney, Agga, Ambrose, Nelson, Mary, Moses; grantor reserves privilege to sell or dispose of any of them except Viney in not to be taken from said children. 27 June 1821. Wit: E. Yancey, J. W. Williams.

261-3 William Tatom to Moses Woody, for $400, 107.3 A on Bold Br adj both men to the VA line. 10 Oct 1822. Wit: C. Holloway, Absolem HBurton. Proved by oath Crowder Holloway.

263-4 Articles of agreement between Isaac Satterfield & Frances Raven(widow of John Raven decd) who have agreed to intermarry; since property of each is under encumbrances, each party shall not be liable to pay debts of the other; Frances Raven to have full power to give or sell her property at all times, and if she is the longest to live, she has power to take possession of her own property. 18 Dec 1822. Wit: Lewis Amis.

264-6 William Robinson (Roberson) to Obedience Pool of Granville Co., NC, for $65, 50 A on Stories Cr adj S. Glenn, Jno Fullar, Solo Clayton. 24 Dec 1822. Wit: Jesse Bumpass, D. Sneed.

266-7 James Williamson to Jno G. A. Williamson, for 200?, 200 A on Rosemary Cr. 25 Dec 1822. Wit: Jno Douglas.

268-9 Thomas J. Moore of Richmond Co., GA, city of Augusta, to McKinzie, Bennach, Gregory, & Harden - two firms as merchants & traders of Augusta - for $1000, 640 A on Flat R, it being tract granted to Robt Dickens & sold by sheriff to William Dickens who deeded it to said Moore adj James Jay, former claim of Ann Pyron, Henry Ford, Joseph Jay former land; said land to be sold to pay debts & mortgages. 26 Mar 1822. Wit: Robert H. Reid, Robt Gumbleton. Proved 6 Feb 1823 in Richmond Co., GA.

270-2 Thomas Winstead (in debt to Edmund Dixon Sen. for $150) to William Dixon, in trust, for $1, 36 A adj Benja Hallibruton, Richd Hallibruton, & purchased of the latter. 1 Mar 1823. Wit: Archd Carnal, Levi Dixon.

272-3 Joseph Royster to Jesse Bradsher, a gift of negro girl Viney to satisfy a certain agreement. 20 Oct 1822. Wit: Wm. H. Royster, Jno W. Royster.

273-4 John Barnett, sheriff, to Nathaniel Norfleet (to satisfy court order against Sackey Marshall for $109.63) 162½ A on S Hyco adj David Mitchell sold to Norfleet for $47.80. 11 Mar 1823. Wit: Wm. McKissack, Jno Lawson.

275-6 Thomas V. Hargis to Robert Blalack, for $150, 150 A on Flat R adj Allen, said Blalack, Terrel. 28 Apr 1823. Wit: H. W. Milner, R. Vanhook.

276-8 Joseph Hargis (in debt to L. V. Hargis & Co. for 2 debts) to E. D. Stanfield & Harris Wilkerson, in trust, for 25¢, a bay horse, hogs, goats; all furniture except 1 bed, loom & wheel; all tools, rifle, crops. 25 Apr 1823. Wit: Robt Stanfield.

278-9 Power of attorney - Gabriel C. Jones to Wylie Jones, trusty friend & brother, to act for him in selling property; to pay & discharge debts & to manage his estate. 3 Apr 1823. Wit: Richd E. Bennett, Ditrion Thaxton.

279-81 John Garner, agent by power of attorney for Hardy Black of State of TN, to sell his undivided interest being one-third of estate of his father Robt Black- to Edmund Dixon Sen., for $96, 38 A on Hyco Cr adj Archd Dunnaway, Edmund Dixon Jun. 29 Apr 1823. Wit: Levi Dixon, Alexr Moore, James P. Harrison.

281-2 Thomas Hargis & Sarah Hargis to Ephraim Hawkins, for $60, 32 A on Bushy Fork of Flat R. 23 Apr 1819. Wit: Wright Nichols.

282-4 Allen Green (in debt to Thomas Webb for $870.57) to Hugh Woods, in trust, for 50¢, 90 A on Castle Cr adj James Woody, Moses Walker, excepting to his mother Sarah Green a life estate in part of the same; horses, wagon, furniture; 5 Negroes Cloe, Milly, Martha, Cate, Jone; cattle; mother to have life estate to Milly. 24 Feb 1823. Wit: Sterling F. Vaughan, Jesse Monday.

284-5 John Brown to Ephraim Hawkins, for $19.75, 7 A & 32 rods on Flat R adj Hudgins. 6 Mar 1822. Wit: Asa Hudgins, James Bradsher.

286-7 John Barnet, sheriff, to Nathaniel Norfleet, for $54, 100 A adj said Norfleet, James Briggs; said land sold by court order against William Moss for debt of $95.64¼. 11 Mar 1823. Wit: Wm. McKissack, Jno Lawson Jun.

Deed Book F
Page
288-90 George Wood (in debt to Andrew B. Woods for $163.36) to James Williamson, in trust, for 75¢, 100 A adj Jesse Bumpass. 20 Mar 1823. Wit: Wm. McKissack, Green Satterfield.

290-4 Div land of Charles B. Winstead decd to legatees:
  1. Margaret Jones 53 A adj Clixby, William Satterfield, Ira Lea, Carter Lea.
  2. Susanna Fuller 53.135 A adj Satterfield, Ira Lea, Margaret Jones.
  3. Penelope Winstead 53.33 A adj Susanna Fuller, Saml Winstead to Fish Trap Br, Ira Lea, & this the tract where Charles B. Winstead dwelt.
  4. Rebecca Winstead 73.75 A adj Seth Winstead, Clixby, William Satterfield.
  5. Seth Winstead 73.75 A adj Clixby, Rebecca Winstead, Barnett Winstead, Jno Westbrook.
  6. Sally Winstead 73.75 A adj Wheeler old line, Barnett Winstead, Rebecca Winstead.
  7. Barnett Winstead 73.75 A adj Seth Winstead, Atkinson or Carter, Westbrook.
Entire value of land is $843.36½; each legatee to get $120.48 value. _ July 1833. Commrs: Isaac Satterfield, Thos Trotter, James Jordan, Cary Williams.

294-5 Hasten Bartlett to Thomas Woods, for $85.52 which he owes Robert McKee of CC) for $1, in trust, horses, colts, cattle; furniture. 24 July 1823. Wit: Wm. McKee.

296-7 Boling Day (in debt to John Y. Parker for $43.80) to Ambrose Day, for 25¢, trustee, sorrel mare, 2 feather beds, furniture; cow & calf; crops. 17 Feb 1823. Wit: Robt Bumpass.

297-8 John Montgomery (in debt to Robert Stanfield for $97.30) to Andrew B. Wood, for 25¢, in trust, negroes Dulee a woman, Sam a boy, Sarah - or whatever negroes come to him in consequence of deed of gift from Edwd Clay decd to his children. 14 Apr 1823. Wit: B. W. Milner, _ Stanfield.

299-300 William Singleton of Person Co. (in debt to Thomas Easley of Halifax Co., VA, for $181.40), to William Thaxton of Halifax Co., VA, in trust for 6/, all right & claim he has to negroes held by his father Wm. Singleton Sen. during his life; furniture; livestock. 6 June 1823. Wit: J. A. Pulliam.

301-2 John Trew to William Williams, in trust, for $1, 74 A on Stories Cr adj John Hudgins, Danl Clayton - deed of trust to satisfy debt due Thomas Shepard for $21,20 & for bonds due Cary Williams; if sold debt due Elizabeth Trew for $30 be paid. 19 Apr 1823. Wit: Alex Williams, Viney Williams.

303-4 Robert Trim (in debt to John Farquhar for $110.83) to Stephen Wells, in trust, for 25¢, a horse, 2 cows, 10 hogs, sheep; furniture; wagon; 2 cotton wheels, 2 flax wheels; saddles. 11 Mar 1823. Wit: W. Nichols, James Wells.

305-6 Nathaniel Norfleet bound to pay $99.50 on judgment obtained by Thomas Phelps against Sackey Marshall; to indemnify Norfleet, Sackey Marshal to Benjamin W. Milner, in trust, for 25¢, a wagon, bay mare; furniture. 15 Feb 1823. Wit: Josiah W. Milner.

307-8 Thomas Brandon Jr. of Halifax Co., VA, to John W. Brandon of Person Co., for love & affection, 96 A adj Geo Elliott, Jno McCain, Charles Willson. 30 July 1823. Wit: Thos S. Brandon, Robt J. Chappel, Wm. Elliott.

308-10 Hiram Holt of Caloway Co., MO; Hiram Holt atty in fact for Abner Holt & James Brooks of same; Jno Holt, Robert Brandon, William Reynolds & Anna Holt all of Halifax Co., VA - all legatees of Timothy Holt decd - to Robert Holt of Halifax Co., VA, for $200, 50 A on Holt mill cr in Person Co. adj Roger Atkinson, Obediah Faulkner, Alexr Cunningham, the VA State line. 14 Jan 1823. Wit: Wm. Warren, Nathl Warren, Obadiah Faulkner.

310-3 Jos Jones of Petersburg, Dinwiddie Co., VA, to his daughter Lucy Ann Lockhead of same, for love & affection & $1, all lands he owns in Person Co., NC known as Castle Cr & Rambo tracts - 1601½ A adj Jno Lawson & crossing Rambo Br;

Deed Book F
Page

310-3 cont - adj Walker crossing Keedles Br & Castle Cr, Dixon, Bailey, Luke
Robertson br at State line crossing Gideon Br, David Brooks, Joseph Harris former
line - said land part of survey of 2041½ A made 5 Dec 1803 by Isaac Oakes;
balance of about 240 A not included as was sold & now owned by Brooks adj State
line crossing Hyco R twice to Luke Robertson br. 5 May 1823. Wit: David Lawson,
Thos Lawson, Wm. Baird, Thos P. Atkinson, Richd E. Bennett.

313-6 Joseph Jones of Petersburg, VA, to his son Joseph Jones of Halifax Co., VA,
for love & affection & $1, two tracts in Person formerly Caswell Co of 455 A on
Hyco R purchased of Roger Atkinson 9 Oct 1790 called Butler's tract adj Jno
Lawson, Lord Lord; see deed from Phillip Hall to Roger Atkinson July 1785 for
full description adj State line, David Brooks, Luke Robertson, land given to
daughter Lucy Ann Lockhead. 5 May 1823. Wit: Thomas Lawson, David Lawson,
Wm. Baird, Thos P. Atkinson, Richd E. Bennett.

316-7 James McFarland of Davis Co., KY, to Thomas McGehee of Person Co., for $60,
the undivided interest in tract on both sides Hyco adj Alex Cunningham, Joel
Newman, James McGehee; said interest was the interest of Robert Wall, Anderson
Wall, & Banister Wall from death of their brother Hampton Wall & purchased by
McFarland 6 May 1823. 14 June 1823. Wit: Stephen Neal, Thos Torian,
Wm. M. McGehee.

317-9 Robert Wall of Davis Co., KY, to Thomas McGehee of Person Co., for $150,
all interest in tract both sides Hyco adj William Woods, Mumford McGehee, George
Gregory; said land devised him by last will of Claud Muirhead decd - is undivided ninth part. 15 Oct 1816. Wit: Wm. R. Griffith, Clerk, Davis Co., Jos D.
JcFarland.

319-21 Anderson Wall, Banister Wall, & Robert Wall all of Davis Co., KY, to James
McFarland of same, for $25, their undivided interest to tract in Person Co. on
Hyco adj William Woody, Mumford McGehee, George Gregory - their interest was
that of their brother Hampton Wall decd who owned one-ninth part under last will
of Claude Muirhead recorded in CC. 6 May 1823. Wit: Ralph C. Calhoun, William
Glenn.

321-3 Alexander M. Long for himself & acting agent by Power of Attorney for
William G. Long & his wife Bridget Long of Person Co. to William Vernon of same,
for $450, 156½ A adj Lipscomb, Lawrence Vanhook, R. Vanhook, Moses Bradsher.
11 Aug 1823. Wit: George W. Jeffreys, Wm. Irvin.

323-5 Thomas Tolbert of Jackson Co., TN, to Brittain Wagstaff of Granville Co.,
NC, 2/3 of 100 A on Henley Mill Cr adj William Trotter, Edmund Henley, Thomas Grant,
James D. Henley decd; price paid $300; said land was devised by last will of
Edmon Henley Sen. to his wife Letitia Henley for her life & to go to Edmund
Henley Jun son of James D. Henley decd. Edmund Henley Jun has 2 sisters & one
brother living at death of Letitia Henley to wit: Nancy Tolbert, Polly Gains, James
D. Henely & they are lawful heirs of Edmund Henley Jun. decd; Thomas Tolbert in
right of his wife Nancy Tolbert who was Nancy Henley & as atty for Polly Gains are
grantors of this deed. 4 Jan 1823. Wit: Thos McGehee, Cary Williams.

325-6 John Brown to loving daughter Polly Brown, for love & affection, negro
boy Green about 6 yrs old & 3 mos. 11 June 1823. Wit: Asa Hudgins, Lavinia Hudgins

326-7 John Brown to daughter Elizabeth L. Brown, for love & affection,
negro girl Clara about 4 yrs & 5 mos old. 11 June 1823. Wit: Asa Hudgins,
Lavinia Hudgins.

327-8 Isaiah Fullar to Lucretia Williams, for $250, negro girl Agga. 24 Jan 1823.
Wit: Wm. McKissack.

328-9 Solomon Cates to Thomas P. Evans & Lawrence Vanhook Hargis, for $160, 160 A
which is all his right & title to quarter section land in territory of Illinois
warrant #7664 - being NE quarter, Section 6, township 13N, Range 4E in land grant

192

Deed Book F
Page
328-9 cont - by Congress to the late army on or since 6 May 1812 for military
bounties. 7 Nov 1823. Wit: Harris Wilkerson, Rufus Cates.

330-2 William Frazer (in debt to Thomas Lipscomb for $10 and as security to note
due Henry Dixon for $55; for judgment on note due James Dollarhide assignee to
Jno H. Jones for $12.60½) to Ira Lea, in trust, for 50¢, 119 A on Hyco Cr adj
Jno Mason, Thos Lipscomb, Geo Inscore; livestock, furniture; growing crops.
13 June 1823. Wit: Jno Rice Jun.

333-9 Allotment of land of Robert Dickens decd among his heirs:
   1. Samuel Dickens - 3 tracts: 200 A on Deep Cr known as Downey tract adj Jno
      Davis, said Dickens, Saml Yarboro; 150 A being ½ of 300 A belonging to
heirs of Yancey Bailey & Robt Dickens decd on Cub Cr & known as the path tract adj
James Kennedy, Jesse Oakley; 200 A on Flat R called the Horton tract adj Horton,
Robt Stanfield, Nathaniel Norfleet - value $454.50.
   2. Edward Donoho & Catherine Donoho his wife 2 tracts: 342 A purchased of Wm.
Waite on Flat R near Farquhar mill adj James Farquhar, Alldridge, Matthew Cates,
Wm. Cocke, Minshew; 200 A on Burd Cr being ½ of grant to Dickens & Waite adj
James Cocke on Orange Co. line - value $452.57.
   3. William Dickens - 638 A called the meeting House tract exempting 2 A for
meeting house on Flat R adj Daniel, Satterfield, Jno Womack, Rankin now Williamson-
value $638.
   4. Jesse Dickens - 2 lots: 404 A on Deep Cr & Rocky Fork adj Jno Bumpass, on
Washington Road, Doctor Hunt, Eli Tapp, Jonas Parker, John Oakley, Bumpass
mountain; Goshen road intersects lot 1; 200 A called the Burford tract on Deep Cr &
Little Cr adj Luke Moore, Merrit Stone, Blalock. - value $463.74.
   5. Mary Clack (now Smith) - 2 tracts: 957 4/5 A known as Brewer settlement adj
John Bumpass, Doctor Hunt, Mann or Suit, Thomas Oakley, Vaughan, Nathan Oakley,
Sacky Moore - value $404; 22 A called Rosemary on road from Roxboro to Bull's
mill - value $415.
   6. Thomas Webb & Martha Webb his wife - 2 tracts: 723 A adj Abner Williams,
Doctor Hunt, Jno Moore, Kennedy, Mann, Mary Clack, John Bumpass; ½ of 261 A on
Cub Cr adj Cozart, Oakley, John Cash heirs, said tract granted to Dickens &
Waite. - value$463.74.
   7. Heirs of Richard Bland & Elizabeth R. Bland his wife decd - 2 tracts: 342 A
known as Step tract; 100 A on Byrd Cr granted to Dickens & Waite on Orange Co.
line adj Michael Robinson, James Smith former line. - value $476.20.
   8. Maryann Moore daughter of Lucretia - 372 A known as east end of Stepp tract
on Orange Co. line - value $465.
7 Aug 1823. Commrs: John Bumpass, Abner Williams, Jesse Lunsford, Robt Sweaney,
Joel Sweaney.
Estate paid Phillips Moore, surveyor, $3 per day for 4 days; funding self & horse
75¢; plotting $9; return to court $1. The 5 commrs. each recd $1 per day plus
75¢ funding self & horse for total of 7 days; William Brown for carrying chain 2
days $2; John Suit $1 & Cas Vaughan $1 for carrying chain for 1 day each.

340-2 Jesse Long (in debt to Williamson & McKissack for $33.07; to Carver &
McKissack for $25; to Josias Carver for $100) to Green Satterfield, in trust,crops
of corn, wheat, tobacco growing on plantations of Carver & McKissack; livestock;
furniture. 14 June 1823. Wit: Wm. F. Smith.

343 Ezekiel Jackson of Granville Co. (in debt to various persons with George Knott,
security) to Lawson Neal & Woodson Daniel, for $1, in trust, 150 A on Cub Cr in
Person Co. adj Hubbard Cozart, Peed; including all his property except working
tools & exemption allowed by law. 3 Aug 1823. Wit: Dicy Huddleston, Wm. Moutry.
Receiving benefits of this conveyance are Howell L. Ridley, Cameron & Young,
Beverly Daniel. Proved 1823.

END OF BOOK F

Page

1-3 Lewis Daniel of Person Co. to Duncan Cameron of Orange Co, for $600, 389 A
in 2 tracts where James Milner now lives on s fork Flat R adj William McKissack,
James Satterfield, Benja Jones, Daniel, Cameron; said land conveyed by Robt Payne
to Robt Wells 22 Mar 1815 & by Him to James Milner 4 Jan 1816 & sold by sheriff
as estate of James Milner to Lewis Tapp & by him to Lewis Daniel 7 Sept 1822.
3 Nov 1823. Wit: J. G. A. Williamson, James Williamson. Signed also by James
Milner as deed was executed at his instance.

3-6 Abner A. Dixon to Stanford Long, for $525, 95½ A adj Jno Rogers, George
Wade, Jno Bailey, Jones. 4 Nov 1823. Wit: Moses Woody.

6-7 Allen Green to Stanford Long, for $543.37½, 58¼ A adj Abner Dixon, Jones,
Mrs. Walker, Rogers. 25 Feb 1823. Wit: M. R. Long, Abner A. Dixon.

8-9 John Humphreys, mortager (in debt to Robert Halliburton, mortagee, for $34)
7 chairs, bed & furniture; one cow & yearling; violin; trunk, shot gun; his
interest in shop books of date 1823; one book "Life of Jackson". 15 May 1823.
Wit: Wm. Davie.

9-10 Robert Harris, exec of last will of Dennis Obrian Sen. decd to Dennis
Obrian Jun., the highest bidder, for $35.50, 50 A part of land where the decd
lived on Stories Cr. 10 Nov 1823. Wit: Sol Clayton.

10-2 Richard Jones (in debt to Alex Winstead for $121) to Isaac Satterfield, for
$1, in trust, 41½ A on Double Cr being part of 83 A which he & his half-brother
Stephen Wilkerson purchased of Jesse Satterfield & first purchased of John Ravens
adj Isaac Satterfield, Alex Winstead. 17 July 1823. Wit: George Satterfield.

12-4 Reuben Jones Jun. & Amy Jones his wife of Granville Co. to Littleberry
Chandler of same, for $200, 204 A on Bluewing Cr adj Gabl C. Jones, Blanks.
27 Mar 1823. Wit: Willie Jones, Jno Y. Wilkerson Jun. Amy Jones examined apart
from her husband and freely consented to conveyance. 27 Mar 1823. Proved
by oath William Jones. Wit: Robt Harris, JP.

14-5 Survey for Genl Jos Jones of 2441½ A adj county line adj Jno Brooks, Jno
Lawson, crossing Rambo Br, Walker old line, crossing Keedle Br & Castle Cr, Dixon,
Bailey, Luke Robertson to county line crossing Hico twice, McFarland. 5 Dec
1823. By J. Oakes, surveyor. Note on bottom of plat: This part I wish to reserve for my son Jos & balance of survey for my daughter DCPD.

16-8 Ira Lea to Laurence V. Hargis, for $200, the highest bid, 193.9 A on Deep
Cr & Flat R adj heirs of Jno Gooche Sen. decd, Phillips Moore, Herbert Sims,
Minshew - sold to satisfy deed of trust of Thomas Minshew to Ira Lea 4 Nov 1811
for 250 A. _ Nov 1823. Wit: Carter Lea, Matthew Daniel.

18-20 Henry Mahan & Martha his wife to Bentley B. Epperson, for $90, an undivided
ninth part of property now in hands of Elizabeth Epperson wife & relict of John
Epperson, Sen. Decd consisting of a negro woman Henny & her 4 children Ben,
Lucinda, Martha, Mary at the death of Elizabeth or at div of estate. 27 Jan 1823.
Signed only by Martha Mahan. Henry Mahan & Martha give power of attorney
to Bentley B. Epperson to receive any possession due them of their ninth part.
Wit: Francis Epperson, Lucinda Mahan.

20-2 Redman G. Seal of Lincoln Co., GA, in right of his wife Eletha, to Bentley
B. Epperson of Person Co., for $90, an undivided ninth part of property in pos-
session of Elizabeth Epperson wife & relict of Jno Epperson Sen. decd including
negro Henny & her 4 children Lucinda, Ben, Martha, Mary. Epperson is lawful
atty for Redman G. Seal. 2 Jan 1823.

2-4 State of NC - #147 - to James Barnett, for $10 per 100 A, 260 & 1/5 A on Adams Cr adj Heggie, Mitchell, Jno Seymore, Reubin Long, Brooks. Entered 2 Mar 1822. Proved Person Co. Nov 1823.

4-6 William McKissack, late sheriff, to Lawrence V. Hargis, for 3 lbs 15/, the undivided part of 230 A or 47½ A on Richland Cr adj Matthew Daniel, James Williamson - sold to satisfy court order against Joseph Clayton for 43 lbs 13/2½ due since 1809 & said sum recovered by Hargis & Williamson, merchants. 11 Nov 1823. Wit: P. H. Mangum, John Barnet.

6-8 John Barnett, sheriff, to Lawrence V. Hargis, for $19.57, 100 A adj Thomas Hargis, Henry Womack - sold to satisfy court order against William Hargis for debt of $15. 12 Nov 1823. Wit: P. H. Mangum, Wm. McKissack.

8-9 John Walker to Moses Jones, for $350, 100 A both sides Castle Cr adj Henry Bailey, James Holloway, Buckly Walker - being part of larger tract deeded by Buckley Walker. 25 Dec 1821. Wit: Ish Edwards, Hugh Wood.

30 Thomas Williams of Orange Co. to Elias Fort, for $500, yellow girl Charlotte. 19 Mar 1817. Wit: William McKissack.

30-2 Benjamin Bowden (in debt to Nathl Norfleet for $226.1275) to William Whitefield, in trust, for 50¢, 57 A on S Hyco where Bowden lives adj widow & heirs of Ezekiel Dollarhide, former land of Henry McNeill, Nicholas Thompson; 50 barrels corn; horses, cattle; furniture; ½ of wagon & gears owned jointly with his son George Bwoden. 9 Oct 1823. Wit: Ann Milner, Jas Renn.

32a-34 George Bowden (in debt to Nath Norfleet for $78.97½) to Benja W. Milner, trustee, for 25¢, present crops of oats, 10 bushels rye, 30 barrels corn; 2 beds & furniture; 200 weight cotton; cow & calf, ½ of wagon possessed by his father Benjamin Bowden. 27 Nov 1823. Wit: Thos L. Douglas.

34-6 Thomas Blalack Sen. to his son Hasten Blalack, for $1 & love & affection, 235 A on Flat R adj Abraham Moore, Thos Blalack Jun - reserving for grantor & his wife Ann Blalack the house & plantation for their natural life. 12 Aug 1823. Wit: H. W. Milner, Lewis Daniel.

37-44 John G. Willson now of Franklin Co., NC, to James Williamson of Person Co., his greatest creditor, for $1, in trust, his house & all property including balances of all debts as set forth in books; 1 share in Person Library at Roxbrough; his proportionate share of estate of his father Robert Willson decd late of CC; lot in Milton; 2½ shares tickets in Maryland State Lottery; 2 lots in Western Territory, warrant #7888 & 7886 and for transfer deeds in office of Sandburn & Tuylor at St. Louis, MO; grant #1241 from State of NC; benefits from all store books of Wilson & Dixon. Willson in debt to James Williamson, Durkin & Henderson & Co., Petersburg, VA, on execution from CC for debts; James Richardson of CC; Benja Stephens of CC for bond; L. & M. Armstead, Petersburg, VA, for debt in hands of Jno E. Lewis of Milton to settle as their atty; to Thomas Jeffreys of the Red House, CC, for balance & as security for note due Lemuel S. Bowers; to Wilcox, Johnson & Co. of Petersburg on bond secured by Rolulus M. Sanders of CC; to Charles Wilson & Wilson & Jeremiah Dixon of Milton; to Jno Garner for taxes on western land. 7 Nov 1823. Wit: J. Person. Proved 19 Nov 1823 before T. L.Taylor, Superior Court, Wake Co., NC.

44-6 John Allen to William Snipes, for $350, 100 A both sides Flat R adj Robt Blalock, George Briggs, Jane Hargis; 3 A of this includes graves of Richd Hargis decd. 29 Nov 1823. Wit: E. D. Stanfield, W. W. Whitefield.

46-7 John Alldridge to Richard R. Moore, for $86, all his interest in tract purchased with Moore as a partnership on 29 Aug 1820 brom heirs of Job Blackard, decd. 10 Jan 1824. Wit: B. W. Milner, John Douglas.

Deed Book G
Page

47-9 William Hargis, atty & agt for Jeremiah Blackard now of Franklin Co., TN, William Blackard, Washington R. Blackard, Nancy Blackard - all heirs of legatees of Job Blackard decd of Person Co. - to Richard R. Moore & John Allridge, for $160, their undivided shares or 4/5 of 176 A on Flat R adj Thos Blalack Jun., Abraham Moore, Thos Person. 29 Aug 1820. Wit: Benja Phillips, David Allridge.

49-53 Richard S. Hackley of Fayetteville, NC, (in debt to Thomas Strode for $1240) to Robert Strange of Fayetteville, for $1, in trust, 320 A in Cumberland Co., NC, on nw br Cape Fear R, it being ½ of 640 A granted to Thomas Lackley 5 Sept 1835; 438 A in Caswell & Person Counties on s bonk S Hyco adj Jno Rainey, Daniel Malone, Henry Burch, Charles Allison, Bartlett, Leml Rainey - said land was sold by Samuel P. Ashe to David Hay & by him to Richard S. Hackley.
1 Dec 1823. Wit: P. T. Taber. Proved by oath Pardem T. Taber 13 May 1824 before Wm. Norwood, Judge Superior Court.
Thomas Strode upon receiving the $1240 assigns all right & interest in said land to Thos C. Hooper. 2 Mar 1824. In Cumberland Co., NC, Dillard Jordan Jr. proved that Richard S. Hackley is not in this State & the signature to this deed is his handwriting. P. T. Taber is out of State & his signature proved by Barnum Beach.

54-5 Lewis Tapp to Lewis Daniel, for $377, 388 A on Flat R adj Duncan Cameron, William McKissack, said Daniel - being the tract where James Milner now lives. 7 Nov 1822. Wit: Ira Lea, Wm. McKissack.

55-7 John Cutillo (in debt to William Baird of Prince George Co., VA, for $93.75) to William Baird, for $1, 3 cows, 6 hogs, bed & bedding, red chest, cupboard, oven, 4 chairs & table; debt to be pd to Thos Hallibruton, legal agt for Baird. 20 Aug 1823. Wit: Jno C. Hallibruton, Margaret H. Meroney.

57-8 William Clayton to John McVay, for $950, 375 A on Flat R adj Taylor formerly Person, Cummins. 7 Oct 1822. Wit: William Yarbrough, McVay Chandler.

59-61 Humphrey Dillard (in debt to Moses Chambers for $80, for $11.67, & for $6) to Nathaniel P. Pool, for 25¢, in trust, furniture, beds, 7 hogs; 4 head cattle; corn, fodder. 31 Jan 1824. Wit: Jos Gill.

61-3 Thomas Hood to John Gravet of Halifax Co., VA, for $315, 209½ A on Mill Cr adj David Allen, Jeffreys, Henderson. 30 Dec 1823. Wit: Wm. Davie, Saml Davie.

63-5 William Brown to William W. Brown, for $420, 105.3 A on Rocky Br adj Jno M. Dobbins, Duncan Rose. 26 Apr 1824. Wit: Saml Brown.

66 Robert Gill Sen. to Thomas Gill, for $250, negro boy about 6 yrs old called Saml Haily. 8 Jan 1824. Wit: Jos Gill.

66-8 Wilson Oliver to Yancy Oliver, for $100, his interest & claim to 107 A adj John W. Brandon, Hugh Hemphill. 2 Jan 1824. Acknd in open court.

68-70 Thomas Lipscomb to Daniel Sergent, for $680, 122 A w side S Hyco as surveyed by James Rainey 29 Aug 1815. 19 July 1823. Wit: Jno Rice Jun., Ira Lea.

70-1 Stanford Long to George Wade, for $280.50, 13.9 A adj Abner A. Dixon, said Wade, Jno Bailey at Bailey bridge on Hyco to Person CH. 9 Feb 1824. Wit: Richd Long.

72-3 Thomas Lipscomb to Daniel Sergent, for $257.50, 57.75 A on Hyco Cr as surveyed by James Rainey Feb 1821 - said land he purchased of George Johnston. 19 July 1823. Wit: Jno Rice Jun., Ira Lea.

73-4 Thomas Lawson to John Phillips, for $75, 100 A adj Hargis, Wilson, Person. 8 Feb 1824. Wit: Robt Blake.

75-6 Edmund Martin (in debt to William Baird of Prince George Co., VA, for $125.25) to Wm. Baird, for $1, in trust, 1 sorrel horse, cow & calf; furniture; crops now growing; debt to be pd to Thos Hallibruton, agt. 20 Aug 1823. Wit: James Woody, Thos P. Atkinson.

Deed Book G
Page

77-8 John Mason to William Royster, for $550, 55 A on Hico at road to conflu-
ence of N & S Hico adj McFarland Oakly. 9 Feb 1824. Wit: Jno H. Jones,
E. D. Stanfield.

78-9 Dennis Obriant to William Burton, for $70, 50 A on Stories Cr. 9 Feb 1824.
Wit: Solomon Clayton.

79-80 Stephen Pleasant to William F. Smith, for $950, 227½ A adj Brooks, Jacobs,
Lipscomb, heirs of Lawrence Lea decd, Gabriel B. Lea, James Johnston. 20 Feb
1823. Wit: E. D. Stanfield, Aaron Scoggin.

81-2 John Pass to Eli Jones, for $900, 2 tracts: 115 A on S Hyco adj Wm. Lips-
comb, Martha Richardson now Nathaniel Torian; 103 A adj Nathaniel Torian, on
road from Leasburg to Hillsborough adj Archd Lipscomb, Elijah Jacobs, Mrs. Combs,
Wm. Lipscomb. 9 Dec 1823. Wit: Jno Douglas, Jas McMurray.

83-4 Cader Parker to William Day of Orange Co., for $230, 100 A on little cr -
said land he purchased of Richard Oakley in 1806 adj William Oakley, Evans.
22 Sept 1823. Wit: Jno J. Carrington, Jno Parker.

84-5 Nathaniel Pass Sen. gives quit claim to Eli Jones & relinquishes all right
to deed from John Pass to Jones; land was conveyed to him as trustee for Thomas
Phelps & William Moore Jun both of CC & known as Thomas land & does not affect
this deed. 13 Jan 1824. Wit: Ch Willson, Nicholas Hester.

85-6 John Rice Senr to Tucker Rice a gift of 100 A on S Hico which is his pro-
portionate part of land of John Rice Sen & he to never claim any other part adj
Lea, William A. Lea, John Mason, Henry Sergent. 2 Nov 1823. Wit: William H.
Royster, Jno Rice Jun.

86-7 William Sears of Newton Co., GA, to Henry H. Allen of Person Co., for $275,
105½ A on Deep Cr adj Moore. 10 Dec 1823. Wit: Nathaniel Smith, Abner Williams.

87-8 Williamson & Lea to William Boswell, for $351, negro girl Nelly. 24 Mar 1817.
Acknd in open court.

88-9 James Warrin of Halifax Co., VA, to William Crawley of Person Co., for
$448, 112 A on Stuart & Holt Mill Creeks adj VA State line, Wm. Reynolds, James
McGehee, Bluford. 11 Aug 1823. Acknd in open court.

90-1 George Broach to David Burch of Orange Co., for $562.50, 112½ A on Double
Cr of Hico adj Jones, John Crisp, Nicholas Thompson. 10 Oct 1818.
Wit: Nathaniel Norfleet, James Martin.

92-3 Thomas Hood to William Brown, for $85, 100 A both sides Mill Cr adj Chs
Moore, Davie Allen, Smith - it being part of tract granted Hood 10 Sept 1819.
29 Oct 1823. Wit: Phillips Moore.

93-4 Henry Lipscomb of CC to Charles Boulton Junr of same, for $850, 104.6 A in
Caswell & Person on S Hico adj Archibald Lipscomb, Jacobs, Archible Lea.
2 Dec 1823. Wit: John Bradsher, Green D. Smith.

94-5 Thomas Clayton Jun. to John Bumpass Jun., for $400, negro boy Abner about
12 yrs old. 31 May 1823. Wit: Robert Bumpass.

95- Power of attorney - William P. Little of Warren Co., NC, to Phillips Moore of
Person Co. to obtain div of 640 A in Person Co. formerly property of Gen. Thomas
Person adj Thomas Hargis, Joshua Cates - it being tract recovered by heirs of
Gen. Person of William Wait; also to sell the one-third part belonging to
Little. 2 Feb 1824. Wit: Thomas Peed.

96-7 Thomas Gowen (in debt to James Holloway for $46.93) to Wilie Brooks, for $1,
in trust, a sorrel mare, hogs; furniture; working tools; crops of corn, fodder,
cotton, tobacco. 19 Mar 1824. Wit: William Springfield.

Deed Book G
Page
97-8 Joseph Farrar to John Walters, for $100, life share in 50 A where Farrar
lives on Bird's Cr adj Timothy Dunnagan; also horse, cattle, furniture; 15
barrels corn. 8 __ 1824. Wit: John Harrington, George Glen. See page 115 for
court approval, May 1824.

98-100 John Walker (in debt to Hugh Woods for $62.56) to Thomas Webb, for 50¢,
in trust, 125 A on Castle Cr adj James Holloway, Moses Jones, Buckly Walker.
25 Feb 1824. Wit: William Webb, Sterling Vaughan.

100-1 Thomas Day, a coloured man, (in debt to Colonel John Day for $14) to Isaac
Day, trustee, a gray mare with one eye about 13 yrs old. 6 Jan 1824. Wit:
Philip Obriant.

101-3 Thomas Dixon to Jesse Walker of CC, for $1231.12½, 201 A on Hico & Cane
Creeks adj Richard Carnal, Jacob Vanhook, Stephen Oliver, Warren Dixon, Robert
Jones. 27 Apr 1824. Wit: Warren Dixon, William Dixon.

103-5 Markus Oakley to Nancy Antiony, for $18, all his right to 9 A on Tapley Cr
whereon she lives adj John Hicks, said Oakley, being part of tract Oakley purchased of Samuel Dickens adj Nancy Antiony's plantation. 18 Apr 1824.
Wit: William Hicks.

105-9 Power of attorney - John Hall, Sarah Hall, Teresa Hall to John A. Howard
of Montgomery Co. to demand & receive from adm or exec of the late William Hughes
of State of NC whatever is payable now or in the future. 12 Feb 1823.
Also signed by Richard Abail & one name unreadable.
Proved Prince George Co., MD, when Jno Hall, Sarah Hall, Teresa Hall, Richard
Abigail & Sarah Abigail appeared in court. Wit: Geo Page, Benja L. Gant.
On 30 Apr 1823 Jno A Howard gives power of attorney to B. Yancey of CC to adjust
with Jno Russell exec of Wm. Hughs to settle all matters. Wit: C. G. Rose.
B. Yancey gives receipt on 12 Apr 1824 for $400 collected from John Russell exec
of Wm. Hughes for the Abigails & Halls. Proved Person Co. 1824.

109-11 John Barnett, sheriff, to Ira Lea (due to court order against Roger Tilman
& Ira Lea for $116.10 which was recovered by State Bank of NC) for $50, 200 A
adj William Satterfield on Henly Mill Cr sold to Ira Lea. 27 May 1823.
Wit: Hosey Carver, Jas McGehee.

111-3 John Barnett, sheriff, to Richard Hargis (due to execution in Orange Co.
against Thos N. S. Hargis for $490.92 recovered by Thos Dunn), for $50, 91 A
adj Nathl Norfleet, Willis Horton, Ann Allen. 27 Apr 1824. Wit: J. W. Williams.

114 Div lands of Daniel Clayton Senr decd to heirs, all of full age:
  1. Homestead 47½ A to Joseph Clayton. 2. Nancy Burton 47 A.
  3. Caty Clayton 47½ A. 4. Thos Clayton 47½ A. 5. Mary Clayton 46¼ A.
All valued at $1.25 per A. Commrs: George Wood, Daniel Clayton, Jno Daniel,
Thos Clayton, Wm. Clayton. Proved May 1824.

115 Attach to pages 97-8: Proved in open court by oath George Glenn.

115-6 Martha Hayes to beloved daughter Isabella L. Hayes, for love & affection,
negro woman named Pat & her 2 children Liza & Jackson. 1 Aug 1822.
Wit: Rebecca Williams, Sally Winstead. Proved in Superior Court.

116-9 Henry P. Womack (in debt to Thomas Sneed for $75 for security for rent
of land where William Cocke decd formerly lived) to William Street, for 25¢, in
trust, all interest in land which he obtained by his wife Frances Womack, the
daughter of Capt. Wm. Cocke decd; she was entitled to land in Western Country
purchased of William Shappard decd of Orange Co. by said Cocke. 30 __ 1824.
Wit: Wm. Blackard, D. Sneed. Proved by oath Dudley Sneed.

Deed Book G
Page

120-1 Jacob Long to Mark Patterson, for 100 lbs, all right & interest to 160 A in Arkansas in NE Quarter, Section 22, Township 1S, range 4W - it being a grant for military service. 6 July 1824. Wit: Hosea Carver, Reuben Love.

121-3 John Austin (in debt to Hugh Woods for $60) to Sterling F. Vaughan, in trust, for 50¢, a bay mare, feather beds & furniture; cattle; household & kitchen equipment. 29 Apr 1824. Wit: Willie Brooks, Jesse J. Parrish.

124-5 Samuel Bumpass to James Webb, for $150, 103 A adj Woods on Dickens road, Thomas Webb. 25 Mar 1824. Wit: Isaac Webb, Harriott Smith.

125-7 Edmund Dixon Junr to James Stuart, for $115, 45 A adj William Dixon on road from red house to Dixon Br. 30 June 1824. Wit: Elijah Morton, William Dixon.

127-9 Edmund Dixon Sen. to James Stuart, for $43.50, 14½ A adj Edmund Dixon Junr. 19 June 1825. Wit: Jesse Bradsher, Warren Dixon, Edmund Dixon Junr.

130-1 William Dixon to James Stuart, for $40, 8 A adj said Dixon. 30 June 1824. Wit: Levi Dixon, Edmund Dixon.

132-9 Trust and marriage agreement between Robert Kennon Jones who intends to marry Lucy Ann Lockhead - Lucy is possessed of land, slaves, & personal property decreed in part from her father & in part from deed of trust of Robt K. Jones for benefit of Wm. J. Barksdale; all said estate shall be conveyed to Thomas Jones & Benson Fearon Jones in trust, for $1 - all property in Person Co. about 1600-1800 A & was deed of gift to her from Genl. Jos Jones; 3 lots of 1 A each in Petersburg, VA, called Prides Field described in deed from Saml Christian to Robt K. Jones in Dinwiddie Co., VA; 8 slaves: Agga, Jenny, Henry, Nancy, Mary, Claiborne, Lazarus & ? ; 6 slaves held by Robert K. Jones namely Leander, Chloe & her 4 children Jenny, Nancy, Hannah, Sally; horses; carriage; furniture as listed in scheucle attached. Lucy A. Lockhead to hold slaves & property during her marriage - then to go to heirs of Thomas Jones & Benson Jones and not to be used for any debts or contracts of her husband. If Robert K. Jones dies first, total conveyance of estate to Lucy & then to any heirs of this marriage according to laws of descent in VA. Plantation in Person Co. to be sold first to pay debts. 15 July 1824. Wit: Thos P. Atkinson, Thos Hallibruton. Proved Dinwiddie Co., VA, 15 July 1824. Schedule of furniture follows. Proved 10 Jan 1825 before Frederic Nash, Judge Superior Court, NC.

139-42 Abner A. Dixon to John Rogers, for $31.80, 5.3 A on Marlowe Cr adj Byrd Rogers. 19 June 1824. Wit: Geo C. Rogers.

143-6 Abner A. Dixon to John Rogers, for $280.20, 46.7 A adj Byrd Rogers. 19 June 1824. Wit: Geo Rogers.

146-7 Isaiah Fuller to Reuben Long, for $511.87½, 292½ A on Stories Cr adj Solomon Clayton, Mary Harris, Rebecca Obriant, Alexr Winstead, tract purchased of John Fuller. 3 May 1824. Wit: Wm. Davie, Jno Hudgins.

147-9 John Halliburton to Francis Wright, for $314, 157 A 2 rods & 39 poles on Bluewing Cr adj Thos Halliburton, Blanks, King. 17 Mar 1824. Wit: Jno King, Moses Cotnam.

149-53 John Priest & Lethy G. Priest his wife of Williamson Co., TN, to James Stuart of Person Co., for $61, 38 A - it being one-third interest in tract of Robt Black decd adj Capt. Edmund Dixon, Wm. Dixon, Edmd Dixon Jun. which Lethey heired from death of her father Robt Black; also the dower of Mrs. Lucy Black in said tract. John Priest signs for self and as atty for Lucy Black; Leathy G. Priest signs for self. 8 June 1824. Wit: John Garner, William Dixon, Jas P. Harrison.
Lucy Black & Hardy Black of Williamson Co., TN, give power of attorney to John Priest to sell said land. 3 Apr 1824.

Deed Book G
Page

153-4 Jesse Ragan to Stephen Jones, for $1, ½ A east bank Bluewing Cr below
red house road adj Lucy Jones. 24 Sept 1822. Wit: Wm. Davie, Jno Lunsford.

154-7 John Barnett, sheriff, (due to court order to sell goods & chattels of
Jas McMurry on debt of $556.74 recovered by Stephen Dodson & Jno M. Dobbins), to
John C. Vanhook, for $50, 90 A on Hyco adj Adam McNeely, James C. Smith.
17 Aug 1824. Wit: J. W. Williams, Moses Chambers.

157-9 Robert Sargent atty of Woodford Co., KY, to Byrd Pulliam of Person Co., for
$80, all claim & interest of the heirs of Ann Sargent decd in 160 A on Gents Cr -
Ann Sargent decd was rightful heir of James Pulliam decd; she has ten surviving
heirs: David Rogers for his wife Elizabeth, Drury Sargent, William Sargent, Mary
Ann Sargent, James P. Sargent. Robert Sargent has power of atty from David,
William, Drury & is guardian for Mary Ann & James - said land adj Cary Williams,
Isham Edwards. 24 Nov 1823. Wit: Jas A. Pulliam, Nany Pulliam.

159-62 John Barnett, sheriff (by court order to sell goods & chattels of Willis
Oliver to collect $135.75 recovered by Alexr Cunningham) to Alexander Cunningham,
for $50, 107 A adj Jno W. Brandon, Hugh Hemphill. 17 May 1824. Wit: Th McGehee,
Ish Edwards.

162-5 John Barnett, sheriff (by court order to sell property of William Evans &
Downey Wade to collect $122.25 recovered by James C. Smith) to John C. Vanhook,
for $130, 72 A on Hyco adj Adam McNeely, James C. Smith. 27 Sept 1820.
Said land was to be sold by Samuel Dickens, former sheriff; deed made 17 Aug 1824.
Wit: J. W. Williams, Moses Chambers.

165-7 William Satterfield to Avery Tilman, for $230, 76 A adj Roger Tillman,
Richd H. Tillman, heirs of Jesse Carter, Barnet Winstead, Jane Clay - said land
was left by Saml Whelor to his widow for her life & then to his son, Saml H.
Whelor. 4 Aug 1824. Wit: James Tilman, William Watson.

167-70 William Trotter to Lewis Amis, Saml Winstead, Byrd Pulliam, & Vincent Lea,
all of Person Co. & Wm. Lea of CC - all trustees, for $8, all his interest in
2¼ A whereon stands a meeting house on the Leasburg Rd. with free use of a
spring & passageway for use of Methodist Episcopal Church. 22 June 1824.
Wit: James Trotter, John Draper.

170-1 John Washington of Granville Co. to Richard Wood of Person Co., for $1000,
277½ A in Person & Granville Counties on Tar R adj said Wood, James Webb,
J. Parker, being part of tract purchased of Wm. Blount Esq. 24 Mar 1824.
Wit: Jas Webb, Alexr S. Webb.

171-3 Robert D. Wade to William F. Smith, for $915, 146 A on S Hyco adj Nathl
Torian, near John Russell; Wade allowed to remove the dwelling house & reserves
24 square feet where grave yard stands. 18 Oct 1822. Wit: Nathaniel Torian,
Downey Wade.

173-4 Ira Lea to Bradsher Fullar, for 5 shillings, release & quit claim to 130 A
on Richland Cr adj Asa Fuller, Richd Atkinson, Moses Fuller, Carter Lea.
13 Mar 1823. Wit: A. D. Murphey.

175-6 Francis Foard to James Sanford of Granville Co., for $850, 200 A on Blue-
wing Cr adj Wm. Loftis on the State line. 1 Aug 1822. Wit: S. L. Pool, Gabl
Jones, James Melton, Wm. M. Sneed.

176-8 William H. Allen of CC to James Allen of Person Co., for $110, tract on
Flat R being the proportionate share of said William Allen in 308 A left by last
will of his father Wm. Allen Sen. decd & to be div equally to his 3 sons John
Boyd & William Allen Jun; land to be left during widowhood or life of Mrs. Nancy
Allen. 8 Oct 1824. Wit: William Snipes, Jno G. Wilson.

178-80 James Clack to Duncan Cameron of Orange Co., for $1000, 991 A e side
Tapley Cr of Flat R adj Cameron, Ben Morrow old field, James Williamson, John
Hicks, Jesse Lunsford - being land whereon Clack now lives & conveyed to him by
William Dickens 5 Nov 1824. 6 Nov 1824. Wit: William F. Smith, Redford
Satterfield.

180-2 James Clack to son William F. Smith & daughter Mary Kennon Brown Smith,
for love & affection, negroes Phillis, Dolly, Leathy & her child Catharine, Ann,
Lizzy, Thomas, Scilla, Horace, Alfred, Martha. 10 Sept 1824. Wit: Downey Wade,
Stephen M. Dickens.

182-7 Benjamin Chambers, by his atty Th McGehee with Cary Williams & William
Williams as securities, to Isham Edwards, for $10, 816 A - several tracts men-
tioned in previous deeds to satisfy deeds of trust & Edwards will pay remainder
of debts. 7 Oct 1824. Wit: B. H. Dillahay, Haywood Williams.
See previous deeds of trust given by Benjamin Chambers.

188-91 Alexander Cummins, Margaret Cummins, William Brown & Mary his wife late
Mary Cummins - to Duncan Cameron, for $435, 145.2 A n side s fork Flat R being
the same tract where John Cummins the elder lived & which he conveyed to the
4 grantors 25 Dec 1820. Plat of survey by Phillips Moore annexed. 16 Sept 1824.
Wit: Andrew Gray, J. Malone. Plat of John Cummins adj land of Francis Epperson
made 19 Aug 1824. Mary Brown examined apart from her husband & freely executed
deed.

191-3 William Dickens of Granville Co. to James Clack of Person Co., for $1, 991 A
e side Tapley Cr of Flat R adj Duncan Cameron, Ben Morrow old field, James
Williamson, Jno Hicks, Jesse Lunsford - it being tract where Clack lives.
5 Nov 1824. Wit: Radford Satterfield, Thos Yancy.

193-4 Jesse Dickens to Jonas Parker, for $450, 404 A adj Jno Bumpass near Wash-
ington fork, Dr. Thomas Hunt, Eli Tapp, said Parker, Jno Oakley, on Bumpass
Mountain - said tract fell to Dickens in div land of heirs of Robt Dickens decd
1823. 16 Oct 1824. Wit: S. M. Dickens, Will F. Smith.

195-6 Thomas V. Hargis to Justices of Court of Pleas & Quarter Sessions, for use
of Person Co. & for $1, a lot of .6 A in Roxbrough purchased at sale of Duncan
Rose adj Williamson store house. 23 Sept 1824. Wit: B. W. Milner, Alexr Winstead.
Proved by oath Benjamin Wells Milner.

196-8 William Lipscomb of Orange Co. to Thomas P. Evans of same, for $1315, 263 A
on S Hyco in Person Co. adj Ebenezer Meeting House, the school house lot, Vanhook.
7 Aug 1823. Lipscomb reserves the grave yard s of the dwelling house where his
wife & other family are buried. 7 Aug 1823. Wit: Thomas Laws, James Cozart.

199-200 William McKissack to Thomas V. Hargis, for $1, .6 A lot adj town of Rox-
brough in line with public square. 23 Sept 1824. Wit: Alex Winstead, B. W. Milner.

200-1 William McKissack, trustee to Thomas P. Evans, 233 1/3 A adj Samuel Gooch,
Robinson; sold to satisfy payment of $1001 to Lewis Daniel for debt due him from
James Cocke. 30 Nov 1821. Acknd in open court.

202-3 William McKissack to Justices of Court of Pleas & Quarter Sessions of
Person Co., for $1, .8 A lot at corner of present public square. 23 Sept 1824.
Wit: B. W. Milner, Alex Winstead.

203-5 William McKissack to James Williamson, for $500, ½ A adj McKissack formerly
William Jeffreys. 23 Sept 1824. Wit: J. G. A. Williamson, R. Vanhook.

206-7 Jno New, trustee to Thomas P. Evans, for $46, tract to satisfy deed of trust
given by William Cates to Thos P. Evans for $50 - said land willed to William Cates
by his father Mathew Cates; mother of William Cates has lifetime on said land
adj Jeremiah Rimmer, James Armstrong on Bird's Cr. 7 Apr 1822. Wit: Saml Johnston, John Y. Parker.

Deed Book G
Page

207-8 Lemuel Rainey of Person Co. to Samuel Woods, of CC, for $500, 170 A on
S Hyco in Person Co. adj.Tho Woods, Bartlett, Gordon at Meggs Br. 3 Sept 1823.
Wit: A. Gordon, Haxelwood Wilkerson.

208-10 Thomas Ruffin of Orange Co. to Thomas V. Hargis of Person Co. (due to
execution issued from Circuit Court of US Dist. in favor of Durkin, Henderson &
Co. & Hinton & Brame against estate of Duncan Rose which Ruffin purchased in
trust for resale for purpose of paying debt of Duncan Rose with Milton Rose,
security - deed of trust already made to Sherwood Haywood), for $500, a 2 story
wooden house in Roxborough where Duncan Rose kept store including the clerk's
office; also 105 A near Roxborough adj William McKissack, Jno Mann, & was purchased of James Payne. 5 July 1824. Wit: B. Yancy, J. W. Williams.

210-2 Downey Wade of Person Co. to John Thomas of CC, for $1600, 2 tracts in
Person Co.: 115 A on S Hyco adj William Lipscomb, Martha Richardson now Nathl
Torian; 103 A adj Nathl Torian on road from Leasburg to Hillsborough, Archd
Lipscomb, Elijah Jacobs, Mrs. Combs. 27 Oct 1823. Wit: James L. McMurry,
Stephen Mason.

213-5 Archibald Lipscomb Junr. (in debt to Nicholas Thompson with William McMurry,
security, & for several other debts) to Charles Mason, in trust, for $1, 60 A
on w prong Double Cr adj James Snipes, Nathaniel Torian, Cammel Vanhook; a gray
mare, cattle, furniture, excepting what law allows him to keep. 7 Feb 1825.
Wit: John Douglas, Jos D. McMurry.

216-7 Jacob Hubbard of Guilford Co., NC, to Josias Dearborn of Geauga Co., Ohio,
for $600, 200 A on Richland Cr in Person Co. adj James Cochran. 28 Jan 1825.
Wit: Thos Lomax, Jno M. Dick. Proved 15 Mar 1825 before F. Nash, JSC.

218-9 John Bradsher to Samuel Bull, for $400, 100 A on Stories Cr adj Isham
Edwards, Robert Brooks, Nancy Graves. 8 Nov 1819. Wit: B. B. Epperson
"I cannot make out name of the other witness." s/BWM/. Acknd in open court.

219-21 James Barnett to Sterling Vaughan, for $376.66 2/3, 112 A on Fishing Br
adj John Barnett, Robt Jones, Henry Bailey, James Barnett. 28 Apr 1824.
Wit: Hugh Woods, Jno Barnett.

221-2 Elizabeth Burton to Cuthbert Wagstaff, for $100, 60 A in Mecklenburg Co.,
VA, on Butcher's Cr adj Joseph Davis, James Eubanks - to be held during natural
life of Elizabeth Burton; all her right & interest to negro slaves. This pro-
perty came to her through death of her husband Charles Burton of Mecklenburg Co.,
VA, as dower right; she contested will for her one-third part. 5 Jan 1825.
Wit: Jno P. Rainey, Cary Williams.

222-3 James Fullar of CC to William Boswell of Person Co., for love & affection,
183 A on Stories Cr adj said Boswell, Richd Atkinson, Walton, John Williams,
Sampson M. Glenn, William Hamlin. 21 Feb 1825. Wit: Jno N.Fuller, Levi Boswell.

224-5 Abraham Hargis to his son Asa Hargis, for 25¢ & love & affection, 79 A on
Double Cr adj James Wisdom, John Moore, John Stanfield. 22 May 1824.
Wit: B. W. Milner, Alex Coleman.

225-8 Thomas Holsonback (in debt to Wright Nichols for 3 notes of $50, $75, &
$75) to Benja W. Milner, in trust, for $1, 124 A on Double Crs of S Hico adj
Jno Moore, Robt Stanfield, Dickens, heirs of Alfred Brown, Ann Graves, McNeill.
12 Jan 1825. Wit: Wm. McMurray, James Wisdom.

228-9 Ira Lea to John H. Jones, for $300, 106 A on Richland Cr adj John West-
brook on still house br, William Westbrook. 15 Nov 1824. Wit: John Rice,
Randolph Westbrook

Deed Book G
Page

230-1 Pursuant to will of Zachariah Lea decd, Vincent Lea & George Lea, heirs
of the decd & both being of age, agree to divide land equally according to will
as follows: 1. Vincent Lea 166 A adj Kindal Vanhook, Jesse Bradhser, George Lea;
2. George Lea 166 A adj James O. Bradsher, Richd Long, John Lipscomb, Archibald
Lipscomb, Kindal Vanhook. 14 Feb 1825. Wit: Jesse Bradsher, Alanson M. Lea.

231-3 James McGehee to John Pass, for $652.50, 145 A on Stuart's Cr adj William
Crawley, Thomas McGehee, Daniel Glenn. 12 Jan 1825. Wit: Th McGehee, Joseph
Yarbrough.

234-5 Harrison Stanfield to Abner Stanfield, for $303, 50½ A on Cain Cr adj James
McCain. 31 Jan 1825. Wit: Obadiah Faulkner.

235-7 John Barnett, sheriff, to Ira Lea, for $45.2375, 100 A on Mill Cr adj Wm.
Satterfield, Ira Lea; said land sold by court order against John Tilman for debt
of $40.19½. ? Aug 1824. Wit: William McKissack, Jno H. Jones.

237-9 Loften Walton to Cary Williams, for $670.40, 48 A on Sergent Cr adj said
Williams, Thos Trotter. 23 June 1821. Wit: J. A. Pulliam.

239-41 Joseph Wallace (in debt to Josias Chambers for $54.07) to B. H. Dillahay,
in trust, for $1, a sorrel mare; crops of tobacco & corn; furniture; farm animals.
2 Oct 1824. Wit: Hugh Woods, James Barnet.

242-4 Samuel C. Brame of Augusta, GA, & John Hinton of Petersburg, VA, late mer-
chants & co-partners in firm of Hinton & Brame (the said Brame acting in behalf
of Hinton with power of attorney) to John F. May of Petersburg, Va, to whom Hinton
& Brame transferred debts due them by Duncan Rose with collection entrusted to
Thomas Ruffin who probably has purchased under deeds of trust certain lands of
Rose - hence all lands conveyed to May with proceedings to collect same.
6 May 1825. Wit: Wm. Holt. Proved Orange Co., NC, 26 May 1825; registered
Person Co. by Wm. Norwood, JSC.

244-5 Ransom Cates & Edy Cates his wife (formerly Edy Sweaney) to Joel Sweaney,
for $900, 112 A both sides Deep Cr adj Samuel Moore (now Sweaney), William
Person, Robert Sweaney Senr to the hollow of the mountain - it being part of
larger tract of Jno Sweaney Senr decd & this part was allotted to Edy Sweaney
as lot #1. Signature is Edith Cates. 10 May 1825. Wit: Alex Winstead, Alfred
L. Moore. Edith Cates examined in private & freely executed deed.

245-7 Nelson Bartlett & Hasten Bartlett to Nathaniel Norfleet, for $145, 110 A
on S Hico adj Thomas Woods, Simeon Cochran, Alexr Gordon - this to satisfy deed
of trust given Alexr Gordon for $145. 27 Sept 1824. Wit: George Broach,
James Burch.

247-8 John Morgan(in debt to Joseph Jones for $700) to William Thaxton, for $1,
in trust, 2 gray mares, 1 colt, cattle, hogs; furniture, crops. 19 Feb 1825.
Wit: Thaxton Puryear, S. M. Abbott, James Faulkner.

248-50 Power of attorney - Nathan Buckley of Sumner Co., TN, to Hiram B. Dollarhide of Person Co., to demand & receive of George Lipscomb (exec of Richd G.
Lipscomb decd) of Halifax Co., VA, any monies due Nathan Buckley in right of his
wife Polly Buckley a legatee of Richd G. Lipscomb decd; the said Polly now decd.
14 Dec 1824. Wit: Jas Dollarhide, Meredith Price. Proved in open court
Feb 1825.

250-3 William Jeffreys & James Williamson to William McKissack, for $1500, 1 A
near Robert Paine's storehouse, near Dickens' house. 23 Sept 1824.
Wit: R. Vanhook, J. G. A. Williamson, Jno Douglas.

253-4 James Barnett to Moses Chambers, for $800, 119.8 A both sides Fishing Br
adj said Chambers, Bailey, John Barnett on the edge of the mountain. 6 June 1825.
Wit: Jesse J. Parrish, Lewis H. Morgan.

254-6 Ransom Cates to Jesse Cothran, for $485.40, 48.64 A on n fork Flat R being
part of land of Robt Cates Senr decd adj Phillips Moore in middle of Hillsboro
Rd., Jno Cothran, near bridge leading to Mount Tirzah. 7 June 1825.
Wit: Phillips Moore, Thomas Burton.

257 Moses Chambers & Josias Chambers to William Davie, for $700, negro woman Betty
age about 19 and her 2 children Anderson & Arthur. 6 Apr 1825. Wit: Kendal Davie.

257-8 Thomas Chandler of Granville Co. to Samuel Yarbrough of Orange Co., for
$230, negro boy Isaac about 7 yrs of age. 28 Oct 1824. Wit: William Yarbrough,Jr.

258-60 Alexander Coleman to William Yarbrough, for $230, 150 A on Tar R adj Jno
Tapp, Thomas Person. 23 May 1825. Wit: Jno Day, Jno Clayton.

260-1 Moses Chambers to Robert Jones, for $1140, 152.? A both sides Fishing Br
adj Henry Bailey, Jno Barnett, Heggie on the edge of the mountain. _ _ 182_.
Wit: Robt Bumpass, James Woodie. Acknd in open court June 1825.

262 Jesse Cothran to Ransom Cates, for $380, negro boy Jim age 14 yrs. 23 Feb
1825. Wit: Newel Cate.

262-4 Arthur G. Dillahay (in debt to B. H. Dillahay(Burrel or Barrie H. Dillahay)
for $25.33) to Willie Brooks, for $1, in trust, 2 feather beds, furniture,
dishes; corn, oats; hogs. 1 Mar 1825. Wit: Jno Dillahay, Joseph Gill.

264-5 Ambrose Davie of Montgomery Co., West TN, to beloved daughter Vallera
Pattern Davie of same, for love & affection, negro woman Sucky & Leathy her in-
fant; Sucky was bought of Robert Downey of Person Co. by William Davie of Person
Co. & sold by him to Ambrose Davie. 19 Feb 1825. Wit: Jones Davie, Robt Davie.

265-6 Bowling Day to Lewis G. Lanier, for value recd, all interest in his
father's estate; Jno Day adm of said estate to convey all title & interest.
1 Mar 1825. Wit: Jesse Lunsford.

266-7 Edward Davis of Orange Co. to James Williamson of Person Co., for $1500,
460 A both sides Dry Cr of Flat R adj Gabriel Davy, John Paine, Robert Paine,
Jno Womack. 18 Oct 1822. Wit: C. Atkinson, J. G. A. Williamson.

267-9 David Hunt of Franklin Co., NC, to James Snipes Jun. of Person Co., for
$660, 212½ A on Double Creeks of Hyco adj William Cocke, Hall now Wisdom.
14 Mar 1825. Wit: F. W. Milner, L. Rainey.

269-71 James Jay & Elizabeth McKissack who shortly intend to be married & each
possesses an estate both real & personal; each desires not to injure their
children; each agrees to pay any debt of estate it possesses but should jointly
enjoy both. At death the estate of each to descend to the children of each.
21 Dec 1824. Wit: William Brown, Stephen Pleasant.

271-3 Francis Lawson (who owes bonds to Cary Williams for $577.25, to James
Williamson & to Wm. McKissack; to William Street as security for bonds) to Hugh
Woods, for $1, in trust, 283 A both sides Mayo & Donaldson Creeks adj Thomas
Lawson, William Street. 6 May 1825. Wit: James Street, William Buchanon.

273-6 Francis Lawson (in debt to John Y. Parker for $633.57) to James Patterson,
for $1, in trust, negro woman Sealy, woman Delilah, girl Sarah. 25 Mar 1825.
Wit: Jas Milner, Jno Hudgins.

276-7 Talton Moton to Mark Patterson, for $150, 75.2 A on Adams Cr adj Charles
Mitchell, Jno Shelton. 20 May 1824. Wit: Robt Jones, Reuben Long.

278-9 Thomas McGehee to James McGehee, for 6½ A, 6½ A adj James McGehee.
2 Apr 1825. Acknd in open court.

279-81 Thomas McGehee to Thomas Sheppard, for $50, all his interest in 50 A on
Hico purchased of Joseph Wood; Thomas Sheppard was partner in purchase, adj

279-81 cont. - Alexander Cunningham towards McGehee mill, Jno McGehee, said Sheppard. 1 June 1825. Acknd in open court.

281-2 James McGehee to Thomas McGehee, for 6½ A, 6½ A on west side of a br from Pass' spring to Thomas McGehee. 2 Apr 1825. Acknd in open court.

282-4 Duncan Rose, exec estate of John Ravens decd, to Stephen Pleasant, for $765, 234 A on Richland Cr adj Alexr Rose decd, Jesse Watson decd, Edwd Clay decd, Richard Jones, James Williamson - said land where John Ravens died, being part of tract granted by Earl Granville to James Talbert 11 Aug 1761. 31 Mar 1825. Wit: Jno Wisdom, Lavinia G. Rose, B. W. Milner.
Frances Satterfield relinquishes her right to said land 31 Mar 1825. Wit: Anne Amis, Elijah Obriant.

284-6 Lewis Ramsay (in debt to Richd E. Bennett for $115.97) to John Holloway, trustee, for $1, & payment of said debt, one wagon, 5 sets gears, horses. 7 May 1825. Wit: Jno Bennett.

286-90 John Barnett, sheriff, (by court order to sell 90 A on John Trew for debt of $31.45 recovered by Claiborne Thaxton) to Peter Thaxton, for $75.25, 90 A on Stories Cr adj John Hudgins, Isaiah Fuller decd. 6 June 1825. Wit: Cary Williams, Saml Davie.

290-2 John Barnett, sheriff (due to court order against Wm. L. Parker for debt of $400 recovered by Hugh Woods & Josiah Oliver) to Hugh Woods, for $306, 160 A adj Wm. McGehee, Harrison Stanfield, Thos M. Hamlet. 7 July 1823. Acknd in open court.

292-3 Henry Sergent of Pittsylvania Co., VA, to Daniel Sergent of Person Co., for $175, 49¼ A on S Hico adj Daniel Sergent, Jno Mason, Tucker Rice. 7 Dec 1824. Wit: John Sergent, Stephen Sergent.

293-5 James Satterfield to Nathaniel Norfleet, for $80.60, a tract belonging to Nancy McKissack who on 24 May 1820 conveyed same to Satterfield by deed of trust; see Book E, pages 331-2. 7 June 1825. Wit: B. W. Milner, Calvin Jones.

295-7 Alexander Winstead to David Painter of Halifax Co. VA, for $3000, 400 A on Richland Cr adj James Holloway, Moses Walker formerly Richd Atkinson, Isaac Satterfield, Reuben Walton; see deed from Edwd Clay Sen. to his son James Clay for further description as Winstead purchased same at sheriff's sale. 2 June 1825. Wit: Jno Barnett, Jno Epperson.

297-9 James Woodie of Halifax Co., VA, to William L. Allen of Person Co., for $1200, 182½ A on Castle Cr of Hyco adj John Dillahay, McFarland old line, Moses Walker, Major Green, Jno Rogers. 28 May 1825. Wit: Jno Barnett, Lewis P. Allen.

299-301 James Woodie & Moses Woodie exec of last will of David Woodie decd to Aaron Woodie (all of Person Co.), release of claim to 50½ A on Bold Br value $252.50 adj Allen Woodie, Moses Woodie, Jno Lawson - said land willed by David Woodie to Aaron Woodie. _ Feb 1823. Wit: Thomas Pool.

301-2 Francis H. Worsham of Granville Co. to Phillips Moore of Person Co., for 50¢, his right, title, & interest to tract known as Gooche mill with 178 A on Flat R belonging to estate of Jno Gooche Senr. decd, adj Julius A. Burton estate, heirs of Robt Cates, Ransom Cates, Phillips Moore, L. V. Harigs, Minshew tract, Gipson mill tract, Herbert Sims. 4 June 1825. Wit: William Moore, Nancy Worsham.

302-3 Judith Elizabeth Worsham of Orange Co. to Phillips Moore, for $1, all her right & claim to tract on Flat R known as Gooche mill tract with 187 A. 11 Mar 1823. Wit: Richd L. Cooke, Wm. Moore.

Deed Book G
Page
304 David Allen, Thomas T. Allen, Drury Allen to Abner Haralson, for ? , 2 A
on Mayo including a house of worship with a spring for use of public worshipers.
1 Sept 1825. Wit: Nathl Smith.

305-6 John Borwn to Stephen Wells, for $116, 2 tracts on Bushy Fork of Flat R:
1.1 A adj John Brown, Ephraim Hawkins, said Wells; 56 A adj Abraham Moore.
9 Aug 1825. Wit: B. W. Milner, Nathl Norfleet.

307 John Chandler to 2 sons McVay Chandler & Washington Chandler, a gift of
negro man Willis, a blacksmith. 1 Sept 1824. Wit: John McVay. Both sons agree
to accept said negro as their part of father's estate.

307-8 Gabriel Davie to Thomas Lawson, for $450, 145 A on Mayo Cr adj Robt Davie,
Ashbourn Davie, said Lawson, Francis Lawson. 25 July 1825. Wit: Thomas Gill,
Jos Gill.

309-12 Shadrack Hargis (in debt to Lawrence V. Hargis & Co. for $56.95 & for
$148.35, to Wilkerson & Hargis for $16.17) to Dudley Sneed & Augustin Vanhook,
for 25¢, in trust, 200 A on Aldridge Cr adj James Wilson, James Williamson -
it being the old mansion place where his father lived & died; horse, cattle;
furniture; crops; a bond on Jonathan Hargis for $220. 5 Sept 1825.
Wit: James Wilson, James Gooch.

313-4 Lawrence V. Hargis, agt. or atty for Elias Fort of Person Co., to Thomas V.
Hargis, for $500, 300 A on Flat R adj Stephen Moore former line, William Cochran
to Dry Br, Cameron. 13 Oct 1824. Wit: Harris Wilkerson, Hezekiah Terry.

315-6 Wyly Jones (Willie Jones) to John Garner, for $1, in trust, 3 negroes
Lewis, Mingo, & Tom; Robt Jones Senr executed bond to Richd Halliburton to
indemnify him as security for Wyley Jones as adm of his decd brother Gabl C.
Jones; this will secure Robt Jones Sen. as his security to Richd Halliburton.
10 June 1825. Wit: Jas Patterson.

317-8 Wright Hichols to Thomas Holsonback, for $200, 124 A on Double Creeks of
S Hico adj John Moore, Robt Stanfield, Dickens, heirs of Alfred Brown, Ann
Graves, McNeill. 12 Jan 1825. Wit: B. W. Milner, Wm. McMurry.

318-9 Nathaniel Norfleet to William Morse, for $50, tract of William Morse which
he purchased at sheriff sale 16 Sept 1822 as Morse has paid debt; see deed recorded in Book F, pages 286-8 for description. 14 June 1825. Wit: B. W. Milner,
(torn) Briggs.

320-2 Sarah Rogers (in debt to Cary Williams for $152.65),to Alexander Winstead,
for 50¢, in trust, the undivided share of negro slaves of Edward Clay decd &
known as negroes of John J. Tribue, decd. 20 Apr 1825. Wit: B. H. Dillahay,
Jos Gill.

322-4 Sterling Q. Trotter to James Trotter, for $500, 172½ A on Sargent Cr adj
James Stuart, Arthur Leath, Thomas Trotter. 30 Aug 1824. Wit: W. Trotter,
G. T. Blaek.

324-5 Susannah Turner to Cary Williams, for $145, 30 A adj Isham Edwards, John
Carver, Currie Barnett, said land she purchased of Cary Williams & Currie Barnett.
22 Nov 1823. Wit: Alexander Williams, Ezekiel Duncan.

325-6 Cary Williams to Sterling Q. Trotter, for $213.50, 172½ A on Hico - said
land conveyed to grantor by James Trotter by deed of trust on 20 Apr 1821 to
pay debts due Ira Lea & Co.; land adj Arthur Leath, Thomas Trotter. 9 Aug 1824.
Acknd in open court.

327-8 Buckley Walker to Jesse Walker Jun., for $215, 93 A both sides Castle Cr
adj Moses Jones, Henry Woody, Jno Dillahay. 17 Feb 1825. Wit: John Rogers,
Hugh Woods.

Deed Book G
Page
328-9 Buckley Walker to Henry Woodie, for $324, 72 A w side Castle Cr adj Henry
Baily, Jones, Jno Dillahay. 17 Feb 1825. Wit: Hugh Woods, John Rogers.

330-2 John Barnett, sheriff, (due to court order from Warren Co., NC, Mar 1825,
to sell goods, chattels, lands of Elias Fort for debt due of $1800) - debt re-
covered by Benja Jones in said court - 1109¼ A on Flat R adj Joseph Lunsford;
said tract purchased by Elias Fort of Benja Jones & purchased by Jones of Solomon
Paid - sold to Duncan Cameron for $428.5 Sept 1825. Wit: B. Yancy.

333-5 John Barnett, sheriff (due to court order of June 1825 to sell goods &
chattels of Henry Day for debt of $131.98 & $119.90 recovered by Gabriel Davey)
to Gabirel Davey, all right of Henry Day in 555 A on Tar R adj James Webb which
was property of John Day Sen., decd, & to which Henry Day was a legatee;
price paid $100. 5 Sept 1825. Wit: Thos Webb, William L. Allen.

336-8 William F. Smith & Mary K. B. Smith to Thomas Oakley, for $162.50, 320 A
adj said Oakley, Mason, Suit - said land descended to Mary K. B. Smith from
estate of her grandfather, Robert Dickens, decd & allotted in 1823. 13 Apr
1825. Wit: Portius Moore, Griffin Jones.
Mary Smith examined apart from her husband & relinquished her claim to said land.
Wit: John Bradsher, Wright Nichols.

338-41 William F. Smith & Mary K. B. Smith his wife, to George Glenn, for $200.25,
215 A adj Thomas Oakley, Vaughan, Nathan Oakley, Suckey Moore - being part of
land descended to Mary Smith from her grandfather Robert Dickens in 1823.
13 Apr 1825. Wit: James Clack, Jas Milner, Portius Moore.
Mary K. B. Smith examined apart from her husband & relinquished her claim to
said land.

341-2 Abraham Moore to William Farquhar as he is known now called William Moore
the natural son of Catharine Farquhar who subsequently married Joseph Moore son
of Abraham Moore, for love & affection, negro man Davy now in Maury Co., TN in
possession of William & was loaned to son Joseph Moore when he moved to TN;
since Joseph Moore is decd, Davy was hired out for benefit of his children.
18 Feb 1826. Wit: Wright Nichols, Stephen Wells.

343-4 Thomas Burton to Jonathan P. Sneed, Dudley Sneed, & Sally Hargis (heirs of
Thos Sneed, decd) for $5, .40 A at mill pond on Flat R adj Saml Cothran & Polly
Cothran - it being part of land allotted from his father's estate to which dam
of Thomas Sneed was joined. 8 Sept 1825. Wit: James Gooche, Caty Sneed.
Proved Dec 1825.

END OF BOOK G

N

Caswell	Richmond	St. Lawrence	Nash
St. David's	Gloucester	St. Luke's	St. James

x

KENDALL

Caswell County 1777-1792 with 8 districts.
X indicates Caswell Court House the name being
    changed to Leasburg in 1788.
Person County was formed in 1792 from the eastern
    part of Caswell. The districts falling into
    Person were St. Lawrence, St. Luke's, Nash,
    and St. James.
The districts in Caswell after 1792 were Richmond,
    Caswell, St. David's, and Gloucester.

208

PLACE INDEX cont.

Barnett(cont'd)
28,59
William,1,3,
4,8,23,25,
33,49,64
Wm,28
BARNEY
John,52
BARROE
Cela,47
BARROTT
Peter,58
BARTLETT
Hartin,89
Hasten,89,120,
126,127,142,
191,203
Hastin,189
Nelson,189,203
BARTON
Nancy,131
William,29
BASS
Christopher,40,
47,48,64,
67,77,79,
81,82,103
BASWELL
James,50
William,49
BAUGHN
Zachariah,4
BAWLEY
Wm.,5
BAYNES
John,46
BAYNHAM
John,65
BAZWELL
David,6,15,
50,60,94,105
William,80
BEACH
Barnum,196
BEADLES
John,25,47
Joseph,6,22,24
Patsy,22
William,22
BEARD
John,3
William,46
BEARDEN
John,54,85
Joseph,27

Nancy,33
Richard,10,24,
29,43,52
Richd,29,39,
46,47
BEARDIN
John,79
Richard,37
Richd,33
BEARDON
Nancy,28
Richd,28
BEDDLES
W,15
BEDFORD
James,72
BEEDLES
Joseph,11,39,
40
Wrice,17
BELL
James,8
John,81
Saml,32,81
Samuel,19
William,67,125
BENEHAN
Thomas,149
BENNETT
Jno,205
Peter,5,10,
16,26,
34,35,
43,18
Richd E.,111,
190,192,205
Sally,50
Thomas,7,114
Thos,148
BENNETTS
Peter,31
BENTON
Jesse,102
BENZIEN
Christian
Lewis,72
BERRY
David,168,187
George,138,145,
156,157
Henry,187
Littleton,159
Patsy,145
Robert,113,126
Susannah,138,

157
BERZEAN
Christian
Lewis,68
BEVIL
Claborn,184
Claburn,106
Claibourne,95
BILBO
William,87,93,
95
BILBOA
William,181
BIRD
Bergoon,161
William,153
BIRK
James,68
BISHOP
Ann,179
Hannah,156,179
BLACK
George,10,
25,26,27,
54,60
Hardy,190
Henry,50,71,79
John,2,9,10,
25,26,28
Lucy,90,92,96,
101,122,199
Nancy,60
Peggy,60
Polly,60
Robert,9,10,
12,26,64,
86,90,92,104
Robt,190,199
Saml,77
Samuel,77
Thomas,10,27
Thorndon,165
Thornton,126
William,60,63,
69
BLACKARD
Jeremiah,196
Job,46,195,196
Jobe,41
Nancy,196
Washington,183
Washington R.,
196
William,196
Wm,198

BLACKLEY
James,13
BLACKWELL
Isaiah,6
James,119
John,75
Saml,56,102,
132
Samuel,96,110,
113,119,156,
162,165,173,
182
BLAKE
John,2,5,8,
15,35,37,51,
61,67,83,97
Robert,172
Robt,196
Samuel,69
BLAKELEY
James,47
BLALACK
Ann,195
Hasten,129,195
John,129
Robert,129,166,
190
Robt,143
Thomas,129,195
Thos,156,195,
196
William,145,157
BLALOCK
Hastin,151
John,32,46,61,
63,153
Millenton,5,56,
75,82,89,
107,117
Millington,9,
11,32,42,47,
48,61,80,93,
181
Millinton,86,
127
Richard,127
Robert,61,
107,127,181
Robt,195
Thomas,46,56,
60,68,82,
109,117,119,
127,151
Thomas F.,9
Thos,85

213

Blalock (cont'd)
  William, 32,
    59, 61, 75,
    82, 107,
    139, 159,
    164
  Wm, 138
BLAND
  Ann, 68
  Edwd, 39
  Elizabeth, 68.
  Elizabeth
    R., 193
  Elizabeth
    Ridley, 68
  Jacob, 179
  Peter
    Randolph,
    68
  Richard, 30,
    31, 39,
    40, 68, 193
  Richard
    Jr., 41
  Sally
    Dickens, 68
BLANKS
  Joseph, 51
  Richard,
    81, 129
  Richd,
    149, 181
BLANTON
  Joshua, 105
    114
BLAYLOCK
  William, 61
BLEDSOW
  Anthony, 102
BLOUNT
  Wm, 200
BOGGUS
  Samuel, 15
BOHANAN
  Thomas, 75
BOHANNON
  Anw, 80
  Thomas, 75, 80
BOHANON
  Thomas, 63
BOLTON
  Edward D., 165
  Saml D., 171
BOMAR
  Alexander, 74

BOND
  Will, 160
BOOKER
  Lowry, 74,
    80, 81
BORING
  David, 10
BOSTICK
  Charles,
    3, 5, 6,
    13, 18, 22,
    25, 28,
    32, 58, 80,
    142, 165,
  Cheslay, 4
  Chesley, 22, 23,
    25
  Richard, 22
BOSWELL
  Elizabeth, 129
  James, 16, 35, 69
  John, 129
  Levi, 202
  William, 127,
    142, 197, 202
  Wm, 160
BOSWORTH
  Obediah, 20
BOULTON
  Charles, 34, 40,
    63, 73, 197
  Joel, 136
BOWDEN
  Benjamin, 195
  George, 195
  James, 185
BOWERS
  Jno, 85
  John, 89, 100,
    103
  Lemuel, 98
  Lemuel S., 195
BOWLER
  John, 4
BOWLES
  John, 9, 47,
    52, 68, 69,
    85, 96,
    125, 180
  Jordon, 47
BOWLS
  John, 56
BOYD
  Alexander, 6
BOZWELL

John, 18
Wm, 168
BRACHEN
  David, 75
BRACKEN
  David, 2
  William, 104
BRADFORD
  Holeman, 134
BRADSHER
  Abner, 63, 68,
    70, 137, 141,
    154, 161, 174
  James,
    139, 167,
    185, 190
  James O,
    163, 203
  Jesse, 49, 88,
    92, 130,
    134, 144,
    146, 154, 155,
    163, 165,
    172, 184, 190,
    199, 203
  Jno, 172, 188
  John, 16, 22, 44,
    63, 88, 97,
    102, 105,
    110, 119, 122,
    136, 146, 147,
    148, 149, 153,
    155, 156, 157,
    161, 163, 169,
    176, 182, 183,
    188, 197, 202,
    207
  Moses, 8, 17, 27,
    54, 63, 65, 68,
    75, 76, 80, 81,
    83, 85,
    88, 103,
    111, 116, 120,
    134, 135,
    139, 151, 154,
    156, 158, 163,
    172, 192
BRAME
  Samuel C., 203
BRAN
  John, 126, 135,
    158
BRANCH
  William, 61, 67
  William S., 60,

77, 83, 87, 90,
    92, 100, 120,
    123, 136, 145
  William Scott,
    76, 88, 91, 93,
    97
  Wm, 87
  Wm S., 128
BRAND
  John, 142,
    151, 159
  Vencent, 68
  Vincent, 19
BRANDON
  Jesse, 147
  Jno W., 200
  John W., 191, 196
  Polly, 147
  Robert, 166, 191
  Thomas, 124, 191
  Thos, 143
  Thos S., 191
  William, 36
BRANN
  Catherine, 29
  Jno, 173
  John, 29, 65,
    135, 143, 173
  Thomas, 16, 29
  Vincen, 37
  Vincent, 13,
    28
BRAVES
  Barza, 130
BRECHEEN
  William, 40
BRECHEN
  David, 24, 28,
    32, 45, 51, 61,
    67, 83, 90, 132
  James, 76
  John, 41
  William, 13, 34,
    38, 41, 49, 71,
    76, 81, 94,
    106
  Wm, 92
BRECKEN
  William, 5, 75
BREESEE
  John, 77
BRESSEE
  Murrel, 160
  Murrell, 98
  Nancy, 160

214

215

Buchanon(cont'd)
Cornelius,147
   David,113,
     114,148
   James,22,18
   James B.,137
   John,110
   William,147,204
   Wm,165
BUCKANAN
   Arthur,57
BUCKANON
   Andrew,32,34
   Artha,33
   Arthur,34
   Dean,32
   James,23,33
   William,34
BUCKHANNON
   Arthur,44
BUCKLEY
   Nathan,203
   Polly,203
BUGG
   Anselem,27,67
   Ansolem,69
BULL
   Elizabeth,170,
     176
   Jacob,15,16,
     22,33,43,
     49,74,86,87,
     92,96,
     98,104,108,
     110,117,122,
     135,147,
     148,153,
     156,170,173,
     176
   Jesse,148,156,
     165,170,173
   Saml,148
   Samuel,93,96,
     122,156,158,
     162,175
     176,202
   William,97
BULLINGTON
   Robert,92
BULLOCK
   Benjamin,89,93,
     149
   Elizabeth,149
BUMPAS
   Saml,133,145

BUMPASS
   Alfred,100,110,
     128
   Augustin,25
   Edward,25,57
   Elizabeth,25
   Gabe,53
   Gabriel,10,34,
     37,74,80,
     95,110,111,
     115
   James,25
   Jesse,75,100,
     108,133,134,
     139,147,
     154,166,176,
     190,191
   Jno,184,201
   John,32,34,
     37,41,52,
     53,56,74,
     75,98,100,
     108,110,
     119,120,128,
     139,150,152,
     157,162,186
     193,197
   Josias,189
   Robert,119,197
   Robt,150,191,
     204
   Saml,48,100,
     107,115,146
   Samuel,19,25,
     56,57,108,
     110,112,115,
     120,134,199
   Sidney D.,152
   William,128
BURCH
   Baylor,20,24,
     36,50,69,
     70,71,74,
     84,103,116,
     119,122,
     128,143,
     155,176
   Betsy,80
   David,197
   Edm,70,71
   Edmd,20,127
   Edmond,36,71,
     101
   Edmund,69,137,
     145

   Geo,20
   George,5,16,
     20,25,37,141,
     145,154
   Henry,49,79,
     81,121,196
   James,10,203
   Jean,80
   John,8,136
   Lucinda,154
   Lucy,154
   Nicholas,103,
     126,146,148,
     150,184
   Pemeberton,7
   Philip,123
   Phillip,56,186
   Richard,20,
     23,25,36,
     37,49,69,70,
     80
   Richd,5,10,42,
     69
   Taylor,46
   Thom,101
   Thomas,71,
     74,77,101,
     119
   Thos,35,39,70
BURFORD
   John,48,68
BURGUS
   Christion,2
BURK
   James,63
   Saml,59
   Samuel,113
BURTON
   Absolem,189
   Allen,88
   Charles,202
   Charles H.,37,
     43
   David,2
   David H.,159
   Dnaiel,124
   Elizabeth,202
   Hutchins,166
   James M.,16
   James Minge,33
   Jas M.,79
   John,147
   John H.,11,163
   Julius A.,205
   Martha H.,34

   Nancy,134,136,
     198
   Rebecca,166,175
   Rebekah,82
   Richard,127
   Robert,48,127
   Thomas,51,204,
     207
   Thomas H.,19,
     34,159
   Thos H.,7,31,
     43
   William,197
   William H.,147
BYAS
   John,6,81
BYASE
   Thomas,149
   Thos,180
BYASEE
   John,106
   Joshua,188
   Thomas,106,142,
     188
BYASSE
   Joshua,172
   Thomas,154
BYRD
   Baylor,50
   James,52,57,
     59,61

       -C-

CADDEL
   Andrew,7,36,
     37,38,40,43,
     49,69
   Eunice,49
   Jean,49
   John,4,33,37,
     40
   William,4,7,
     23,36,155
CADDELL
   Andrew,4
   John,41
CADEL
   Andrew,2
CAERNS
   Alexander,141
CAIN
   William,89
CALDWELL
   Andrew,138

217

218

Davy(cont'd)
 Gabriel,10,46,
  69,106,144,
  145,146,184,
  204
 James,1
 Jane,146
 John,46,106
 Nancy,184
 Polly,106
 Robert,46,146
 Saml,151
 Samuel,176,187
 William,46,77
 Wm,109
DAY
 Ambrose,139,
  143,153,168,
  191
 Boling,191
 Bowling,204
 Elijah,109,110,
  138
 Francis,52,
  86,110,148.
 Henry,51,77,
  101,122,
  126,132,207
 Isaac,16,22,
  42,79,96,
  162,198
 Jno,157,168,
  204
 John,16,21,22,
  26,42,49,51,
  73,76,80,86,
  96,116,121,
  123,139,143,
  158,161,
  162,198,207
 Phillip,116,
  139
 Roben,153
 Thomas,3,198
 William,21,197
 Wm,30,130
DEARBORN
 Josias,202
DEBCE
 Benjamin,8
DEBOE
 Benj,42
 Fred,42
 Frederick,8,42
 Solomon,14

DEBOW
 Benj,66
 Benjamin,105
 Benjn,12
 Frederick,11,
  12,14,19,
  21,77,104,128
 John Allen,11
 Lucy Rogers,12
 Milley Rogers,12
 Nancy May,11
 Rachel,11,12
 Sol,56,61,113
 Solomon,12,46,
  102
DEGRAFENRED
 Vincent,11
DELAHAY
 Edmund,38
 John,22,38
DELAMAR
 Chruchwel C,147
 Churchil,161
 Churchill,165
 Churchwel,162,
  170
 Churchwell C.,
  182
DELK
 David,10
DELONE
 Edy,43
 Frankey,43
 Nicholas,8,26,
  32,43,
  44,50,54,
  65,110
DENBY
 Elijah,12,13,
  15,32,37,144,
  145
DENEY
 Thos,161
DENNIS
 Abraham,116
DENNY
 Ben,128
 Claborn,106
 Clayborn,51
 Elizabeth,143,
  153
 Nancy,143
 Thomas,171
 Thos,143
 Zachariah,50

DER SCHWEINITZ
 Lewis,130
DESHAZO
 Clembernet,129
 Clement,102
 Clement Barnet,
  129
 Edmond,75
 Edmond Bennett,
  10
 Edmund,32,75,
  129
 Richard,5,41,
  75,77,80
 Richd,90
 Robert,41,47,
  58,59,60,69,
  77,87,102,
  124,129,160,
  162,172
 Robt,171,174
 Robt Bohannon,
  129
 William,5,129
DESHAZZOR
 Edmond,18
DEURAST
 Hezekiah,104
DEWESE
 Hezekiah,41
 Isaiah,35
DEWEST
 Isaiah,49
DICK
 Jno M.,202
DICKENS
 Frances,141
 James,152
 Jesse,3,9,14,
  20,25,32,
  33,45,46,48,
  52,53,
  55,56,
  62,68,
  79,80,84,
  85,87,103,
  107,112,
  115,116,119,
  120,123
  126,128,
  139,
  141,142,147,
  148,160,168,
  170,175,
  181,193,201

Martha,68
Parthenia,68
Robert,1,2,
 3,4,6,
 8,9,11,12,
 14,15,19,
 22,23,
 25,27,
 28,29,30,
 31,32,33,
 34,35,36,
 37,39(6),
 41,43,45,
 46,48,49,
 50,51,
 52(5),53,
 56,57,59,
 60,61,
 62,66,68,
 71,84,85,
 86,90,94,
 103,104,
 105,121,132,
 144,151,
 168,175,
 193,207
Robert A.,1
Robt,24,25,77,
 81,86,138,
 147,155,
 170,193,201
Sally,32,68
Saml,41,48,
 50,62,81,100,
 120,123,124,
 132,137,
 141,147,148,
 154,158,
 159,160,164,
 166,175,180,
 184
Samuel,32,
 52,53,55,
 56,67,68,
 69,79,84,
 86,89,92,
 93,95,102,
 103,107,108,
 109,114,
 115,116,
 118,119,122,
 124,126,127,
 128,138,144,
 147,152,153,
 159,163,

222

228

GWYN
John,58

-H-

HACKLEY
Richard S.,
196
HAGGIE
Thomas,63
HAGIE
Thomas,144
HAILBURTON
Thos,129
HALL
Addison,119,
173,183
Ann,82
Geo,48
George,6,26,
30,33,34,
49,58,64,77
Jno,15,26,
28,177,198
John,3,15,43,
44,49,61,96,
114,198
John S.,77
Jon,149
Joseph,43,
51,56,58,
96,122,128,
145,162
Joseph Addison,
133
M.,12
Philip,3,12,
60,81,90,108
Phillip,44,58,
82,87,89,92,
100,104,106,
192
Sarah,198
Teresa,198
William,81,85,
89
William
Pleasant,169
Wm,60,82,87,
90,152,188
HALLIBRUTON
Richd,165
Thos,199
HALLIBURTON
Allen,117,120

Benja,159,188,
190
Benjamin,151,
161,165,175
Charles,3,6,7,
10,29,46,49,
77,82,94,104,
147,149,183
David,10,103,
149
Humphries,149
Jas C.,181
Jno C.,196
John,10,11,12,
21,27,31,
58,66,81,
110,132,137,
146,165,
188,199
John C.,132,147
Letty,188
Martha,6,31
Martin,66
Mary,154
Mary A.,154
Richard,120,
127,151,152,
159,161,
165,172,175,
188
Richd,146,155,
190,206
Robert,58,76,
154,194
Robt,132,147
Sarah,7,147
Susanna,149,183
Thomas,6,7,
11,49,58,
70,91,104,
110,132,147,
149,160,183
Thos,43,56,
83,132,
146,196,
199
HALLYBURTON
David,76
Martha,76
Thomas,76
HAMBLEN
Joseph,88
Nathaniel,88
Richd,88
William,95,138

HAMBLET
Frances,25
James,17
james,25
Thomas M.,25
HAMBLETT
Betsey,56
Fanny,43
Frances,56
James,20,26,
43,53,56
Thomas M.,20,58
HAMBLIN
Benj,106
Joseph,107
Nathaniel,
106,107
Richard,46,58,
70,107,128,
162
William,46,
58,70,77,
88,103,
106,107,
116,128
Wm,160
HAMILTON
James,127
John,8
HAMLEN
Nathaniel,88
William,27,152
HAMLET
Frances,163
Geo M.,185
James,75,96,
122
Jno,163,183
John,164
Robert,118,
163,183
Thomas M,164
Thomas M.,183
Thos M,163
Thos M.,205
HAMLETT
Frances,128
James,1,25,
26,101,128,
145,162
John,101,133,
145,163
Robert,101,119,
128,133
Robt,145

Thomas M,163
Thomas M.,1,133
Thomas Moore,
26,119
HAMLIN
Joseph,88,150
Nath,182
Nathaniel,145
Nathl,121,182
Richard,164,179
Richd,138,147,
153,180
William,27,
30,64,109,
115,121,125,
175,188,202
William Jr.,6
Wm,125,168,184
HAMPHILL
Hugh,50
HAMPTON
William,76
HAMRIC
Henry,58
HANKS
John,32
HANNAH
James,126,127,
134,135,
142,143,173,
187
Jas,177
HANSON
Richard,114,148
HARALSON
Abner,17,109,
130,206
Anderson,38,41
Archd,82
Benj,15
Benjamin,7
Bradley,17,25,41
Burges,8
Burgess,1,4,33,
34,35,55
Burgus,22
David,130
Elizabeth,4
Elkanah,8,35
Eunicy,17
Ezekiel,11,14,
15,17,
23,25,29,
33,35,41,47,
55,57,58,59

229

230

Harris(cont'd)
  Robt,29,80,84,
    133,156,177,
    179,194
  Saml,148
  Samuel,26,28,
    97,148,153
  Sarah,130,
    142
  Starling,50,55,
    61
  Sterling,74,87
  William,147,162
  Willis,130,
    142
  Wm,130,172,177

HARRISON
  Ailsey,160
  Anna,13
  Benjamin,19,
    96,160
  Eleanor,109
  Elender,106
  Ellen,79,110
  Ellin,105
  James,144
  James P.,190
  Jas P.,169,181,
    199
  Vincent,79

HART
  Joseph,180
  Saml,106
  Samuel,109
  William,64
  Zachaus,76,
    109
  Zacheus,58

HASKENS
  Creed,90

HASKINS
  Aaron,64,83
  Aron,84
  Christopher,185
  Creed,64,72

HATCHER
  Benj,2,12
  Benjamin,10,54,
    101,106,111
  Benjn,8
  Charles,101
  John,101
  Mary,90,145,
    155,156
  Polly,101,111

Thomas,101,111
Thos,101
HATCHET
  Bartley,144
HATCHETT
  Bartlett,93,98
  Bartley,116,
    118,126,129
  Polly N.,118
HAUXHURST
  Eliza,151
  James W.,131,
    151
HAWKINS
  Ann,84
  Elizabeth,176
  Ephraim,1,4,
    31,41,45,
    51,54,61,
    67,68,69,
    76,84,107
    122,136,
    153,172,
    176,190,206
  Ephriam,69,
    123
  John,66
  Thos,153
  William,6,35,
    117,129,176
  William Jr.,6
HAWKS
  Joseph,149,154
HAWXHURST
  James W.,132
HAY
  David,196
HAYES
  Bartholomew,
    164,189
  Bartholomew L,
    155,156
  Isabella,189
  Isabella L.,
    189,198
  Martha,155,164,
    198
  Saml,98,99
  Wm. L.,189
HAYNE
  William,1
HAYS
  Martha,182
HAYWOOD
  Rufus,180

Sherwood,166,
  186,202
Will H.,180
HEGGIE
  Archibald,50,
    119
  Fannie,131
  James,102,113,
    119,122,124,
    125,131,133
  Jas,123
  Thomas,50,72,
    80,124
HEMPHILL
  David,37,50,
    55,96,114,
    122,124,
    128,145,162
  Henry,162
  Hugh,21,23,26,
    29,37,41,53,
    69,77,94,
    101,105,
    114,129,182,
    196,200
HENDERSON
  Leonard,45,
    127,185
  Pleasant,187
HENDLEY
  Darby,38
  Edmund,19
  James,68
  James D.,4,13,
    37,79
  Jas D.,19
HENDLIE
  James D.,143
HENDON
  David,5
HENELY
  Edmund,192
  James D.,192
HENLEY
  Darby,18
  Edmon,192
  Edmund,31,192
  James,48,57,
    133
  James D.,6,55,
    94,163,170,
    192
  James Dunbar,
    6,33,34
  Jas D.,81

Jno,124
John,148
Letitia,192
Lettuce,179
HENLIE
  Darba,25
  James
    Dunbar,25
HENLY
  Edmond,94
HENSHAW
  Thomas,58
HESTER
  Elijah,101,
    118,142,
    145,150,
    184
  Nicholas,119,
    127,142,197
  Nihu,101
  Robert,5,28,
    69,71,118,
    119,127,133,
    137,154
  Robt,101,123,184
  William,28,
    111,118,123
HICHOLS
  Wright,206
HICKS
  Daniel,3,15,
    31,32,52,66
  Fanny,32
  James,15,31,53
  Jno,183,201
  Joel,82,137,
    139,166,175
  John,32,46,66,
    82,109,112,
    138,198,201
  Joseph,47,189
  Toler,52
  William,25,32,
    66,68,137,
    138,179,198
  Wm,52,183
HILL
  James,185
  John,117
  Samuel,24
  Zachaiah,20
HINTON
  John,203
  Thomas,5,91
  William,1

HIX
Daniel, 15
Danl, 15, 57
John, 66, 184
HOBSON
Betsy, 98
William, 33, 40,
73, 94, 98, 136,
172
Wm, 112, 143
HODD
Thos, 85
HODGE
David, 45
Isaac, 45
John, 45
Samuel, 45
HODGES
Archibald, 13
HOLDER
James, 63,
101, 129
Sally, 101
HOLDMAN
Charles, 42, 60
Chs, 6
Richard, 60, 65,
70
HOLEMAN
Charles, 89, 92,
100, 107, 110,
111, 116, 120,
166
Chas, 37, 82,
95
Jane, 31
Richard, 31, 120
Richd, 158, 166,
179, 181
Samuel, 128
HOLLARD
Richard A., 47
HOLLOWAY
Crowder, 135,
151, 170, 189
James, 65, 86,
97, 110, 111,
129, 137,
148, 150, 153,
169, 170, 195,
197, 198, 205
Jane, 106
Jno, 120, 177
John, 26, 30, 38,
59, 64, 80, 83,

94, 97, 104,
106, 109, 110,
111, 116, 129,
133, 135, 161,
170, 182,
186, 205
Richard, 26, 39,
40, 59
Richd, 47
Robert, 104, 118,
123
Thomas, 118
William, 26, 30,
46
HOLMAN
Charles, 164, 188
Richard, 162,
164, 188
Richd, 164, 188,
189
Samuel, 186
HOLOWAY
John, 19
HOLSOMBACK
Abraham, 40
Richard, 13, 15
Richd, 37, 46
HOLSONBACK
Delpha, 39
Richd, 89
Susan, 165
Thomas, 202, 206
HOLT
Anna, 191
Hiram, 191
Hyram, 166
James, 33
Jno, 191
John, 166
Michel, 115
Robert, 6, 191
Timothy, 7, 24,
33, 74, 127,
129, 191
William, 33
Wm, 203
HOOD
Peter, 135
Thomas, 28, 70,
91, 97, 107,
129, 132, 133,
157, 196, 197
Thos, 94
William D., 137
HOOPER

John, 8
Thos C., 196
HOPE
Mims N, 161
HOPSON
William, 73
Wm, 173
HORLEY
James, 94
John, 85
HORLY
John, 113
HORTON
Anthony, 146
Jas, 23
Willis, 94, 103,
120, 131, 143,
198
HOUSTON
William, 8, 9
HOWARD
Abel, 1, 6,
10, 11, 71
Allen, 81
Devina, 66
Francis, 27, 36,
38, 50, 68, 122
George, 65
Groves, 38, 50,
71
Henry, 6, 11,
16, 21, 35,
38, 50,
65, 66,
68, 71, 103
Henry W., 84
Hiram, 6, 12, 68
Jno, 71
Jno A., 198
John, 65, 71
John A., 198
Johnston, 38,
50, 119
Larkin, 38, 50
Nancey, 38
Nancy, 38, 50
Peggy, 66
Robert, 12,
30, 65,
66(5), 68,
71, 72, 97,
102, 103, 109,
119, 122
Robt, 69, 84
Sarah, 66

William, 36, 38,
50
Wm H., 68
HOWELL
Francis, 45
Jos, 32
HOWERTON
James, 90
HOWSON
Peter, 50
Richard, 5, 42,
43
Richd, 97, 98,
121
HUBBARD
Elizabeth, 96
Hardy, 59, 97
Jacob, 120, 147,
161, 202
Jeremiah, 75, 85
Joseph, 62, 63,
65, 75, 82,
85, 91, 96,
120, 139, 147,
161, 183
Susannah, 96
Woodson, 53, 87,
95, 96, 100,
102, 108
HUDDLESTON
Dicy, 193
HUDGENS
Ambrose, 40
Asa, 164
John, 139
Thomas, 102, 107
HUDGEON
Ambrose, 18
HUDGINS
Ambrose, 23, 141
Ann, 153
Asa, 153, 176,
190, 192
Carter, 46, 48
Jno, 170, 175, 179,
182, 199, 204
John, 128, 137,
147, 153, 162,
164, 169, 179,
180, 191, 205
Lavinia, 192
Starling, 51
Thomas, 46, 48,
56, 66, 91, 124,
153, 162

233

Lawson (cont'd)
Lucy, 133, 141,
  185
  Thomas, 72, 81,
    84, 98, 103,
    105, 128, 149,
    164, 176, 188,
    192, 196, 204,
    206
  Thos, 146, 161,
    192
  William, 141, 185
LAYTON
  James, 34, 57,
    72, 109, 133
  John, 52
  Joseph, 55
LEA
  Abner, 39, 45, .
    48, 54, 63, 75,
    80, 108, 130,
    132, 134,
    135, 165,
    172, 176, 186
  Alanson M., 203
  Ambrose, 45, 76,
    176
  Andrew, 41, 42,
    45
  Archer, 157
  Archible, 197
  Barnet, 40, 142,
    159
  Barnett, 23, 40,
    48, 62, 63, 81,
    113, 125
  Benja, 150, 165
  Benjamin, 54,
    132, 134, 135
  Carter, 25,
    40, 68, 92,
    111, 123,
    128, 129,
    131, 137, 138,
    149, 164, 165,
    173, 176, 179,
    183, 187,
    191, 194, 200
  Edmond, 9
  Edmund, 42
  Elizabeth, 176
  Gabl, 99
  Gabl B, 158
  Gabl B., 155
  Gabriel, 41, 44,

58, 67, 91, 108,
  118, 152
Gabriel B,
  165, 197
Gebl B, 161
Geo, 17, 39, 40,
  54, 62, 65,
  67, 73, 76,
  125, 172, 186
George, 11, 17,
  33, 44, 48, 58,
  66, 68, 75, 77,
  80, 88, 89,
  91, 103, 108,
  111, 135, 137,
  148, 156, 159,
  165, 176, 183,
  188, 203
George J., 135
Henry, 85, 148,
  151
Ira, 84, 91, 92,
  98, 101, 104,
  105, 107,
  108, 109,
  111, 114,
  115, 117,
  118, 119,
  122, 123,
  124, 125, 127,
  128, 129, 132,
  137, 138,
  141, 143, 144,
  145, 149,
  150, 152,
  154, 160,
  165, 167,
  169, 170,
  172, 173,
  175, 177,
  179, 180, 181,
  182, 185,
  186, 187, 191,
  193, 194,
  196, 198,
  202, 203, 206
James, 23, 29,
  41, 54, 62, 87,
  123, 165
Janet, 75
Janett, 66
Jennet, 39
Jno, 184
John, 9, 11, 29,
  42, 44, 45, 48,

60, 88, 115
John B., 54,
  75, 79, 81,
  82
L, 17
Laurence, 96, 155
Lawrence, 96,
  103, 146, 197
Namah, 16
Owen, 149, 173,
  176
Polly, 176
Rachel, 151
Reuben, 45, 50
Richard, 9, 29,
  42, 54, 63, 132,
  135, 165
Sally, 148
Susanna, 172,
  186
Susannah, 108
Vincent, 44, 50,
  54, 81, 91,
  98, 99,
  103, 108, 118,
  121, 126, 134,
  137, 144,
  145, 151, 152,
  156, 158,
  161, 200, 203
Will, 10, 17
Will A., 147,
  149, 185
William, 2, 4, 5,
  8, 11, 16, 18,
  19, 23, 32, 33,
  38, 39, 44,
  45, 48,
  50, 55, 58,
  61, 63, 66,
  67, 68, 75, 76,
  77, 79, 81,
  91, 108, 110,
  120, 138, 184,
William A., 91,
  111, 131, 138,
  172, 184, 186,
  197
William Archer,
  108
Wm, 63, 74, 83
Wm A., 148, 157
Zachariah, 68,
  151, 163, 172,
  203

LEAN
  William, 34, 97
  William A., 125
LEATH
  Arthur, 104, 130,
    133, 134, 148,
    151, 177, 206
LEDBETTER
  Daniel, 41, 42,
    48
  Henry, 53, 57
  Joel, 13, 37, 57
LEE
  Ira, 176
LEMAY
  John, 27, 142
LESTER
  George, 112
LEWIS
  Bressie, 82, 111
  Edmond, 6, 52
  Edmund, 1, 19,
    28, 37, 91
  Edward, 166
  Elisabeth, 93
  Elizabeth, 97
  Fielding, 14, 15,
    18, 32, 50, 64,
    73, 82, 83, 87,
    90, 94, 97, 98,
  Hiram, 52, 75,
    82, 85, 88, 126,
    127
  James, 50, 64, 83
  Jno E., 195
  John, 72, 73, 82,
    97, 98,
    99, 176
  John B., 84
  Joseph, 8
  Martha, 39
  Mary, 37
  Nicholas, 73
  Warner, 75
  William, 66, 97
  Zachariah, 82,
    90, 97, 98
LIGON
  James, 77
LIMPSOMB
  Archd, 82
  Archibald, 129
LINGO
  John, 31, 56, 61
  William, 56

236

LIPSCOMB
Arch,118
Archd,132,184,
197,202
Archer,149,157,
182
Archibald,65,
68,82,88,94,
126,127,
134,135,
144,145,
146,148,
150,164,176,
197,202,203
Archiblad,183
Benion,131
Benion P.,
176,183
Binion,88,127
Bynion,126
Comma,88
Delpha,183
Dorothy,
164,176
Elisha,126
Elivira,88
Eloisa,127
Emma,126,127,
131
Geoffra,131
Geoffre,88
Geoffrey,126,
162
Georffrey,127
George,203
Henry,137,
144,145,
146,148,161,
163,172,182,
197
Jeoffrey,128
Jeofrey,162
John,203
Louisa,126,131
Matilda,88,126,
127,131
Polly,94,150
Richd G.,203.
Sally,148
Thomas,88,94,
126,127,131,
134,144,
146,150,183,
193,196
Thos,134,187,

193
Willaim,97
William,98,
108,137,146,
155,163,
187,201,202
Wm,172,185,197
LITTLE
William P.,197
Wm,174
LOCKHART
Saml,44
Sarah,7
William,7
LOCKHEAD
Lucy Ann,191,
192,199
LOFTEN
William,182
LOFTIS
William,176,
180,187
Wm,200
LOMAX
Thos,202
LONG
Abner,16
Alexander M.,
192
Alexr M.,184
Ambrose,35,65
Benj,18
Benjamin,4,5,
34,43
Benjamin G.,83
Benjn,8,16
Bridget,192
Jacob,199
James,2,6,
16,20,21,
31,43,64,
65,92,93,98,
110,135,142,
143,147,156,
165,173,176,
182
Jesse,74,92,
96,98,102,
119,148,193
Jessey,88
John,16,28,
35,40,83,
97,109,122,
176
Martha,20

Marthew,16
Moses,118
Rebecca,95
Reuben,4,5,
28,34,90,98,
135,145,
148,149,156,
166,173,174,
195,199,204
Reubin,26,34,
40,43,59,79,
96,100,118,
123,148,158
Richard,83
Richd,113,196,
203
Ruben,162
Stanford,188,
194,196
William,2,6,
16,77,156
William G.,154,
192
Wm,20,28,29,
172
Wm.,20
LORD
Lord,97,127,
154,192
LOTT
Christian,68
LOVE
Alen,16
Allen,6,15,20,
21,26,30,31,
39,40,44,55,
59,64,66,71,
74,75,124
Allin,21,65
Fanny,75
Hugh,74,75
John,111
Reuben,199
Samuel,38
LOW
Edmund,20
LOWHEAD
William,28,29,
37
Wm,31
LOWTHER
William,14
LUMKIN
Anthony,55
Edmund,68

Wm,127
LUMPKIN
Anthony,68
LUNSFORD
Elizabeth,106
Jesse,32,45,
74,80,88,
89,109,112,
116,119,123,
150,151,
158,159,
160,170,
175,176,
189,193,
201,204
Jno,200
John,158,
159,160,
170,186
Jos,68,84,167
Joseph,32,37,
55,69,80,
88,106,109,
110,123,139,
150,151,161,
183,207
Samuel,106
LYON
Elisabeth G,
123
Elizabeth,100,
146,152,169
Elizabeth G.,
114,123,124
Henry,17,20,39
Jane or Jean,34
John,24,100,
104,105,107,
114,123,124,
146,152,169
Peter,71
Richard,24,39,
91,104
Richard T.,31,
105
Richd,34,45,
59,67
William,71
LYTLE
Robert,21

-M-

MABRY
Lewis,33

237

238

239

Malone(cont'd)
Stephen,118
Thomas,40,50
William,13
Wright,118
MAN
Charles,119
John,2,38,84,
132,18
Thomas,58
William,8,18
Wm,119
MANGUM
Josiah,77
Willie P.,149
MANN
David,1,2
James,182
Jane,72,149
Jno,84,115,202
John,10,72,
112,149
Robert,115,
145,149,164
Thomas,72,145,
147,182
William,23,72,
84,112,115,
149,176,182
Wm,62,101,145
MANSFIELD
John,176
Wm,70,71,84
MARET
Thomas,143
MARR
William Miller,
90
MARRABLE
Hartwell,85
MARSHAL
John,149
Wm,84
MARSHALL
Frederic William,
48,72
Frederic Wm,68
Frederick
William,51,64
Joseph,160
Lackey,141
Sackey,190,191
Thomas,48
William,141
MARSHEL

William,37
MARTIN
Alexr,2
Edmund,110,196
Edward,90,166
James,86,119,
120,128,168,
179,187,197
Jas,168
Wm B.,158
MASON
Charles,202
Jno,74,88,103,
115,170,183,
187,193,205
John,29,34,41,
64,69,77,79,
87,89,98,99,
100,106,113,
125,129,132,
142,143,148,
152,153,184
197
Stephen,40,202
Thomas,4,68
MASSEY
Nathan,82
MATHEWS
Samuel,14
MAXWELL
David,19
MAY
John F.,203
MAYLER
Thomas K.,179
MAYO
Wm,114
MDGEHEE
Mumford,192
MEADERS
Daniel,109
MEADOWS
Abraham,141
Daniel,56,116,
117
Jesse,10
MECALISTER
Neal,32
MEDARES
Abraham,25
MEDARIS
Abraham,128
MEDEARES
Abram,166
MEGEE

William,98
MEGEHE
John M.,29
Joseph,29
Munford,29,33
Thos M.,59
MEGEHEE
J.M.,15
Mumford,14
Munford,47
William,64
MEINUNG
Frederick,72
MELEAR
John,27,44
MELONE
Isham,18
Mark,98
Pomfort,101
MELTON
George,105
James,200
John,165
MENCHEW
Thomas,54
MERCER
James,46
MERIT
Daniel,145
Thos,172
MERITT
Daniel,147
Polly,182
Thomas,182
MERONEY
Margaret H.,196
MERONY
Margaret H.,183
MERPHIN
Benjamin,90
MERRIT
Danl,62
Thomas,187
MERRITT
Daniel,59,68,
103
Danl,81
Thomas,180
Thos,171
MESSER
James,9,80,84,
86
METCALF
Charles,48,64,
68,72

MICHEL
Samuel,129
MICHELL
David,45
Wm,54,145
MILAM
Lewis,35
MILES
Abraham,43
Abram,49
Betsy,21
Byrd,21
Fanny,21
Heartwell,21
John,51,54,
67,68,70,
73,80,81,
100,103
Nancy,21
Patterson,21
Tho,1
Thomas,21,27
MILLER
Allen,62,83,95
James P.,82
James
Paine,
4,31
MILNER
Ann,195
Benj,134
Benj A,183
Benj W.,182
Benja,162
Benja A.,195
Benja W,129,139
145,151,
185,202
Benjamin,181
Benjamin W.,136,
143,174,176,
188,191
Benjamin Wells,
201
Jacobina,176,
188
James,113,137,
152,157,166,
168,169,179,
180,188,
194,196
Jas,32,39,
125,131,174,
204,207
Josiah W.,191

240

241

Moore(cont'd)
Richd,114
Ro,62
Robert,6,15,
25,47,51,
59,63,66,
70,91,94,
95,97,105,
119,120,
126,128,135,
150,161,162,
171
Robt,14,24,
103,141
Sacky,193
Saml,141
Samuel,120,134,
159,161,203
Seth,3,10,13,
23,85,87,90
Sidney,120,134,
141,161,
170,181,182
Solomon,65
Stephen,3,13,
14,15,21,
28,32,41,
42,47,48,54,
62,87,91,112,
120,141,153,
162,168,206
Stephne,80
Suckey,207
Tarlton,98,112
Thomas,4,10,
11,33,60,62,
84,101,116,
122,147,157
Thomas H.,72
Thomas I.,67
Thomas Ivy,67
Thomas J.,64,
67,77,79,82
86,123,190
Thomas Jay,87,
89
Thos,42,91,
102,123,128
William,25,37,
61,66,76,81,
82,83,84,
89,109,125,
128,146,151,
176,181,197,
205,207

Williamson,150,
158
Wm,83,85,127,
151,153,205
Yancey,170,182
MORGAIN
John,18
MORGAN
Allen,52,69,
110
Ezl,189
Jno,130
John,112,181,
203
Lewis H.,203
Phillip,24
Saml,104
Samuel,86,94,
102,105,118,
121,122
Thomas,109
MORRIS
Leonard,60,170
MORROW
Archd,187
Archibald,189
Ben,169,201
Benja,169
Benjamin,42,
69,77,79
Ebenezer,147,
186
John,9,69,186,
187,189
Mary,186,189
Thomas,15
William,5,9,
26,51,57,77,
115,121,
187
MORSE
William,206
MORTEN
Thomas,29
MORTON
Elijah,199
George,108
Hezekiah,169,
170,185
Joseph,77,81,
176
Martin,173,
187
Talton,163
Thomas,5,46

Thos,75
William,5
MOSELEY
Frances L.,122
Francis L.,121
MOSS
Ebenezer,44
William,190
MOTEN
Thomas,29
MOTON
Talton,204
MOUTRY
Wm,193
MUIRHEAD
Claud,105,106,
114,192
Claude,192
Elisabeth,106
MULLENS
James,42
MULLINS
James,29
MUNDAY
Jesse,129,137
MURDOC
David,175
MURDOCK
Robert F.,189
MURPHEY
Ad,24,26
Alex,26,132
Alexander,155
Alexr,27
Arch,11
Archd,9,12,
14,60,87,
123,128
Archibald,1,
20,25,27,
43,56,60,
64,67,75,
77,136
Archibald
D.,155
Archiblad
D,161
Nancy,56
Nicholas,161
Smith,130
MURREY
William,21
MURROW
Ebeneser,161
Ebenezer,183,

186
William,75
MURRY
Abraham,9
William,4,5
MUTTER
John,20
MUZZALL
Jas W.,
104,108
Jos W.,
109,113
Joseph W.,113
W.,40
William,41

-N-

NALTINES
Henry,52
NASH
Edwd,38
Frederic,189,
199
Thomas,1,58
William,8
NCNEEL
Henry,99
NCNEILL
John H.,157
NEAL
John,6,18,77,
90
Lawson,98,115,
149,173,176,
193
Stephen,192
Thomas,173
NEALY
Garnet,81
Thomas,109,115
NEEL
John,10
NEELEY
Garnet,20
Garnett,49,53,
79,80
Isaac,57,66
Joseph,67
Samuel,1,57
Tho,27,33,66
Thomas,4,6,7,
21,23,25,34,
44,49,53,66,
67,77,80

242

243

Negroes(cont'd)
Philis,20
Phill,79,169, 170
Phillis,12,16, 28,94,113, 169,170,181, 201
Piety,188
Polly,89,92, 157,181
Price,111
Prince,12,63
Punch,11
Quiller,51,118
Rachael,181
Rachel,1,51, 89,92,111, 144,155, 169,171,175
Ralph,106,109, 110,114
Randel,75
Randill,53
Randolph,169, 170
Reuben,108,177, 181,187
Reubin,87
Rhoda,91,112, 168
Rhody,87,93 ·
Richard,93,169, 174,181
Richd,167,171
Ritty,176
Robin,75,113
Roger,16
Rosanne,65
Rose,12,98, 111,175,176
Russell,168
Ruth,28
Sall,39,108, 167
Sally,166
Saluda,70
Sam,61,74,81, 115,157,177, 187,191
Saml,157,166
Saml Haily,196
Sancoe,46
Sarah,2,22,30, 62,157,169,

171,175,176, 181,191,204
Scilla,201
Scot,169
Scott,59,171, 181
Sealy,204
Seth,28
Shadrack,108
Sharper,44,48
Shedrick,91
Silvia,14,91, 111
Simon,93, 109,169,171, 181
Sine,166
Smith,62,174, 182
Sol,12
Solomon,45
Sook,153
Squire,118
Stephen,45,89, 92,108
Suck,161,170
Sucke,11,76
Sucky,169, 171,181,204
Susa,74
Susanna,171
Susannah,90
Sylvia,182
Tabb,157
Tamar,183
Tamer,109
Tempey,108
Tempy,87,98
Terry,12
Theny,178
Thomas,62,155, 201,18
Till,22
Tiller,91,93
Tom,12,28,47, 55,68,72,93, 107,114,160, 186,206
Traveller,76
Tresey,28
Tulip,92
Ursuly,157
Venus,2
Veny,157
Vilet,54

Vines,76
Viney,160,189, 190
Washington,157, 166,169,170
Will,83,111, 112,165
William,118, 144,186
Willis,206
Willy,144
Winny,89,92
Winters,2
Yancy,118
Zack,87

NELONE
Nicholas,21

NELSON
James,91

NEW
Jno,201
John,175

NEWMAN
Joel,49,58,66, 85,103,114, 120,187,192
Jopel,127
Kichen,175
Kinchen,109, 120,188
Robert,101,109

NEWTON
Ben,71
Benjamin,4,6, 19,21,30
Henry,2
Jno P,158
John,4,6,17, 54,63,68,79, 88,137,158
John G.,105
Reuben,2,6,88, 132
Reubin,20,21, 159
Robt,174
Uriah,91,132
Ursula,92

NICHOLAS
Micajah,47
Richerson,184
Willis,149,167
Wright,38

NICHOLS
Amos,152

John,136
Mathias,86, 131,149,153
Micajah,13,15, 32,51,57,58
Nicajah,95
Priscilla, 13,24
Richd,180
Richison,131
Susanna,122
Willis,13,15, 24,32,51,86, 87,95,108, 131
Wright,24,53, 116,122,123, 124,144,145, 157,159,184, 190,202,207

NIVEN
Margaret,74

NORFEET
Nathaniel,100

NORFLEET
Edwd,174
James,53,62
Nath,39,100, 161,176
Nathaniel,32, 39,61,72, 76,91,104, 105,108,109, 113,134,143, 171,172,174, 177,184, 190,191, 193,197,203, 205,206
Nathl,41,48, 62,80,83,91, 113,115, 125,137,141, 142,143,150, 151,168, 188,195,198, 206

NORMAN
John,56
Thomas,106

NORRIS
William,143

NORSWORTHY
Bethsheba,62
William Noyal,62

245

Paine(cont'd)
Robt,38,57,58,
137,164
Solomon,135,
137,179
Thomas,80
William,2,7,
10,11,
16,38,46,47,
52,80,86
PAINTER
David,205
Jane,144
Martha,144
Nathaniel,55,
95,115,152,
173
Patsy,144
Saml,144
Samuel,144
Wyatt,115,
151,181
PALHAM
Atkn,170,171
PALMER
Joseph,7,12,
15,16,23,32
Thomas,7,23,45
Thos,67
PANNELL
William,123
PANNILL
George,105
Jeremiah,105
Samuel,105
Wm,121
PARISH
Abel,24,47,55,
130
Abel L.,153,
172,174
Canor,9
Eleanor,43
Elkanah,36
Jno,172,177
John,9,29,36,
37,43,47
Nathan,31
Overton S.,
153
PARKER
Abner,47,49,
51,75,107,
115,119
Abraham,117

Amos,79
Anne,2
Bird G.,96
Blackmore,10
Byrd G.,98,99
Cader,117,197
David,47
Doctor,64
Jno,106,197
John,88,90,
92,94,103,
105,106,108,
109,110,
116,121
John Y.,191,
201,204
Johnathon,27
Jonas,16,22,
49,133,152,
166,189,193,
201
Jones,77
Josias,103
Nancy,84,103
Powel,16,22,77
Powell,47
Richard,65
Robert,1
Sarah,2
Stephen,49,51
Thomas,77,99,
103,106,109,
115
William L.,89,
177
Wm L.,128,205
Wm S.,73
PARR
John,128
PARRISH
Abel,31,74,
79,80,87,
117
Caner,31
Charles,100
Eleanor,47
Jesse J.,199,
203
Jno,180
John,31,73,79
William,61
PARROT
John,103
Lewis,18,
56,72,

Reuben,25,176
Reubin,18
PARROTT
John,33,89,128
Lewis,1,50,76,
84,100
Reuben,149,173
PARTACE
Hubbard,112
PARTAIN
Hubbard,112
John,112
PARTEE
Benj,53
Benjamin,9,
27,37,42,
59,93,107,
109
Benjn,21,139
Earbe,37
Earle,27
Joshua,71
Yearbe,93
Yearby,59,109
PASCHAL
Saml,149
PASKILL
Jacob,113
PASS
Holloway,8,35
John,184,
197,203
Nathaniel,197
PATTERSON
Elizabeth,144
Gideon,1,9
21,32,
62,124
James,1,4,5,
6,10,11,
20,21,65,68,
109,204
Jas,206
Mark,199,204
PAYNE
James,186,202
John,16,30,45
Robert,24,30,
84,123
Robt,194
William,57
PEACHY
Thomas G.,114
Thomas Griffin,
113

PEAD
George,128
PEARCE
Obadiah,26,
122,145,163
Obediah,35,38,
45,51,61,68,
69,71,72,
117,134,138,
161,162,168,
182
Sally,71,72
PEARSON
John,23,26,42,
61,62,64,86,
104
PEDE
Thomas,154
PEED
Andrew,60
David,185,189
George,170,
189
Jesse,128,170
John,125
Leory,161
Richard,60,154,
166
Richd,60
Thomas,125,154,
197
PEEDE
Andrew,88
PENDERGASS
Richard,65
PENDERGRASS
Richard,33,63,
64,66,70,76,
89
Richd,40,76,
103
Robert,66
PENICK
William,42,87
105
Wm,23,29,69,
76,87,127
PENINGTON
Catherine,76
Ezekiel,76
PENN
Elizabeth,188
John,139,143,
188
William,44,54

247

253

Vanhook(cont'd)
  Kendal,146,150,
    172
  Kindal,61,137,
    156,203
  Kindel,16,20,
    44,54,81
  Kindle,16,73,
    99,100,136,
    187
  Laurence,16,17,
    146,154,
    155,185,187
  Law,6,172
  Lawrence,3,4,
    7,11,36,45,
    49,50,52,54,
    72,73,83,99,
    100,133,134,
    137,138,184,
    192
  Loyd,8,14,22,
    25,36,41,43,
    44,45,
    49,50,
    59,61,64,66,
    67,68,69,70,
    73,74,
    75,76,79,
    80,81,82,83,
    84,86,88,
    92,96,97,
    98,101,102,
    103,105,107,
    115,116,117,
    134,137,139,
    154,184,185
  Margaret,154
  Mary,157
  McDaniel,118
  Parthenia,157,
    165,166
  Richd,129
  Robert,16,54,
    98,99,139,
    149,151,
    154,157,
    158,159,162,
    163,165,
    166,171,173,
    176,184,186
  Robt,70,137,
    144,148,154,
    156,161,
    174,186

Rovt,185
Sally,165
Samuel,54
Sarah,76,103,
  109,110
Thomas,1
William,149,
  173,176
VARMILLION
Wilson,6
VASS
Philip,5,6,7,
  11,40,77
  24,51,129
Thomas,51,65
VAUGAN
John S.,117
VAUGHAN
Aris,158,189
Arris,169
Cas,193
Caswel,169
Caswell,92,148,
  158,161,163
Dicy,158,161,
  169
Dilly,148
Drucilla,148,
  158,169
George,17,69
Lewis,103
Milly,148,158,
  169
Sterling,198,
  202
Sterling F.,190,
  199
Tabitha,106
Thomas,66
Zachariah,161,
  163,169
VAUGHN
George,41
Granville,45,
  46,88
Susannah,107
Zachariah,68,
  89,106,107,
  117
VEAZEY
Anne,27
James,27
John,27
Zebulon,25,
  27,31,36,

  42
VERELL
Jno,137
VERLINES
Abraham,79
VERMILLION
Wilson,18,
  19,25,
  28,37,177,
VERNON
William,192
VILLINES
Abraham,57,79,
  91,99
Edward,166
Thomas,79
Thos,187

-W-

WADE
Allen,58,63,
  112,113,117,
  120,126
Ann,144
Benjamin,179
Benjn,172
Betsey,54
Charles,148,
  184
Charles D.,
  176,178,187
Chs D,164
Downey,81,86,
  98,143,153,
  157,164,168,
  171,174,177,
  178,184,
  187,200,
  201,202
Edmund Tinsley,
  168
Edwd,42,43
Elisabeth,31
Elisabeth
  Henriette,106
George,136,188,
  194,196
James,168
Jane Mary,168
John G.,109,
  129,144,145,
  146,148,168,
  171
Josiah,69,81,

  119,143
Lucey,3
Mary,187
Nancy P.,104
Patsey,55
Robert,3,55,
  60,70,73,79,
  85,86,
  87,94,107,
  110,121,
  144,156,184
Robert D.,155,
  157,171,184,
  200
Robt,62,73,
  132,142,
  143,145,
  146,147,
  148,153,168
Robt D.,144,
  145,177,178
Sally,168
Thomas,87
Tinsley,1,5,
  144
WADKINS
Philip,44
Phillip,26,50
Sally,26
WAGGONER
Jacob,135,
  167
WAGSTAFF
Brittain,192
Cuthbert,202
John,92,105,
  128,152
WAIT
William,5
WAITE
George,110,
  132,150,
  151,156,
  158,159,
  160
Jno,177,180
Robert,57
William,1,2,
  3,4,8,10,
  15,19,24,26,
  34,35,36,37,
  40,46,48,49,
  51,52,56,57,
  61,62,
  68,71,74,

260

261

www.ingramcontent.com/pod-product-compliance
Lightning Source LLC
Chambersburg PA
CBHW070355270326
41926CB00014B/2561